Bureaucracy in Traditional Society:
Romano-Byzantine Bureaucracies
Viewed from Within

by
T. F. Carney

Coronado Press   1971

Published by
Coronado Press
Box 3232
Lawrence, Kansas 66044

Standard Book Number
87291—033—4

Manufactured in the USA

Dedicated to

The Faculty of Arts
University of Sydney

TABLE OF CONTENTS

Book One: A Survey of Roman and Byzantine Bureaucracies

Maps

Appendix

LIST OF ABBREVIATED TITLES

CAH — *Cambridge Ancient History*, Cambridge U.P., 1934 ff.

CMH — *Cambridge Medieval History*, Cambridge U.P., 1966.

De Mag. — John the Lydian's *On the Magistracies of the Roman Constitution* as translated in Book III.

De Mens. — R. Wünsch, *Ioannis Lydi de Mensibus*, Teubner, 1898.

De Ost. — C. Wachsmuth, *Ioannis Laurentii Lydi liber de Ostentis*, Teubner, 1897.

Eisenstadt — S. N. Eisenstadt, *The Political Systems of Empires*, Free Press, 1963.

Hammond — M. Hammond, *The Antonine Monarchy*, American Academy in Rome, Papers and Monographs 19, 1959.

Homo — L. Homo, *Roman Political Institutions from City to State*, Routledge & Kegan Paul, 1962 ed.

Jenkins — R. Jenkins, *Byzantium: The Imperial Centuries A.D. 610 to 1071*, Weidenfeld & Nicolson, 1966.

Kunkel — W. Kunkel, *An Introduction to Roman Legal and Constitutional History*, Clarendon, 1966.

LRE — A.H.M. Jones, *The Later Roman Empire 284-602: A Social, Economic and Administrative Survey*, Blackwell, 1964.

MacMullen — R. MacMullen, *Soldier and Civilian in the Later Roman Empire*, Harvard Historical Monographs 52, 1963.

Millar — F. Millar, *The Roman Empire and its Neighbours*, Weidenfeld & Nicolson, 1966.

RE — A. Pauly, G. Wissowa & Co., *Real-Encyclopädie der classischen Altertumswissenschaft*, ed. 2, 1894 ff.

Riggs — F. W. Riggs, *Administration in Developing Countries: The Theory of Prismatic Society*, Houghton Mifflin, 1964.

SEHRE — M. Rostovtzeff, *The Social and Economic History of the Roman Empire*, Clarendon, 1957.

Wittfogel — K. A. Wittfogel, *Oriental Despotism: A Comparative Study of Total Power*, Yale U.P., 1957.

BOOK ONE

A Survey of Roman and Byzantine Bureaucracies

•

BOOK TWO

Byzantine Bureaucracy from Within

•

BOOK THREE

John the Lydian
On the Magistracies of
the Roman Constitution
(De Magistratibus)

BOOK ONE

A Survey of Roman and Byzantine Bureaucracies

PREFACE

This book had its beginnings in 1963-5 in the University of Sydney when I tried to cope with a request from a very lively and intelligent body of students that we explore together the workings of political institutions in antiquity. These students all had some background in ancient history and many of them had done work in political science too. Together we surveyed democracy at Athens, oligarchy in Rome and bureaucracy in Byzantium. It rapidly became apparent that the books available in Byzantine bureaucracy tended to fall into two main categories, comprising either highly detailed specialist studies or a chapter or two in some general survey. It also emerged that the specialists, whether classicists or historians, tended to think very much in terms of work produced within the confines of their own disciplines.

In 1965-6 I had the good fortune to be a visitor at the Center for International Studies at M.I.T. where I participated in Fred Riggs' seminar "Studies in Comparative Bureaucracy" and in the "Man and Society" course run by the Department of Political Science. Books One and Two are largely based on work produced for these courses. The emphasis in this teaching was on an inter-disciplinary approach, which seemed to prove highly meaningful and stimulating to all involved. My subsequent experience in lecturing to survey courses in ancient history and in working with history method seminars at the University of Manitoba indicates that there is a very great deal of interest indeed in this inter-disciplinary method.

This book in consequence is neither a specialist historian's treatise nor yet a general survey. It aims to indicate systematically how a particular set of bureaucratic institutions affected its society, and it lets the bureaucrats involved tell their own story about this relationship. In so doing it employs concepts and methods of analysis which originate in several neighbouring disciplinary fields. So the discussion in this book can be related to the wider contemporary debate on the issues involved.

The readers for whom the book is written are primarily students in History and Political Science, secondarily those in Classics. However, the division of the work into three Books is meant to enable readers to select within it if they so desire. Classicists, for instance, should be particularly interested in the second Book. Hopefully, the work as a whole should prove of interest to those of the general reading public who read in the areas of history and the social sciences. Its bibliography has been evolved with this kind of readership in mind. It indicates something of the richness and variety of the disciplinary fields related to this subject. It should enable readers to go more deeply, or range more widely, into various of those fields. For the reader's convenience, every attempt has been made to cite works available in paperback and in English. Specifically, the book deals with the working of Byzantine bureaucracy and of the significance of that bureaucracy for its host society and times. "Bureaucracy" has been interpreted so as to include the ecclesiastical and military as well as the civil administrative hierarchies of officials. All three groups were bureaucratically organised, equally vital to the empire's existence, and competed in common for their resources of money and manpower. Each developed in a symbiotic relationship with the others. So to examine any one in isolation is to present a lopsided picture. Systems approaches now enable us to avoid this, by considering the interactions of all three as an on-going process.

Book I starts with an overall survey, to give a general impression of trends and environmental influences and so on. Book II concentrates on a shorter period, within that covered by the survey, so that readers can review the subject via the specificity of a case study. It is not a specialist treatise, but it has gone into detail where this is necessary to show the situational pressures on, or the life space surrounding, the bureaucrat on whom it largely centres. An original document is provided in translation (Book III), so that readers may themselves assess how that bureaucrat felt about his work. Relatively little work has been done on this bureaucrat. By making his writings available, together with a commentary, the work thus provides new data against which to check the various theories current on the working of bureaucracy in pre-industrial society.

It is my pleasant duty to record my debts to the people who have helped me. My thanks go to Edwin Judge and Dick Spann of the University of Sydney. But the major part of the stimulation for this work came from the scholars who made my stay at the Center for International Studies at M.I.T. so rewarding. I went there to work with Fred Riggs, to whose work I am deeply indebted for a series of insights.

At M.I.T. however there resided the most genial company of intellectual iconoclasts it has ever been my good fortune to fall in with. Dan Lerner taught me about multi-variate analysis; Ithiel Pool was always worth listening to on people's perceptions of communications; Harold Isaacs went about revealing the scratches on our minds. All stimulating in different ways were Amy Leiss, Tom Fisher, Bart Whaley and, in Classics, Harald Reiche. This is not an attempt to implicate any of these people in the infelicities which reviewers will no doubt find in this work, but simply a vote of thanks to them.

I am glad also to record my gratitude for the assistance which I have had from various foundations, and for the spirit in which that assistance was tendered. A Fulbright Fellowship made the year at M.I.T. possible. A summer research fellowship from the University of Manitoba's Faculty of Graduate Studies helped bring this book to publication. An award from the Killam Fund has given me the time, motivation and energy to write it up. One is always reading thanks in prefaces for such help; one has to toil under the work load of a departmental headship for a year or two before one fully appreciates their true significance.

To Miss Carol Clerihew, Mrs. Jean Birch and Mrs. Sherry McQuarrie go my thanks for turning a voluminous and untidy manuscript into the typescript copy for a book in the short time available. My editor and publisher John Longhurst is a kindred spirit. His brand of irreverent iconoclasm has somehow got me through the labour of writing up the various studies on which this book is based. If my thanks to him come last in this preface, they are certainly not thereby least.

T. F. Carney
Winnipeg, October, 1971

Chapter 1
Problems Involved in Studying Bureaucracy in Antiquity

Bureaucracy is one of those words, like democracy, which mean so many things to different persons. It can, for instance, mean the power of the bureaucrat, often his *undue* power, in everyday life. Or it can mean entangling red-tape. Or it can even, I suppose, mean the rational organization of group endeavours in a non-charismatic or non-family-dominated way. Such definitions all look to the functions of bureaucracy, how it works or affects people. Less controversially, one can define by structure, and say that a bureaucracy exists where one meets with a hierarchy of positions which constitute the offices of an organization. Now, clearly, such a definition will encompass other bodies than the civil administration of a state.[1] An army is, in these terms, bureaucratically organised. So is a church that can have a thousand officials associated with a huge building under an archbishop, and which includes archbishops, bishops and lesser clergy in a more territorially widespread disposition of its officials.[2] The focus of this book, accordingly, is upon all three organized hierarchies which were to be found from the late Roman world onwards: church, army and civil administration (the group for which alone the term "bureaucracy" is normally reserved).

There is no one study, to my knowledge, which provides a survey of the Roman and Byzantine bureaucracies when they are defined in this way. However studies which focus on any one of the three organized hierarchies involved have always to deal, at some point or other, with the other two.[3] For all three drew upon the manpower and financial resources of the Empires which supported them, and which they, in turn, supported. One writer on bureaucracy speaks of the scanty surpluses which these non-industrial, agriculturally based societies could wrest from their toiling rural populations as 'free floating resources.'[4] Any group which had the crucial role of allocating these scarce resources was inevitably subjected to what can at best be euphemistically described as 'influence attempts' by its fellow groups, who were, after all, competitors for those same resources. Thus the fortunes of all three were closely intertwined. Consequently to look at any one of the three on its own will produce all the distortions proverbially associated with a one-sided view of a situation.

There are three major sources of difficulty involved in attempting a survey of this nature. One is the complexity of the bureaucracies themselves. The second is their tangled inter-relationships. The third involves new insights in regard to interpreting the above. Firstly there is the sheer historical complexity of the three organizations involved. Although bureaucracies often seem to the outsider to be unchanging, unresponsive monolithic structures, actually they have a sort of dynamic equilibrium. That is to say, they are constantly shifting and changing their inner organizations the better to cope with pressures which they perceive to be coming from within and without. So posts, titles and functions constantly shift into new patterns in each group, in response to an equally fluctuating pattern of pressures upon the Empires which were the host-societies for these groups. A survey can at best hope to trace the major trends in all of this. Especially as, then as now, much that goes on within a bureaucracy received little publicity, making the historian's task in reconstructing events more than usually hazardous.[5]

The inadequacy of the source material does in fact pose real problems. Roman history under the Empire centres on warfare, diplomacy, court intrigue and, in general, on the doings of those in high places. Writers take knowledge of how the administration worked for granted in their readers. It was a dull subject on which no one who wanted a reputation for readability would write. One has usually, as a result, to glean evidence from references made in passing, and piece these together, to reconstruct the workings of that administration. One is however helped in attempts at reconstruction by the Roman habit of leaving a full record of a man's career on his tombstone. Enough such evidence remains to enable career sequences and patterns to be traced. The law codes, produced though they were in the *subsequent* era, also yield insights into the operations of various governmental departments — if only by indicating their defaults, very often. Legends (i.e. brief public-relations type catch-phrases) and mint-marks on the imperial coinage add a few more scanty clues. Reconstruction of a garment which is in such a state of rags and tatters allows considerable diversity of interpretation, readers must be warned.

If one takes Byzantine history to begin with the foundation of Constantinople (and this is probably the most reasonable and widely agreed upon starting point), then the situation is somewhat better. After all, this world was bestridden from the outset by large organized bodies and so thought in terms of them. To this period, in fact, there date several documents which are specifically concerned with the detailed working of the various bureaucracies. The *Notitia Dignitatum (List of High Offices)* details the civil and military officials, their staffs and insignia and, in the case of the military, their stations. The *De Magistratibus (On the Magistracies)* of Count John of Lydia, on which the present work is largely based, gives a history of his own particular department. Lord Cassiodorus' *Variae*, a collection of official correspondence and documents, preserve some of the actual business done by a senior bureaucrat. There are various treatises on ceremonial, including Philotheos' *Kletorologion*, a sort of official order of seating for official occasions. There is a treatise on imperial administration (whose contents do not fully live up to the expectations roused by its title as it contains much historical narrative). And there are various military treatises on tactics, even one on the themes, as the military administrative zones dating from seventh century Byzantium were known. To the Byzantine period too date the various collections of laws; and seals, indicative of trade and customs practices, are also extant in fair numbers. The writings of the church fathers, and histories by churchmen, shed light upon the organization of the ecclesiastical bureaucracy too, though such writings have been more thoroughly investigated for their doctrinal than for their historical implications by modern scholars.

It is worth noting that modern scholarship, the invaluable secondary sources whose reinterpretation does so much to shape our views of the past as transmitted by the original sources, has given most of its attention to the Roman Empire, especially the early Empire, and far less to Byzantium. As discussions of the Pirenne Thesis showed,[6] the Middle Ages have also tended to be viewed from the perspective of the Latinized West, with Byzantium and Islam receiving less than their proper share of attention. However, culture-boundedness varies from one national group to another, so there have always been some scholars for whom Byzantium was more important than the Latin West. But, as the Slav and Middle European scholars have neither the language medium nor communications outlets which would carry their work most readily to an English-reading audience, this has not helped until of late, when Byzantine studies have been receiving a little more prominence.[7]

Another two major difficulties have already been foreshadowed. There is the business of tracing the complex interweaving of such a set of on-going inter-relationships. Then there is the matter of doing so

- 3 -

while keeping in mind the insights and interpretations suggested by current scholarly work on bureaucracy as a phenomenon. Naturally a topic as important as bureaucracy is to twentieth century hyper-organized man receives a good deal of attention. It is not easy for a non-specialist to pick (or even find) his way through the profusion of studies and schools of thought which have resulted. So there will be no pretence to an exhaustive survey of the field. Rather, this chapter will set out ideas, produced by specialist workers on bureaucracy, which have particular importance for the understanding of assumptions then held as to what bureaucracy was all about or should be doing.

But first let us look at the second problem, that of tracing the tangled relations of the three bureaucratically organized groups as their fortunes waxed and waned across the period. One cannot simply as it were slice through the middle of the sixth century, the period upon which this book is focussed, and reveal a cross-section of the current balance of forces, then extrapolate backwards and forwards. This will not give a sense of the developing situation, since developments took the form of massive changes which altered the course and nature of the bureaucracies and host society involved. And if our particular bureaucrats cannot be seen by us as in a field of forces generated by the on-going situation in which they were caught up, then it will be impossible to appreciate their position and their feelings.

There are at least three levels of relationships that need to be considered, and simultaneously at that. The first involves change within any one bureaucracy itself. The second involves change in the relations of the three bureaucracies with one another. The third involves change in the environment within which all three operated. Change in the latter would necessarily bring changes in the other two, and so on. A brief review of some developments at each level will illustrate what is involved.

The first *Princeps*, as the ruler of Rome's Empire and director of her government was initially known, could not wholly depend upon the Senate, the aristocratic class which had hitherto run Rome's affairs, to administer under and for him. So he used the freed slaves of his extended household to perform some functions, and created new posts, for trusty creatures, to perform others. With governing powers increasingly devolving upon the *Princeps*, the functions (and numbers) of his various officials grew. Emperors came and went. There were four in one year in 69 A.D., an unusually rapid turn-over. Imperial dynasties, too, passed away. The imperial officials, however, stayed on, and grew in effective (implementing) power, especially when the tempo of the game of imperial chairs was rapid or their holders incompetent. These officials regularized their positions, and extended and rationalized their functions. Hence the 'model' administrative bureaucracy of the Antonines, anonymous and competent. Then various among the officials came to be empowered over others (the Praetorian Prefect by the Severan dynasty for instance), so power constellations built up within the bureaucracy. Hence our word 'Pretorianism': by the third century these Prefects were so influential that they could make and unmake Emperors. Constantine dealt with this problem by raising another official, the Master of Offices, in importance; considerably weakening the Praetorian Prefect; and setting the two in a relationship wherein they inevitably conflicted with (and thereby controlled) one another. Justinian seems to have tried to do away with the built-up aggregations of power within the civil administration. He tried to make that administration into a series of minor functionaries and instrumentalities rather than a few large constellations of office and power. And so it went. Each of the bureaucracies was kept internally seething, as it were, in this way. If it was not departmental empire-building that was going on, then it would be power-plays or court intrigues. Morale and code of ethics varied with the fortunes of one's department, bishopric or unit within each overall bureaucracy. Thus the internal histories of the bureaucracies were records of ups and downs, rejoicings and despairings.

The balance of power between the various bureaucracies was no more stable. This will emerge from the following brief review of the ups and downs they individually experienced. At the outset of the period under consideration the Senate had just been edged aside from power by the Emperor. Senatorial influence was still very considerable however. It would appear that not till after the death of the first Emperor did contemporaries fully appreciate how great a shift of power there had in fact been. At one stage it was fashionable among modern scholars to speak of a 'joint rule' of Senate and Emperor at this point. By the second century the Emperor was clearly in control, but the moral influence of, and administrative assistance rendered by, the Senate was considerable. In the third century however the Senate was pushed aside from power by the military. Though it enjoyed something of a recrudescence of power and prestige under Constantine the Great in the fourth century, it never again was effectively to wield power.

It was the growth in power of the military that had brought the Republic down and led to the establishment of the Principate. Perhaps the greatest achievement of the first *Princeps* was that he changed the nature of the armies of the late Republic. These had become the political instruments of the men whose charisma had brought them together, somewhat like giant free-booting expeditions. They were transformed into docile long-service units of professionals, safe and a-political upon distant frontiers. Identification with the regions in which they were based begins later in the century, and seems to have grown during the deep peace of the Antonines. The time of troubles in the third century saw an enormous increase in military numbers and political power. This growth was maintained in the reorganization (involving a frontier militia, a central strategic reserve of professionals, and a yet further increase in numbers) at the turn of the century. In the fifth century, in the West the military became all-powerful, and after a series of puppet-Emperors Odoacer, a barbarian military man and king-maker, finally seized control. In the East the civil administration managed to increase the number of military commanders and, by producing a situation of counter-vailing powers, to bring them under control. Justinian's wars in the sixth century, however, involved dangerous mandates of power, and to combat Islam in the seventh century a themal organization was created which henceforth threatened to carve the Empire up into an assemblage of feudal baronies.

As we will see in more detail later, the power of the civil administration grew piecemeal in the first century, consolidated in the second, gained immense strategic importance in the third and developed into a mammoth bureaucracy in the fourth. It was to weaken in the West in the fifth but continued to be of central importance in the East for that century. Thereafter a diminution in its powers is probable.

Most striking however is the organizational history of the Christian Church. It started out as a congeries of groups of believers in this town and that, with only the link of a common faith to help the faithful if they moved between towns. It grew in the second century, after the Jews had been scattered, into a flock guided and guarded by bishops with long range connections. In the third century its organization, modelled on that of the Roman Empire — for it too was comprised within the organizational divisions of that Empire — became equipped with doctrine, learning and bishops with powers of discipline and intermediacy. In the fourth century it was first officially recognised and established, and then it became the sole religion of Empire. As the Church came to be identified with the Establishment, dissidence grew within its ranks. By the fifth century the Church was heavily involved in the world, in administering law, and with its growing affluence. Its power was to continue to grow, as were its schisms.[8]

- 6 -

This survey does not mean to suggest that this kind of change terminated after the sixth or seventh century. Such is far from the case. It is merely designed to show, by reviewing a period relevant to the issues upon which this book is centred, how extensive and how continuous such change was. Thus the first century A.D. started with the Senate in a strong power position, relative to the other groups, the army in a moderately strong one, and the nascent imperial administrative bureaucracy in a weak, or at least undeveloped, position. The Christian Church did not as yet exist. By the second century the Senate's position of power had slipped to one of moderate influence only; the army's remained constant, or had developed somewhat. It was the administrative bureaucracy which had grown enormously in power, probably almost attaining equal importance with the army. The Christian church was by now definitely a factor, if only a minor one, to be considered. By the third century the Senate had fallen catastrophically from power, the army was dominant and the administrative bureaucracy, although enjoying less prestige, came a very close second to the army. The Christian Church was by now an organized body which had to be given very serious consideration — in the form of persecutions — indeed. By the fourth century that Church had moved dramatically forward to prominence and power within the Empire. Possibly the administrative bureaucracy was the most important entity in this organizational complex, but army power was still high. The Senate's position had by now deteriorated beyond recovery; it was to have only social importance for the future.

Admittedly, such generalizations are impressionistic, but they merely represent received opinion in each of their several areas and thus simply collect and compare a number of summaries which are generally made independently. There is something of a feud for pre-eminence, initially between the Senate, the military and the administrative bureaucracy; then between the latter two; then between these two and the Church — which, after all, like the other two, was exerting its claims on men's bodies and their labour. So the power position of any one group varies with the total, overall patterning of the mix of groups.

Finally, and on the third level, the environment of these groups changed also. We are apparently simply being twentieth century chauvinists in assuming that massive rapid change is a feature of modern, rather than of traditional, society. Even a cursory survey of the period already reviewed will indicate this. The survey will consider socio-economic change within the Empires of Rome and Byzantium. It will also consider technological change, and changes in what might be called the state of international relations.

The first century A.D. saw the institution of a new order, called 'the Principate' by contemporaries. This had the effect of altering the composition of the ruling echelons of Roman Society: in place of metropolitan Roman nobles it came to be wealthy provincials who ran Rome's government. The deep plough was introduced in Europe, altering the kind of farming and land usage possible. Gaul throve, with the advent of Roman roads, banking techniques and new flora and fauna — and the money poured into the paying of the legions along the Rhine (where Rome's crack legions were stationed in force). Italy began to go into a recession. Glass blowing was discovered about the beginning of the first century, and superior wares began as result to be produced, in Egypt and Syria. Later, the monsoons were discovered and trade out of Egypt with India and Ceylon and parts further East built up rapidly. The Parthians, who were not an aggressive people, were the only civilised foe beyond the periphery of the Empire.

The second century saw Roman society in effect change from one consisting of a spectrum of statuses — Senator, Knight, citizen, freedman (ex-slave), provincial and slave — to one consisting of two groups only: *honestiores* (the 'better people,' constituted, virtually, of those with the property qualifications for Knighthood, 200,000 *asses*) and *humiliores* (the 'humbler kind,' i.e. everyone else). It saw a shift from big estates run by slaves to share-cropping 'free' tenants on smaller estates. Both of these developments lessened the ignominious plight of the slave, if only by making it less distinguishable from that of the poor citizenry. Slaves were by now, after all, harder to come by. This change in the basic forces of production was not unconnected with a growing man-power shortage within the Empire. Marcus Aurelius seems to have brought back from the East something like small-pox, and the disease wrought horrendous ravages among the Empire's population. The Danube was now recognized as the most threatened military zone and wars were fought away in the East to establish control of the lucrative caravan routes.

The third century witnessed a series of attacks on the Danubian frontier by barbarians who were now well trained and equipped and massed into large ethnic units. Weakened by the civil wars of the end of the second century, Rome's defences were breached. The invaders were eventually driven back, but only at enormous cost. Between them the military and the civil administration extracted so much from the town population of the Empire that the towns of the West anyway never recovered. Not that the rural population fared better; indeed uprisings and what was termed (from the government's viewpoint) 'banditry' became endemic and threatening in the countryside. But anyway, peasant and rural landowing elements (army occupations upon retirement) were advanced in society at the expense of the more cultured and literate townspeople. The currency collapsed and Rome reverted to dealings in kind. A new dynasty, the Sassanids, took over from the (Arsacid) Parthians in the East and proved a much more aggressive neighbour.

By the fourth century a new system of government, called the Dominate, had appeared. It had all the pomp and circumstance traditional to the despots of the ancient Near East. Men were forced to remain in their professions, trades or callings. A form of caste system resulted, with the labourers on the land as a type of serf. Whole tribal units of barbarians were admitted into the Empire as *Foederati* (federates): in return for the land granted them they were to provide military service. As towns in the West shrank in size, roads deteriorated and large private estates centred upon villas built up, so there seems to have been some migration of erstwhile Western commercial and manufacturing populations (often Syrian in origin) to the East. Asia Minor, Syria and Egypt now became the centres of trade and manufacture for an empire which, with the building of Constantinople, was dividing increasingly into Latin-speaking Western and Greek-speaking Eastern sections. Christianity, with its non-Classical world-view and values, now triumphed. New art-forms came to predominate.

The fifth century saw the West invaded, the Mediterranean over-run by Vandal fleets (so that fortifications now became necessary if towns fronted on to what had for so long been a Roman lake). It saw Attila on the move, probably much assisted by the breast-strap harness, which considerably augmented the potential of the horse power available, and probably not so much assisted by outbreaks of anthrax. Rome was sacked and a thrill of horror ran through the civilised world. Antioch in Syria, by way of contrast, had its streets lit by street lights at night: the East had not suffered by being over-run by the invaders. The waterwheel seems to have made its appearance in the West, probably in response to critically low levels of man-power supplies.

Again, this is not to suggest that the rate of change in subsequent centuries was less. Such was not the case. But, clearly, the resources upon which the various bureaucracies could draw were undergoing violent changes and enormous strains and stresses came to bear upon the empire as a whole. So it could not but be that the positions and fortunes of the bureaucracies too should undergo a like buffeting. For

- 9 -

instance, the collapse of the currency in the third century, and spiralling inflation both in that and the following century, made nonsense of the pegged official salaries of the administrative bureaucracy and led directly to all sorts of excesses in bribery and corruption. The whole moral and ethical code of this once proud group changed.

Perhaps a criterion which may help in cross-comparing the bureaucracies at various periods is that involved in classifying power relationships in the political scientist's terms of weight, domain, range and scope. By 'weight' is generally meant the ability of a governor or government or what have you to change the outcome of events. Thus the weight of an Emperor's power varied greatly across the period: when an Emperor could call upon readily available feelings of patriotism and could easily command and discipline his bureaucratic instrumentalities he was clearly in a better position than when he could do neither of these things. It is illuminating to compare, say, Augustus and Severus Alexander in these regards. By 'domain' is meant the area over which an Emperor's word was law. A glance at the maps of the Roman and Byzantine Empires, century by century, will show immediately how much this area fluctuated. By 'range' is meant the kinds of rewards and penalties which an Emperor could administer. Both escalate across the period, the latter dramatically. By 'scope' is meant the sorts of things which are regarded as subject to the exercise of power. The Church was increasingly to circumscribe these and so were the border barons, though there were *reprises* of imperial power. So this criterion too indicates the variable nature of the power position of the government with which our bureaucracies were associated.

Change thus came from inside, in between, and from outside the three hierarchically organized groups under consideration. It was often of very considerable proportions, though this could be obscured by the habit which these groups all had of retaining traditional forms. An attempt has just been made to indicate the extent of change by providing, in succession, chronological accounts of changes occurring at each of the three levels. But this method of exposition cannot relate the overall configuration, at all levels simultaneously, of one period so that it can be contrasted with a similar overall configuration at another.

An attempt will be made to delineate this complex inter-relationship by reviewing the relative power-positions of all the groups concerned. This will be done at each of a series of what are by general agreement historical turning points; points, that is, which involve major changes either for the bureaucracies or for their environment. To give us a vantage point from which to view the data I will attempt to follow the fortunes of the Praetorian Prefect and his staff, or their bureaucratic descendants, amid all of this. This procedure will provide a form of measure against which to assess the magnitude and direction of changes and developments. But, inevitably, such a survey will necessitate some attempt to isolate out the more important aspects of the various bureaucracies or their operations. The insights generated by the specialists who work on bureaucracy are most helpful in directing one's attention to what these may have been. For we have now to deal with the third of the problems mentioned at the outset, that of identifying those issues likely to have been of particular importance in bureaucracies of the kind involved, i.e. those within an agriculturally-based society with pre-industrial technology and family systems.

The following discussion is, then, an attempt to appraise the political culture[9] of Byzantium, for Byzantium *was* its various hierarchically organized groups. First it will briefly review the institutional background, and will try to indicate how Byzantine institutions as it were locked that Empire into a situation wherein there was little opening for progress and development. Secondly it will examine the political process, which did not engender an over-riding concern with the advancement of what moderns would define as the public interest. Finally it will attempt to suggest something of the climate of popular feeling within which Byzantine government operated, showing something of the political vision of the man in the streets of this traditional society.

In the history of the Greek and Latin civilizations of antiquity the periods of democratic governance were in fact short-lived. The major upsurge of democratic institutions in Greece is generally associated with Athenian democracy. This lasted from the 450's to 323 B.C. The Roman Republic, which seems actually to have been something of a *façade* behind which small aristocratic cliques ran the government, allowed freedom of speech and debate from 287, when popular meetings gained unfettered freedom to vote, until 31 B.C. These periods produced such an outpouring of genius at the time, and have engrossed so much attention subsequently, that it is not fully realised how authoritarian, by and large, were the civilizations, especially that of Rome, which produced them. The Minoans and Mycenaeans operated through a hierarchically organized system on bureaucratic lines, which they borrowed from the older and more developed civilizations of the ancient Near East. Dark Age, Archaic and Classical Greece (democracy occurred within the latter period) were unusual in their independence from influences emanating from that region.

Hellenistic Greeks were governed under bureaucratic institutions taken therefrom, or lived on the periphery of kingdoms so governed. Initially Rome, far away in the more backward West, was run under city-state institutions. But once Egypt and the fertile crescent was firmly in her grasp, she too contracted therefrom an autocratic form of government backed up by a bureaucratic apparatus. And Byzantium simply carried this structure over when Rome fell, in the West. Wittfogel has made his case well.[10] The apparatus which bureaucracies evolved to cope with the great riverine civilizations of Mesopotamia and Egypt were organizationally superior to other forms of government produced in this culture area and in that comprised by the ancient and to a large extent medieval Mediterranean. Certainly they repeatedly exported themselves Westward to the latter area. They constituted the form of governance to which the peoples of their time and area repeatedly reverted, the background, as it were, of their political thinking.

If one reviews the various forms of political organization which occurred in this whole general culture area during antiquity, one finds three in particular: tribal, autocracy with a bureaucratic apparatus, and city state. A fourth, feudalism, appears, at least in embryonic form, before the middle ages: there were the Spartan helots, the *coloni* or share-croppers attached to the Roman *villa* and the *foederati* or *laeti* (conquered peoples, transported *en masse* across the Empire's borders and settled on Roman lands to provide various services without full citizen rights).[11] Now even modern political systems, and they are admittedly by no means perfect, do not have many sorts of political machinery with which to go about their business; but the communities under consideration had still less. Moderns operate with some form of executive, bureaucratic instrumentalities, legislatures and political parties. Each of these institutional forms enables the community which possesses it to do certain things. The Romans and Byzantines had only the first two. The legislature, involving majoritarianism, the concept of the rule of law, and representation, was an invention of the Western middle ages. Of the related concepts, only that of the rule of law (in the form of constitutionalism) dates to Graeco-Roman antiquity, and it flourished only when democracy did. Political parties, which are quite different from factions, are only about two hundred years old.[12] Without a legislature and political parties, two things happen. Executive — priest-king and trader, kingly overlord, champion of wandering tribe, hereditary king, tyrant, dictator, *Princeps* or *Dominus Noster* (Our Lord), to list forms relevant to the experience of the societies which produced the Empires studied here — and bureaucracy cannot be checked, and they attract all political talent to themselves, for there is nowhere else for it to go and be effective. Hence an all-powerful government. Secondly it is very difficult indeed, under these circumstances, to produce an informed citizen body which feels it to be its duty actively to participate in politics.[13] In a crisis popular support *may* be mobilized behind the government, but such a state of affairs is very far from being usual. More commonly the feelings engendered in the lower orders of society varied between apathy, aversion, dread and hostility.

The non-availability of legislature and political parties had other consequences too, which affected the bureaucratically dominated Empires in a variety of ways. For instance, these Empires were bedevilled by the dangers of over-centralization and of fragmentation simultaneously. Too great a mandate of power and an Emperor would raise up a subject too dangerous to be controllable. Pretorianism would result, as we have already seen. But if distant officials were given even moderate mandates of power, in an effort to disperse power-centres and avoid over-centralization, then, with the poor transport and communications facilities of this level of civilization, 'frontier feudalism' resulted. A German commander with his *comitatus* (sworn following of fief holders) on his *villa* in land assigned to his *foedorati* would not meekly submit to the tax collectors of the administrative bureaucracy. Nor would an Alexandrian archbishop, nor a border baron, lord protector of this themal area. Feudalism is thus not a form of relationship which only occurs later in the medieval West, but rather a type of relationship which co-exists with apparatus bureaucracy, ever ready to start up on its further or more impenetrable fringes. Hence resort was frequently had to the device of setting two or more powerful bureaucratic groups organizationally at odds with one another, by allocating to them overlapping spheres of influence or the like. The aim of this arrangement was to prevent either the building up or the hiving off of powerful groups. Its consequences, however, were that the bureaucracy was hampered in its activities and could neither be deployed nor controlled (as responsibility would be difficult to locate). Indeed, often the resultant chaos would eventually necessitate a concentration of power somewhere within the bureaucracy to reorganize the administration back into a state wherein it could function effectively.[14]

As the autocrat (for want of a better word) who governed one of these empires through his apparatus of bureaucrats could not depend on solid popular support, it was crucial that he should control certain resources and facilities. Most basic were man-power and taxation resources. Army recruitment was always an area which received ample official attention: promotions, incentives, privileges, pay-scales and pensions loom large in the literary, legal, inscriptional and numismatic records. *Corvée* or forced labour of one type or another was readily had recourse to; from the very beginnings of Empire Augustus, for instance, could impress other people's slaves for government service,[15] and this was the mildest form which such impressments were to assume. Taxation engrossed a like amount of attention. In a way confiscation acted like a kind of super-tax upon the very rich. From the earliest times, Emperors badly in need of money (Nero for instance, and Domitian) secured it in this way.[16] In fact the growth of large estates always meant difficulties for the central government and its tax extracting agencies. In this respect it is probably true to say that the Emperors loved the more defenceless 'little man.' Anyway confiscation was always a very sensitive issue around which powerful forces played. A government which habitually practiced forced labour and the confiscation of large fortunes did not provide an environment within which large-scale mercantile business could grow and flourish. So vested interests of a business nature could exert only a weak countervailing pressure against the government's massed bureaucratic might.

In ancient society there seems to have been a tiny literate elite and a huge illiterate mass.[17] Skills and wealth were not dispersed across the population as they are, to a certain extent, in a modern industrialized society. Rather a small group engrossed all the advantages of wealth, education and organizational skills. Such men were needed for the armies, for the administrative bureaucracy and for the local town councils through which so much on-the-spot administration was channelled. When the Church began to make inroads into this pool of man-power, taking men off into monasteries and so forth, the inelasticity of this resource rapidly became apparent. From the autocrat's point of view, it was of the utmost importance that the 'right' men be available and be placed in the upper echelons of the army, administration and Church; thereafter they could be depended upon to look after other junior appointments. It was also essential that the main religious bodies and their administrative apparatuses should be loyal to his rule. Hence persecution of the Christian church when it was a weak out-group and Caesaropapism (the rule over the Church by the Emperor from within it) when it had grown to become a powerful in-group. Hence too the fact that religious issues rapidly become political. In societies prior to the age of belief in pluralism there could only be one authority and one directing purpose. The upshot, in any case, was that the three hierarchically organized groups of the government took to themselves all of the Empire's resources of skilled man-power. Hence politics was much dominated by the in-fighting of the Establishment wherein nearly all the skill and talent was located.

If power is like the musculature of a horse, say, and institutions resemble its skeletal structure, then communications are the nervous system which stimulate the rest to action. In an age without mass media, telecommunications and rapid transit systems, speedy communications conferred enormous strategic advantages on those who had access to them. Hence imperial care was lavished upon the upkeep of the roads and upon the imperial pony express which could travel so rapidly along them, switching horses at stations positioned along the way. Hence also special transportation services for those travelling under the Emperor's orders, whatever the cost to dwellers along the route, whose labour, foodstuffs, beasts or conveyances might be impressed at need. And the ministry charged with the upkeep of these facilities, which appear in most text-books under the innocuous name of the Public Post (a direct translation of *cursus publicus*), was generally also charged with supervision of the secret service and *agents provocateurs* who complemented such an information network. Thus the sector of the civil administration which is charged with looking after the communications network is of the utmost importance to the Emperor. Any growth in its facilities, any organizational improvement, means a direct augmentation of that Emperor's power — as long as he could control the head of the department containing the secret police, of course.

Major building operations take capital, planning and man-power. They can pump-prime a flagging local economy or add an instrumentality which changes the whole potential of a region. They assemble and deploy large groups of able-bodied men. They provide employment and give high prestige to those responsible for initiating the programme of building. They are political, that is; so it is the Emperors who are the great builders.[18] After the fall of the Republic there came an end to the practice whereby aristocrats had the roads or the temples which they had built named after them. As any urban renewal project can show you, a major building programme is never merely a matter of the economics of bricks and mortar.

Now an Emperor's agents are more essential to him than he is to them. For, observably, Emperors can come and go without much impact on the bureaucracies massed around and beneath them, whereas a major breakdown in a key sector of a bureaucracy may cost an Emperor his life. Claudius, for instance, was almost stoned to death early in his reign because of a breakdown in Rome's grain provisioning services.[19] Interests of Emperor and his apparatus bureaucrats need not, then, coincide. In fact surveys of bureaucracies of the traditional type in pre-industrial societies of different cultural backgrounds show that there are certain recurring friction points and lines of strain, or, so to say, a political process and style which go with such bureaucracies. Let us now turn to take a look at these things.

First of all, the bureaucracies with which we are dealing here had a kind of life cycle. This appears most clearly in the case of the civil administrative bureaucracy.[20] Initially it is the tool which a usurping autocrat, and his immediate successors, build up to help in carrying out the basic administrative tasks with which they are faced. The former administrators, an aristocratic group, will not cooperate in a venture which can only lead to their own further undoing. The problems of this stage of the cycle involve the attraction of suitable men and the most effective identification and execution of strategically important functions and tasks. Then, as the dynasty regresses and the bureaucracy progresses, the bureaucracy reaches functioning maturity. Problems of this stage involve its own regulating of the services which it itself provides and of its own inner workings. Finally comes a struggle by various highly-placed interest groups to take over the no longer disesteemed bureaucracy. This struggle, if successful, carves the bureaucracy up into an often embattled array of, as it were, little fiefdoms. Problems of this stage concern the competence and integrity with which the bureaucracy functions, and its overall direction and effectiveness.

The different stages of this struggle see different parties participating in it. Initially the struggle is between the autocrats and the old guard of aristocrats or previous power holders. The term bureaucracy can sometimes at this stage overly dignify the nascent organization, which may as yet be a motley collection of members of an extended family and various creatures of the autocrat. It is a docile tool of the autocrat, functions as yet imperfectly and has little social esteem. By the time the second stage is reached, the struggle is between the bureaucracy and the various social groups whose activities it is regulating. It is an effective instrumentality and is seen as such. It is beginning to create a prestigeful image for itself. The final stage sees one social group fighting with another for control of a now much esteemed prize, namely the monopoly of positions of control within the bureaucracy. Landowning military men and wealthy townee aristocrats both now feel such positions not to be beneath them, indeed to be vital to attain.

Attitudes have shifted. In the initial stages the question was: what shall be the relation between the governed (the ex-power wielders) and the governors (the new apparatus of administration)? Later it is: Who (shall govern) Whom? Though apparently assuming more acceptance of the established order of doing things, the latter question can result in as much political change as can the former. In a society which had not as yet realised the advantages of a pluralistic interest-group and value system, a monopoly of power in the hands of the apparatus was accepted. The whole background of thinking about human relationships, in a society dominated at its upper levels by extended families and a backward looking educational system, was authoritarian. Hence the posture of the bureaucracy towards the general public was one of officials towards a subject population. On one side were massed all the advantages of wealth, skill and education, for there were no bureaucracies outside the governmental to countervail against them. The corporation was as yet in a rudimentary stage of evolution, there was no independent judiciary (far less an independent press), and the Churoh was part of the Establishment. The psychic costs of this situation for the lowly were alienation and apathy, if not when times were bad, downright *anomie*, i.e. a condition of not being able to identify common values or reasons for group identity. And the alienation of the subject population increased as the bureaucracy became increasingly engrossed in advancing its own interests, for such was what was happening in the latter stages of the cycle which is under discussion.

In contrast to the humble folk, however, other members of the elite from which the men of the apparatus were drawn had inner lines of communication through an 'old-boy' net-work or circle of acquaintance. They were brought up in the same culture, the Great Tradition of Graeco-Roman literature (whereas the humble had only their diverse local peasant customs and popular beliefs), so could readily communicate with the bureaucrats. Dog did not eat dog. Disciplining such men from above was as difficult as it was easy for them to obtain special treatment. In fact the people who effectively shaped imperial policy were those clustered in strategic sub-departments dealing with the vested interests of their peer groups outside the bureaucracy. Such men, at the very least, would look forward to a dignified retirement as a country gentleman and would consequently favour policies not inimical to such a goal. Hence under-exaction from those who could most afford to pay (and over-exaction from those who could least afford to do so) was not unusual. This was a further reason for alienation in circles outside that of the sub-elite enjoying such favoured access to the men of the apparatus of government.

If one wishes to control a bureaucracy, the critical issues are those of recruitment and discipline. According to the practices followed in these matters, bureaucratic morale rises or falls. Whoever controls discipline retrospectively controls the actions of the bureaucracy. It is consequently of the utmost importance that bureaucrats should themselves staff, and make the decisions in, any disciplinary body. If they cannot, prestige and morale drop away, for the bureaucrats may be tried by criteria other than those on which they must act in their work. If they can, then the possibility of control from above, or indeed outside, the bureaucracy is severely limited. There was no independent judiciary in antiquity, yet this is the only way out of the above dilemma, which follows along with 'political' justice.

Equally crucial is the matter of recruitment and, going along with it, of promotion. An Emperor could pack the higher reaches of an administration with his own men. If he did so by ignoring promotion patterns favoured within that administration, morale would crumple. The guidelines by which to direct a career would be gone and men with different values than those endorsed by the bureaucracy would be running its affairs. The strategies that pay well in the long, grim, grey haul step by step upwards within the bureaucracy are not those of the courtier. Yet it was the latter type of strategy which won a man access to a top-level position, for this was a matter in which the Emperor was likely to be involved. Consequently it often happened in antiquity that, just as there was a gulf between the men of the apparatus (who were a literary elite) and the populace in general, so there was also a gulf between the lower and middle echelons of the bureaucracy and its more rarified upper levels. At the very top were the aristocrats; elsewhere there were worthies from lower down the social scale, if still among the 'top people' — small town big-wigs for example. Anyway, the conferring of titles was a matter around which powerful forces played: whether these involved recruitment, promotion or even final reward upon retirement, they shaped policy, prestige and preferment within the apparatus. Purchase of office was another equally important issue area. Sale of an office could bring in money which a ruler might desperately need and might well simultaneously thwart a creeping power build-up within a department. But it did so at the cost of immediate efficiency and of long-term control and responsiveness within the administration. The main point, however, is that there were tensions within the ranks of the bureaucracy for an Emperor to play upon.

The autocrat had an obvious strategy to use. He could build up an inner court, men in but not of the bureaucracy, loyal to him and strategically situated within it. He could, for instance, favour the use of eunuchs. The latter could hardly found a dynasty within their bureaucratic domain, so could be employed without casting a shadow over the administrative future as it were; and, as they generally came from outside the social circles held in esteem, they were the autocrat's 'men' in a very special way. But the bureaucrats too had a strategy, that of using the *camarilla*. When the monarch is above the law, the succession tends very much to be a tricky business involving court intrigues and coldly calculated power politics.[21] A small but strategically located group could thus abuse their position in the inner workings of the court and administration to prepare the way for an Emperor of their choice. And a 'good' Emperor in the eyes of such a group might well appear a very young or docile or incompetent ruler to outsiders. More than one Emperor was thus pre-selected by the apparatus in anticipation that he would prove malleable, if not incompetent.

The distinction which moderns tend to make between politics as decision-making and administration as 'mere' implementation of those decisions made even less sense then than it does now. The setting of priorities and amounts of resources committed to each are 'political' decisions readily taken within the 'administrative' process even in this age which can check on such things. The Byzantine law-codes contain instance after instance of attempts by the Emperors to legislate against bureaucratic malpractices which still recur, for all their efforts. Manifestly, the bureaucrats *could* take the law into their own hands with impunity. There was no representative or 'participatory' bureaucracy in these Empires. The administration was uniformly staffed by men of an elite which constituted only a fraction of the total population. Hence outcry against social injustice from within the bureaucracy was not forthcoming. Furthermore the overlapping spheres of influence which abounded within the civil administration led to the build-up of super-departments, combining a multiplicity of services. This happened if only to triumph over tendencies to paralysis and entropy when there was a major, urgent task which just had to be done. The development of the Praetorian Prefecture, which provided manpower and food supplies for the Empire in general in the chaotic second half of the third century, is a case in point. Such super-departments were virtually beyond discipline. For all these reasons, all too frequently the various bureaucracies were each individually, on more than one occasion, 'a law unto themselves.' Basically they were all, and not least the civil administration, in a very strong power position. The latter for instance was the mediator in the allocation of its society's scarce surplus resources. And in striking contrast to the power of the bureaucracies is the extreme weakness of the constraints upon the exercise of that power.

This all conjures up a picture of a bureaucracy which is a far cry from the neutral, a-political, public-service-oriented instrumentality, with goals of rationality and efficiency, posited by Weberian theorisings on the 'ideal' bureaucratic type.[22] It is difficult to draw organizational charts of these bureaucracies in ways that would be meaningful to an advocate of scientific management. But this does not mean that these bureaucracies did not function effectively. There is in fact every indication that they were all too efficacious when it came to tax extraction, for instance.[23] Even in the modern world there are situations in which nepotism and the promotion of men with aptitudes and background ill-suited to career bureaucrats manifestly pay off well.[24] These traditional bureaucracies were adapted to their environments. Features which moderns regard as corrupt or irrational were very often necessary adaptive mechanisms.[25] The standards applicable to nineteenth century Prussian bureaucracy or twentieth century American corporate administration are those which tend, unconsciously on our parts, to shape our thinking[26] — as does psychoanalysis when we thing about personality, or Marxism when we think of economics. So a brief indication will be attempted of the ways in which their background of thought and action, as a coherent cultural whole, as it were, differed from what we moderns assume to be 'normal.' The contrasting depictions will be set out in two parallel columns to make the comparison easier for the reader to find his way around in them.

A difficulty which meets us at the outset is that 'the voices of antiquity speak to us in cultured tones'; that is, we are presented with those aspects of antiquity that were important in the eyes of its literate elite. But more is becoming known about how the other ninety percent lived. Archaeological finds of artifacts keep mounting up; so do papyrus finds documenting the trivia of everyday life on the Nile. The Fathers of the Church, when used as *historical* sources, offer many a glimpse into the life of the lower orders. And cross-cultural studies of other societies at similar stages of development[27] have suggested a good deal more. The following, then, is a reconstruction based on findings from all of the above sources or studies and also upon hints in the more obviously historical source-material of the periods concerned. Its aim is to outline the ways in which the attitudes of a traditional society towards its apparatus of government most probably differed from our attitudes to our bureaucracies.

In a traditional pre-industrial society the general orientation of the mass of the population towards the government seems to have been that of subjects.28 Though they might have considerable 'spectator expertise' in interpreting the subtleties of power plays, they did not expect the government to be sensitive to their wishes or controllable by them.

In a modern industrialized society the general orientation towards government is that of the citizen. Quite large numbers of people actively participate in the decision making process in one form, or at one stage, or another. People in general have opinions on major issues and expect such popular opinion to be taken into account. In the West governments will fall if they do not pay heed to this feeling.

The man of the apparatus of administration has a punishment orientation towards his clientele. He is an official, in a society wherein officials are top people. The clientele is composed of subjects and inferiors to be regulated and disciplined. There is one law for the rich, another for the poor. The bureaucrat is not answerable to his clientele and regards it at best as a golden-egg-laying goose, a resource to be carefully managed to ensure maximum productivity.

The bureaucrat thinks of himself as a civil servant. He is a member of a public instrumentality which is engaged in rendering a public service in a form which can and will be evaluated in one way or another. Public servants can be held in some disesteem in contrast with men of the wealth-producing corporations. The bureaucrat is answerable to the same legal processes as is everyone else, and is watched by an alert press.

The prevalent mood in the masses is one of apathy. The aim is to escape the attentions of officialdom. But the disparities in society and hopelessness of the lot of the lower orders can easily lead to disorders. There is a feeling of regression from a golden age, and more mysticism than materialism in general views on life.

The generally prevalent mood is one of some agreement on basic issues such as the conduct of labour negotiations and the need for a form of social security. There is acceptance of several definitions of the aims of society, considerable ability to manage conflict without escalation into disorder, and a feeling of having a stake in a community. Ideals of progress and of improving standards of living are widespread.

The prevalent motivations involve putting one's own or one's family's interests first. Little is known about personality and life is seen as lived amid a mass of blind, amoral forces, unless one has some form of religious belief to give meaning to it. Little awareness of 'social forces' or the like is evident. Great men everywhere bestride this world. Entering a client-relationship subordinate to a great man is the only way in which a poor man can obtain any form of social security.29

The prevalent motivations involve a market morality and nationalistic beliefs. Owing to the former many relationships are defined in economic terms involving maximization of profit, and competitiveness is an accepted norm.30 Owed to the latter is much of the individual's sense of identity in a complex and confusing world. General knowledge about personality dynamics means some disenchantment with hero figures.

Communications are mainly oral. There is mass illiteracy. Formal education is mostly open only to the more well-to-do. It is literary in orientation, and aimed at producing gentlemen steeped in its Great Traditions. Information is difficult to come by and information levels are low. The range of interest in public affairs demonstrated is restricted. Biased and emotional presentation of information is usual and words are thought to 'stand for' things.31

Communications mainly occur via the mass media, in such enormous quantities that people rely on 'experts' within their circle of acquaintance to interpret them. Each man is expected to be informed and to have an opinion. There is mass literacy and a technologically-oriented educational system, open, at least at the lower levels, to all. Ideals of a neutral, social scientific corps of communicators are widespread.32 There is some awareness of the tricks that words and rhetoric can play.

This is not a society which can easily be mobilised33 into action except within a narrow range of issues. Governmental authority is strongest in the centre of Empire, weakens on its fringes. The amount of compliance is in inverse proportion to the influence wielded by the individual, very often.

This society can be speedily mobilised to act upon an issue by publicity campaigns. A wide range of issues is felt to concern the public good. Governmental authority extends right up to the frontiers and all alike must comply.

One is recruited into e.g. the civil administration on the basis of a literary training and as a generalist. Belonging to a particular ethnic, local or religious group is generally of considerable importance. Status attained by birth is equally important. Progress comes through personal connections, largely.

One is recruited into a specialized slot because one has technical competence in the area. Recruitment is professedly impersonal, often by examination. Racial, religious and local connections should be irrelevant. Progress is for merit, which should be in some way measurable.

Change is negatively viewed; the social and educational system is essentially involved in maintaining the *status quo*. Society is authoritarian; there is little geographic, social or psychic mobility for most people, and constricted world views are everywhere evident. Officials tend to group into small in-groups, linked by locality- and kinship-connections, and to aim at furthering their own interests by working through the bureaucracy.34

Novelty is positively viewed and social change is planned for. A man plays many roles and the ability to empathise with others is valued. Norms are egalitarian and democratic, ideally at least. Pluralistic values militate against over-identification with any one cause and informal groups are likely to be composed of erstwhile strangers. Dedication to the bureaucratically defined 'good' is valued and career advancement can be gained by advancing it.

Without strongly developed criteria of efficiency or of rationality, the bureaucracy is likely to suffer from goal displacement, i.e. to be actually pursuing goals other than its nominal objectives. Resources are regulated via a 'trickle-up and trickle-down' process, in which o.g. all sorts of fees find their way into tax extractors' personal money-bags during collection, and much money is irregularly retained during redistribution of tax-resources within the governmental system. There is a culturally-set ceiling on expectations and within these limited desires a life of ease is sought.35

With highly developed criteria of efficiency and rationality, the bureaucracy prides itself on its out-put of services. There is much evaluation of its overall progress and of changes necessitated to match changes in the environment or clientele demands. As a public instrumentality, the bureaucracy is audited and kept under general surveillance. Hence, in general, high (and well directed) productivity. Set in a society which puts a high value on work and which is oriented to a rising ceiling of expectations, the bureaucrat expects to work hard and to be appropriately rewarded by his society. Ease is connected with retirement, *not* a positively regarded period in life.

The concept of 'the state' was not available to any of the writers of these empires, for nationalism was as yet unknown. Neither did they have the concept of 'bureaucracy' as such. Clearly this lack of terminology does not mean that things very like what we mean by 'states' and 'bureaucracies' did not then exist. But it should serve as a warning that people then did look upon what they had rather differently from the way in which we customarily regard such things now.[36]

FOOTNOTES

1. See F. W. Riggs, 'Bureaucratic Politics in Comparative Perspective,' *Journal of Comparative Administration* 1, 1969, pp. 5-9.

2. *LRE*, pp. 910-11 and 873-85.

3. For some readily available general surveys, see N. H. Baynes and H. St. L. B. Moss, *Byzantium*, O.U.P., 1961, chaps 4 (church) and 10 (administration); J. M. Hussey, *The Byzantine World*, Hutchinson, 1967, chaps. 5 (administration) and 6 (church); S. Runciman, *Byzantine Civilization*, Methuen, 1961, chaps. 4-6 (administration, church and army respectively). All these are paperbacks. Basic reference works are G. Ostrogorsky, *History of the Byzantine State*, Blackwell, 1956 and part 2 of volume 4 of the *Cambridge Medieval History*, Cambridge, 1966.

4. Eisenstadt, p. 27.

5. See Millar, p. 72.

6. See A. F. Havighurst (ed), *The Pirenne Thesis*, in the series 'Problems in European Civilization,' Heath, 1958, p. 106.

7. Shown by, for instance, R. Jenkins' *Byzantium: The Imperial Centuries*, Weidenfeld & Nicolson, 1966. But the period is very poorly served in comparison with that of Greece or Rome. Translations and editions of literary works, for example, are not nearly so numerous, and this is typical of the whole apparatus of scholarship involved.

8. R. H. Bainton, *Early Christianity*, Van Nostrand, 1960, part 1, provides a concise and readable survey.

9. For this concept see L. W. Pye & S. Verba (eds.), *Political Culture and Political Development*, Princeton, 1965, pp. 7-11; chap. 12 contains a more extended discussion. On the breakdown into institutions, process and culture see L. W. Pye, *Aspects of Political Development*, Little, Brown, 1966, pp. 47-48.

10. See K. A. Wittfogel, *Oriental Despotism*. For the superiority of agro-hydraulic despotism over other organizational forms, see pp.

161-2; for the Greek, Roman and Byzantine experience, see pp. 195 and 207; 197 and 208-12 and 178. The remainder of the chapter is much influenced by Wittfogel's book, as qualified by Eisenstadt's *The Political Systems of Empires*.

11. MacMullen refers to such developments as 'incipient feudalism' p. 21; cf. P. Oliva, *Pannonia and the Onset of Crisis in the Roman Empire*, Prague, 1962, pp. 32-92.

12. A. de Grazia, *Politics and Government*, Collier, 1962, lists and dates the emergence of what he terms the 'basic ideas of political science' at volume 1, pp. 16-54; see pp. 32-34 in particular. There is a discussion of the evolution of the political party at pp. 188 ff.; see pp. 188-90 in particular.

13. See D. Lerner, *The Passing of Traditional Society*, Free Press, 1958, pp. 38-51.

14. For a good discussion of the pathology of bureaucracies in the historical empires see R. G. Wesson, *The Imperial Order*, University of California, 1967, pp. 285-320; see pp. 290-291 with reference to overlapping spheres of responsibility.

15. See the *C.A.H.* X, pp. 371 and 376.

16. Nero expropriated half of the estates in the Roman province of Africa by executing six large landowners all at once: H. H. Scullard, *From the Gracchi to Nero*, Methuen, 1963, p. 321.

17. See G. Sjoberg, *The Pre-Industrial City*, Free Press, 1960, chaps. 5 and 6 on class and family patterns in antiquity. Pages 321-28, incidentally, contain a synopsis of the findings of the book and give an outline of how such a city differed from a modern one in its political and socio-economic structure.

18. In time of peace an Emperor had between 300,000 and 500,000 (military) men to employ gainfully, as the cost of paying them, the most important item in his governmental expenditure, must have reminded him. And the Roman belief was that hard work was good for discipline. Hence the mighty works of construction wrought by the Roman army. See MacMullen, chapter 2, especially pp. 32-33.

19. Suetonius, *Life of the Divine Claudius*, 18, 2.

20. On the life-cycle (and friction points) see S. N. Eisenstadt, 'Political Struggle in Bureaucratic Societies,' *World Politics* 9, 1956, pp. 15-36 (the life-cycle thesis of this article is expanded in *The Political Systems of Empires*, pp. 282 ff., esp. 288-9, 291 and 297).

21. See Wesson, *The Imperial Order*, pp. (277-) 285.

22. See e.g. M. Weber, 'The Essentials of Bureaucratic Organization: An Ideal-type Construction' in R. K. Merton & Co., (eds), *Reader in*

Bureaucracy, Free Press, 1952, pp. 18-27.

23. *LRE*, pp. 468-69.

24. E.g. a newly independent nation may require a tycoon who is a novice at civil administration for development administration rather than a civil servant trained under a colonial administration which aimed at regulation and the maintenance of the *status quo:* see J. LaPalombara (ed.), *Bureaucracy and Political Development*, Princeton, 1963, 12; cf. also pp. 11 and 55.

25. Cf. Riggs, pp. 100-237. As Riggs indicates, to view the phenomenon of Byzantine bureaucracy as a series of corrupt failures to measure up to a Weberian model obscures the fact that one is dealing with an integrated set of practices based on values foreign to Weber's but well adjusted to a wholly different political and socio-economic background.

26. The hyper-critical attitude of moderns who write on Byzantine bureaucracy contrasts strikingly with the views of other moderns who are engaged upon the comparison of Byzantine institutions with those of the contemporaries of Byzantium. From such contrasts it speedily becomes evident that Byzantium had an enormous advantage in her bureaucracies: see e.g. A. B. Bozeman, *Politics and Culture in International History*, Princeton, 1960, pp. 318-23; cf. Wittfogel, *Oriental Despotism*, pp. 59-67.

27. Such as E. E. Hagen, *On the Theory of Social Change*, Dorsey, 1962; see especially chap. 4 and 5.

28. For the terms 'subject/citizen orientation' see G. A. Almond and S. Verba, *The Civic Culture*, Little, Brown, 1965, pp. 13-26.

29. A high death rate, lack of the social insurance provided by the extended family (which seems to be located rather in the upper echelons of society in antiquity) and adverse property holding conditions result in what has been termed 'amoral familism' in the modern Mediterranean: E. C. Banfield, *The Moral Basis of a Backward Society*, Free Press, 1958, pp. 9-12 (see also chap. 6). A chronic melancholy affects the wretched who feel themselves 'in' but not 'of' their society: *ibid.*, pp. 63-67. The lot of the poor in the towns and especially in the countryside (rustics were exploited and held in low regard) must have been much like this. Hence the long continuance of the *patronus-cliens* (patron-client) relationship in all its varied forms and the *coloni* (share-croppers) who submitted to the lord of a villa. Such forms of dependency would at least ensure a claim on the support of a man of influence if one were in dire need.

30. For the psychological significance of the advent of a market mentality see E. Fromm, *The Fear of Freedom*, Routledge & Kegan Paul, 1960, pp. 34-36; 40-45 and 49-53. For the personality dynamics involved in successful entrepreneurship, see D. C. McClelland, *The Achieving Society*, Van Nostrand, 1961, pp. 191-97; cf. 46-57 on the 'need for achievement.'

31. On the thought world of pre-print man in a manuscript culture see M. McLuhan, *The Gutenberg Galaxy*, University of Toronto, 1962, pp. 110-111 and 124-33; on the semantics involved see T. D. Weldon, *The Vocabulary of Politics*, Penguin, 1953, chap. 2.

32. See L. W. Pye (ed.), *Communications and Political Development*, Princeton, 1963, pp. 24-25 and 78-79.

33. For the concept of 'mobilization' see F. W. Riggs' study 'Agraria and Industria' in W. J. Siffin (ed.), *Toward the Comparative Study of Public Administration*, Indiana University, 1957, pp. 74-76.

34. Cf. Riggs, pp. 164-73.

35. There have been many disquisitions on the 'wantlessness of the impoverished'; but peasant economics are geared to the harsh realities of subsistence living and include little provision for luxuries: see E. R. Wolf, *Peasants*, Prentice-Hall, 1966, pp. 12-17. In relation to notes 27 and 21, see Wolf, pp. 77, 87-88 and 93-94.

36. The only work of antiquity whose central themes were the relations between states and the relations between a ruler and his bureaucracy was the *Arthashastra* attributed to Kautilya, the adviser of Chandragupta, the Indian King of the fourth century B.C. (at whose court was the Greek writer, Megasthenes). Even if it was elaborated over the years, this document in its various forms was available to a succession of rulers and peoples who had close contacts with Hellenistic, Romanized and Byzantine Greeks. Its contents could well have been learned by practical experience of the policies it advocated. It assumed an amoral expediency and a balance of power mentality that was truly Byzantine (if not Machiavellian) in the worst sense of these adjectives. Such is likely to have been the formative influence upon Byzantine thinking in these matters, as it held the field uncontested by other theorisings thereupon. See Bozeman, *Politics and Culture in International History*, pp. 118-26 and 327-68; for a translation, see R. Shamasastry, *Kautilya's Arthasastra*, Mysore, 1929. Moreover, if one starts with a charismatic autocrat whose grip on power becomes institutionalized via an apparatus of government which regulates a population having no effective countervailing power, a ruling class of office-holders results. A rational-legal instrumentality servicing a plural-

- 27 -

istic society does not evolve from such an apparatus. Rather it is a totally different bureaucratic entity (and social order). See H. Constas, 'Max Weber's Two Conceptions of Bureaucracy' in *American Journal of Sociology* 63, 1958, pp. 400-409, especially 403 ff.

Chapter 2
The Prelude: The Bureaucratic Structure
of the Early and Middle Roman Empire

In 31 B.C. the battle of Actium, which Antony and Cleopatra lost to Octavian (later to become Augustus), brought about the end of Republican government in Rome. It was followed by the limited monarchy which the Romans knew as the Principate.[1] The first *Princeps*, Augustus, laid the foundations of what was to develop into the imperial administrative bureaucracy. But this is not to say that no bureaucratic structures existed before his day or that they first came into existence as a coherent body of organization during his reign. The case is rather that there was a patch-work growth, in which very striking developments occurred during this time. Possibly this growth might be best described by likening it to an old shrub (the Senate), alongside but separate to which there springs up first one then another fast-growing new shrub. The first of these would be the new imperial officials (prefects, legates, procurators) and the career patterns in which these posts formed stages. The second 'shrub' would be the Emperor's freedmen, managing the affairs of his 'household,' affairs which had become inextricably intertwined with those of the empire. Meanwhile yet another shrub, which has got out of control (the army), is cut back to size and some of its cuttings replanted, so that it forms a more effective windbreak as it were. Augustus was, that is, more like an old gardener operating with patient, loving care than an advocate of management science with an organization chart as his planning blue-print.[2]

Prior to Augustus the machinery of government was that usually found in a city state: annually elected magistrates plus a council of life members.[3] Diagram 1 (below, pages 31-32) illustrates; it is taken from the hey-day of senatorial government, before the troubled times of the late Republic.[4] Running the civil administration there were, in 31 B.C., in ascending order, an annually elected hierarchy of 40 quaestors (who acted as paymasters), 6 aediles (who looked after municipal affairs), 16 praetors (who conducted the business involved in lawsuits), and 2 consuls (the top executive officials). Every five years a pair of censors was elected for eighteen months. These officials registered citizens in their tribe (voting ward), their census rating and their *ordo* (the three orders were those of the Senate, the equestrians and the populace or commons)[5], and let governmental contracts (many taxes were farmed out to the equestrian big-business syndicates). These were the sought-after magistracies in the career of honours (*cursus honorum*). Standing outside this *cursus* was the tribunate. For ten tribunes of the people were also elected annually. Their functions changed with time and by 31 they had come to be little more than political agents for more important people — consuls, generals or cliques of senators or equestrians (the latter were men of considerable wealth; it may help to think of them as knights).

There were also various minor posts, known as the Twenty-Man-Board *(vigintivirate)*, which normally preceded the *cursus.* This board comprised mint-officials *(monetales)*, whose names appeared on the coins which they struck. A body of four officials looked after the streets of Rome, another of three looked after crimes among the lowly,[6] and yet another, this time of ten, looked after lawsuits in which a citizen's freedom was involved. The higher orders of Roman society, where extended families were common, were used to taking council before acting upon a matter of moment. So senior magistrates would act in concert with an advisory body or *consilium* of friends, amongst whom those with a reputation for knowledge of the patchwork quilt of Roman law[7] *(juris prudentes)* were much sought after.

To cope with the management of business other than that of the metropolis, i.e. provincial matters, the institution of the promagistracy had been evolved. After his year of office a magistrate could be 'prorogued' or continued in an acting *(pro-)* capacity. As a *propraetor* he could go out to a province where he would direct the civil administration. A province with more than one legion or where warfare would be involved necessitated a *proconsul.* Both officials took their paymasters, in the form of *proquaestors*, with them. They also took a group of friends (*comites* or companions) in a semi-official capacity — to act as a *consilium* and so on.

Also, the Roman government relied heavily on local town councils to run their cities' business. If this were done efficiently, a city might be spared the attentions of the provincial governor, and there were grades of privileges which cities enjoyed to mark their competence in this regard.

This annually changing body of officials was underpinned, however, by a permanent clerical and sub-clerical staff (*scribae* and *apparitores*

respectively).[8] It was, for instance, a matter for comment that Cato Uticensis, a stickler for doing the job properly, understudied his quaestor's post for months before entering it. The result was that his staff had the (apparently unusual) experience of not being able to bamboozle this young aristocrat when he took up his post.[9] The *scribae* were citizens of some standing (though such a profession was not for a gentleman who might aspire to a magistracy), of the equestrian order in fact. They held their jobs for life and prided themselves upon their competence. They were a distinct cut above the sub-clerical staff of *apparitores*, which comprised messengers *(viatores)*, heralds *(praecones)* and lictors (a guard of honour while in Rome; gaolers and executioners in the provinces).[10]

These underlings, both clerical and sub-clerical, were organized into decuries or panels of ten; each college of magistrates had a pool of decuries, upon which the individual magistrate drew. Appointment was initially by the nomination of a magistrate of the college served. Once appointed one was immovable. One purchased one's post and was subsequently on the established paylist of the *aerarium* or state treasury (hence, owning the post, one could depute someone else to perform its tasks). The salary was small but was well supplemented, apparently, by the perquisites which went with the job (a prisoner would have to pay well to die painlessly, for instance).

The army too was officered by annually elected magistrates. A young aristocrat would commence his career by obtaining election as a Military Tribune chosen by the people *(tribunus militum a populo)*. Later he might serve as paymaster (as *quaestor* to a consul, whence he might be continued as *proquaestor*). Rome's wars were fought under her consuls (or acting consuls, if fighting dragged on).

This amateurism at upper levels was only possible because of the professionalism of the other ranks and certain of the other officers. A commander could for instance appoint his own military tribunes (when so appointed, they were known as *tribuni militum rufuli*). He could also select a senior man as legate *(legatus)*, to perform more demanding duties. After all, there was provision for a magistrate to make a personal appointment, of one of his freedmen, to his clerical staff (such a man was termed an *accensus*).

But the army really ran on its centurions.[11] Since Caesar's campaigns in the 50's B.C. the legions had had permanent numbers and a regular promotion system. It worked as follows. A legion comprised 6,000 men in 60 centuries. Each century was commanded by a centurion; an *optio* was second in command, and a *vexillarius* bore the century's standard (the legionaries took their dressing from this). The centuries were grouped six to a cohort. Thus the Legio III Augusta, [12] for instance, would have 10 cohorts; of these the first cohort was the senior one, the tenth the most junior. There was seniority of centuries within the cohort, too. Cohorts were divided into front *(prior)* and rear *(posterior)* ranks, and into the divisions *pilus, princeps* and *hastatus.*

The order of seniority among centurions ran: *pilus prior, pilus posterior, princeps prior, princeps posterior, hastatus prior* and *hastatus posterior.* This only mattered within the first cohort apparently: i.e. if one started as centurion as *hastatus posterior* in the tenth cohort, one would keep that position on promotion, but be promoted to the *ninth* cohort and so on up. The same went for a *princeps prior* in the tenth, who would be promoted *princeps prior* in the ninth, etc. But when one reached the first cohort, one moved first to the position of *hastatus posterior*, and then went up rung by rung from there.

The centurions of a legion's first cohort were very important troops. They were seasoned veterans of demonstrated steadiness. They were part of the commander's council of war. From their ranks were chosen the *aquilifer*, or bearer of the legion's standard, the sacred eagle: [13] the prefect of the camp (and Roman campaigns have been described as 'mobile trench warfare' because the troops dug in every night); and the prefect in charge of the engineers. Also, the legions were flanked by mercenary troops, known as auxiliaries *(auxilia).* These comprised foot (organised in cohorts of 1,000 with their centuries under their own centurions, etc.) and horse (in squadrons of 500, known as *alae*, each consisting of 16 *turmae*, each with 3 *decurions*, 3 *optiones* and a *vexillarius*). There was a prefect in charge of each auxiliary cohort and of each *ala*. He was often a former Roman centurion.

Moreover, a provincial governor had a staff *(officium)* of *officiales* which was headed by a centurion as *Princeps praetorii* (Head of the General's staff). He and the 3 *cornicularii* and 3 *commentarienses* comprised the higher grade of this staff. They each had assistants, *adiutores.* The lower grade comprised 10 *speculatores* and 60 *beneficiarii.* It is not known precisely what all their functions were, but *commentarienses* and *speculatores* took custody of prisoners and carried out executions. Also on the staff were clerks *(exceptores, exacti, librarii)*, equerries *(stratores)* and a bodyguard *(pedites/equites singulares).* Service among the *officiales* was a promotion for an ordinary *legionarius*, who would stay there, rising from lower to higher grade, unless he was promoted to centurion therefrom (as happened frequently, apparently): pay was good, and there were plenty of perquisites. An *officialis* was permanently attached to his province.

However strong the underpinning, however, Rome's superstructure of city state magistrates proved unable to support the weight of an empire which was, by 31, almost the size of Alexander's. A succession of special overriding military commands (the *imperium maius*), resuscitations of the long-defunct dictatorship (by Sulla and Caesar), and the emergence of something rather like a *junta* (the Triumvirates of 60 and 44) finally culminated in the permanent one-man-rule of Augustus.

The Roman aristocracy was likely to strive as hard to bring this *régime* to an end as it had striven to end the others. For the families comprising that aristocracy had monopolised power and office for centuries. The monopoly was maintained as follows. Most elections were won by the sons of senators. Elections for the higher offices went almost automatically to certain of them: for about 200 to 44 B.C. there had been only 15 'new men' *(novi homines)*, as men from outside the small circle of families ennobled by holding the consulate were disparagingly termed. Ex-magistrates (and suitable others adlected by senior senators) went into the Senate for life. The Senate in effect controlled all decision-making, but under rules of house procedure such that only men of consular rank from the 'great families' *(gentes maiores)* normally participated in debate.[14]

Such an oligarchy would not cooperate as servants with a man whom they contemptuously regarded as an upstart Italian, especially as his success could only mean their ruin. Yet they comprised most of Rome's top-level administrative talent and Octavian (the Augustus to be) had been brought to power by the breakdown of the administrative system. He had consequently both to provide an improved and expanded administration and simultaneously to find new administrators to run it.

It is difficult neatly to delineate the outline of Augustus' solution, for solution, as stated, did not come by way of a blue print but by a series of opportunistic and expedient moves which only gradually revealed their directing purpose (to judge by contemporary reactions).[15] But if one looks at the four areas which have been shown to be crucial to an autocrat's power — financial and man-power resources, communications, and building activity — the main outlines of the newly forming organization stand out clearly. And these outlines foreshadow the bureaucratic development that was to come under later emperors.

First, finance. Up to now the Senate's *aerarium* or treasury had been the main source of governmental monies. But now a new concept developed, that of the fisc. Each province had its own *fiscus* or pay-chest. These now only paid in their *surplus* to the Senate's *aerarium* (from which Augustus could be authorized to make withdrawals).[16] But the biggest concentration of funds was in the Emperor's *patrimonium*, or privy purse, which was swollen by the pickings from the civil wars. In fact it was from this that monies went out to subvent the senatorial treasury and provincial pay-chests on more than one occasion. One huge grant in particular established an *aerarium militare* or military treasury to serve as a source of pensions for the soldiery. Thus whoever controlled the privy purse controlled the entire finances of government, in the long run. For the imperial system of revenue collection was rigid, barely met annual expenditures and could only be expanded to meet financial crises by extraordinary measures.[17]

Now the controller of the privy purse was Augustus' own freedman accountant. He was known as the *(procurator) a rationibus*, the Treasurer. As a freed slave he owed a client's duties to his patron, the Emperor who had freed him. Thus he could be proceeded against with the fullest rigour of the law, and had no social or political influence beyond that gained from association with the Emperor. Another freedman was soon to control the Emperor's correspondence — the activities of his ministry are evident under Tiberius, the next Emperor. Thus a solution had been found to the problem of securing able direction for these critically sensitive matters while yet maintaining control of the directors.

In the matter of the issuing of coinage, too, the Treasurer had great influence. This was an important matter because, as the coins were overvalued in relation to their metallic value, the issuing of coinage, particularly in precious metals, paid the issuing authority handsomely. And only the Emperor issued such metals — indeed from the reign of the next Emperor every effort seems to have been made to acquire all gold and silver mines for the privy purse (by confiscation). Moreover the coins were the only mass medium of antiquity. They spoke with legend — wording — and symbol (to a people who thought in terms of symbolism), with many different legends and symbols appearing on the same denomination within the same year in some cases.

True, the Senate's *monetales* were nominally in charge of Italian issues. But they were young, transitory and inexperienced. Moreover, the Emperor kept a careful eye on young men at this particular point in their careers. The mint-master, or *exactor auri argenti et aeris*, effectively ran the mint. He was directly under the *a rationibus* and was a freedman. True, he leased the manufacturing of the coinage to

contractors. But they too were either freedmen or slaves (and operated in little bureaucratised shops called *officinae*). What is more the mint-master bore the military rank of *optio*, so he could constrain obedience from such people. Below him in the mint were *conductores* who saw to the contracted minting; some were in charge of precious metals, some of bronze and *orichalcum* (a mixture of bronze and zinc). Then there were *nummularii*, who put the coins on the market, and accountants, *dispensatores*, to audit the whole operation. The Emperor was never to lose direction of this source of revenue and publicity.[18]

An Emperor's household had many mansions indeed, and it is not to be imagined that the enormous task of coordinating all these finances was carried out by one man. In point of fact, the Treasurer had a considerable staff below him. All were freedmen from within the Emperor's household. The higher grades were termed *proximi* (nearest to the treasurer) and *mello-proximi* (destined to be nearest to the Treasurer), and had assistants to help *them*. The lower grades comprised cashiers *(dispensatores)* and accountants *(arcarii, tabularii)*. A very considerable number of men seems to have been involved. Moreover the numerous imperial estates in the provinces were looked after by freedmen procurators, who reported in to the central Treasurer, but who each had his own staff of underlings.

These were men of a real power which far exceeded their apparent status. This was an apparatus state with a redistributive economy (i.e. wealth was obtained by removing surpluses from primary producers and channelling them around the various governmental instrumentalities rather than by producing wealth through industrial productivity). So wealth went along with power. Those in the apparatus, in however lowly a position, have both, and are thus sharply set off from the vast majority of those outside.[19] Thus, under the next Emperor, a certain Musicus, himself a lowly cashier in a Gallic province, had a household of sixteen slaves to wait upon him, as well as a costly wardrobe and silver plate. His wealth, presumably, came from fees and perquisites, Not that the Emperor paid over-lavish salaries — in fact he made a profit from his slaves and freedmen, so much so that he had a *fiscus* to handle the sums they paid him to purchase their liberty, or which accrued to him in their wills as their patron. The point is, however, that such service was hereditary. Men were not freed until they left sons behind them. Consequently, once initiated, these ministries were self-perpetuating (or rather, they grew apace).[20]

Next for consideration is the matter of manpower resources. It had been the emergency armies of the late Republic which had brought constitutional government to an end. Raised by a charismatic military adventurer, they had followed him into politics after their wars were over to gain land allotments in lieu of pensions. It was Augustus now who provided the pension, and without need of politicking on the soldiers' part. Moreover he established the army at 25 legions, strung out along the borders of empire, with an equal number of auxiliaries (recruited from provincials) at their side. Fleets, too, now rode permanently at their stations, manned by freedmen. After their service provincials and freedmen gained full citizen status. In this way a union of hearts with the central government, on the part of the rank and file, was contrived. But officers, too, alienated from the central government, had followed the military adventurers. Augustus now interwove military and civilian career lines so that no one could rise to high command without long involvement with the civil administration and Establishment.[21]

In so doing he 'restored the Republic,' as he put it. To this point the senatorial elite had monopolised control, and thus a faction had taken over the commonwealth, had taken it away from the mass of the worthy citizenry. Now effective control of that commonwealth, of the Republic, was given back to those worthies.[22] Provincials could serve as prefects in the *auxilia*; equestrians could serve as prefects in the fleets. But greater openings yet were available to the latter: new types of prefectures, too dangerously powerful to entrust to a senator in some cases, and too suspiciously close to service under a master to be attractive to a senator in others.

Augustus, that is, created new positions. Patently, administrative needs were going unmet; speciously, precedent was pressed into service to give an aura of respectability to the new-found dignities. There were some senators whom Augustus could rely on. After all he had the power to make instant senators, instant patricians even, by fiat. A newcomer to politics, without connections and disdained by the old nobility, could advance furthest and fastest by loyalty to an Emperor. After all, that Emperor was both the sole source of patronage and the man who was purging the Senate from a throng of 1,000 persons (containing, he claimed, many disreputable elements) to a more proper 600 (containing only the 'better' elements).[23] A starveling equestrian, too, could best advance his interests by becoming a member of the apparatus of government, that source of wealth and power.

Consequently, the highest ranks of the Emperor's service, whatever people might say of the positions involved, came to be filled with senators, another restoration of the Republic's practices. New careers opened up in governmental service for equestrians, and numbers of them were found ready to occupy these, intermediate as they were. As all posts were equipped with their due quotas of clerical and sub-clerical staffs, many new opportunities for employment were opened up for humbler folk, citizen and freedmen. There was always a shortage of employment at this level, so here too posts were filled.

Augustus had been left in command of all troops after the civil war and did not intend to arm potential aristocratic opponents again by farming out army commands among them. So he took over responsibility for the provinces where fighting was likely. This gave him 7 provinces to the Senate's 10 (and 24 legions to the Senate's one). For these provinces, and for Rome — where, as e.g. in Spain, extensive building operations were carried out — he created a new set of official positions *and career lines to go with them.* He wanted experienced administrators, not *dilettante* politicians. In doing this, he laid the foundations for Rome's greatest traditions of public service.[24]

The position of legate now became an official step in a regular career sequence: there was a *legatus legionis* or legate in charge of a legion, and a *legatus Augusti pro praetore* or provincial governor. The prefectship, also, was extended: there were now prefects of the fleet, in charge of the various naval detachments; there was the prefect of the *vigiles* or night watch in Rome, and the prefect of the *annona,* or task of provisioning Rome with grain. There was the Urban Prefect, a sort of chief of police for Rome, with 3 urban cohorts and powers of summary jurisdiction. Lastly, there were the two great prefectures which gave more power than any other positions anywhere in government — the prefectures of Egypt (the Emperor's special preserve; no senator was allowed entry to the country) and of the Praetorian Guard (comprising 3 cohorts in Rome and 6 in various towns within Italy).

The post of *procurator* now also became an official one in a career sequence. A *procurator* might oversee the collection of direct taxes in a regular imperial province or he might even command auxiliary troops as governor of a minor one. Curatorships were likewise to become official career positions: there were for instance *curatores viarum,* curators to look after the roads leading into Rome, a position connected with the 'Public Post.' Curators looked after public works, waterworks (with a staff of 240 trained slaves) and the banks of the Tiber (flood control and prevention of illegal extensions of building were involved here). These officials all had their staffs, of course. There were the usual *beneficiarii* or seconded soldiers serving as *officiales* or administrative staff for provincial governors. For the metropolitan officials there were *scribae* and *apparitores* (including *geruli* or porters in some cases !); the curators even had lictors — and *architecti* (surveyors) too, where necessary.

There were now *careers* in the Emperor's service. A senator's son, if he were of good repute and a millionaire (i.e. possessor of 1,000,000 *sesterces*) would commence as a military tribune or prefect of an *ala*. He then held a post in the *vigintivirate* (as *monetalis*, if he wished to ensure imperial favour). At 25, when elected *quaestor*, he officially became a member of the senate. Unless he were a patrician, he would then hold either a tribunate of the people or an aedileship. At 30 he could hold a praetorship, which qualified him to be a legionary legate or a legate governing a small imperial province. At 42 he could become consul (from 5 B.C. and regularly from 2 B.C. there was an extra pair of suffect, or 'replacement,' consuls elected every year, doubling the number of consulates available). His consulship qualified him for a governorship of an important imperial province, a curatorship in Rome, even for the Urban Prefecture, summit of a senator's career in the Emperor's service.

There were careers in government for equestrians too, now, for the first time in Rome's history. Free birth, possession of 400,000 sesterces and a good character were the qualifications. Commencing as prefect or military tribune in charge of an auxiliary cohort, an equestrian could proceed, as *procurator*, to become the financial comptroller of an imperial province, then the governor of a minor imperial province. Then, for the best of them, came the prefectships — of the fleet, the night watch, the grain supply. The summit of an equestrian career came in holding the prefectship of Egypt or, ultimately, of the Praetorian Guard in Rome.

The Emperor's service thus comprised trained and experienced men as his governors; and prefects and *procurators* stayed at their posts for several years at a time, a practice which was an administrative improvement on the senatorial system of one year's tenure. It was effective. Provincial government improved in competence and integrity, military command in professionalism. Rome, in 31 B.C. the most unruly and violent city in the Empire, was the best policed and serviced city therein at the end of the reign (14 A.D.). Augustus could boast that he 'found it a city of brick and left it a city of marble'; its services — police, flood and fire control, building regulations — and facilities (aqueducts, baths, parks, a library, covered shopping areas, improved sewerage, even some urban renewal) were so improved as to be of another order.

All this was done with complete security. There were no mandates of concentrations of military power to senators; and everywhere equestrian *procurators* (or freedmen *procurators* of the estates of the privy purse scattered through the provinces) reported back upon senatorial governors and officials. Such arrangements, involving institutionalized countervailing official powers, were to be a feature of bureaucratic machinery for the future and to be considerably developed. All army officers had links with both civil and military establishments.

A new order was coming into being: the consulship, once the supreme prize and zenith of political ambition, was now a mere qualifying stage in a career sequence. The very meaning of the terms which had so long been dominant in the political culture of the Republic was to be unknown to the Romans of the generation after Augustus' death.[25] The next imperial dynasty was to come from a family trained and brought to prominence in this service, and such was also the origin of Trajan, who inaugurated what was to be the Golden Age of the Antonines.

The old city state institutions, too, were now overpassed. In 31 there had been Rome and Italy, the provinces and some protectorates. Now there was a Rome of 265 precincts and 14 districts, within an Italy comprised of 11 administrative regions. There were the inner, older and wealthier senatorial provinces and the armed ring of imperial frontier provinces. Then there was Egypt (containing the oldest and most well developed bureaucratic system of the ancient Near East, incidentally, and the Emperor's special charge) and the protectorates. In place of some 14 plus legions and a succession of hand-to-mouth emergency expeditionary forces, there was a standing army of some 350,000 effectives strategically positioned. And for the first time there were troops in Rome: 3 Praetorian cohorts, 3 urban cohorts, 7 cohorts of *vigiles* — one for every two urban districts — and 2 of *classiarii* or marines.

Indistinctly, the shape of the great bureaucracies of the future looms into view. There are the central prefectures — the Praetorian, the Urban and that in charge of the food supply; the central secretariate is just about evident in the shape of the minister of the treasury and (beginning to be apparent) another minister, of correspondence. A whole financial complex is emerging: senatorial and military treasuries, fisc and privy purse. Typically, there is confusion and overlapping of spheres of competence. Not a transitory phenomenon. There is a *concilium principis*, the *Princeps'* Council, a standing liaison committee between Emperor and Senate, soon to develop into a form of inner court. This is the central organizational machinery, as it were.[26] In the provinces there are prefects (of Egypt, the fleets and the armies), legates (as governors and as generals) and *procurators* (as minor governors and as financial comptrollers). And this whole top level of the administration is underpinned by highly organized and well staffed clerical and sub-clerical services.

A review of the decision-making process will point up the changes which had come about and indicate developments which were to come. Legislation, in 31, had been by vote of the assemblies. Such votes still made law: the Emperor, by virtue of his tribunitial powers, could put a bill before the assembly (e.g. the *leges Iuliae*). On occasion, too, a decree of the Senate could become law (e.g. the *Senatus Consultum Silanianum*). But there were now new sources of law, and these were far more used: the Emperor's edicts; *decreta*, i.e. judicial decisions handed down by the Emperor; *mandata*, i.e. the Emperor's instructions to officials; and rescripts, i.e. the Emperor's replies to petitions. There would soon have to be a central secretariate to handle this mass of decision-making activities.

Jurisdiction of old had been either a matter for the standing courts or was settled by an appeal to the people, *provocatio ad populum* (for the highly placed; the lowly were more cursorily dealt with via the police-type officials of the *vigintivirate*). Now there was 'appeal unto Caesar,' *appellatio ad Caesarem*. Cases involving men of high standing came now before two new courts: the Emperor in Council or the Senate. These had primary jurisdiction and there was no appeal allowed, either to the people or from one court to the other. Also, with the spread of Roman citizenship in the provinces (a marked change in its territorial distribution that came with the Principate), provincial governors came to have some criminal jurisdiction. The Urban Prefect began to take over from the courts of law. New areas of law began to be developed in regard to business contracts and inheritance matters. The Emperor gave certain jurists the *ius respondendi*, the right to give opinions on vexed questions in the law. The magistrates' courts and Senate, that is to say, begin to yield to the Emperor and his officials as an influence in creating law. And, as in legislative matters, administrative rulings or officials are the shaping force behind the changes, very often.[27]

Elections of old had been decided by the people; there was no dearth of candidates, and competition was fierce. Now the Emperor could name *(nominatio)* or commend *(commendatio)* to a certain number of magistracies. Also a practice known as *destinatio* was introduced, by which a preliminary vote of 10 special centuries of senators and equestrians (i.e. the very topmost people) gave a strong lead to the assembly. Things had changed by now, it is evident. Sometimes there were not enough candidates for the annual vacancies. Little glory, even, was left to the older magistracies: one might rebuild a road or temple, but it would not bear the name of one's family as result. Real power was elsewhere, in the Emperor's service; and men seem to have followed it thither. As for the people, they might (occasionally) legislate — though Augustus, with his tribune's powers, could block even this. They did go through the motions of elections, though nomination, commendation and *destinatio* robbed such motions of much meaning. In fact Augustus' instruction to his successor was that the latter should hand over elections to the Senate, and this was done. The people's judicial powers too were increasingly lost. To Augustus' reign dates the development of the craze for following the colours *(colores)*, as the various racing stables of the *Circus Maximus* were known. The craze was to grow apace.[28] So was the engrossment by the apparatus of the various decision-making functions listed above.

Further major developments of the bureaucratic apparatus are generally associated with the Emperor Claudius (41-54 A.D.).[29] Upon the assassination of his predecessor Caligula, the Senate fell to discussing the possibility of discontinuing the principate. Their deliberations were broken off upon tidings that the praetorian guard had set a new emperor, Claudius, upon the throne. After Claudius' reign there could be no question of reversion to republicanism. Debate centred rather upon how to secure the best *princeps*; the system of the principate was taken for granted.[30] Popular legislation disappeared after this reign, and legislation via the Senate decreased markedly. The central administrative apparatus had assumed the form and importance which it was, by and large, to retain for well over a century.

It was no accident that it was the praetorian guard which took the devisive step in this succession crisis. The Praetorian Prefect had emerged as the most powerful figure in the apparatus in the reign following Augustus', when its holder, Sejanus, came very close to setting himself upon the imperial throne. Sejanus had brought all 9 cohorts together into one camp at the gates of Rome, where their military presence could dominate the capital. Sejanus had come to deputise for the Emperor, as the latter withdrew to Capri. He took over security powers, acted as deputy at meetings of the Imperial Council *(consilium principis)*, and tried cases which came before the Emperor. The position was in fact so influential that there were normally two prefects, one to check upon the other; Sejanus had managed to become sole prefect. Moreover the guard itself was an influential body. It carried out police- and security duties in and from the capital, centre of empire. It acted as an officer training corps for men from the most Romanised provinces. Such men subsequently went out to the frontier armies, to maintain Roman traditions therein, despite tendencies towards provincialization inherent in their frontier life and situation.[31]

However, the pre-eminence attained by Sejanus was owed to a unique combination of circumstances, rather than an institutional power base. There was a still inchoate apparatus of government, an out-of-town Emperor and Sejanus' own strength in guile and opportunism. There were to be other prefects with great influence, especially in succession crises, but no further such would-be usurpers until the great increase in the power of the prefect's staff in the third century.

Now, two emperors later, Claudius was to develop the freedmen ministers into an enormously powerful central secretariate.[32] The prominence attained by several of these secretaries (Pallas, the *a rationibus*; Narcissus, the *ab epistulis*; Polybius, the *a studiis* and Callistus, the *a libellis* for instance) indicates that the secretariate was still at an early stage of development where the men were more important than the offices.[33] Contemporaries certainly seem to have thought that these secretaryships were the positions of real power, from Claudius' reign onwards.[34]

Four major new departments are generally identified. From of old there were the *a rationibus*, the Treasurer, and the *ab epistulis*, Correspondence Secretary (with both a Latin and a Greek section). Newly prominent, if not newly initiated in all cases, were the *a libellis* or Secretary in charge of Petitions; the *a cognitionibus*, Secretary in charge of Inquiries; the *a vehiculis*, Transport Secretary, and the *a studiis*, Secretary on Briefings. Claudius had transferred security functions, that is to say, to less powerful servants than his Praetorian Prefects. He had also extended the scope of his activities in jurisdiction, another strategic area.

His activity in regard to jurisdiction in fact occasioned much adverse comment from contemporaries. Trial before the Emperor's own court now became more frequent, apparently. The *consilium* rather than any one person normally gave the verdict, but Claudius was notorious for having the final say. And all this while the jurisdictional power of the Urban Prefect was growing apace. He was a mature, experienced man

with long tenure of office, often a jurist. Naturally, then, his court was more effective than that of the *tresviri capitales*, who were after all youngsters at the beginning of their careers, holding office for a year only. Also the Urban Prefect controlled the urban cohorts and the night watch and was, after a fashion, the equivalent of a police-chief. Observably, he processed cases faster than did other courts. He could take cognisance of several offenses together and of offences not covered by statute. Hence his jurisdictional powers grew, even at the expense of the regular jury courts.[35] In the provinces, too, imperial *procurators* were empowered to take cases from the governor where treasury matters were involved. On the other hand the four senatorial *quaestors* who had seen to the administration of law and order in Italy disappear during this reign.[36] Presumably the functioning of the Urban and Praetorian prefectures made them otiose.

But, as with Augustus, change under Claudius was a matter of a patchwork of adaptations, fumblings[37] and minor innovations or developments of precedent rather than total renovation to a blueprint. This does not mean that it was inconsiderable in extent, however, as a review of a major decision will indicate (see Diagram 3 above, pages 45-46).[38] For the matter of provisioning the capital with grain, upon which action had long been deferred owing to the enormous costs involved, was now effectively tackled by Claudius. The whole operation, owing to its size and complexity, was not completed until Nero's reign (in regard, for instance, to the building of the new harbour at Ostia), but the overall direction was Claudius'. The sum total of all the minor changes involved constitutes very considerable change indeed. It would appear that some kind of centralized control over the various treasuries was now established in the form of a central *fiscus*. Roads and waterways into Rome came under the control of the Emperor's men. So did all essential services: provisioning, water, police, fire and flood control. Huge building projects, such as the draining of the Pomptine Marshes and the building of a large new port at the mouth of the Tiber, physically and politically close to Rome, were executed by the Emperor.

Perhaps the fiscal situation merits somewhat fuller discussion. When the provisioning of grain was apparently made a charge upon the new, central *fiscus*, the Senate lost the major sources of income — grain from the provinces of Sicily and Africa — for its *aerarium*. Imperial procurators were given judicial competence in contested claims involving the provincial *fiscus*, even in senatorial provinces. The *a rationibus* now got control of the 5% tax on legacies and manumissions (i.e. the freeing of slaves); new types of *procurator* appear to look after these taxes. The goods of the condemned (and 35 senators and 300 equites had their estates confiscated during the reign) now reverted to the *patrimonium*, which was given a special *procurator*, of equestrian status, to look after it. There was much fudging of the boundaries of spheres of competence: a complaint made at the end of the reign was that the senatorial and imperial finances were hopelessly entangled.

For instance the *aerarium* reverted to quaestorial control. But it was not a case of one *quaestor* elected annually by the Senate. Rather the Emperor selected pairs of *quaestors* and they had a three-year tenure of office. Again, the new *Procurator Ostiensis*, the *procurator* who took over the handling of grain at the bar of the river from the senate's *quaestor*, had under him a *praepositus mensae nummulariae fisci frumentarii Ostiensis*, an Overseer of the Accounts for the Grain Treasury at Ostia. This official must also have been subordinate to the Grain Treasury itself. Momentous decisions were taken in regard to the coinage, too: the weight of the gold piece was reduced; much plating of the silver ensued; the bronze coins — nominally in the control of the Senate — were discontinued because their metallic quality could apparently not be maintained.[39] The result is typical of Claudius' activities: new officials, either freedmen or the Emperor's appointees, each of course with their staffs, encroaching upon senatorial administrative preserves. Coordination of hitherto unconnected activities led to centralization.

At the beginning of the next reign, during Nero's short honeymoon with the Senate, his initial programmatic speech promised to avoid what the Senate had most objected to in Claudius' reign. There was to be no selling of favours or of offices. Freedmen were not to intervene in the affairs of government. The powers of the Senate were to be maintained: the consuls were to preside, according to republican usage. Specifically, the Emperor was not to encroach on the jurisdiction of other courts or try cases within his own court, and cases concerning Italy and the senatorial provinces were to be tried before a consular court. Also, as appears from the coinage, the Senate (briefly) struck gold and silver coins and directed what kinds of public relations imagery should appear upon its bronze coinage, too.[40] But the trends apparent in Claudius' day could not be reversed and were soon all evident, in heightened form, in Nero's administration too. There were even more trials of senators, more confiscations of huge estates.[41]

As far as the army was concerned there were two developments of note. Claudius rewarded the praetorian guardsmen who had effectively conferred the throne upon him by making them a donative, or cash payment on top of regular pay, of 15,000 *sesterces* apiece. This grant initiated the practice by which an Emperor was to be expected, at the beginning of his reign and upon auspicious events within it, to make such grants to his troops. Practice came eventually to be that Praetorians should receive three times the amount given to the rest of the soldiery (actually however they generally received a far larger amount than this). Pay scales were a sore point with the rank and file of the army: Tiberius, who succeeded Augustus, had been confronted with riotously pressed demands for a *denarius* (16 *asses*) rather than 10 *asses* as the daily unit of pay and for cash (not land situated at the emperor's discretion) as pension.[42] The donatives thus constituted one way of tacitly meeting these demands. The demands were explicitly met, however, when Domitian, some thirty years later, raised the basic army pay from 225 to 300 *denarii* p.a. But this particular grant made by Claudius probably had the immediate effect of furthering the resentment, which was building up among the frontier units, of the privileged position of the Praetorians.

Secondly, the army under Claudius over-ran Mauretania and occupied part of Britain. Two protectorates, Thrace and Lycia, were annexed as provinces. Another fleet, the British *(classis Britannica)*, was added to the six already in existence. This meant new fields for the military to conquer, and then develop and exploit. It also meant something of an increase to the overall military and naval establishment. Thus, all in all, the army did very well out of the reign.

At this point the Christian Church was evolving from a missionary ministry to a local and pastoral ministry. Within two generations it moved from being a group of apostles, prophets and teachers to become an organization with bishops, presbyters and deacons. Probably at this stage there were two distinct orders, namely bishops and presbyters as opposed to deacons. The presbyter-bishop administered the holy services, while the deacon looked after church property and administered charitable relief. Each order was lifelong. The Church at this stage consisted of groups of believers in the cities of Syria, Asia Minor and Greece. It was also established in Rome. It aimed to look after the poor, widows and orphans, and visit the sick and those in prison or sent to the living death of labour in the mines. It provided hospitality to Christians who were travelling; it provided for burials. Its churches and their adornments were simple, its officials poorly paid.

Christianity was a revulsion against the inhumanity of the brutality and lasciviousness of Graeco-Roman civilization. It proposed to base life on faith rather than reason. It brought in stricter standards of sexual morality for men as well as women, along with the concept of original sin. It was a religious movement of revolutionary potential, but without political aims. Its devotees could not serve in the imperial armies or join in the unifying cult of emperor worship; they could not hold civic office (in case they might be implicated in responsibility for torturings or executions), and would not become involved in non-Christian festivals. Their stand-offishness was misunderstood and misrepresented by the generality; as far as officialdom was concerned their association and gatherings were illegal.

However, at this point the Christian Church was as little known to officialdom as it was little understood. Its major enemies were orthodox Jews, some of whom looked upon the Christians as encouraging the perversion of the Jewish law and therefore fit to be done to death. The Roman authorities were, if anything, looked upon as protectors, for they prevented Jewish attacks upon Christians, if only to maintain law and order. There may have been some kind of conflict in Claudius' day in Rome between Christians and Jews (whose religion was recognised by the Roman authorities as being an old one, and one with whose devotees it was best not to tamper). But, by and large, the church seems to have been beneath attention at this point. Nero's persecution of the Christians, when he attempted to make them the scapegoats for the great fire in Rome, seems to have found them totally unprepared for such a visitation of imperial wrath. Yet now the precedent had been set, and the attention of the authorities drawn to them for the future.[43]

But by Claudius' reign another, different major social change within the empire has become evident. That empire had once been dominated by, and run in the interests of, the metropolitan nobility of Rome. It was now beginning to become a universal world empire run by its upper classes — who were all, however, equally subjects of the Emperor. Augustus had thrown the Senate and the machinery of government open to *tota Italia*, men from anywhere within Italy. Claudius was to extend such access to prestige and power to provincials. The reactions of Italian senators and equestrians seem to have been markedly adverse to this extension of privilege.

Claudius advanced Gallic noblemen into the Senate. He seems to have done so acting as *censor*, by *adlectio*; i.e. he conferred senatorial status upon them without requiring them to go through the normal succession of minor offices. Now these men came from a part of Gaul which had long been heavily Romanised — 'the province' (*provincia/*

Provence). Only the province of Baetica in Spain (whence came Trajan, the first provincial emperor) could boast of longer or heavier Romanization (however, unlike this part of Gaul, Baetica could not boast that Claudius had been born there). Nonetheless the Senate objected mightily. Claudius went on to constrain the Senate to rule that Roman citizens from the area could stand for office in Rome. And Claudius seems to have been generous, if cautious, in conferring citizenship on provincials in general.

By Claudius' reign the Senate could elect magistrates, pass laws, act as a high court of justice. It had a prestige of long standing. It seems to have been able to imbue many of its new members with republican sentiments. But Claudius had shifted the balance of power between Senate and imperial apparatus of government decisively in favour of the latter, especially of the latter's central secretariate and major prefectures. From 47 A.D. on, Claudius seems to have been forced by senatorial intransigence into a policy of putting 'safe' men into the Senate and then into key positions and magistracies within the apparatus.[44] Who safer than provincials, under such circumstances? [45]

By Claudius' reign too Italy was in something of a recession. Exports of Arretine pottery, once a major source of income, had dropped away. Asia Minor and Alexandria prospered mightily in the East (this was the reign in which the monsoons were discovered and trade with India consequently expanded). Spain flourished in the West. Striking economic development seems to have taken place in Gaul.[46] Money and material went out to the legions on the frontiers, especially to the eight along the Rhine.[47] Hence, relatively, the plight of Italy must have seemed even worse that it actually was.

The funny money produced in the latter part of the reign cannot have pleased the Italian business community. And it cannot now have been easy for Roman businessmen to exploit the provinces as of old. The Emperor's agents were everywhere. Roman citizenship was increasingly widespread. In many out-back communities Roman centurions had been settled, upon demobilization, to Romanise those communities. They would not make a very exploitable upper layer of such communities. Moreover the despised Easterners were being advanced into the equestrian order. Many Greeks, who, with the Syrians, seem to have formed the backbone of the trading communities of the eastern Mediterranean, appear to have been admitted. Then again some junior procuratorships were going to freedmen.[48] Thus, in spite of the fact that Claudius took careful thought for, and added to the prestige of, the equestrian career, he seems to have met a marked degree of opposition from Italian equestrians as well as senators. Rumour had it that as many as 300 equestrians were executed during his reign.

At the end of the reign, however, there was a distinctive equestrian career, probably containing a much increased number of provincials, comprising three stages.[49] First came the *tres militiae:* service as Prefect or Tribune of an auxiliary cohort, then as Tribune of a legionary cohort, then as Prefect of a wing of cavalry. Then came the financial procuratorships and higher procuratorships (as governor of a province). And here Claudius added the newly formed provinces of Thrace and Judaea to the equestrian career: they were to be governed by an equestrian *propraetor.* Finally came the great prefectures. It was an impressive and important career. A man could feel proud of having served within it. Many did. Rome's enemies could — allegedly — charge that 'the provinces were won with the blood of provincials.' There could be no nationalism when everywhere the upper echelons of society were to come to see themselves as an integral part of the Roman system.

Hadrian (117-138 A.D.) is the next emperor to whom major changes in the Roman system of government are attributed. His reign might be said to mark the transition to the middle empire, imperfectly defined as this period is. The second and third centuries A.D. are poorly represented by surviving literary historical remains. Consequently, much of the account of his and later reigns is patched together from gleanings from inscriptions, coins, passages in (later) law codes, and asides in literature focussed primarily on other themes. Nonetheless there is ample evidence of major change.[50]

If one judges politics by the criterion of 'Who gets what, when and how?'[51] it would appear that the army is the dominant bureaucracy within the apparatus of government to this point. It had been an army man, Vespasian, who had founded the next imperial dynasty, that of the Flavians, after Nero's death brought the Julio-Claudian dynasty to its end. And, after the demise of the Flavian dynasty, another army man, Trajan, inaugurated what has been described as the silver-plated age[52] of the deep peace of the second century. Trajan was followed by Hadrian, his son (some said) by adoption; yet another man reared up within the career and traditions of army service. Both were provincials, from the oldest and most Romanised part of Spain — more 'Roman' by now than Rome itself, which had become something of an ethnic and cultural mosaic. It was even thought that Hadrian was overly sympathetic towards Greek culture. For the future there were to be more provincial than Roman or Italian Emperors, though Hadrian's reforms did produce, for a short while, Emperors who had come up through the civilian sector of the apparatus. But, clearly, by now the empire was being run by the upper classes of its provinces.[53]

Equally clearly, the army's voice was loudly heard in the topmost deliberations of the government. Hadrian had to extricate Rome from a prohibitively expensive eastern war, which had over-extended her military resources in the East, involving an epidemic of local uprisings behind the front. The change of policy seems to have necessitated executing and replacing four top military men. Embattled with the Senate, this Emperor had to pay dearly for army support with which to make crucial decisions stick. For instance, when he adopted L. Aelius Caesar, thus designating the next Emperor, he gave each legionary a donative of 225 *denarii*. The praetorian guardsmen received 5,000 *denarii* apiece, a fact which well illustrates the effective power of the Praetorian Prefect and his staff.

At the local level army interests were too well entrenched for the Emperor to do much but foster developments desired there. By now the army establishment had risen to 30 legions, whose pay had been increased by one-third by Domitian.[54] Legions were now encamped in 'single' camps, i.e. one legion only (not two) to a camp. This was to prevent uprisings against the central government. The legions now tended to be stationed in stone-built camps. Domitian had initiated what was to become known under Hadrian as the *limes* policy, that of a static line of permanent frontier defence works. He had also shifted the centre of military gravity from the Rhine to the Danube.

The resulting build-up of legionary forces on or near the Danube (there were 10 legions in the area in Hadrian's day) rapidly advanced the area to importance within the empire. Men, money and material were poured in. There were, for instance, 9 fleets by now within the empire, and two of them were located on the Danube. Population tended to grow up around the camps. Each had its own encirclement of *canabae* or dwellings of traders or of the women with whom the soldiers were living (marriage was not allowed). Farms sprang up along the routes leading into what were in effect towns. So did potteries to serve them, and the officers' villas also added to the farming community. Trade lines relocated accordingly. A pool of man-power ideally suited for military service came into being. In fact the next century was to see some of the best Emperors Rome ever had come out of this region.[55]

Faced with this situation, Hadrian's options were limited. The regional affiliations of the troops had been evident since they had fought with the hated Praetorians in the 'Year of the Four Emperors' (68-69 A.D.), themselves going into the king-making business. The policy of frontier defence works was extended. A stone or earthern curtain went up, to shut the 'barbarians' out of the Roman empire — the wall in Britain, an earth rampart with palisades, forts and signal towers in Germany and the Dobrudja, a ditch in north Africa. There seems to have been more local recruiting. The auxiliaries had always been brigaded with the legions; now Romans and non-Romans alike were to be found in both types of service. Small contingents of barbarian troops, known as *numeri*, were incorporated into the auxiliaries while retaining their own native arms, equipment, language and methods of fighting. An improved form of the old Macedonian *phalanx* reappeared too. Ex-centurions commanded. Local men and local influences were being allowed their way.

The inclusion of such units broke up the homogeneity of the men in the ranks, who by this time otherwise tended to be locally recruited and retained on the spot. Casualties or replacements gave an opportunity to introduce other non-local elements here too, and care was taken to have a core of Latin-speakers at the level of the centurionate. Such men might come originally from the older provinces, such as Spain. The officers had, up to this time, been politically neutralized by rotating them, from posting to posting, to one district after another as they advanced in their careers. This prevented any one man's lengthy retention of a command, with the risk of his building up strong local support and becoming a security hazard. But Hadrian now allowed the recruiting of officers, too, on a local basis. All that consequently stood in the way of the provincialization of the legions was the fact that many officers still came from the praetorian guard, the chief officer training corps of the empire, to fill vacancies in the frontier legions.[56]

Hadrian granted to the sons whom the soldiers should not rightly have had, the legal right to inherit from their fathers. All in all, his reforms tended to make out of the army something of a border militia, officered by landowners and manned by peasants. Military life had always tended to be a life apart;[57] now a split between the military and the townee population of the older, inner richer empire was foreshadowed.

The more so because it apparently became possible under Hadrian to go right through a career in the civilian part of the apparatus of government without military service. For equally epochal changes occurred within this sector of the bureaucratic apparatus also in this reign. The equestrians, for instance, took over the ministries of the central secretariate from the imperial freedmen.[58] The great classical age of Roman law developed, with the Emperor's officials shaping it — and, as a consequence, most of the centralised decision-making process as well. The Emperor's council became the key policy-making body of government. And government finances were extensively reorganised. As a result, the composition of the Senate altered and its effective power dropped still further away.

This was the reign which inaugurated the great age of the imperial civil service, which now came to knit more cohesively together. The *consilium principis*, or Imperial Council, was now the chief policy-making body, the supreme court wherein top people were tried, and the originator of new laws. Its members, the *consiliarii*, most probably comprised the Heads of major departments, the senior prefects and distinguished jurists. Specifically these seem to have been the Treasurer *(a rationibus)*, Correspondence Secretary *(ab epistulis)*, Justice Secretary *(a libellis)*, the Secretary in charge of Briefings *(a studiis)*, and two new posts, the *Praefectus vehiculorum* and *procurator hereditatium* (see below). The Praetorian and Urban Prefects were probably members, as were the Prefects of the Watch and of the Grain Supply. Distinguished jurists were also invited on as salaried members.

Augustus had had a council, the *consilium semestre*, as a liaison with the Senate, but this seems to have come to an end with the death of the next Emperor, Tiberius. Since then, other Emperors had called in friends to counsel them, after the Roman fashion. But Hadrian's council was more formal, although the changes which he introduced seem to have consisted largely in merely carrying existing practice to its logical conclusion. Its members, the Emperor's friends *(amici)*, aides *(comites)* and jurists *(juris consulti)* were approved by the Senate. The body was somewhat like a privy council. It was to have an important part in government for the future, now that it had been more formally constituted.[59] And, in the Emperor's (frequent) absence, the Praetorian Prefect deputed for him by taking over the chair at Council meetings.

Other important developments of an institutional nature were that the 'Public Post,' or communications services, were placed under the direction of a central bureau at Rome headed by a Prefect, the *Praefectus vehiculorum* (Prefect in charge of Vehicles) mentioned above.[60] A records office, under the *a memoria*, was also set up. Information and communications services seem in fact to have been greatly augmented by this reign. Hadrian was notorious for having his security officials check even upon his friends.

Communications had been something of a problem since Domitian's day, it would appear, for to the latter's reign date a new concept and the new and untoward influence of a personal attendant. The concept was *fumus* or 'smoke,' by which was meant inside opinion on the Emperor's mood on the day in question. The person who sold it was the *(libertus) ab admissione*, or freedman in charge of admissions to the Emperor's presence. That such a gatekeeping role had become so important is a sign of the distance the Emperor had moved from 'parity' with the Senate. Senators had not purchased gossip from a chamberlain in Augustus' day! But the growth in importance of the Emperor's Council will have perpetuated the breakdown in communications between the latter and the Senate.

Something of a departmental feud may have built up by this time between the Urban and Praetorian Prefects.[61] The latter were normally soldiers, the former often — and increasingly from Hadrian's reign — jurists. Already by the end of the first century the Urban Prefect had apparently taken over the administration of justice within Italy; he also appears to have preempted the functions of the aediles; and he was increasingly to influence the formation of law. The Praetorian Prefect had designs on the first and third of these functions, as will appear in due course. Both of these officials were, however, by now of enormous importance within the apparatus of government. It was Attianus, Hadrian's kinsman and Praetorian Prefect, who had had the four generals — all of consular rank — executed at the beginning of the reign in the controversy over pulling out of the eastern war. Hadrian even alleged that Attianus had acted of his own initiative in so doing.

Equally important changes had occurred, as stated, within the central secretariate, where equestrians replaced freedmen in command. All of the hallmarks of bureaucracy are evident: serried ranks of titles and pay-scales — and an anonymous officialdom. This is the reign in which the equestrians move decisively forward to take over effective power in running the government. New posts are created for them and they gain new functions too. Nowhere is this more evident than in regard to financial matters. The newly reorganised bureaucracy, paying salaries of 300,000, 200,000, 100,000 and 60,000 *sesterces* p.a. to its four major ranks (this when the pay of a man in the ranks, better off than the commonality, was 1,200 *sesterces*) cost 50 million *sesterces* p.a., apparently.

Yet it paid its way, it would appear. Hadrian had had to write off 900 million *sesterces* in bad debts to the government at the beginning of the reign. The new machine was designed to collect taxes more effectively. Equestrian tax-farming companies (elaborate organizations with Masters, *Magistri*, heading provincial branch-offices) were replaced by these officials. A new official, the *advocatus fisci* or Public Prosecutor, replaced informers (who had retained a quarter of properties confiscated upon a successful prosecution) as the means of dealing with tax evasion. The central bureaucracy now sent its bright young men, with the styling 'Overseer of the Commonwealth' or the like *(curator rei publicae)*, to regulate the affairs of cities in the provinces if such cities conducted their financial affairs amiss (taxes were largely collected through the intermediacy of local city councils). A department was established to collect a 5% succession tax; this was that of the *procurator hereditatium* already mentioned.

There were other new functionaries, too. The imperial court had had a special account to meet its expenses, the *ratio castrensis*, since Domitian's day; an imperial freedman looked after this. After Domitian, Nerva had initiated a new scheme for feeding the poor children of Italy, the *alimenta Caesaris*; a *procurator* looked after this. Trajan, whose Dacian campaign (the last war of the empire to pay for itself) had brought in vast amounts of bullion, had instituted a *procurator monetae, procurator* of the mint. Since Claudius' day, and more especially since the extravagance of Nero's court (the most expensive of the empire), the coinage had been becoming increasingly debased. Hadrian halted the downward trend during his reign. He also put out a great series of coins advertising the provinces.[62]

Meanwhile the Senate's treasury had shrunk almost to the status of a regional treasury. The Emperor's privy purse, the *patrimonium*, was now looked after by a *procurator*; its proportions were far more considerable. The idea of considering the *patrimonium Caesaris* to be attached to the position, rather than the person, of the reigning Emperor seems to date to this time,[63] possibly because of the crucial importance of that patrimony in the overall financial scheme of things. It is therefore small wonder that the director of imperial finance now received the title of *procurator fisci* instead of *a rationibus* (later in the century he was to be termed the *rationalis*, Officer in Charge of Accounts) and to rank high within the equestrian career in status and salary.

Perhaps a brief outline of such status and salary rankings might not be inappropriate at this point. For a semantic field of bureaucrat's jargon had by now evolved. A senator was known as a *vir* (gentleman) *clarissimus*, an inheritable title. There were three grades of titles for equestrians. A *primus pilus* or top centurion, prefect of a wing of cavalry and a minor *procurator* was known as a *vir egregius*. Then, in ascending order, came the important *procurators*, the Prefects of the Watch or Grain Supply, and men like the *a cognitionibus* or Procurator in charge of Judicial Investigations. Such a man would be known as a *vir perfectissimus*. A Praetorian Prefect was truly described as a *vir eminentissimus*. Equestrian titles were for life only. Incidentally, it is to legal documents datable to this reign that the first conceptual distinction of the citizen and other population of the empire as *honestiores* (the better class of people, i.e. equestrians and their superiors) and *humiliores* (the humbler sort) is owed. Status lines were obviously becoming more sharply drawn, as citizenship (now rapidly expanding) became less of a criterion of demarcation.

Salary rankings reveal both the hierarchical nature of the apparatus, its formalism and its piecemeal growth.[64] The lowest salary level, that of the *sexagenarii* (officials in receipt of 60,000 *sesterces* p.a.) comprised assistants of various sorts (e.g. the *adjutor* to the Prefect of the Grain Supply; the vice-director or *subcurator* of Sacred Buildings and Public Works). Here too were the assessors, *consiliarii*, of the Praetorian and Urban Prefects, the Correspondence Secretary for Greek, and the minor procuratorships — of Pavements, for instance, or of regional parts of the Emperor's patrimony. Here also were the financial *procurators* of minor provinces, prefects of unimportant fleets, provincial *procurators* of the Public Post and provincially operating Public Prosecutors.

The next grade up, that of the *centenarii* (officials on 100,000 *sesterces* p.a.), comprised the Correspondence Secretary for Latin; *procurators* such as those of the Mint, Water Services, and Public Works — and the *a commentariis* of the Praetorian Prefect. It is a mark of the power of an official that his underlings receive preferential treatment and by this criterion the various Praetorians all bear witness to their master's preeminence within the apparatus. Also at this level were the Public Prosecutor, the subprefects of the Grain Supply and the Watch, and the financial *procurators* of large or strategically important provinces, of important fleets, of imperial mines and of big imperial estates.

The next grade, the *ducenarii*, (officials on 200,000 *sesterces*), comprised those *procurators* who were heads of departments, or who served in imperial provinces of consular rank or conjoint provinces of praetorian rank. The topmost grade, the *trecenarii* (officials on 300,000 *sesterces*), included the Praetorian Prefect and the Prefects of the Grain Supply and the Watch; the Heads of the central secretariate, and the

Directors of Finance (the *fiscus*) and the patrimony.

Such posts might be held only for a few years' duration and there was no provision for a pension scheme. They were tax exempt, however. So a succession of them, as one's career wound to its close, could make one's family fortunes. Pay was good and prestige was high in this, the hey-day of the bureaucracy of the civil administration. Its pervasive influence can be seen in the political style of the empire in its dealings with outsiders for much of the rest of the century. In striking contrast with, say, the foreign policy of a militarist *régime* such as Septimius Severus', the politics of administrators supervene. A defensive posture is maintained, and attention is focussed upon managing the internal affairs and resources of the government.[65] Certainly all the sinecurism and feather-bedding which civilians are wont to associate with a peace-time army seems to have been allowed to develop among the military.[66] It looks as though the interests of the central administrative apparatus were more carefully looked after by those bureaucrats than were the interests of their officials in the provinces. For there is no comparable innovation in the types of instrumentalities provided there, though, naturally, appropiate extensions of central departments were appended.

A review of decision-making will indicate the effective power of this apparatus of government. For instance, eminent jurists came to work more closely with the administration. This is the classical age of Roman law, and Hadrian's reign stands as the high-water mark of the age.[67] Its principle achievement was the producing of collections of decisions and simple, general treatises ordering masses of legal material. Thus the praetor's Edict, a sort of on-going accumulation of decisions based on precedent, was codified. Henceforth magistrates could not add to the law by interpreting it, and change comes through imperial decisions, guided by the advice of the jurisconsults of the administration and taking the form of *constitutiones* or imperial regulations. This is also the great age of trials before the Emperor's court. Possibly, too, the concept of the municipality as a legal entity, allowing an expansion of business activities, is owed to this reign.[68] Certainly owed to it is the practice of having four *juridici* or judges of consular status go on circuit to administer the law around Italy. The latter was an unpopular innovation with the Senate, as it reduced Italy to procedural parity with the provinces.

In fact, however, the overall trend of Hadrian's activities was to reduce discrepancies of status between Italy and the provinces.[69] The body of law produced by the apparatus represented an impressive intellectual achievement and something of a social revolution. It was essentially reasonable, based on ideas of equity and the premise that men are reasonable beings, entering into contractual and reciprocal obligations of their own accord. True, theory outran practice, for slavery and the *honestior: humilior* distinction (which involved, e.g. different penalties for the same crime according to status) remained.[70] But Roman law is a creation unique within the world of antiquity, fitting product of a governmental system which maintained peace and prosperity over more of Europe, and for a longer time, than ever before or since.

The Senate was much changed, too, by now. On top of the advancement of new *élites* by the Emperors there had been the blood-lettings of the Year of the Four Emperors and then of Domitian's reign. Virtually none of the aristocratic lines which had dominated centuries of the history of the Republic survived the first century of the empire. Nor did the new nobility raised by the Julio-Claudian Emperors do much better.[71] Everywhere provincials were coming forward to power. Hadrian spent almost half his reign touring the provinces. He advanced their cities in status. He made lavish grants of 'Greater Latinity' *(Latium maius)*, under which all future members of the town council of the town which had been made such a grant became Roman citizens. There was much building, financed by the imperial government, in the provinces. More was spent on Athens than on Rome, an unprecedented occurrence. More easterners than ever before were admitted to the Senate (there was prejudice against "Orientals," westerners being preferred). It was a very different Senate from that of Augustus' day which Hadrian attended. The old families, with their proud traditions, and hostility to the *princeps*, had gone.[72]

The Senate's aims in government had changed proportionately. Senators wanted to secure the best *Princeps* possible, an Emperor who would not put senators to death and in whose selection they had some say. Succession was managed by adoption — of a candidate "favoured" by the Senate — from Nerva (96 A.D.) to Marcus Aurelius (died 180 A.D.).[73] Even so, Hadrian's engrossment of power left even the weakened Senate of his day bitterly resentful. From this reign on, however, it was to retain little but prestige. A brief glance at the relative power positions of Senate and imperial administration in regard to their respective fields of influence in the provinces is highly informative in this regard. In 27 B.C., at the beginning of the Principate, the Senate had had 10 provinces, the *princeps* 7, better than a ratio of 5 to 4 in favour of the Senate. At the beginning of Hadrian's reign, the Senate had 11 provinces, the *princeps* 33, a ratio of 3 to 1 in the latter's favour. Thus of the 27 provinces added in the interval, on balance, 26 had gone to the Emperor and only one to the Senate.

However, there was one non-imperial bureaucratically organised group which *had* grown in influence. This was the Christian Church. [74] This was partly due to adventitious factors. The Jews, the Christians' bitterest enemies, had fallen foul of Rome. There had been a rebellion in 66 A.D. which was stamped out in 70 by Vespasian's son, Titus, the tenth legion building its camp upon the ruins in Jerusalem. All Jews were required to pay their two *drachmae* in yearly dues not to the temple at Jerusalem but to Jupiter of the Capitoline — and the *fiscus Judaicus*. Then Trajan's eastern campaigns ruined eastern trade, in which Jewish interests were heavily involved, when it was at its most prosperous. [75] There was another uprising under Bar-Cochbar. After fierce fighting Jerusalem fell and the Jews were banished from Judaea in the "scattering," or *diaspora* (135 A.D.). They were thus in a poor position for proselytising, or for campaigning against other religious groups.

Christianity fared better, relatively speaking. Christians would not participate in pagan cults — including the imperial cult, failure to make obeisance to which meant death. They would not serve in the armies. They were thought to practice secret vices. But officialdom found them harmless and law-abiding. Thus, although the cult was illegal, official-dom was generally slow to persecute. Anonymous indictments were ignored; sacrifice to the Emperor would clear a man actually on trial. Unless both local mob and provincial governor wanted a witch-hunt, action was not taken against Christians. There were some martyrs and even a drastic persecution in 177 in the Rhône area under Marcus Aurelius (here appearing as a philosopher killer). But sporadic police action actually provided a stimulus to the growth of the Church, which spread apace in the second century. It went up the Rhône valley, up the Nile valley and to North Africa. By the end of the century it had spread upwards in society, too, winning converts among the womenfolk of the highly placed. Christians felt that the spread of their religion was proof of its divine origins.

Organizationally, too, the Church advanced in this century, far surpassing other popular cults within the empire in this respect. Each city now came to have a bishop, with some presbyters below him, and some deacons below them. The bishop ordained, corresponded with, and visited other Christian communities, and provided guidance against theological error (such as that of the Gnostics, Valentinians or

Montanists). The bishop came also to be the lineal successor of an apostolic founding father of his city's church. By his correspondence with, and travels to, other cities, the Church came to be webbed together in a net of long-range connections. Presbyters, by now a distinct rank below the bishops, could celebrate communion and teach. A strongly moralistic tone was beginning to emerge in teaching. Deacons looked to almsgiving and handling property, as of old.

It was a century of standardisation in other ways too. A Rule of Faith was hammered out for guidance of the faithful; a New Testament began to be defined — the gospel according to Matthew, Mark, Luke and John. The Church had long been the only organised group to attempt to speak to the little people in the direct colloquial language which they could understand, couching its message with dignity and without condescension. Now the attempt was made to present the Christian case to the upper order, educated in the Great Tradition of classical literature, by adapting Platonic metaphysics and Stoic ethics.

This organisation was built up among the disadvantaged and was tempered by times of tribulation. It was to come into its own in the chaotic second half of the third century when the upper classes in the cities, together with their institutions, were to be mauled, if not broken. The organizational base built in the second century was then to put Christianity in a most competitive position.

The next major changes within the apparatus of government occur in the reign of Septimius Severus (193-211 A.D.). In fact, changes occurring within the brief course of the dynasty he founded brought about massive overall reshaping of the complex of institutions we have been considering. In many cases changes occurring under one of his successors are so manifestly the working out of developments set in train by his activities that it would be perverse not to mention them. So mention will briefly be made of such striking and immediate consequences under his successors. Those successors were, incidentally, Caracalla his son (211-217); Macrinus, a usurping Praetorian Prefect (217-218); Bassianus or El Gabal ("the priest of Ba'al"), Caracalla's alleged natural son (218-222); and Severus Alexander, the latter's cousin (222-235).[76]

Perhaps however we should first note certain changes in the environment within which the Roman apparatus of government functioned. Marcus Aurelius' armies had brought back a plague from the east in 166. It may well have been smallpox. The primitive hygienic conditions under which the poor lived in the cities made the empire a splendid breeding ground for infectious diseases. Mortality was enormous and a decline in population seems to have set in.[77] On top of this, pressing upon the northern frontiers there was now a new and unprecedentedly dangerous barbarian menace. The barbarians were no longer a quarrelling mass of tribal splinter-groups but organised and in ethnic federations. They had accumulated Roman technical skills, implements and organizational know-how (when it came to fighting). And, behind them, the east Germanic peoples were on the move, setting the whole demilitarized zone along the Rhenic and especially the Danubian frontiers in motion.

This was the time the Romans chose for a 4-year long bout of particularly ferocious civil wars, involving 5 "Emperors" and two major campaigns, one in the East, the other in the West. This in turn triggered an uprising within the empire (in Britain) and an attack from the Parthians. The latter were soundly defeated. So weakened were they, as a result, that one of their own subject peoples, the Sassanids, overthrew them. So it was that the poorly organised and relatively pacific Parthian *régime* came to be replaced by an effective and aggressive Persian empire. Shapur, son of the Ardashir who founded this empire in 227, was even to take the Emperor Valerian prisoner in 260.[78]

Upon plague, civil war, uprising and invasion famine naturally followed; and it may well be that malaria spread across the depopulated and unworked lands of the empire.[79] Such were the conditions which prevailed while El Gabal dined off nightingales' tongues dusted with powdered pearls and his divine mother introduced the Roman court to ritual prostitution. In their own ways the various sectors of the apparatus of government comported themselves with equal discernment and discretion. The Severi were to be followed by a failing economy,[80] massive social change and fifty years' military anarchy.

There is no doubt that the most powerful sector of the apparatus was the army. When the murder of Commodus, last and least of the Antonines, put the throne up for grabs, various army units played at king-making. Septimius Severus, who won the throne, is alleged to have advised his sons on his deathbed: "Enrich the soldiers and despise the rest of the world." Now the army had the faults of an overly powerful bureaucracy in a tendency to inter-departmental feuding, as it were, and an arrogant attitude towards its *clientele*, the population of the empire. The Praetorians put Pertinax on the throne as Emperor, killed him when he attempted to discipline them, and then offered the throne to the highest bidder. It went to Didius Julianus, who offered 100,000 *sesterces* apiece as a donative from atop a ladder leaning against the wall of the Praetorians' camp. But by now the provincial armies of Illyricum (near the Danube), Syria and Britain had put up their candidates. It was the crack Danubian troops who, in the sequel, set their candidate, the African Septimius Severus, on the throne.

The rival groups paid dearly. The Praetorians were disbanded and dismissed from the service; for the future those so disciplined were not to approach within one hundred miles of Rome. The guard was then reconstituted. It was no longer drawn from Romans or Italians from the long Romanized provinces of Noricum (near the top of the Adriatic), Spain or Macedonia. Instead it was to be composed of legionaries from the frontiers, whose spell of duty in the guard was to groom them for promotion to positions as frontier officers. This meant that the last barrier to the provincialization of the legions had been removed.

Syria and Britain were split into two provinces each, thus for the future scattering their concentrations of legionaries. This was to be a general security measure: no province was henceforth to have more than two legions, and "new" provinces were made to bring this about. But civilians too, like these provinces, had (perforce), chosen the wrong side. As result whole cities — Antioch, Byzantium and Lyons — were given over to the fury of, and despoliation by, the soldiery. Living apart in their cantonments along the frontiers, the soldiery had by this time apparently come to think of themselves as the masters, rather than the guardians, of the rustic drudges on the land and the despised townee populations of the soft inner provinces.

They drove a hard bargain as their price for putting Septimius upon the throne. There was a pay increase, of course — or rather a series of them. Commodus, the last of the Antonines, had increased legionary pay to 375 *denarii* p.a. (from the Domitianic figure of 300); to the Praetorian guardsmen he gave 1250 *denarii* p.a. Septimius Severus increased these sums to 500 and 1700 *denarii* respectively, and his son Caracalla increased Septimius' rates to 750 *denarii* p.a. for legionaries and presumably stepped up praetorian pay proportionately. If the ordinary legionary's pay had increased by 100% under the Severi, it should be remembered that a top centurion received 50 times this amount and higher officers proportionately more. Donatives now came more frequently, too. And they increased in amount. Caracalla, for instance, recipient of a greater fortune than any Emperor before him, squandered it all in one day on a donative to keep the troops loyal after his murder of Geta, his brother and co-Emperor.

The army establishment, moreover, went up from 30 to 33 legions. What is more, veterans were given precedence in appointments to the provincial staffs of the administrative bureaucracy, after their period of army service — and, with the creation of new provinces by subdivisions in Africa, Britain and Syria, large numbers of minor staff posts must have been created. New terrain, that of Mesopotamia, was also overrun and the army settled in to look after the area as a province, and its own commercial interests as well. For, apparently, business dealings on the side were characteristic of all ranks in the army by this stage.[81]

Occupation of Mesopotamia, to round off the Roman hold on the Fertile Crescent with its busy trade, was only to be expected once Syrian interests were well represented in army circles. And there were very strong Syrian influences acting upon this dynasty. Its highly influential womenfolk, worshipped as divinities and "Mothers of the Camps," were Syrians, not to speak of El Gabal and Severus Alexander, their offspring. Meanwhile, upon the Danubian frontier, Marcus Aurelius had given freehold land to the soldiery in return for an hereditary obligation on their part to provide military service. This arrangement was extended to other such troops by Severus Alexander. Such soldiers were apparently very much aware of their propertied interests in the area; they killed Alexander, in the event, rather than have his policies harm those interests.

Army interests were looked after in other ways, too. The ban on soldiers' marrying was now lifted. The status of their inevitable dependents was thus regularised, giving the latter access to all of the privileges enjoyed by the soldiery — Roman citizenship, for instance, for a start. Also the soldiery, and ex-service men, gained exemptions from the spate of taxes and related obligations which now came to fall crushingly upon residents within the empire. Combined, such privileges were all that was needed, in these circumstances, to make a separate caste out of the soldiery.[82]

There is ample evidence of goal displacement in all this. The army was putting its own interests as a group ahead of its duties to the community it was supposedly safeguarding. This becomes evident from the sequel to the Severi, when the monetary economy collapses, due to over-exaction from a dwindling tax base, and the *limes* fails to contain pressures from without. But the army was fast becoming almost a race apart from the citizenry and was defining its interests and duties accordingly. Military families supplied much of the man-power for what was rapidly becoming an hereditary career. Under Septimius Severus the centurionate became the required first stage in that career. This meant that senators, and even equestrians (such as were not sprung from the military), were to be excluded from military service. But centurions' sons were now to become of equestrian rank, as the ranks of the equestrian order were expanded to incorporate more and more soldiers. Increasingly the traditional split between "gentlemanly" officers and other ranks drawn from the commonality was to vanish as promotion upward through the ranks became institutionalised. Maximin, the first Emperor after the Severi, had been a Thracian peasant originally, a striking demonstration of army service as an avenue for improvement of one's social standing.

There was a change, too, in army religion. Instead of worshipping the legionary *aquila* or eagle as representing the *numen* or divine in-dwelling force of the legion, the Emperor was worshipped as divine, along with his wife, who became the *Mater Castrorum* or Mother of the Camp. Other links with the past vanished too. The Severi were supported by a non-Italian army. The three new legions which were raised were recruited in Illyricum, now *the* military centre of the empire. One of them, the *Legio II Parthica*, was subsequently stationed upon the Alban Mount near Rome, thus reducing Italy's status to that of a province. No longer were the men of Italy or the long-Romanised provinces to predominate in positions of authority throughout the armed forces, apparently. The fate of the Praetorians was symptomatic.

This democratization and provincialization of the army's command structure meant that the men of the great tradition of Graeco-Roman culture were increasingly replaced by men of the peasant-traditions of little communities. More than literary predispositions were lost. Respect for constitutionalism and the Roman tradition of service weakened. Stoicism seems, for instance, to have vanished in the third century. In its place came increasing reliance on, and latent enmity towards, more autocratic forms of government.[83] It was to be an increasingly authoritarian age, but discipline was gone and the Emperor came to be commanded rather than to command.

There is some evidence of new institutions within the army. The *scholae*, for instance, seem to have originated at this point. Initially they were a form of social insurance: burial clubs, or community chests into which one could contribute against the possibility of the expenses involved in a move for promotion. The *scholae* were to develop almost beyond recognition from these humble beginnings. But the most striking development occurred in the build-up of the powers of the Praetorian Prefecture. True, one set of guardsmen had been scattered; but the institution remained. It was located within both military and civil administrative bureaucracies and, as these both advanced in power, its total gains were to make the Praetorian Prefect second only in power to the Emperor himself. This is the great age of this prefecture's power, the age to which we owe the concept of "Praetorianism." In the time of the Severi alone, for instance, the Praetorians put Pertinax on the throne and cast him down again; they put Didius Julianus on the throne; Macrinus, the first non-senatorial Emperor, stepped from the Praetorian Prefecture to the throne (he was to have his imitators later in this century); and El Gabal was overthrown by the Praetorians.

The Praetorian Prefect's increased powers came largely from developments within imperial financing and taxation, to which the discussion will accordingly turn. Signs of financial strain had been evident as early as Marcus Aurelius' day (161-180). His reign had commenced with a donative of 20,000 *sesterces* apiece for the Praetorians. He had had to hold an auction of imperial heirlooms and furniture, later, to meet imperial expenses. Rumour had it that his wastrel son Commodus left only 25,000 *denarii* in the treasury upon his demise. Yet Septimius Severus, after giving out 220,000,000 *denarii* in donatives to the Praetorians and in hand-outs *(congiaria)* to the populace at Rome, was able to bequeath to his sons a full treasury, fuller, in fact, than any inherited to this date.

By Septimius' time the Senate's treasury, the *aerarium*, had shrunk to become a mere municipal treasury for the city of Rome. The patrimony, *patrimonium*, was inherited with the empire. By a retrospective adoption ceremony Septimius had declared himself the "son" of Marcus Aurelius, and thus inherited all the property of the Antonines and the Emperors before that back to Nerva. This patrimony consisted of imperial estates all over the empire and royal estates in Egypt. It was thought to be attached to the position, rather than the person, of the Emperor, and its incoming revenues were fed into those of the *fiscus* or imperial treasury. Even in combination, however, these were now proving to be inadequate to meet expenses.

Recourse was had to various devices. The property of opponents in the civil wars was confiscated. This happened without loss of life in the sequel to the first bout of civil wars, but the second bout was followed by the arraignment of 64 senators, of whom 29 were condemned to death as well as having their estates confiscated. Caracalla, Septimius' son, improved on this by confiscating the estates of 20,000 persons who had supported his brother Geta (whom Caracalla murdered to obtain sole control of the empire). The huge fortune accrued by confiscation, however, went into a new treasury, the *Res Privata*, looked after by a *Rationalis* or Accountant who ranked among the highest *echelons* of the civil bureaucracy. The *Res Privata* was held to be the property of the individual, not of the office of Emperor. It made that individual easily the wealthiest man in the Roman world. It drew the attention, later in the third century, of military adventurers, representing as it did a golden prize that went with the position of Emperor. But it did not help imperial financing as such.[84]

Help for the latter came in various forms. Taxes were increased. Towns which were "supporters" of the losing side in the civil war had been forced to pay up to four times the amount which they had contributed to the coffers of that side. This principle, as it were, seems to have been extended; for subsequently the cities and towns of the empire were required to contribute voluntary gifts of precious metal (aurum coronarium or oblaticium) to the Emperor on appropriate occasions. Such gifts would be required upon accession, for instance, or in the event of "victory" in war. Thus were the expenses of the troops' donatives met.

As will become evident, the tenor of Septimius' legislation was such as to lessen discrimination within the empire based on the lack of possession of citizenship. By the Constitutio Antoniniana of 212, one year after his father's death, Caracalla extended Roman citizenship to all but the dediticii* within the empire. Caracalla then doubled succession duties and manumission taxes to 10 percent. All Roman citizens had to pay such dues. Also, prior to the Constitutio Antoniniana, Roman citizens living in a tax-paying city had been exempt from the tax-related obligations of non-citizens. Now all alike had to meet those obligations. Thus was the tax-base widened.

The reason for the introduction of these "obligations" was that the coinage was dropping in buying power. In 198, Septimius had allowed the bronze alloy in the silver currency to increase to 40-60% so as to produce enough denarii to meet the payment of the troops, the government's main financial out-going. By 200, imperial currency was in forced circulation within the empire, and the peoples outside of the empire would not accept imperial "silver," only gold (and even the gold pieces dropped in weight). Caracalla in 215 took the step which was to lead by the 260's (when the "silver" was 97.5% bronze) to a breakdown of the currency system. He introduced a new silver coin, the Antoninianus. It was one and a half times the weight of the denarius, consisted of 50% silver, and was tariffed at two denarii. This set the

---

*Dediticii were barbarians who had been transported en bloc and put on deserted land within the empire; they had to farm that land, and defend it under arms at need, but they were not given citizen status.

pattern for the future when Emperors could not make financial ends meet: weight and precious metal content were dropped while simultaneously declared value was increased. People began to hoard the good old coins; a black market in gold developed; counterfeiting became prevalent.

As taxes were pegged at set financial levels whereas inflation was everywhere evident, the imperial administration now began to exact payment in kind at its own valuation, which ignored inflationary price increases. Increasing use, too, was made of *corvée* labour as a form of taxation. Hence the above-mentioned tax-related obligations. These were of three kinds. There were *munera personalia*, which were largely menial tasks performed by the poor, involving provisioning, portage and so forth. There were *munera patrimoniorum*, which fell on the wealthy. These involved providing billets and transport, holding local office (with its requirements to provide public services), and collecting taxes for the government (any shortfall to be made good from the local collector's own purse). And there were *munera mixta*, which normally involved an obligation to perform some form of service personally for the government, but which could involve the payment of money in an emergency. But still it proved increasingly impossible to pay the soldiers' wages in (an increasingly worthless) money. So it was that exactions in kind, the *annona militaris* or "grain for the soldiery," came to provide both the military and the civil apparatus of government with their food and clothing. And to the Praetorian Prefect fell the task of seeing that this was done.

The *alimenta* scheme, which involved making provision both for poor children and indirectly, poor farmers within Italy, was now more necessary than ever it had been (it had been suspended, as an economy measure, in Commodus' reign). A strong hand, too, was needed to see to the *annona*, which involved provisioning Rome with grain by using a Mediterranean-wide network of services. The Praetorian Prefect had come to control both of these functions of the government (in the latter case the Prefect of the Grain Supply merely handled the doling out of grain in Rome now). It was only reasonable, under the circumstances, to combine with these duties the procedurally interrelated duty of overseeing the provisioning of the army. This meant, of course, that the Praetorian Prefect needed an appropriately empowered seat in the inner counsels of power. He was given the right to hear appeals from the provincial governors, in all of whose provinces his agents were, after all, negotiating. Likewise he took over all criminal cases in Italy beyond a 100 mile radius of Rome.

This meant that the feud over spheres of authority between the Urban and the Praetorian Prefects had now been decided decisively in favour of the latter. The Urban Prefect was in fact never to recover from this set-back until the seventh century. He was equipped with 14 subordinates, of consular status, to "help" him look after Rome's 14 city regions. As the Tribunate of the People and the Curule Aedileship seem to have been dropped from the senatorial *cursus honorum* at this point, it is extremely doubtful whether such a move was meant to strengthen the Urban Prefect's position. Traditionalists in the Senate, with whom the Urban Prefect would have to work, would resent both moves, for they devalued tribunate, aedileship and consulship.

The Praetorian Prefect in this way took over the Urban Prefect's position as the chief legal luminary in the administration. Leading jurists begin to be appointed to the position. It is held, for instance, by Papinian under Septimius Severus and by Ulpian and Paul under Severus Alexander. The latter gave the Praetorian Prefect senatorial status. This made him a peer of senators, whom he could consequently try before his court. And, as of old, he presided over the Imperial Council in the absence of the Emperor. He was now second in power to the Emperor alone.[85]

The Imperial Council seems to have developed into the effective decision-making body of government. Certainly Septimius did not allow the Senate to make decisions, whether these involved decrees or the election of magistrates or provincial governors. For him, the Senate's function was merely to acclaim imperial decisions. Trials occurred only before the imperial court. It was the decisions of the latter which now shaped policy and law. We have now arrived at the late classical age of Roman law. The *juris prudentes* are now mostly equestrians. They hold high office and their duty is to administer justice and give legal advice to the Emperor. Their incorporation within the Establishment seems gradually to have stifled progressive elements within the law. It was Septimius' legal advisers, for instance, who conveniently put forward an opinion that the Senate had surrendered its powers to the Emperor. In Severus Alexander's day the Imperial Council was established at a membership of 70. There were 20 equestrian, salaried jurisconsults, the inner ring of the body, and 50 senatorial *amici* of the Emperor, who seem to have functioned as mere figure-heads.[86]

It was the equestrians who now surged forward to power. The newly created province of Mesopotamia was put under an equestrian Prefect. The three new legions were put under equestrian officers. Senators are in fact not found in positions of command in the army from this point.

Now for the first time equestrians become companions, *comites*, and *consiliarii* (advisers), of the Emperor. A whole range of administrative posts hitherto the monopoly of the Senate opens up to them. For senatorial governors went unappointed and in their place equestrian deputies *(vicarii* or *praesides)* governed. The power of the provincial governors grew too, for they all now had criminal jurisdiction. Moreover there seems to have been an increase in the number of the officials sent out to investigate city affairs; these were known as the *curatores rei publicae.* All had their staffs of underlings, of course. In fact the size of the apparatus of the civil bureaucracy must have grown somewhat. For three new provinces, with all their apparatus of administration, had been created by subdivision. Moreover the size of the local staffs seems to have swollen too, because of their increased duties. New types of minor officials are found, as well. Army numbers, and related commissariat problems, had increased. Repairs to the *limes*, whereon stone forts replaced the former wooden ones in Caracalla's day, had also increased.[87] Hence the need for an increase in the administrators' numbers.

With these developments came an increase in the numbers of the equestrian order. Most of the newcomers probably came from army men, what with inflation on the one hand and increased pay and donatives on the other. Moreover, given the nature of services being provided by the provincial administrative staffs, there was a trend to appoint ex-soldiers to them. The *fiscus* had taken from the cities the cost of maintaining the public post. Its functions were too important to be left to the vagaries of local financing. Secret service agents, known as *speculatores* and *frumentarii,* drawn from the legions, swarmed in the provinces under Caracalla, hunting down former supporters of his brother. From Septimius' day a network of troop-stations had been set up in each province to cope with "banditry," as the authorities termed the endemic civil disturbances resulting from alienation within the population in general.[88] Thus the civil apparatus became increasingly involved in the operations of the military and came to adopt a more military image, involving ranks and titles and insignia of office. It was probably from the changes which commenced now that service therein came to be known as *militia*, "the (military) service."[89]

Meanwhile the influence of the Court was growing. There was no question now of adoption of the best *princeps* or constitutional monarch after consultation with the Senate. Commodus' autocratic reign had shown the hollowness of pretensions to constitutional rule or joint rule with the Senate. The new *régime* was an open dynastic succession. Rulers were now undisguisedly autocratic. They and their household (the *domus divina*) were "divine." Their womenfolk likewise were divine rulers. Politics were in consequence dominated by court intrigues. Thus the Praetorian Prefect Plautianus, Septimius Severus' favourite, came to exercise enormous power, dispensing with a colleague in his tenure of the prefecture. Under Caracalla a eunuch, Sempronius Rufus, was notorious for his influence. The reigns of El Gabal and Severus Alexander were in fact master-minded by the ladies of the imperial household, Maesa, Soaemias and Mammaea.

As the military and civil apparatus of government grew in power they had thus brought about a climate of politics dominated by bureaucratic infighting. More constitutional forms of governance were swept to one side. The Senate lost even its illusory prestige. It was treated with open hostility (by Septimius Severus) or contempt (by Caracalla). Its members were tried before the Emperor's court and, in many cases, condemned to death. Under the Severi there was, as has been seen, a movement to make all equal before the law. As far as concerned the Senate, this meant that senators too were, like *humiliores*, liable to torture and death penalties. The Severan law was no respecter of persons. A provincial Afro-Syrian dynasty, the Severi were cosmopolitan in outlook. Italy was brought down to the status of any of the provinces (Septimius stationed a legion therein), and provincials, especially the formerly disdained easterners, were advanced to senatorial status. So were many equestrians and military men. The Senate now had no semblance of authority. It had no control over finances, could not pass decrees or even act as a court of law when its own members were on trial. Senators disappear from army commands and provincial governorships. Its values and beliefs were repudiated, and, indeed, trampled upon in the reign of El Gabal.

The local senates, the town councils of the cities of the empire, were to undergo a like diminution in privilege and power. Under Septimius Severus boards of the ten foremost local citizens, the *decem primi*, begin to appear. These boards were charged with responsibility of seeing to it that the various obligations or *munera* were met. Both the local *bureau* of the central government and the *curator* of their particular township were there to see that the local worthies undertook these onerous and expensive responsibilities. The local worthies were the most important of the people with money. When taxes (such as the succession tax for instance) went up, they paid. When a "voluntary" gift of *aurum coronarium* was required, they gave, and there were no special privileges for Roman citizens now; all were equal before the law of the Severi.

Some citizens were, however, more equal than others. In view of their public service to the government, for instance, the men of the apparatus were exempt from these other public obligations. And the "men of the apparatus" were defined to include ex-soldiers, agents collecting taxes for the imperial estates, *coloni* or share-croppers on the imperial estates, and the *collegia* or guilds (e.g. ship-owners, firemen). Thus, as the incomes and the privileges of the local worthies shrank, heavier and heavier obligations were imposed upon them. Meanwhile the status of guilds of commoners increased markedly, and the domains owned by men connected with the apparatus flourished under fiscal exemptions. That the Roman empire survived the third century, with its military anarchy and foreign invasions, was owed to the price that the imperial tax extracting machine compelled this sector of society to pay.

But the costs to the empire were high. A participant style in politics stems, apparently, from activity in and identification with the affairs of local government. Such activities provide a body of politically active and competent people from whom government can draw for civic-minded politicians at regional or higher levels.[90] Such men and such local loyalties were readily forthcoming in the first and second centuries A.D. After the third century, however, the supply of both seems to have dwindled. This could only mean government from the top down, and through an apparatus, at that, which viewed residents within the empire as subjects rather than citizens.

The rural population does not seem to have fared much better than the urban upper class. The lowly went into service under local men of influence as *coloni* or share-croppers, becoming in effect bound to the land and indebted to a local lord — but protected from the imperial tax-collectors and the soldiery (who were empowered to commandeer food, clothing and beasts of burden at need).[91] This meant the end of the big ranches run on slave labour. Indeed, the position of the slave seems to have improved. The days when Rome's wars brought in huge hauls of slaves had ended, so slaves were becoming rarer and more valuable. The intent of Severan laws was to protect the weak and powerless, including slaves, against other elements in society. But in effect what this seems to have meant was that the position of the lower orders and the slaves merged into the one disadvantaged status, that of the *humilior*.[92] For instance the words for slave *(servus)* and rustic *(rusticus)* now become apparently interchangeable. And large groups of other disadvantaged persons, the *dediticii* (transferred aliens lacking full civil rights) had been interspersed among this rural population, as were the men broken by confiscation and fleeing the swarming security forces. Alienation in town and countryside thus rose to ever higher levels. Bulla "the bandit" maintained himself for 20 years against the forces of the government *in Italy*. Such "banditry" seems to have been widespread and on the increase.

Amid all this, the growth of the Christian Church went on apace.[93] The rural population of north Africa, for instance, racially different from the Roman upper and citified classes who were exploiting it, probably embraced Christianity all the more because that religion was banned by the government. And, to the punishment orientation of the apparatus of government, the Church opposed the Christian concept of charity, *caritas*, which involved succour for the weak and downtrodden. Certainly, as a relief institution, the Church had little official competition. Septimius Severus forbade conversion to Christianity and there was a persecution in Alexandria in 200 and in Carthage in 202. But the Severi were not active persecutors. El Gabal may have been attempting to win over the Christians, and other cults within the empire, by imposing his own set of syncretistic beliefs that would encompass all others. Severus Alexander was actually friendly disposed. Christianity thus experienced only sporadic persecution and a good deal of tolerance. So it was that, by 251, when even the government was in financial straits, the Church in Rome — and it was still the organ of an illegal cult — had a bishop, 64 presbyters, 7 deacons, 7 subdeacons, 42 acolytes, 52 exorcists, readers and doorkeepers and was feeding 1500 widows and other needy persons.

It is difficult to date these developments more specifically, as we are dealing with an underground organization whose writings concern its belief, rather than its organizational, system. Still, under Septimius Severus and his dynasty the following developments seem to have been in train. Within each province the bishop of the leading city of the province, the Metropolitan, came to have more influence than the bishops of the other cities and towns. Within the empire as a whole the Metropolitans of certain highly important cities — Rome, Antioch and Alexandria — came to have precedence over other Metropolitans. There were meetings of bishops, or synods, on Church governance, meetings run on the house-rules of procedure of the Roman Senate. The power of the bishops was growing. The Church was now conceived as a school for sinners (rather than as a community of the elect of god) and the bishops were to gain the power to forgive transgressions of the Christian code. They could also discipline extravagance, whether this involved theological speculation or the urge to prod governmental authorities into proceedings which could speed a man, as a martyr, straight to the ranks of the departed blessed.

The faith was spreading too, both geographically and socially. It had grown to considerable proportions in Rome by 251, a date by which there were 100 bishoprics in Italy. Christians seem to have become numerous in Africa by Septimius' day. They were present in quantities in Spain then, too, in all probability, and the expansion of the Church in Britain seems to date to the first half of the third century. Members of the higher *echelons* of society were being attracted in by the beginning of the third century. Indeed, the Church is thought to have had a powerful friend at court, in the person of Marcia, concubine of Commodus, as early as the time of the last of the Antonines. To Septimius' reign dates the first Christian literature in Latin, the writings of Tertullian (160-225 A.D.). This is evidence that the Church was now addressing itself to the Latin-speaking upper reaches of society in Rome and the West. By the mid-third century, in Novatian's day, such writings had a poise and assurance which bespeaks effective communication. As early as the reign of Severus Alexander, in fact, there were Christians in the Emperor's own household; and this Emperor was friendly in his attitude, as has been indicated.

In regard to communications, indeed, the Church was as superior to the other cults which flourished within the empire as it was in regard to its bureaucratic organizational structure. In respect of organization it had in fact learned much from the imperial apparatus and legal corpus, and its own hierarchy was becoming educated and literate. So, just as the empire was ordering and codifying its law, the Church produced its own basic body of lore, the New Testament, and a creed to give the essentials of that testament and guard against erroneous interpretations thereof. To Septimius' reign dates Tertullian's enunciation of the doctrine of the Trinity. For, just as the Roman law had evolved over time, so uniformity of belief was only reached within the Church via the elaboration of doctrines, such as that of the Trinity, taught by neither Jesus Christ nor Paul. Christian doctrine by now had enough intellectual standing to draw upon it the attacks of pagan intelligentsia. It also had enough resources at its command to produce Christian apologists who could argue in sophisticated terms in defence of their beliefs. Christianity was producing a literature of its own. It had the only developed theology of any contemporary cult. In a world where others' beliefs were failing, it claimed to provide an answer to life's problems. This vigorously expounded counter-ideology will have acted as a catalyst in a society in which revolutionary social change was already under way.[94] Contemporaries certainly seem to have thought Christians responsible for many of their troubles. After all, Christians would not serve the apparatus (which they regarded as like a chain-gang, in that it did good works though it consisted of bad individuals) either in a civil or a military capacity. They would not attend shows, purchase meats which could have come from a beast which had been sacrificed, produce work which might go to adorn a non-Christian temple, and so on. The public baths were immoral, so uncleanliness was equated with godliness — in times beset with plagues, many borne by body lice (not that this was realised). They eschewed personal ornaments, because such vanities weakened resolve and, should there be a persecution, a Christian would need all the fortitude he could muster. Hence, in a society which did not distinguish religious from secular issues at all clearly, the Christians were readily identified in times of adversity as the source of the wrath of the divinities of the empire (who were, it was believed, producing such adversities as consequence of that wrath). The third century was to be the century of the great persecutions, "great" in that they were extensive and shrewdly directed. Trajan Decius in 249 required that all citizens certificate the fact that they had made sacrifice to the gods (a source of apostasy and subsequent schism over the treatment of those whose nerve had failed). Valerian attacked the bishops, for they were the crucial element within the bureaucratic structure of the Church. By the third century they had become a self-perpetuating hierarchy instructing their flocks. Even as early as the time of the Severi such instruction could run counter to Roman law. In the case of marriage between upper-class women and men of inferior social status, for instance, Roman law attached heavy penalties to such a union. Callistus, ex-slave and bishop of Rome in 217, gave such unions recognition (Christians made small distinction between slave and free within their own ranks). The Church was now a state within the state, as it were. Its continued growth could only lead to a major confrontation, as Church and government were issuing contrary instructions to, in many cases, the same set of people.

FOOTNOTES

1. The basic work of reference on Augustus is the *C.A.H.*, vol. X; see chapters 7 and 8 in particular. A good paperback reference is Scullard's *From the Gracchi to Nero*; see chapters 11 and 12. For the general socio-economic background to the period, see *S.E.H.R.E.* chapter 2.

2. For the difference between the modern concept of "government" and ideas on the subject in Augustus' day, see Millar, pp. 52 ff. For a concise treatment of the apparatus of government at this stage see H. Mattingly, *The Imperial Civil Service of Rome*, Cambridge, 1910. Though old, this book is a veritable mine of well-laid out information and makes a most convenient short work of reference on its subject.

3. The basic survey is contained in L. Homo's *Roman Political Institutions: From City to State;* see chapters 1 to 4 for the factual background to diagram 1.

4. The date of 134 B.C. was chosen for the diagram because, from the time of the Gracchi (133 and 123-2 B.C.) onwards, developments of an administrative nature (such as the *Senatus Consultum Ultimum* or declaration of a state emergency) and all kinds of enlargements upon political practice (such as the extension of client relationships to include soldiery and provincials) increasingly make for difficulty in describing Roman politics by such diagrams. On the *S.C.U.* see K. von Fritz, *The Theory of the Mixed Constitution in Antiquity*, Columbia U.P., 1954, pp. 232-4 and 282-3; on developments of *clientela* relationships, see E. Badian, *Foreign Clientelae*, Clarendon, 1958, pp. 159-60, 196-200, 266 and 272-73.

5. By the end of the Republic the military, known as *homines militares* (military men; *viri militares,* "military gentlemen," is of later occurrence), had virtually become a fourth estate, though not officially recognised as such, with their own distinct vested interests. See R.E. Smith, *Service in the Post-Marian Roman Army*, Manchester U.P., 1958, pp. 51-52 and 62-69.

6. On the *vigintivirate* see Scullard, *op. cit.*, p. 428 n. 21 and Homo, pp. 312-345. Even at this early date there was, effectively, one law for the rich and another for the poor. For members of the upper *echelons* of society were tried before a court of inquiry or *quaestio* and allowed to flee into exile to avoid a death sentence. In the case of a member of the commonality, however, a capital offence brought summary retribution from a police court (deprivation of liberty did not yet exist as a punishment for a criminal offence). See Kunkel, pp. 61-65.

7. At this date Roman law involved an early code, known as the Twelve Tables; a hazy background of custom; practical innovations adopted because they worked (also known as "custom," *mos maiorum*); an aggregation of laws on specific (constitutional) issues, and an accumulation of guidelines and case-precedents known as the *edictum tralaticium*. Jurisprudents were aristocrats whose hobby, as it were, it was to make themselves knowledgeable in various areas of this patch-work and piece-meal conglomeration (the "classical" age of Roman law came only with the professional lawyers of the middle principate). See von Fritz, *op. cit.*, pp. 174-77 and 440 n. 36, and Kunkel, chapters 5 to 7. The underdevelopment of the legal institutions of the Rome which Augustus took over appears strikingly from the discussion in A. W. Lintott, *Violence in Republican Rome*, Clarendon 1968, part three.

8. For all the details on the various civil and military subordinate officials see A.H.M. Jones, *Studies in Roman Government and Law*, Blackwell, 1960, chapter 10; cf. Millar, pp. 61-62, and Parker, *The Roman Legions*, Heffer, 1958, pp. 205-207.

9. Plutarch, *Life of Cato Minor*, chapters 16-18.

10. This is a summary description; many other minor officials also were to be found on these staffs. See Jones' study cited above in note 7.

11. See Parker, *The Roman Legions*, pp. 30-36 and 196-205 on the centurionate. A centurion was to be paid at 15 times the rate of pay of an ordinary legionary; some of the higher centurions received 30 times this basic pay. This book is a mine of information on army movements, recruiting and conditions of service, incidentally.

12. The legions, with their individual members and titles, had each their own distinct traditions and identity and their doings can be followed, in some cases, through hundreds of years of imperial history. See Parker, above. The *Legio III Augusta* has been picked out for mention because it was the only legion controlled by the Senate and it literally built, to a very large extent, the Roman province of Africa, over the years. See Millar, pp. 105, 170-171 and 173.

13. The Institution of the cult of the eagles was owed to the Marian army reforms (of 105 to 101 B.C., probably). The penalty for the loss of an eagle was decimation. Generally, however, the legion was lost along with its standards (as happened at Carrhae in 53 B.C. and in the Teutoburg Forest in A.D. 9). In such cases the legionary number was never replaced; a gap was left in the series when a supplementary legion was raised.

14. On the aristocrats' monopoly of office behind the *façade* of republicanism, see R. Syme, *The Roman Revolution*, Clarendon, 1952, chapter 2. On senatorial rules of debate see H.H. Scullard, *Roman Politics 220-150 B.C.*, Clarendon, 1951, chapter 1, especially pp. 25-26.

15. There was much talk at the time of a *respublica restituta* or "republic restored to the citizenry" and of a first citizen or *princeps* who surpassed his peers only in moral authority or *auctoritas*. This, and the able use of constitutional precedent and institutions, seems to have done much to conceal the shift in the locus of power. See von Fritz, *op. cit.*, pp. 304-305 and 464; Homo, p. 248; C.G. Starr, *Civilization and the Caesars*, Cornell U.P. 1954, chapter 3, especially pp. 37-42. There is a good analysis of the basic ambiguities of the position of the *princeps* (and of modern attitudes thereto) in K. von Fritz, "Tacitus, Agricola, Domitian and the Problem of the Principate" in *Classical Philology* 52, 1957, pp. 73-97, especially 85 ff. For an aristocrat, long versed in the realities of politics, this new settlement meant servitude: see Ch. Wirszubski, *Libertas as a Political Ideal during the Late Republic and Early Principate*, Cambridge U.P., 1960, pp. 90-91.

16. The objective of this procedure was to prevent loss of bullion through shipwreck or piracy during trans-shipment.

17. See Hammond, pp. 454-457.

18. I have attempted to give a history of the Roman mint, its coinage and its policies in *Roman and Related Coins in the Courtauld Collection*, U.C. of Rhodesia and Nyasaland, 1963; see pp. xvi-xviii. For a study of the coinage as a public relations medium see C.H.V. Sutherland, *Coinage in Roman Imperial Policy 31 B.C. − A.D. 68*, Methuen, 1951. Millar at p. 69 details some important matters about the procedures involved in handling official monies, about which nothing is known.

19. See Wittfogel, pp. 301-307, especially 302-304.

20. On Musicus, see Jones, *Studies in Roman Government and Law*, p. 160. On the imperial freedmen, see A.M. Duff, *Freedmen in the Early Roman Empire*, Heffer, 1958, chapters 7 and (especially) 8.

21. See Smith, *Service in the Post-Marian Roman Army*, chapter 6.

22. See Syme, *Roman Revolution*, p. 513, and Wirszubski, *Libertas*, pp. 100-106.

23. See Syme, *Roman Revolution*, chapters 25 ("The Working of Patronage") and 32 ("The Doom of the *Nobiles*"). Basically two kinds of Emperor were (initially) possible. One variety (e.g. Tiberius) viewed the position of *princeps* as that of a kind of care-taker under whom governmental affairs should proceed with the minimum of encroach-

ment on senatorial or constitutionalist preserves. The other wished to increase the Emperor's powers. He might be a believer in centralization (like Claudius, say) or a despot (like Caligula or Domitian). See O. Kuntz, *Tiberius Caesar and the Roman Constitution*, U. of Washington Press, 1924, pp. 25 and 44-45. From either type of Emperor, a different set of highly placed personages stood to gain. Hence an unfailing source of intrigue.

24. Syme discusses the ideals of the new aristocracy of imperial service (*obsequium:* "rational deference to authority") at *Tacitus*, Clarendon, 1958, pp. 25-28. See also D. Earl, *The Moral and Political Tradition of Rome*, Cornell, 1967, pp. 90-94.

25. I discovered this when trying to reconstruct the picture of a prominent Roman of the late Republic held by an important writer who flourished in the reign of the next Emperor after Augustus. See "The Picture of Marius in Valerius Maximus," *Rheinisches Museum* 105 (4), 1962, pp. 293-5, whence it appears that Valerius thought *popularis* (which meant something like "an advocate of popular policies") meant something like *humilis* ("man of the people").

26. In the pre-industrial empires the capital city far outstripped any other in importance. See the discussion of the "primate city" of historical societies in contrast to the "rank-size rule" of modern industrial society, wherein other major cities more nearly approach the capital in size and importance: E. Jones, *Towns and Cities*, Oxford U.P., 1966, pp. 81 and 83-84.

27. See Kunkel, pp. 100-102 and 118-123.

28. See H. Mattingly, *Roman Imperial Civilisation*, Arnold, 1957, pp. 37-88 and 166-7.

29. The basic work of reference is, again, *C.A.H.*X; see chapter 20, especially section 6. Scullard's *From the Gracchi to Nero* is likewise a good paperback reference work; see chapter 14, sections 1-6. For the general socio-economic background to the period see *S.E.H.R.E.*, chapter 3.

30. See Wirszubski, *Libertas*, pp. 126-129.

31. On Sejanus see F.B. Marsh, *The Reign of Tiberius*, London, 1931, 126-127; cf. A. Boddington, "Sejanus: Whose Conspiracy? " in *American Journal of Philology* 84, 1963, pp. 1-16. On the Praetorian Prefect and his men see Homo, pp. 225 and 306-7 and Hammond, pp. 176-9; 249 and 453. On praetorianism, i.e. soldiers setting themselves up as the arbiters of politics via intrigues or *coups d'état*, see S. Andrzejewski, *Military Organization and Society*, Routledge & Kegan Paul, 1954, pp. 104-107.

32. See Homo, pp. 308-310 and Scullard, *From the Gracchi to Nero*, pp. 302-303. Service in this secretariate long bore the stigma of service rendered to the master *(dominus)* of an extended household *(familia)* by his dependents. As this implied a master: slave relationship, members of the top *echelons* of Roman society were not prepared, initially anyway, so to serve: see Homo, pp. 309-310, and Hammond, p. 451. Other positions, however, could be associated with the rôles of *amici* or *comites* (friends/counsellors or companions) of a great man acting as magistrate under the Republic, and so were socially acceptable: see Millar, pp. 52 ff.

33. The fact of Claudius' dependence upon them, however, indicates their strategic importance to this embattled *princeps*. This is something new and bespeaks a critical development during the reign. See Eisenstadt, pp. 158-72, for analysis in terms of bureaucratic politics.

34. See, for instance, S.I. Oost, "The Career of M. Antonius Pallas," in *American Journal of Philology* 79, 1958, pp. 113-139.

35. Homo, pp. 313-4 and 326; cf. 253. Homo notes the significance of the lack of an independent legal profession at 372-3; see Kunkel, pp. 66-7. This development of the powers of the Urban Prefect was to bring friction with the Praetorian Prefect, for, while the latter had no court of his own, his security duties led to his screening of and acting upon charges laid by informers *(delatores)*, who throve in this period. Hence overlapping spheres of activity. For the political consequences of the absence of an independent judiciary, see Wittfogel, pp. 145-6, Eisenstadt, pp. 98-99 and Riggs, p. 235.

36. Homo, p. 325.

37. Claudius seems to have been a spastic; his "idiocy" is a product of the distaste of Roman polite society for such physical defects combined with the maliciousness of an alienated senatorial class close to court circles and gossip. See P. Leon, "The *Imbecillitas* of the Emperor Claudius" in *Transactions of the American Philological Association* 79, 1948, pp. 79-86.

38. In regard to the specific administrative changes depicted in the diagram, see *C.A.H.X.*, pp. 218-22; 293-4; 304; 674-75, n. 1; 689-90; A. Momigliano, *Claudius: The Emperor and His Achievement*, Clarendon, 1934, pp. 41-43; 45-46; 49-52; T. Frank, *An Economic Survey of Ancient Rome*, Pageant, 1959, vol. V, pp. 41; 251; 268-9; R. Meiggs, *Roman Ostia*, Clarendon, 1960, pp. 45; 53-56; 62-63; Carney, "The Helops," in *Phoenix* 21, 1967, p. 217; cf. Sutherland, *Coinage in Roman Imperial Policy* p. 129.

39. See Carney, *Roman and Related Coins in the Courtauld Collection*, pp. xxi-xxii, and Sutherland, *Coinage in Roman Imperial Policy*, pp. 132-3.

40. On the speech from the throne, see Homo, p. 249; *C.A.H.*X,p. 697 and Frank, *Economic Survey of Ancient Rome*, V, 42-3; on matters of coinage, see Carney, *Roman and Related Coins in the Courtauld Collection*, p. xxii.

41. On the confiscations in Claudius' day, see e.g. *C.A.H.*X, pp. 671-73. On the functioning of confiscation within a traditionalist despotism, see Wittfogel, pp. 72-73. Riggs speaks of "Pariah Capitalism" at pp. 185-95. Without the protection of governmental institutions there can be no security of private property or, consequently, powerful mercantile interests to countervail against ruler and apparatus.

42. Other demands were for the shortening of the term of service and for abolition of the requirement of further service, on a territorial basis, after discharge. See Millar, pp. 120-122.

43. See H. Chadwick, *The Early Church*, Pelican, 1967, chapters 1 to 3, and Bainton, *Early Christianity*, pp. 20-23. For the general background to Christian daily life see E.A. Judge, *The Social Pattern of Christian Groups in the First Century*, Tyndale, 1960, especially chapters 3 to 6.

44. The plotting of a die-hard opposition group of nobles seems to have implicated certain families in a standing feud with successive *principes*. See D. McAlindon, "Senatorial Opposition to Claudius and Nero" in *American Journal of Philology* 77, 1956, pp. 113-33 and "Claudius and the Senators," *ibid.* 78, 1957, 178-87.

45. See Syme, *Tacitus*, chapter 43 ("The Rise of the Provincials").

46. The various regions of the empire in this century are discussed in Frank's *Economic Survey of Ancient Rome*, vol. V; see also Millar, chapters 7 to 12.

47. See R. MacMullen, "Rural Romanization" in *Phoenix* 22, 1968, pp. 237-41.

48. Hammond, p. 452.

49. Homo, pp. 346-7; Parker, *The Roman Legions*, 189.

50. The basic reference work is *C.A.H.*XI; see chapters 8 and also 10, 11 and 21. A.E.R. Boak's *A History of Rome to 565 A.D.*, MacMillan, 1954, is now in paperback; see pp. 313, 320-23 and 344-70. Syme (*Tacitus*, chapters 20 & 36) is well worth reading on Hadrian. For the general socio-economic background to the period see *S.E.H.R.E.*, chapters 4 to 8.

51. H.D. Lasswell, *Politics: Who Gets What, When, How?* Meridian, 1962, sets out a framework within which comparative analysis can proceed. D. Easton's *A Systems Analysis of Political Life*, Wiley, 1965, shows the central importance of the decision-making process (or "authoritative allocation of values" or what have you). The discussion proceeds in terms of this kind of frame of reference.

52. The phrase comes from T.B. Jones' *The Silver-Plated Age*, Coronado, 1962. Jones' thesis is that the education in vogue stultified the intellect and thus contributed to the decline in creativity which proved to be the downfall of Graeco-Roman civilization (see p. 9). See Q. Wright, *A Study of War*, U. of Chicago Press, 1965, p. 604 as an illustration. This is in fact a perennial problem in traditional autocracies. See Sjoberg, *The Preindustrial City*, pp. 297-318; Riggs, pp. 149-56, and Hagen, *On the Theory of Social Change*, pp. (69-) 78.

53. Rather abrasively put by P. Oliva, *Pannonia*, p. 118; see Syme, *Tacitus*, chapters 43 and 44, and Starr, *Civilization and the Caesars*, pp. 91-95.

54. There is an excellent synopsis of the development of the army and of its conditions of service in Millar, chapter 6; see also Homo, pp. 243-45 and 346-7; *C.A.H.* X, pp. 218-35; XI, 310-13 and Hammond, p. 170.

55. For conditions in general on the Danube, see Oliva, *Pannonia*, chapters 3 and 4.

56. See *C.A.H.* X, pp. 225 and 230-31; XI, p. 311. On the officer's career see in general Parker, *The Roman Legions*, pp. 187-96.

57. There was by now a complete hierarchy of military positions, in two major sections, one for officers, another for the ranks: see n. 56 (officer's career) and Homo, pp. 351-53 (ranker's). On the "military mind" in antiquity, see MacMullen, pp. 174-6.

58. This meant that the image of this part of the apparatus must have considerably improved: see note 32. Also the equestrians were by now long used to the idea that governmental activity should involve careers for their order, and they were numerous enough to desire the greatest possible expansion of career opportunities. There seems to have been some antipathy between senatorial and equestrian orders; this would have steeled the latter in their bid to take over this highly important area of governmental functions. See Hammond, pp. 450-53 and Homo, p. 248. On the positions still held by freedmen and slaves, see G. Boulvert, *Les esclaves et les affranchis impériaux sous le Haut-empire romain*, Aix-en-Provence, 1964 (doctoral thesis), vol. 1, pp. 278-314; cf. 389-456.

59. Homo, p. 260; Hammond, pp. 370-79, especially 375-9 (see also notes 33-38, pp. 398-400 and n. 47, p. 404).

60. Homo, pp. 260 and 308; for the significance of the "public post" in a traditional autocracy see Wittfogel, pp. 54-59.

61. This seems indicated by the stage which their quarrellings over spheres of jurisdiction had reached later in the second century. See in general Homo, pp. 259-60, 328 (cf. 309-310), and 313-14 (with 326) on the Urban Prefect and 306-307 on the Praetorian Prefect; Hammond, pp. 426-28, 453 (cf. 387-90); Kunkel, pp. 66-7 (cf. 102).

62. Carney, Roman and Related Coins in the Courtauld Collection, p. xxvii; "The Political Legends on Hadrian's Coinage: Policies and Problems" in The Turtle 6, 1967, pp. 291-303.

63. Hammond, pp. 456-57.

64. The list given in the text is a skeletal outline only; see Homo, pp. 349-51.

65. See Wright, A Study of War, pp. 592 and 595. Christians, though averse to warfare on religious grounds, did serve in the army in the second century, apparently because there was little likelihood of killing anyone in consequence: see Bainton, Early Christianity, pp. 54-5. Many a Roman soldier will have lived out his service career without experience of battle in this age: cf. MacMullen, pp. V, 32.

66. Hadrian was renowned for his determination to stop the soldiery turning their camps into market gardens: see MacMullen, p. 2.

67. Kunkel, pp. 97-115, especially 108 ff.

68. See J.A. Crook, Law and Life of Rome, Cornell, 1967, p. 235; for the importance of the concept, see de Grazia, Politics and Government, p. 33.

69. See H.J. Muller, The Loom of History, Galaxy, 1966, pp. 200-212.

70. See H.J. Muller, Freedom in the Ancient World, Bantam, 1964, pp. 285-6.

71. See M. Hammond, "Composition of the Senate, A.D. 68-235" in Journal of Roman Studies 47, 1957, pp. 74-81, and Syme, Tacitus, pp. 572-83.

72. See Wirszubski, Libertas, pp. 167-70.

73. Op. cit., pp. 129, 135-8 and 152-8.

74. Cf. Chadwick, The Early Church, chapters 2 and 3, and H. Mattingly, Christianity in the Roman Empire, Norton, 1967, chapter 3 for what follows.

75. On Rome's eastern frontier see F. Stark, Rome on the Euphrates, Murray, 1966, chapters 9 and 10; see also pp. 248 and 251-54.

76. The basic reference work is *C.A.H.* XII; see chapters 1 and 2 (sections 1 & 2); cf. also 3-5 & 7. H.M.D. Parker, *A History of the Roman World A.D. 138-337*, Methuen, 1958, part 2, is a good, shorter work of reference. MacMullen in *Soldier and Civilian* indicates the pivotal importance of the Severi. See also R. Rémondon, *La crise de l'empire romain de Marc-Aurele à Anastase*, Paris, 1964, chapter 2. For the general socio-economic background to the period, see *S.E.H.R.E.*, chapter 9.

77. Most prominently associated with the thesis of declining man-power is Boak; see M. Chambers (ed.), *The Fall of Rome: Can it be Explained?*, Holt, Rinehart and Winston, 1963, pp. 21-28 (but cf. Finley's *riposte* on pp. 29-36). On the city of the times as a "necropolis" see L. Mumford, *The City in History*, Secker and Warburg, 1961, chapter 8; cf. Sjoberg, *The Pre-industrial City*, chapter 4. On the nature and consequences of the plague introduced by Marcus Aurelius see H. Zinsser, *Rats, Lice and History*, Bantam, 1967, chapter 7, especially pp. 100-102, and F. Henschen, *The History and Geography of Disease*, Delacorte, 1966, pp. 52-3. For the difference between ancient and modern population structure, see A.R. Burn, *"Hic Breve Vivitur"* in *Past and Present* 4, 1953, pp. 1-31.

78. See Stark, *Rome on the Euphrates*, chapters 11 and 12 on the happenings in this area under the Severi.

79. On the chain of disasters and their psychological effects see P.A. Sorokin, *Man and Society in Calamity*, Dutton, 1942; in particular pp. 288-92, 225-26 (cf. 145-53). On malaria, see R. Fiennes, *Man, Nature and Disease*, Signet, 1964, chapter 5, especially p. 64, and Henschen, *The History and Geography of Diseases*, pp. 138-9.

80. Carney, *Roman and Related Coins in the Courtauld Collection*, pp. xxviii-xxxiii. Possibly more accessible are two important articles: A.H.M. Jones, "Inflation under the Roman Empire," in *Economic History Review* 5, 1953, pp. 293-318 and T. Pekary, "Studien zur romischen Wahrungs- und Finanzgeschichte, von 161 bis 235 n. Chr." in *Historia* 8, 1959, pp. 443-89. See also MacMullen, p. 93.

81. See MacMullen, chapters 3 to 5; it is particularly noteworthy that it was the Severi who seem to have given a big impetus to the employment of soldiery on police and tax-collecting duties (pp. 53, 59-60, 161); allowed them to hold land in the province where they were serving (pp. 2, 10, 11, 17); encouraged manufacturing by the military (pp. 26, 30), and allowed soldiers to trade (pp. 109, 154).

82. See MacMullen, pp. 126-7 (consequences of legalising marriage for soldiers on service); p. 69 (dominant position of army officers in

society); pp. 172-76 (militarization of social practices); cf. pp. 154-56. See also Parker, *A History of the Roman World,* pp. 86-7, 113.

83. The normal authoritarian syndrome: see Hagen, *On the Theory of Economic Change,* pp. 71-74, 97-98 & 107-108.

84. It has been argued that the huge build-up of imperial domains played havoc with the socio-economic life of the empire: Frank, *Economic Survey of Ancient Rome* V, pp. 300-302. On the *res privata* see Parker, *A History of the Roman World,* pp. 76-77, 91.

85. On the Praetorian Prefect, see Parker, *A History of the Roman World,* pp. 73, 107-8; Kunkel, p. 113; Homo, pp. 306-307 & 326. On the Urban Prefect, see Parker, *A History of the Roman World,* p. 108; Homo, pp. 313-14.

86. On the Imperial Council, see Parker (above), pp. 106-107; Homo, p. 304.

87. On the advance of the equestrians, see Parker (above), pp. 73, 84, 116; Homo, p. 347. On the increase in the types and numbers of minor bureaucrats see MacMullen, pp. 67 and 157; Rémondon, *La crise de l'empire romain,* pp. 84-85.

88. On general unrest, popular alienation and civil disorders involving elaborate security measures, see Parker, *A History of the Roman World,* pp. 72, 119, 128; Oliva, *Pannonia,* pp. 113-26, and Starr, *Civilization and the Caesars,* pp. 95-99. See also R. MacMullen, *Enemies of the Roman Order: Treason, Unrest and Alienation in the Empire,* Harvard, 1966, chapters 5 to 7 and appendices A and B.

89. On the increasing militarization of the equestrian order and administrative bureaucracy, see MacMullen, pp. 49-50, 106, 162-73; Homo, p. 353; Parker, *A History of the Roman World,* p. 85.

90. See G.A. Almond and S. Verba, *The Civic Culture,* pp. 346-47; cf. 365-69 and 117-45. Compare Wittfogel, pp. 102-103 and Eisenstadt, pp. 198-207. See Starr, *Civilization and the Caesars,* pp. 101-113; Rémondon, *La crise de l'empire romain,* pp. 89-91 and 113, and Parker, *A History of the Roman World,* pp. 123-26.

91. On *coloni* see Oliva, *Pannonia,* pp. 82-88; the variety of forms of lease-hold entailing services being evolved at this time (see MacMullen, pp. 15-16) indicates the pressures working to affix men to the land. On military patronage see MacMullen, pp. 115-17; on the requisitioning system, *angareia,* see Millar, p. 98; and on the hatred felt by the commonality for the soldiery, see Oliva, *Pannonia,* p. 130. See E.T. Salmon, "The Roman Army and the Disintegration of the Roman Empire" in M. Chambers, *The Fall of Rome,* pp. 37-46.

92. See Oliva, *Pannonia,* pp. 88-95.

93. See Chadwick, *The Early Church*, chapters 3 to 6; Mattingly, *Christianity in the Roman Empire*, chapter 4; Muller, *Freedom in the Ancient World*, pp. 323-34, and A. Harnack, *The Mission and Expansion of Christianity in the First Three Centuries*, Harper, 1962, pp. 431-44.

94. See C. Johnson, *Revolutionary Change*, Little, Brown, 1966, chapter 5, especially pp. 105-112. On the crumbling away of the Graeco-Roman classical tradition and its related belief systems see Starr, *Civilization and the Caesars*, pp. 274-308.

Chapter 3
Proto-Byzantine Times: The Late Roman Empire

Cutting history up into periods is always an unsatisfactorily subjective process. But there does seem to be some sort of a consensus that the establishment of the dominate marks the advent of the Late Roman Empire; that the dominate and the foundation of Constantinople together inaugurate the early Byzantine age, and that the advent of Islam marks the beginning of the middle Byzantine period.[1] Certainly all these events mark definite turning points in the history of their times, as will appear. However, the establishment of the dominate dates, largely, to the reign of Diocletian (284-305 A.D.) whereas Constantinople was only founded in 330, late in the reign of his successor, Constantine I the Great (306-337 A.D.). But it took the reforms of both these Emperors to establish the dominate firmly, so they will here be considered as constituting, in overall terms, one single process of reform. The period under consideration, then, dates from 284 to 641 A.D.[2]

The empire of the year 284 was situated in a markedly different field of forces from the empire of Septimius Severus' day.[3] Military anarchy had followed in the wake of the Severi. Besides attempted usurpations, of which there were many, 26 militarists succeeded in their bids for the title of Emperor, *Augustus*, within the period 235 to 284. The chaotic conditions which resulted made the empire an easy prey for barbarians and Persians alike. Both were more effectively organised, anyway, in this period than they had been before. Consequently the Visigoths had overrun Dacia; the Vandals had invaded Moesia, Pannonia and Illyricum; the Franks had raided into Gaul, Spain, Greece and Italy, and the Persians had thrice successfully warred with Rome. Under the strain Rome's monetary system had collapsed, with a reversion to much trading and taxation in kind. Massive inflation resulted. All sorts of internal divisions within the empire were precipitated in process. To some extent the military anarchy was due to regional separatist impulses. In Christianity a powerfully organised religion rejected much of the Graeco-Roman tradition. It met fierce opposition.

Latin-speaking West and Greek-speaking East were drifting apart. The bases of peasant production were such as to encourage the build-up of domains or *villae* across the Alps and on parts of the Danube, whereas they encouraged single-family plots around the Aegean.[4] Hence the imperial bureaucracy had a much easier job administering the latter area than it did with the other two. Asia Minor and Egypt, centres for manufacturing and commerce, had gone unscathed by invasion and its side-effects of plague and famine. So the eastern trading centres had won relatively much greater preeminence within the empire. In short, the end of the empire as an integrated whole seemed imminent.

It was preserved by the institution of the system known as the dominate. *Dominus* was the Latin term for "lord" or "master," whereas *princeps* had the connotation of "first" (among peers). If the principate had been a disguised autocracy, the dominate meant outright despotism. The Emperor and all about him was sacred. One prostrated oneself on approaching him. To do so meant going through all the pomp, ceremony and seclusion of his court. He was the fount of law and was served by an all-powerful apparatus of government. The dominate did not spring up overnight, however. Diocletian seems rather to have formalised a number of practices which had been developing during the third century.

Prior to Diocletian the administrative apparatus had consisted of various clusters of officials and institutions. There were the Imperial Council, the Secretariate, the various prefectures, the financial officials and the provincial governors. The military apparatus involved legates, prefects, tribunes and even some procurators. All these high officials had *officia* or departmental groups subordinate to them. The latter were becoming increasingly militarized in stylings, dress and even inductees.

Diocletian built upon this complex of institutions and officials, further extending developments already in train within them. Constantine carried this process a little further. The result of their activities, in overall terms, took the following forms.

Diocletian instituted a Tetrarchy (joint rule by four rulers) to off-set regional separatism and attempts at usurpation. It consisted of an *Augustus* for the West, with a *Caesar* under him, and a similar arrangement for the East. On the retirement of an *Augustus* his *Caesar* was to become *Augustus* and adopt the best available man as his *Caesar* in turn. All decisions by either *Augustus* (West or East) were to be upheld by his colleague throughout the empire. The provinces of that empire had by now increased enormously in numbers, to 96 in 197 A.D. in fact, as the original areas had been "chopped up into slices," as contemporaries put it. The aim behind this was partly to prevent the build-up of troop concentrations, but still more to enable closer administrative supervision. These "sliced" provinces were grouped into regions of intermediate size, known as dioceses and roughly equivalent to the original provinces of the early empire.[5] This procedure allowed of the coordination of activities on a regional level. There were 6 dioceses in the "West" (which included Africa), 3 in the Balkans and 3 in the East. The dioceses were administered by Vicars, under the overall direction of the Praetorian Prefect. The Vicars deputed for him at the diocesan level and controlled troops. In this way the Praetorian Prefect came to the zenith of his powers, as he controlled the organizational infrastructure. But the tetrarchs split the empire into four huge zones and one governed in each: the western *Augustus* split the West into two and gave one part to his *Caesar* and the other *Augustus* did likewise in the East. Diocletian chose to be *Augustus* in the East.

The Tetrarchy simply did not work, as things turned out. When it came to standing down, or passing over their own sons for promotion, Diocletian's colleagues failed to play their parts. Moreover, the Tetrarchy had dangerously empowered the Praetorian Prefect. And even without such empowering three Prefects had used their office as a springboard in a successful bid to become Emperor since Macrinus' day.[6] Hence the sequel to Diocletian's reign turned out to be a protracted bout of civil wars. These ended with one man, Constantine the Great, controlling the empire and the Praetorian Prefect half stripped of his powers. Yet Constantine's new order was built within the framework which Diocletian had laid down for the Tetrarchy. This came about in the following way.

To neutralize the power of the Praetorian Prefect Constantine disbanded his guard and made of him a purely civil official. He also increased the numbers of Praetorian Prefects. He retained the great administrative zones of the tetrarchy. These were to become Prefectures (initially three in number, later four), each administered by a Praetorian Prefect. The latter was thus no longer an official operating solely out of the capital city and at the Emperor's side. There were other changes, important if not quite as dramatic, in the group of high officials who surrounded the Emperor.

Each *Augustus* and *Caesar*, under Diocletian's dispensation, came to have his own secretariate. Along with his own "household" of attendants, the *cubiculum*, and his advisory council, the secretariate accompanied the ruler on his travels. Hence it came to be known, along with his military attendants, as the *comitatus* or Retinue. The financial ministers regained some importance under Diocletian in spite of the enormous growth in the powers of the Praetorian Prefect. Responsible for the collection of money taxes, mines and mints was the *rationalis rei summae*; he also saw to the expenditures of incomes from these sources. The imperial lands were looked after by the *magister rei privatae*. Both these officials had their representatives at the diocesan level. The various bureaux *(scrinia)* of the secretariate were also now headed by *magistri* or Masters. As Diocletian had little time for senators, all these posts went to equestrians.

Under Constantine the financial ministers gained immensely in importance. As will appear, Constantine gained access to huge amounts of bullion and began to end the use of debased currency. He also acquired vast estates from opponents in the civil wars. Hence these finance ministers were of great strategic importance in his reign. The former came to be known as the Count of the Sacred Largesses *(comes sacrarum largitionum)*, the latter as the Count of the Private Estate *(comes rei privatae)*. The Praetorian Prefect would retain the secretariate of the former tetrarch to administer his prefecture. But something had to be done to re-centralise the various *comitatus* or Retinues.

Under Constantine one central administration was to coordinate all these functions. Naturally, there were changes. Possibly the most dramatic was the institution of the position of Master of Offices, *magister officiorum*. This official's sphere of influence overlapped that of the Praetorian Prefect's at several points, a fact which automatically generated tensions between the two positions, neutralizing their power potential. The Praetorian Prefect was now responsible for army recruitment, supply of rations throughout the apparatus and control of the arms factories. The Master of Offices, so called because he was the head of all the official bodies resident in the palace, controlled the central secretariate, now made into a mere group of service *bureaux* (the *scrinia* — of the *memoria* [Records] , *epistolae* [Correspondence] and *libelli* [Petitions]). He also controlled audiences with the Emperor (via the Office of Admissions), and the public post — which the Praetorian Prefects, by the nature of their job, had to use. In this way the imperial couriers, the *agentes in rebus*, and the inspectors, or *curiosi*, came under his control. They seem rather rapidly to have acquired a bad name for their security activities, to which the Praetorian Prefect and his men were as lamentably liable as any other group.

Other new officials appear, too, pre-empting yet more of the

Prefect's functions. New to the apparatus was a group called the Notaries. These kept the minutes of the imperial council, now known as the Sacred Consistory *(sacrum consistorium)*, and issued codicils of office to civil officials and commissions to the military. They rapidly became highly influential within the apparatus because of these crucial gate-keeping functions. A further innovation was the establishment, in the person of the *Quaestor* of the Sacred Palace, of an official to oversee all legal and judicial matters.

To a modern mind these overlapping functions seem merely confusing. They jar upon our ideals of efficiency. For Constantine however a more overriding consideration was that of providing against officials' having too much power. Thus precautions were taken against the Master of Offices in his turn. Although he had just been raised as a counterweight to the Praetorian Prefect, provision was made that he should control the staffs of the *bureaux* but not the Masters in charge thereof. This gave the Emperor a means of cross-checking upon the Master of Offices. It also encouraged the Masters of the various *bureaux* in the habit of poaching upon one another's preserves, however, thus making the functions of the different *bureaux* shift and change.[7]

Constantine called the officials in attendance upon him the *palatini,* the "people of the palace." They consisted of the *Castrensis Sacri Palatii* (Head Steward), the *Praepositus Sacri Cubiculi* (Head Chamberlain) — i.e. the heads of the Emperor's household staff; the Consistory; the Master of Offices and Praetorian Prefect of the East; the *Primicerius* (or Officer in Charge) of the Notaries, the *Quaestor* of the Sacred Palace, and the Counts of the finances. Also there were the Count of the Domestics and the Masters of the Soldiery, on whom see further below. Though the Urban Prefect was a very senior official, ranking second only to the Praetorian Prefect, he was primarily the chief representative of the Senate and so not of this group. Constantinople did not in fact receive an Urban Prefect of its own until 359. The *palatini* were a very privileged group, enjoying exemptions from tax obligations and having the status of soldiers. Constantine also made an official title out of what had formerly been a mere appellation. His *comites,* or Companions who formed his *comitatus* or Retinue, were now known as Counts. Counts came in three classes: counts of the first, second and third rank. Constantine was fond of ceremonial. The court of the dominate, with its hierarchies of statuses, grew apace in his day.

Diocletian's reforms had made for greater efficiency, but at considerable cost in additions of man-power. The institution of the *comitatus* meant that the central secretariate was quadrupled. There were 40 to 50 new diocesan officials. The provinces had almost been doubled in numbers. True, inflation had reduced the pay scales of officials severely: they now received, effectively, more modest salaries than under Hadrian, say. But the total cost probably came to about what it would have cost to maintain two more legions. And each official had his own *officium*, which had by this time been increased by the addition of new minor financial officials. A provincial governor's staff totalled some 100 men, a vicar's 300. This amounted to the equivalent of 3 more legions of officials.[8] It provided, moreover, a mass of career opportunities ideally suited to men at the level of the local town council, or *curiales*. But these men were needed in their local towns, as will appear in considering Diocletian's taxation measures.

Constantine's reforms made the split between the military and civil careers complete. In the positions of the former now were many rough barbarian soldiers; those of the latter were filled by city-bred intelligentsia, many of them lawyers. But Constantine may well have aimed at winning over influentials of all kinds in order to weld the empire and his new regime solidly together. He had no aversion to senators in his service; they were no longer a menace to an Emperor. They were consequently allowed access to equestrian positions, and swarmed back into prestigeful posts in consequence. He promoted Germanic officers. He advanced Christians. Hence a new aristocracy of service locked into position behind and around his throne. To demarcate and legitimate this new *élite* there was a whole range of titles. Senatorial status now went along with the title of *clarissimus*. One could inherit such a title. Certain offices conferred it, in some cases during, in others after, tenure. Or the Emperor might confer it by a grant. But within the senatorial order itself a hierarchy of titles now sprang up. In ascending order, there were *spectabiles* (Honourables), *illustres* (Illustrious), and Patricians. The latter, which was sparingly given, was the highest title conferred upon those not of the imperial family. For these the stylings *Caesar* and *nobilissimus* (Most Noble) were reserved. A title in most cases came with the attainment of an official position, which was, appropriately, known as a "Dignity" *(dignitas)*.[9] Men of all types and from all quarters thus came to have a vested interest in Constantine's new dispensation.

Diocletian's reforms of the administrative apparatus were part and parcel of his taxation reforms. The *ad hoc* system of requisitions (and extraordinary superimpositions) in kind was now turned into a flexible taxation system known as the *iugatio*.[10] This regularised such requisitions and produced the first annual budgeting instrument in antiquity. It was based on a *iugum*, or taxable unit of land. This might be 5 *iugera* (a *iugerum* was about 2/3 of an acre) of vineyard; or it could be 20 *iugera* of first class seed land, 40 of second class, 60 of third; or 225 olive trees of first class yield, 450 of second class, etc. Along with this went a poll tax, *capitatio:* 5 adult humans *(capita)* comprised one *iugum;* so did 20 cattle; an official could assess implements by value and compute them by the *iugum* too. All that needed to be done was classify the land and register its complement of humans, stock and instruments; then an *indictio* (assessment of the rate to be paid *per iugum*) gave a simple, global tax, variable by yearly need and applicable empire-wide.

This arrangement meant, however, that the worker on the land could not be allowed to shift domicile or employ. The local upper class *(curiales, decuriones),* who could be made to meet any shortfall from their own produce, would naturally be most suited to the unpleasant task of keeping the local boy down on the farm. So every effort was made to prevent such local worthies going into military or administrative service. With Constantine's recognition of the Christian Church, and his grant to it of various privileges and immunities, another haven for the hard-pressed *curiales* opened up. Even members of the governors' staffs, the *cohortales*, faced with the *primi pili pastus* (see below) were showing reluctance to meet their obligations, and had to be kept at their stations in life. Hence, with Constantine's resolute attempts to hold all groups to their duties, a caste-like system grew up in which all were tied to their father's status or profession.[11] As the Church simultaneously imposed (a certain amount of) celibacy, coupled with voracious demands for man-power, however, this caste system could never work perfectly or without strain.

Along with Diocletian's tax reform went an *Edict*[12] laying down maximum prices for wares, food etc. The edict was quite ineffective. Some anti-inflationary results were, however, produced by a currency reform involving the *follis* (a new bronze piece), a *denarius argentarius* (a *silver denarius*, 96 to the pound weight and as pure as Nero's *denarii* had been), and a gold piece (at 60 to the pound weight). The Severi had encouraged army manufacture of swords, nails, bricks etc. Diocletian introduced government-run factories. He also provided that the head *(princeps)* of each local governor's *officium* should, on being promoted to the position of *primipilus* (top centurion — a position whose numbers had been much increased), convey to the military on the border the grain levied as a tax on the province. This burden, known as the *primi pili pastus*, was to be met from this official's own pocket. It was a huge expense, so the post came to be avoided. This combination of measures provided a tax-base wide enough to support the expenses of government without further recourse to *ad hoc* emergency measures.

Constantine thus had some well laid financial foundations upon which to build and he it was who produced, in the *solidus*, a coin which was to remain stable in weight and purity for the next 700 years. Actually the word "coin" is a misnomer. The *solidus*, which weighed one seventy-second part of a pound, was rather a piece of bullion, stamped with an official emblem, to which the almost worthless bronze and other goods related. Constantine achieved this remarkable feat by amassing vast quantities of precious metal. He did this in various ways. He invented two new taxes. The *collatio lustralis* was paid by traders (city folk had prior to this escaped direct taxation) and the *collatio glebalis* was paid by senators on their landed estates. But income from such sources was meagre. The traders had little enough to spare and senators belonged to a powerful group which had ample opportunities to obtain tax exemptions. More productive of gain was the removal from the cities of the incomes which they had enjoyed from their surrounding lands or their customs dues. These monies now went to the Emperor, easing his position at the expense of the local *curiales*. As victor in a series of civil wars Constantine had amassed a fortune in booty. But the largest windfall came as a side effect of the Emperor's conversion to Christianity. The pagan temples were despoiled of all their ornamentation, right down to the gilt work. And, of course, compulsory gifts of gold were still required, from time to time, from the cities.

So it was that precious metals came out of their hoarders' hands and into circulation. And circulate they did, with a vengeance. Constantine was lavish in gifts to his friends and his Church; his building activities were even more prodigious than those of the other Emperors considered to date, and his apparatus of government was larger than Diocletian's. And all the while, though the mint poured out vast quantities of its debased coins, the tax-men took taxes only in kind or in *specie*. Inflation consequently surged forward at a dizzying pace under Constantine. A measure of wheat, priced in Diocletian's *Edict* of 301 A.D. at 100 *denarii* went for over 10,000 by the end of Constantine's reign. A *solidus* was worth 4,250 *denarii* in 324, over 250,000 by the end of the reign.

There were changes, too, within the military apparatus. From the years of military anarchy Diocletian inherited a border militia, the *limitanei*, of indifferent performance, and the nucleus of a central strategic reserve. This comprised soldiers of good quality who had come to be part of the Emperors' retinues. There were the *promoti* or Horse-guard; the *scholae*, an imperial body-guard, possibly formed by Diocletian himself, and the *protectores*, a corps of officer cadets. Diocletian seems to have sent many of these men to the frontiers, where he may have instituted a new type of military commander, the *dux* (Duke). Late in his reign he increased the legions, adding about 35 to the 34 that had been in existence since the end of the Severan dynasty. Given the existing manpower shortage, this increased military enrolment meant pressing barbarians into service, using conscription, and compelling veterans' sons to serve. Even though a soldier's pay was now relatively low, mostly consisting of food, clothes and equipment, the total additional burden on the taxpayer was very heavy indeed.

If Diocletian was an administrator, Constantine was a military man, and he it was who solved the problem of giving the army of the dominate an effective central strategic reserve. This meant that even if the border militia could not contain an attack at a set point, the army of the interior could speedily reach and despatch a group of invaders as they moved deeper inside the empire. This army of the interior, known as the *comitatenses*, was built up by the inclusion, in addition to the units already mentioned, of *auxilia*. These seem to have been irregulars of various types from rough provincial or border areas. Constantine apparently raised some new forces to bring the *comitatenses* up to strength. But he also drafted in some of the better frontier units, known by this time as *ripenses*.

He did not do this at the expense of weakening the frontier defences, however. New formations of *auxilia* are found there too, as are new types of cavalry units, called *cunei*. Constantine furthermore adapted the army's command structure to the three-tiered system of provincial administration. In command of the *comitatenses* were two Masters of the Soldiery, a Master of Horse *(magister equitum)*, and a Master of Foot *(magister peditum)*, in ascending order of seniority. The *protectores* now seem to have acted as an officer corps, much as the Praetorians had of old. Some were drafted *(deputati)* to the frontiers or on special missions within the empire. Constantine made of others his own personal staff officers. These were known as "the Domestics" *(protectores domestici)* and were under a Count. In the border areas Dukes *(duces)* commanded — provincial governors no longer exercised any but civil administrative functions. A Count *(comes)* could be put over a regional force (at the equivalent to the diocesan level) if such an intermediary course proved necessary.

Constantine's reorganisation involved the raising of additional forces. This seems to have meant probably less than a 25 percent increase, but the additional burden on the manpower and financial resources of the empire forced the latter even further into the straight-jacket of the semi-caste system which had been evolved. The problem which arose as a consequence of the new style army was that the palatine posts commanded so much prestige and influence that there was great pressure to get into them. This meant that the establishment tended to grow, that more place-seekers than soldiers accumulated there, and that all the abuses of sinecurism were to creep in.

The two frontiers regarded as most important by this date were the Danubian and the Armeno-Syrian. Effectively, the Emperors had been moving their capital away from Rome towards them. Maximian had ruled from Milan, Diocletian from Nicomedia. Constantine now took an epoch-making step. Since Septimius' fury had fallen upon it, Byzantion had lain humbled, a shell of its former self. Yet it lay on a geo-political strain line and had an almost impregnable site. Constantine now capitalised upon its strategic position by making it his administrative centre. A new model city was built on the model of Rome, having fourteen regions, one outside the city proper, and so on. It also was to have its own Urban Prefect. Thus the Urban Prefect in Rome dropped in status and power, as he was now for the first time equipped with a colleague and as that colleague's city outstripped his own in importance.

In six years a huge city sprang up. It was far bigger than Byzantion had ever been: 40,000 *foederati* had laboured *helping* to build it. Money and *materiel* were poured into the venture. There were two outside walls; pagan monuments from all over the empire were brought in to embellish the streets; private building was encouraged. So was immigration. The result, Constantine's *polis* or city, did not share Rome's status. It had not the traditions or the senatorial nobility for that. But it had the new nobility of empire and a much larger middle class than Rome, for this was an administrative centre, an Ottawa or Canberra, not a major manufacturing city. Rome was never again to be the capitol of empire. However this relocation of the administrative centre reinforced the inequalities of the population and skill-structure of the empire, heavily overweighting the Greek-speaking East. Also, it produced, in a new city without the taint of pagan traditions, a splendid environment in which Christianity could grow up around this first Christian Emperor.

For under Constantine, the "thirteenth apostle," the fortunes of the Christian Church were to undergo a revolutionary transformation. Confronted by the most rapidly growing and most powerful single organization within the empire, Diocletian had resorted to oppression and religious syncretism to counter it. The last and greatest of the persecutions occurred in his day, for instance. Diocletian, now *dominus et deus* (Master and God) instead of *princeps*, styled himself *Jovius* and his Caesar Maximian *Herculius*. This verbal symbolism linked the religion of the sun god, classical mythology and a monotheistic divine father and son relationship with the imperial cult. All to no avail, as far as Christians were concerned. If the Christians had not been broken by a massive confrontation in time of peace, no one of the seven contestants in the subsequent bout of civil wars was likely to cope with them by a like strategy. And, though they may have comprised as little as one-tenth of the empire's population, they were an organised, city-dwelling tenth, living mostly in the economic heart-land of that empire. Constantine's solution of the dilemma was that of joining them.[13]

The Church was legally recognised. Christianity was zealously propagated. Strikingly pagan symbolism disappeared from the imperial coinage and other public insignia. Its place was taken by ambivalent symbols which could be interpreted as pagan or as Christian. The new army standard, for instance, the *labarum*, was as much a Mithraic as a Christian symbol (Mithraism was the major army religion). A pole with a transverse bar, from which there hung a silken, gold-embroidered cloth, it was topped with a golden wreath containing a monogram which believers recognized as symbolizing Christ. Everywhere a more formalised, symbolic art begins to replace classical realism.[14] A different concept of the world came with this new art.

Constantine's "fatal gift" of recognition changed a religion of the poor and dispossessed into the religion of the well-to-do, and resulted forthwith in the emergence of a powerful and wealthy established Church.[15] There was retribution for the confiscations of the days of persecution. Lands and properties were restored. To these the Emperor added rich gifts: he built churches, granted endowments to churches, made distributions of money to clergy, and freed them of obligations, even of those which went with curial status. This was in 312; fifteen years later the latter benefaction had to be rescinded: too many had taken advantage of it. Bishops were given the right to use the facilities of the public post. Their courts of law were legally recognised. Such courts were not merely for clergy; lay persons could bring business before them. Churches were enabled to accept legacies and became wealthy corporations. Certain notoriously immoral pagan temples were destroyed. All pagan temples were stripped of their treasures. Christians were advanced in society. There was a rush to join the Church. Though pagan religions were not banned, Christianity thus came overnight into an overwhelmingly superior competitive position. Not all Christians saw this as an unmixed blessing.

Shortly before Constantine's day there had been a movement within the Church to withdraw from the dangers and temptations of the worldly life into the solitude of the desert.[16] St. Anthony is associated with this phenomenon. He was among the first of the hermits in the deserts round the Nile. Increasing numbers were attracted to such a life, as the Church became heavily involved in the world in Constantine's day (and as restrictions on *curiales* who entered the Church were eased). As this trend spread, its practices too, developed. A group of novices would congregate in the vicinity of a great hermit, forming a *lavra*. Then a soldier Pachomius, converted to Christianity, found that, although the demands of an anchorite's life were beyond most Christians' abilities, a group could live a common life *(koinon bios)* of "holy athleticism."

Hence the *coenobium* was formed and the monastery came into being. In a great complex of buildings near the Nile there was an assembly hall, refectory, offices, and cells for the monks, who lived a directed life of work and prayer under their superior. Soon Pachomius presided over a group of nine such institutions, as well as two for women. More than 3,000 souls came to be among the chosen. And Pachomius did not accept all comers. Indeed on one single occasion he is reputed to have turned away 100 would-be entrants as unsuitable. But in this way even the revolt within the Church against its Establishment came to have an organizational form like that Establishment. The monks however always stood especially high in popular esteem for their renunciation of worldly things.

But, if the Church had been drawn into the world, the government now found itself embroiled in the feuds within the Church. Believing in a god who was both a being and a person, static and dynamic, one and many, and being subject to a variety of interpretations of their religious beliefs from a variety of linguistic, social and cultural backgrounds, Christians of the fourth century came to subscribe to many (possibly as many as eighty) varieties of Christianity. In Africa and Egypt there were serious schisms. The country folk, who were ethnically different and not overly well disposed to the townees, had resisted the persecution manfully. They were hardy, long inured to police actions on the part of the authorities, and had some opportunities to flee from them. The townees, enjoying none of these advantages, had not done so well. Now the former groups, Donatists and Militians respectively, were against the acceptance of apostates, of whatever sort, back into the Church. But the main controversy, known as the Arian controversy, centred around the relation of Christ to God: was He a *subordinate* divine being? Was He a mode of God's activity? Constantine thought it his duty to bring unity to the Church and faith, as he had brought it to the empire.[17] Church and empire were now becoming so close-linked that a feud within the former could have serious repercussions upon the latter.

Constantine accordingly convened a council of the Church in 325 A.D. in Nicaea. A formula was reached that enabled those gathered (overwhelmingly from the East) to reach a consensus. It was the Nicene Creed: the son was distinct from God, but there were not two gods. The Son was of the same essence *(homoousios/consubstantialis)* as the Father. Described as "uncharitable, unscriptural, uncatholic and unanimous," the formula was as effective as Diocletian's *Edict* had been in dealing with the problem against which it was directed. But the Church had now set the precedent of having the Emperor convene a synod of its senior administrators to solve its problems. It operated under senatorial house-rules and the Emperor had been chairman and convenor there.[18] The Church, moreover, now recognised the Emperor as god's vice-regent upon earth: that is to say, god's will was seen as working through the Emperor. So Constantine was as "sacred" and as absolute a ruler as ever Diocletian had been. The difference was that now the Christians were the staunchest upholders of such a situation. For them the Kingdom of God had relocated. It was now "of this world" rather than "of the world to come," a major shift in their viewpoint. Christians would now fight for their faith in the imperial armies. They were to give, in fact, more support for warfare than any other of the higher religions save Islam. And, all the while, their Church was spreading, to become coterminous with the Roman empire and adopting many of the organizational forms of the dominate (vicars and dioceses, for instance). At the local level, a new official, the *oeconomus* or business manager, was proving a necessary innovation to cope with the tremendous increase in property and business transactions within the Church. For clerics could (and did) trade, taking advantage of their privileged position in regard to immunities and so on. A countervailing power to that of the administrative bureaucracy was building up.

Such was the new dispensation brought about in society by the establishment of the dominate. Diagram 4 (below, pages 105-106) attempts to depict the organizational structure of the apparatus of government graphically. Comparison with the first diagram (above, pages 31-32) will reveal at a glance that all decision-making has been relocated within official ranks. It will not, however, show the increasing barbarization of the army, militarization of the civil administration, divinization of the ruler and Christianization of the background culture. This new world was bestridden by the giant organisations of army, Church and civil administration. All still had largely different value systems. German "barbarian" elements dominated within the army; (Athanasian) Christians within the Church. Considerable numbers of the civil administrators, however, had been brought up within the Great Tradition of Graeco-Roman culture and, equally with the other two groups, held those others' values inferior to their own. Adjustments thus still lay ahead for the men of the apparatus, and hence for the empire.

The next series of major changes is associated with the reign of Theodosius I, the Great (379-95 A.D.).[19] The leading sectors, as it were, in regard to change were the army and the Church.

Theodosius was raised to power after the Romans had been shatteringly defeated by the Gothic horsemen at Adrianople in 378.[20] The fighting of the previous reign had run Roman army strengths perilously low. In raising new units to bring the *comitatenses* and the frontier troops up to strength, Theodosius seems to have found the army reduced to half strength. And within the army the power and influence of barbarian officers, who staffed many of its higher command positions, was considerable. For instance, when the city folk of Thessaloniki lynched his Goth Master of Soldiery, Butheric, in a riot triggered by the latter's imprisonment of a popular charioteer, Theodosius had in reprisal to organise a wholesale massacre of the citizenry by the Gothic troops.[21]

In these circumstances the best that Theodosius could do to deal with the victors of Adrianople was to admit them within the Roman empire as "federate allies" *(foederati)*. Under this arrangement the Goths received land in northern Thrace against an obligation to field army units for the imperial government on request. However, they entered as an organised group owing fealty only to their own leader. It was he who undertook to provide the empire with men upon request. This was an unprecedented step. Formerly such transplanted peoples had either been scattered about in penny numbers under individual Roman landowners or brought in in small detachments of *laeti* under a Roman commander. The *foederati*, however, constituted a little feudal enclave within which the writ of the administrative bureaucracy did not run. Army interests were thus clearly getting precedence over those of the empire as a whole.

This phenomenon was to spread in the West, weakening the efficacy and reducing the income of the administrative bureaucracy there. For it was in the West that the barbarian inroads were being made; in the East the invaders could not get past the impregnable city of Constantinople to strike into Asia Minor, heartland of the empire. Moreover, in the West pagan administrators were trying to employ Arian Goths to fight Arian Goths on behalf of orthodox townees; whereas in the East a Christianized administration was employing mingled Arian and Orthodox forces to fight Persian unbelievers. Hence Gothic influences were less in the East. For instance, as a sequel to Adrianople there, Julius, the Master of Soldiery in the Eastern Prefecture, had had all Gothic units brought out of the cities as for a pay parade and massacred. The operation was executed without fail simultaneously throughout the prefecture on a given day. Roman commanders were to predominate in the East for the rest of the reign, among a judiciously blended top level staff containing Germans, Goths and Orientals. German Masters of the Soldiery, however, were the prominent group in western army circles.

The power and influence of the Church were demonstrated equally strikingly.[22] Theodosius was a devoted Christian. Moreover he had followed the contemporary practice of receiving a death-bed baptism — and then recovered. Hence spiritual sanctions could be applied to sway his judgement. And it happened that his reign coincided with the bishopric of Ambrose of Milan, who had the resolution to apply such sanctions. The majority of the clergy seem to have been of curial stock: men of aristocratic or military rank seem to have been much less common among those entering holy orders. Ambrose was the son of a Praetorian Prefect. He was a Consular, or provincial governor, when drafted (against his will) into the bishopric of Milan. He compelled Theodosius to do public penance for the carnage at Thessaloniki. His influence is suspected of being behind the Emperor's decision to ban paganism and Christian heresies. All churches were to be handed over to bishops of the Nicene Creed. Though the Jewish religion was tolerated (despite pressure from Ambrose), Christianity was now the official religion of the empire. This decision was reached because Constantinople was the "New Rome" and administrative center of empire, not

NOTES ON DIAGRAM 4

The name of the office, or group, of officials is everywhere capitalised. Above it, in lower case, there appears the title of the official in charge.

1. The distinction between Masters of the Soldiery in the Presence (of the emperor) and Masters of the Soldiery in the various prefectures, each with an army of *comitatenses*, dates to a time after Constantine.

2. All officials in charge of offices etc. within the central government are *ex officio* members of the Consistory.

3. The Notaries provide all officials with their codicils of office and all army officers with their commissions. They are also sometimes given secret agent type assignments.

4. The hatched lines indicate that officers from this *corps* could be sent to serve in outlying units or seconded for special duties anywhere in the empire.

5. One of the Praetorian Prefects, the P.P. for the prefecture of the Orient, was in the Presence and thus a member of the Court and Consistory.

because of its apostolic tradition. Prior to this Alexandria had been the dominant see in the East, and Antioch had long-established claims to seniority. Strong regional interests lay behind these claims to seniority; and position within the empire-wide hierarchy of the bishoprics of the Church commanded extensive power and influence by this time. This was the century, however, which produced the greatest writers amongst the Greek Fathers of the Church, and consequently the influence of Greek Orthodoxy was predominant in Theodosius' reign.[23]

Events within the administrative apparatus were of a less epoch-making character. The power struggle between Praetorian Prefect and Master of Offices took an interesting turn, however. Rufinus, a Master of Offices who enjoyed great influence with Theodosius, succeeded in having control of the imperial arms factories transferred from the prefecture to his department. He also managed to bring a Praetorian Prefect, Tatian, into public disgrace and to step into his post. Moreover, prior to Theodosius' reign, the Master of Offices had brought it about that his agents, the *agentes in rebus*, should staff all posts of *princeps* in the *officia* under the Praetorian Prefecture, except at the provincial level, where there was reluctance to undertake the post because it involved the *primi pili pastus* upon termination.

This development meant that the topmost position on every office-staff serving a Vicar or Praetorian Prefect was occupied by an agent of the Master of Offices. The latter thus had access to information on all business transacted within the Prefect's sphere of operations. The agents were well rewarded for their services: in this reign they were made senators of consular rank upon holding the position of *princeps*. Many, however, seem to have been men of such slender financial resources as to have had to give up such a title for lack of means. But, however they fared, there could be little doubt by this time as to which high official had the greater effective power, so much did they empower their Master. Others of their number went, year after year, to fill the position of *princeps*, in like fashion, on the staff of the Urban Prefect. Meanwhile the Notaries had gained so much in importance that they were above the more mundane scribal duties of their positions. The Master of Offices sent in men under his control, the *memoriales*, to do the tedious humdrum work for them. He thus gained control over establishments.[24]

Such cross-appointments were however one way of keeping controls upon officialdom, and the administrative bureaucracy under Theodosius I seems to have been kept under extremely effective control. Praetorian Prefects were men of proven ability. Promotion came to them after they had displayed their competence at lower levels in the administration. As a tax-extracting machine the Praetorian Prefecture seems to have done its job all too well, for an Emperor who made very heavy demands upon the tax-payer.[25] Such faithful servants did not go unrewarded. All of the higher Palatine officials were given senatorial status, a status which meant by now more a mark of social distinction (with attendant immunities from tax-related obligations, of course) than any form of decision-making capability. The *proximi* or second in command in the *scrinia* or *bureaux* were given the status of Vicars, not just Consulars (*provincial* governors). Rank seems to have become an issue of major importance during this reign. There is an imperial constitution differentiating between the status of those who have actually held a given position and those who merely enjoyed an honorific grant of the title pertaining thereto (and further variations upon this theme). The result was an enormous growth in the numbers of officials of the central government. For instance, the *corps* of Notaries grew from 4 (under the Emperor Julian) to 520 members. Agents teemed in profusion on all sides. Many poor men were admitted to Senatorial status as a result.

The other side of this picture involves the *curiales*. They seem to have been trying desperately hard, and pretty successfully, to achieve entry into the administrative apparatus and the Church. The Emperor was equally indefatigable in his (equally successful) attempts to keep them out or to return those who had managed to change status.

It was a reign, then, in which the men of the apparatus saw their interests advanced. The military fared best, as was their wont. But the orthodox Church made great strides. What political struggle there was largely took place within these three bureaucracies or between one of them and the Emperor, ultimately the resource person for the allocation of privilege within the empire. And, as the success of the military in exerting such pressure had forewarned, it was the last reign over a united empire.

In the fifth century, the century, that is, in which Rome in the West collapsed, there is no one reign which stands out as a turning point. But perhaps the reign of Theodosius II most dramatically illustrates the power and workings of the apparatus.[26] These workings led, by the end of that reign, to a new environment within which that apparatus operated. Basically what happened was that the western part of the apparatus virtually collapsed, and extensive disintegration followed upon the failure of its redistributive servicing activities. The eastern part of the empire, on the other hand, had more defensible frontiers and a wealthier and more taxable population. Coping with the lesser task and the greater resources, its apparatus performed effectively, developing as it did so. East Rome developed with it.

The invasion tracks on any map of the invasions (see Map 3) tell much of the story. Asia Minor, Syria and Egypt passed through the period unharmed. But, with the dreaded Huns behind them, Goths and Germans broke in everywhere upon the empire in the West. Alaric and his Visigoths invaded Greece, then Italy, taking Rome in 410 A.D. His people eventually established themselves in Aquitania, on the Atlantic coast of Gaul, first as federate allies then, by 450 under Theodoric, as an independent kingdom. By 450, too, there were Burgundians occupying Savoy as federate allies and Franks holding the lands by the channel in a like capacity. Eastern Britain was lost to hordes of Angles, Jutes and Saxons. The Vandals had passed via Italy, Gaul and Spain — where they left the Suevi in control of what is now Portugal, to establish a kingdom in north Africa. Their fleet was abroad upon the Mediterranean, ending centuries-long peaceful trading conditions. On top of all this came the Huns. Under Attila, the "Scourge of God," they struck into the Balkans, against the Goths and the Franks, and down into Italy. Of all these attacks only those into Greece and the Balkans were directed against East Rome, and these regions were not at the economic centre of the eastern empire. But Rome in the West came effectively to lose hold of much of Gaul, Spain and Africa.[27]

The western taxation system broke under the strain. Lands had been lost to barbarian kingdoms or "federate allies." The road system could not be maintained. Everywhere villas were springing up; and the local lords with their private armies who controlled them withdrew the lands in the vicinity of such villas from the control of the tax-collector. The effects of all this dislocation were evident in famines, the dying-back of the towns, and the dropping away of trade. For the major centres of production in the West, of Gallic or Rhenic glassware for instance, had also been involved in the general ruin.[28]

In a way, then, the invasions actually gave an advantage to eastern traders, by eliminating such competition in manufactured articles as the western part of the empire had formerly afforded them. But the commercial resources of East Rome were immeasurably greater even had it not had peace in which to develop them. The major trade routes channelling spices and luxury items from the Far East, that is, from India, Ceylon and China, debouched via Egypt and Syria. Besides Rome, there were no cities in the West now to match the populations and resources of Alexandria, Antioch or even Constantinople. And the former were no mere market towns but bustling centres of manufacture and commerce in a symbiotic relationship to the countryside around them. The eastern administration seems to have given more thought to the development of its internal and trading resources than to military matters. But it had ample money to finance and train its armies. It also had, in the Isaurians of Asia Minor, a pool of man power on which to draw for those armies. And it could afford the high cost of city fortifications. So it was that the century which saw Rome taken twice — by Visigoths in 410 and Vandals in 455 — saw Antioch enjoying the first street lighting by night of any city in antiquity and Constantinople's huge, cistern-based, urban water supply system.

Large estates, moreover, were a less prominent feature of the countryside in East Rome: small-holders abounded everywhere. Thus the administrative bureaucracy in the East had a larger tax-base on which to draw than did its western counterpart, and less refractory and independent subjects from whom to do the drawing. It seems to have gone to some pains to see that the monies which it extracted in taxes were redistributed wisely and that its gold coins should be the currency in which international trade was conducted.[29]

Theodosius' death left his two sons in power. Arcadius was seventeen years old, Honorius, ten; neither seems to have been a forceful or an able personality. The Emperor's death also left a variety of powerful officials. The Vandal Stilicho, Master of Soldiery and the Emperor's trusted favourite, was with the bulk of the army in the West. Rufinus, another favourite and at this time Praetorian Prefect, dominated the apparatus in the East. The intrigues which ensued within the apparatus exercised a decisive and lasting influence upon the empire.

In the West Stilicho, regent for the ten-year-old Honorius, equipped himself with authority to cope with the situation by changing the nature of his Mastership of the Soldiers. He had been Master of Foot and had precedence over his colleague the Master of Horse. He now made himself Master of Both Services *(magister utriusque militae)* and thus turned his former colleague into his subordinate. Also, the positions of *princeps* (head of the office staff), *commentariensis* (in charge of disciplinary matters) and two *numerarii* (accountants) in the *officium* (office staff) of every Count and Duke now came to be filled by men from the Master's central *officium*.[30] This concentration of power in the hands of the Master of Both Services gave him control of the apparatus and of the Emperor. Hence the Master comes to have the title of Patrician; he often married into the imperial family and was very much the power behind the throne. The military, moreover, dominated the civil apparatus. The major institutional innovation concerned the setting up of various Regions under control by Counts. All the great names within the apparatus were those of military men: Constantius, Castinus, Aetius, Boniface. And a series of puppet Emperors commenced: Honorius, for instance, was succeeded by a six-year-old, Valentinian III.

In the East things worked out differently. Rufinus, the Praetorian Prefect, was executed, probably at Stilicho's instigation, by Gainas, the Goth commander of the eastern troops who now returned from the West. This won Gainas his Mastership of the Soldiery but control of events was taken over by Eutropius, a eunuch Chamberlain *(praepositus sacri cubiculi)*, who had meanwhile attained influence over Arcadius. Eutropius proceeded to institute 7 Masters of Both Services, two of whom were In the Presence *(presentales)*, that is they resided in Constantinople with the Emperor, one commanding on the European, the other on the Asian side of the strait. There were mixed forces of cavalry and infantry under each Master. This arrangement meant that no one Master could attain predominance, via a *coup*, as others could always be moved against him. A signal demonstration of this was given by the sequel. Eutropius exiled two of Theodosius' top commanders. Gainas toppled him, but was himself toppled. Thereafter the big names in the politics of court intrigues are not those of soldiers. Moreover Goths were increasingly dispensed with in army service from 400; and German generals are scarce until the 420's. When they do return, they do not exercise any untoward influence upon the non-military life of East Rome.

Increasingly the palace forces seem to have been controlled by, and taken their tone from, the civil administration. Their numbers swell, their ranks and titles augment, their code is professional. Thus the *protectores* put out an off-shoot in the *protectores deputati*, as officers from the *corps* were seconded to units and tasks everywhere in the eastern empire (which now claimed to include Illyricum). This measure increased the control over outlying forces exercised from the centre. The Domestics split into an infantry and a cavalry section. The post of *Spatharius* or Captain of the Emperor's Bodyguard seems to have been instituted by Theodosius II. And there is every evidence that place-seekers in their multitudes strove for access to positions in these units, as to the other civilian staffs of the palace.[31]

In the East the struggle in high places for power seems in fact to have been that between the Praetorian Prefect for the East and the Master of Offices. For, here as in the West, a powerful officialdom had installed a minor on the throne in the religious and bookish Theodosius II, aged seven upon his accession. His sister Placidia and later his wife Eudoxia exercised considerable influence over him, and behind them stood a series of powerful officials. The first two, in this series of great men of the apparatus, were Praetorian Prefects (Aurelian and Anthemius); then there was a long interval with Helio, the Master of Offices, dominant; finally a Chamberlain, Chrysaphius, won to precedence in conjunction with Nomus, the Master of Offices. It was men such as Anthemius and Helio who became Patricians in the East. The civil administration held the military in control.

A review of the accomplishments of the respective governments in the age of Theodosius II will indicate what these new power-balances within the two apparatuses meant for the governed. In the West there was a series of attempted *coups*, as the military men strove with one another for dominance. Alienation and unrest reached new highs in the countryside, as far as can be judged by the activities of the *Bacaudae* or bandits, as they were styled by the Establishment.[32] The West proved unable even to defend its own capital. Rome fell to Alaric the Visigoth, and a thrill of horror ran round the civilised world at this portentous event.

In the East, by way of contrast, the Theodosian Code was produced. This was an authoritative and exhaustive collection of all legislation since 312 A.D. and produced relative order in what had hitherto been an unmanageable profusion of accumulated rulings on a mass of unrelated topics. This codification and classification was a great blessing to commerce, jurisdiction and administration. It was also a project which had been seen as desirable since the days of Julius Caesar. Yet not until this reign were resources and business needs such as to bring this long-desired event to fruition. A university was established at Constantinople. Now there were better facilities for producing and training the lawyers and intelligentsia needed by the apparatus of government. And Constantinople was equipped with walls adequate to withstand the fiercest assault (as Attila was able to attest). The way into Asia was barred to invaders from the North. The commercial and administrative activities of the capital were rendered immune from disturbance. Taken together, these three achievements meant increased prosperity for the eastern empire.

But perhaps matters relating to finance and status-seeking tell an even more revealing story. For the easterners had been hard put to it financially in this reign. Although Attila could not take Constantinople or cross the strait into Asia, they had not been able to withstand him in battle. Thrice they had to buy peace from him before they managed, as they had done with Alaric the Visigoth, to "pass him along" to the West. The money seems to have been raised from the wealthy, those who could most afford to pay. There were compulsory refunds of tax rebates or remissions of arrears; immunities and exemptions were cut back. Yet the cost of tax extraction amounted, in 258, to only one silver piece or *siliqua* per tax *iugum*.

In the West, officials made two gold pieces (48 times the cost in the East) in the process of extracting taxes from each *iugum* in their far less affluent domains. Moreover, in the West, fiscal immunities were liberally granted and remissions of tax arrears were enormous and frequent. For after Honorius the top positions in the civil apparatus had gone increasingly, not to seasoned and experienced men promoted from lower down within that apparatus, but to aristocrats, many of whom were young and untrained in administrative matters. To such men, fellow aristocrats could successfully turn with pleas for special treatment. In the East, on the other hand, only tried and experienced administrators rose to the top; and they did so after proving their competence in related but subordinate postings. So it was that although in both parts of the empire *adaeratio* (payment of taxes etc. in gold, not in kind) increased during this century, it was in the East that financial recovery was made. The authorities had largely ceased their huge issues of copper coins, so inflation began to recede. By the end of the century a stable relationship between bronze and gold coins seems to have been reached there.

At the focus of attention in the East are the politics and concerns of bureaucrats: size of establishment (which kept creeping up), speed of promotion, ranks and titles. A major development, and hence preoccupation, of the fifth century, seems to have concerned access to an established position as a civil servant. A huge number of supernumeraries awaited a vacancy within the established positions *(statuti)*; like those positions, the supernumeraries were graded in three ranks. Theodosius II was to regulate carefully against queue-jumping and define who might go forward in the event of a specific vacancy. Equestrian rank had by now become so cheapened by ready access as to be worthless, and so had the lower *echelons* of the Senate. Effectively only *illustres*, the topmost rank of "senators," now had senatorial privileges. Hence the intense competition for those offices which would confer this top rank. For those who secured office a critical issue concerned the court before which officials could be tried for alleged misconduct. It was all-important to an official that this should consist of his colleagues. *Palatini* could by this time be tried only before the Counts of the Sacred Largesses or of the Private Estate. But the Master of Offices extended his jurisdiction — a sign, this, of his increased power — to include the members of the bedchamber: *cubicularii*, *castrenses* and *silentiarii* (Silentiaries were ushers within the court in attendance upon the Consistory).[33]

There were significant, if not dramatic, developments within the religious apparatus in this reign, too.[34] However, in this case, it was the West where greater order reigned. As the western apparatus of government broke up under the strain, in many areas the Church took over some of the responsibilities defaulted upon;[35] and a weak Emperor meant less imperial influence upon the Pope of Rome. After Ambrose's death and with the accession of two strong popes, Innocent and Leo the first, the see of Rome came increasingly to dominate western Christianity. And, if the western Emperors lost administrative and military influence over Illyricum to those of the east, the Pope won religious control over the area from the Patriarch of Constantinople. He managed this by making the Bishop of Thessaloniki a Papal Vicar with the right of consecrating all bishops in the two dioceses concerned.[36] With the writing of Augustine's *City of God* Christian literature in Latin rose to be fit for comparison with classical literature.[37] A strong, well regulated and articulate Church was in being.

In the east the Church was much more subject to imperial controls and much less subject to unity of command from within. The Emperor for instance could (and did) appoint Patriarchs and summon Oecumenical Conferences (there were two, in 431 and 451 — the latter, the fourth, just after this reign). But, though Constantinople might successfully assert its claim to second place within the sees of the empire, that claim was not recognised in Alexandria. Nor was the Patriarch imposed by the Emperor. Ethnic differences underlay this struggle for pride of place. The local bishop of Alexandria effectively controlled the Church in Egypt. He was supported by the hordes of Coptic monks, the *parabolani*, unkempt, unwashed and riotous masters of the streets.[38] As Byzantine man was more of a religious than a political animal, regional and ethnic differences had a habit of emerging as heretical interpretations of the nature of Christ. Hence Nestorianism came from Antioch, semitic and rivalrous, and Monophysitism from

Coptic Alexandria. These views clashed in schism with the Orthodoxy of Greek Constantinople.[39]

There were other conflicts within the Church, too. Feeling was growing against the use of money by clerics to win power, place and influence. Objections were also springing up against clerical traders. The intensities of the feelings roused show how much their Church was at the centre of contemporaries' thoughts and concerns.[40] Certainly the Emperor had his work cut out to prevent *decurions* (men from town councils) transferring their talents and other resources thereto. The power of the established Church inched steadily forward. In this reign it became law that, if a cleric died intestate, his property went to the Church. The churches and monasteries thus gained considerably in wealth. They seem to have put it to highly practical use by the building of hospitals. The first of these had apparently been established by Basil the Great, Bishop of Caesarea, in 372 or thereabouts. St. John Chrysostom now erected several in Constantinople. It was in fact the Church which largely provided welfare and relief services and on a scale, at that, hitherto unknown in antiquity.[41] Shortly after the reign (in 457), and due to a feeling that must have been welling up during its course, coronation by the Patriarch of Constantinople came to be considered necessary in an Emperor's accession to the throne. The eastern Emperor was thus within, not above, the Church.[42]

Of the remaining reigns in this period Justinian's (527-565 A.D.) was the most productive of change for these varied bureaucracies.[43] Justinian influenced the government of Rome for a long period, inasmuch as he enjoyed high favour with his uncle Justin (Emperor from 518-526) before his own accession. Moreover there was considerable change at this time in the background environment in which the bureaucracies operated.

The empire went over to the attack in its dealings with the Germans. North Africa, Sicily, Italy, Dalmatia and part of Spain were recovered (see Map 4). A 50% increase in territory resulted, which made the Mediterranean a Byzantine lake. However the campaigns involved over-strained even the enormous financial resources of Byzantium. And, as ill-luck would have it, one of Persia's ablest rulers, Chosroes I (531-579), appeared in the East. Devastating Persian raids into Syria resulted. Huns and Slavs took this opportunity to come across the Danube and down into the Balkans. But, simultaneously, missionaries were going out into Arabia and the Sudan, the Caucasus and southern Russia. Two monks smuggled silkworm eggs back from China in a bamboo staff; the silk trade consequently began to relocate.

If international affairs, as it were, brought major changes, there were equally dramatic happenings on the domestic scene too. Justinian was almost overthrown by a gigantic riot, the Nika Riot of 532, which brought extensive arson and carnage to Constantinople. There were a series of highly destructive earthquakes and repeated outbreaks of what was probably bubonic plague. Antioch, destroyed first by earth tremors then by Persian assault, was slow to recover. Rome, five times captured in the wars in Italy, was ruined. Athens saw her philosophical schools closed. Constantinople thus came to be commercially, intellectually and administratively the centre of empire.

In 518 the Emperor Anastasius had left his successor the moŝt well-filled treasury any incoming Emperor in Romano-Byzantine history was ever to take over: 320,000 pounds weight of gold. Constantinople at the outset of Justinian's reign was not only the world's wealthiest city; her empire probably disposed of over half of the trade and wealth of the world of those times. Justinian's main problems seem to have been those of regulating trade and of regulating an apparatus of government swollen to giant proportions and teeming with abuses. Trade and apparatus of government were interconnected matters, as was to be the case from this time onwards. For upon the economic prosperity of the empire depended imperial tax resources and those resources were necessary to pay the armies and fund the diplomacy which protected an increasingly beleaguered Byzantine world.[44]

The missions went out in an attempt to build up Christian communities in areas such that, by having influence over them, Byzantium could reroute the trade lines to the East and cut out the Persian middle-man. These areas lay north of the Caspian and along the Red Sea, respectively. The wars of the reign gave Byzantium control of Mediterranean commerce and retained her control over that of the Black Sea.[45] A government monopoly in the purchase of silk, regulating the prices and the (three) places at which it might be bought, was set up. And customs barriers appear, organised on a scale and with a thoroughness that was something new to the Mediterranean world. There was a new tax, the *dekate* (10%): there were three customs zones; houses for the collection of customs dues were built.[46]

Collected on this scale, customs dues brought in considerable resources from a form of taxation which formerly had not been so productive. But they also required a framework of services to facilitate commercial dealings. The law, for instance, had to be readily intelligible and accessible. The administrative bureaucracy had to be supportively, rather than rapaciously, redistributive.

Justinian's top legal expert, Tribonian, the Quaestor of the Sacred Palace, was given the task of bringing order out of the confusion which had accumulated since the compilation of the *Theodosian Code*. His task force produced the *Justinianic Code*. Its twelve books compiled all the legislation of the period from Hadrian to Justinian, in process revising the earlier *Theodosian Code*, systematising it and eliminating obsolete material. A *Digest* did the same for all the interpretative work of the jurists; there were to be no further commentaries. A handbook of civil law, the *Institutes*, was produced as a manual for training law students. Only the Emperor could add to this body of law; he did so in new laws *(novellae leges)* published as the *Novels*. These publications now constituted the sole valid "law" for the courts of the empire and the class-rooms of the three great law-schools (of Beyrut, Constantinople and Rome). Changes in the laws produced in course of editing made them reflect Christian values and sixth century problems. Together these publications constituted a giant step forward toward a better-integrated commerce and society.

They also made it easier to bring defaulting officials to book. Effectively to proceed against them, however, was another matter. The legal documents themselves show this. *Novel* after *Novel* provides sanctions against the same bureaucratic malpractices. Rioting against officials indicates how serious this problem was. Townspeople, not just the country-folk, long inured to bureaucratic oppression, now felt the pressure, as the customs dues worked upon their cost of living. But the tax-gathering machine was inexorable. Unfalteringly it extracted its dues *(and* its perquisites) no matter how severe these, or the agitation against them, might be.

The trouble was basically rooted in three inter-related bureaucratic practices.[47] The maintenance of these practices was vital to the interests of the men of the apparatus while the operation of the practices was frustrating to the Emperor and prohibitively expensive to the tax-payer. Wages were not high, so fees paid for services rendered expedited service. The step from fee-exacting to the taking of *douceurs* was easily taken; and from there to influence peddling, and thence to downright bribery, the progress was easy. The term *sportulae* ambiguously covers this whole area of transactions. Given an ethos which sanctioned *sportulae* it was all important for an official that he be tried only before his peers. Such after all was the custom for senators, and most officials now had pretensions to senatorial status. This form of trial, known as *praescriptio fori*, made the individual official virtually unassailable and the bureaucracy *en masse* very hard to discipline. Official position came in this way to be eagerly sought after. There were many more applicants than there were positions. Applicants consequently tried to establish preemptive rights upon desired positions by negotiation with the holder prior to his retirement. A holder might thus sell the reversion to his office. A series of such sales could easily lead to a situation in which offices were thought of as saleable, or as one's purchased property. Hence absenteeism was rife; this led to sinecures, which in turn led to increased establishments. And, of course, to an expectancy that one could legitimately recoup one's initial expenditure via fees. In this way a vicious circle was created.

Justinian, efficiency and equity oriented, directed his untiring energies to rectifying this situation. The results of his endeavours were probably as unanticipated to the bureaucracy as they were to him. The military seem to have been more manageable than the civil administrators, so let us first consider his activities in regard to the army. By this time posts in the Palace could only be obtained by purchase. The imperial guard had become a mere parade-ground corps, if that. Justin had bought supporters, after the intrigue which had unexpectedly placed him on the throne, by (amongst other things) raising four additional regiments, or *scholae.* Justinian disbanded them. Moreover, he transferred the other *scholae* and the *protectores domestici* to frontier duties, allowing them to opt out of the latter if they would forego their pay.

Auditors from the Pretorian Prefect's staff *(discussores)* fanned out to the frontiers. Here the names of men long since defunct padded the pay-rolls, and lined the money-bags of local Dukes or their office-staffs. The *discussores,* not without some blackmail, rectified this position, receiving for themselves one-twelfth of what they thus saved the government. Justinian even went so far as to dock the border militia of its pay upon the signing of a "perpetual peace" with Persia. This was a policy for which he was to pay dear. The militia melted away; the Persians broke in and extorted protection money from the cities and Justinian had eventually to purchase renewals of the "eternal peace" by heavy subsidies.

A variety of devices was adopted to deal with abuses within the civil administration. Provincial governorships were made no longer saleable. Discontinuance of sales of these posts cost the Emperor not only the price which would have been paid for further posts, but also sums paid in compensation to those who had acquired the right of appointing to certain posts and with it the *suffragia* paid for them. As the men of the *scholae* had not received such recompense, it is clear which group had the greater real power within the apparatus. For the future provincial governorships were to be granted upon the recommendation of the neighbouring bishop and local authorities. Governors were given an elevation in status, to the rank of *spectabiles*, and empowered to try all cases involving sums of up to 750 gold pieces. The office of "Champion of the Community" *(defensor civitatis)*, given to officials descended from the *curator rei publicae* who looked after the affairs of each provincial town, was empowered to try all cases involving sums up to 300 gold pieces. The "public post" had its activities restricted. Various officials had acquired the right to use its services or give others the right to use them. It had thus come to impose a heavy burden upon the lives and properties of those who lined its route and from whom services could be requisitioned.

Justinian also tried to dispense with the various Vicars. They had come to serve little purpose within the administration as, between them, Praetorian Prefect and provincial governors had coped with all matters arising. Vicars were, moreover, poorly paid and hence corruptible, and so an obvious target for removal. Too many bureaucratic vested interests were at stake, however. Vicars reappear again even before the reign is over.

Justinian had relied heavily on the making of certain appointments in his attempt to bring the administrative bureaucracy under control. John the Cappadocian and Peter Barsymes were financial experts who were elevated to the post of Praetorian Prefect without regard for the normal internal procedures of promotion. Thus they were in, but not of, that bureaucracy. Confronted by a hostile staff, whose tastes and manners clashed with their own, these "provincial upstarts" were prepared to apply the sanctions which a "sound" man, put forward by the central office itself, would have connived at ignoring. The problem merely took another form, however, in the long run. For these men, too, proved as corrupt as the sound men, but in different ways. And they were even harder to discipline. For the abolition of many of the services of the public post and the transaction of much business at the local level made it difficult for the Master of Offices to check up on the Praetorian Prefect now. It has even been suggested that the Emperor's attempts at reform of the administration were restricted to areas in which his advisor, the Praetorian Prefect, did not feel that his own vested interests were vitally affected.[48]

The fact, however, was that Justinian persisted in his support for such appointees despite pressure for their removal. John the Cappadocian, for instance, was ousted at the demand of the Nika Rioters, but later (in the same year) returned to office. This time it took the Empress, who had access to sources of information not open to the Emperor, to secure his removal. In the meanwhile new officials were created, partly to deal with the security problems caused by discontent with the exactions of the administration, partly as a consequence of the growth in importance of Constantinople as a centre within the empire. The old Prefect of the Watch was superseded by a Prefect of the Demes. Such was the name by which the circus factions (colores) of old were now known. They were by now organised into claques and groups for corvée labour, and needed careful supervision because of the potential for violence given them by this organization. Then there was the Quaesitor, an official who kept records of those entering the city. The office was probably an extension of that of the Master of Records established by Constantine. This Master had come to have a variety of duties, such as registering students, of a nature akin to those of the newly instituted Quaesitor.[49] Finally there was the biocolytes or "Preventer of Violence," a police official. Several of these posts were established for the countryside of Asia Minor. All this meant a growth in the power and importance of the Urban Prefect.

Justinian seems, in fact, to have dealt more effectively with the lower orders than with the men of the apparatus. Before the reign was out he seems to have had to revert to the sale of offices once again. It is interesting to see what the bureaucracy could (or would) do or not do. It could impose new taxes. It could sell monopolies to shop-owners. But it had to reverse itself hastily when it tried to debase the currency. And it gave itself a new range of titles; certain high officials now were dubbed gloriosi or "glorious." As illustres seem by now effectively to have been the only senators proper, a need for a hierarchy of precedence within the senatorial order was thus met.

Justinian also introduced changes affecting the structure of the apparatus of military officials and their relationships with the civil administration. As has been seen in his treatment of the scholae, he does not seem to have felt threatened by the military establishment. Indeed, after the victory of his general Belisarius over the Vandals in north Africa, a victory which brought in a huge haul of booty for the treasury, he allowed Belisarius to hold a triumph in the capital. This was the first triumph held by a subject of the Emperor since Augustus' day. But Belisarius seems eventually to have grown too powerful for Justinian's comfort. Justinian seems to have starved him of men and supplies, at the imminent risk of losing the war in Italy, in order to raise another general, the eunuch Narses, as a counterpoise there. For Masters of the Soldiery like Belisarius now posed a considerable potential threat. The army was by now entirely composed of mercenaries and such men maintained their own little standing armies, known as *bucellarii.* Belisarius, for instance, had 7,000 such troops. Justinian might well have misgivings about the loyalties of an army of this nature.

In spite of this, Justinian was prepared, on occasion, to merge the duties of military commander and civil governor in the one man. This happened in Pisidia and Lycaonia, where the Counts took over. There was a similar arrangement in one of the two Cappadocian provinces. A new post of Quaestor to the Army *(quaestura exercitus)* was created. This official seems to have had the duty of seeing to the supplying of troops situated in Thrace by drawing upon resources in the littoral of Asia Minor and the Aegean Islands and Cyprus. These innovations had within them a growth potential that was to cause them rapidly to eclipse the institution of the Master of the Soldiery. By 584 combined civil and military powers granted to the distant governor of Italy brought about the institution known as the exarchate. From this, given the quaestorship of the army, it was but a step to the theme or border region designated as under the administration of its military commander. There were naval themes, too. One coincides strikingly with the area of authority assigned to the Quaestor of the Army. All this lay in the future, in a world shaped by the advent of Islam. But Justinian had initiated the movement towards this empowering of the military by his cession to them of powers of civil administration.[50]

Some idea of the precariousness of the balance of bureaucratic forces achieved prior to Justinian's day and wrecked by this compounding of the functions of high military officials can be obtained by reviewing the accessions of the Emperors who follow him. His immediate successor was a Count of the Excubitors (a military unit attached to the Palace). Then there were three men put up by military interests. The last two in fact owed their advancement to successful insurrection. In this respect, as in his overcommitment of men and money to his goal of recovering the West, Justinian left a legacy of trouble behind at his death.

Justinian's reign marks the high water mark of Caesaropapism in Byzantine times.[51] Justinian was an Emperor who was prepared to maltreat and imprison a Pope because the latter would not agree with his imperial decisions on Church dogma. Eastern clergy knew better than to oppose their Emperor in such matters. "Nothing whatsoever may be done within the Church contrary to the wish and order of the Emperor" was how one of them put it. This situation, imperial control over matters more properly clerical, was mainly caused by two things. The first was that issues had arisen concerning the organizational infrastructure of the Church and of such a nature that only settlement by the Emperor would lead to general agreement. The second was that the Emperor had to coerce an Orthodox and Monophysite east Rome to pay for a crusade on behalf of an unwilling Catholic west Rome; hence an initial strategy involving conciliatory policies, a strategy which had later to be reversed to avoid widening schisms.

By Justinian's day the numbers of the clergy, their collective incomes, and the endowments funding churches, monasteries and hospitals engrossed more of the resources of Byzantium than did the upkeep of the administrative apparatus of government, gigantic though the expenses of the latter were. Take the establishment of the Great Church of Constantinople (at the *reduced* figures brought in by Justinian):

60 priests;
100 deacons and 40 deaconesses;
90 subdeacons;
110 readers;
25 singers;
100 doorkeepers.

This staff of 525 (which does not include gravediggers whose services the Church shared) serviced four only of the multitude of churches in the capital. Staff were on fixed stipends not the dividend system, yet the establishment had been allowed to exceed the Church's endowment, running it into debt. This kind of problem was widespread apparently. When a metropolitan bishop received a salary of forty pounds weight of gold each year, it was not difficult to run into financial problems of this kind — and a priest in a great and well endowed church could easily receive more than a bishop in an impoverished see.

Hence the need for the Emperor himself to intervene. This was a highly sensitive area. Justinian forbade what were known as *insinuativa*, fees exacted by clergy from newcomers admitted to the establishment of their Church. He regulated the consecration fees demanded from a bishop upon his ordination. He ruled against married bishops, or bishops with children, and also against the alienation of Church property by bishops.

Then there were the matters of recruitment and promotion. As the Church prided itself on being modelled upon the administrative bureaucracy, imperial rulings in this area, though frequently disputed, do not seem to have been thought improper. The recruitment of slaves or share-croppers *(coloni)* into the clergy was, in certain circumstances, permitted. *Curiales* and *cohortales* (office staffs of provincial governors) were stringently excluded. This was the major status group from which recruits came, apparently, and the frequent repetition of prohibitions on such recruits shows how unsuccessful the Emperor was in this regard. Bishops were now required to have six months standing as genuine clerics prior to their ordination as bishops. There are repeated rulings against irregular promotions or the "migration" of clergy from one area into another. Also, the areas of jurisdiction of the various Patriarchs were demarcated. Greater control over their unruly monks was legislated for abbots. Thus were the issues related to *sportulae, suffragia* and *praescriptio fori* regulated for the clerical bureaucracy. Information on these topics first becomes available in bulk in the sixth century, indicating that this was the period in which that bureaucracy was first confronted with the major problems of having acquired an Establishment.[52]

There is other evidence too, that this was so. What with Roman conquests, barbarian or Persian attacks and earthquakes, this was a reign which saw much rebuilding. Along with fortresses on the frontiers and reconstruction in the towns, went the building of many Christian churches. After all, the custom was to leave the Church something in one's will, and bubonic plague had occurred in two mass outbreaks. Hence there were ample funds for building, from inheritances. The building of Church-run hospitals also seems to have reached a new level in numbers and size of buildings. Symbol of the age was the great Church of the Holy Wisdom, deservedly one of the wonders of the world, in Constantinople. The Roman world put on an appropriately Christian architectural garb.[53]

Justinian, whose aim was "one Church, one Faith, one Empire," strove for a like uniformity in matters of belief, too. Intolerance for unorthodox beliefs had been growing since the time of Theodosius I. It reached a new high in this reign. The fate of heretics whose small numbers made them politically unimportant — Manichees, for instance — was death. Arians and Donatists had to turn their churches over to Orthodox clergy, and were placed under civil disabilities. Jews and pagans had severe legal disabilities imposed upon them. The powerful Monophysite Church was conciliated at one time, persecuted at another.

These events had two important consequences. An African cleric, Facundus, protested that the Emperor had no business meddling with Church dogma; this marked the beginning of the outcry against Caesaropapism. Secondly, widespread alienation from Orthodoxy occurred wherever deviant beliefs coincided with non-Greek ethnicity. Syria and Egypt in particular became so full of separatists that they were to welcome the invading Mohammedans.

But these events lay in the future. Even during the reign, however, signs of disaffection towards the Emperor and Orthodoxy were evident. There were by now five major (and rival) Patriarchates: Rome, Constantinople, Alexandria, Antioch and Jerusalem. In the East, Alexandria was not prepared to yield pride of place to Constantinople. And the Patriarch of Alexandria exercised absolute control over the Church in Egypt, commanding a loyalty which gave him, as the century wore on, more wealth and power than the official governor.[54]

The fact was that Christianity, in its various forms, by now extended beyond the coercive control of any despot residing in Constantinople. In the West the Popes had never ceded the point that the Christian Church was a federation of Patriarchates. The *bouleversements* and even scandals associated with the growing series of Oecumenical Councils bore out, in their opinion, their contention that the Church needed firm direction from Rome, its ruling see. Moreover, there were semantic problems. Rome did not have the linguistic tools nor the sophistication fully to explore the complexity of the issues posed in the East.[55] But the Byzantine victory in Italy led to the disbanding of the bureaucratic apparatus in the West, and the exhaustion which followed upon the war with the Goths was to allow the Lombards to pour into Italy before the century was out. The Pope of Rome thus came to have unquestioned religious supremacy in the Latin-speaking West, the only well-elaborated apparatus of government there, and considerable freedom from control by the eastern empire.

Moreover, in Justinian's time, monasticism in the West underwent a change which was to make of it a potent force for religious and social development. Eastern monasticism had already a fixation upon asceticism and mysticism. The *Rule* of St. Benedict, however, founder in 529 of the monastery of Monte Cassino, prescribed physical work. Cassiodorus' monastery, the *Vivarium*, was a centre for the copying out of manuscripts which must otherwise have been lost in the chaos of the times. The western Church was to have in such institutions disciplined bodies of men (and women). Monks went out and reclaimed lands, spread literacy and converted souls. They were the *corps d'élite* of a vigorous and independent movement. There was nothing like them in the East.[56] Thus, in the religious as in the military field, signs of a new order to come were evident by the end of Justinian's reign.

The fact that this chapter closes with the account of Justinian's reign should not be taken to imply that nothing of significance occurred between 565 and 641. Such a supposition would be very far from the truth.[57] But enough has been said to give an outline of the main trends of the period; and such is all a survey can do, in the nature of things. When compared with the trends in the following two periods, those of this one show some striking disparities. Church and military were more compliant in this than in the later periods, the civil bureaucracy less so. This is a striking feature of the period, as is shown in Table I (page 126).

As early Byzantium is the age of (in)famous eunuchs and powerful civil bureaucrats, these phenomena will be briefly considered at this point. There were at least three major advantages, from an Emperor's viewpoint, in employing eunuchs. They had difficulty in using their official positions to build up an intra-bureaucratic power constellation of descendants or relatives ensconced in strategically located positions. As they were alien to their host society they were unlikely to act in collusion with the landowning aristocracy, for this was the group from which they met with most disdain. This was also the sub-elite from which most of the senior civil administrators originated. Hence use of eunuchs freed an Emperor from dependence on this group.[58]

The rise of powerful civil bureaucrats seems to indicate that Constantine, in his preoccupation with the threat posed by overpowerful military men, had not anticipated the consequences which were to follow from his erection of a system of bureaucratic checks and balances. His dispensations had several consequences, in this period. One was the prevalence of bureaucratic infighting which seriously impaired the functioning of the civil apparatus. Another consequence was that, periodically, individuals had to be allowed to aggregate powers so as to make concerted action possible within an apparatus otherwise hamstrung by its many overlapping spheres of authority. And it was far from easy to get the apparatus to discipline itself. Justinian's attempts to cope with these last two problems did not have beneficial results. The *morale* of important sectors of the civil bureaucracy suffered disastrously and control of outlying districts increasingly went to local officials along with dangerous mandates of power to the military. Problems of "frontier feudalism," the hiving-off of border commands as independent baronies, seem to have bedevilled traditional

TABLE 1

A cross-comparison of the prominence of the administrative, ecclesiastical and military bureaucracies* in Early, Middle and Late Byzantium

SECTOR	EARLY	MIDDLE	LATE
Administrative	Difficult key ministers. Intriguing & powerful eunuchs.	Very little indeed is known about personalities within this bureaucracy at this period.	After battle between civil and military bureaucracies, the military aristocracy take over key titles and positions from the eunuchs.
Ecclesiastical	Emperor convenes synods, appoints Patriarchs, rules on dogma, acts in case of schism.	Emperor's right to rule on dogma challenged by monks. Iconoclasts dishonour monks, take over Church property. Iconodule victory. Important missionary activities.	Patriarchs discipline Emperors. Bans on Church estates lifted. A Patriarch appoints Emperors, decides on schism against imperial wishes.
Military	Generals disciplined and controlled. Some eunuch commanders.	Uprisings smashed.	Military aristocrats take over the throne, establish the *Pronoia* system and build up their baronies.

*A plot-out of "famous names" would show eunuchs and administrative bureaucrats largely clustering in the fourth to sixth centuries (cell one), "political" Patriarchs and Abbots in the seventh to ninth centuries (thinly spread) and in the tenth and eleventh centuries (where they would be thicker). This involves cells five (mostly) and six. Military aristocrats largely occur in prominent positions from the eleventh to fourteenth centuries (cell nine).

empires, since the latter lacked telecommunication facilities and the technology and institutions necessary to mobilise public opinion behind the central government.[59]

Early Byzantium contrasts very strikingly with the Roman empire which preceded it in that the empire no longer bestrode "her" world but co-existed uneasily with a number of other powers. Hence there was now a need for a sophisticated diplomacy which had been unnecessary, and therefore poorly elaborated, in that previous age. In turn, there were also new and heavy demands on her administration, which now had to provide the money, information and men to operate this diplomacy. Byzantium thus existed in a much more complicated external environment, to which she related via a much more complicated internal organizational structure. So a change made within the latter could very easily result in unforeseen consequences. Especially when, as in Justinian's reign, misfortunes — bubonic plague, Chosroes, earthquakes — occurred in rapid succession, thus overloading the system in its attempts to cope with them. Consequently, by the next period, Byzantine affairs were in a very different state.[60]

FOOTNOTES

1. Thus the major modern work on the late Roman empire, *LRE*, dates the period as 284-602 A.D., i.e. to commence with Diocletian. Muller, in *The Loom of History*, chapter 7, characterizes what the new order meant for Asia Minor by focussing on its development of the city of Byzantium into Constantinople. On the significance of the founding of Constantinople for Byzantine history, see *ibid.* pp. 11-13 and Hussey's time-divisions in her book *The Byzantine World*.

2. The basic reference work for the purposes of this chapter is A.H.M. Jones' *The Later Roman Empire 284-602: A Social, Economic and Administrative Survey (LRE)*. As well as the chapters on Diocletian (chap. 2) and Constantine (chap. 3), parts of chapters 12, 16, 17 and 22 will be found relevant. In *CAH* XII, chapters 11 & 20 (and also 19) refer; in Parker's *A History of the Roman World*, chapters 4 to 6 of part 5; pp. 25-44 of Ostrogorsky also refer. Boak's *History of Rome to 565 A.D.* is likely to be the most suitable general reference in paperback; see chapters 22 and 23. On the general socio-economic background see *SEHRE*, chapter 12. On the various high officials, see M. E. Cosenza, *Official Positions after the Time of Constantine*, Dissertation, Columbia, 1905 (especially chapters 2 & 7); A.E.R. Boak, *The Master of Offices in the Later Roman and Byzantine Empires*, Univ. of Michigan Studies, Humanistic Series XIV, NY, 1924; L. L. Howe, *The Praetorian Prefect from Commodus to Diocletian*, Chicago, 1942, and W. G. Sinnigen, *The Officium of the Urban Prefecture during the Later Roman Empire*, Papers and Monographs of the American Academy in Rome, XVI, 1957, pp. 10-69.

3. Rémondon gives a good brief review of intervening events in chapter 3 of *La crise de l'empire romain*. For the general socio-economic background to the times see *SEHRE*, chapters 10 and 11. Chapter 13 of Stark's *Rome on the Euphrates* gives a vivid picture of events in the East; for the West see E. A. Thompson, "Peasant Revolts in Late Roman Gaul and Spain" in *Past & Present* 2, 1952, pp. 11-23; for the Danubian area see chapter 6 of Oliva's *Pannonia*, and for the peoples pressing in upon the empire from without see Millar, chapters 16 & 17 (see 13 on the third century in general).

4. On the different ways of life and production of the peasants in these two areas see Wolf, *Peasants*, pp. 32-34.

5. On the diocesan arrangement see *LRE* pp. 373-77. See maps 1 and 2.

6. They were Philip the Arab and Carus, Emperors in 243-49 and 282-83 respectively; and Aper, whose bid for the throne was unsuccessful. Aper executed the Emperor Carus and his son Numerian, only to have the troops elevate Diocletian to the purple. See Hammond, pp. 175-84, for a general review of their activities.

7. On the notion of "counterweighting" see A.E.R. Boak, "The Roman *Magistri* in the Civil and Military Service of the Empire" in *Harvard Studies in Classical Philology* 26, 1915, pp. 83-84. Riggs comments on "overlapping" and "functionalism" at pp. 13-19. For the relations of the Master of Offices and the Masters of the various *bureaux* see Boak in *Harvard Studies*, p. 102; on "poaching," see pp. 94 and 96; as to what the individual *bureaux* did, see pp. 92-100 & 108-110. The title of "Master," incidentally, seems first to have been used for relatively powerful officials in the third century (prior to this it was applied to the less important posts). It was first systematically employed by Diocletian and Constantine, apparently: see *ibid.* pp. 112-15 & 161-62.

8. *Tabularii* (accountants) and *actuarii* (originally quartermaster sergeants), seem to have originated as soldiers serving in a military *officium*, then been either added as a new type of post in a civil *officium* or demilitarized. See *LRE* pp. 564 and 626-28 & 674 respectively; cf. MacMullen, pp. 72 & 74 on *actuarii*. As to the additional costs, this is Jones' estimate: cf. *LRE* pp. 51-52. Too much can however be made of this increase in the size of the apparatus. Light taxation does not necessarily make for a strong community, nor heavy taxation a weak one. Indeed, it was the larger bureaucracy of east Rome which kept that part of the empire secure and wealthy. See A.R. Lewis, *Naval Power and Trade in the Mediterranean A.D.*

500-1100, Princeton, 1951, pp. 39-40 on taxation and, on the services rendered by the bureaucratic apparatus, Bozeman, *Politics and Culture in International History*, pp. 318-23.

9. Most concisely set out in Boak, *A History of Rome*, pp. 458-59.

10. *LRE* has an enormous amount of detail on this, but somewhat scattered (see n. 2 above; add chapter 13 to those cited there). For a clear, concise survey see A. Segré, "Studies in Byzantine Economy — *Iugatio* and *Capitatio*" in *Traditio* 3, 1945, pp. 101-127.

11. On the *curiales* see *LRE*, pp. 724-34 & 737-57. On the caste-like society resulting from these regulations see part 3 of J. Gagé, *Les classes sociales dans l'empire romain*, Payot, 1964, especially chapters 2 to 4.

12. Translated in Frank's *Economic Survey of Ancient Rome*, V, pp. 310-421.

13. This does not necessarily mean that his conversion was any the less genuine because it was opportune. Psychoanalysing the long-since dead rarely convinces others than the would-be psychoanalyst. Moreover, in this case we have (a) no autobiographical writings from our subject, (b) biassed (i.e. Christian and pagan) accounts of him, and (c) an imperfect idea of the religious thought-world of the fourth century with which to go about any analysis. Modern historians seem to be as impartial on this topic as they are in writing about the impact of Christianity at this time, so no bibliography is given.

14. The concept "pagan" first appears in the fourth century. On the gulf between Christianity and classical culture, see Muller's comments in chapter 10 of *Freedom in the Ancient World*, especially pp. 318-23 & 340-44; more fully C.N. Cochrane, *Christianity and Classical Culture*, Galaxy ed. 1957, chapter 6; H.O. Taylor, *The Emergence of Christian Culture in the West*, Harper ed. 1958, *passim*. The non-Christians are at this point thinking in terms of defending *Romanitas*: see D. Earl, *The Moral and Political Tradition of Rome*, chapter 5. On symbols on the coinage, see Mattingly, *Christianity in the Late Roman Empire*, pp. 62-63; on art forms, see Taylor, *The Emergence of Christian Culture*, pp. 316 ff.; H.St.L.B. Moss, *The Birth of the Middle Ages*, Oxford U.P., 1963, pp. 87-89, and Runciman, *Byzantine Civilization*, pp. 254-58.

15. On the recognition of Christianity as a licit religion and the consequences of such recognition, see Chadwick, *The Early Church*, chapter 8 and pp. 163-64; *LRE* pp. 89-93 and chapter 22; *CMH* vol. IV, part 2, pp. 118 ff.

16. The strictures of the monks were such as to replace the old pagan cry "The Christians to the Lions!" with a new Christian one: "The monks to the Tiber!"" See Chadwick, *The Early Church*, chapter

12; Bainton, *Early Christianity* pp. 71-76, and Hussey, *The Byzantine World*, chapter 7.

17. Two major controversies appeared in Constantine's day, Donatism and Arianism. On the Donatists see Bainton *Early Christianity*, pp. 64-67 and Chadwick, *The Early Church*, pp. 123-34; cf. 219-25. Among the Arians were barbarians who had been converted to Christianity by Wulfilas, a follower of Arius. They believed that Christ was a deified man. See Bainton, *Early Christianity*, pp. 67-70; Chadwick, *The Early Church*, chapter 17; H. Daniel-Rops, *The Church in the Dark Ages*, Dutton, 1960, vol. 1, pp. 151-56.

18. See F. Dvornik, "Emperors, Popes and General Councils" in *Dumbarton Oaks Papers* 6, 1951, pp. 1-26.

19. On Theodosius see *LRE* pp. 156-69, Ostrogorsky, pp. 48-51 and Boak, *A History of Rome*, pp. 444-47. J.B. Bury, *A History of the Later Roman Empire from the Death of Theodosius I to the Death of Justinian*, Dover ed. 1958, commences with an excellent survey of the state of the apparatus of government, Constantinople and the international scene at the close of the reign of Theodosius I: see chapters 1 to 4.

20. This victory is generally seen as heralding the advent of the barbarian horseman as the decisive element in battle: see e.g. C.W.C. Oman, *The Art of War in the Middle Ages*, Cornell U. P. ed. 1953, chapter 1, especially pp. 4-7. Lynn White has argued against this view (in *Medieval Technology and Social Change*, Clarendon, 1962, chapter 1, especially pp. 6-14) but misapprehends the importance of the stirrup in cavalry tactics. See J.D.A. Ogilvy, "The Stirrup and Feudalism" in *University of Colorado Studies, Series in Language and Literature* no. 10, 1966, pp. 1-13. The case seems to be that cavalry skills are extraordinarily difficult to acquire and maintain (see Andrzejewski, *Military Organization and Society*, p. 49). Hence they involve a large commitment of a society's resources, which in practice takes the form of the domination of areas of its terrain by a mounted squirearchy (*ibid.* pp. 141-45). See pp. 56-57 for a survey of changes in Byzantine social stratification over time caused by its changing forms of military organization.

21. Graphically described in A.P. Vacalopoulos, *A History of Thessaloniki*, Institute for Byzantine Studies, 1963, pp. 24-26.

22. See Cochrane, *Christianity and Classical Culture*, chapter 7. For the general background to the reign, see A. Momigliano (ed.), *The Conflict between Paganism and Christianity in the Fourth Century*, Clarendon, 1963.

23. On regional interests behind dissident theological views, see Bainton, *Early Christianity* pp. 64-68 and 79-82; on the great Greek Fathers, see Chadwick, *The Early Church*, pp. 287-88.

24. On the cross appointments to the staff of the Praetorian Prefect see *LRE* pp. 128-29 & 162; on those to the staff of the Urban Prefect see Sinnigen, *The Officium of the Urban Prefecture during the Later Roman Empire*, chapter 3; on the take-over of some of the duties of the Notaries by the *memoriales*, see *LRE*, pp. 574-77.

25. See *LRE* p. 163.

26. See *LRE*, chapter 6; Bury, *History of the Later Roman Empire*, chapters 5-9, especially 7; Ostrogorsky, pp. 51-56 and Boak, *A History of Rome*, chapter 24.

27. See J.B. Bury, *The Invasion of Europe by the Barbarians*, Russell & Russell's 1963 reprint, and C.D. Gordon, *The Age of Attila: Fifth Century Byzantium and the Barbarians*, U. of Michigan, 1960.

28. There is general agreement on the major contributory causes of the collapse in the West. See e.g. F.W. Walbank, *The Awful Revolution: The Decline of the Roman Empire in the West*, Liverpool U. Press, 1969, pp. 88-93; W.C. Bark, *Origins of the Medieval World*, Doubleday, 1960, chapter 3; S. Katz, *The Decline of Rome and the Rise of Mediaeval Europe*, Cornell U. P., 1955, pp. 96-112; N.H. Baynes in D. Kagan (ed.), *Decline and Fall of the Roman Empire: Why did it Collapse?*, Heath, 1962, pp. 78-85. On the general background to these events, see S. Dill, *Roman Society in the Last Century of the Western Empire*, Meridian ed. 1960.

29. For a contrast of the resources of western and eastern Rome see Bark, *Origins of the Medieval World*, pp. 45-66; Hussey's conclusions at p. 133 of *The Byzantine World*, and Lewis, *Naval Power and Trade in the Mediterranean*, pp. 7-13. But too much should not be made of the wealth of the average city: A.H.M. Jones, *The Greek City from Alexander to Justinian*, Clarendon, 1940, pp. 267-69. As to the contention that the Byzantines were not primarily predisposed to aggression, see Wright, *A Study of War*, p. 572 (under "Orthodox"). On how the easterners viewed developments in the West, see W.E. Kaegi, *Byzantium and the Decline of Rome*, Princeton, 1968; cf., e.g., chapter 1. On Byzantine gold pieces and international trade, see Lewis, *Naval Power and Trade in the Mediterranean*, pp. 15-16.

30. On the cross appointments see *LRE* p. 174. For a full discussion of the history of this Mastership, see Boak, "Roman *Magistri* ..." in *Harvard Studies in Classical Philology*, 26. Pp. 118-19 discuss the use of the Master as a counterweight to the Praetorian Prefect; pp. 120-24 the

emergence of regional divisions of the *comitatus*; pp. 124-25 the Master as King-maker; pp. 133-37 the Master's increasing prestige, and pp. 146-51 & 159-60 his jurisdictional powers and prerequisites respectively.

31. See e.g. *LRE* pp. 567, 614, 639-40, 643 & 647-49.

32. E.A. Thompson, "Peasant Revolts in Late Roman Spain and Gaul," in *Past and Present* 2, p. 20.

33. On the points raised in the text, see *LRE*, pp. 528-29; 535; 570-72 & 584-86. For a good discussion of ranks and titles see Cosenza, *Official Positions after the Time of Constantine*, pp. 4-9. Among titles, apart from gradations of rank, there were the following distinctions: *in actu positi* or officials actually holding the office; *honorati* or *ex officio* holders of the office; *vacantes* or officials who had been given a title superior to the actual office they had last held, and *honorarii* or those not in official circles but awarded the outward insignia of an office along with its title. The latter two groups were further differentiated accordingly as they were present in Court or absent from it in the provinces. Cosenza also gives, in chapter 12, a list of all official positions in descending order of status, and lo, the Praetorian Prefect's name leads all the rest.

34. For a vivid depiction of the Orthodox Church from the death of Theodosius I to this period see Daniel-Rops, *The Church in the Middle Ages*, pp. 177-201.

35. Even extending to repelling barbarian attacks upon occasion: See Duff, *Roman Society in the Last Century of the Western Empire*, pp. 217-18, or, more fully, Daniel-Rops, *The Church in the Middle Ages*, chapter 2.

36. See *LRE* pp. 211-216.

37. Augustine attracts a variety of comment: compare Daniel-Rops, *The Church in the Middle Ages*, chapter 1 with Earl, *The Moral and Political Tradition of Rome*, chapter 6 and Muller, *Freedom in the Ancient World*, pp. 346-55. For general reference see F. Van der Meer, *Augustine the Bishop: Church and Society at the Dawn of the Middle Ages*, Harper ed. 1965, and H.A. Deane, *The Political and Social Ideas of St. Augustine*, Columbia Univ. Press, 1963.

38. Graphically described in E.M. Forster, *Alexandria: A History and a Guide*, Doubleday, 1961, pp. 54-57. More fully in E.R. Hardy, *Christian Egypt: Church and People; Christianity and Nationalism in the Patriarchate of Alexandria*, Oxford U.P., N.Y. 1952. Hardy speaks of the Patriarchs of Alexandria with their enormous powers and following as "The Pharaohs of the Church": see chapters 3 & 4,

especially pp. 84, 92, 104-5 and 108-10. The monks were held in even higher respect than the other clergy because of the exacting spiritual exercises *(askesis)* through which they put themselves so as to become pure in the sight of God. For a glimpse of the thought world of the monks, and of the masses who held them in such awe, see E. Dawes and N.H. Baynes, *Three Byzantine Saints*, Blackwell, 1948, pp. ix-xiv and pp. 1-71 on St. David the Stylite.

39. Nestorians hesitated to recognise Mary as Mother of God, "finding it difficult to conceive of God as two or three weeks old"; hence they thought of Christ as a dual personality, both God and man. Monophysites believed, to state their case in its simplest and most extreme form, that Christ had only one nature, the divine. See Chadwick, *The Early Church*, chapter 14; Bainton, *Early Christianity*, pp. 80-82 and Daniel-Rops, *The Church in the Dark Ages*, pp. 190-201.

40. This can be seen, too, in the extent to which religious matters engross the attention of the writers of the time: see Hussey, *The Byzantine World*, pp. 86 and 100-101. M.Rokeach examines the various synods and their anathemas for evidence of authoritarianism within the Church at *The Open and Closed Mind*, Basic Books, 1960, chapter 21.

41. See D.J. Constantelos, *Byzantine Philanthropy and Social Welfare*, Rutgers, 1968, pp. 154-56.

42. Hence Hussey prefers to speak of "interdependence" rather than of Caesaropapism (the domination of the Church by the Emperor): see *The Byzantine World*, pp. 83-87.

43. The master work on Justinian is B. Rubin's *Das Zeitalter Justinians*, De Gruyter, 1960; vol. 1 is all that has appeared to date. For basic reference works on Justinian see Bury, *History of the Later Roman Empire*, Vol. II, chapters 15-23; *LRE* chapter 9 and also the relevant parts of chapters 12-14, 16-17 & 22, and Ostrogorsky, pp. 63-72. Available in paperback are Boak, *A History of Rome*, chapter 25 and Moss, *The Birth of the Middle Ages*, chapters 4-6. For general background see G. Downey, *Constantinople in the Age of Justinian*, Univ. of Oklahoma Press, 1960 and E. Barker, *Social and Political Thought in Byzantium from Justinian I to the last Palaeologus*, Clarendon, 1957, chapters 1 & 2.

44. On the interrelationship of trade and the apparatus of government see, in general, Riggs, pp. 139-49 & 222-28; cf. also pp. 100-116. See also K.Polanyi & Co., *Trade and Market in the Early Empires: Economics in History and Theory*, Free Press, 1957, chapters 13 & 18 (the Byzantine empire is based on instrumentalities which redistribute wealth with some reciprocity, rather than on maximization of profit

economics). See next note. Specifically, see Bozeman, *Politics and Culture in International History*, pp. 318-22.

45. See Lewis, *Naval Power and Trade in the Mediterranean*, chapter 2, especially pp. 25-28 and 32-38; cf. Stark, *Rome on the Euphrates*, chapter 16.

46. See H. Antoniadis-Bibicou, *Recherches sur les Douanes à Byzance*, Colin, 1963, pp. 39 and 91-95; cf. R.E. Lopez, "The Silk Industry in the Byzantine Empire" in *Speculum* 20, 1945, pp. 1-42.

47. See *LRE*, pp. 484-94 for *praescriptio fori*, 496-99, 602 & 605 for *sportulae*, and 391-400 & 603-605 for *suffragia*; cf. R. Guilland, "Vénalité et favoritisme à Byzance" in *Revue des études byzantines*, 10, 1953, pp. 35-46.

48. See chapters 9-11 of this book on this bureaucratic in-fighting. For the "suggestion" see *LRE* pp. 282-83.

49. On the "Blues" and "Greens" see G. Walter, *La vie quotidienne à Byzance au siècle des Comnènes (1081-1180)*, Hachette, 1966, pp. 62-66 (and cf. chapter 6); G.L. Seidler, *The Emergence of Eastern Europe*, Pergamon, 1968, pp. 109-117, and, more vividly, B. Diener, *Imperial Byzantium*, Little, Brown 1938, chapter 5. On the records office see Boak, "Roman *Magistri* in the Service of the Empire" in *Harvard Studies in Classical Philology* 2-6, pp. 103-110. Cf. also chapter 10, n. 19 to section 4.

50. On the ethnic composition of the army see J.L. Teall, "The Barbarians in Justinian's Armies" in *Speculum* 40, 1965, pp. 305-322. Boak, *op. cit.* pp. 127-28 notes that the importance of the Masters of the Soldiery diminishes markedly after Justinian's day. On the exarchate see *LRE* p. 312; on the new Counts and the *Quaestura Exercitus*, see p. 280 and Lewis, *Naval Power and Trade in the Mediterranean*, p. 31. On the foreshadowing of the later themal organisation by these measures of Justinian's see J. Karayannopoulos, "Contribution au problème des 'thèmes' byzantins" in *L'Hellenisme Contemporain* 10, 1956, pp. 482-83 & 501-502.

51. On the religious background to the reign, see, in addition to the works cited in note 40 above, Daniel-Rops, *The Church in the Dark Ages*, pp. 208-238 and Barker, *Social and Political Thought in Byzantium*, pp. 7-12 on Caesaropapism.

52. See *LRE* pp. 934; 911, 903 & 906; 909; 905; 929; 897-88; 921 & 925-26; 895 & 933.

53. On architecture generally, see D.T. Rice, *Art of the Byzantine Era*, Praeger, 1966, pp. 9 & 47-60; on hospitals, see Constantelos, *Byzantine Philanthropy and Social Welfare*, pp. 158-68. On the Great

Church, administrative centre of Orthodox Christianity, see G. Walter, *La vie quotidienne à Byzance,* pp. 51-59.

54. On the Patriarch of Alexandria, see E.R. Monks, "The Church of Alexandria and the Economic Life of the City in the Sixth Century" in *Speculum,* 28, 1958, 349-62. The basic reference work is E.R. Hardy, *Christian Egypt.* See chapter 4, especially pp. 127 ff.

55. Latin lacks the definite article and thus cannot compete with Greek in the building up of multiple-level abstractions. Greek does this by inserting a string of prepositions, verbs and substantives and making one concept out of this composite whole. It is also much easier in Greek to build words by compacting different word-roots and/or prepositions. Justinian was the last Latin-speaking Emperor, and knowledge of Latin was already poor in the Constantinople of his day. Greek was equally little known in papal circles in the West. Hence ample opportunities existed — and were taken advantage of — for simple linguistic confusion.

56. See Daniel-Rops, *The Church in the Dark Ages,* pp. 346-61. Works on western monasticism are legion. Easily accessible and relevant to the approach taken here is C. Dawson, *Religion and the Rise of Western Culture,* Doubleday ed. 1958, chapter 3.

57. As is evidenced by P. Joubert's recent three-volume work on the period; see *Byzance avant Islam sous les successeurs de Justinian,* Picard 1951, 1956 & 1965.

58. The contrast between Claudius and Hadrian in their reliance on freedmen illustrates similar problems and strategies in an earlier period. On the eunuchs see Runciman, *Byzantine Civilization,* pp. 92 & 203-204 and Barker, *Social and Political Thought in Byzantium,* p. 33. For more general considerations see Wittfogel, pp. 354-58 and Eisenstadt, 282-87.

59. Ostrogorsky says (*History of the Byzantine State,* p. 33): "The real interest of the development of the administrative system of this period turns on the internal struggle between the different instruments of government." The tendency towards bureaucratic feuds, empire-building and other forms of goal displacement is caused by the institutional structure and social values current, rather than the personality dynamics of this or that individual. See Riggs, pp. 164-73, 196-202, 222-37, 263-85 & 312-18, and cf. Wesson, *The Imperial Order,* pp. 285-308.

60. On the importance of the sequence and the spacing out of problems to a country's development, see R.E. Ward and D.A. Rustow, *Political Modernization in Japan and Turkey,* Princeton, 1964, pp.

440-41 & 465. For the concept of demand overload see Easton, *A Systems Analysis of Political Life*, pp. 58-59, 82-83 & 119.

Chapter 4
The Middle and Late Byzantine Empire

The bureaucrats on whom this book is focussed lived in the age of Justinian, so the period covered by this chapter postdates them. The survey continues, in order to set the Justinianic age in its context of on-going trends and evolving developments. But the same depth of coverage cannot be accorded events which followed the age, as these contribute far less to our understanding of the situation. Constantinople fell to the Osmanli Turks in 1453; so the period of this post-script, as it were, is a lengthy one. Within this lengthy period, however, two centuries stand out: the seventh and the eleventh. Events in each of these centuries were of such a nature as to give shape and direction to the centuries which followed. This chapter will illustrate what is meant by reviewing the fortunes of the bureaucratized groups against the background of events in both of these centuries in turn.[1]

Within 40 years of Justinian's death most of Spain was lost to the Visigoths and large parts of Italy were lost to the Lombards. By the seventh century, in fact, the piecemeal division of Italy which was to persist until the nineteenth century was already in being, in one of its earlier forms. Byzantium controlled an area round Venice, a strip from Ravenna to Rome, an area round Naples and the heel and toe of Italy. The remainder of the peninsula was made up of a mosaic of Lombard duchies. Behind to the West lay the barbarized Gaul of the Merovingian Dark Ages.

The lands beyond the Danube were stirring, too. Slavic peoples under Avar (Hun) masters poured down into the Balkans and Greece. Behind them, along the southern bank of the Danube, the Bulgars, a Turkish people, established their kingdom. Dimly discernible in the yet remote background were the terrible Turkish Khazars whose movements seem to have caused the Slav, Avar and Bulgarian folk wanderings.

But the major changes came with the advent of Islam. Syria fell to the Muslim Arabs in 636, Palestine in 638, and Egypt in 641. North Africa was to fall in 698.[2] This produced an entirely new state of international affairs. An eastern power now controlled the Fertile Crescent and Egypt. It had access to the Mediterranean and took vigorously to the seas. Saracen raiders were to strike everywhere, and by the eighth century Spain, Sicily, and Cyprus were to be in their grip. As early as the seventh century, however, the balance of power was irremediably changed by the appearance of this huge and rapidly growing Islamic Empire.[3]

These changes restructured the Byzantine Empire. Byzantium was never again to be *the* power which bestrode her world. She was, in fact, almost confined to the Anatolian *massif*. Hence a new posture and set of institutions appeared. These were to set their stamp upon this, the great middle period of the seventh to eleventh centuries. Vital territories had been lost. Syria and Egypt were formerly the major centres of manufacturing and commerce of the empire, and Egypt had been its bread-basket. The Balkans and Greece were now *Sclavinia*, the land of the Slavs. An effective barrier to overland travel to the West, this area now came to constitute "the West" for Byzantium. Against the great walls of Constantinople, or Micklegarth as the northmen termed it, many an expedition was to sally forth from these lands, bent on plundering that city of gold. The Muslims too were animated by similar desires.

There was another important consequence which followed from the losing of these territories. With Syria and Egypt went the Monophysites, with north Africa the Donatists, with Italy the Arians and, effectively, the Roman Catholics. Thus the hallmark of Byzantine civilization was to be Orthodox Christianity; and the Patriarch of Constantinople was disencumbered of his quarrelsome fellow Patriarchs from Alexandria, Antioch and Jerusalem. Furthermore, the language of these new Romans, as the Byzantines saw themselves, became, from the seventh century, Greek. Peoples of many races and from many lands filled the Byzantine empire. Hellenistic culture and Orthodox Christianity welded them together, for the possession of both of these was the criterion for acceptance within the empire.[4]

Now, once Antioch and Alexandria were lost, Constantinople became the commercial, as well as the administrative, centre of empire. No longer fed by Alexandria, she disgorged some of her military population, spreading the logistical load. The Orthodox had fled from invaded countries to the Byzantine heart-land, so there was an accession of people with commercial and manufacturing skills. With the invention of the lateen sail a class of small ship owners came into prominence. As trade and manufacturing picked up and population density increased, there was some abatement of the caste-like system which tied people to hereditary occupations. One could leave a guild in a city now; there was some easing of the restrictions of the colonate, allowing a limited amount of mobility. Free peasant communities were numerous.[5]

Thus the Byzantine of the seventh century lived in a remarkably different world from that of the East Roman in the sixth. The West — whether this involved the Balkans, Italy or Spain and Gaul — was alien and barbarised. There learning was almost lost; tra le and commerce were in sad disarray; life was crude and unsophisticated. The East was over-run by the forces of Islam, virile but rude and inexperienced at administration (Byzantine practices were readily adopted). Wealthy, civilized and sophisticated, the empire was ringed around by warrior peoples fresh to power who eyed her like a gleaming prize. Something of a besieged mentality seems to have set in. War with Islam partook of a crusading fervour, which furthered the Church-state union of hearts.[6]

And the Byzantines had good cause for their preoccupation with war. There were no safe inner provinces now. All alike were open to attack. So all were mobilized to defend themselves. The cost of survival was high. In effect it involved something like a state of martial law throughout the empire. For the empire was now divided into a number of zones. In each an army regiment or *thema* was settled, and each was administered by the resident army commander. The zones were called "themes," the word for a regiment being extended to connote the region wherein the regiment operated.[7] The zones took their individual names, as well as their general designation, from those of the regiments quartered within them. There was *Armeniakon* for instance, the theme of the Armenian regiment, and *Anatolikon*, theme of the *Anatolikoi* or forces of the former Count of the Orient.

Each soldier was allotted a peasant-type small-holding of medium size, big enough to enable him to feed and equip himself as a heavily armed horseman. The holdings were hereditary and involved an hereditary obligation to provide military service. The holding was the trooper's main recompense for service. Pay was low. A soldier commenced at a rate of one gold piece per year. This increased annually for eleven further years, till it reached the maximum rate of 12 gold pieces. Officers' rates of pay were much higher, the General in charge of an important theme receiving as much as 40 pounds' weight of gold per year (see Table 2, pages 140-141).

The General acted as both military commander and governor in his

TABLE 2

Tagmatics (Troops in Constantinople)

OFFICER	UNIT COMMANDED
Domesticus	Scholarii (mounted)
Domesticus	Excubitors (mounted)
Domesticus	Hikanatoi (mounted)
Domesticus	Numerus (infantry)
Drungarius	The Arithmos of the Bigla (Latin vigilia; the palace guard)
Count of the Walls	Troops on the extreme wall
Hetaireiarches	Hetaireia (Imperial bodyguard)

TABLE 2 (cont.)

Thematics (Troops of the themes)

OFFICER	UNIT COMMANDED	PAY—SCALE
Stragegos/General Subordinates:	Thema (10,000 men)	24-40 lbs. depending on importance of theme*
Domesticus/Equerry Chartularius/paymaster	consisting of	
Field commanders:		
Turmarch	2 Turmai each of 5,000	12 lbs.
Drungarius	5 Banda each of 1,000	6 lbs.
Comes	5 Pentarchies each of 200	3 lbs.
Pentecontarch	5 Pentecontarchies each of 40	2 lbs.
Dekarch	4 Dekarchies each of 10	1 lb.

*The Strategos of the theme Anatolikon held the most senior position in the army. Next in standing to him was the Domestic of the Scholarii.

district. On the borders of his theme there might be a *Kleisurarch* and his men, defending a key strategic pass (hence the name: the "Commander of the Key"). In the open country, as descendants of the *limitanei*, were the *Akritai*, "Lords of the Border Marches" or Margraves, with their skirmishing frontiersmen. The latter were the folk-heroes of Byzantium.[8] They might occasionally be put under the command of the General of the theme.

The system of themes produced an army which was, in its day, the best in its world. It was well rewarded, if pay and land grants are taken together. It was well established. There is a figure of 120,000 men for the ninth century; in the sixth Justinian, ruling an empire almost three times as large, had made do with 150,000. The army was superbly organised: there were medical orderlies, maps, a commissariat. There was also a Byzantine art of war: literature on the armament, tactics, strategies and even on the psychological background of the various different peoples with whom warfare was possible. Byzantine officers were trained, sophisticated professionals. No romantic chivalry for them. Their men were often fighting for their own soil (mercenaries were few) as well as the one true God. This made the *caballarius*, or heavily armed Byzantine horseman, a fearsome foe. In the seventh century a Byzantine army held off, then destroyed a huge Islamic force attacking Constantinople in 678. This campaign marked a turning point in history. It showed that the forces of Islam could be beaten. It stayed their advance. It saved Christendom from destruction.[9]

There were political dangers in so empowering the military. The constant *razzias* (skirmishes) along the border with the Arabs to the South were a school for generalship. They bred a race of warrior lords, who lived on estates remote from the capital. Armenians, the finest fighting stock within the empire, predominated therein. Thus there came to be a military aristocracy of the countryside with interests and values quite distinct from those of the city-bred Greeks of the central civil administration. The Iconoclast Controversy which wracked the empire from the eighth to tenth centuries has been attributed to military dislike of "images" (representations of Christ and the Saints) and of ecclesiastical power and privilege. The key to control of the military lay in the preservation of the peasant small-holdings of the themal troops. If the local General could convert these small-holders into serfs on a great estate, then the resultant baronies would dissipate Byzantine military resources, destroying centralized unity of direction.[10] Thus the central administration was locked in a life or death struggle to control the big estates.

The new model army could, however, do things which were not possible under the previous dispensation. It could transport *en masse* populations of productive farmers to lands denuded of people. Hence in the seventh century several hundred thousand Slavs were brought across from Greece and the Balkans and settled in Anatolia, where they and their agriculture flourished. With this higher population density went increasing numbers of free small-holding communities.[11] The Armenian region was won for Byzantium in this century too. Not only for the gold in its hills; with the loss of the Prefecture of Illyricum, Constantinople had lost her best recruiting area for soldiery. In Armenia she gained another such recruiting area, within the Anatolian heart-land of empire. The sons of that area were to write many a glorious chapter in Byzantine military history.[12]

There were other novelties, too, in the organization and deployment of Byzantine forces in the seventh century. Many of the attacks which now fell on the empire were sea-borne. Byzantium consequently now first organised a standing navy, on the themal principle, to contain these attacks. There were five, possibly six, fleets. Based on Constantinople was the Imperial Fleet, the Karabisians, armed with the dreaded "Greek Fire" which ignited as it was shot through the air and burned upon the water.[13] Then there were the themal fleets: that of the Aegean (Cyclades and Dodecanese Islands), and the Kibyrrhaeots (from the southern coast of Asia Minor). There was a fleet based on Ravenna, which controlled the upper reaches of the Adriatic. Another, the Sicilian, patrolled that region and southern Italy; and there may have been an African fleet controlling the Balearics as well as the north African coastline. The *strategos* or Lord High Admiral of the Imperial Fleet was the superior of all the admirals of the themal fleets.[14] The navy was, however, in the eyes of the military men of the empire, the junior of the two services and always tended to get second best in terms of recognition despite its crucial strategic importance. There is in fact some evidence of inter-service rivalry, as will be seen.

Pirenne thought that the victory of Islam destroyed the unity of the Mediterranean, ended the Roman world, and facilitated the growth of a wholly different Carolingian society in the West.[15] This seems not to have been the case. The unity of the Roman world in the Mediterranean disappeared in the fifth century and there was no break in trading patterns with the advent of Islam in the mid-seventh. The Arabs encouraged in their subjects the well established commercial lines which filled Arab tax-coffers. They retained the Byzantine administrative system, the Greek language, and even some Byzantine administrators to run their affairs. As desert nomads they were not, initially, skilled in such things. But in 692 the Caliph Abd al-Malik struck the first Arabic gold dinars, halted the export of papyrus, and replaced Greek Christian emblems on appropriate products with Arabic ones. This was an assertion of independence from Byzantium and was met by warfare.

Now the Byzantines seem already to have been controlling trade in the Black Sea, where they made the Khazars channel all trade through Cherson in the Crimea, a city in which both sides could exercise controls on through traffic. They seem now to have applied such a strategy to the trade lines of the Mediterranean, using their sea power to compel vessels to use harbours under Byzantine control. The full effects of such a policy were not immediately apparent in the closing years of the seventh century, of course, but by the end of the first quarter of the eighth they were very much in evidence. Syria, Egypt and north Africa appear to have been suffering from seriously deteriorated economic conditions. Spain and France were likewise in the doldrums. Only Italy, or rather those parts of it which were under Byzantine control, flourished.[16] Mediterranean trade was seriously inhibited and both Frankish and Muslim powers moved their centres of government inland from the Mediterranean.

This meant that some Byzantine seafaring interests were being sacrificed in the interests of military strategy. Also those seafarers, good Orthodox Greek Christians, were confronted by the demand of the military Iconoclasts that their beloved holy images be dispensed with. Hence revolts by the naval themes against the central government, such as those of 726, 821-3 and 978 for instance.

Clearly, then, this change in the organization of the military apparatus, involving as it did consequential changes to the administration of the provinces, had pervasive influence upon the whole balance of forces within the apparatus of government. There was, for instance, an end to the system of *limitanei* and *comitatenses*. Not that this meant that the *Palatini* were dispensed with (see Table 2, above). Vested interests of long standing are not so quickly dissipated. Besides, the capital needed forces for its own defence. So, although the forces of the Masters of the Soldiery in the Presence went out to the provinces to settle them as themes, the Palace Establishment retained its proud position. And its previous practices. The Imperial Bodyguard, for instance, was very well paid (whereas the going rate for the other tagmatics was 16 gold pieces per year) and large admission fees were required of would-be entrants. The officials who felt the effects of the change most severely were the Praetorian Prefect and his staff.[17] Gone now was the three-tier provincial system. Gone too was much of the business of the *annona militaris*, or tax in grain applied to feeding the soldiery. The Praetorian Prefecture had in its hey-day over-reached itself by the acquisition of a conglomeration of functions. Its *morale* had subsequently been broken in Justinian's attempts at reform. It was now dismembered and vanished. Much the same fate befell the Master of Offices, too. The Urban Prefect, however, or rather the *Eparch* as he was now termed, witnessed a recrudescence of his powers and status. There was only one Eparch now, with Rome gone. Moreover Constantinople had become a bustling commercial centre. Looking after the guilds, provisioning of the city, surveillance of visitors and police and fire-fighting, the Eparch came now to be the highest judicial official of the central government. He had under him a Logothete of the *Praetorium* who saw to judicial business and a *Symponus* who supervised the administration of the capital. Also within his general area of competence were the *Quaesitor*, whom Justinian had instituted, and the city *Praetor* who dealt with marital disputes and questions of wills and guardianships.

In terms of civil administration the bureaucracy of the seventh century was confronted by a much different set of problems than those which had confronted its predecessors in the sixth century. For one thing the area to be administered was much smaller, more compact and more homogeneous. Much more, too, now depended on the flow of trade and upon controlling that flow. Customs were at a new high level of importance. Vestments, the beautiful and precious garments produced by the imperial workshops, were of critical importance for trade (which specialized in precious goods) and diplomacy. And Byzantium now supplied its world with gold currency, and the Mediterranean with the coppers in which small scale retail trade was conducted. The important duties of this administration, then, were financial ones. The population of the empire was eminently taxable: small-holders were flourishing and the large estates had not obtained a stranglo hold upon the countryside. Trade and commerce were vigorous. So a network of customs posts sprang up. Some posts controlled trade with the East, as at Nisibis and Daras. Constantinople regulated trade with the Bulgars and, via Cherson, with the Khazars. The empire was divided internally into trading areas via customs zones.[18]

But it had other important duties, too. If the system of military small-holdings were to be engulfed by large estates, as has been observed, then Byzantine security and prosperity could be destroyed. There had to be cross-checks, as ever, upon high officials and the owners of large estates, to prevent this. Consequently what seems to have happened[19] is that, in place of the old decentralized system in which officials clustered in groups under a few high officials of considerable independence (such as the Praetorian Prefect or Master of Offices), there now appears a scatter of co-ordinated — rather than subordinated — officials. These are all, however, under much stricter central control from above than before.

The cross-checks worked in the following way. The opposite number of the *Eparch*, or top judicial official, was the *Sacellarius*, or chief financial official. He controlled the various treasuries. For these had now proliferated into a number of fiscs each under its own Logothete or Accountant.[20] In each of these treasuries was a Notary who reported to the *Sacellarius*. Moreover every themal *Strategos* had under him a *Chancellarius* or Paymaster who was answerable to the Logothete *tou Stratiotikou* (of the military), whom the *Sacellarius* controlled, and a *Protonotarius* or Head Notary who was a member of the staff of the *Sacellarius*. The *Strategos* also had a *Praetor* under him to act as Judge in his theme, and any bishop in the theme could have appeal made to him in a lawsuit. Every attempt was thus made to prevent the various Financial Heads from assuming too much authority and to prevent the General from becoming a law unto himself in his theme and building up an independent centre of power there.

Strong central controls entail a powerful central secretariate and information-cum-security forces. Both groups do in fact now appear to move forward to power. The Head of the Imperial Chancery, or *Protoasecretis*, now becomes one of the most important officials within the apparatus (in striking contrast to the senior Master of the *scrinia* of the sixth century who had been a subordinate to several higher officials, it will be remembered). He had under him the Custodian of the Imperial Inkwell (i.e. Head, Records) or *epi tou Kanikleiou*; the Emperor's Private Secretary, or *Mysticus*; and the Director of the (gigantic and heavily-endowed Constantinopolitan) Orphanage, or *Orphanotrophos*. The "Public Post" of old was now known as the *Dromos* or "Course." Its Head, the Logothete of the Course, took over many of the powers which the Master of Offices had exercised, and others besides. He it was who now instituted high dignitaries in their positions and supervised the security forces and important visitors to the capital. He too was an extremely influential official.

The most influential dignitaries, however, seem to have been the eunuchs of the Palace. For they were the gatekeepers at the crucial channels of communication which led to the Emperor himself. Eunuchs were employed in these strategical positions for reasons already explained:[21] they were generally not members of powerful families, so could not readily aggregate powerful groups around them. Most important was the Grand Chamberlain, the *Parakeimomenos* ("the One who Sleeps beside the Emperor"). Then there was the *Protovestiarius* or Controller of the Royal Wardrobe — and Treasury thereto. A *Praepositus* was Master of Ceremonies for the Court and a *Papias* was its Castellan. They were the inner ring around the Emperor, fount of all power within the empire, and their influence was proportionately great.

This central administration thus comprised some very powerful dignitaries and officials. Not all of them men (as it were) of whom the rude lords of the border marches would entirely approve. Yet they could, and did, exercise surveillance over the most powerful themal overlord. There was thus constituted a Court and administrative aristocracy of the capital institutionally involved in frictions with the military aristocracy of the themes. Dominance exercised by either group over its rival resulted in disaster for the empire. What was needed was a balance of power. This was struck in the seventh century. It was disturbed in the middle of the eleventh, as we will see.

The preoccupations of the bureaucrats of the capital seem to have involved titles and all the perquisites which rank brought with it. This is a complex topic[22] and mere lists of names will not help much in grasping the general outline of what is involved, so discussion will mostly be in terms of trends. A major difficulty is that most of our knowledge comes from the ninth century, when these trends had been operating for some time. However most of the offices and procedures involved were already extant in the seventh century, so we may take it that the situation in the ninth century merely represents a somewhat more advanced stage in an on-going trend.

The Emperor personally granted all "dignities," as the Court titles of rank were known. Some went with the conferring of an actual office by an edict. Others were honorary; that is to say the beneficiary merely obtained the insignia pertaining to the office without actually holding it. Titles acquired by dint of actually holding the position named outranked honorary titles to such status. One retired with the rank of the highest title achieved during one's career.

There were three groups of titles. The first, containing four degrees of rank in this early period, were conferred only upon members of the imperial household. They included a title for women. The second group went to eunuchs. There were seven degrees of rank within it in this early period, for most of which only eunuchs were eligible. When a eunuch and a man both held the same rank (i.e. Patrician status or that of *Protospatharius*), the eunuch outranked the man. There were fourteen degrees of rank for other officials. The top one was that of *Magister*, a reminiscence of the high position formerly held by the *Magister Officiorum* or Master of Offices. The last two were those of *Stratelates* and *Apo-Eparch*. These had formerly been the titles of the Master of Soldiery and the Praetorian Prefect. The low status of the latter titles shows how those once mighty offices had fallen in repute in their declining years.

Titles, however, seem to have become cheapened with time. This phenomenon is most marked from the eleventh century onwards, but can be discerned earlier. For instance *Nobilissimus*, originally reserved for members of the imperial family, came to have the title *Proto-nobilissimus* set above it. In the twelfth century this revised title too had become cheapened, so it was again stepped up to *Protonobilissimo-hypertatus*. By the end of the empire the latter piece of grandiloquence had become a title borne by a mere provincial official. Titles, then, tended to become cheapened as more and more officials gained access to them. They might then be stepped up by an impressive prefix, or they might be dropped. It eventually came about that the original meaning of the title and the functions of the position with which it was initially connected were unknown to the holder, because it had for so long merely designated an honorific rank rather than a set of functions to be performed. However, the elaboration and repeated re-elaboration of a vocabulary to demarcate minute distinctions within a given area shows how very important that area was to the society of its time.[23]

The administrative bureaucracy of middle Byzantium seems to have been a hard-working, relatively anonymous group of men who performed their regulatory and redistributive functions with thoroughness and effectiveness. To them was largely owed the internal stability of the empire. But there is another side to the picture. Officials still had to purchase access to office, hence needed to recoup subsequently by exacting fees or securing *douceurs*. Yet they now had no powerful Head of *Corps* to carve out a bureaucratic empire within which his word was law and his jurisdiction prevailed. They could not, that is, now rely on being tried before their colleagues in the event of an accusation. And the law was now more accessible to all, for Justinian's codifying activities were followed by others in the centuries which followed. Also the whole apparatus was enmeshed in a criss-cross pattern of cross-checking officials. So the officials of the civil administration were caught in a set of cross-pressures which were built into the workings of their bureaucracy. Hence there is no more of the *esprit de corps* which had marked the civil bureaucrats of the proto-Byzantine period. The military have a high morale, as do the clergy; but the civil administration shows little sign of having a comparably ebullient self-image.[24]

The seventh century was a momentous one for the ecclesiastical apparatus.[25] The Emperor Heraclius (610-41) found Byzantium so ringed around by enemies that he proposed to transfer the capital of empire to north Africa. The Patriarch Sergius opposed this plan and put the wealth of the Church behind a holy war upon Persia, in 622, which was to prove dramatically and conclusively victorious. But even as the Emperor took over the title of *Basileus*, or Great King, upon the destruction of Persia, long the only comparable other great power in the Byzantine world, the Mohammedans swept over the Near East, replacing the Greek ruling class which had existed since Alexander's conquests by an Arabic one. So it was that unity came at last to the Orthodox. Syria, home of Nestorianism, and Palestine with its Jewish population, were lost. As well as these Aramaic-speaking peoples, the Copts of Egypt and their Pharanoic Monophysite Patriarch were lost to the empire,as were the Berbers of north Africa later. So, though having the styling of Oecumenical, or world-wide, the Orthodox Patriarch now had to deal with only one of the five original patriarchates.

For the western Church, under Pope Gregory the Great (590-604), was thrown upon its own resources, very largely, in a Lombard Italy, and decided that Western Christendom was to develop under the strong central authority of Rome. Separatist tendencies were enormously accelerated when Latin was abandoned as the language of administration in seventh-century Byzantium. Rome and Constantinople now no longer spoke the same language, and imperfect communications, coming atop other causes of friction, were to sunder the eastern from the western Church.[26]

The influence of both the Orthodox and the Roman Catholic Churches spread far beyond the areas physically controlled by Constantinople and Rome. While Islam was winning converts via the *jehad* or holy war in the East, Orthodox missions to the Slavs began the

Christianization of the northmen of the steppes. A new area of influence opened up to the Patriarch of Constantinople. Meanwhile the Church of Rome was experiencing dramatic success with its mission to Britain. The world of western Christendom began to build up. It was to encompass the German, Scandinavian and Magyar peoples.

Within the empire the Orthodox Church flourished. Bishoprics within territories secured by the *Basileus* were of course assigned to the Patriarch of Constantinople. So Rome, for instance, lost the see of Thessaloniki. The wealth and influence of the Orthodox Church also grew. For instance, the establishment of the Great Church of Hagia Sophia (the "Holy Wisdom") rose to even larger numbers than in Justinian's day. From this Church were chosen the secular clergy whom the *Basileus* designated as successive Patriarchs of Orthodoxy.[27] A new senior position was instituted, that of *Syncellus* ("He who shares the same cell"). The *Syncellus* was to act as *liaison* between Basileus and Patriarch. Church estates were growing apace and *Oeconomi* or (Ecclesiastical Property) Managers now become a striking and influential feature of the apparatus of ecclesiastical government. They were joined by *cancellarii, ecdici*, and *referendarii*, officials who could manage archival, legislative and judicial matters.

Monasteries abounded. In some cases, as for instance upon the hills around Chalcedon, they clustered in such numbers that people spoke of "Republics of Monks." They were wealthy, for the cult of their sacred (and richly decorated) images had reached fantastic proportions among the commonality: one used an *ikon* to swear by, as prophylaxis or healer in disease etc. Moreover swarms of long-haired, unkempt monks readily took to the streets and violence to impose their definition of the will of God, often in matters which appear secular rather than religious to a modern.

In regard to decision-making, in fact, the power of the Orthodox Church seems to have been growing. In the seventh century it rejected the claims of the secular authorities to intervene in doctrinal disputes. Heraclius tried to paper over the gulf yawning between Monophysitism and Orthodoxy by a ruling on the single will of Christ. Though at first this compromise position proved acceptable, hard-line dogmatists on both sides were soon to have it condemned as the damnable heresy of Monotheletism.

The Orthodox Establishment also cast off other forms of intervention by secular authorities in their affairs. Bishops, for instance, were from this century on to be selected by bishops; no laymen were to participate in the selection process.

In cases where there was a conflict of civil and ecclesiastical jurisdictions, the sphere of competence of the ecclesiastical authorities was extended. Theoretically, if a cleric should be found guilty of a serious crime, he had first to be deposed by his bishop before the secular authorities could proceed against him. In actual fact, however, the secular authorities were given to proceeding against clergy in a much more arbitrary and high-handed fashion than this. But Heraclius in 629 passed a law which provided that all clergy and monks in Constantinople could only be tried before its Patriarch; clergy and monks from around Constantinople could also have their cases heard before the Patriarch rather than the civil authorities if they so wished. In such cases the secular authorities were prohibited from intervening and the Patriarch was responsible for sentencing. In the provinces the Metropolitan had like authority. Thus a cleric would normally take his case before his own bishop. If dissatisfied with the verdict he could appeal to his metropolitan and from there to the Patriarch. Thus was the time-honoured principle of *praescriptio fori* triumphantly established by the ecclesiastical bureaucracy.

This growing power, affluence and independence of the Church seem to have brought it into conflict with the army authorities, for both apparatuses were imposing heavy demands for men and money on the selfsame community. Conflict came in the following century, in the form of the Iconoclast Controversy (725-843).[28] Like so many other conflicts in Byzantine history, religious and secular issues were mingled in the genesis and working out of this one. The Armenian and Isaurian army *élites* needed men and money. They saw wealthy monasteries teeming with able-bodied men who not only were playing no part in defence of a hard pressed empire but were active dissidents within it. Wealth, desperately needed for military *materiel*, was being poured into the embellishment of ikons which seemed idolatrous to men of their Armenian and Syrian artistic and cultural backgrounds. The fact that the Iconoclasts (Breakers of Images) lost to the Iconodules (Slaves to the Images) gives some idea of the power and influence of the Church in the hearts of the Hellenised population of the empire.

The world of the peoples around the Mediterranean had changed very considerably indeed by the eleventh century. Perhaps the most far-reaching changes had occurred in western Europe, where the first agricultural revolution in history had occurred. The prime mover was no longer human muscular power, but rather animals and water-power. This was a true iron age, for the metal was now plentifully available. Ploughing practices, field system and crop rotation had all changed. Secondary proteins were more abundant than had ever been known. Hence the pattern of population decline of Roman times altered to one of population growth. A new dynamism imbued the peoples of the area.[29]

What is termed the renaissance of Islam had occurred in the tenth century. In that century, controlling the Balearics, Sicily and Crete, the Saracen corsairs wrested control of the waters of the Mediterranean from the Byzantines. Their trade and commerce flourished, especially in north Africa. This area now, as the Mahgreb, reached unprecedented affluence: caravan routes opened up the Sahara, industrialization proceeded apace, and there was a vigorous Mediterranean commerce. The Arabs introduced the citrus fruits, cotton, rice, the silk-worm and the sugar cane into the lands they controlled. They also brought in the manufacturing of paper, and a range of sophisticated banking techniques.[30]

But Islam was split by dissension among the believers. Its harem system encouraged internecine warfare. It indulged in social victimization of the infidels on whom its commerce so largely depended. Hence Muslim power receded in the eleventh century.[31] However, by that time the renaissance of Islam had restructured the trading patterns of the Mediterranean and allowed new carriers, the Italian cities, to come to the fore. In the eleventh century the latter took over the sea lanes and rerouted trade. Constantinople was to become the traded with rather than the trader. This shift had catastrophic consequences. Byzantine wealth had come from the exercise of monopolies and privileges maintained by regulating trade. That of the West came from the development of internal resources. Now the West began to add to those resources by itself regulating trade. The Byzantine response was to invest a larger proportion of its waning resources in large estates, to the detriment both of its sea power and its small holders, the twin pillars which upheld the Byzantine empire.[32]

Meanwhile new and terrible foes had appeared to assail the Byzantine and Islamic empires. From the East came the Seljuk Turks; from the North, over the Danube, came the Patzinaks, Uz and Cumans; and from Italy in the West came the Normans. Resolute government could have contained even enemies such as these; and until the death of Basil II in 1025 Byzantium had such government. But in the 46 years thereafter no less than 10 "rulers" were put upon the throne, either by *camarillas* of Constantinopolitan bureaucrats or by *coups* engineered by border barons from the great military families. Sectional interests, now of one faction, now of the other, triumphed. Precious military resources were allowed to drain away. The upshot was the Seljuk rout of an enormously numerically superior Byzantine army at Manzikert in 1071. This gave the Seljuks control over a large part of Anatolia, the heart-land of the Byzantine empire, and this meant the end of Byzantium as a great power.[33]

A brief outline of Byzantine history in the eleventh century will act as a background frame of reference for the analysis of the fortunes of the various parts of the bureaucracy. At the outset Basil II (976-1025) was on the throne. This man of iron kept all three of his departments of government — administration, army and Church[34] — under firm control in the eleventh century. The Byzantine empire reached its greatest extent since the days of Justinian in this reign. After Basil's death, however, popular affection for the Macedonian dynasty suffered a series of incompetents to attain the throne. These were the *protégés* of influential Constantinopolitan bureaucrats and they dealt harshly with the military aristocracy of which those bureaucrats were by this time inveterate enemies. They also squandered the immense treasures which Basil had amassed (15,000,000 gold pieces), and impoverished the central government.

Eventually, however, the border barons rose and put one of their number, Isaac Comnenus, upon the throne. Now it was the turn of the administrative and ecclesiastical bureaucracies to receive harsh treatment. But Isaac, an ailing man, was forced into retirement within two years, in 1059. Thereupon Constantine X, a supporter of the townee aristocracy, was hastily manoeuvred on to the throne. It was another eight years before, in response to obvious signs of declining military capability, another military man, Romanus IV, was put upon the throne in 1068. It was too late. Byzantine military capability had dropped below a level at which effective resistance to the Seljuks was possible. The military family of the Comneni again won to power in 1081, and their brilliant and talented dynasty (1081-1185) was to give Byzantium over a hundred years' reprieve. But it did so by dint of building upon the power of the military barons. The small-holders were made serfs and lost their will to fight. Separatist tendencies went along with feudal baronies. The empire fell to the fourth crusade in 1204. It was never thereafter to recover its former power and prestige.[35]

There is no one point in the eleventh century from which one can review the fortunes of the three bureaucratic groups: they all fluctuate too much for this. One can however contrast the period in which they were *under* control with that in which one or others of them was *in* control. In this way one can see how decision-making was affected, particularly as far as the vital matters of taxation resources and the great estates were concerned.

Basil's reign[36] shows what had to be done to make these three great divisions of the apparatus of government subordinate their own interests to those of the empire as a whole. As contemporaries saw it, what he had to do was to appoint no magnates to high military commands; to tax the magnates' estates so savagely that all their thoughts would be preoccupied with their personal affairs; and to allow no women to exercise power within the government.[37] Certainly the attempts at usurpation early in his reign by two of the great military aristocrats, Bardas Sclerus and Bardas Phocas, must have brought home to Basil the power given to the great military families by their huge estates and their monopoly of military skills. But he managed to put the would-be usurpers down without extirpating their leading support-ers, thus preserving the military sub-*élite*.

Basil now proceeded to build up the central forces of the government while decreasing the power of the individual themal commanders. This was, however, done without weakening the over-all power of the military. At Constantinople Basil established his own Varangian Guard. This comprised 6,000 men sent by the Russian Vladimir of Kiev. The commander of the troops in the capital, the Domestic of the Scholarians, was already a military man of immense power, ranking second only to the General of the Anatolian theme. To neutralise the effect of giving an official who was already so powerful control of such a strategically located body of troops, Basil gave him a colleague. Henceforth there were two Domestics, one for the East, the other for the West.

In the course of the eleventh century the themes were much increased in number by slicing them up into ever smaller pieces. Basil will have done some of the slicing, as a security measure: each border baron will now have commanded a smaller force and have co-existed with a larger number of rivalrous peers. Basil also added Bulgaria to the empire, increasing the western themes. This will have done something to counterbalance the power potential residing in the eastern themes. The transplantation of Bulgarians, too, must have affected the population structure, and hence the loyalties, of these eastern themes. There was annexation of territory in the eastern frontiers, too, and in consequence new lands for the border barons to take over. The recently evolved military rank, of *Catepan*, outranking the *strategos*, was given to commanders in a series of newly acquired regions. It went to the commander of the most important theme in Bulgaria. It went also to the commanders of the new frontier themes in the East. An occasional commander here received the even higher new-fangled styling of *Dux*. And the title of *Catepan* went also to the commander who was now put in charge of all Italian territory controlled by Byzantium. By contrast the commanders of the themes dominated by the long-established military aristocracy were down-graded in importance.

It would take time for a military over-lord to build a power base in these new and turbulent lands. So the military *élite* were encouraged to look to the new areas for dealings in land. Basil commenced a ruthless harrying of the long established great estates elsewhere in the empire. The security of the empire depended upon a plenitude of military small-holders in the themes. The security of the Emperor depended upon massive support for him emanating from small-holders. Basil consequently proceeded to make the large landowners disgorge lands expropriated from the peasantry; and he forced the wealthy to bear the brunt of the taxation. To retain his large estate the landlord had to produce valid documents proving his title to the land and of at least 75 years' standing (1,000 years in the case of crown lands!). He had also to prove unbroken tenure since commencement of ownership. Failing this the land reverted to the original owner, without recompense to the landlord. To terrorise the latter group into submission, an example was made of two important military families. The Phocas family saw its properties grievously cut back. The Maleinus family was impoverished. Moreover any large estate in the vicinity of a peasant community was made responsible for making good any shortfall in taxes on the part of any member of that community. The great estates died back and small-holding flourished as a sequel. Bulgarians were transplanted, in large numbers, to swell the growing numbers of small-holders.

A naval contingent had joined the usurper Sclerus in 978. Basil never forgot an enemy, or his power base. He consequently weakened the power of the themal fleets by ignoring them during his lengthy campaigns against Bulgaria. Also he gave the Venetians a favoured status in regard to Byzantine tolls in return for their performing policing and carrrying duties in the Adriatic. Prior to this, favoured status had been given Byzantine Greek shipping interests; now the Emperor was advancing a countervailing mercantile interest. This is one area in which Basil's policies are open to criticism; he seems inadvertently to have eroded Byzantine naval capabilities.[38]

Relations between the Emperor and his civil administration need not detain us long. There is little that calls for comment. This part of the apparatus of government seems to have given Basil little trouble, and that little involved the exercising of untoward influence by powerful officials. For this, one of them, Basil the eunuch, was overthrown and exiled and had his property confiscated (985). This eunuch had been the all-powerful *Parakoimimenos* at the beginning of the reign.[39] Later Philocales the Protovestian was humbled to the status of peasant by the Emperor, and the Musele family, large landowners from the class of the civil bureaucrats, was treated likewise. The disciplining of senior members of this group seems to have kept the rest in order.

With the Church, which this Emperor regarded as another department of the governing bureaucracy, there is more evidence of conflict.[40] It involves Church properties, in the first instance. In 988, when Basil was reduced to desperate straits by an attempted usurpation, the Patriarch forced him to repeal Nicephorus' legislation on Church estates. This legislation had prohibited the alienation of land to the Church on the grounds that so much Church-owned land had already passed out of cultivation through poor management. It further stipulated that any monies donated might only be used for the restoration of ruined monasteries, not the founding of new ones.[41] Once Basil was securely in power his harassments of large Church estates were particularly severe. Repeated protests from the Patriarch Sergius were brushed aside. Indeed the Emperor's *novels* specifically legislate against privileged Church estates.

It took a strong Emperor to deal with the Orthodox Church in this way. For an Emperor could not generally deal with opposition from both Church and military aristocracy simultaneously. Normally, in fact, he was forced to make concessions to one group for its support against the other, as in 988 (above). In doing so every concession made reduced his own resources while increasing the joint bargaining power of Church and army. Hence the steady drift towards the dominance of the latter groups. This trend was furthered by the fact that the extent and complexity of ecclesiastical properties was such as to lead to the development of the concept, and the powers of, the corporation.[42]

Basil controlled his Church by controlling its topmost personnel. He appointed three Patriarchs of Constantinople in his day. One was a layman; the other two were nobodies. He deposed a Patriarch of Antioch and put his own creature in his place. He detained the Patriarch of Jerusalem from 1000 until his death in 1004. In the settlement of Bulgaria he provided that its Archbishopric should be in his own gift; this arrangement was clearly meant to curtail the power of the Patriarch of Constantinople. In consequence of such a policy he ruled an amenable Church.

It took a strong Emperor to dictate to the Orthodox Church in regard to property rights and appointments to sees; both were highly sensitive areas.[43] But then, with Heraclius, Basil II was the strongest Emperor middle Byzantium had. The sequel to the reign shows dramatically what the men of the apparatus could do when they had lesser Emperors to contend with.[44]

Once Basil's controlling influence was removed by death, the full bitterness of the hostility between civil bureaucrats and military aristocracy was starkly revealed.[45] The civil bureaucrats had the upper hand. The military aristocracy had been sternly suppressed by Basil and was demoralised and disunited. The civil bureaucrats, on the other hand, were close to the quarters where decisions were taken. Thus it was they who took control (1025-81). Only when it became clearly apparent that without a renaissance of her military might Byzantium could not survive did the military aristocracy win to power (1081-1185, the dynasty of the Comneni).

No decision could be of more fundamental importance than that as to who should be Emperor. It was the civil bureaucracy which in the event decided this, and their choices reveal their aims and interests. Basil's death left his aged and ineffectual brother Constantine VIII and three sisters, supported by blind popular devotion to their great Macedonian dynasty (867-1056). The eldest sister, the pock-marked Eudocia, was in a nunnery. The youngest, Theodora, was induced to go there likewise This left the pretty, empty-headed and ageing Zoe. Her husband would be the next Emperor.

The military aristocracy rose *en masse* at Basil's death. But he had left a divided military aristocracy and a strong army, and the latter put the former down piecemeal. Besides, the main objective of the military aristocracy was that the imperial war on large estates should end. As the civil bureaucracy too invested in large estates, this matter was dealt with with alacrity. However, the civil bureaucrats round the dying Emperor Constantine VIII (1025-1028) induced him to pass over the capable Dalassenus, a military man, in favour of the Eparch Romanus. Romanus III (1028-1034), as the latter now became, was elderly and ineffectual; but he represented the cream of the bureaucratic aristocracy.

Close to the Empress, however, and knowing her tastes, was the influential eunuch John the *Orphanotrophos* (Keeper of the Orphanage). He made his brother her lover, toppled Romanus, and put that brother on the throne as Zoe's second husband, Michael IV (1034-1041). When Michael IV fell from favour, after an illness which made him bloated and ugly, John got Zoe to adopt his nephew as her son. The latter reigned as Michael V (1041): he had neither the background nor the capacity for the job, and was speedily put down. These two Emperors, however, are products of the intrigues of the non-aristocratic elements in the civil bureaucracy.

It was now the turn of the ecclesiastical bureaucracy to put their candidates on the throne. The influential and able monk Michael Cerularius induced Theodora to leave her nunnery and reign jointly with Zoe. This gave ecclesiastical interests a powerful friend at Court. A third husband was chosen for Zoe, the senator who became Constantine IX (1042-1055). By 1056 only Theodora remained alive and she was induced to choose the Logothete for the Army as the next Emperor. This man, Michael VI (1057), was a dotard; but he possessed the vital qualification of being a bitter enemy of the military. He proved so disastrous, and the military forces of the central government had by now been so weakened, that a military usurper, Isaac Comnenus, forced his way to the throne (1057-59). Cerularius had foreseen Comnenus' success and swung his support behind him, for a price, before his accession. Once in power, Comnenus reneged on his agreed price and had Cerularius ousted. But Cerularius' influence was so great, especially as a "martyr,"[46] and Comnenus' health so poor, that the latter was himself forced to resign in the sequel.

By now the military situation was truly desperate and Isaac Comnenus was able to hand power on to another military man, Romanus IV (1068-1071). But the feud between military and civil aristocracies was so bitter that a civil aristocrat betrayed his Emperor at Manzikert and won to the throne as Michael VII (1071-78). But Michael had been supported to greatness because he was a nonentity and his Logothete Nicephoritzes now came to control him in the interests, if of anyone other than himself, of the non-aristocratic civil bureaucracy. This alienated the ecclesiastical powers and the bureaucratic aristocracy. They consequently swung support behind the usurpation of Nicephorus Botaneiates. The latter ruled for 3 years (1078-81) as Nicephorus III, and was succeeded by Alexius I Comnenus (1081-1118) who, as the founder of the Comnenian dynasty (1081-1185), set the military aristocracy in power for over a century.

As can be seen from the above, the civil bureaucracy was not one monolithic pressure group. Moreover groups which were usually hostile, such as the military and ecclesiastical élites, could on occasion unite, when mutual interests were threatened. Each interest group, however, at some point or other in the eleventh century managed to introduce its own nominee as Emperor. So all special interests were catered to. A survey of trends will show what these were and where they clashed.

The interests of the military and of the civil buroaucracy will be considered together because, as is shown by the bitter hostility of these two groups, the one set of interests is often diametrically opposed to the other. On some things, of course, the interests of both groups were in accord. Such interests will be considered first. Then the case of interests which were in conflict will be considered. Finally there will be a brief review of the special interests particularly dear to a specific interest-group. To start with mutually shared interests, then, all the high officials of the apparatus planned to retire on to their large estates. So the harassment of the large land-owner ceased upon Basil's death. Titles to ownership simply ceased to be investigated. The law making the neighbouring large estate liable to meet tax defaults of peasants nearby was rescinded. Immunities were once again extended to large landlords. The change in policy coincided with several years' plagues of locusts. Everywhere the numbers of small-holders began to thin out, as the great estates spread and proliferated.

This meant that expenses had to be met by extracting taxes from a shrinking number of tax-payers. The reaction of the non-aristocratic bureaucrats was to increase taxes, regardless of how the magnates were affected. This happened under both John the Orphanotrophos and under Nicephoritzes, and brought the hatred of the powerful and ruin upon them both. The Orphanotrophos, for instance, vastly increased the number of taxes. He also compelled the Bulgarians to pay taxes in cash instead of in kind, thus causing a rebellion. The aristocratic bureaucrats met this problem, as early as the time of Romanus III, by "farming out" the taxes in certain areas. Under this arrangement the tax farming company paid the government the taxes due and then itself extracted them from the citizenry. "Expenses" of 100% of the taxes involved could be extracted in process, for the government turned a blind eye to the methods used by the tax farmers. Presumably many of the tax farmers were of the same class (if not the same persons) as the aristocratic bureaucrats.

Both of the above strategies had a similar result. Confronted with inexorable demands for payments of sums yet larger than those which he was already incapable of meeting, the small-holder either sold out to the large land-owner or put himself under the latter's "protection." As the tax collector could not coerce the large land-owner, he tried to extract still more from the surviving little men. So it came about that ruin fell upon the small-holders in this period. And the whole themal system depended upon the existence of a large and flourishing class of small-holders.

As things became critical, hand-to-mouth expedients were used. Positions were sold; a popular move, no doubt, with bureaucratic beneficiaries. Included among the posts which went for sale were the very financial posts themselves, through which the much-needed money had to be raised. The result was corruption which became so deeply and pervasively rooted that even a fanatical campaign against bureaucratic malpractice by a military Emperor, Andronicus I Comnenus, was unable to eradicate it.[47]

The weaker Byzantium became, the more her enemies pressed in upon her. As she could not trust the levies from the Armenian and Georgian regions, these were allowed to buy their way out of future military service by paying for the steadings which obliged them so to serve. But the sums thus gained were soon spent upon the mercenaries upon whom Byzantium had now increasingly to rely. To retain the services of these mercenaries, the civil administration consequently evolved the system of *pronoia* or "Forethought." Under this system a mercenary was paid by being given the usufruct (tax-income, etc.) of a tract of land. He took forethought for this and in return rendered military service to the empire. Once the military got into power their Emperors made this system hereditary. It was similar in practice to their own system of large estates and bolstered that system. Alexius moreover took advantage of the inflation occasioned by the debased currency to increase both the range and rate of taxation. Further, he imposed all kinds of obligations to provide services, or materials below cost, upon the lower orders. So it was that the empire changed from reliance on a system of free small-holders to dependence on a congeries of feudal baronies.

In all this it is difficult to determine where unconscious self-interest stops and corruption commences. The civil aristocracy were not prepared to apply curbs to estatism, although the growth of estates encroached upon taxation revenues; and the vicious consequences attendant upon the introduction of tax farming can have come as no surprise to them. Failure to act in the matter of estatism may simply have involved self-centred passivity. But establishments had increased, so there was little justification — in terms of the *public* interest, that is — for turning over the collection of taxes to others' personnel.

The non-aristocratic *echelons* of the bureaucracy seem to have tended to think in terms of the well-being of the men in the machine rather than of anything else. The sale of offices was a practice long sanctioned by custom. Raising more taxes meant more work, thus more establishments and fees. Even Nicephoritzes' regulation of the grain traffic seems to have benefited the bureaucratic regulators rather more than either producers or consumers: both these groups suffered from this regulation. Yet these may have been the unthinking responses of the trained incompetence of administrators bent on producing remedial measures which also would be conducive to the welfare of the bureaucratic machine.[48]

The military *élites* seem to have thought that only the great baronial estates which were so dear to their hearts could effectively deploy the empire's resources for self defence. They certainly worked to bring about this form of social order. They may well have done this in all good faith: the Comneni, indeed, made a gallant effort to preserve Byzantium.

So much for mutually shared interests. In some things, however, the interests of the central government were diametrically opposed to those of the military aristocracy in the outlying areas. If the latter gained too much power they could pass beyond control of the former. They could set themselves up as, virtually, little independent principalities: the sequel to the sack of Constantinople in 1204 is informative in this regard. This hiving-off would mean that the regulatory functions of the central bureaucracy could not be exercised and it would lose power, prestige and establishment — and the empire, too, in consequence. Consequently the civil bureaucrats of the capital set vigorously about putting the military *élite* in its place.

Lulled into a false sense of security by Basil's successes, they cut

- 161 -

military supplies back. The themes were sliced ever smaller. The *Praetor* in each theme was given authority overriding that of the *Strategos* in civil matters. The military elite were ranked into *Duces, Catepans* and *Strategoi*, in descending order of seniority. This introduction of invidious distinctions must have caused rifts and dissension amid the military *élite*. "Untrustworthy" elements were disciplined. Thus the Armenians, long the flower of Byzantine military might, underwent religious persecution and were transplanted from their homes.[49] Army size, military equipment, morale and loyalty all declined catastrophically in consequence.

Meanwhile the status of the officers commanding the Constantinopolitan forces was upgraded. The erstwhile Domestics of the Scholarians now became the Grand Domestics and moved to pride of place within the military command. The central forces were increased in numbers, effectiveness and — it was thought by the central bureaucrats — dependability by recruiting foreigners as mercenaries. Thus there was inadvertently produced a situation ideally suited for outbreaks of pretorianism.

Instead of being disposed in themal fleets, the navy now came to be controlled from the centre.[50] Thus the importance of the Lord High Admiral increased, and he was upgraded to the status of *Dux*. There was also much reliance on naval mercenaries, and the Venetians advanced their economic interests yet further by customs-exemptions gained as their price for such service. These exemptions made yet further inroads into Byzantine tax-income, so that there proved to be no other way of paying the mercenaries than by the desperate expedient of debasing the *solidus* or gold piece. A 700 year old tradition was thus terminated. The "bezant," as it was known to contemporaries, had been the currency of international trade. All the advantages accruing to Byzantium from having such a coinage were now lost. The shepherding and cultivation of the empire's financial resources by the imperial bureaucracy had safeguarded the empire to this point. Now collapse was imminent.

It came sooner than anyone anticipated. A demoralized and disloyal army was pitted, at Manzikert in 1071, against the Seljuk Turks, the most capable foe Byzantium had faced since the early days of Islam. The ensuing disaster was to put Asia Minor, the heart-land of the empire, under foreign domination. From this loss recovery to former strength simply was never to be possible. The Comneni rallied the resources of empire by subjugating the citizenry to a military (baronial) *élite*. But from this time on the empire needed a succession of supermen as Emperors to maintain its position, and the workings of the apparatus upon the succession were not such as to accommodate this need.

The fortunes of the military altered, of course, under the Comneni. Clearly, they had to, for the empire had been dismembered by the loss of the Anatolian heart-land. As has been seen, these Emperors, true to their class, encouraged the build-up of baronial estates. But they also retained firm control from the capital over the now sadly depleted outlying areas of empire. Naturally, however, the military *élite* was the group which was now rewarded by prestige and dignities. Lower rankings tend to disappear. Provincial commanders are known as *Duces*, with the occasional *catepan* as a regional subordinate. The Lord High Admiral is elevated to the status of *Megas Dux*. Military men now begin to attain to dignities and titles formerly monopolised by the civil aristocracy, even to those which only eunuchs had enjoyed to date. The logothete of the Army was to be removed from his supervision of the military *élite:* the post simply disappears in the twelfth century. And the military were to have the gratification of seeing the bureaucrats in their turn harried by an Emperor (Andronicus I).

Now even the great Basil II had appreciated the significance of naval power, if somewhat imperfectly. Between the military aristocracy and the naval men there seems always to have been something of a gulf. The latter were, quite simply, regarded as inferior to the military. Their topmost ranks bore lesser titles. They were the first upon whom retrenchment was practiced; indeed they were regularly neglected in time of peace. And Alexius I Comnenus came of military stock. He was, moreover, antipathetic toward the civil bureaucracy, and mercantile interests were quite foreign to him. So it was that he was prepared to pay the price which the Venetians demanded when he needed their naval assistance against the Normans. In 1082, by his Golden Bull, he granted the Venetians exemptions from Byzantine customs dues throughout the Mediterranean, with the exception of the harbours of Crete and Cyprus. In addition Venice was allowed control of certain warehouses and quays in the capital. These were privileges which no Byzantine merchant enjoyed. They broke long-standing Byzantine traditions in regard to exacting customs. They were to lead to enormous prosperity for Venetian carriers, a consequent increase in Venetian naval strength, and thus to the dependence of Byzantium upon Italian naval power, by this time dominant upon the seas.[51]

In regard to special interests particularly dear to one group or the other, there were, of course, areas in which the civil bureaucracy was the main, or even the sole, party interested. These mostly concern positions and titles. The inner ring of bureaucrats chose Emperors favourable to the civil administration and these Emperors spent lavishly upon that administration. Its establishment increased vastly in numbers, apparently. So did the size of the senate, which was thrown open to a much wider range of social groups.[52] There was in consequence tremendous pressure to obtain titles, and these proliferated. The university was refounded and with it a law school, to provide facilities for training the increased numbers of bureaucrats. There was an increase in legal activity which was so marked as to require the Head of the Chancery *(Protoasecretis)* to set up a new department under the Secretary for Petitions *(epi ton deeseon)*.

Within the central administration administrative boards with powers of jurisdiction, the *sekreta*, came to the fore. They were represented in the themes by a *krites* or Judge, but executive power lay with the central boards. These now directed the various aspects of governmental activity, in regard to customs, taxation, jurisdiction or what have you. Others, independent of the above, looked after imperial estates, one board attending to each region. Their activities were coordinated by a prime minister or Vizier, who was to come to be known as the *Mesazon*.[53]

When the *régime* of the military aristocracy supervened, the military *élite* gained access to these positions and titles. Many of the latter had been cheapened into valuelessness by their proliferation. So there was a further round of coining of names.[54] Amid the tangle of terminology which resulted, confusion came upon the bureaucracy itself. Its hierarchy of rank and its coordination were no longer clearly demarcated. Removal of the Logothete for the Army, for instance, might placate the military, but it left important functions still to be fulfilled. They were fulfilled, but by a *sekreton* or board, loosely coordinated with other such boards, rather than by an official at a determinate point within an official hierarchy. Hence Alexius I retained the "prime minister." He put Logothete *ton sekreton* over the entire civil bureaucracy, to act as its chief minister and specified as such.

The ecclesiastical bureaucracy was not a whit less involved in this scrimmage to defend or advance special interests. In fact it has been reserved for separate, and climactic, consideration because the part which it played had such momentous consequences. The eleventh century produced, in Michael Cerularius (Patriarch 1043-1058), the most powerful Patriarch in the history of Constantinople. He boasted that he could make and unmake Emperors, and this was little short of the truth. Church interests advanced accordingly. The harassment of imperial estates terminated with Basil's death. In the period of the dominance of the civil aristocracy, with which it had strong links, the Church was to gain immunities for its estates; all limitations upon acquisition of property by ecclesiastics were removed; and, in Cerularius' day, many gifts were made to it, and some enormously expensive churches built for it in Constantinople.

But, beyond this, Cerularius was to assert the principle that the affairs of the Church were more important than those of the government, and that none but churchmen were to have a say in those affairs. His price for forcing Michael VI to retire and sponsoring Isaac Comnenus was in fact an agreement that the Church alone should administer the Great Church of the Holy Wisdom and that the Emperor should not interfere in Church affairs. Although Comnenus interpreted this agreement by going immediately about the deposition of Cerularius once he was himself installed as Emperor, so much odium resulted from his treatment of Cerularius that he had to retire — to a monastery. By no means all the gains made for the Church by Cerularius were lost.

The jurisdiction of the Church, for instance, was extended in this period to cover questions involving marriage (formerly dealt with by secular courts). All matters of dispute concerning charitable foundations were also now to go before ecclesiastical courts for decision.

But more important yet was the new ecclesiastical ministry developed by Cerularius.[55] Ecclesiastical titulature suffered the same fate as other bureaucratic titulature in the eleventh century. The title *Syncellus* went by now to all Metropolitans; indeed so cheapened had it become that a superior rank of *Protosyncellus* had come into use. Cerularius provided that the five *syncelli* who lived with him in the Great Church of the Holy Wisdom should be appointed by the Patriarch, be known as *exokatoiloi* and have their own *sekielon* or ministry.

Their titles and functions were as follows. There was the Great *Oeconomus*; he looked after the property of the Great Church and of the Patriarchate. The Great *Sacellarius* was to supervise the monasteries. The Great *Skeuophylax* was in charge of all Church vessels and equipment. The Great *Chartophylax* was responsible for the library and archives of the Patriarchate; he came to have disciplinary control of the clergy, take decisions on referral from ecclesiastical courts and act as Vicar-General of the Orthodox Church. This was a most important post. Appointment was made of the Great Chartophylax Leo to the Archbishopric of Bulgaria, for instance, thus undoing all Basil's attempts to scale down the power of the Patriarch of Constantinople. The fifth member of the group was the *Syncellus* of the *Sakellion*. Parish churches everywhere were in his care. This meant he dealt with appeals for ecclesiastical protection when a peasant took refuge from a landowner and so on. As the metropolitan and episcopal *curiae* (administrative offices) were organised along similar lines, and as the Church now existed in areas outside the Emperor's control, the ecclesiastical apparatus of government thus came to have enormous influence.

Once the military aristocracy succeeded in setting their Emperors upon the throne the fortunes of the Church ceased to flourish quite so vigorously. Alexius I on two occasions confiscated ecclesiastical treasures to finance his campaigns against the Normans. He also employed the device of *charisticium*. By this the Emperor could hand over monastic property to a layman to be developed. The Emperor could thus remunerate a supporter and cut back the growth of monastic estates. However, as the clergy were forbidden to engage in trade and could not alienate Church property, only such a device could prevent monastic estates from falling out of use. The device could work in the interests of the Church and some of its leaders were shrewd enough to see this. Protests at Church councils, however, show that the practice was not in general appreciated.

By and large, for all that, Emperor and Church did not come much into conflict. Both were engaged, after all, in propagating the one true faith, and large estates. In fact, under the Comneni important privileges were bestowed upon the Church. The gift of first fruits by peasantry to the local bishop, heretofore sanctioned only by custom, was made compulsory and regulated by law. The scale of fees which a bishop could exact from those he ordained was likewise regulated, as were the fees he could charge for officiating at a marriage ceremony. Priests who lived as *paroikoi* or taxpaying farmers on a great estate were given some remissions of taxes. All in all, then, the military Emperors tended to see to it that the members of the ecclesiastical apparatus received the kinds of perquisites and privileges that officials of the apparatus were wont to receive.

The Church in the West had by now long been outside of the

boundaries of the Byzantine empire.[56] It had managed to continue in existence without the Emperor's protection — cooperating with the Carolingians, almost overwhelmed by the Vikings, under German masters in the case of Otto I and II. It was in fact by now unique in the West for its complex and sophisticated bureaucratic structure, and in that its adherents and agents transcended all regional boundaries. Moreover its monasteries contained, not self-centred ascetics but outspoken critics of wrongdoing and champions of the weak and oppressed. Though this or that monastery might come to ruin, from one or another of those remaining revolt would break out against un-Christian behaviour among the wielders of power. The western Church thus had an independence unknown to that of the East.

In the eleventh century the western Church was situated within a feudal society whose local lords were inclined to treat its properties as theirs to dispose of. A movement of resentment against their secularization built up in the monasteries. At Rome the papacy, administrative centre of the western Church, sympathised with and espoused the movement (this was under Pope Leo IX: 1048-54). Under Cardinal Humbert the first statements of the reform movement were articulated: there should be free election of Church leaders by churchmen without lay intervention or control. By the time of Pope Gregory VII (1073-1085) the revolutionary implications of the reform movement were becoming clearer to many. It meant an end to the concept of a sacred monarchy and made of the Pope the supreme leader of a bureaucratic organization, with its own code of law and law courts, which transcended regional boundaries.

As Humbert was thus championing the cause of papal independence in the West, Cerularius rose to dominance within the apparatus at Constantinople. He chose this time to attempt to bring western Church practices into line with those of the (implicitly superior) eastern Church. This act of bureaucratic in-fighting touched upon a raw nerve at Rome, for the westerners claimed that leadership and direction of Church affairs within the Church lay with the Pope. Humbert had himself despatched to Constantinople to discipline Cerularius. With two such personalities involved, compromise was out of the question. So it was that in 1054 each Church anathematised the other.[57]

In its way this incident was as dire in its consequences as was the conflict at Manzikert, though contemporaries did not at first, apparently, realise its full significance. The short-term sequel was that the papacy was to defy Byzantium by allying with that empire's Norman foes. The long-run sequel was that bitter feelings of hostility built up between the Christian communities of East and West. No conciliation was possible. The Orthodox Church accepted its dependence upon its Emperor while claiming equality with the papacy. The Roman Catholic Church rejected control by temporal powers while asserting its sovereignty over all of Christendom. Already by the end of the century western Christendom was beginning to menace Byzantium. The fleets of the Italian city states were increasingly dominant in the Mediterranean. The first crusade, that blend of holy war, mercantilism and military adventuring, had struck out of the West.[58] This internecine feud within the ecclesiastical apparatus was to cost Byzantium dear.

The sequel was a fourth crusade which diverted itself to Constantinople and took and pillaged the city (1204). A Latin Empire sprang up in what had been Byzantium. It was to pass away, and a faint resemblance of past glories returned in the reconstituted "empire" of the Palaeologi (1259-1453). The end did not come until the city fell to the Ottomans in 1453; but the city which fell to them was a far cry from that which had been mistress of the world in the days of Basil II.[59] As has been shown, the years which followed his death marked a turning point for the empire. They brought feudalism, and with feudalism this book is not concerned. Hence this survey closes at this point, without rehearsing the sorry tale of the centuries of decline.

FOOTNOTES

1. The basic reference work for the period is *CMH* IV, parts 1 (pp. 27-42) and 2 (chapters 20, 22 & 23); see also Ostrogorsky, *History of the Byzantine State*, chapter 2 and Jenkins, chapters 2 to 4. For greater detail see J.B. Bury, *A History of the Later Roman Empire (395 A.D. to 800 A.D.)*, vol. II, MacMillan, 1889; see pp. 207-398. For a vivid description of the city of Constantinople see B. Diener, *Imperial Byzantium*, Little, Brown, 1938, chapter 4.

2. The causes which underlay this turmoil of peoples on the move around the Mediterranean are difficult to discern and variously identified. Recently the case for a minor climatic change, which would affect the course of trade winds and storm tracks, has been persuasively put. See R. Carpenter, *Discontinuity in Greek Civilization*, Cambridge, 1966, pp. 12-15 & 77-80.

3. See Jenkins, pp. 8, 10-13 & 30(-35). The Mohammedans appear to have been treated with even more unmerited bias and disdain by

modern western historians than are the Byzantines. Forster's *Alexandria* (pp. 58-63) provides a highly readable corrective to such views. For a study of the general background to the rise of Islam, see W.H. McNeill, *The Rise of the West*, Mentor, 1965, chapter 9.

4. Thus it was that Hellenised Armenians were to fight in and lead Byzantine armies and Hellenised Slavs to repopulate Anatolia, filling the heart-land of empire with a loyal, industrious and free peasantry. See Jenkins, pp. 24 & 52.

5. Vol. 13 (1959) of the *Dumbarton Oaks Papers* comprises a series of studies of changes within seventh-century Byzantium. See J.L. Teall, "The Grain Supply of the Byzantine Empire 330-1625" (pp. 87-140) and R.S. Lopez, "The Role of Trade in the Economic Readjustment of Byzantium in the Seventh Century"(pp.69-85).For the peasantry see P. Lemerle, "Esquisse pour une histoire agraire de Byzance" in *Revue historique* 218, 1958, pp. 32-74.

6. The Orthodox Church had actually turned her treasures into gold pieces to finance Heraclius' campaigns against the Persians after the sack of Jerusalem (Jenkins, pp. 21-22). Hence Heraclius has been termed "the first crusader." Subsequently the Arabs, who denied Christ's godhead, waged holy war upon Byzantium. Hence the fighting between these two peoples came increasingly to be seen against a religious background by the Byzantines.

7. On the themes see *CMH* IV, 2, pp. 35-41; Ostrogorsky, *History of the Byzantine State*, 87-90; Walter, *La vie quotidienne à Byzance*, pp. 267-8, and Jenkins, pp. 16-18, 22-23 & 53-54. The themal system seems to have been gradually evolved. Justinian had given military commanders in certain areas gubernatorial powers. Maurice had developed the exarchate, under which the commander-in-chief of a distant region (in Ravenna, say, or Carthage) took over the functions of governor. See discussion to n. 50 of chapter 3, and chapter 13 of Bury, *A History of the Later Roman Empire (395 A.D. to 800 A.D.)*, vol. II.

8. It is around the activities of such a Margrave that the great Byzantine epic is written: see *Digenes Akrites*, ed. J. Mavrogordato, Clarendon, 1956.

9. In general see Oman, *The Art of War in the Middle Ages*, chapter 3, *CMH* IV, 2, pp. 43-45. On the defeat of the Muslim attack on Constantinople in 673-8 see Jenkins, pp.(42-)44.

10. See Andrzejewski, *Military Organization and Society*, pp. 56-57. For a discussion of the basic significance of the patterns of property holding see K.M. Setton, "The Importance of Land Tenure and

Agrarian Taxation in the Byzantine Empire from the Fourth Century to the Fourth Crusade," *American Journal of Philology* 24, 1953, pp. 225-59.

11. See P. Charanis, "Ethnic Changes in the Byzantine Empire in the Seventh Century" in *Dumbarton Oaks Papers* 13, 1959, pp. 25-44 and "The Transfer of Population as a Policy in the Byzantine Empire" in *Comparative Studies in Society and History* 3, 1961, pp. 140 ff. and cf. Jenkins, pp. 52-4.

12. See P. Charanis, *The Armenians in the Byzantine Empire*, Bertrand, Lisbon, 1963, pp. 18-21 & 34ff., and cf. Jenkins, p. 18.

13. On "Greek Fire" see *CMH* IV, 2, pp. 49-50; the reference work on the subject is M. Mercier, *Le feu grégois*, Paris, 1952. Oman (*The Art of War*, p. 55) points out however that Greek Fire was merely an (admittedly important) individual item in the sophisticated war machinery ably deployed by the Byzantines.

14. See *CMH* IV, 2, pp. 45-50; Lewis, *Naval Power and Trade in the Mediterranean*, pp. 73-4, and H. Ahrweiler, *Byzance et la mer*, Paris, 1966, pp. 17-28.

15. The Pirenne Thesis is most usually associated with H. Pirenne's book *Mohammed and Charlemagne*, Meridian ed. 1961; cf. pp. 147 ff. For a discussion of the current status of the theory see Havighurst, *The Pirenne Thesis*, especially pp. 102-106.

16. See Lewis, *Naval Power and Trade in the Mediterranean*, pp. 78 ff., especially 89-97.

17. On the Court and administrative bureaucracy in general see *CMH* IV, 1, pp. 35-7 & IV, 2, pp. 19-34, and Ostrogorsky, *History of the Byzantine State*, pp. 220-23. On the seventh century date for these changes, see C. Diehl, *Byzantium: Greatness and Decline*, Rutgers, 1957, pp. 64-68.

18. On the currency, see Lewis, *Naval Power and Trade in the Mediterranean*, pp. 78-9 & 83-88; on small-holdings see *CMH* IV, 1, pp. 38-41; on customs-posts see Antoniadis-Bibicou, *Les Douanes à Byzance*, pp. 197-210 (especially 208-210) & 219-222.

19. A dark age occurred in Byzantine literature from 650 to 850 A.D.: see Part B of the Appendix. The Byzantines were engrossed first by a life and death struggle with the Muslims, then by the Iconoclast Controversy — after which literature produced by the losers was destroyed. Hence restricted literary productivity and unusually low rates of survival for what was produced. See Baynes & Moss, *Byzantium*, p. 114 and Barker, *Social and Political Thought in*

Byzantium, p. 46. Consequently our knowledge of the bureaucracy of this age is largely based on the *Kletorologion* or *Handbook of the Order of Seating at Official Functions*, which post-dates the seventh century. Arguments as to developments in the bureaucracy of the seventh century are thus based partly on inference, partly on snippets of surviving contemporary information, partly on deductions from the *Kletorologion*, and partly on comparisons between this and an analogous document of fifth-century date, the *Notitia Dignitatum* or *List of Official Positions*. For instance, the *Notitia Dignitatum* records 22 officials for the East, to some of whom all the others are subordinate. The *Kletorologion*, on the other hand, records some 60 officials for a fraction of the fifth-century East, and most of these officials are in co-ordination. On the *Notitia* see O. Seeck, *Notitia Dignitatum*, Minerva reprint, 1962; on the *Kletorologion* see J.B. Bury, *The Imperial Administrative System in the Ninth Century; with a Revised Text of the Kletorologion of Philotheos*, Franklin, N.Y., no date.

20. There was a Logothete *tou genikou* (of the Land Tax), for instance; another *tou stratiotikou* (of army pay and commissariat); another *epi tou eidikou* (over state factories supplying equipment for the troops). There was a *Chartularius* (Actuary) *tou Vestiariou* (of the state wardrobe, described above) and a Logothete *ton agelon* (of the Herds or imperial stud farms, remnant of the *Res Privata*).

21. See chapter 3, n. 58. The monograph to which reference is always made in this connection is R. Guilland, "Les eunuques dans l'empire byzantin," *Etudes byzantines* 1, 1943, pp. 197-238.

22. See *CMH* IV, 2, pp. 19-23.

23. You do not, for instance, have 20 different words for "snow" unless you are an Eskimo or a skier. On "semantic fields" (clusters of terms all related to one another like the pebbles of a mosaic) see S. Ullmann, *Semantics: An Introduction to the Science of Meaning*, Blackwell, 1962, pp. 243-53.

24. These officials will try proceedings against officials of the other two parts of the apparatus, for this is part of their dog-eat-dog *ethos*. But they do not seem to want to write *memoirs* on beloved Departments as John the Lydian did. On this view the propensity of such officials for intrigue (or of Byzantines for diplomacy) is a function of the situational pressures bearing upon them, rather than the result of some psychological quirk of national character. See Wittfogel, pp. 137-60.

25. For background reference on the Church at this time see *CMH* IV, 2, chapter 23; Daniel-Rops, *The Church in the Dark Ages*, vol. 1, pp. 287-305 and 11-49 of vol. 2.

26. Jenkins, p. 7.

27. After the success of the Iconodules in the Iconoclast Controversy, which was largely owed to the monks, it became the normal practice for a monk to be selected for this position. Hence a breed of more recalcitrant Patriarchs. *CMH* IV, 2, p. 113 gives an account of the establishment to which Heraclius *reduced* the personnel of the Great Church of the Holy Wisdom. This now stood at 713 and included 5 new *types* of post. It was the nerve-centre of the bureaucracy of the Orthodox Church. And, with the Palace and the Hippodrome, it was one of the three centres of activity in Constantinople, the mistress of the contemporary world. See G. Walter, *La vie quotidienne à Byzance*, pp. 51-59.

28. For background on the controversy, see G.B. Ladner, "Origin and Significance of the Byzantine Iconoclast Controversy" in *Medieval Studies* 2, 1940, pp. 127-49 (where the struggle is seen as a confrontation between the Emperor and the Church). On the immense wealth and estates of the Church see Charanis, "Monastic Properties and the State in the Byzantine Empire" in *Dumbarton Oaks Papers* 4, 1948, pp. 51-119. On the political activities of the monks see Diehl, *Byzantium: Greatness and Decline*, pp. 131-5 & 165. On the confusion of religious and secular issues see *ibid.*, 58-59 & 73-78 and Barker, *Social and Political Thought in Byzantium*, pp. 5-12. On the actual theological issues involved, see Ladner, "The Concept of the Image in the Greek Fathers and the Byzantine Iconoclastic Controversy," in *Dumbarton Oaks Papers* 7, 1953, pp. 1-34, and Jenkins, chapters 6 & 7.

29. See White, *Medieval Technology and Social Change*, chapter 2, especially pp. 40, 54, 56-7, 61, 66-76 & 78; see also pp. 83-5 & 110. F. Cottrell, *Energy and Society*, McGraw-Hill, 1955, pp. 21-3, 32 & 37-8 indicates some of the constraints on the societies of this level of technology.

30. On the renaissance of Islam see Lewis, *Naval Power and Trade in the Mediterranean*, pp. 134, 156, 163-72; cf. P.K. Hitti, *History of the Arabs*, MacMillan, 1961, pp. 343-52.

31. See Hitti, *History of the Arabs*, pp. 484-6 (and chapters 30-32 for greater detail); cf. Lewis, *Naval Power and Trade in the Mediterranean*, pp. 183, 196-8, and especially 259-62.

32. See Lewis, *Naval Power and Trade in the Mediterranean*, chapters 6 & 7, and, in more general terms, P. Charanis, "Economic Factors in the Decline of the Byzantine Empire," *Journal of Economic History* 13, 1953, pp. 412-25.

33. See Jenkins, chapter 26 on Manzikert. For the period in general, as basic reference-works see *CMH* IV, vol. 1, pp. 177-92 and chapter 5; vol. II, pp. 17-54; Jenkins, chapters 22-27, and Ostrogorsky, *The History of the Byzantine State*, pp. 264-333. For a survey of the socio-economic background to the period, see Walter, *La vie quotidienne à Byzance*, especially chapters 1-4 of Part 1.

34. On Basil's treatment of the Church as a department of his apparatus of government, see Jenakins, pp. 329-330 & cf. 81 & 353.

35. For a readable survey in general terms see Hussey, *The Byzantine World*, chapter 3.

36. In the nature of things incidents occurring early in the reign are touched upon in the following discussion, so events of the tenth century occasionally will be mentioned in the following narrative. The central focus is, however, upon the reign as a whole and its contribution to Byzantium of the eleventh century. This boundary problem recurs later in the discussion of Alexius I Comnenus (1081-1118); to point up the contrast between the administration under the civil aristocracy and that under the military *élite* reference has to be made to the entire reign. Again, however, although there is some mention of events in the twelfth century, the focus of attention is upon the eleventh.

37. See Jenkins, p. 310.

38. On the maritime problems and policies of Basil II see Lewis, *Naval Power and Trade in the Mediterranean*, pp. 189-90, 201-202 & 217. On previous policy, which had even gone so far as to grant monopolies to Byzantine traders — who had grown in affluence and influence in the tenth century, see Antoniadis-Bibicou, *Les douanes à Byzance*, pp. 140-3; cf. 40, 55 & 220. The values of a mercantilist society are different from those of a society dominated by an apparatus of bureaucrats given to landowning. Mercantilist values require a different social structure for their support. Consequently they may not be acceptable to a member of a differently structured society, even should he be able to appreciate their value. See Cottrell, *Energy and Society*, chapter 4, especially pp. 58-62, 72 & 76-7. Hence the persistent undervaluing of maritime affairs by the bureaucratic and military *élites* of Byzantium.

39. He was, moreover, the great-uncle of Basil II.

40. On the general course of developments within the eastern Church at this time see *CMH* IV, 2, chapter 23.

41. On the legislation of Nicephorus II see Jenkins, p. 281.

42. See *CMH* IV, 2, p. 119.

43. On the sensitivity of the Orthodox Church in regard to its property rights see Jenkins, p. 118.

44. Jenkins (p. 315) indicates the series of dominating "protectors" and "advisors" from whom Basil managed to win free. Only a man of his fantastic iron will and sense of purpose could do so. At Basil's accession it was 70 years since a legitimate Emperor had been in full control of all departments of the apparatus. Even Basil took some time in finding out how the bureaucracy worked (Jenkins, p. 305). An aged or inept Emperor simply could not prevail against his ministers.

45. On this hostility see *CMH* IV, 2, p. 33; Hussey, *The Byzantine World*, p. 44; Jenkins, pp. 334 & 378 (cf. 273-4 & 280-1 on the reason for the civil aristocrats' dislike of their military peers), and Ostrogorsky, *History of the Byzantine State*, pp. 283-4.

46. Cerularius was so infuriated by Comnenus' treatment of him that he seems to have had some sort of stroke; he died before he could be deposed.

47. Hussey gives his working principle as "If you do not cease from maladministration, you can cease from living." It went along with wholesale execution: *The Byzantine World*, p. 64; cf. *CMH* IV, 2, p. 34.

48. On Nicephoritzes, see Ostrogorsky, *History of the Byzantine State*, pp. 306-308. On the concept of trained incapacity, see Merton, *Reader in Bureaucracy*, pp. (360 &) 364.

49. See Charanis, *The Armenians in the Byzantine Empire*, pp. 50-53.

50. See Ahrweiler, *Byzance et la mer*, pp. 151-63 (this is the only study, of all those cited here, which shows the *rationale* behind the actions of Constantine IX, who was making a serious attempt to cope with a desperate administrative situation).

51. On the Golden Bull see Lewis, *Naval Power and Trade in the Mediterranean*, p. 238; for the rise of the Italians as carriers in the sea trade, see pp. 131, 160-1, 165 & 214-5; on the build-up of their sea power, see pp. 198-201, 238 and 246; for its effects — Italian control of the sea lanes and the re-routing of trade — see pp. 225 & 245.

52. See Ahrweiler, *Byzance et la mer*, p. 143.

53. *Ibid.*, pp. 140-2.

54. See Ostrogorsky, *History of the Byzantine State*, pp. 325-7.

55. See *CMH* IV, 2, pp. 114-5.

56. For the general background see Dawson, *Religion and the Rise of Western Culture*, chapters 5 and (especially) 7, and Daniel-Rops, *The Church in the Dark Ages*, II, chapters 8 and (especially) 10; see also Jenkins, chapter 8, especially p. 112.

57. On the schism of 1054 see Daniel-Rops, *op. cit.* pp. 242-68 and Jenkins, chapter 25.

58. The Crusades are too vast a topic for any attempt at providing an outline bibliography in this note. However, from the point of view of the discussion in the text see Lewis, *Naval Power and Trade in the Mediterranean*, pp. 239-42 & 245.

59. This last, declining age of the Byzantine empire is portrayed in G. Walter, *La ruine de Byzance 1204-1453*, Michel, 1958.

MAPS

NOTE ON MAPS

Reference has been made to this collection of maps at appropriate points in the text. They have been grouped together here in order to make it easily possible for readers to review the changing circumstances of the empires involved by leafing through the maps all together and in sequence. See Appendix A for an estimate of the various territorial and population sizes of the empire.

In Chapter 2 of Book II, there are three additional maps. These reconstitute the geographical references of John the Lydian in the *De Magistratibus.* They are:

1. The Classical Map
2. The Map of the Dominate
3. The Contemporary Map

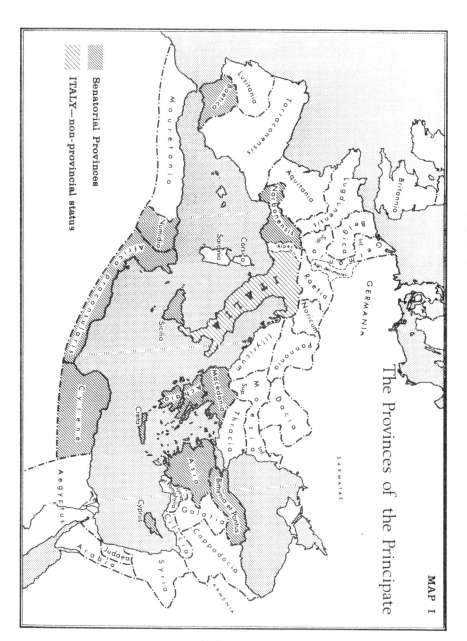

The Provinces of the Principate

MAP I

Senatorial Provinces

ITALY—non-provincial status

Lusitania
Baetica
Mauretania
Tarraconensis
Aquitania
Numidia
Sardinia
Corsica
Alpes
Narbonensis
Lugdunensis
Belgica Inf.
Sup.
agri decumates
Germ.
GERMANIA
Britania
Raetia
Noricum
proconsularis
Africa
Sicilia
Illyricum
Pannonia
Dacia
Sup.
Moesia
Inf.
SARMATAE
Macedonia
Creta
Thracia
Cyrene
Asia
Bithynia et Pontus
Aegyptus
Cyprus
Pamphylia
Lycia
Galatia
Cappadocia
Cilicia
Syria
ARMENIA
Judaea
Arabia

- 179 -

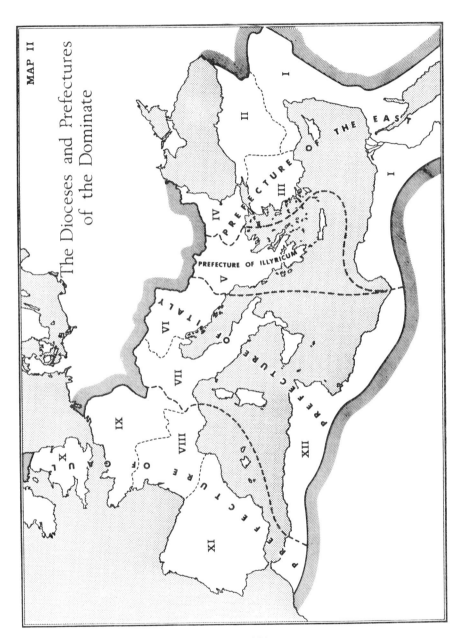

MAP II

The Dioceses and Prefectures
of the Dominate

PREFECTURE OF THE EAST

PREFECTURE OF ILLYRICUM

PREFECTURE OF ITALY

PREFECTURE OF GAUL

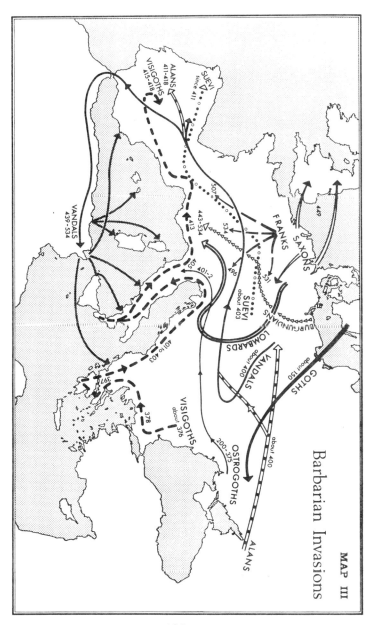

MAP III

Barbarian Invasions

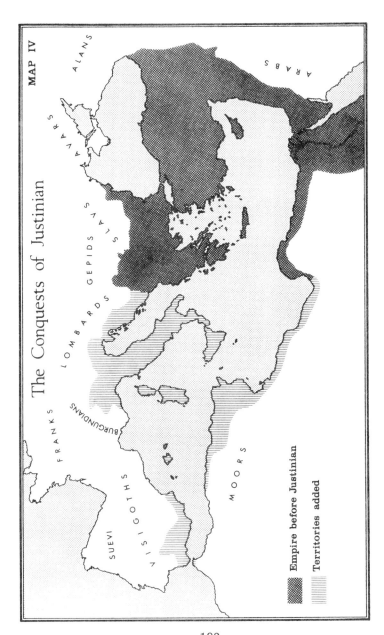

MAP IV

The Conquests of Justinian

ALANS

ARABS

AVARS

SLAVS

GEPIDS

LOMBARDS

FRANKS

BURGUNDIANS

SUEVI

VISIGOTHS

MOORS

Empire before Justinian

Territories added

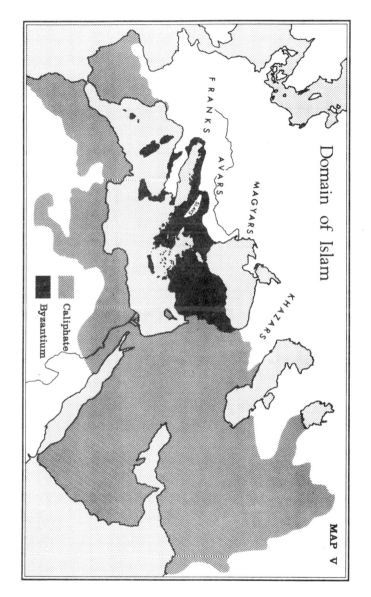

Domain of Islam

Caliphate

Byzantium

FRANKS

AVARS

SLAVS

MAGYARS

KHAZARS

MAP V

- 183 -

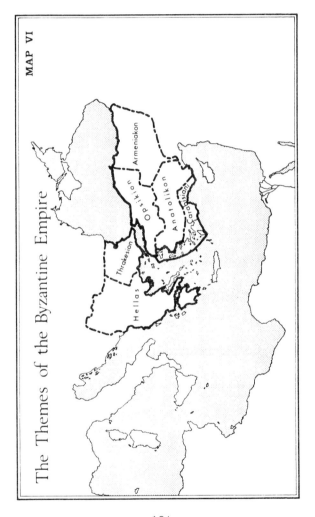

MAP VI

The Themes of the Byzantine Empire

Armeniakon

Opsikion

Anatolikon

Caravisian

Thrakesion

Hellas

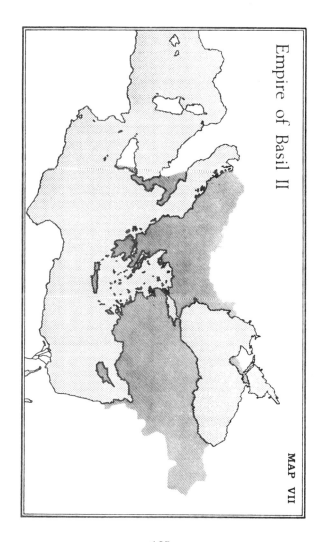

Empire of Basil II

MAP VII

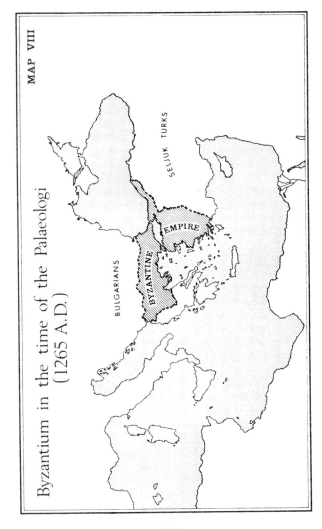

MAP VIII

Byzantium in the time of the Palaeologi
(1265 A.D.)

BULGARIANS

BYZANTINE EMPIRE

SELJUK TURKS

APPENDICES

Appendix A

Territorial and Population Sizes of the Empire[1]

Date	Territorial extent	Population numbers
First century	4,000,000 km	70,000,000
Fourth century[2]	4,000,000 km	50,000,000
Fifth century	1,600,000 km[3]	26,000,000
Sixth century (after Justinian)	2,350,000 km	30,000,000
Eleventh century	1,100,000 km	20,000,000
Twelfth century	650,000 km	10-12,000,000
Michael VIII Palaeologus (1261-82)	250-350,000 km	5,000,000

1. Figures are based on E. Stein, "Introduction à l'histoire et aux institutions byzantines," *Traditio* 7, 1949-51, p. 154; see however D. Jacoby, "La population de Constantinople à l'époque byzantine: une problème de demographie urbaine," *Byzantion* 31, 1961, pp. 81-110 for an argument that such population figures are too high.

2. In the following proportions:

	Territory	Population
Eastern Empire	1,600,000 km	26,000,000
Western Empire	2,400,000 km	24,000,000

(The fifth century figures are deduced from these.)

3. See maps for changing frontiers.

Appendix B

Table of Influential Writers or Documents
Spanning the Byzantine Period (330 - 1453 A.D.)

GREEK MEDIUM

Century	Historians	Church Fathers, Clerics	Documents	Other
330 4th	Eusebius*	Athanasius		Julian (Letters) Libanius (Rhetorician)
475 5th	Zosimus	St. John Chrysostom		Nonnus(last paganepic) Proclus (Neoplatonist)
6th	John Malalas . . . . . . Procopius Evagrius			Cosmas (geographer) John Lydus; Greek Anthology Romanus (Hymns) Paul of the Silentiary (on Church of Holy Wisdom)
632 7th		John the Monk Barlaam and Iosaph	Farmer's Law Miracles of St. Demetrius	
725 8th			Rhodian Sea Law Ecloga (law)	Leo (military art)
800 843 9th	George the Monk . .	Theodore of Studion		Philotheos (Formal Order of Invitations) Photius (Encyclopaedist)
961 10th	John Camieniates Constantine Porphyrogenitus Leo Diaconus		Basilica (law) Suda (lexicography)	Palatine Anthology
1054 11th 1071	Psellus	Michael Cerularius		Cecaumenos (military art) Digenes Akritas (epic) Attaliates
12th	Nicetas Acominatus Anna Comnena Cedrenus John Cinnamus John Zonares			
1204 13th 1261	Nicetas Choniates George Acropolites			
14th	George Pachymeres John VI Cantacuzenus	Gregory Palamas	Hexabiblos Syntagma (legal compilations)	Palatine Anthology (re-edition) Nicephorus Gregoras (polymath)
1453 15th Dates of years indicate battles or events of importance.				Plethon (philosopher)

* The line of dots . . . . means that the writer falls into the adjacent category as well.

Table of Influential Writers or Documents (cont.)

Century		LATIN MEDIUM			OTHER LANGUAGES
		Historians	Church Fathers	Documents	
330	4th	Ammian Eutropius . . . . Orosius	Jerome		
475	5th			Codex Theodosianus Notitia Dignitatum	
	6th	Gregory of Tours . . . Jordanes	Benedict Boethius	Codex Justinianus Cassiodorus (Letters)	
632	7th				Barlaam is Life of Buddha as Greek Novel Koran
725	8th				Beowulf
800 843	9th				
961	10th	Liutprand			Tabari
1054 1071	11th				
	12th				
1204 1261	13th				Geoffrey Villehardouin
	14th.				
1453 Dates of years indicate battles or events of importance.	15th				

* The line of dots . . . . means that the writer falls into the adjacent category as well.

Bibliography to Accompany Table of Writers

Readers may be interested to know of the availability of the following sources in translation:

The Theodosian Code, translated by C. Pharr, Princeton, 1952.

The Institutes of Justinian, translated by J. B. Moyle, Clarendon, 1955 (5th ed.)

The Digest of Justinian, translated by C. H. Monro, Cambridge, 1904 & 1909 (2 vols.)

Procopius, *History of the Wars; Secret History; On the Buildings of Justinian*, translated by H. B. Dewing, Loeb, 1914-40

The Greek Anthology, translated by W. R. Paton, Loeb 1916-18

Paul the Silentiary, *Description of the Church of St. Sophia:* see W. R. Lethaby & H. Swainson, *The Church of Sancta Sophia*, London, 1894.

The Farmer's Law, translated by W. Ashburner, *Journal of Hellenic Studies* 30, 1910, pp. 85-108 & 32, 1912, pp. 68-83

The Book of the Prefect, translated by A.E.R. Boak, *Journal of Economic and Business History* 1, 1929, pp. 597-619

Constantine Porphyrogenitus, *De Administrando Imperio*, G. Moravcsik (ed.) & R.J.H. Jenkins (translator), Budapest, 1949; *De Cerimoniis*, translated by A. Vogt, Bude, 1935-40

Three Byzantine Saints: Contemporary Biographies of St. Daniel the Stylite, St. Theodore of Sykeon and St. John the Almsgiver, translated by E. Dawes & N. H. Baynes, Blackwell, 1948

Michael Psellus, *Chronographia*, translated as *Fourteen Byzantine Rulers* by E. R. A. Sewter, Penguin, 1966

* * *

The following volumes contain collections of translated documents bearing on their themes:

R. S. Lopez & I. W. Raymond, *Medieval Trade in the Mediterranean World*, Columbia, 1955

E. Barker, *Social and Political Thought in Byzantium from Justinian to the Last Palaeologus*, Clarendon, 1957

* * *

There is a very exhaustive bibliography of Byzantine source material in D. J. Constantelos, *Byzantine Philanthropy and Social Welfare*, Rutgers, 1968, pp. 291-304.

BOOK TWO

Byzantine Bureaucracy from Within

TABLE OF CONTENTS

Book Two: Byzantine Bureaucracy from Within

Part One

The World of a Bureaucrat in Ancient Times

Introduction

First, I had better define the subject. I am taking "The World of the Bureaucrat" to mean "how a bureaucrat perceived his environment." That is, we are not out looking for new facts or more precise dates. Rather, we will take a look at the facts our bureaucrat chooses to present. By so doing, we will see *what* he saw — and what he did not see — and *how* he saw it. And we are not going to try to think of some mythical creature (*the* "typical" bureaucrat). We are going to look at John the Lydian, because:

(a) he was a career bureaucrat and wrote a monograph on his beloved Corps

(b) his is the *only* such writing to have survived from all Romano-Byzantine antiquity.

The work is the *De Magistratibus*. It was written in the 550's A.D. and reviews the history and antecedents of the Praetorian Prefecture (which means, given our bureaucrat's pride in his Corps, the entire history of the magistracies of Rome). It is a rambling and discursive work. Consequently, it throws light on many other aspects of concern to its author besides its professed subject matter. It is, in fact, ideal for the sort of treatment that it will be given.

John's picture of the world he lived in is important because it is the sort of picture that the vast mass of bureaucrats had to guide their conduct. And for centuries of the Roman and Byzantine empires it was men like John who kept those empires in being. We are thus, in a way, catching a glimpse of the thought-world of the mass of administrators in the great administrative machine. These men, and John in particular, were the products of the highest levels of the educational system of their day. John has a lot to tell us, albeit inadvertently, about literary history and the transmission of the Classics. Also, his will be, very probably, another world to the ones with which readers of the usual ancient authors will be familiar. He is no shrewd historian, sensitive poet or keen critic of society. Nor, despite John's fond imaginings, is he a master of prose style. He expresses himself in a pedestrian fashion, in fact. He rambles. He shows little capacity for incisive analysis or far-ranging synthesis. We are, that is, not presented with the highly a-typical viewpoint of a literary genius but with a glimpse of an unremarkable, though highly educated, mind at work.

I will go about looking for his picture of his world by looking at some of the things a scholar normally looks at in his texts, and counting heads to see if generalizations are possible. There will be some illustrations to help explain my points. I am proposing to look at (1) what features in the physical world around him John saw fit to notice; (2) what sorts of things he considered Rome's history to be made up of; (3) the world of books and teachings available to him; and (4) the feuds and factions that for him made up life in "the Service." To let the overall implications in all this stand free from the welter of details necessarily thrown up in the course of these four inquiries, they will be followed by a summary indicating the trends and implications involved.

First, however, a thumb-nail biography of our subject. I have pushed the source-evidence to the utmost in an attempt to produce as full a biography as I possibly could. The biography will also, I hope, suggest such of the problems and preoccupations of a sixth-century civil servant as may well have influenced his attitudes towards the world around him.

Chapter 1
John the Lydian: A Biography

John was born in Lydia, in Philadelphia below Mt. Tmolus, in 490, of well-connected curial stock.[1] He received secondary education in Greek and Latin and had such a reputation for proficiency in his studies that, *at the age of 14*, he served as temporary secretary to the dreaded *commentarienses* in their travels to the East to discipline Appion and his following in 504.[2] He travelled via the Public Post at least as far as Antioch in process. He also sojourned in Cyprus, probably at some time after 540.[3]

At 21 he came to Constantinople, where a cousin was already doing well in the clerical service of the *comitatus*, to seek his fortune. While awaiting an opening in the *memoriales* (Establishments Board), he studied philosophy at the university level. Both were shrewd decisions. The *magistriani* (Staff of the Master of Offices), amongst whom the *memoriales* served, were *the* corps within the civil bureaucracy and the Emperor Anastasius had favoured men with literary training. But John's fame had already preceded him, and an influential distant connection, named Zoticus, currently serving as Praetorian Prefect, pressured him into the *praefectiani* (Staff of the Praetorian Prefect), where there seems to have been something of a need for Latinists.[4]

Since switching Corps was impossible, John's lot was irretrievably cast. This was a fatal mistake for his career, though in the short run the decision paid off handsomely. Soon John was to be socialized by his work-*milieu* into identifying fully with the *praefectiani*. He served close to his patron for a year, taking a massive haul of *sportulae* ("fees") — 1,000 gold pieces. At the end of the year he received an unheard of promotion, which put him many rungs up the interminable clerical career ladder: he was appointed first secretary to the Heads of the Department of Civil Law Suits (*chartularius* to the *ab actis* — see discussion of the career ladder below), and this without having to pay a fee to receive the appointment. His skills in Latin were much in demand, and he won great intra-departmental popularity for expeditiously completing the *suggestiones* (legal reports to the Senate). Doubling up on his posts in a frenzy of work, he also served as a free-lance secretary and an Assistant Secretary in the courts of law of the Prefecture — a brilliant start for a young man of 22. A review of the career ladder will indicate what lies behind John's preoccupation with promotions and positions (see Diagram 1, following).

The *officium* of the Praetorian Prefect at Constantinople probably had an establishment of about 2,000 positions in the sixth century. Below the Prefect himself his men were in three great divisions. First there was the Establishment. This consisted of the Heads of the Corps, *primates officii*, and the Heads of Departments, *promoti*. Then there were the groups (*scholae*) of clerical staff (*exceptores*); this division was known as the *litterati*. Lastly there were the sub-clerical staff — criers, messengers and the like; this group was known as the *illitterati*. We are here concerned with the top two strata only.

The *primates* consisted of a *princeps officii* (Head of the *Corps*), who was an ex-secret service man *(agens in rebus)*, a member of the *magistriani*. He supervised the entire operation of the *corps*. His duties involved keeping an eye on the *matricula*, to see that no improper persons made their way on to the staff; deciding which cases ought to come up for trial; and general security duties — he would report any transgressions of the law to the Master of Offices, for instance. Next came the *cornicularius*. He had been Head of *Corps* until the *princeps* inserted himself. He was responsible for the actual conduct of cases at law (and shared the fees arising therefrom with the *princeps*). Then came the *primiscrinius* or *adiutor* or *primicerius adiutorum*, as he variously is styled. He appointed the *executores*, the officials who were to see to the carrying out of decisions of the *corps*; John attributes to him general responsibility for tax assessment in his day.

The *promoti* or Heads of Departments consisted of the following officials (in descending order of prestige and standing): the *commentarienses*, the *ab actis*, the *curae epistolarum*, the *regendarii* and the *numerarii*. The *commentarienses* were two in number and saw to matters involving criminal prosecutions. There were likewise two *ab actis*; they saw to the conduct of cases involving civil law. The Judicial Branch of the *corps* outranked all other branches in standing. There were two *regendarii*, also. They saw to the issuing of warrants authorising use of the facilities of the Public Post. As the *praefectiani* had lost control of the Post, this job had declined in importance and was something of a sinecure. Hence the *regendarii* were inferior in status to the *curae epistolarum*. The latter were eight in number. They were, by this time, in charge of correspondence. Two each looked after

the administrative areas of *Asiana, Oriens, Pontica* and *Thracia.* The *numerarii* were the Heads of the accountants and bookkeepers. Despised by the *litterati,* they had only with difficulty secured recognition as members of the *praefectiani* and were in, but not, of its establishment. Their numbers and importance were to grow dramatically during John's career (and to ruin his prospects in consequence). At the outset of that career, however, they do not seem to have counted for much. But this was before the *a secretis* and the *scrinarii,* all financial officials, came to the fore, as John tells us.

Supposing you are a young man of the "right" background for service with the "Prefect's men": you have a sound training in literature. Your parents will probably have registered you, as a child, as a *supernumerarius* or supernumerary. Registration is effected via the *matricularius* or Head, Personnel Records, an official associated with the departments under the *cornicularius.* There are over 1,000 enrolments each year. You are entered among the *exceptores* (clerks). You await your turn for eligibility for a vacancy. If your background is satisfactory, if you do your work well and if you can afford the purchase price for a clerk's position, you will purchase the vacancy when your turn comes.

You are now enrolled in a *schola* or division of clerks. There are 15 divisions; each is headed by a *primicerius.* There seem to have been 15 Departments (not counting the *numerarii,* who were not *litterati* and who were organised in *scrinia* or *bureaux*). After nine years as an *exceptor,* presumably one in each of the different types of department, you are eligible to become an *adiutor* or assistant. *Adiutor* has a variety of meanings. It can mean Assistant to the *cornicularius,* i.e. the *primiscrinius;* it can mean the *aide* to the *promotus* or Head of Department; or it can mean an assistant to the *aide.* The latter post is that of *chartularius* or secretary, and this is the type of assistantship now open to you. The nine years' service as *exceptor* need not be consecutive. Generally, in fact, it will not be; for you have to await the occurrence of a vacancy in each position. Although the posts are held only for a year, there are queues for the vacancies. The climb up the career ladder is to be a tedious business.

However, after this nine years' training, you are eligible to become an *aide,* and this is an established post. You receive your *probatoria* from the *memoriales* (the Notaries deal only in commissions and dignities, not these lesser appointments). You are now admitted to the *militia* or Service, as it is known. You are also at a parting of career-ways. If you have shown promise in the eyes of senior members of the clerical staff and if you now make a good showing in the *boethura* or year as assistant to the *primiscrinius*, you may be allowed to enter the *augustales*. This is a college of 30 of the most senior, capable and experienced assistants serving the Judicial Branch. If you do not wish for, or cannot achieve, acceptance into the *augustales*, you will remain as a secretary/assistant in the Administrative Branch (the Departments of the *curae epistolarum* and *regendarii*). What this parting of career-ways means for your future is the difference between (relatively) speedy affluence and a very slow progress through a less rewarding series of posts. Via service in the *augustales* you will rise to finish your career with the post of *cornicularius*. And the *augustales* are retired at the rate of two per year. The other type of service leads only to the post of *primiscrinius*. Because the number of your colleagues is larger and the retirement rate (one per year — the *primiscrinius*) slower, in this branch of the Service promotion is slower, even though there are two Heads in each Department (one for promotions from either branch).

Suppose you are fortunate enough to become an *augustalis*. You can now hold assistantships (at the level of *aide*) in the Judicial Branch — each *commentariensis* had three *aides* (and three assistants to those *aides*), for instance. There are other posts, too, open to you in this branch: that of *cancellarius* (confidant, assessor, intermediary to the judge in the court of law), of *subadiuva* or deputy assistant, or of *instrumentarius* (archivist), or *matricularius*. The position of *aide* was an important one; an *aide* could sign for his departmental head. Only senior *augustales* held such positions — for the *augustales* were themselves split into two sections of fifteen, the senior group being known as *deputati* (originally so-called because they were sent on secondment to the very highest courts when business required).

After holding all fifteen posts of *aide* (the primiscriniate is not open to you) in due order of seniority, you now at last become eligible to proceed through all the corresponding Headships, in like order. Given the limited size of the establishment of the *augustales*, their retirement rate, and the fact that these posts were all of one year's duration, promotions would come almost in succession at this stage. Holders of the position of *cornicularius* became *comites*, Counts, and gained senatorial rank. They also gained a huge haul of fees, for their signatures on documents. All the more senior headships, in fact, were likely to bring in large sums of money in this way. Thus was retirement provided for; government pensions were on a very modest scale, even for an official who had reached this level of eminence.

In terms of time one could, ideally, complete one's career in 41 years: a year as supernumerary; nine years as secretary; one year in the *boethura*; 15 in the various assistantships of the stage of *augustalis*, and 15 as head of the various departments. Clearly, few will have got round the course in par, as it were, given the numbers queueing for posts along the way. Moreover, the various bureaucratic malpractices involved entailed bottlenecks in promotions. Purchase of office leads to absenteeism and sinecurism, which in turn encourages pullulation of further offices — partly to get the work done, partly to provide more saleable offices. This is clearly a vicious circle tending to perpetuate this form of administrative pathology.[5]

But let us return to John. The preferential treatment he had been accorded because of the influence of Zoticus as Praetorian Prefect had brought him, in his second year of service and at the age of 22, to a career point only three years, or stages, away from admission to the *augustales*. Well might he comment on his youth in contrast to the advanced years of the colleagues with whom he shared this level of seniority within the service!

This early period was the happiest and most promising of John's life. He was rapidly advanced within the judicial branch, key sector of the Prefecture, and formed lifelong bonds of comradeship with his colleagues in the Corps. In a career where advancement came by seniority and to attain one's appropriate rank at the earliest year allowable was a seldom-attained ideal, John was ahead of the game. His ex-patron secured for him an advantageous matrimonial alliance, one fine June day, one which brought a handsome dowry of 100 pounds weight in gold. John seems to have been genuinely devoted to his bride. But this marriage did not last for long; his wife soon died, and John seems never to have remarried.[6] However, as far as his career was concerned, John felt so confident that his future lay solely within his Corps that he resisted overtures from Court society in order to concentrate all his energies on departmental work.

This, like his excessive respect for aristocratic large landowners,[7] was to prove a serious misjudgement. For a reforming Emperor imported a series of new brooms to sweep the prefecture clean. Efficiency was the order of the day. Rhetoric and red tape, together with John's beloved filing systems and use of Latin for its effect, went out, and skills in accountancy were advanced in their stead.[8] This meant the worst thing possible for a skilled man: mid-career skill obsolescence. Prospects of pay, perquisites, and dignities receded. John's hatred for John the Cappadocian, the efficiency expert who carried these reforms through, knows no bounds. It culminated in an act of bureaucratic suicide, at least so far as his career was concerned: John associated himself prominently with the aristocratic Phocas, with whom Justinian was forced, because of the Nika Riot (532), to replace the Cappadocian as Praetorian Prefect. In the upshot Phocas was speedily retired. Aged 42, John's prospects for advancement were at an end, for the Cappadocian came back into office as Prefect before the year was out.

John now[9] gave himself over to books, as he puts it. He remained, for the most part, in Constantinople and close to Court circles, being acquainted with the Empress Theodora and the Master of Offices, Peter the Patrician.[10] In — but not of — the academic community, towards which he occasionally exhibits an animosity never shown towards his fellow bureaucrats,[11] he built up a considerable reputation as a scholar.[12] When the Cappadocian finally fell in 541, John's connections secured him recognition from Justinian,[13] who instructed the then Prefect to count John's teaching service in lieu of service actually within the bureaucracy. John was by now in his early fifties. He may have done some lecturing at a military academy at this stage of his career.[14] Whether this is so or not, the post he now attained was the equivalent of a university professorship: John's academic abilities and achievements were thus very amply recompensed. Some of his prize lectures from this period are probably included in the digressions in his subsequent books.

John wrote three books that have survived.[15] There is the *De Mensibus (On the Months)*, a work on the calendar and related matters of historical and antiquarian interest. Then there is a book *On Portents (De Ostentis)*. And finally there is his work *On the Magistracies of the Roman Constitution* (whose short Latinised title is the *De Magistratibus*), with which this study is so largely concerned. It is difficult to date their composition to stages in John's career, but internal evidence suggests the following order and timing of composition. John probably wrote the *De Mensibus* in the 'thirties, the period when he "gave himself over to books," as he puts it. About 540, when his fortunes were at their lowest ebb, he came to subscribe to the influence of the stars upon human destiny and to write on the subject. Such a non-Christian belief would well accord with his revulsion from the policies of the highly Orthodox Christian reforming Emperor. Certainly both the *De Mensibus* (in the concluding chapters of which the writing of the *De Ostentis* is promised) and the *De Ostentis* (in the opening chapters of which the *De Mensibus* is cited) are dedicated to the Urban Prefect Gabriel, an aristocratic opponent of John the Cappadocian and of the Emperor himself. John was possibly in Cyprus when he commenced work on *De Ostentis.* [16]

His new convictions were to be dramatically vindicated by events, in this case. The Cappadocian was struck down and John's friends at Court secured his return to imperial favour. This striking *bouleversement*, however, left John with a most impolitic piece of writing to his credit, for he now enjoyed the Emperor's favour. He seems to have reacted by attempting to keep the matter as dark as possible. Though he frequently cites his earlier work (the *De Mensibus*) in his later writings (the *De Magistratibus*, written after his retirement), he never mentions the *De Ostentis*, even when the subject matter brings it strikingly to mind. Nor does he give any but the slightest indication of his knowledge of astrology and the lore of portents in his subsequent writings. During the 'forties, however, his work at the university seems to have kept him too busy to write: it was not until he was once again out of the service that he produced another book.[17]

And so John came to the end of his official career. But his last years coincided with the prefecture of Hephaestus, an economy expert specializing in retrenchment and manipulating monopolies.[18] So, though John held the (normally lucrative) concluding career positions, he did not amass the *sportulae* that, accruing at this point, should have enabled him to retire in financial comfort. He retired in 551 A.D., with the title of Count (of the First Rank), and with senatorial status. His seems to have been a "model" career: all career stages seem to have been attained at the minimum ages respectively allowable. He was now 61. But he retired to a life of penury, and had to find occasional employment to make ends meet. Together with the writing which he had deferred until his retirement this kept him busy and preoccupied.[19]

The *De Magistratibus* was written at this stage.[20] John may have done some of the writing of the first two books of this three-volume work before retirement. At all events, Book III, the *addendum*, is different both in style and in spirit. Books I and II are rather formal; book III is a backstage view, "blowing the gaff":[21] John makes no secret of his resentment at the way in which his services had been rewarded. The *De Magistratibus* does not mention the recapture of (parts of) Spain (552 A.D.), the settlement of Italy (554), the earthquake at Constantinople (557) or the second visitation of the plague (558), though touching on matters such that one would expect reference to these had John known of them. There is much evidence of either haste in compilation or of the absence of a final editing.[22] Probably the *De Ostentis* was written before this work,[23] and the *De Magistratibus* was thus the sole work of John's latter years. Probably, however, John died relatively soon after his retirement.[24] The *De Magistratibus* has all the imperfections of a first draft which never received a thorough editing, a fact which suggests that John's death came soon and at an untimely moment after his retirement. The disappointment and anxiety of his declining years have certainly left their mark in the sombre and gloomy imagery and assumptions with which the *De Magistratibus* is written.

We now turn to look at this work to see what it has to tell us of the life and preoccupations of its writer and men like him.

FOOTNOTES

1. *De Mag.* III 26, 1 & 4 (all references to the *De Magistratibus* are keyed to my translation; see Book 3; cf. also n. 4. References to John's other writings are keyed to the editions listed in the short titles under *De Mens.* and *De Ost.* Most of the autobiographical detail given by John occurs in the passage III 25, 2-30, 10. Substantiation by footnote is provided hereafter only for items not mentioned therein.

2. This appears from the following passages: on the date, see III 17, 1-3 (which firmly dates the event to 504) and III 67, 3 (which is an oblique reference to this early period of service — see also I 28, 5, commented on in n. 4). On the functions of the *commentarienses* see III 17, 1-18, 5. Travels are implied at III 17, 1; cf. also n. 3 below. Bury (*History of the Later Roman Empire*, vol. 2, p. 471) records a tradition that Appion went East to Edessa as Praetorian Prefect; this would explain John's references to journeying *commentarienses*.

3. On his trip to Antioch see notes 10-12 in Chapter 2, and discussion thereto in text. On his sojourn in Cyprus see *De Mens.* IV, 47; as he did not become interested in omens until after 540 (*De Ost., Pref.* 1), the incident should date after that year.

4. On his first choice (the *memoriales*) and actual entry-point (the *praefectiani*), see III 26, 1 & 4. The reference to Zoticus' "having the

power to compel" John to join his branch of the "service" is most easily explicable on the understanding that John is of curial stock, and thus is evading his responsibilities by fleeing into the less onerous service of the *comitatus* (cf. *LRE* pp. 743 & 748-55). Certainly, John is very silent about his family connections (which would give him away — he only mentions kinsmen who are in the Prefecture). He can personally remember the curial councils before Marinus did away with them (I 28, 5; III 49, 2 refers — and would date Marinus' measure, with Borghesi, to "after 498," as John was in Constantinople from 511: cf. Bury, *op. cit.).* He unthinkingly associates *"boule"* with the *curial* council (rather than the senate). And he identifies with people who seem from their relative wealth to be tax-evading *curiales* when he tells of action taken against them by the Cappadocian (III 57, 4-7; 59, 1-60, 4). As the Prefecture extracted taxes, collusive practices may well be involved (the Cappadocian had to discipline his staff: II 21, 2; III 65, 4; possibly III 57, 4-7 relates to this). In this case Zoticus would be building up a group to represent the local interests of Philadelphia within the prefecture, a typical maneuver in a traditional bureaucracy (see Riggs, "Agraria and Industria, Toward a Typology of Comparative Administration," in *Toward the Comparative Study of Public Adminis- tration*, Siffin, pp. 40-42). The ostensible reason for pressing John into this branch might well, however, have been its need for Latinists, indicated by III 27, 3-5 (and also III 20, 5-9). John seems already to have enjoyed a considerable reputation as a Latinist (III 67, 3).

5. This reconstruction of the career pattern of the *litterati* in the *praefectiani* is based upon a scatter of passages in John's *De Magistratibus.* It is also based upon other attempts at reconstructions of the interrelationships between these posts. I submit it with some hesitation. John's references are far from providing a clear picture. The reconstruction is supported by John's text and is in line with the ideas of modern specialists on the subject. Hopefully, it will provide a reasonably firm chopping block for further inquiry into this topic. For specialist studies see Jones, *Studies in Roman Government and Law*, pp. 153 ff., especially 166-75 (cf. also the Appendix, pp. 213-6); *LRE*, pp. 586-92, and Sinnigen, *The Officium of the Urban Prefecture during the Later Roman Empire*, pp. 10-69, especially 63 ff. The following table sets out the relevant passages in the *De Mag.*

6. John does not give the date of the marriage but his description of his career successes indicates either a date before the death of Anastasius in 518 (*litterati* throve under Anastasius, and John had exactly the qualifications preferred: cf. III 50,1-5) or certainly before Justinian brought the Cappadocian in as Praetorian Prefect (531 at latest). For the death of John's wife see *De Mens.* IV, 88.

7. Zoticus seems to have supported the interests of large estates: Bury, *History of the Later Roman Empire*, I, p. 445 and n. 1. John's acerbic comments on Demosthenes may well be connected with the latter's tightening up of tax requirements bearing on landowners: III 42,4 and Bury, *op. cit.*, n. 2. Phocas, a "true" aristocrat according to his admirer John, seems to have been prosecuted as a pagan (Bury, vol. 2, p. 55 and n. 2) and may even have been hounded to suicide later (*ibid.*, p. 368): he was very probably foisted on Justinian by aristocratic pressure — i.e. that of the large landowners — acting through the Nika

Riot (cf. *LRE*, pp. 271-2). Moreover, the aristocratic Urban Prefect Gabriel, who opposed both the Cappadocian and Justinian (*De Mag.* III 38,3-5), was a friend of John's: the latter dedicated both of his other works to him (Suidas, on Ioannes Philadelpheus Lydos).

8. This is indicated by John's laments on (a) the dying away of rhetoric, Latin and filing (coupled with criticisms of the Cappadocian on this score), and (b) his fulminations against the advancement of accountancy staffs: see respectively (a) III 19,1-4; 20,5-9; 28,3; 54,1-2; 66,1-2; 68,1-4; 76,10; and (b) III 10,3; 21,2; 36,1 (cf. 35,4-5).

9. John does not date this retirement, but a content analysis of his references to affairs within the Prefecture reveals that all his detailed references to its activities cease with the prefectship of Phocas (all references to the Cappadocian, significantly, antedate the Nika Riot). His view of the Prefecture prior to this is that of an insider — however dim-sighted — within the corridors of power; after 532 A.D. his view is that of a Constantinopolitan close to Court circles — he talks of the new law codes, of the triumph of Belisarius and the spectacular displaying of the captive king Witigis, and of "the" plague — the Great Plague of 542-3; he does not seem to have lived to know about the second visitation of 558.

10. III 69,2 was written by someone close — in official contact as well as in sympathy — to the Empress; as his "Contents" indicate (III 15,4), John wrote a laudation of her. John is equally laudatory when speaking of Peter the Patrician; II 25,3-26,5 (*not a critical view: cf.* Procopius, *Secret History* 16 and Bury, vol. 2, pp. 164-67).

11. III 47,1 indicates his underlying contempt for academics (cf. also II 26,4); he identifies with his fellow bureaucrats throughout the work: I 15 (4); III 30, 10&67, 4-6.

12. Besides III 29, 1-4 & 30, 4-8, see 73,2; as Chapter 4 on "The Literary World of John the Lydian" will indicate, this was probably inflated beyond John's merits; even he felt qualms about living up to it, on occasion: II 26,5.

13. Again, John gives no precise indication of date, but the Cappadocian fell in 541 and we find Justinian requesting John to write up an achievement of his (Justinian's) that dates to 540: see III 28,5, where it is specifically stated that the *last* attack made on Daras is in question — on this see Bury, vol. 2, p. 98. As the treaty of 545, which ended the war, is not mentioned (the repulse of the attack on Daras being considered Justinian's major achievement to date — contrast III 55,2), the incident may well antedate that year. It rather looks as

though the powerful intermediacy of Theodora and Peter the Patrician secured speedy restitution for the Cappadocian's foes after his fall.

14. In Chapter 2 it will be shown that the maps in terms of which John views his world are those of a military strategist; in Chapter 3 it will be shown that he has a marked predilection for military heroes; Chapter 4 will show that the largest single body of his reading involves military treatises. This is not merely a reflection of the temper of the times: Agathias, a historian proper (i.e. not a writer on *civilian* institutions) does not, as does John, introduce major digressions on military topics (cf. e.g. I 46,1-47,4 and III 51,6-53,4). On the institution in which John taught, see Barker, *Social and Political Thought in Byzantium*, p. 16. John certainly seems to have been present at the major occasions at Court in which the military establishment was fêted (see II 2,5 & III 55,3-4) and seems to have been thought of by Justinian as primarily a writer on *military* matters, for the latter gave John (rather than Procopius) the job of writing up his Persian war (III 28,4-5).

15. We know of three which have not survived: a panegyric on Zoticus, another on Justinian, and the history of Justinian's Daras campaign: III 27,2; 28, 4 & 28, 5 respectively. See Rubin, *Das Zeitalter Justinians* pp. 168-9.

16. He may have been in Antioch, a city he appears to know well, and have repaired thence to Cyprus in view of the danger of a Persian attack: see chapter 2, note 11.

17. The internal evidence for this reconstruction is as follows. *De Mens.* IV, 79 end promises that a book on portents will soon be written. *De Ost.* 7C cites the *De Mens.* as already written. John connects his new convictions about prodigies with those foretelling the Persian advance to the Orontes in 540 at *De Ost.*, Pref. 1. The latest identifiable historical event related in the *De Ost.* occurs in 535 (*De Ost.* 9c) which is described as recent (see also note 31 in chapter 3). John came on material for the book while in Cyprus (*De Mens.* IV, 47) and its geographical horizons centre on the Levant — they are in fact distinctively more southerly in their orientation than are those of the *De Mag.* On the dedication to Gabriel, see note 7; on the lack of cross-citation in the *De Mag.*, see note 23 below. The works are usually put in the manuscript order *De Mens.*, *De Mag.*, *De Ost.*: see Wünsch's introduction to his edition of the *De Mens.* pp. v-vi (but cf. his comments at vii) and Klotz on Lydos no. 7, in *RE* 26, 1927, column 2211. See also discussion in text preceding n. 38 in chapter 4.

18. After his disastrous association with Phocas in 532, John does not seem to have had close relations with another Praetorian Prefect until the touching scene when Hephaestus honoured him on his retirement (see III 30,4). This recognition, tardy but all the more gratifying for that, may well have coloured John's feelings. Hephaestus certainly seems to have been prominently associated with retrenchments and fund-raising (Bury, vol. 2, p. 358 and *LRE*, p. 296), so John's favourable attitude is otherwise difficult to explain.

19. On the title accruing to a *cornicularius* see III 4,2, and on John's holding of the post and acquisition of the title, see III 25,2 & 30,10. This was a *comitiva primi ordinis* and conferred the clarissimate, i.e. senatorial rank: *LRE*, p. 548. John stresses that he completed his service in 40 years and 4 months (III 30,10). This seems meant to be a significant combination of facts, and represents a remarkable achievement, if the career-pattern reconstructed at Diagram 4 is accurate. On his penury, see III 25,1-6; 30,10; 66,5-6 & 67,5 (John did however receive, upon his retirement, an Order on the Treasury entitling him to a daily allowance of provisions: III 30,4). On his pre-occupations see I 23,3.

20. Dating of (the stages of) composition poses complicated problems. The work was clearly *completed* after retirement in 551 (I 15 (3)-(4); 23,3; III 25,6; 30,10 & 67,5). The error at III 54,5 fits with this assumption: it is an old man's memory slip concerning an incident in his younger days. But John would seem to have been working on I 2,6 in c. 545 A.D., and the length of the work plus its elaborate digressions (e.g. on the dictatorship, the legion and the Caspian Gates) argue for a lengthy production. John states that book III was an afterthought (III 1,1): certainly the structure of its vocabulary is quite different from that of the previous books (see also n. 21). The digressions show something of a development: there are no biographical or autobiographical digressions in book I; these commence in book II and are most frequent (and picturesque) in book III. On the other hand, in regard to non-biographical digressions book III is closer to book I:

I	II	III
23 Roman names	4 the *Limbus* (dress)	25-30 autobiography*
40-41 Roman comic poetry	13-14 Prefect's regalia	32 Rhine and Danube
42 Scorpions	19 the *fasces* (rods)	52-53 Caspian Gates
46-47 The Roman legion	21 John the Cappadocian*	62&65 John the Cappadocian*
	26 Peter the Patrician*	62-63 Pheasants & the *Helops* (a fish)
		64 the *sandyx* (dress)
		72-75 Phocas*

* indicates biographical or autobiographical writing.

However, again, the digressions become more and more oriented to contemporary issues as the work progresses.

Internal evidence from the self-citations suggests the following resolution of these difficulties (see also n. 23). In I, John refers to the *De Mensibus*, has a cross-reference to I and a hazy forward reference (but *no* specific forward refs. to III). In II there are frequent references to the *De Mensibus*, back references to I, numerous cross-references to II, and four forward references (of varying degrees of imprecision). In III there are back references to the *De Mensibus*, (hazily) to I and (clearly) to II, plus a mass of cross-references to III and some very hazily general back references. It looks as though the structure of the work only emerged as John worked on it (e.g. III 11,2 refers forward to III 36-37 as to "the end of the work"). He seems to have worked hard on one book at a time, completing them fairly fully. By the time of writing III, part I was dim in his memory, II much clearer (the pattern of self-citations of II resembles that of III much more than that of I).

21. The spirit of I, 15 (4) and III 25,6-7 & 67,6 is remarkably dissimilar, the former passage breathing benevolence, the latter pair of passages full of acrimony. Though inconsistency is not involved (the former concerns colleagues — on whom see III 30,10 — the latter conditions of service), the iron seems to have entered more deeply into John's soul by the time of writing III (cf. the relatively mild I 23,3). See previous note and Chapter 5 on John's picture of the bureaucracy, and cf. R. Wünsch, *Ioannis Lydi de Magistratibus Populi Romani*, Teubner, 1903, p. viii.

22. Striking evidence of this is the duplicated passage II 10-12 & III 40-42. Faulty cross-referencing further substantiates: see Wünsch's comments *(Ioannis Lydi De Magistratibus Populi Romani)* to III 3,6; 7,6; 8,7 & 9,8. The same legislation is attributed to Theodosius I (II ii (4)) and Arcadius (III 41,3); and, quoting Junius' "direct words," John reproduces a passage claiming Junius as its authority (I 24,4; cf. *Pref.* 6). "Palestine" occurs instead of Palaeste at III 46,8; like the anachronism at III 54,5, such slips should have been removed by a final editing.

23. John's habit is to refer back to earlier work and (less frequently) forward to work about to be commenced. The sequence of composition: *De Mens.*, then *De Mag.* I, II and finally III, is clearly borne out by such self citations. But the *De Ost.* is nowhere cited in the *De Mag.*, even when a cross-reference might well have been expected (as at *De Mag.* III 50,2). Clearly, however, *De Ost.* was written just after *De Mens.* (cf. note 17 above), and *De Mens.* so long before *De Mag.* that John had no idea that he was going to write the latter work (the *De Mens.* has no forward references to the *De Mag.*). The most economical explanation of this anomaly is that John published the *De Ost.* when he had nothing to lose from official disfavour (i.e. when his career was in ruins) and tried not to draw attention to it when thereafter he was unexpectedly returned to official favour (even in retirement he would have his little pension to lose if he fell from grace, presumably).

24. Wünsch dates the *De Mag.* somewhere between 554 and (before) 565: *op. cit.* pp. vi-vii. W. Ensslin moved it back to *after* 565 (*Phil. Wochenschrift* 62, 1942, 452-4), only to have F. Dölger bring it forward to "before 554" (*ibid.* 667-9). Certainty is unattainable in such a semantic morass, but the balance of probabilities seems to favour dating it to before 554.

Chapter 2
John's Picture of the World Around Him

If one is going to look at the pictures inside a man's head, one had better look for something that he thought of pictorially. This means his geographical environment. Let us look and see what areas John thought about most in writing the *De Magistratibus*, what specific places he noticed (and what, in these, drew his attention), and where the gaps and fuzzy bits are. True, he is not writing a geographic treatise, but he *does* have a lot to say about the world around him (some 390 references are involved), sometimes going out of his way to do so. There is ample evidence to show the whereabouts, from his viewpoint, of the blind spots and of the prominent places.

John's frame of reference was formed by Ptolemy, if internal evidence from citations is anything to go by: he cites him three times in the *De Mens.*, twice giving the titles of specific works; cites him again three times in the *De Ost.*, and once in the *De Mag.* The other geographers whom he might have mentioned, Strabo and Pausanias, are nowhere mentioned. John should, therefore, think of his world in terms of Ptolemy's map. The question is: what parts of or places on it were salient for John? In order to let such details emerge, all John's geographical references, divided up according as they refer to peoples and places in one or the other of three periods of time, have been plotted on to three identical base maps. We thus have maps for each of the following periods:

(a) prior to the Dominate (285 A.D.); called the "Classical Map" (Map 1);

(b) under the Dominate up to Justinian (518 A.D.); called the "Map of the Dominate" (Map 2);

(c) of contemporary times (519-550's); called the "Contemporary Map" (Map 3).

So that it will be easier to see how the details mass into patterns, heaviness of shading has been employed to indicate areas in which John shows most interest; light hatching indicates notice in passing, and

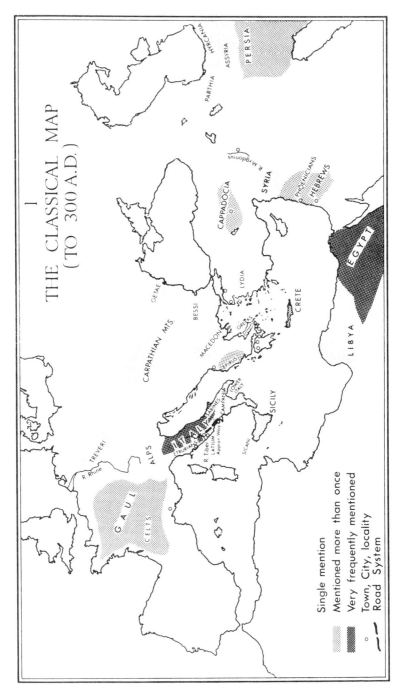

1

THE CLASSICAL MAP
(TO 300 A.D.)

PERSIA

HYRCANIA

ASSYRIA

PARTHIA

R. Mygdonius

CAPPADOCIA

SYRIA

PHOENICIANS

HEBREWS

EGYPT

LYDIA

CRETE

LIBYA

GETAE

CARPATHIAN MTS.

BESSI

MACEDON

GREEKS

EPIRUS

LOWER ITALY

CAMPANIA

SICILY

SABINES

ETRURIANS

LATIUM

R. Tiber

Appian Way

SICANI

ITALY

ALPS

TREVERI

R. Rhine

GAUL

CELTS

Single mention

Mentioned more than once

Very frequently mentioned

Town, City, locality

Road   System

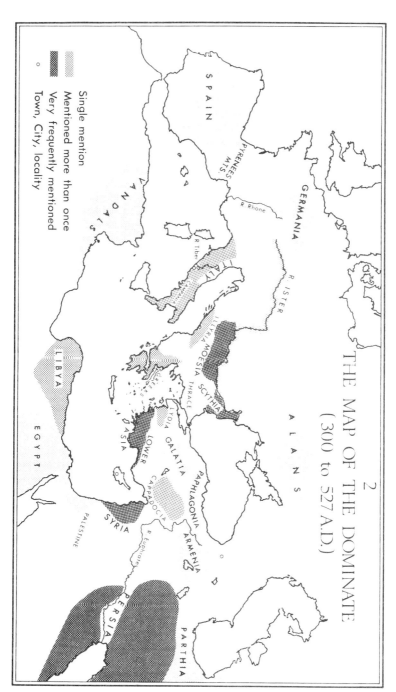

THE MAP OF THE DOMINATE
(300 to 527 A.D.)

Single mention
Mentioned more than once
Very frequently mentioned
Town, City, locality

SPAIN
PYRENEES MTS.
GERMANIA
R Rhone
VANDALS
R. Tiber
R. ISTER
ILLYRIA
MOESIA
SCYTHIA
THRACE
ALANS
LIBYA
LYDIA
GALATIA
PAPHLAGONIA
EGYPT
ASIA
LOWER
CAPPADOCIA
ARMENIA
SYRIA
PALESTINE
R. Euphrates
PERSIA
PARTHIA

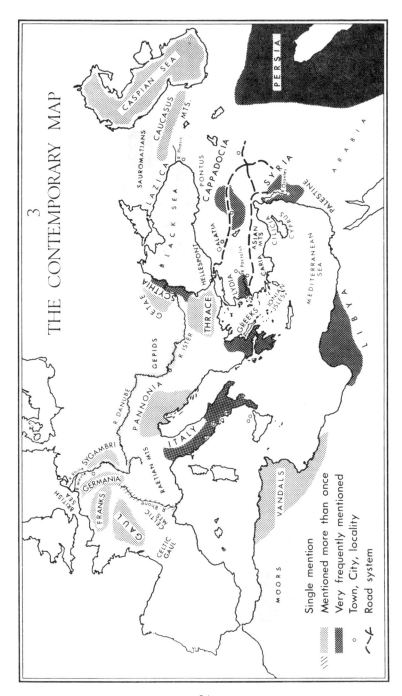

THE CONTEMPORARY MAP

3

PERSIA

CASPIAN SEA

SAUROMATIANS

CAUCASUS

LAZICA

MTS.

R Phasis

PONTUS

CAPPADOCIA

SYRIA

Orontes

PALESTINE

ARABIA

BLACK SEA

GALATIA

CARIA

ASIAN
MTS

CILICIA

CYPRUS

SCYTHIA

GETAE

HELLESPONT

LYDIA

R Pactolus

GREEKS

IONIAN
ISLES

MEDITERRANEAN
SEA

THRACE

GEPIDS

R ISTER

LIBYA

PANNONIA

R DANUBE

ITALY

RAETIAN MTS

VANDALS

SYGAMBRI

R Rhine

GERMANIA

CELTIC MTS

FRANKS

R Rhone

GAUL

BRITISH
SEA

CELTIC
GAUL

MOORS

Single mention

Mentioned more than once

Very frequently mentioned

o   Town, City, locality

Road system

blank spaces indicate that no reference at all has been made.[1] These maps reflect the preoccupations of their times. John is making references to crucial issues across the flow of years and is thus merely reporting, rather than consciously selecting his data, when he gives the background to these events. Thus what was important to the writers of their times appears through the intermediacy of John.

Judging by where the thickest clusters of details are, in the Classical Map John's attention has focussed on Italy, Mainland Greece, the Eastern Mediterranean and Persia, in that order. In the Map of the Dominate he focussed on the Eastern Mediterranean, Persia, the Balkans and Italy. In the Contemporary Map he focussed on Asia Minor, the Balkans, the Caucasus and the Franks in that order. Dissimilarities that strike one are that Italy is seen as a regionally differentiated complex *only* in the Classical Map; in the Map of the Dominate Mainland Greece drops out and no islands are visible; in the Contemporary Map Italy is seen only in overall terms as a unit, the North African coast looms into view, Egypt drops out and the seas (Black, British and Caspian) and islands emerge to prominence. The Classical Map concentrates on the Mediterranean seaboard, a civilized complex dominated by towns. In the other two attention moves outwards to the west, north and east, and rivers, natural features of the landscape and mountains become the dominant reference points. The Balkans, Asia Minor and the Caucasus are seen accurately and in detail; Gaul is largely but erroneously visible; Spain and Britain are invisible. The Crimea nowhere appears.[2] Only two bishops are mentioned and these in such a way as to indicate that John did not think, primarily at least, of the territorial organization of the Church. Nor does he appear to think predominantly in terms of commercial interests; rather, this is a strategist's map.[3]

Think back, if you will, to the areas on which John's attention focussed. Supposing you were to draw *in heavy outline* a map of those regions, indicating the most salient areas by the heaviest shading. You would find yourself with a Classical Map that looked from Italy towards the Eastern Mediterranean; with a Map of the Dominate that looked from the Eastern Mediterranean towards Persia and towards the Balkans, then towards Italy. But the Contemporary Map would look, from Asia Minor, first at the Balkans, then at the Caucasus, then at the Franks — i.e. the Mediterranean would cease to be the centre of attention.

But maybe readers may be dissatisfied with such an impressionistic

TABLE 2.1

Number of Times Features in Each Area are Mentioned

AREA	CLASSICAL MAP	MAP OF THE DOMINATE	CONTEM- PORARY MAP	TOTALS
North	3	15	12	30
South	17	9	31	57
East	16	38	61	115
West	6	4	21	31
Mediterranean	87	22	48	157
TOTALS	129	88	173	390

survey, and would prefer substantiation of the above impressions by some form of quantification of the evidence. One can simply count numbers of mentions of places, as in Table 2.1. The snag is that many places (e.g. Rome, Constantinople and Italy) will occur again and again with relatively little geographic significance — as opposed, say, to a mention of the Caspian Gates; an administrator thinks in terms of his administrative centres. So one can also count specific places mentioned as in Table 2.2. The frequency count will give us John's relative emphases, whereas the count of specific *places* mentioned will indicate striking features in his environment. Let us break the "world" down into *the ancients'* North, South, East, West and Mediterranean[4] areas. We can now compare these, from Map to Map, firstly in terms of sheer numbers of references, and secondly in terms of towns, tribes, rivers, mountains etc. allocated to each.

Actually the two lots of resulting statistics correlate, to a large extent (Table 2.3). In the Classical Map the *oecumene* (the settled, civilized world of cities) dominates, engrossing the largest bulk of references and of specific places singled out for mention, in the pattern: Mediterranean, E, S, W, N.[5] And the *oecumene* so dominates John's thought-world that, in overall terms, this is the pattern of priorities *if you go by sheer bulk of references*. In the Map of the Dominate, again, parallel patterns emerge, whether you rank by simple bulk of references

TABLE 2.2
Number of specific items cited in each area

Map I		Roads	Districts	Countries	Tribes	Towns	Natural Features	Rivers	Mts.	TOTALS
	N				(2)				(1)	3
	S			(3)	(2)	(2)				7
	E		(2)	(4)		(4)		(1)		11
	W			(1)	(1)			(1)	(1)	4
Med.—		(1)	(3)	(5)	(5)	(12)	(4)	(1)		31
TOTALS		1	5	13	10	18	4	3	2	56

Map II		Roads	Districts	Countries	Tribes	Towns	Natural Features	Rivers	Mts.	TOTALS
	N		(2)	(1)	(1)	(1)		(1)		6
	S			(3)	(1)	(1)				5
	E		(7)	(3)		(1)	(2)	(1)		14
	W			(2)				(1)	(1)	4
Med.—			(1)	(2)	(1)	(3)		(1)		9
TOTALS		0	10	11	3	6	2	4	1	38

Map III		Roads	Districts	Countries	Tribes	Towns	Natural Features	Rivers	Mts.	TOTALS
	N		(3)	(1)	(2)	(1)	(1)	(2)		10
	S		(5)	(2)	(2)	(1)		(1)		9
	E	(1)	(7)	(4)	(1)	(5)	(3)	(3)	(3)	27
	W		(1)	(3)	(1)		(1)	(3)	(2)	11
Med.—			(1)	(1)	(1)	(3)	(3)			9
TOTALS		1	12	14	7	10	8	9	5	66

TABLE 2.3
Relationships of Frequency of Reference to Specific Items Cited
KEY
(See Note 5 in text)

	Frequency of Reference					Specific Items Cited			
Rank- ings	Overall	I	II	III	Rank- ings	Overall	I	II	III
1	Med.	Med.	E	E	1	E	Med.	E	E
2	E	S	Med.	Med.	2	Med.	E	Med.	W
3	S	E	N	S	3	S	S	N	N
4	W	W	S	W	4	W&N	W	S	S&Med.
5	N	N	W	N	5		N	W	

- 27 -

or by individual places mentioned: E, Med., N, S, W. East Rome, that is, was the centre of both literary and historical worlds for John. His writings simply reflect the fact that it is the literary output of this complex that underlies and shapes his focus of attention. The only exceptional pattern comes in the Contemporary Map. Here the mention of *specific places* indicates that the Late Empire is situated in a *new* world (by which is meant field of political forces). There is an entirely new pattern: E, W, N — then South and Mediterranean, on a par and *last*. But the proportions of specific places named on all three maps, when counted as an *overall* total, agree with the pattern of proportions formed by a straight frequency-count of references on the Contemporary Map: E, Med., S, W, N. Contemporary events, that is to say, had led John to single out the places in the news from the rest of his environment, and he had noticed these when they had cropped up at any (time-)point in his work, *if you go by specific places singled out for mention.*

What this means, if you block out the areas mentioned, is a shift of attention upwards, from an oblong strip reaching from Italy and North Africa to Persia (the frame of reference of the first two Maps), to an oblong strip reaching from the Caspian Gates via the Danube to the Meuse (that of the third, the Contemporary Map). This is John's "real" (i.e., not his "literary") world.

A striking fact indicated by comparing these two sets of statistics is the re-emergence of the West into the attention area of John's day: it had dropped out in the Map of the Dominate. The recession from attention of the Mediterranean world is again in evidence when the maps are examined in this less impressionistic way.

Looking at the sorts of things that John's attention focusses on from map to map, a count reveals a shift of attention from the complex (in order of precedence):

TOWNS	to that of:	COUNTRIES
COUNTRIES		DISTRICTS
TRIBES		TOWNS
DISTRICTS		RIVERS

(see Table 2.2, p.27)

You would expect some such focus in an administrator bent on tax-extraction. But, for a *Corps* charged with securing the taxation income for the maintenance of the *Cursus Publicus*, roads come low in the scale of attention. Where, moreover, have the TRIBES gone to? Actually, they are still about, but as properly constituted *countries*, in contemporary times. John's first map is a Map of Rome's Empire. His last is a World Map in which Rome is merely one of many powers.

In a key passage (III 55, 1-56, 2) John tells of what happens when Justinian overestimates the strength of Byzantium: a wave of attacks from all around is triggered off. Not by accident does John repeatedly speak of his state in the metaphorical language of flood and inundation (in fact, the only metaphors in which he thinks of it are those of a ship tossed by a storm), of a tornado, or darkness, rushing down, or of floods pouring over a land.[6] He lives in a beleaguered world. Attacks come out of the Caucasus into Lazica, Armenia and Syria; or out of Persia into the last two areas; from over the Danube come wild-beast-like creatures to dash against Constantinople; the Franks sweep down into Italy, and the Moors come out of the hinterland against the civilized littoral of north Africa. Egypt alone goes unthreatened — and unnoticed, consequently. Equally, Byzantium may attack down from Lazica into the Persian heart-land, or strike from Syria either towards the headwaters of the Tigris or south towards the Euphrates. It all depends on the pressures on any one of the participants, in this harsh strategist's world.

It is a world of *Machtpolitik*. No quarter, or respite, is anticipated for the weaker party. Yet John does not have a concept of nationhood to rally to. He has no consistently used name for the peoples whom we know as Byzantines; the terms "Greek" and "Roman" shift uneasily in his usage when he refers to them.[7] His is in fact a thoroughly uneasy world. He even has two focal points for his loyalties: Constantinople and his home-town and its environs, Philadelphia below Mount Tmolus. The former was a Christian city *par excellence*; the latter seems to have taken a pride in its pagan traditions. The double loyalty cannot have been without its problems of identification for John.[8]

Two final points seem worth mentioning. The first is this. John has a habit of seeing things in clusters: a river, say, with a town upon it and two districts named nearby — all against a blank background. He visualizes the city in which he spent most of his life, Constantinople, in terms of streets and houses oriented against the backdrop of the hills upon which the city is built.[9] This is how he thinks of his home-town Philadelphia.[10] It is also how he thinks of Antioch. Little details like the shadow of the crags reflected in the river simply are not found elsewhere in his topographical references.[11] Now the only road of which he speaks at any length is the imperial highway running across the Anatolian *massif.* He tells of vegetables in the fields beside it, women and children trudging along it, economic disaster when army supply-routes moved away from it.[12] Such trivia are rare in John's work. Moreover he assumes familiarity with regions abutting onto the line of road, as he does of those around his home town, Philadelphia.[13] From map to map a line of towns along or adjacent to the main roads appears and every district through which they pass is mentioned. No comparable lengthy tract of connected detailed knowledge appears elsewhere in the work. It is a fair assumption that John had travelled over this area.

The second and final point is simply this. Although John cites Ptolemy as his geographical mentor, the data John provides will all plot on to Strabo's map. Plotted on to Ptolemy's map they leave much larger blank areas, as well as not fitting into the configurations so readily.[14] It looks as though John is claiming the superior source, whom he ought to have used, while actually employing an inferior but more readily available and useable source. It certainly would not be the only time that he makes such misleading claims about his literary sources. However, this happening suggests what has been suspected by moderns, that Ptolemy's impact may have been as transitory on the Easterners as it was on the Westerners.[15]

FOOTNOTES

1. I must acknowledge my indebtedness to Miss Helen Baker, a student of mine at the University of Sydney in 1964-5, who dated the periods to which the various geographic references related and plotted out place-names and numbers of mentions on to Mercator's Projection. The editions of John's various works contain indices listing place names; that of Wunsch's *De Magistratibus* was used for the maps cited here. The size and detail of the resultant maps were such as to involve difficulties in reproduction in this series and to obscure what was at the focus of John's attention. So I adopted a form of cartography used by K. Lynch (*The Image of the City*, M.I.T. Press, 1960; cf. e.g. pp. 18-21, 69-72, and 85-91) in a somewhat analogous situation. On the methodology underlying this chapter, see my study "Looking for a Writer's Picture of Reality" in *Revue* (Journal of the International Organization for Ancient Languages Analysis by Computer) 2, 1968, pp. 36-81.

2. These findings support contentions that, during the sixth century, there occurred a "ruralization" of towns in general and the irruption of a Slavic "Wedge" in the Balkans that was henceforth to represent "the West" for Constantinople: see G. Ostrogorsky, "The Byzantine Empire in the World of the Seventh Century" in *Dumbarton Oaks Papers* 13, 1951, pp. 1-21, and "Byzantine Cities in the Early Middle Ages," *ibid.*, pp. 45-66.

3. It is the strategically, not economically, important areas that are foremost in salience: one can easily compute invasion routes from these maps, but not trade-lanes; the "invisibility" of Egypt is striking. Professor G. Bagnani suggested that this might be because Justinian had withdrawn it from the Praetorian Prefecture of the East to ease his religious-administrative problems.

4. The "Mediterranean" for the ancients is here taken as Greece, Italy and the Islands. The terms North, South, etc. refer to areas situated to the North, South etc. of this central complex.

5. Key to Table 2.3: "Frequency" means simply the number of times a place is mentioned. "Specific Items" means the number of actual individual *places* mentioned (i.e., 17 mentions of Rome count as 17 units under "Frequency" but only as one under "Specific Items"). The comparison is run as a control on the places mentioned as geographical entities proper as opposed to those mentioned for convenience of reference when e.g. they actually stand for an administrative concept and not a place. "Rankings" — top number of mentions under either of the above categories rates rank 1 in its column for the area so mentioned. Lowest number of mentions rates rank 5, and so on. The columns (I to III) represent the relative rankings of the five areas for each "map" under either category plus (under the heading "Overall") rankings obtained when the overall statistics for all three maps, again under either category, are correlated. This is a configurational analysis: the object is to find patterns (rather than check on individual placements), as in each case the individual area can only be ranked in relation to the other four. Perfect correspondence of patterns is all the more significant as it is unlikely to be merely coincidental.

6. Ship of state metaphor: III 44,1; probably 51,6; 69,2 & 76,1; "as a tornado/darkness falling upon a state": III 33,4 & 34,5; floods and inundation: III 45,1 & 3; 56,1. Once "hamstringing" is used metaphorically: III 46,1. The idea of blind, amoral elemental forces buffeting his state is very prominent in John's imagery.

7. "Hellene" may mean the user of the Greek (rather than the

Latin) tongue: I 2,6 & 11,5; a non-Greek speaker is tacitly equated with a barbarian at I 5,2. "Itali(ans)" may be contemporary dwellers in Italy (I 50,1; II 4, (2); 20,2) as opposed to the "Romans" — who lived there of old (I 3,2), or it may simply mean "speakers of Latin" (II 27,2; III 59,3) — a frequent meaning. "Roman" has a variety of meanings: citizens of the time of the Republic or Empire (respectively I 17,4, and I 12,6 & III 41,3); Latin speakers (I 9,3; 10,1); members of the Empire — as opposed to Persians or barbarians (*Contents* III 13); inhabitants of the city of Rome (I 16,2; 28,5); we in Constantinople, of the contemporary Roman Empire (III 47,4). Conflict of identity shows most clearly at a culture clash: II 1,7 speaks of "the peoples of the East (with Pompey)" versus "the barbarians of the North and West (with Caesar and the big battalions)." In communications terms, the community is not "mobilized" and has no conscious national identity: on the strains involved see Riggs, pp. 157-64, on "Poly-Communalism and Clects," or D. Lerner, *The Passing of Traditional Society*, pp. 68-73 and 96-101.

8. On Constantinople see nn. 29-30, and discussion thereto in text, in chapter 3, " 'Roman History' for John." On his home town and its environs see *De Mag.* III 58, 5-61, 2. But his local patriotism goes further than this: the Tuscans, who instructed the Romans in the arts of kingship, thus helping to establish Rome were, according to John, *Lydians* (*De Mag.* Pref. 1-4); i.e. he claims for his fellow-provincials responsibility for assisting in the foundation of "Holy Rome." On the attachment of the people of Philadelphia to their pagan traditions see *De Mens.* IV, 58 and cf. 2 & 71.

9. III 70, 3-4; cf. 62, 5.

10. The mountain: III 26,1; the buildings: III 59,3 & 7.

11. III 54,3. By contrast, Rome's hills are mentioned as the sites of historically famous incidents (e.g. I 34,8 — the Aventine), without indication of topographical knowledge. The Persian attack on Antioch in 540 seems to have been a traumatic experience for John (*De Ost.*, Pref. 1), suggesting strongly that he was in the city at the time (and withdrew to Cyprus before the threat? cf. *De Mens.* IV, 47).

12. III 61, 7-8 & 70, 1 at the beginning. The only other road mentioned — the Appian Way (I 23,2) — occasions merely a passing literary reference.

13. Ethnic and regional stereotypes are evident: III 46, 7; 49, 2 & 54, 4&6 (Syrians); III 57,2&3; 58,3&6; 61,9; 62,5 (Cappadocians). He mentions the following places or areas: Syria, the Orontes and Antioch;

Cilicia, Cappadocia, Mazaka and Pessinus; Galatia; Chalcedon. He also mentions the Asian Mountains, Caria, Lydia, the Pactolus, Mount Tmolus and Philadelphia. This makes it appear that he was familiar with both of the main lines of road. These have been represented on Map III so that readers can see what is meant. For John's familiarity with the Lydian area see *De Ost.* 53 and *De Mens.* IV, 115.

14. See also n. 5 to chapter 4, "The Literary World of John the Lydian."

15. See H. F. Tozer, *A History of Ancient Geography*, Biblo & Tannen, 1964 reprint, p. 367.

Chapter 3

"Roman History" for John

John's picture of Rome is built around a chronological framework
of which the following are the key stages:

Aeneas' arrival in Italy; .1169 B.C.
the building of Rome; .752 B.C.
the expulsion of the kings; . . . . .509 B.C.
(Consular rule to) the time of Caesar; . . . . .44 A.D.
the time of Constantine; . . . . .331 A.D.
the death of Anastasius. . . . . .555[1] A.D.

There is no sign of awareness of the fact that the abbot Dionysius
Exiguus (who died about 540 A.D.) had, within John's lifetime,
introduced the Christian era as a system of dating. Such a system would
have helped him enormously with his time-reckoning. As things stand,
chronological errors are too well substantiated in the historical details
mentioned by John here, there and everywhere in his writings to be
simply the result of textual corruption.[2] His grasp of Roman history is,
quite simply, imprecise and superficial.

If one plots out all John's references to historical personalities and
events, it emerges strikingly that his is a very patchy awareness of
Rome's history: see Table 3.1. For John the "Late Republic" really
means the first century B.C. (the Gracchi, for example, are not
mentioned), of whose personages the following are named: Marius,
Sulla, Cicero, Verres, Catiline, Pompey, Crassus, Caesar, Lepidus,
Antony, Octavian and the ladies Antistia, Atia, Fulvia and Julia.[3] This
is quite an impressive roll-call, under the circumstances. Of the
Julio-Claudian period are mentioned the Emperors Augustus, Tiberius,
Claudius (and the latter's Admiral Optatus), and Nero (and the latter's
General Corbulo). Of the Flavian period, we find Titus and Domitian
(and the latter's Praetorian Prefect Fuscus). All of the *Eastern*
Emperors of the Dominate are mentioned, with many of their
Praetorian Prefects, Masters of Offices and even, occasionally, consuls.
John's knowledge of this period, clearly, is full and detailed, and his

TABLE 3.1

The Depth of John's Knowledge Concerning
The Various Periods of Rome's History

(John's) Historical Turning Points	SCANTY	FAIR	FULL
Building of Rome		Foundation & Kings	
Expulsion of Kings		Early Republic	
Reign of Caesar	Middle Republic		Late Republic Early Empire (Julio-Claudians)
		Early Empire (Flavians)	
	Middle Empire		
Reign of Constantine			Late Empire = the Dominate (in the *East*)
Death of Anastasius			Contemporary times

assumptions and allusions indicate that he expects his readers to have similar acquaintance with the period. This is one of the (relatively) brightly-lit patches in his picture of Rome's history. The third century A.D. is the least visible period for him, if one wishes to contrast patches of the overall picture which are spotlit and in darkness, as it were.

This patchiness is not a mere by-product of the subject-matter of the *De Magistratibus:* it reappears in the *De Mensibus.* In both works there are four "great" (in the sense "very frequently cited") historical figures: Romulus, Caesar, Augustus and Constantine. These dominate an historical frame of reference which agrees very closely with the periodization John claims to be using. These Great Men also, in John's mind, dominate Rome's history (see Table 3.2). Then comes a much less salient group of secondary and tertiary key-figures. These receive much less frequent mention than the Great Men, but are cited significantly more often than the generality of historical personages (whom John generally does not mention more than once). They are, in chronological order, Tarquin, Brutus, Antony, Nero, Domitian, Trajan, Diocletian and Julian. These are all names which recur with more frequency than chance among the historical personalities repeatedly cited by contemporaries. It looks as though a (text-book) framework of history underlies these uniformities.

Now this is a reasonable division into periods: Regal Rome, Republic, Principate, Dominate and contemporary times. At first blush, however, the saliency of the Late Republic seems odd: "*the* Civil War," for instance, is that between Pompey and Caesar; *the* (Roman) history is, for John, Livy's; and, when he mentions the name Catiline, it is with the caution "the writer, *not* the conspirator."[4] But, as we shall see in chapter 4, this saliency is a function of the salience of the literature which their age produced. However, the key personalities which peg the whole arrangement together do seem a motley lot, at all events if one looks at the secondary and tertiary heroes. Two factors seem to be operating here: a predilection for military heroes[5] — possibly in keeping with the tastes of the time, possibly because John lectured in a military academy — and the distorting effect of seeing history from the viewpoint of how the vested interests of the Praetorian Prefecture were affected.

Looked at from this point of view one rather striking fact emerges. The Praetorian Prefecture, "the first of magistracies," as John habitually terms it,[6] turns out to have originated with Romulus (an improvement on Cassiodorus, who has Joseph as its originator!)[7] The trick is managed by having the *hipparch* (Master of Horse) become the *eparch* (Praetorian Prefect). John assures us that the minor verbal change need not confuse us as to the fact that essentially the same office (changing, naturally, in scope with time) is concerned.[8] He repeatedly urges this contention.[9] He does so because it is vital that he establish a key point: the Prefecture has to have a pedigree stemming from a Republican magistracy, because the magistracies created by the Emperors were held in far, far lower esteem.[10] Hence John's

TABLE 3.2

Priority rankings of historical personages by frequency of mention

	De Mensibus	De Magistratibus†	Overall++	(Overall)
HIGH (over 10 mentions)	Romulus (22) *Caesar** (16) *Augustus* (11)	Caesar (20) Romulus (17) Augustus (16) Constantine (15)	Romulus (39) Caesar (37) Augustus (28) Constantine (22)	CATEGORY I HIGH (over 20 mentions)
MEDIUM (4 to 8 mentions)	*Constantine* (5) *Aeneas* (5) Brutus (4) Tarquin (4) Nerva (4) Trajan (4) Julian (4)	Marius (8) Theodosius II (8) Aeneas (8) Pompey (6) Leo I (6) Brutus (5) Domitian (5) Rufinus (5) Tarquin (4) Sulla (4) Lepidus (4) Theodosius I (4)	Aeneas (14) Brutus (9) Tarquin (8) Domitian (7) Trajan (7)	CATEGORY II MEDIUM (9 to 7 mentions)
LOW (2 or 3 mentions) — Listings are chronological where numbers of mentions are the same	Fabius (2) Antony (2) *Claudius* (2) *Nero* (2) Domitian (2) Hadrian (2) Diocletian (2)	Celer (3) Antony (3) Tiberius (3) Titus (3) Trajan (3) Evander (2) Numa (2) Marcius (Dict.) (2) Nero (2) Fuscus (2) Licinius (2) Diocletian (2) Julian (2) *Zeno* (2)	Nero (6) Julian (6) Antony (5) Diocletian (4)	CATEGORY III LOW (6 to 4 mentions)

† Contemporaries omitted.

++ Only personages mentioned more than once in *both* works are included (e.g. Marius gets 9 mentions, but in the form 1+8, so is not included).

* Italics indicate mentions in the *De Ostentis* (added to overall totals — e.g. Constantine).

N.B. High, Medium and Low are differently computed for the "Overall" than for the "Individual Works" columns.

preoccupation with regal Rome and its mythology.

The following are the Emperors whose reigns, in John's estimation, saw marked changes in the fortunes of the Praetorian Prefecture: Augustus, Domitian, Constantine the Great, Constantius, Valens, Arcadius, Theodosius the Second, Anastasius and Justinian. They are not all heroes (e.g. Domitian), though sometimes it is the Praetorian Prefect himself (e.g. Rufinus) who is cast in the villain's rôle.[11]

From all this it is easy to see where John stands in regard to the Great Men v. Social Forces interpretations of historical causation. John sees personalities rather than issues. Thus the history of early and Republican Rome is seen in terms of kings, dictators, the "rule" of consuls, and tyrants (military adventurers: Marius and Sulla are seen with an insight that has been affected by the events of the third century A.D.).[12] The Senate does not feature as a formative influence — in fact the word *boule* is almost exclusively associated with municipal councils in John's associational field.[13] "The people" are viewed throughout by Count John the Lydian as lower orders in need of direction and correction by their aristocratic betters.[14] The history of the Empire is shaped by individual Emperors or top bureaucrats. John's unconscious assumption of political insignificance on the part of the Senate under the Empire is all the more telling inasmuch as the political activities of the people of the capital in their demes *do* in fact occasionally obtrude upon his attention.[15]

The Great Men are seen in stereotypes: highly simplified in regard to careers or achievements, they often typify qualities — Augustus piety and the modest way of life, Titus gentlemanliness, Trajan feats of arms, Aurelius intellectual brilliance (II 28,3). They are credited with enormous influence: a single Emperor can bring the Empire to the verge of ruin (Zeno) or raise it to affluence immediately therefrom (Anastasius): III 45,1-3. Larger forces work more confusedly behind the scenes. Fortune, who deserted Rome, possibly, with the discontinuance of Latin as the official language (John was a Professor of Latin),[16] occasionally vents her spite on the Empire or on the Prefecture.[17] God seems always to be there to prevent final disaster, however: time and time again he intervenes to save the city to which he has given mighty power.[18] The epithet "god-founded" does not occur in any of John's many comments on Constantinople. But this is merely one amongst many indications of his ambivalence in regard to the claims of Orthodox Christianity. If one considers the similes and metaphors in John's discussions of historical developments, one finds that his imagery is full of the theme of rebuilding — and of the rebuilding a *lesser* dwelling out of the ruins of a more magnificent predecessor. His is a world that is on the defensive and no stranger to adversity. It is also the threatened world of an authoritarian personality.[19]

And his world and the Rome we are accustomed to think of are poles apart. He has to tell his readers, for instance, where Ostia is (after mentioning it in connection with Rome) and *what* the Appian Way is.[20] He refers to a current *Persian* custom to explain a custom of the Early Principate. Persia in fact predominates in his thinking when his thoughts turn to the relationship of the Empire with external powers.[21] This "distance" from the Rome with which we are familiar has two causes. One is sheer lapse of time. Things have got lost in the mists of antiquity or are distorted when seen through the preconceptions of the sixth century A.D.

A good instance of such distortion is John's idea of *clientela*.[22] The development of this body of practices is telescoped. Later practices are assumed to have been the norm throughout. In general, however, John's picture of (for example) the Late Republic and Early Empire is a blurred one. He has a good grasp of the first centuries B.C. and A.D. in outline, and he knows a good deal of facts about them. But, on close inspection, the facts just do not quite fit together correctly. There are lots of minor anachronisms and *minutiae* are rarely correctly integrated.[23]

Secondly, "distance" was also caused by emotional factors. John is a Greek and an easterner, who looks with some disdain on the barbarous Latin West. As he sees it, in the death-throes of the Republic, Caesar and "all the warlike barbarians of the West" mass against a (heroized) Pompey and the civilized peoples of the East.[24] Rome could never have withstood Alexander (*the* hero for any man of Greek culture in antiquity) and, in her heart of hearts, she knew it.[25] John thus dismisses the claims of West Romans to military preeminence. Rome took her legal institutions, her electoral system, and even her satire from the Greeks.[26] John thus strips from Roman literature the only achievements for which Romans regularly claimed *sole* credit. As we have already seen, Rome's pagan tutelary deity — *Fortuna* — had abandoned her, John (and others) believed.[27] Together, these negative stereotypes add up to a thoroughgoing depreciation of the achievement of western Rome.

Perhaps this feeling can be best appreciated by contrasting the sentiments of Cassiodorus, a contemporary western bureaucrat, with those of John in regard to the relative positions of Rome and Constantinople in the two writers' worlds. For Cassiodorus — or his masters — the somewhat hysterical and rather devious inhabitants of Constantinople fail to appreciate the grandeur of Rome and all that is owed her as a centre of *civilitas*. Holy Rome is ever at the centre of his attention, Constantinople somewhat menacingly on its periphery.[28] For John the "blessed" Constantinople, "centre of Empire," "whose streets are lined with gold," "has passed beyond the jealousy of a rival";[29] "Holy Rome," "the elder Rome," "mother of our civilization" has been abandoned by her famed pagan *Fortuna*; Constantinople has far surpassed her, bringing her into obscurity — but Justinian "has preserved for Rome what was Rome's."[30] Constantinople is at the heart of a complex which engrosses John: poor faded Rome is a minor concern, held in reverence but put in her place. She is not important enough to merit *animus*, when he does think of her and her claims.

Finally, on this topic, what of contemporary history? Actually, except insofar as concerned his beloved Prefecture, John does not seem to have been highly politically conscious. There is mention of the Nika Riot,[31] of course, and occasional asides on disturbances caused by the factions.[32] Apparently the plague drew his attention (presumably he had to measure literary skills with Thucydides).[33] Peter the Patrician appears in a remarkably different light to the monster Procopius depicts.[34] John clearly preferred Anastasius, the Emperor of his — and the Prefecture's — balmier days, to Justinian.[35] But Justinian's campaigns receive only their formal meed of attention (and his Spanish conquests are not singled out for comment).[36] This is, in effect, a bureaucrat's thought-world. It is centred upon life in the administrative capital, and so preoccupied with bureaucratic in-fighting that only major outside events register. The intellectual life of the capital, in fact, was far more salient than political events in John's consciousness; and to consideration of this intellectual life we now turn.

FOOTNOTES

1. The schema underlying John's picture of Roman history is given at I 2,1-6. John reckons by time-periods elapsing between events which were turning points in Roman history, thus: "from Aneas' arrival in Italy to the building of the city of Rome, 439 years passed." The best way of showing the shaky foundations upon which John's reconstruction is based is simply to set out the data as John presents them, with a commentary.

Events	Time inter-vening in years	John's dates No.1	No.2	Traditional dates
Arrival of Aeneas		(1227 or) 1205 (or 1191)	1169	1183
Building of Rome	439 or 417	788	752	753
Expulsion of Kings	243	545	509	510
Consular rule until Caesar	466 or 465	80 B.C.	44 B.C.	44
Time of Constantine	375	295 A.D.	331	337
Death of Anastasius	215 or 224	519	555	519
	= 1746 years			

Reckoning no. 1 was achieved by the simple device of counting backwards from the last datable event cited by John and using the traditional date for that event. Reckoning no. 2 was achieved by starting the count from each of the historical turning points in series and trying out John's (various) dates until a combination emerged which produced a relatively close approximation to traditional dating. Only by reckoning from Caesar's assassination can anything resembling a historically accurate set of dates be produced. This, however, produces a date for the death of the Emperor Anastasius which John, as a contemporary, must have known to be wrong. Wünsch (*Ioannis Lydi De Magistratibus*, pp. vi-vii) consequently emends the text slightly. The last stage is thus made to date to the year in which John wrote the *De Mag.* as result of the reading in the emended text.

2. John clearly had difficulties in reconciling the different systems of dating he found in his authorities: see I 38, 8 (two dating systems) and III 17,3 (three). Close scrutiny of I 38, 1-13 will indicate the haziness of his chronological frame of reference. John is frequently guilty of anachronism in regard to details (in book I, see 11,4; 12,1; 17,2; 18,1; 23,2; 34,3; 35,1; 38, 10 & 11; 46,2 and 50,2). He does not seem to have considered this a matter of crucial importance (see I 6,5), so it would be prudent not to blame textual corruption for this or that particular error on his part before we have a *total* plot-out of *all* his chronological assumptions. On Exiguus see L.W. Jones, *An Introduction to Divine and Human Readings by Cassiodorus Senator*, Columbia U.P., 1946, p. 33; the earliest use of the system of dating by the

Christian era occurs in 562 A.D., a fact which adds somewhat to the arguments for dating the composition of the *De Magistratibus* to the 'fifties.

3. For substantiation of the frequencies given in the tables, readers are referred to the *Indices nominum* in editions of John's three works. For the methodology see my article on Content Analysis: "Construing Literature as History," in *Mosaic*, 1 (1), 1967, pp. 22-38.

4. Respectively: I 38,13; 34,2 (where see Wünsch's note); 47,1.

5. This is much more marked than Table 3.2 suggests, as there are e.g. minor digressions on the military activities of Marius, Pompey, Leo I and Zeno.

6. See the description of II 4,3 in the *Contents*; in the body of the text, see II 17,2; 29,1; III 1,1; cf. II 7,2.

7. I 14,2-6. A similar lofty pedigree is claimed for the senior clerical staff of John's office at II 3,8! On Joseph, see Cassiodorus *Variae* VIII 20 (p. 367 in T. Hodgkin, *The Letters of Cassiodorus: being a Condensed Translation of the Variae Epistolae of Magnus Aurelius Cassiodorus Senator, with an Introduction*, London, 1886).

8. On the change of name: I 14,2 & II 6,1; on the functional realities underlying the change of name: II 23,2-3.

9. See I 15,1-(2); and II 13,1; a good instance of special pleading occurs at II 6,1-4.

10. II 27,2.

11. In fact his references to Domitian and Rufinus provide, in a nutshell, the evidence on how the "trained incompetence" of a bureaucratic specialist could distort events by seeing them through its own restricted perspective. See I 49,2 (especially), II 19,3 & 9 and III 22,3 & 23,1 on Domitian; II 10,3; III 7,5; 23,1 & 3 and 40,2 on Rufinus. For the concept "trained incompetence" and its implications, see I. Lewis, "In the Courts of Power," in P.L. Berger (ed.), *The Human Shape of Work*, MacMillan, 1964, p. 138.

12. Personalities rather than issues seen: II 10,3 (actually this is the occasion rather than the cause); III 38,2-5; 61,2-8 & 68,2-5; Marius and Sulla as military adventurers: II 1,1-4.

13. At II 9,2 John explains to his readers "what the Senate was" (!)

14. The classical instance of his punishment orientation is III 70,5; see also I 38,6 & 44,3, and II 30,6. In general, John associates the concept "the people" with others such as "the mass," "the (unlearned) men in the street" and "the subject population." "The people," as he represents it, is either a passive object to be manipulated or else a body

which is up to some nefarious practice or other. In any case, it is not a favorable picture.

15. II 15,2; 29,3; III 70,1-2.

16. There is an allusion here to the "Fortune of the Roman People" which, pagans claimed, had left Rome — hence her troubles — because of the activities of the Christians. On the alleged abandonment, see II 12,2 & 42,2; II 10,2 & III 40,1; and on John's profession in teaching: III 19,1-4 & 73,2.

17. Spite vented on the Empire: III 46,1; on the Prefecture: II 12,1-2. But beneficent activities are asserted: III 45,3 & 55,1.

18. III 69,1; 71,1; 72,2; 76,4 & 9.

19. II 5,1; 7,3; 11,(2); III 41,2. On the background to John's life see Wittfogel, "Total Submission," pp. 149-156 (and compare III 39,2-5 with the latter pages).

20. Ostia: I 20,6; Appian Way: I 23,2. See note 9, and discussion thereto in text, in chapter 4, "The Literary World of John the Lydian."

21. II 3,6; cf. also I 7,1. On the "orientalization" of life in Constantinople, see Barker, *Social and Political Thought in Byzantium*, pp. 32-33. The threat of a Persian attack haunted John's thoughts: see Wachsmuth's ed. of the *De Ostentis*, p. xxxiv. To judge by sheer frequency of mention, the Persians loom larger on John's horizon in the *De Mag.* than do all the "barbarians" put together.

22. I 20,1-7 refers. Another instance of this kind of confusion in regard to social history is this. John is unaware that there is a difference between the Patriciate (a superior caste which monopolised the magistracies in early Rome and later was regarded as the epitome of blue-blooded aristocracy) and the *nobilitas* (men who had held the consulship and their descendants).See I 16, 1&44,3 as contrasted with I 20-1, 4&6.

23. For a classical instance see I 1,2-6.

24. II 1,7; Caesar is conceived as the villain of the piece: cf. I 38,13 & II 2,2-3&7.

25. I 38,9-10. Alexander's *mana* for a man of Greek culture came from the fact that he had conquered the civilized eastern world for men of this culture and left them running it for the next 1,000 years (until after John's day, that is). Hence hero worship. Hence also a *Kulturkampf* as to how Alexander would have measured up to the cream of Roman generals.

26. Respectively: I 34,3; 47, 5-6 & 41,2.

27. See n. 16.

28. All references to Cassiodorus are to his official correspondence as a bureaucrat, the *Variae*, in Hodgkin's edition, *The Letters of Cassiodorus*; citations refer to Cassiodorus' book and letter and Hodgkin's page. On Constantinople and her denizens, see I 16, p. 153; 31, p. 161 & 43, p. 167. For expressions of patriotism for Italy, see I 27, p. 159, VIII 31-33, pp. 378-83 & X 19, p. 431; on Rome: X 18, p. 430; 32, p. 445. See also chapter 6, "Two Contemporary Views of a Traditional Bureaucracy", for further illustration of how the identification of each bureaucrat with the great city in which he worked led to some depreciation of the other city.

29. Respectively: III 26,1; 38,3; 44,3 & II 30,5. Even more indicative of the writer's emotional attachment to his city, however, is his fury and distress at damage done to it, and joy over its further beautification: III 70, 3-71, 1 & 76, 6-9.

30. Respectively: III 22,2 & 55,1 (holy); 28,4 (elder); 1,2 (mother); 40,1 (Fortune); II 30,1-5 (surpassed); III 55,1 (preserved for Rome...).

31. III 70,1-5 & 76,6. It is noteworthy that John's references to contemporary events in the *De Mag.* are, by and large, to a later set of incidents than those referred to in the *De Ost.*, where the striking allusions are to events of the 'teens, and where allusions peter out in dealing with the 'thirties of the sixth century.

32. II 15,2 & 29,3.

33. *Contents* III 16 adumbrates a disquisition on the plague.

34. Contrast II 26,1-5 with Procopius, *Secret History* 16,2-5.

35. Anastasius' name is mentioned 17 times to 12 (specific) mentions of Justinian in the *De Magistratibus*, quite a feat in view of their relative impacts upon the state. In the *De Ostentis* Anastasius merits 3 mentions while Justinian's name does not occur. Though John conforms by giving Justinian his meed of formal eulogy, this does not contain the warm affection which he sometimes bestows on Anastasius: see III 45,3 & 47,3. See F. Cumont, "Lydus et Anastase," *Byzantinische Zeitschrift* 30, 1929/30, pp. 31-35.

36. The relevant passages are: II 24,5 & 28,2-29,1; III 1,2; 28,5; 55,1-56,2 & cf. 54,5.

Chapter 4

The Literary World of John the Lydian

Our subject had the good fortune to receive education at all levels available in the east Rome of the sixth century. He was, we know, a child prodigy in terms of learning; and, as a man, was felt by contemporaries to be unusually widely read, and proficient in both Latin and Greek.[1] Proficiency in Latin was clearly unusual in the literary circles of east Rome, to judge by the exaggerated regard in which John's (very modest) control of the language was held. John is much aware of the literature and thought-world contained in the Hebraic languages, but has to reach them through translations. He is *not* living in a mono-lingual world and is well aware of this.[2]

Primary level education taught John the "3 R's"; secondary level brought the grammarians, and acquaintance with the Latin as well as the Greek literary classics (see Table 4.1). The grammarian's approach was to remain a feature of John's attitude to literature and was possibly reinforced by his training in archival systems as a civil-service clerk.[3] In the major cities facilities for further education were available. Law and philosophy could be studied in Constantinople, for instance, at this level. John chose philosophy. But acquaintance with literature did not end when a man left university and entered the civil bureaucracy. The service traditions encouraged literary endeavours and there was an expectation that a man would continue his reading. The *litterati*, as John's grade of officials were termed, were aptly named. Their lives were passed in a world of books and of literary figures and events. Theirs was a cultivated, studious *milieu*; an abstemious life and dedication to literature were prized.

Let us consider first the readings upon which education at the level of the grammarian was based. For this level, after all, was the highest that was feasible for all but a few wealthy or gifted young men. It provided the common intellectual culture that served as a background to the life of the upper *echelons* of citified society. In Greek, education at the secondary level seems to have centred on "the classics." Both John and a number of contemporaries[4] seem to regard the following as writers whom "every school-boy knows":

Homer*	Sophocles*	Thucydides*	Ptolemy*
(the poet)	Euripides*	(the historian)	(possibly)[5]
	Aristophanes	Diodorus*	
		Plutarch*	
		Arrian*	
		Cassius Dio*	

An asterisk indicates that the author is cited elsewhere in John's writings as well as in the *De Mag.* The following observations seem to be in order. "Homer" seems to have meant the *Iliad* for John and his contemporaries. There are no references to the *Odyssey.* Also there seems to have been something of a tendency to go in for large-scale, general histories at the sixth century equivalent of the high school level.

In Latin there was a similar body of "classics": e.g. *"the"* Latin poet, historian and philosopher are respectively: Vergil,* Livy* and Apuleius* (!) "Vergil" for John seems to have meant the *Aeneid;* the *Eclogues* and *Georgics* are nowhere mentioned. Other writers with whose work familiarity is assumed are:

Horace	Cicero (*Verrines*)
Lucan*	Caesar* (*Gallic Wars*)
Juvenal	Suetonius (*Lives, On Famous Courtesans)*[6]

However, the Greek-reading grammarians and their pupils of east Rome seem to have approached these works through the intermediacy of commentaries: e.g. Aemilius Asper on Sallust and Polemon on Lucan. In fact, in John's case references to Sallust and Lucan could well *all* be at second-hand through such commentaries.[7]

John's grip on Latin is shaky and his claims to have read many Latin writers are misleading, being based on second-hand acquaintance with their work in more general "potted" works.[8] In regard to Vergil, his citations come from books 6, 7 and 8 only of the *Aeneid.* All references to Livy seem to come through an abridgement, possibly in a Greek translation. References to Caesar, Cicero and Horace are fleeting and could well have been at second-hand.[9] As elsewhere in John's work, there is some disingenuousness behind his claims to wide reading in this area. That he could build a reputation for being a great and widely-read Latinist on *his* degree of familiarity with that language and literature shows how little was known of either in the Constantinople of his day. Yet Latin was the official language of the empire and the Latin-

TABLE 4.1
The "Classics" of John's Day:
What every (Eastern) schoolboy read

Greek	*Roman*
Homer *(Iliad)* — "the" poet	Vergil *(Aeneid)* — "the *Latin* poet"
Sophocles	Horace
Euripides	Lucan (in Polemon's commentary)
Aristophanes	Juvenal
Thucydides — "the" historian	Livy—author of "the" history of Rome
Diodorus	Cicero
Plutarch	Caesar
Arrian	Suetonius
Dio Cassius	Apuleius—"the Roman philosopher"
Ptolemy	
Local literary celebrities who also	*Christian religious works seem also*
formed part of the curriculum	*to have been studied*
Poets:	Daniel
Peisander (wrote on Lydia)	The Hebrew prophets
Claudian	Eusebius' History

speaking Justinian tried to extend its use, though apparently with little effect (see note 32).

Several other influences played upon the educational system at this level, predominant among which were ecclesiastical pressures and those of local patriotism. The influence of the Church can perhaps be seen behind John's assumptions that his readers "know all about":

Daniel
The Hebrew prophets
Eusebius' *History*
The poetry of Cyrus (Bishop—but also Praetorian Prefect)[10]

This is all the more striking as John makes rather few references to religious matters for a contemporary (and seems in fact to favor

Monophysitism)[11] and dwells lovingly on the immoral pagan "Greats" (Aristophanes and Apuleius for instance).

Writers from Asia Minor seem to have been included in the syllabus, even if their claims to fame were rather tenuous, out of a kind of local patriotism. John refers to the following such writers:

Claudian (from Paphlagonia)
Peisander (who at least *wrote* on Lydia)
(Possibly) Capito (of Lycia, who translated Eusebius' abridgement of Livy and wrote, under Anastasius, on Lycia and Pamphilia).[12]

This local feeling continued in John as an adult: though he does not generally cite contemporary writers, he *does* cite the Lycian poet Lycophron (who is otherwise unknown).

John was, however, one of the fortunate few who proceeded to the tertiary stage of the educational process. He was to treasure his memories of this stage. For at this level, in Constantinople, he had access to the works of the following philosophers:

Aristotle — who was regularly the prime authority studied.
Plato — who was rather infrequently lectured on, apparently, as *Proclus'* Neoplatonism seems to have been more to the taste of the times.

There were "fashions" in lecturing — Agapius was "all the rage" in John's undergraduate days — and "schools" of philosophical thought were lionized: e.g. Christodorus' wrote up that of the disciples of Proclus.[13]

Service in the bureaucracy, with its great literary traditions, seems further to have provided a species of in-service training. An interest in "The Service" and its traditions was assumed. Specialist monographs written upon its various branches were eagerly read. John mentions the following:

Peter the Patrician: *On the Master of Offices*
Cyrus (Praetorian Prefect): poetry
Ulpian (jurisconsult): *On the Quaestorship.*

Also read were the works of scholar-Emperors Constantine the Great (!) and Julian.

Furthermore, as an official within the judicial branch of the prefecture, John was expected to be familiar with the law. He in fact shows familiarity with both the great law codes — the Theodosian, which was of fifth century compilation, and the Justinianic. The Justinianic Code did not achieve its final form until 534 A.D., so clearly John's legal expertise was acquired while he was in the service. John did not receive formal legal training. Indeed, he may actually have harboured some animosity towards the legal specialists, who had forsaken the prefecture upon its decline, hastening its ruin by so doing.[14] Yet he was expected, as stated, to be familiar with the law. Such familiarity ought, moreover, to have involved not only the law codes themselves, but also the works of the great masters of jurisprudence.

Possibly this was expecting too much, under the circumstances. John clearly knew who some of the great jurisprudents were. He names them, at one place or another between chapters 14 and 50 of book one of the *De Mag.*: Paul, Pomponius, Gaius, Ulpian and Aurelius. But he probably laid claim to an intimacy of acquaintance with such writers which he did not, in reality, possess. He most likely knew of their work only at second-hand through the legal compilations. All of John's references to the jurisprudents can be reconstituted from part of book 1 of the Justinianic *Digests*. References to the jurisprudents are, moreover, confined to book one of the *De Mag.*, occurring nowhere else in John's writings. Gaius and Junius he knew of only at second-hand and four of his quotations from the jurisconsults are inaccurate (a sign, in John, of quotation at second-hand). John in fact cites as "greats" those legal luminaries who had been the favourites for excerpting in constructing the Justinianic compilations.[15] It is a fair presumption that the pressure to save bureaucratic face has outrun John's bibliographical resources in this matter.

Another bibliographical area wherein John was expected to be familiar with the "greats" of its literature involved antiquarianism. Here again John seems to have laid claim to a first-hand acquaintance with Latin writings with which he was in fact only familiar at second-hand. His citations of Nepos and Varro are examples of this; so, in all probability, are those of Capito and Fonteius.[16] Yet Capito, Fonteius and Varro are three of the small group of six writers (Ptolemy, also suspected of being only consulted at second-hand, is another) who are cited in each one of John's surviving works. There was, evidently, great pressure to show that one had read *the* authorities.

It seems in fact to have been expected also that a writer upon a particular topic should have consulted the relevant specialist treatises and monographs in the appropriate subject area. The apparatus of scholarship had been quite well elaborated by this time, and writers were expected to be familiar with it and to use it. Works of this narrow, specialist nature featured very largely in the readings of an expert on a subject, apparently. John seems to have felt that a display of such erudition was called for at important points in his work, in dealing with *cruces* or digressions, for instance.[17] One is left with the impression that these paradings of authorities are largely opportunities for name-dropping, to preserve the author's status as the "most learned" John.

So here we find our subject in the exciting bustle of the literary circles of Constantinople. We get little snapshots of the day-to-day life of such circles: men won fame by their oratory; there was competition to publish and to produce work of eminence (III 76,10). Linguistic skill, especially in Latin, was highly regarded, as, indeed, was scholarship in general.[18] This seems to have led to some competitiveness amongst academics (III 47,1) and to some pretensions, which were challenged on occasion: John remembers with embarrassment a grilling he had himself undergone at the hands of a senior bureaucrat who was an accomplished *litterateur* (II 26, 3-5).

We can even go a little way in exploring the motivations and aspirations which animated these literary circles. For internal evidence gives us some indications of John's aims in writing and of his target audience. The *De Magistratibus* is meant as a thank-offering and tribute to fondly remembered colleagues (I 15(4); cf. III 30,10). It aims to acquaint readers with the (now bygone) glories of what John loyally sees as "the first of offices" (III 1,1) and to excite the proper pity for its decline. An important secondary motive, growing in strength across the work, is to call attention to wrong-doing.[19] Moreover activity and industry were well thought of, and indolence considered a vice, from the point of view of the *litterati* of the Prefecture (II 22,1; cf. III 11,1 & 20,9-10). These are views with which John agrees.[20] He is also motivated by the thought that the book may well bring the immortal fame which contemporary writers strove for (III 76,10; cf. 75,4). It would certainly be welcomed by the reading public who were interested in antiquities (III 9,1; cf. II 19,1 & 26,4-5).

Evidence of the high value put upon literary training by the pre-Justinianic civil bureaucracy is clear. John reminisces yearningly of the good old days, when the *bureau*-chiefs, business completed, resolved *cruces* of word-meaning (John carried the tradition on) for the academics who flocked to them to discuss such points (III 13,4; cf. 11,3). The skills of the *Augustales*, the most accomplished of the *litterati* had been of exhibition winning quality in rhetorical competitions (III 50,2&5). Something like a mandarinate of bureaucratic *litterati* seems to have dominated the literary and academic life of the capital in the latter years of Anastasius' reign.

Internal evidence tells us also something about the library facilities available in Justinian's Constantinople: see Table 4.2. No longer available were: Junius Gracchanus and (probably) Varro —e.g. *Latin* writers of the Republic.[21] Works available then but not now were as follows: Aeschylus' *Etna*, Apuleius' *Erotica*, Arrian's *History of Parthia*, Callimachus' *Aitia*, A. Cornelius Celsus in full, Constantine the Great's *Discourses*, Dicaearchus' *Journey round the World*, Euripides' *Peleus* and *Hypsipyle* (only five of Euripides' plays are in fact ever cited; these two and *The Bacchae*, *Hecuba* and *Helen*), Ephorus' *Histories*, Frontinus' *On the Officium of the Legatus*, Julian's *To the Jews*, Livy's *History of Rome*, Nicanor's *Biography of Alexander*, Peter the Patrician's monograph upon the Master of Offices, Sallust's *Histories*, Suetonius' *On Famous Courtesans* and Ulpian's *On the Officium of the Quaestor*.

Not all of the above works are cited in the *De Magistratibus*, this is a composite list of citations of major writers (or important writers on the apparatus of government) in all of John's surviving works. The list gives no idea of the plethora of minor authors whose works seem to have been available to John. Among these writers Greek is, naturally, much better represented than Latin. As far as Greek literature is concerned there is little sign that texts were going out of existence at the rate at which they were being lost in the contemporary western world. Greek literature was not, in fact, to be confronted with this situation until the advent of Islam and the subsequent Iconoclast controversy.

Many writers have been totally lost: Sinnius Capito, Lepidus, Lycophron and Patron. It was not hitherto known that literary works were produced by these men, unless I am mistaken (see nn. 12 and 29 and text thereto). In other cases, only the writer's *name* survives: for instance, the Catiline whom John describes as "not the conspirator."

A great number of secondary writers (commentators, antiquaries, lexicographers and writers of abridged histories), now lost, were then readily available. There seems in fact to have been a plethora of

TABLE 4.2
Genres of works actually read by John the Lydian

	Encyclopedists & Antiquaries	Commentaries	Bodies of contemporary lit.	Erotica & satire	Historians	Juristic Literature	Lexica	Philosophers	Poets and Playwrights	Specialist Treatises
	4	2	3	6	12	3	4	3	10	11
B.C.										
VIII-VII									Homer & Hesiod	
VI									Peisander, Sophocles, Euripides	
V					Thucydides					
IV								Plato, Aristotle	Aristophanes	
II	[Cato the Elder]				Castor					
I	[Varro]				Diodorus, Caesar, [Sallust]		Philoxenus		Vergil	
A.D.										
I	Celsus			Persius	[Livy]			Philo	[Lucan]	
II		Polemon, ?Aemilius		Apuleius, Juvenal	Arrian, Plutarch, [Crito]		Herennius, ?Asper, Diogenianus			Apollodorus, Ptolemy, Frontinus
III				Suetonius	Suetonius Cassius Dio [Ulpian]					Paternus, Ulpian, (Constantine the Great), [Fonteius], [Julian]
IV					Eusebius	Codex				
V						Theodosianus Codex		Proclus	Cyrus	
VI		Hephaestus	Justinian	Epigrams, (Lycophron)		Justinianus			Claudian	Peter the Patrician, (Christodorus), (Agapius)

KEY: [ ] Possibly at second hand   ( ) Probably best in this column   ? Not datable: assigned to complete list of citations treatises to hand, and this may have induced "specialists" to claim a wider bibliography than in fact was theirs (see nn. 8, 33 & 34 and discussion thereto in text). The works of "famous" men, such as, for instance, Cyrus, Praetorian Prefect and Bishop, cited by Evagrius, John's contemporary, also seem to have had a high survival potential. Of the "classical" authors, now-vanished playwrights may well have been to hand: Cratinus, Eupolis etc.[22] As the list above indicates, works which have since been lost, by writers still represented by surviving works, were available in the sixth century A.D. Abridged histories and collections (of epigrams as of jurisprudence) were pushing the classics into oblivion, however. The Latin classics were probably not over-readily available, as has been suggested.

Internal evidence also tells us something of the literary tastes of the readership of the time, by indicating what was the sort of thing that was expected in the work of this particular *genre*. A number of striking digressions, in this and in other comparable works, identify these as a taste for the exotic and for a sardonic kind of humour. The following, for instance, is a list of such digressions in the *De Mag.*

There is one on exotic fish; this also occurs in Cassiodorus *Variae* I, 35.

Another concerns table delicacies, for example the pheasant, also mentioned by Agathias.[23]

Another involves exotic places, such as the Caspian Gates.

A prominent feature of the work is epigram-collecting: John's quotations of famous verses anonymously circulated and of notorious lampoons, which he obviously "collected," foreshadows Agathias' collection in 570. The latter was to form the basis of the Palatine Anthology which has come down to us (see n. 32). There must have been a vogue for such collections.

A similarity in historical points touched on and in illustrations (for instance the repeated use of the case of Sardanapallus), indicates that one text-book history of the Late Empire underlies much of the writings which have survived. Probably this was a school book in use at secondary level.[24]

Also, the society for which John was writing had an avid, if *dilettante*, interest in military matters. John was obviously expected to make numerous allusions to military treatises. They are, oddly enough, the most frequently cited type of specialist monograph in this work, which after all concerns the *civilian* bureaucracy.[25] He never fails to develop an allusion which had a bearing on military matters. Presumably Justinian's conquests had aroused a warlike fervour in the citizenry. Maybe, however, John could not refrain from displaying the bibliography and virtuosity acquired in the course of writing his (now lost) *History of Justinian's Persian War.*

Such, then, were the external literary influences which exercised their formative influence upon John's mind — the various levels of the contemporary system of education, the behavioral code of a bookish bureaucracy, the aims and pretensions current in the literary circles in which he moved, the library resources available and the push and pull of literary fashions. Let us look to see how that mind made use of this sophisticated and highly literate *milieu*, to see just what was the intellectual furniture, as it were, with which John equipped himself.

A simple catalogue of all the authors whom he quotes anywhere in his surviving works, arranged by *genre* and date of composition (Table 4.3), gives a frame of reference. These are the works which he could have read. It is a relatively simple matter to distinguish, among these, between those writers whom he cites with every indication of familiarity and those whom he seems to know of only at second-hand. In the first case one has to deal with quotations of a writer's actual words, or of titles of his works; with allusions indicative of an expected shared knowledge in the reader; with frequent references, in more than one of John's works; with writers also quoted by other contemporaries; or with combinations of several of these characteristics. In the latter case one occasionally meets with an admission that the work was not available at first-hand to John: at other times quotations involve errors or anachronisms which make it impossible that he had the source before him when he quoted from it; then there are vague or very unspecific citations, or isolated citations; and, again, combinations of these characteristics appear. In this way one can select out another catalogue, arranged as the first one had been but containing only such works as internal evidence suggests to have actually been read (Table 4.4). The second table will enable some cross-comparisons to be run.

Even if one distinguishes between the works which John claims to have read and those which he probably did read (Tables 4.3 and 4.4 respectively marshall the details), it is the writers whom we would consider secondary or derivative that loom largest in either bibliography. If one counts names dropped — that is to say, the reading that John's "ideal" reader ought to have been familiar with — the second

TABLE 4.3 (Part 1)
Names dropped: centuries B.C.

Century	8th	7th	6th	5th	4th	3rd	2nd	1st
GREEKS	Homer	Hesiod	?Peisander (Heraclea)	Eupolis, Cratinus Aristophanes (Acharnians, Frogs) Euripides (Peleus, Bacchae, Hecuba) Sophocles (Ajax) Sophron (literary mimes) Thucydides (History, book 1)	Aristotle (History of Animals) ? Patron (Military treatise) Plato Rhinthon (comic poet)	[Aristaeus] Aristophanes of Byzantium (Or. Fish) Blaesus (comic poet) Sciras (comic poet)	Castor (Chronica)	[Aristaeus] Diodorus (World History) Philoxenus (Lexicon)
ROMANS							Cato the Elder M. Junius Gracchanus (De Potestatibus) Lucilius Titinius (comic poet)	Caesar (Gallic War) Cicero (Against Verres, actio 2) Sallust (Histories) Sinnius Capito Horace Decimus Laberius (poet — on acipenser) Lepidus (On Priesthoods) Cornelius Nepos (on the acipenser) L. Cornelius Sisenna (Histories) M. Terentius Varro (Antiquities) Vergil (Aeneid, books 6 to 8)

TOTALS

	8th	7th	6th	5th	4th	3rd	2nd	1st	
Greek:	1	1	1	5	4	[6]	1	[2]	= 21
Roman:	–	–	–	–	–	–	4	11	= 15
Overall:	1	1	1	5	4	[6]	5	13	= 36

TABLE 4.3 (Part 2)
Names dropped: centuries A.D.

Century	1st	2nd	3rd	4th	5th	6th
G R E E K S	Herennius Byblus (lexicographer) Onasander (On Strategy) Plutarch (Pompey)	Philon Aelian (On Tactics) Aeneas (On Tactics) Apollodorus of Damascus (On Sieges) Arrian (The March up Country; Hist. of Parthia) Athenaeus (Sages at Banquet) Marcus Aurelius Crito (On the Getae) Diogenianus (Lexicon) Polemon (commentator on literary texts) Ptolemy	Africanus (Chronicon) Cassius Dio (History of Rome)	Eusebius (Chronicon) Julian (Mechanics)	Cyrus (poet, bishop, Praetorian Prefect) Proclus Diadochus	Agapius (philosophy) Christodorus (On Proclus' Disciples) Hephaestus (Decree on John the Lydian) Lycophron (poem on John the Cappadocian) Peter (treatise on the Master of Offices)
R O M A N S	A. Cornelius Celsus (encyclopaedist) Fenestella (History of Rome) ? Livy Lucan Persius Petronius C. Trebatius Testa (jurist) Turnus (satirist)	Apuleius (Erotica) Frontinus (On Strategy) Gaius (On the Law of the Twelve Tables) Juvenal (Satires) Paternus Tarruntenus (jurist: On Military Practice) Paul (jurist) Sextus Pomponius (jurist) Suetonius (Augustus, Courtesans) Ulpian (jurist: On the Office of the Quaestor)	?Q. Samonicus Serenus (On the Getae)	Fonteius Aurelius Arcadius Charisius (legal treatise) Sextus Aurelius Victor (On Famous Men) Vegetius (Military Institutions) Constantine the Great (Discourses)	Theodosian Code Claudian (Encomium on Stilicho)	Justinianic Digests

TOTALS							
Greek:	1	11	3	2	2	6	= 25
Roman:	8	9	2	5	2	1	= 27
Overall:	9	20	5	7	4	7	= 52

TABLE 4.4 (Part 1)
Writers whom John probably had read

Century B.C.	8th	7th	6th	5th	4th	3rd	2nd	1st
G R E E K S								
	Homer	Hesiod						
		------Peisander------						
				------ Aristophanes ------				
				Euripides	Aristotle		Castor	Diodorus
				Sophocles	Plato			Philoxenus
				Thucydides				
R O M A N S								
							[Cato the Elder]	[Caesar]
								[Lepidus]
								[Sallust]
								Vergil
								[Varro]
TOTALS								
Greek:	1	1	1	3	3	0	1	2 = 12
Roman:	0	0	0	0	0	0	[1]	1 [6] = 1 [7]
Overall:	1	1	1	3	3	0	1 [1]	3 [9] = 13 [19]

NOTE: Brackets [ ] mean that John's acquaintance with the bracketed writer was most probably at second-hand. Brackets [ ] around numbers indicate number of authors claimed as read.

TABLE 4.4 (Part 2)
Centuries A.D.

Century	1st	2nd	3rd	4th	5th	6th	
G R E E K S		Herennius Byblius Philo Apollodorus of Damascus Arrian Plutarch [Crito] Diogenianus Polemon Ptolemy	Cassius Dio	Eusebius [Julian]	Proclus Cyrus	Agapius Christodorus Hephaestus Justinian Lycophron Peter	
R O M A N S	Celsus [Livy] Persius [Lucan]	Apuleius Frontinus [Juvenal] Paternus Tarruntenus Suetonius [Ulpian]		[Fonteius] Claudian Constantine the Great [Codex Theodosianus]		Digests	

--- PLUS TWO UNDATABLE IMPERIAL SOURCES: AEMILIUS ASPER & ASPER (THE GRAMMARIAN) ---

TOTALS	1st	2nd	3rd	4th	5th	6th	
Greek:	0	7 [8]	1	1 [2]	2	6	= 17 [19]
Roman:	2 [4]	4 [5]	[1]	1 [2]	1 [2]	1	= 9 + 2 [14] + 2
Overall:	2 [4]	11 [13]	1 [2]	2 [4]	3 [4]	7	= 26 + 2 [31] + 2

NOTE: For brackets [ ] see note opposite — Table 4.4, Part 1.

century A.D. with 20 names comes easily first, followed by the first century B.C. with 13, then the first century A.D. with 9, and the sixth and the fourth centuries A.D. with 7 each. If one counts what John actually *did* read, the second century A.D. with 11 names still tops the list; but it is followed by the sixth century A.D. with 7; and then come the fifth, fourth and first centuries B.C. plus the *fifth* century A.D., *all* as equal third-place holders with 3 apiece.

The different ranking of priorities is caused by the fact that John read with more facility in Greek, so did not read even the later Latin writers whom he "ought" to have read. Thus, when it is a matter merely of name-dropping, Latin authors outnumber Greeks for the first century B.C. (11 to 2) and the first and fourth centuries A.D. (8 to 1 and 5 to 2 respectively). But when it comes to works actually read, Latin authors only outnumber Greeks in the first century A.D., and then by a much smaller margin (2 to 0). The conclusion must be that, for John at any rate, despite his unusual bibliographical assiduity and proficiency in Latin, only the Golden Age of Latin literature edged Greek literature aside from predominance at *any* age of writing in either language. Moreover, the prominence of the fifth century A.D. indicates that proximity in time, rather than literary merit or volume of productivity, had become an important factor: older works were probably going out of existence.[26]

"The classics" seem to have been a part of secondary-school existence, not followed up in adult life. Thus, if one considers works cited in every one of John's extant writings to be an indication of the fibre of his literary thought-world, as it were, then none of the works selected by this criterion seems to be one of these school texts. The books which thread through all the written work of his adult years are those of Aristotle, Capito, Fonteius, Proclus, Ptolemy (on whom see note 5), and Varro. Now, of these, four — Capito, Fonteius, Ptolemy and Varro — were probably only "read" by John at second-hand. They are cited frequently because they are often apposite, and were, bibliographically speaking, expected, given the nature of his work. The remaining two authors, with whose works John repeatedly shows signs of great familiarity, date to his lovingly remembered years of university study. John's literary furniture, so to speak, was largely made up of recent, rather than antique, pieces. But, though he employed (besides the more recent specialist monographs) abridged histories and encyclo-pedists, it would seem that the thing to do was to claim acquaintance with the "classics" on which they were based. In spite of this literary convention, however, the evidence suggests that the period which was most read by and influential with the literary world of John's day was that of the Early Empire (Augustus to the Antonines, especially the latter), that is to say, the Silver Age of Latin literature. The Classical and Hellenistic Ages came next in importance, and that of the Dominate and contemporary times third (see Table 4.5). But the Silver Age of Roman literature markedly shaped both the writers who followed it, and John's understanding of the Rome which had preceded it. And, although this results in his having a very blurry picture of Rome, his picture of Greece is even more blurry yet.[27] Fundamentally this is a fault caused by the dominant influence of the Silver Age Latin literature, which played such a prominent part in the makeup of John's bibliography.

This plethora of bibliographical and literary information which can be reconstituted from John's work can thus tell us a good deal, obviously, about both John and his times. But it can also render a further service. For it contains amid its multitudinous details some hitherto little noticed facts about the literature of the Graeco-Roman Great Tradition. Here are the new things which John has to tell us. They are listed in point form for the sake of brevity and clarity.

Aemilius Asper wrote a commentary on Sallust (as well as on Terence and Vergil): III 8,4.

Castor *did* in fact write a great chronological work: III 70,3.

Christodorus the poet wrote a treatise on Neoplatonism concerning Proclus' disciples: III 26,3.

Crito now becomes datable: a contemporary of Trajan's, who wrote on his wars: III 28,2.

Fenestella wrote *not* from the Punic Wars but from the Founding of Rome: both events referred to (at I 24,4 and III 74,1) *antedate* the Carthaginian Wars.

Content analysis of Fonteius' *Tonitruale* indicates fourth century preoccupations: new occurrences of diseases (*De Mens.* 40B) and loss of areas in the East to barbarians (*De Mens.* 40C) from the *basileia* or Roman empire; the Roman peace troubled by disputes over dogma, and military insurrections originating in the West (*De Mens.* 39B). This confirms the case for a late date, and would make him a fourth century writer on Roman antiquities and on divination from omens.[28]

Lepidus wrote a treatise on the priesthoods: I 17,5.[29]

Lycophron, a Lydian poet contemporary with John, wrote an

TABLE 4.5
Number of authorities cited — by time periods

Periods	Comments	Relative rankings	Absolute numbers
Pre-classical	Bottom	10	2
Classical	Equal 4th level of popularity	5	7
Hellenistic	Next to top	2	18 < 11
Republican	With next to top	*(2)	11
Augustan	High, for its shortness	(7)	6
Early Empire	Low, for its length	7	31 < 6
Antonines	Top	1	19
Middle Empire	Next to bottom	9	5
Dominate	Third level of popularity	4	10
Contemporary	Equal 4th level	5	17 < 7

*Brackets indicate that more "possibly at second-hand" authors are involved, so ranking is 2, (2) [=3], 4.

Boxes indicate major literary periods.

---

attack on John the Cappadocian; this occurred in his *Alexandra*, a work apparently written in iambic trimeters: III 61,1; cf. *De Mens.* IV 6,7.

Patron, possibly the Phocian mercenary commander of Alexander's day, wrote a military treatise: IV 47,1.

Autonius Polemon wrote a *Commentary on Lucan's "Pharsalia"*: III 46,7.

Finally, John's practice of liberally besprinkling his works with literary allusions, self-citations and so on makes him unusually self-revelatory. There is enough internal evidence to enable a modern to deduce a fair amount about John's procedures of composition. As John is so steeped in the literary traditions and conventions of his time, knowledge of his working methods provides an *entrée* into those practised in his day. What is known about him can be cross-compared with the lesser amounts known about various of his contemporaries in regard to working methods of composition. It should thus be possible to assess the shaping influence of the conventions which governed the actual process of getting books written, and which thus, to a certain extent, regulated the contents of those books, in the sixth century A.D. The obvious place to make a start upon such an undertaking is with John's citations, where his literary behaviour is very conspicuous. John's citations come in clusters, not spread evenly throughout his writings (see note 17). Before establishing an important date or launching out upon a digression, John parades his authorities. This would appear to be model practice. Unfortunately, however, it would also appear that conforming to what was ideally desirable led John into some disingenuousness. For it would also appear that a writer was held to be bound to go back to the original first-hand authorities in such bibliographies. For Roman antiquities this meant Varro. So John cites Varro in such a way as not to make it at all evident that he in fact had only consulted the latter's works at second hand. Even if one tests John's references to Varro using the variety of criteria indicated in the discussion above on the construction of Table 4.4,[30] it still appears as though John was familiar with his work. Yet he at one point admits to never having seen one of Varro's major works.[31]

Moderns have been led by such disingenuousness into assuming that contemporary academic standards in the sixth century led John into making pretentious bibliographical claims. He laid claim, that is, to having read originals which were actually only known to him through references in secondary sources. The matter is not quite so simple however. For instance, a quotation which simply gives a snatch of phrase from an unacknowledged source indicates the utmost familiarity with that source, both in John and in his audience.[32] In such a case John is not pasting on a snippet culled from a secondary source, but making an allusion which he expects to be so readily identifiable by his readers that it would be *gauche* to identify it for them. This indicates that those readers were themselves very well read. Moreover John's digressions have all the appearances of being elaborately written prize essays for which place had subsequently been found within the body of works to which they were only marginally relevant. The topics involved were, as has been indicated above, much to the tastes of the times. John, as an eminent *litteratus*, subscribed both to the tastes and to the literary competitions of the times. The bibliography could thus have been as well prepared as the essay-digression. John can on occasion, moreover, be very modest in regard to references to writers with whom he was extensively familiar (see notes 13 and 37).

However, all indications are that John's actual reading was much less than his total of bibliographical names dropped: see Tables 4.2 and 4.4. From this it would appear that John does in fact "pad" his actual reading by claiming some of the authorities which he found cited in his reading as having been read.[33] It also appears that John prefers *not* to name compilatory work on which he is drawing, claiming instead the more prestigious readings which the compiler had predigested. John seems to have been at pains to live up to an overgrown reputation: he claims a bibliography which is vastly in excess of his contemporaries' claims.[34]

Self-citation is a marked feature of John's writing and thus would appear to have been allowable by the literary conventions of the day. John's self-citations refer not merely from work to work (e.g. from the *De Magistratibus* back to the *De Mensibus*), but within the one work. From this it appears that the chronology of his works most probably is *De Mensibus*, *De Ostentis* and *De Magistratibus*, and that *De Mag.* III is something of a singleton added to the first two books as an afterthought.[35]

This chronology is borne out by the internal evidence of the background bibliography to John's three works. Six authors, as has been observed, are common to all three works. These we may take as representing either works of seminal significance for John or else basic reference works. Seven authors are common to the thinking which went into the production of the *De Mensibus* and *De Ostentis*: Anaxagoras, Hipparchus, Labeo, the Hebrews, Tages, Thales and Zoroaster. Most of these works are either abstruse or recondite. Only one author, however, links the *De Ostentis* with the *De Magistratibus*, and this is Eusebius, whom every sixth-century schoolboy probably knew. If one thinks of this in terms of a Venn diagram with its overlapping circles, clearly the former two works are much more closely interconnected than the latter pair.

John had quite an apparatus of scholarship to hand. Cross-reference was facilitated by working with membranaceous (*not* papyric) volumes.[36] He had encyclopaedic collections of antiquities to draw on, as well as commentaries, abridged histories, collections of laws and epigrams, *lexica* and an abundance of specialist treatises. For the *De Mag.* his bibliography was largely made up of historians, followed by specialist treatises. Oddly, poets come next. Part of the intellectual furniture of a properly educated man, the poets could often be drawn upon for illustration. And there seems to have been something of a vogue in satiric poetry, to which reference was, accordingly, in order. John obviously had a predilection for philosophy, but he mutes it, largely, in this work.[37]

John's eagerness to cite authorities does not extend to the works of contemporaries, from whom he keeps himself somewhat aloof. After all, an antiquarian might well with propriety concern himself primarily with the older writers who were contemporary to the events with which he dealt. This does not mean that he does not conform to the contemporary literary conventions and affectations, merely that he does so tacitly. He seems preoccupied with maintaining his high reputation as a scholar. And to do this he has to conform carefully to the literary and academic conventions of his day. In so doing he has, as indicated above, given us an outline of what they were like.

Possibly Barker's point is worth re-making in conclusion. In a literary world as preoccupied with "classical" canons of excellence as was this one of John's, the relentless focus on the past meant that John and his like had to think through the forms and concepts of that past when faced with the problems of present-day change.[38] The concept of "Strategic Learning"[39] is immediately relevant: the autocrat presiding over the empire had little to fear from a bureaucracy staffed by men who accepted traditional forms as unquestioningly as this, and whose attention had been so effectively side-tracked from serious thinking about political and social issues. Thus Aristotle, for instance, despite his salience for John, is not thought of as a political thinker.[40] Equally, however, such a bureaucracy could never become "service-oriented"[41] in the modern sense. And it is to its actual orientations that the narrative now turns.

FOOTNOTES

1. See chapter 1, note 2 and discussion thereto in the text.
2. Non-Graeco-Roman languages mentioned in the *De Mag.* are Celtic (I 12,1 & 23,2; II 13,5), Hebraic (I 31,5), Persian (III 52,4), Phoenician (I 12,1 & 23,2), and Thracian (III 32,5). This may not mean much however: all but the Hebraic occur in connection with observations about individual words and may be culled from lexicographers (e.g. Diogenianus: cf. I 17,1 and II 13,6). Still, there is mention of Zoroaster in both other works by John. Hebrew was, clearly, much more salient. John speaks of translators of it (Aristaeus and "in Ptolemy") at I 31,5-6, where he may be referring to the Septuagint and

mentions Daniel. The writings of "the Hebrews" are mentioned in each of John's works (mentioned in the *De Mensibus* are Isaiah (IV, 24), *Psalms* (III, 11) and Leviticus (IV, 53)), and Moses is specifically cited. The influence of the Church may be behind this. Possibly, however, John's sojourn in Syrian Antioch may have something to do with it: see chapter 2, notes 10-12 and text thereto. As a professional translator (from Greek into Latin), John was presumably well aware of the difficulties and value of the art: see III 27,5 and concluding sentence of next note, below.

3. The grammarian's approach can be seen in John's predilection for etymologies, which are often digressive, and in his elaborate and allusive digressions, very much the product of a *litterateur*: see my article "The *Helops:* A Case-study of the Transmission of a piece of (Natural) Scientific Knowledge by the Scholarship of Antiquity," in *Phoenix*, 21, 1967, pp. 46-64. The bureaucracy's archives required a similar type of fine writing, involving word-glosses and high style: III 11,2-3; 13,4; 20,5-9 27,3-5, and 68,3-4.

4. These conclusions are based on a comparison of the authorities cited or used by John, and his contemporaries Evagrius and Procopius; for the *curriculum* in Latin John was compared with Jordanes, a contemporary in the Latin-speaking West. This comprised the sum total of *indexed* editions of contemporaries available to me at the time of making this study. However, even cursory acquaintance with the writings of Cassiodorus confirms the present hypothesis: in the three books on which the content analysis underlying chapter 6 is based, Homer, Ptolemy, Cicero, Horace, and the Church fathers are mentioned (and Plato and Aristotle). The work "*On Divine and Human Readings*" mentions Apuleius, Cicero, Claudian, Eusebius, Homer, Ptolemy and Vergil, as well as Aristotle and Plato. In the Preface (section 4) to the "Human Readings," *the* poets and orators — Latin and Greek — are detailed: they are respectively Vergil and Homer and Cicero and Demosthenes. We have to do with the common culture of the Great Tradition: see Riggs, "Agraria and Industria" in Siffin, *Toward the Comparative Study of Public Administration*, pp. 74-78. When an authority whose use as a school text is probable (see n. 32) is cited by all the writers concerned, it is assumed that the authority was in fact so used, especially if John cites him in works with different subject matter to the present one (indicated by an asterisk).

5. In view of the strong possibility that John, while claiming to use Ptolemy as his authority, actually employed Strabo (see chapter 2, n.

15), it is interesting to observe that *all three* other writers claim to be using Strabo.

However, Ptolemy — otherwise cited only by Jordanes and Cassiodorus — is unique among the Greek authors suggested here as being on the school *curriculum*, inasmuch as he alone (among this group) is cited in *each* of John's works.

6. For substantiation consult the index of authors contained in each of John's three surviving writings. For Apuleius as *the* Roman philosopher, and Suetonius' *On Famous Courtesans*, references which assume considerable familiarity on the part of John's readers with what could be regarded as pornography see II 64,5; and cf. 59,5; 64,1, and 65,2-3, passages which cater to a similar class of reader. But works of a philosophical nature did go under Apuleius' name: see Cassiodorus *"(On Divine and) Human Readings"* III 12.

7. All references contain only fleeting allusions: *Pref.* 3 (Sallust) and III 46,3 & 7 (Lucan — the second citation avowedly at second-hand through Polemon). Klotz (*RE Lydos* no. 7) believes that John read Vergil with Servius' *Commentary* (column 2213) and read a commentator on Horace (column 2214), cited at I 41,3.

8. On John's (small) ability to translate Latin see III 3,1. Klotz is of opinion that John knew Latin words but not their meanings (column 2216); Wachsmuth (p. XXXIX of his edition of the *De Ostentis*) is even harsher, terming him *"homine Latini sermonis misere gnaro"* ("a fellow with a wretched knowledge of Latin"). More recently, however, Rubin (*Das Zeitalter Justinians*, p. 427, n. 386) has indicated that detailed examination of John's etymologisings shows a considerable feel for, and knowledge of, Latin. Both Klotz and Wachsmuth are of the opinion that John does not cite his immediate sources but *their* authorities and that, for all his wide reading, he introduces many errors, when citing, through carelessness and faulty understanding (respectively columns 2212 & 2216 and pp. xxv & xlvi).

9. On Vergil and Horace see n. 7. The references to Livy are unusually vague, suggesting some such intermediacy: I 34,1 & 2 and 35,2 (where see Wünsch's notes). Klotz is of opinion that John owes the reference to Caesar at III 32,1 to Pliny: a general treatise on the subject is mentioned at 32,6 — Sammonicus', which John misdates (see Klotz, column 2216), a sign elsewhere that he is misreporting an unmentioned intermediary source — see n. 16. The aside on Cicero at I 13,2 could well come from a lexicographer.

10. On the influence of the Church on the intellectual life of Constantinople, see Barker, *Social and Political Thought in Byzantium*,

pp. 12-15. I cannot agree with A.H.M. Jones in his contentions (at *LRE* pp. 1005-1007) that Church influence in these matters was slight. The most perfunctory reading of Cassiodorus' *Divine and Human Letters* shows that the Church had e.g. its own historians (see section XVII of *Divine Letters*) who had given a Christian interpretation of history. Saint Augustine had had a marked influence on the school *curriculum*. In terms of organization, the Church was in fact the only section of the community with a specific policy in the educational field. See the comments on Cassiodorus' foundation of the Vivarium, in chapter 6. It is difficult to decide whether John read Cyrus because he had been a Bishop or because he had been Praetorian Prefect, but probably the latter is the case: see II 12,2 (=III 42,2).

11. He speaks highly of the Monophysites Anastasius (III 47,3) and Theodora (III 69,2) and of the (crypto-pagan?) Phocas (III 74—see Bury, *The Later Roman Empire*, vol. 2, pp. 55, and note 2, and 368). He never comments adversely on Julian, though he well might do so at III 52,3 (he has only recently castigated Leo and Zeno for military failures—43,1 and 45,2). Furthermore, he gave a highly sympathetic account of Julian's Persian War and death at *De Mens.* IV, 118. Moreover, passages such as *De Mag.* I 38,10 and III 33,4-34,3 are imbued with an irreligious spirit, and the anecdote at III 59,5-6 hardly redounds to the credit of the Bishop mentioned. In fact, the only two Bishops who are mentioned are both negatively presented, and John approves of the disciplining of Macedonius for his tenacity to Orthodoxy at III 17,3. The contrast with the religious fervour, and religious writers, informing Cassiodorus' equally bureaucratic writings is most striking: see the following chapter, "John's Picture of the Bureaucracy." What is more, John's predilection for omens (openly avowed at *De Ost., Proem.* 1 — not that such avowal is necessary in the writer of a treatise on the subject) was in direct opposition to the teachings of the Church: see Cassiodorus *(Divine and) Secular Letters* VII 4.

12. It is in fact uncertain just who is the Capito mentioned by John. It is unlikely that he is the famous lawyer. The latter is not cited at first hand in the Justinianic *Digests*, which seem to be the source of John's legal knowledge (see notes 14 & 15). In the *Digests* this lawyer is referred to as Ateius in any case. Moreover John never cites him in regard to a point of law. It is also unlikely that John's contemporary is the man in question (the view of *RE*, Capito no. 10, column 1527): as *De Ost., Proem.* 2 & 3 indicates, John really knows very little about this

writer (a point substantiated by the fleeting nature of *all* John's references to Capito), a lack of knowledge which would be out of character if Capito were a contemporary. The case for identification with Sinnius Capito seems the most plausible (against Wachsmuth pp. xxiv-vi, it is easy to assume that John "inferred" that Capito was a priest): a commentator is just the sort of writer who might well appear in the lists of authors cited at *De Mens.* 1,37 (= *De Mag.*, *Pref.* 3) & frag. 6. Citations of Capito are most probably at second hand, in view of the above. Association with Fonteius (in three of the five passages where Capito's name is mentioned) is natural in view of their names, the common ground on which they touch (see n. 28), and John's imperfect acquaintance with either of the two.

13. III 26,2-3. Internal evidence amply bears out John's claims to acquaintance with these writers. Plato, if all three of John's works are considered, is far and away the most frequently cited author, followed by Aristotle. Their works are obviously well known to John, who cites titles and passages from them. Apparently, Plato was rather little known, as John implies (see Barker, *Social and Political Thought in Byzantium*, p. 14). The great accuracy and modesty of John's statement (and the fact that this is the *only* mention of Plato in the *De Magistratibus*) makes one hesitate before impugning others of his bibliographical claims (see also notes 30 & 37). Proclus, like Aristotle, is cited in every one of John's surviving works, a distinction shared with only five other writers (Capito, Eusebius, Fronto, Ptolemy and Varro).

14. He seems in fact to have some knowledge of the legal handbooks, enough to tell when the compilers of the Justinianic Code have omitted something from the Theodosian: II 10,6; III 20,4; 23,3 & 40,5. But as these omissions all concern functions (and consequent powers) lost by the Prefecture, this may mean no more than that John was acquainted with sections of the law relevant to his work. Klotz, in *RE Lydos* no. 7, column 2215, is of opinion that John was acquainted only with the more recent juristic collections of his day; cf. notes 12 & 15. As to John's attitude towards lawyers, see II 16,2-3; 17,1-2; III 66,1-3; cf. 25,4-5. A series of negative or disparaging observations upon lawyers is a marked feature of books II & III of the *De Mag.* There is now no incentive for lawyers to enter the service of the prefecture: III 9,10; though they once thought highly of it, they do not any longer: III 20,9-10. A story is told in terms that redound to the discredit of a lawyer who had headed the *Corps* at II 21,1. Clearly, the presence of leading lawyers at its head made all the difference to the prestige of the

Prefecture: III 50,2. This may explain why John professes such a low opinion of contemporary barristers: III 20,9.

15. John's quotations are as follows:

Lawyer	John's Ref.	Error Present	Passage occurs in Justinianic Compilations at	Use of lawyer by Justinian's compiler's
Aurelius	I 14,2		Dig. I 1,11	✓
Gaius	I 26,2	†(from Pomponius) †(from Pomponius)	Dig. I 2,22,33 Dig. I 2,24	Frequently
Junius	I 24,2 cf. Pref. 6*	†(from Ulpian) †	Dig. I 1,13	✓
Paul	I 50,6-8		Dig. I 1,15	Second most used source
Pom- ponius	I 48(4)		Dig. I 2,34	Third most used source
Ulpian	I 28,1 cf. I 24,6 (Not legal I 48(5) texts as such)		Dig. I 1,13	Most used source

† Slight inaccuracy
* A statement that Junius' work was by now only found in writings of compilers of law codes.

The matrix shows that all John's references to the lawyers can be reconstituted from book I of the *Digests* (actually, from I 1,11-15 & 2,22-34.

16. E.g. at III 63,5 Nepos and another writer of the first century B.C. are cited as authorities for an anecdote concerning the following century (Klotz says that John is using Pliny here without acknowledgement — *RE op. cit.*, column 2214). Varro, the third most frequently cited authority in John's writings, seems to be cited at second hand: see n. 31. Varro was clearly "the" Roman antiquary: see Cassiodorus, *(Divine and) Secular Letters* II 17. On Capito and Fonteius, see note 12.

17. Generally, John's citations of authorities occur in clusters, rather than being sprinkled across his work. For example, of the 35

authors named in book I, 30 are named in two chapters: I 41(13) & 47(17). Likewise, in book III, citations cluster within the digressions: 6 in chap. 25-26; 4 in 32-33; 5 in 63,3-5 (a *crux*) and 3 in 64,3-5. Klotz, however, is of opinion that the roll-call of authors of military treatises at I 47 comes from Vegetius, with an occasional addition by John — *RE op. cit.*, column 2214.

18. See III 20,7; 27,4-5; 29,1-2; 30,4-7; 73,2-7 and Barker, *Social and Political Thought in Byzantium*, pp. 16-17, 42-45 & 49-50.

19. The progression is from the idea of writing an honorific memorial as a tribute to colleagues (I 15(4)), through that of writing an *addendum* on his own *officium* (III 1,1), to that of expressing indignation at the misbehavior of officials (III 39,2-5) and at the failure to recognize his desserts and those of his colleagues by recompensing them with adequate pensions (III 25,6-7; 30,2 & 10 and 67,4-6). The latter is, in fact, the main source of grievance and is a theme foreshadowed earlier in the work (I 23,3).

20. On contemporary values in regard to hard work, see III 76,10 & 51,1-4; John clearly approves of hard workers: II 15,3; 26,3; III 9,5-6; 13,4; 27,5; 47,1 & 55,1.

21. This is specifically stated: *Pref.* 6 & III 74,1 (see further, on Varro, n. 31). However, the disparity between claims and actual bibliography is much greater in Latin than in Greek:
Greek: *Books claimed* — 46. *Books read* — 29.
Latin: *Books claimed* — 42. *Books read* — 12.
Though this is no doubt partly due to John's greater facility in Greek, this must reflect the non-availability of many Latin texts (John *never* comments on the disappearance of a Greek author, for instance). See n. 26.

22. I 41,3 *assumes* knowledge in John's readers of "the characteristics of Cratinus and Euoplis." However, the names do not recur elsewhere in John's works.

23. It is clear that abstemiousness rated high in John's system of values and that excess was anathema to him (contrast II 20,3 & III 72,4-5 with II 21,1-4 and III 62,3-5 & 65, 2-4; see also III 51,1-4) and to the society of his day (cf. II 28,3; I 42,1-43,1 reveals similar value judgements to those in Justinian's *Institutes* I 23,3). Thus his taste for satire in general (Juvenal: I 20,2 & 41,4; Persius: I 19,2; 32(4) & 41,3) may well have been in reaction to some of the extravagances of his day (in particular III 62,3-5 & 65,2-4 mentioned above; he quotes the contemporary satirist Lycophron as criticizing such extravagance: III

61,1), and thus be the expression of a more widely-shared taste (see n. 6, on pornography, for evidence of other shared preoccupations of an authoritarian society).

24. See discussion of Table 3.2 in chapter 3, " 'Roman History' for John."

25. The figures on names of monographs claimed as read show military treatises (10 instances) leading from specialist historical monographs (9) with the omnibus category "commentators and antiquaries" (8) next. However, Klotz is of opinion that the bibliography consisting of authors of military treatises at I 47,1 is all taken, at second hand, from Vegetius: *RE Lydos* no. 7, column 2214.

26. The tables record the following facts:

Pre-Christian writings: *Claimed as read − 52. Actually read − 28.*

Post-Christian writings: *Claimed as read − 51. Actually read − 30.*

I.e. about a third of the earlier works are readily available as opposed to three-fifths of the later works. In the West, John's contemporary Cassiodorus was organizing the copying out of older works because of their rapid decline in availability across the fifth century: see Jones, *An Introduction to the Divine and Human Readings*, pp. 27-28.

27. The Athens of Solon's day is interpreted as though similar in social background to the sixth century A.D. at I 47,4. It would also seem that John imagined that the Twelve Tables and tribal system of Early Rome were derived from (Solonian?) Athens: cf. I 34,2-3 and 47,5-6.

28. A well known *crux*. Wachsmuth reviews the evidence in his edition of the *De Ostentis* (pp. xxvi & xxxix). Actually, apart from the *Tonitruale* (allegedly Fonteius'), John might well know of Fonteius only at second hand: in one case the same passage recurs three times (*De Mens., Frag.* 7; *De Mag.* II 12,1 & 42,1), in another twice (*De Mens.* I 37; *De Mag., Pref.* 3); elsewhere Fonteius is cited amid a list of names (*De Mens.* IV 2; *De Ost., Proem.* 3C), or in conjunction with sources read at second hand but claimed as John's direct authority (IV 80 − Numenius: q.v. Klotz, *RE* 26, 2212).

29. This is the only reference to the work in all of John's writings. It occurs in an aside upon an unusual word, and concerns the Tuscan (i.e. for John, "Lydian") antecedents of Rome, and so has all the hall-marks of being a citation at second-hand. The obvious candidate for identification as author is the *triumvir* Lepidus, the well-known *Pontifex Maximus*, who had ample time to write the subject up in his latter years when he was rusticated by Augustus. This would explain

why this relatively minor historical personage is mentioned so frequently in the *De Mag.* (at I 38,13; II 3,8 & 6,1).

30. I.e. authorities cited more than once in the *De Magistratibus*; authorities also cited in John's other works; authorities from whom titles of works or actual words are quoted (the latter are both rare practices, only 15 writers being in fact quoted verbally). A record has been kept of authors whom John indicates he has knowledge of only at second hand. This provides a cross-check.

31. There is some doubt that John did in fact consult Varro at first hand. Problems are that, while John claims to have seen Varro's *On Divine Affairs* (*De Mens.* IV 2: Wachsmuth, p. xxxii-iii, is dubious), he admits to *not* having seen *On Human Affairs* (*De Mag.* III 74,1; I 2,1 *should* come from this work — yet the passage implies first hand acquaintance with Varro). Actually, the (single) work in question is styled *On Human and Divine Matters Pertaining to Antiquities.* There is anachronism in the claim at *De Mag. Pref.* 3 to acquaintance with Varro: see n. 28. The citation of Varro's *De Imaginibus* (*De Mag.* I 12,1) could well come from the lexicographer mentioned in connection with it (Klotz, in *RE*, column 2213, suggests that the passage comes from the *Commentary* to Vergil — *Aeneid* I 312 — which John uses). The reference to the *De Ling. Lat.* at II 13,6 could well come from a lexicographer. So, although Varro is John's third most frequently cited authority (with 18 references; after Plato and Aristotle, who rate 35 and 19 respectively), and although John mentions the titles of four of his works, the balance of probabilities is against John's having used him at first hand.

32. In such anonymous or allusive quotations, Greek authors massively predominate, indicating how much less familiar contemporaries were with the Latin classics. Writers concerned are Homer (I 30,2; 36,1 & II 7,1 & 3), Hesiod (III 67,1), Thucydides (III 46,3), Aristophanes (III 7,1), Plutarch (III 15,3) and apparently the collection of Greek verse which finally reached modern times as the *Palatine Anthology* (III 18,1 & 56,4; Klotz emphasizes John's interest in oral traditions: see *RE* column 2216). Latins are Livy (possibly: I 34,2 — see Wünsch's note), Vergil (possibly: I 21,3), and the compilers of the Theodosian Code (*Pref.* 6). Some indication of the extent to which even writers who were widely read in the sixth century have not survived occurs in the fact that four other such "as every school-boy knows" allusions cannot be identified: I 43,2; II 10,1; III 59,4 and 69,1. This means that moderns do not even know the names of authors

whose works were then known by heart.

33. A comparison of Tables 4.3 and 4.4 will give an idea of the specific writers and the general amount of disingenuous claims respectively involved. This finding corroborates that of others who have worked on John: see n. 8.

34. Proportions are:

Number of times by which John's alleged bibliography is larger

CONTEMPORARIES	GREEK SOURCES	LATIN SOURCES
Evagrius (Greek)	$3^{2/3}$	19
Jordanes (Latin)	22	3
Procopius (Greek)	$13^{1/2}$	14

But it should be observed that Procopius adopts the reverse practice in source-citation, affecting considerable reticence as to his authorities.

35. See n. 17 in chapter 1 and discussion thereto in the text. Wünsch at p. viii of the Preface to his edition of the *De Mag.* gives his reasons for inferring that the *De Mag.* was initially planned as a two-volume work and that this original plan was later altered to allow for the addition of a third volume sometime afterwards.

36. This seems indicated by III 14,1 (where see note in my translation); moreover, the facility of reference lauded at III 20,4-5 would seem to indicate volumes with pages, rather than rolls.

37. E.g. there are only two mentions of Aristotle and one of Plato in the *De Mag.*, masterly restraint in view of John's familiarity with their works. This is yet another feature of his practice in making bibliographical claims which, as in the case of his honesty in regard to Varro (see n. 31), compels caution in rejecting them (see n. 13).

38. *Social and Political Thought in Byzantium*, pp. 16-24, esp. 17; II 26,5 provides a splendid illustration of the mental blinkers imposed by this type of education and its values. It should be noted, however, that John's bureaucratic jargon had immensely expanded the range of concepts currently available. For instance, the word *pleroma* had developed from its meaning "a filling-up" (e.g. as of a bucket with milk) in Classical Greek through "a filling out" (of a tax-return) in Hellenistic Greek, into "Plenitude of God" in the ecclesiastical jargon of the Church bureaucracy, to become the "last official position which fills up and rounds out a career sequence" in John's writings (III 6,1; 9,1 & 2; 67,5).

39. See Riggs, pp. 149-56.

40. On the side-tracking: see e.g. I 3,5-7 & 6,5-6, classical instances of the Orwellian "double-think." Aristotle's political works are nowhere mentioned by John; they do not seem to have formed part of his studies in Aristotle — and this although he had specialised in him at the equivalent of university level.

41. See Eisenstadt, pp. 285-99, esp. 293-4.

Chapter 5
John's Picture of the Bureaucracy

We are confronted with difficulties of two kinds. First, the wealth of detail and the plethora of issues raised in John's writings mean that one can easily lose sight of the wood unless one tries carefully not to become engrossed in individual trees. So analysis here will be "in-the-big" and confined to a limited number of issues. Secondly, one must be careful not to import into the analysis modern preconceptions of what bureaucracy is or does. I propose to cope with this difficulty by contrasting John's views with those of his contemporaries, in such a way as to highlight how his occupationally conditioned preoccupations cause his impressions to differ from theirs.

Let us start by seeing whether the view looked different from a room at the top of the bureaucratic hierarchy. The official correspondence of the occupant of such a room, Lord Cassiodorus' *Variae*, survive, indicating something of the thought-world of such a high dignitary, a political appointee. John's works, in contrast, are those of a professional clerical officer, who rose by dint of expertise and length of service to a responsible but intermediate position of authority.

At first glance there is a good deal of similarity in the thought-worlds which appear (despite the different *genres* in which these are conveyed). Both complain of overwork and lack of time; both stress the great influence that a Praetorian Prefect could exert over a ruler; both careers end in disillusionment with and alienation from the bureaucracy, and in both there is a withdrawal from "the world."[1] Job-selection of a particular personality type may be behind this. Similar literary pretensions emerge (in topics for and types of digressions).[2]

But these similarities only serve to enhance the latent differences. A Head of a *Corps*, such as the Praetorian Prefecture, for instance, headed up a *series* of different *corps* across his career. His staff served *all* their lives in *one corps*. The Head was a generalist, not a specialist. Though he might have respect for the traditions of a *corps*, he did not identify with it as his staff did. Cassiodorus, for instance, does not lament the decline of the Prefecture from past glories; and he sees to the writing of a history of the Church, not of "his" *Corps*.[3] His reference-group was his fellow-aristocrats, *not* bureaucratic colleagues.[4] His career problems were different, too. First among them was *getting* his job: this was effected by political "pull," not length of service. Second among his problems was that of *running* a *corps*, not securing promotion within Departments. He worries about the loyalty of subordinates and whether commands will be faithfully implemented. In a word, his view of the bureaucracy is *strategical*, whereas John's, a subordinate's, is *tactical*.

Consider the preoccupations of the two writers. John is concerned about *suffragia* (purchase of offices) and *sportulae* (fees) where Cassiodorus worries over speed of promotions for his subordinates and establishing "proper" career patterns. John is concerned that recruits have proper literary background training and advance after showing evidence of expertise. Cassiodorus calculates advancement in terms of relative pedigree strengths. John worries over the pension his job will confer; Cassiodorus uses his job to look after the interests of his local barony.[5] Cassiodorus' world is not bestraddled by giant bureaucrat heroes or villains; it *does* however contain incompetent intermediate-level officials.[6] John constantly refers to inter-departmental or inter-*corps* feuding; Cassiodorus is sensitive only to the envy and detraction emanating from his peer-group. John speaks of the mechanics of tax-extraction; Cassiodorus' pages are concerned repeatedly with legal decisions handed down in test-cases against large estates bent on tax-evasion.

But perhaps the constricted horizons of the underling's world show most clearly in the differing attitudes taken towards the working of the Prefect's court of law. John's attention is engrossed by issues connected with *praescriptio fori*, such as special privileges for his group, the Prefect's Men, before the law; the standing and scope of the Prefect's court, and the amount of lucrative business going through it.[7] It is *the* instrument of power in a world of inter-*corps* feuds. Cassiodorus is concerned that there be respect for "the Law" in principle, for equity in its administration and for moderation rather than strict insistence on the letter of the (tax-extraction) law. For him popular demonstrations of unrest can have *two* sides; he shows something of a spirit of *noblesse oblige*, in contrast to John's exclusively punishment orientation.[8]

Similar differences show up in regard to the two writers' concepts of responsibility. John's is a regulative bureaucracy; Cassiodorus' has *some* service functions. John is oblivious to the cross-pressures of the world of high policy; Cassiodorus thinks in terms of policy problems.[9] He is aware that commerce needs encouragement ("economic" thinking for John is restricted to the presence or absence of taxable subjects), and that timely organization can eliminate food shortages. John, however, is conscious of the unanticipated consequences that can result when the well-intentioned ideas of his superiors are translated into practice. Both writers make suggestions aimed at improving organizational problems. In both cases paper-work is concerned, a consequence of their almost exclusively literary education.[10]

Finally, the two writers differ sharply in their ability to distinguish between the myths and the actuality of contemporary politics. John subscribes uncritically to the official picture (the "greater part" of the West recovered; Rome "rescued" and given her "due"). Cassiodorus, more realistically, knows that, in Goths and Romans, two nations are living in Italy, and that Rome's world and that of Constantinople are *two* quite separate worlds.[11] The room at the top afforded, it thus appears, a clearer overall picture.

Now let us contrast these insiders' pictures with that of someone outside the bureaucracy. Both bureaucrats have their misgivings about their Emperor Justinian and about their times. So for a comparison we should not look to one of Justinian's panegyricists or for a generally euphoric writer. Let us take Procopius' depiction of Justinian and his times, as given in *The Secret History*. This posthumously published indictment certainly cannot be charged with presenting an uncritical depiction! However, it merely strips off the mask worn by the writer in his published works, wherein close examination reveals similar, if muted, disenchantment with the Emperor. Procopius, then, delivered himself freely of his opinions in *The Secret History*. Let us contrast his picture with John's, to see whether any patterns of difference emerge.[12]

The first thing that strikes one is that the writers choose somewhat different parts of Justinian's activities for comment and that, when both comment on the same thing, their relative emphases differ (see Table 5.1). In general, John's attention is preoccupied by changes affecting the bureaucracy: he has over 50 percent more references to changes in this area than to those in all other areas combined. Whereas changes elsewhere receive uniformly adulatory comments — sometimes vague, sometimes specific, in this area John makes fine distinctions — between trends resulting in changes affecting the bureaucracy,

TABLE 5.1

Aspects of Justinian's activities upon which there is comment

Activity	Procopius		John the Lydian
Changes within the bureaucracy	$\overline{36}$	Seen largely in terms of political intrigue involving personalities.	24	Trends seen operating across time; (unanticipated) influence of imperial agents distinguished; adverse (unplanned) side effects seen as such.
Military action	$\overline{33}$	Emphasis on loss of life and money and on scandals involving people in high places.	$\overset{+}{8}$	Generalized references to successes and conquests.
Taxation	$\overline{14}$	From the viewpoint of a landed aristocrat.	1	
Real estate	11		0	John carefully dissociates
Trade	11		0	Justinian from John the
Legislation	5		$\overset{+}{1}$	Cappadocian in comment
Public relief	4		0	upon these matters.
Currency control	3	Error of fact here	0	
The Church	$\overline{9}$		0	
Building activities	$\overline{3}$		$\overset{+}{3}$	
Literature & education	$\overline{3}$		$\overset{+}{3}$	Highly laudatory on specifics, but undercurrent of criticism in generalized references.

KEY: Numbers indicate the number of times the point is discussed.
     + means that discussion is couched in highly favorable terms.
     — means that its terms are most unfavorable.

NOTE: As the source citations upon which this table is based are almost identical with those provided for the similar table in chapter 7, they are not reproduced here.

happenings resulting from the influence of agents, and adverse consequences arising out of side-effects.[13] Such niceties of discrimination are not for Procopius, who emits a uniform howl of execration. Though changes to the bureaucracy engross more of his attention than changes to any other single aspect of imperial affairs, his comments thereupon only comprise just over a quarter (27 percent) of his total comment. Moreover Procopius' comments really wax hottest in connection with the cluster taxation, finances, property holding, and, to a lesser extent, reforms affecting trade; these, as a theme, together net more comments than does the bureaucracy. In John's writings, on the other hand, this theme passes all but unnoticed. In fact John has *no* comments in five areas where Justinian's activities aroused Procopius' ire; these areas involve finances, property holding, trade, public relief and the Church. In terms of relative emphasis evident in these writers' discussions of changes affecting the bureaucracy, Procopius exhibits most heat when he is scandalized by political intrigues involving bureaucrats (over a third of his references). On the other hand John's ire is most apparent when he is discussing changes in the standing of the Prefect's Court of law, of the Prefect's staff, of recruitment patterns or career lines, and of prefectural financial activities. Such matters, in fact, make up over two-thirds of all his references to changes affecting the bureaucracy.

Now Procopius and John are much the same in having a traditionalist's outlook, negatively adjusted to change (see Table 7.2).* The outside world is seen as more sombre, irrational and threatening by Procopius, but this is only a matter of degree. It is therefore surprising to find a very marked difference in their estimates of Justinian's motivation (see Table 7.3).*

For Procopius Justinian is driven by a lust for blood and money, in a passion for novelty and turmoil. Treacherous, unstable, incapable of matching circumstances with appropriate action, in thraldom to a vicious female, Justinian hounds senators, taxpayers, the city poor and the soldiery, favoring the Blue faction, the church and the barbarians. He works with unnatural activity, displaying inhuman abstinence from food and sleep, and is, it is popularly believed, a demon.

---

*The present passage synopsizes a detailed discussion in chapter 7, where this Table, together with its apparatus of source-references, is integrated into that detailed discussion. Hence the forward reference, to avoid repetitiveness.

For John, Justinian is aiming to be a model Emperor, seeking to maintain institutions in decline and to increase efficiency. Ably assisted by his wife, he is benevolent to the lower orders and encourages literature. It is, however, not safe to disregard his wishes. He cannot control *all* aspects of his agents' activities, and some of his measures have had unfortunate and unplanned side-effects. If he is a hard-driving taskmaster, this is only because he expects of others what he expects of himself. There is some empathy behind this picture: John can understand the pressures of work and of frustration involved in getting things done through a bureaucracy. However, one must not make too much of this. John's work is not a posthumous publication, and it must consequently pay lip-service to the official line even if dissatisfaction with that line lurks, easily discoverable, between the lines of John's writings. Still, he can "see" Justinian in a light in which Procopius *cannot* see him.[14]

It is perhaps worth noticing that John appears to know nothing of a collapse of army morale or of undue preoccupation with religious issues on Justinian's part. In the early 'fifties, at any rate, these do not seem to have been serious problems.

Something of the behavioral code of the bureaucracy of John's day emerges from all this. An outline sketch is as follows. First and foremost came devotion to one's *corps* and to one's colleagues.[15] The current Prefect was not necessarily encompassed in this. The office of Praetorian Prefect was distinguished from its incumbent: there were "good" and "bad" Prefects — "good" and "bad" from the viewpoint of the *corps*, that is.[16] There was strong feeling against disciplinary boards.[17] The first loyalty of a *Praefectianus* was to his *corps* and to his Prefect; the Prefect was expected to reciprocate this feeling and to act upon it.[18] Criticism of imperial policy seems to have been rife, though open political opposition was not, apparently, contemplated.[19] Appearances were highly valued; these involved special dress, special verbiage, even special paper and writing-style.[20] Strict protocol was observed on official occasions. There was an "Establishment" within the Department.[21] There was also a code of "proper" behaviour. This involved moderate and abstemious living and devotion to intellectual pursuits; it was firmly set against empire building — in bricks and mortar.[22]

Crucial vested interests are readily identifiable. They involve the maintenance of the system of fees, with which pensioning was inter-connected. This complex of practices had as its consequences pluralism and sinecures.[23] Yet no one item in the complex could be tampered with without disrupting the whole system, around which the lives of John and his friends were adjusted. Consequently, it was with regard to these conditions of service as a frame of reference that they viewed and evaluated developments affecting the bureaucracy. Changes negatively affecting these vested interests were bitterly resented, however salutary such changes might be in regard to other groups or other matters.

The Service was no stranger to hard work, and John places a high value on energy, drive and expertise.[24] His attitude to promotions is that these ought to come, as a reward for merit and service, to the "right" people, i.e. those who have an appropriate background of sound literary training.[25] There is an efficiency oriented professionalism about this section of the bureaucratic code, as it was practised by John and others like him in the middle *echelons*. Good and bad working conditions and practices (e.g. lunch-breaks and archives) were known to be connected with the output of work of quality.[26] A work overload, it was realised, could cripple a Department or *Corps*.[27] But, as against this, John realizes that taking on a workload of wider scope can be strategically desirable in the interests of improved perquisites and conditions of service for the staff, both of the *Corps* in general and of specific Departments within it in particular.[28] It is even realized that some functions are structurally inter-connected, so that inefficiency results from a takeover by another *corps* of part of a work-area.[29] But this is a realization that only occurs to John when his own *corps* is adversely affected by such a development (cf. III 37,3). In the main, he does not seem capable of a strategist's approach to takeovers of this nature.

Beside the self-centred assumption implicit in all this (that staff convenience has first call on administrative arrangements),[30] there are two other key assumptions. One concerns the atmosphere of antagonistic cooperation in which John passed his bureaucratic life. He assumes the omni-presence of a quite ruthless, unintermittent condition of inter-*corps* feuding, in which the chief and, he has reluctantly to confess, the more successful antagonists are "the Master's Men."[31] He also assumes a similar condition of intra-departmental feuding, between the clerical and judicial staffs on the one hand and the accountancy staffs on the other.[32] Again, he has to give the other side best, an admission made with much acrimony. His branch and its Departments had once comprised the most prestigeful section of a *corps* which far outstripped all other *corps* within the civil bureaucracy in standing. Its members had had a *morale* and a self-image commensurate with such preeminent status (see II 9,1-2 & III 13,1-4 for instance). But, by John's time, both branch and *Corps* had fallen far from that former high estate, and there is a sad defeatist spirit about them. The spirit and *morale* of the "Prefect's Men" had, in fact, been broken.

Two assumptions were mentioned. The first has been detailed. The second concerns the public. They are expected to be interested in, respectful towards, and grateful for the regulating services provided by officials such as John (III 9,3 & 18,5). Again, however, it is realized that the relative standings of the various *corps*, and even of branches and Departments within the bureaucracy, are reflected in the respect which they are severally accorded by the public.[33] And John's branch does *not* enjoy the awe and esteem in which it once was held in the "good old days."[34] This is, in fact, not merely the imaginings of an embittered and harassed elderly man. An era was ending. It was the era of the dominance of *Corps*-Heads disposing of semi-autonomous constellations of power. The bureaucracy was not to see their like again.[35]

FOOTNOTES

1. As this part of this section summarizes findings from chapter 6 on "Two Contemporary Views of a Traditional Bureaucracy"*(q.v.)*,it is not proposed to duplicate source evidence cited there. Consequently substantiation is provided only for points additional to those established there. In regard to the "withdrawal from 'the world'," in John's case this took the form of abandoning his judicial functions in favor of teaching; Cassiodorus retired from public life to found a monastery: see Jones, *An Introduction to Divine and Human Readings*, pp. 19-24.

2. The most striking similarities are the digressions on fish (*De Mag.* III 62,5-63,5 and *Var.* I 35), and on "the stage" (*De Mag.* I 40-41; *Var.* I 20); less striking, perhaps, is the theme of the blessings conferred by book-learning on a head of state (*De Mag.* II 28,2 & III 33,3; *Var.* X 3). Etymological digressions abound in both writers and there is the same practice of parading literary authorities in both (*De Mag.* I 47,1 & *Var.* I 45). A key assumption held by both writers is that the activities of a scribe are in themselves of the utmost importance (see *De Mag.* III 11,2-3; 14,1 & 20,5-9 and *On Divine (and Human) Readings* XXX, 1). See also n. 10 on "Strategic Learning."

3. The monk Epiphanius seems in fact to have produced the collation known as "The History of the Church in Three Parts" at the prompting and under the sponsorship of Cassiodorus: see Jones, *An Introduction to Divine and Human Readings*, pp. 28-29.

4. Detailed substantiation can be found in chapter 6, "Two Contemporary Views." This finding emerged by a serendipity effect in the course of the content analysis on which the interpretation of Cassiodorus is based: entries had to be made under the cluster of interrelated headings Nobles, Patriciate, Pedigree, and Senate (for specific remarks on reference groups see *Var.* I 13 & 42) with quite exceptional frequency. For John, in contrast, the key term is *hetairos* ("comrade"); it is used, with great emotional fervour, of fellow-members of his *officium*: see *De Mag.* III 30,12.

5. Again, for details see chapter 6. In overall terms, it is striking that the themes which arouse the most heartfelt emotion in the two writers are quite different. In John's case the theme which arouses far and away the most emotive writing is that of the failure of the state to provide an adequate pension (*De Mag.* III 25,1-7; 29,4-30,2; 30,10; 66,3-67,6). In Cassiodorus' case it is that of his home district which he controlled (*Var.* VIII, 31-33).

6. In general Cassiodorus speaks in terms of the office rather than of individual occupants:

Office	Individuals Mentioned	General Discussion
Praetorian Prefect	1	11
Master of Offices	1	3
Prefect of the City	4	7
Bishops	0	5

"Loyalty" is something one owes a king (only one — *Var.* VIII,17 — or at most two — VIII,18 — references concern "friends and colleagues" out of sixteen references in this connection). His image of the Prefecture is essentially that of a stewardship (*Var.* VIII 20 & X 27). This emphasis is, presumably, inevitable in a writer of official correspondence (rather than a gossipy *memoir*). However, in regard to staff-relationships Cassiodorus' dominant preoccupation seems to be with discipline. Apparently his experience as a Head of a *corps* led him to take a less exalted view of the importance of such Heads than did John, whose view of the world around his *Corps* was largely blotted out by the (for him) towering figure of its Head.

7. This point is fully discussed in chapter 7, "Problems in Effecting

Change in a Traditional Society"; see notes 27 and 31 to 33 and discussion in the text of that chapter.

8. In just this fashion, as was indicated in the biography of John in chapter 1 (n. 4 and discussion thereto in text), Zoticus watched over the local interests of John's home town Philadelphia and its environs. This type of regional particularism should not be seen in romanticized or sentimental terms (it led to the ruin of John's life, for instance): it is a "clect." For the term and its meaning, see Riggs, pp. 164-73 & 274-76.

9. Cassiodorus had administered three different *corps* (as *Quaestor* of the Sacred Palace, Master of Offices, and Praetorian Prefect) under the immediate directions of four different rulers (Theodoric, Amalasuntha, Theodahad and Witigis). John had served in (various Departments of) one *corps* under what was, for the most part, only the remotest direction of three rulers. Effectively, for all but the *primates*, the most senior members of a *corps*, the Head of that *corps* was their lord and master. Hence John's picture of the Emperor Anastasius is a sentimental stereotype, dating as it does to his earliest years of service (511-518). The Emperor Justin barely registered on him — probably Justinian had more influence upon the men of the apparatus even in his uncle's reign. Justinian becomes more salient in John's later, senior career stages; but he is nowhere as vividly seen as are the various prefectural Heads under whom John served at this date. John thus sees only one side of part of the picture, whereas Cassiodorus sees both sides of several parts of that picture. Hence Cassiodorus is much more conscious of "images," by which is meant other people's conceptions of what it means, for the holder, to hold a particular post and so on. There is, for instance, his self-image: *Pref.* p. 136 (the page references are to the appropriate page of the translation in Hodgkin's *The Letters of Cassiodorus*, and are given to pinpoint the passages concerned) & X 22, p. 434. Then there is his image of "the King": VIII 4, p. 350; 9, p. 352; X 31, p. 444; of "the Emperor": X 8, p. 423; 23, p. 436; of Theodora: X 20, p. 433; of "the barbarians": X 29, p. 440; of the Praetorian Prefecture: VIII 20, p. 367 & X 27, p. 438 and of how the bureaucracy appeared to a Goth: X 31, p. 444. This consciousness produced an awareness of extra-bureaucratic interests and viewpoints, or, if you like, an objectivity and sophistication, less evident in John's more constricted world (on the latter concept see Lerner, *The Passing of a Traditional Society*, pp. 72 & 47-56).

10. John's recommendations concern the reintroduction of archival

systems of proven utility for reference and cross-checking purposes (III 19,1-2; 20,4-9 & 68,2-5) and of work-breaks for junior staff (III 15,3). Cassiodorus produced a model official letter conferring high office so as to save subsequent incumbents of the Master's post the labor of writing these out afresh and differently for every conferment of a high dignity; see *Pref.* p. 138. These are essentially changes of detail and do not affect the bureaucratic (still less the political or social) system. That our authors are so immured within this system is, in this regard, the result of the operation of an in-built feature, "Strategic Learning" (see n. 39, and discussion thereto in text, of the previous chapter).

11. For the details, see chapter 6. Basically this disparity seems to be caused by the fact that Cassiodorus is further from the centre of government and therefore from the official "truth." Discrepancies between myth and actuality were less concealable from such an official. "Further" is used here in psychic, rather than geographic, terms: for Cassiodorus *"the"* centre of legitimate government was Rome. But he was well aware that this was only the formal centre, as final power and responsibility lay at the Gothic centre of government in Ravenna. And this he knew to be the case only for Italian affairs. Intervention by the overriding authority of Constantinople was always a threat. That threat materialized in Cassiodorus' day, and brought about the abolition of his civil bureaucracy of western Rome in the sequel. Western bureaucrats could only lose in any merger with the bureaucracy of east Rome. Thus Cassiodorus' world is the amoral strategist's world which John assumes to underlie international or intra-bureaucratic relationships (see chapter 2, notes 6 & 7, and discussion thereto in text; see also n. 32 below). But for Cassiodorus, unlike John, his fellow Romans in the other part of the empire were little better than the outright enemies who abounded in this strategist's world of power relationships. Hence his bleakly realistic picture.

12. As this part of this section summarizes findings from chapter 7, "Problems in Effecting Change in a Traditional Society," it is not proposed to duplicate source evidence cited there (see comments to n. 1, above).

13. Trends are discussed at II 23,1-3 & 29,1-3; III 35,1-36,2 & 54,1-2; the influence of agents is discussed at III 38,3-5; 39,2-4; 50,5; 62,3 & 69,2-3; unanticipated consequences are discussed at II 10,2 (cf. III 31,5); 21,1; III 56,2; 67,2-4 & 68,2-4.

14. This holds for Anastasius too: John can be sympathetic towards his attempts to bring about change (III 47,3; cf. 17,3), although critical

of him on occasion (III 46,2-3 & 51,1-4); he can also see an administrative problem as it must have appeared to this (bureaucrat) Emperor: III 45,3. In this respect John's picture of the situation is akin, in its more restricted frame of reference to be sure, to that of Cassiodorus, another bureaucrat: see n. 9.

15. On devotion to one's *corps* and colleagues, see I 15(4); III 30,10; 66,4-6 & 67,4-6. Other *corps* are seen in an inimical light: III 9,10 & 23,2. There is hostility towards a competing skill group, in a different Department but within John's own *corps*: III 10,3-4 & 36,1-2. There is also depreciation of other professional groups: III 20,9 & 47,1. Palace society, moreover, is seen as "different": II 4(2) & III 28,2.

16. The classical instances of a "good" and a "bad" Prefect for John are represented by Phocas and John the Cappadocian, who are represented as polar types: see respectively III 72,2-75,10 and II 21,2-4 & III 57,1-72,1. Other classical examples of "bad" Prefects are Rufinus (II 10,3; III 7,5; 23,1-2; 40,2-3) and Marinus (III (36,1) 46,2-3 & 49,1-5); the activities of these men lessened the power, prestige and perquisites of the Prefecture in general.

17. See II 21,2; III 17,1-2; 65,4-5 & 68,4.

18. John unhesitatingly carries out an illegal action for Phocas at III 75,1-2. The Prefect was *not* expected to "truckle" to the Emperor's authority: II 17,2; III 42,3-4 & 50,4-5. In practice, the Prefect, for his staff, was all-powerful: III 69,2-3.

19. There is (an account of others') open criticism of Anastasius at III 46,2-7 (the point behind the concluding anti-Epeirote remarks is that Anastasius was an Epeirote by origin) & 51,2-4. There is implicit criticism of Justinian at II 18,2; III 2,3-5; 11,1; 29,4; 30,2 & 10. There is criticism of the new law code at III 14,2 and 20,4. John apparently felt that even such oblique criticism should be offset by precautionary circumspection. He goes out of his way to state specifically that any criticisms of his were aimed at imperfections in individuals, not at imperial institutions or the Emperor: III 39,2-5. The bureaucratic code did not allow for political activism. Downright non-cooperation (the most extreme form of opposition contemplated) was regarded as too dangerous: III 76,2.

20. Dress and regalia: II 13,2-14,2; 16,1-2; III 14,3; verbiage: III 11,3; cf. 17,4; writing paper: III 14,1; cf. 68,4 (see n. 2 above on this issue).

21. On protocol see II 16,4 (cf. 9,2) and III 35,5; on its underlying belief system, see II 27,2 (& cf. 7,2 & 6). Note 10 and text thereto in

chapter 3, " 'Roman History' for John," relates to this issue. On "the Establishment" see III 35,3-5 & 67,2.

22. The — deliberately contrasted — pen-pictures of Phocas and John the Cappadocian detail the behavioral code (see n. 16 above). Every Head of a *corps* was expected to conform to it. John goes out of his way at II 26,1-5 to sing the praises of a Master of Offices who was, from the viewpoint of a bureaucratic *litteratus,*an exemplary instance of all that a Head should be. A similar code pertained in Cassiodorus' bureaucracy over in the West: *Var.* I,7; I,8: cf. VIII 17. However, in regard to empire building in terms of *manpower*, it would seem that something like Parkinson's Law seems to have operated (II 21,1), despite this code.

23. The syndrome is detailed in *LRE* pp. 601-606; this is Riggs' "Prismatic Society" (see pp. 99-240, and in particular 207-214). For the implications of the syndrome see S. N. Eisenstadt, *Essays on Comparative Institutions,* Wiley, 1965, pp. 223-24.

24. See n. 20 in chapter 4, and discussion thereto in the text.

25. Generally the combination of qualifications involves the "right" people, i.e. *litteratti*(for an example of the "wrong" people, see III 62,3), who have the appropriate abilities and experience: II 18,2-3; III 2,3-5. Each of these qualifications is vital in John's view. Prospects for promotion must be of the right type (cf. II 17,1); they must have ability (see III 67,3) and be equal to the work (III 6,1; 9,5-7); and experience is necessary (III 14,2). The model syndrome occurs at III 20,2. These standards were also applied to Heads of the *Corps* by their subordinates. The latters' appraisal was critical and widely ranging; see II 20,2 & III 38,5 and n. 22 above.

26. Lunch breaks: III 15,3-4; archives: III 19,2-4 & 20,5-9; see also III 68,4 (a system of cross-checking necessary) and II 10,5 and III 40,4 (a criticism of duplication of work).

27. See II 29,2; III 44,2 & 56,2-4.

28. An instance of the effects of a takeover of authority on the relative strengths of the senior posts concerned in the two competing *corps* occurs at III 24,1-2 in conjunction with 25,4-5. Functions may be wrested away from another Department to increase the power of one's own Department within one's own *corps* (III 38,3-4); or such a wresting-away may downgrade another *corps* (III 49,3-5). When a *corps* loses functions there is a deterioration in its conditions of service (III 40,3), as actual duties, rather than a formal role, empower (III 21,2).

29. See II 10,5 and III 40,4.

30. See III 10,1; 24,2; 25,4 & 27,1(!) and cf. 76,10. The doing away with the lucrative bureaucratic perquisites described here enormously improved the position of the lower orders; in fact, it brought the processes of justice within the reach of their purses. The counterpart of this preoccupation with their own vested interests on the part of John and his like is Cassiodorus' (i.e. the Head of *Corps'*) repeated injunctions to his staff to be "moderate."

31. See III 24,1-25,5 and n. 15 above.

32. The key passage is III 35,1-36,2. The amoral atmosphere which John assumes as the norm for such inter-*corps* (and intra-departmental!) interactions is strikingly similar to that which he assumes to underlie all relationships between the Empire and the Persians: see III 33, 2-34,5 and cf. n. 11 above.

33. See III 16,3 & 42,5.

34. The passing of "the good old days" is sadly remarked upon at II 16,4-17,2. John was not alone in noticing this; both Anastasius (III 50,1-2) and Justinian (III 39,1) had tried to put the clock back — but in vain, so all-powerful were the workings of the bureaucracy's internal dynamics.

35. See Book One, chapter 4, note 19, and discussion thereto in the text.

SUMMARY OF THE FINDINGS OF PART ONE

One's first impression is of the overwhelmingly *literary* nature of the world in which John lived. Distant periods are more real to him than those which are nearer, if those distant periods had had marked impact upon the stream of literature over the centuries and been well written up by the writers who dominated John's bibliography and thought-world. Literary pretensions were such that John felt obliged to lay claim to the reading of works which he had not, in fact, consulted at first hand. He had to do so to maintain his much-prized reputation for learning. For he lived in a society which set tremendous store by wide reading in the literature of which it was so proud. Further, even within the bureaucracy, a literary education was expected to make the most effective training for a high official; and literary skills were necessary if a bureaucrat wished to advance within the apparatus. Along with this preoccupation with literature go limited political, professional and social horizons, marked selectivity in perception — and little of the broadening influence of travel.

A second general impression is that the bureaucracy by no means presents us with one uniform viewpoint. Bureaucrats obviously differed in attitudes according to rank, *corps*, even branch or Department within a *corps*. Moreover these attitudes shifted in the course of time. But the mass of the bureaucracy will have had John's viewpoint, rather than Cassiodorus'. This means that we cannot presume that they had a service-orientation. Rather they saw their functions as regulative and were punishment oriented. Administrative technology was static; there were shifts of emphasis, large and small, but no structural innovations.[1] Alienation, formalism, overlapping, and goal-displacement are strikingly visible, a classical syndrome for a traditional society caught in a developmental trap.[2]

As we have seen, Cassiodorus, as Head of *Corps*, felt it necessary to keep checking upon his subordinates to see that they carried out his instructions to them. As we have also seen, a mere Emperor — Justinian for instance — had even greater difficulty in dragooning his civil bureaucracy into actions which it felt to be against its professional interests. Thus the civil bureaucracy (or the ecclesiastical or military bureaucracies, for that matter) cannot be thought of as though it were a kind of black box automatically translating inputs in the form of instructions from the Emperor into outputs in the form of actions which are in perfect accord with those inputs of instructions. The "black box" is equipped with a scrambling device. That device is the bureaucratic code which we have examined in such detail. Instructions are implemented according as this code dictates. Actions coming out of the box do not, therefore, automatically correlate with the instructions fed into it.[3] Hence *Novel* after *Novel* from the Emperor vainly legislating against (often the same) bureaucratic malpractices.

In a way, too, a modern working on Byzantine bureaucracy himself operates in a way somewhat similar to this black-boxing process. In his case, the "box" consists of his set of assumptions and preconceptions as to how a bureaucracy worked in the sixth century A.D. These assumptions process (and scramble!) his inputs, as it were, of reading materials, to produce "outputs" consisting of interpretations of those materials shaped by his assumptions and related processing procedures. The modern, that is to say, needs to be as aware as is possible of the assumptions which he is bringing to bear, and of their ramifications and consequences, if he is himself to avoid a scrambling process analogous to that described in the preceding paragraph.[4]

FOOTNOTES

1. Introduction of special bureaucratic Departments to carry out specific servicing functions (for example, coordinating agricultural development) is the kind of thing that is meant by structural development. S. N. Eisenstadt, "Political Orientations of Bureaucracies in Centralized Empires," in *Essays on Comparative Institutions*, pp. 223-24, indicates the true background to the developments which we have been considering in the bureaucracy of John's day. The Emperor is trying to bring under his control a bureaucracy which has shed off that control in many of its activities.

2. On the syndrome see Riggs, "The Prismatic Model," pp. 99-318. The concept of a "developmental trap" is owed to a mimeo-ed paper by Professor Riggs on "The Comparison of Whole Political Systems," given at a seminar in the Center for Comparative Political Analysis in the University of Minnesota, 1967. By the concept is meant a situation in which the institutions of a society assume a set position, prevent evolutionary change (from within) and generally lock the society into a static state by creating an intermeshing complex of practices such that piecemeal amelioration is impossible.

3. On the "input output model" see Riggs, pp. 195-96.

4. This entails awareness of the conceptual frameworks currently

designated as models. On the problems involved in choice of models, see Riggs, "The Prismatic Model: Conceptualizing Prismatic Societies," pp. 3-49, esp. 5-12. For a survey of the varieties of models currently available, see now O. R. Young, *Systems of Political Science*, Prentice-Hall, 1968; cf. for example pp. 10-11 & chapter 7.

Part Two

Two Contemporary Views of a Traditional Bureaucracy:
John the Lydian and Magnus Aurelius Cassiodorus Senator

Chapter 6
Two Contemporary Views of a Traditional Bureaucracy

Section 1. Introduction

The aim of this chapter is to see how a bureaucrat in traditional society conceived of his job. This will be done by taking what two such bureaucrats have written about their work and looking to see what themes are uppermost in their writings, and what areas of concern or disinterest occur in both. The writers concerned are Cassiodorus and John the Lydian. A biographical sketch of John the Lydian will be found in chapter one, and will not be repeated here. A biographical sketch of Cassiodorus will, however, be given here.

Magnus Aurelius Cassiodorus Senator (born about 480 A.D.[1] and dying 95 years later) came of distinguished lineage: his great-grandfather, the *Illustris* Cassiodorus (c. 390-460) had governed Sicily; his grandfather (c. 420-490) had been Tribune and Notary under Valentinian III, close friend of the influential Aetius, and highly successful ambassador to Attila. His father had served King Odovacar as Count of the Privy Purse and as Count of the Sacred Largesses; under King Theodoric he had been Governor of Sicily and of his own home area of Bruttii and Lucania; then he had been Praetorian Prefect and, finally, had received the highest honour it lay with the king to bestow, that of the Patriciate. In the East, Heliodorus, a cousin of the Cassiodori, had had a brilliant 15-year tenure of the post of Praetorian Prefect in Theodoric's day.[2] His father had been wealthier than King Theodoric.[3] In its way (i.e. in traditions of holding administrative office, as opposed to Gothic traditions of tribal aristocracy) Cassiodorus' family was at least as distinguished as that of any of the transient Gothic kings under whom he served. Thus in Lord Cassiodorus we have a representative of the top *echelons* of the civil administrative bureaucracy.

Cassiodorus was born on the family estates, at Squillace in Bruttii, southern Italy. Albeit paternalistic, his affection for this region is one of the most deeply-rooted emotions in his entire makeup.[4] In 503 his father, as Praetorian Prefect, took the young Cassiodorus (aged 23 and fresh from his legal and literary studies) on to his council as a legal assessor. The young man made such a favorable impression on the Gothic King Theodoric, on an occasion when he presented the latter with an honorific address, that he was made *Quaestor* of the Sacred Palace in 507. This post involved acting as spokesman for the semi-literate Goth. Cassiodorus, who seems to have seen the union of Goth and Italian as the only hope of peace and stability for Italy, aimed to further the best interests of Italy in this way.[5] Service as Quaestor terminated in c. 512, and in 514, at the age of 34, Cassiodorus enjoyed the signal honour of being made *Consul Ordinarius*. The distinction was enhanced by the facts that troubles in the East kept him without a colleague and that he secured the election of Hormisdas to the Papacy, ending an *impasse* produced by ecclesiastical faction. In the following year he was made a Patrician and, probably, governor of his home area of Lucania and Bruttii.

At this point came a break in his career. In (probably) 519 he wrote the *Chronicon*, a rather hastily compiled Universal History, *not* one of his better works and, subsequently, not well thought of by him. About 520 came his *Gothic History*, which equipped the Goths with splendid traditions and a place as a force in Graeco-Roman civilization. In 523 came his appointment, aged 43, as Master of Offices, a post held until 527. He had then to wait until 533, when he was 53, for appointment as Praetorian Prefect, a post he held until 537, when he seems to have retired, at 57 years of age, from service in the administrative bureaucracy.

By now literary activity was coming to the fore as a preoccupation. His *Variae*, letters composed as *Quaestor*, Master and Prefect, were probably edited in 537 and he seems to have busied himself with his writings on the soul, the *De Anima*, at about this time. Religion, always important in his life, seems to have become a dominant force as he grew older.[6] A commentary on the *Psalms* and *Epistles* was commenced. It was to occupy him for many years. In 546 he may well have fled before Totila to Sicily; he seems to have come to Constantinople with the refugees who fled from there in 547. In 552 came the final Byzantine conquest of Italy and, with its destruction of the Gothic nobility, the end of many of Cassiodorus' hopes. In a Romano-Gothic state the Roman bureaucratic aristocracy was indispensable to their Goth war- and overlords; Byzantium had no such shortage of trained administrative personnel.[7] Cassiodorus, now in his sixties, decided that his life work would be the foundation of a monastery, Vivarium at Squillace, for the study of the scriptures.[8]

Surrounded by grammarians and translators, he applied all his administrative skills to this project, creating a splendid library and establishing a *scriptorium* for the copying of manuscripts, by now fast going out of existence through war devastation and failure to recopy. His writings continued. Sometime after 551 came a text of Jerome's version of the Scriptures, divided into 9 volumes, with chapter, titling and synopses. Then came his *Institutiones*, an outline of divine and human literature to be used by his monks.

His stay in Constantinople had not been wasted. This work, plus that which he caused to be produced,[9] did for the lore of the Church what Justinian had done for the Law of east Rome: it established the official version of the ecclesiastical law (in approved texts of the Scriptures and of the "proper" synods); it defined who the "correct" commentators on that lore were; and it provided for the training of future expounders of that lore. After writing a work on Orthography at 93, Cassiodorus died at 95, having achieved his objective of instituting a formal system of higher education for the Church in the West like those he had so much admired in the East.

Section 2. Problems in the Interpretation of the Evidence

Owing to the dearth of source material, this study is based upon what is available rather than what would be desirable. It involves the only pair of bureaucratic contemporaries writing upon their bureaucracies to have come down to us from antiquity. Thus only one pair of writings is suitable for comparing the viewpoints of different levels within the bureaucracy. Unhappily, they are far from parallel:

Cassiodorus: Westerner — Head of *Corps* — Official letters
John the Lydian: Easterner — Section head, clerical staff — History of the Praetorian Prefecture

It would, in fact, clearly be desirable to have two variables held constant; in this case, all three vary.

Cassiodorus' work involves a selection of official letters. Now, these are not merely the presentation of the one uniform official viewpoint. Cassiodorus *selects* letters written for kings who sometimes were hostile to one another. So critical notes are not lacking in his work. But it is in the nature of official correspondence that something of a public relations heartiness pervades such writings. John wrote in disgruntled retirement, and therefore a negative tone is pervasive in his writings. But Cassiodorus was yet to go on and produce his major writings, indeed even what many would consider his life work, after withdrawing from the bureaucracy. Quite simply, he had less reason for feeling depressed than did John (who had every reason for such a feeling). With only two writers, one cannot show trends in attitudes at their respective levels. Still, John's feelings can hardly have been atypical, given the declining fortunes of the clerical staff of his day.

The *genres* differ, so the focus of the writers' attention and the constraints upon them differ too. But both works are extraordinarily discursive, as the literary fashion of the time apparently required. They both have digressions on similar *exotica*, employ similar historical *exempla*, and so on. Neither work is narrowly focussed or narrowly confined by *genre*. The same general literary constraints manifestly exercise a major influence on both. The influence of their literary times, in fact, lies very heavily upon them, as is evident from the highly mannered formalism common to both sets of writings. As has been seen, the bureaucracy itself expected its mandarins to be steeped in its literature and common academic values. There is consequently much that is similar in these two writings, for all their differences in *genre* and official status.

Moreover, analysis is focussed upon basic underlying issues of a very general nature. What is considered is official attitudes about authority figures, human interrelationships, and social change. Views on such fundamental issues are beyond conscious control, certainly in the society under review here. They permeate all writings by officials, irrespective of the *genre* of the writing involved, because such views are taken for granted and simply underlie the writing as assumptions. Expressions of such views can be investigated using methods suggested by findings on how authoritarians (the personality type engendered by this form of society) perceive such things. Consequently the investigation is focussed on issue-areas which are known to be of central importance to both writers, and on modes of perceiving them which are outside the writers' conscious control. We are looking at the basic assumptions of the men in the administrative bureaucracy of the sixth century.

And, after all, "the Service," as the bureaucracy was known, in its framework and much of its detail stemmed from the one origin and was markedly similar in both cases. Both writers are schooled in the one "Great Tradition" and hold many values in common.[1] In both cases there is alienation and withdrawal from administration, entailing the writer's immersion in the world of letters. Finally, the decisive factors in both careers are changes wrought by Justinian upon the bureaucracies in which they served. Thus there is enough parallelism to make meaningful comparison possible, in the terms employed here, at any rate.

A second undesirable element basic to this analysis is that it is based, for the greater part of its findings on Cassiodorus, on a content analysis[2] of Hodgkin's "translation" of (three books only of) the *Variae*. Hodgkin has not given a word-for-word translation; because of the verbosity and repetitiveness of the Latin, he mostly abstracts. He has nonetheless been used because of his intimate knowledge of this period and because his is the only "translation" to which readers are likely to have access. My contentions are urged in the light of an overall reading of the *Variae*, of course, but the books analyzed in detail are three only: I, VIII and X (plus the Preface). These books give an excellent coverage of the influence on Cassiodorus of different jobs combined with different superiors. The short run of data avoided a number of problems involving uniformity of selective criteria across the analysis.

Actually only certain types of inference can be drawn — by me — from the *Variae*. Having translated John's work I am at home with his bureaucratic jargon. This does not hold for Cassiodorus, where the problems are no less formidable.[3] Consequently, I have not attempted any comparative analyses of semantic fields. Upon consulting the mazy verbosity of either author, however, readers may nonetheless feel grateful for the content analyses involved. At least the latter enable one to form an idea of the relative proportions in mentions of the various items and of the gaps and special emphases.

The content analysis of the *Variae* was based on the indices to the *De Magistratibus* of John the Lydian. A card-index composed of similar entries was built up, and analysis of the *Variae* proceeded in terms of this. Unused and additional cards showed up areas of divergence. By a form of serendipity effect, groups of *much*-used cards gave access to clusters of issues which formed underlying preoccupations in Cassiodorus' writing. This choice of indicators seemed least likely to impose my own perceptual frame of reference on the source material. The indicators were initially simply salient points that had emerged in course of translation of John's work. They were later refined by further use of John's writings in critical evaluation of modern histories of the sixth century, and cross-checked against Procopius, another contemporary source. However, no one is without a frame of reference and, in dealing with bureaucracy in traditional society, mine has been much influenced by the work of F. W. Riggs. In particular, in attempting to assess issues which were salient for men such as John, I have been guided by Riggs' work on "Prismatic Society." In looking for clues in the writers' views on change, causation, time-focus and in their use of judgement-scales, what I know of work on authoritarianism has informed my questioning.[5]

Figure 6.2 is appended in the belief that some form of diagrammatic explanation may facilitate understanding of how the micro- and macro-analyses used in this study relate to one another. Figure 6.2 shows how an individual issue would be analyzed (duplicate of the same matrix being used for the other author):

Figure 6.2

ISSUE AREA	AUTHOR'S TREATMENT How perceived and emphasized				
Dysfunctional bureaucratic perquisites	Notices: Yes/No?	How much comment?	Pro/Con?	How intense?	Reference in general terms or special pleading?
praescriptio fori					
suffragium					
sportulae					

Now, clearly, it is a relatively simple matter to compare the findings of a study of one author, set out as above, with those of a study of another, set out in the same way. One can thus compare not just individual details but *patterns* in one's findings. And one can move on to do the same with another "issue-area," and then another, and so on. In this way, one moves away from the analysis of detail, the micro-analysis, of the individual issue, to search for the larger patternings in the source material, to macro-analysis, that is. This is the technique of analysis which has been used to allow the trends to emerge from the welter of details sifted.[6]

Section 3. Specific Issues as seen by
the Two Bureaucrats

In regard to the role and influence of the Head of the *Corps* the two writers have much in common, if allowance is made for the fact that one sees the post from the viewpoint of an occupant, the other from that of an underling. But this difference in viewpoint produces, when their total impressions are concerned, radically different overall views of the real power of such headships.

John is in no doubt that the fate of a *corps* lies in the hands of its Head.[1] Effectively the Prefect, by the way he implements the Emperor's instructions, can execute a policy in direct contravention of those instructions — and no one dare inform the Emperor in such a case.[2] The Prefect can exercise considerable initiative in his administrative actions — which do not necessarily require the Emperor's knowledge or consent.[3] In cases where the wills of an Emperor and a Head of a *Corps* are at cross purposes, the Emperor has considerable difficulty in making his will prevail.[4] Not surprisingly, the first loyalty of a member of his staff went to the Head of *Corps* as a consequence.[5] If the Prefect does not care for his staff, they can be ruined;[6] if he does, the world is at their feet.[7] But a Prefect can ruin his *Corps* by becoming so powerful that he constitutes a threat to the Emperor. In such a case he is personally destroyed and the power complex he has built up is shattered.[8] A Prefect can also ruin the fortunes of a *corps* by making a wrong decision which costs that *corps* power and authority,[9] or he can pursue a policy detrimental to the long-range interests of the *corps*.[10] It was in fact a series of such Heads that brought ruin to the Prefecture.[11] Responsibly run, the Prefecture should be the guardian of the Empire's finances.[12] But officials are wont to indulge in illegal activities,[13] and few are the Heads who care enough to make up the ground that has been lost.[14]

Hence John's world is bestridden by a series of giant figures, Heads of *Corps* whose decisions have shaped Rome's destiny.[15] He has strict views on what constitutes behavior appropriate for a Head of *Corps*, and the reverse. And, in regard to this code, his normal balance of judgement deserts him: the stereotypic thinking of an extreme authoritarian prevails.[16]

Cassiodorus' *Letters* differ from John's monograph in that they set out the official line on the issues concerned, whereas the former study aims at presenting an inside-dopester's view. However, critical comment is possible in Cassiodorus' writings because succession struggles produced, in Witigis, a King who was critical of his predecessor.[17] Also, in editing, Cassiodorus indulges in tacit criticism by including letters from a King (Theodahad) whose duplicity was shown up by subsequent events.[18] Consequently, the negative aspects of the picture, though glossed over, are there to give a modicum of balance. Certainly, the picture that emerges of the powers and duties of a Head of *Corps* is not a mere official stereotype.

As in John's case, Cassiodorus recognizes that there is a behavioral code for Heads: "A sort of religious holiness is required from those who hold office under a righteous King."[19] This official line recurs elsewhere: righteousness, moderation and care for the public weal are the qualities expected in a Praetorian Prefect.[20] The need for the publicization and repetition of this approved version stirs doubts as to whether it represents a code whose practice subjects took for granted. Certainly Cassiodorus presents us with instances of breaches of the code which are not portrayed as exceptional occurrences.[21]

And, again as in John's case, a Head saw himself as having the Emperor's ear[22] — and was so seen by outsiders.[23] His influence could be decisive in a crisis. A typical crisis occurred when the succession was to be decided. At such a time the men of power at the centre of government could influence selection processes, and men of power in the provinces could ensure that the king selected gained local support.[24] This degree of access and of strategic importance to his king on the part of a minister would tend to create what the letters show us to have existed — ministers who were difficult to discipline and who were in consequence given to lawless self aggrandizement. Hence the apparent anomaly of (a) official emphasis on the highly moral code to which bureaucrats operated, combined with (b) their actual practice in abusing official power in their own interests. This is the formalism typical of prismatic society.[25]

The real difference between Cassiodorus and John was that the former had been privy to the engineering of consent at a disputed succession[26] and had seen the bargains struck between the mighty behind the façade.[27] Loyalty was less readily and totally given in Cassiodorus' world: The King was subordinate to an Emperor[28] and "ruled" insecurely over powerful barons.[29] Hence the succession was a far more severe testing time for "loyalties" in the West than in the East.[30] Consequently, succession arrangements and protestations of loyalty to the King figure largely in Cassiodorus' letters.[31] That this is far from meaning that a Head of *Corps* conceived his first loyalty to be to the King is evident. There is a — surely tongue-in-cheek — letter in which a (weak) ruler protests his capacity to do anything, just prior to complying with a request from a dissident group of subjects[32] that he swear an oath to them.[33] This monarch had to practice dissimulation to rule.[34]

From Cassiodorus' letters there emerges something of what the aristocratic order, to which they were addressed, expected of their King.[35] The King was not to abuse his position and he was to keep his officials in hand.[36] "Kind promises" were looked for upon accession;[37] powerful subjects had honors to look forward to on such an occasion[38] — and the Goths would respect none but a warrior King.[39]

It further emerges that Cassiodorus is in no doubt as to the fact that, among the administrative, ecclesiastical and military bureaucracies, it is the latter which takes pride of place.[40] Though an administrative Head of *Corps* might have the ear of the King, it was the voice of his military chief that, by and large, prevailed in his counsels.[41] It is true that nearness to the King's counsel-chamber brings honors,[42] but the chief amongst these is intermarriage with royal Gothic stock, *not* high administrative office.[43] Moreover, appointments to the top administrative offices are made at the suggestion of the military advisers.[44] And the authority of the latter seems to have overridden that of civil or ecclesiastical bureaucrats if a clash of authorities occurred.[45] Still, the expectation was that posts which were the object of ambition would go to the King's intimates,[46] and that tried supporters would be honored.[47] Once access to honors had been achieved, a man could expect to progress higher.[48] But there was no time sequence or pattern that could be depended upon.[49]

There is little in this depiction of the position of an administrative Head of *Corps* at court that would encourage in Cassiodorus the belief that such an official's decisions shaped the fate of the state.[50] And in fact "great" bureaucrats do not loom large in his depiction of the play of politics in Italy: the only two mentioned are Easterners.[51] He does talk about the posts themselves, however, if he does not celebrate their incumbents. There is, effectively, nothing on the Chamberlain's post or on that of the Master of the Soldiery or the Count of the Privy Purse. But the post of Count of the Sacred Largesses was clearly important,[52] as was that of the *Quaestor* — in a minor way[53] — the Urban Prefect (a "prestige" post),[54] and the Praetorian Prefect. The latter was quite clearly the most important and influential administrative post in the West;[55] that of the Master of Offices is far less salient.[56] There is ample evidence that a powerful Head of *Corps* who had the good will of the King could take over functions which were normally performed by the Head of another *Corps*. Such aggrandizement of his sphere of authority was regarded by a Head as fit source for pride. The overlapping of functions thus caused, however, must have wrought confusion within the administrative machine.[57]

What is striking about this depiction of the realities of official power is not so much that its "weight"[58] is felt to be far less by Cassiodorus than by John,[59] but that the sub-*élite* (i.e. persons like John) simply form no part of it. If John does his Head of *Corps* the honor of imputing to him more power than actually was his, Cassiodorus does not reciprocate by preoccupation with his staff. Goth nobles, "Roman" Patricians, and Senators comprise his reference group, and, for him, the class which, under the King, ran his world.[60]

Another obviously important issue area[61] concerns what are here called the crucial (dysfunctional) perquisites of *officiales* (as the Head's subordinate clerical staff were called): *praescriptio fori, sportulae* and *suffragium*.[62] The first involves the privilege of the Head's staff to have business concerning them brought before the judicial court run by their own *Corps*. The second concerns fees and tips of various types which accrued to those strategically placed to expedite or frustrate the execution of business. The last concerns purchase and "ownership" of one's office.

This cluster of practices forms a syndrome, because their interaction involves a complex of consequences such that piecemeal reform is impossible.[63] Thus *praescriptio fori* results in overlaps of judicial functions and a justice that is as good as one's purse can buy. *Sportulae* result in the "trickle-up and trickle-down"[64] form of tax-collection that overexacts from the subjects and underreturns to official coffers. *Suffragium* involves nepotism, sinecure posts, pluralism and extended career ladders (to maximize payoff opportunities for purchasers of posts). Such formalism, combined with overlapping and the "trickle-up" process, makes for difficulties in control, directing and disciplining of the bureaucracy by the monarch.[65]

Of these issues, the one which attracts most comment from John is

- 106 -

praescriptio fori.[66] He does not dwell specifically or at length on the privilege of trial before the law court of one's own *corps*, it is true. But this is an issue which would not normally be discussed by an official benefitting under it in these terms, which are a hostile, negative description of the practice, in such a man's view. He notices the following matters, which all assume the operation of *praescriptio fori.*

What he most deplores is intervention within the sphere of competence of the law court of a *corps* by outsiders.[67] Even when his own Prefect does so, to the considerable advantage of the Prefecture's staff, John cannot refrain from bitter adverse criticism.[68] John is particularly outraged by the successful intervention of the Master's Men (to be precise the *principes*, on the staff of the Master of Offices) in the process of deciding upon the recipients of postal warrants.[69] These allowed free travel on the imperial post-horse system; they had at one time been issued at the discretion of the Prefect's court. The resulting abuses well indicate the irresponsibility to which *praescriptio fori* could lead in such cases.[70]

Ordinarily, it would appear, a Head of *Corps* exercised, and was believed rightly to exercise, exclusive control in regard to "his" court, even deferring when the Emperor's intervention was invoked as result of abuse of the Head's powers.[71] He was expected vigilantly to maintain his sphere of authority at its widest extent.[72]

John's basic assumption in maintaining these views is that the welfare of a *corps* depends on the importance of its law court, which is viewed primarily as a weapon of power rather than an instrument of justice.[73] It is the scope of its field of judicial competence, and the amounts involved in individual decisions, which produce the vast flow of administrative business necessary for the economic well-being and prestige of its staff. An immoveable backlog of business was thus regarded as a status symbol (and a source of additional emolument) rather than an indication of administrative inadequacy.[74]

The next most frequently mentioned issue is that of *sportulae.* These are seen solely from the bureaucrat's viewpoint. Thus, the fact that a suit cost an appellant 37 gold pieces (rather than "the miserable pittance" which a poor man, earning a few gold pieces a year, could pay) was considered commendable, desirable (in the days of the miserable pittance), and appropriate.[75] Quite simply, fees made the difference between affluence and penury for men like John. With inadequate pensioning[76] and nominal wages,[77] only fees could provide the dignified retirement to which such men aspired.[78] John clearly did

- 107 -

not attain his desire.[79] The most bitter note in his entire work occurs when he criticizes the bureaucracy for its lack of provision of adequate pensioning.[80]

John's views on the purchase of office, an issue which comes up least frequently of these three in his writings, are confused by a desire to have his cake (i.e. secure rapid promotion for penurious merit) and eat it (sell offices attained).[81] The issue is seen in terms of recruitment and promotion policies within the bureaucracy. Recruits should be the "right people," which for John means men who have shown themselves proficient in their literary training.[82] After recruitment they should show merit and application, and be promoted only after becoming duly experienced.[83] Aged sinecurists are likely not to measure up to the demands of their high office (and so are provided with capable middle-aged assistants),[84] and simple purchase of office has adverse effects upon staff competence.[85] But officials should be able to sell their offices, if this is done at a moderate price and the *corps* retains control.[86] Moreover pluralism, the reverse of the coin featuring sinecurism on its obverse, is considered a financial and career aid for the capable rising man.[87]

This is the blinkered view of the middle-level official. He is alive to issues which affect the welfare of himself and the "comrades,"[88] with whom he identifies himself closely.[89] He is far less sensitive to the ways in which procedures favorable to his interests affect those of the clients of the bureaucracy or the working of the larger bureaucratic system. Obsessed with the world of his *officium*, what passes outside barely impinges on him.[90] He can visualize the politics within the bureaucracy without, apparently, comprehending those of the larger society of which the bureaucracy is a part.[91]

It is striking how differently Cassiodorus, as a Head of a *Corps*, views these issues. He has no references to *sportulae* (or pensions!) and only one to *praescriptio fori*.[92] But John's references were often tangential, and Cassiodorus does have comments on these issue areas, if they are broadly interpreted.

Actually, he is much preoccupied with legal issues.[93] To judge by frequency of reference, the aspects which are uppermost in his mind are: appeals, actual criminal cases to be decided, the maintenance of judicial equity, the promulgation of legal rulings, and the disciplining of (top) officials. It is the big issues of the Law, rather than jurisdictional problems involving courts within the bureaucracy, which concern him. Moreover, cases are seen not as just so much more grist for the administrative mill — which Cassiodorus does not wholly trust to implement his orders faithfully[94] — but as human problems involving human consequences. Consequently the process of decision making brings high emotional costs.[95]

And there is a hint of the embarrassment that a Head, who was, after all, a political appointee, could feel when faced with more professionally competent subordinates.[96] He is well aware that his staff may have a far higher opinion of the man he has replaced.[97] But his reference group is elsewhere (as is the peer group before which alone he can be tried),[98] so the fortunes of the Prefecture do not engross his whole attention — he is, in fact, rather relaxed on this score.[99] As in John's case, his loyalty is to his friends; but Cassiodorus' friends are fellow aristocrats.[100] So he feels no remorse about invading the sphere of authority of another *corps*. He had, after all, run that *corps* in another capacity.

Thus *praescriptio fori* is a wholly different issue for such a Head of *Corps* than it is for a staff member of that *corps*. Not that intervention was regarded with indifference. Inter-bureaucratic "adjustments" were vigorously dealt with.[101] And extra-bureaucratic intervention was equally vigorously discouraged.[102] Cassiodorus could not fail to be aware of the (potentially ruinous) resentment of a nobleman denied access to "his proper court."[103] But there was another side to the matter, when one had some notion of how the machinery of government ran. The endless prolongation of litigation which could result from it might have deleterious political consequences.[104] Heads, absolute masters within their own bailiwicks, could go too far; and this is in fact what is most frequently deprecated in Cassiodorus' letters.[105] Moreover, despite John's beliefs,[106] they could be dismissed in disgrace.[107] Cassiodorus pleads for moderation.[108] In view of the problems which arose when an influential man had to be disciplined, this need not simply be a good public relations gambit.

Cassiodorus has no references at all to *sportulae*, wages or pensions. Clearly, men such as he did not look upon their *dignitates* (the technical term for appointment to a high position) primarily as wage-paying "jobs." There could be no mincing of words if a "tip" were offered a judge: it was bribery.[109] Possibly John's reaction to the lack of consideration shown to men like him in regard to pensioning had been generated by the indifference to such matters exhibited by top bureaucrats.

Though there is little comment on *suffragium* as such, the related issue of promotion is at the centre of Cassiodorus' focus of attention: well over two-thirds of all comments that can possibly be regarded as concerning this whole issue area have to do with this aspect of it alone. The most cogent reasons for promotion seem to have been claims arising from high birth.[110] Appropriately, for this view of "merit," official position is not regarded as the highest objective of ambition: marriage with a maiden of royal blood is felt to be the highest aspiration.[111] The feudal viewpoint of the Gothic nobility seems thus to have interpenetrated the topmost *echelons* of the bureaucracy. *Dignitates* are regarded by Cassiodorus, with some detachment, as items for routine distribution.[112]

The next most cogent reason for the conferment of high office is that of services rendered; office rewards these.[113] Mere intimacy with the King was felt to constitute a reason for expecting high office, if not speedily:[114] one of the norms of this society seems to have been that acquaintance involved good will.[115] There is a strong undertone of assertion of the need for training (especially for military positions) or experience (especially for legal posts).[116] Much less stress is laid on ability, which does not anywhere feature as the sole reason for promotion.[117] There is some notion of an official career sequence,[118] but as many mentions of unexpected delays within such sequences or of inversion of the sequence.[119]

High offices, clearly, were not felt to be positions through which one could calculate on proceeding, via merit, in a predictable career pattern. The King had thus broken the identification with bureaucratic principles which *élite* bureaucratic personnel might have maintained. Promotion was regarded as coming unpredictably for ascriptive qualities (birth, intermarriage), or loyalty, or proximity. The topmost level of the bureaucracy had veered toward the norms of feudalism.[120]

In regard to recruitment, Cassiodorus' sole specific comment is that a careful check was necessary in the case of would-be entrants into the Senate. Other classes, he says with indifference, may have "the middling men."[121] One is jarringly reminded of John's laudations of his fellow bureaucrats, whose whole value system differs from that of the aristocrats. In John's case professional competence was felt to entail literary training, administrative expertise and industry. In Cassiodorus' case the claims of lineage seem to have been felt to entail a somewhat paternalistic attitude of responsibility towards the lower orders.[122]

Only once does Cassiodorus deign to mention positions at John's level. This occurs when he guarantees certain appointees in their tenure.

His motives are interesting: contracts must be secured because their stability is essential to the smooth running of high administration.[123] Pluralism and sinecurism are beneath his attention. Presumably these matters were so salient to John and his like because, if they did not arrange them for themselves, no one else would. Cassiodorus' concern for the doings of his underlings seems confined to seeing that these recalcitrants did as they were bid.[124] There seem to be two different worlds here, within the one bureaucracy. Cassiodorus' view of the bureaucracy is rather like that of a man who considers only the portion of an iceberg which is above water.

A third major area of concern for John is that of the status and prestige of his dearly-loved Praetorian Prefecture. He is very sensitive to its position relative to other sections of the various bureaucracies, and feels its decline keenly. If his laments on this score do not have the emotional intensity of those he makes about lack of pensioning, they are sometimes put with great force for all that,[125] and their constant repetition makes of them the dominant theme that threads through his work.[126]

John views the situation in terms of a balance of power between the Prefecture and the Master of Offices: what the former has lost has accrued to the latter, empowering that *corps* in proportion as the Prefecture has been enfeebled.[127] There were, in John's view, two historical turning points: the realignment of bureaucratic powers in the days of Constantine the Great,[128] and, more ruinously, the empowering of the Master to countervail against the Prefect by Arcadius.[129] By giving the Master's Men key strategical positions within the judicial departments of the Prefecture,[130] the latter redistribution of powers had set these two staffs at one another's throats, apparently. John always speaks with great bitterness of the specific group of Master's Men involved.[131] He assumes competitive hostility between the two groups,[132] and makes much of another instance where the ambitions of a department within the Master's *corps* had brought complete ruination upon a department within the Prefecture.[133]

The picture is complicated by the co-existence of a power struggle within the Prefecture itself, where the accountancy department had gradually displaced the judicial and records departments, bringing to the members of the latter departments humiliation and poverty.[134] With all the bitterness of a man whose career skills have been rendered obsolescent in mid-career, bringing a distinguished career to an

- 111 -

ignominious close, John rounds upon this upstart group.[135]

Such experiences in the course of his career projected a stark grimness into John's world view. Change, for him, means a decline from past glories.[136] "Time" is "inherently destructive."[137] Hence the recurring image of the building of a (lesser) building out of the crumbling remains of a once proud edifice.[138] Causation is a bewildering play of amoral forces,[139] made all the more confusing because of the fact that John is able to see that the monarch is not always responsible for the way an agent carries out his instructions, and that some consequences were not those which had been anticipated.[140] John thus infuses intra-bureaucratic dealings with the ethics of balance-of-power politics: stark amoral expediency prevails in the interrelationships between bureaucratic groups.[141] Hence John's total and emotional identification with his own ingroup of colleagues involves hostility to all outgroups. Thus he is antipathetic, to say the least, towards the academics amongst whom his lot for a time had been cast.[142] The Urban Prefecture has two tales told to the discredit of its prestige.[143] He only records two stories concerning members of the ecclesiastical hierarchy, and both place them in an embarrassing light, while showing the superior standing of the Prefecture.[144] And, in the good old days, even the army chiefs had bent the knee before the Prefect.[145]

Such views could only make for a highly antagonistic state of cooperation within the rank and file of the bureaucracy, and they help to explain the distance which a Cassiodorus maintained from that rank and file. For his part, John has a profound respect for aristocratic birth and its claims,[146] and reconciles his *animus* against Prefects (which is inconsistent with this view) by erecting stereotypes of "good" and "bad" Prefects.[147]

The picture which Cassiodorus presents of the field of forces in which the Prefecture is situated is not simply a mirror image of John's picture of it, for all that both works are composed when the author's career has terminated in disappointment and disillusionment.[148] Cassiodorus' letters are official correspondence, so cannot give the backstage view[149] with which John's third book in particular is concerned. But they are carefully edited, and show signs that tacit criticism is intended.[150] Reviewing the promotions and demotions, official praises and reprimands and "meritorious" actions and malpractices there depicted, one can construct a strategy for a King (as opposed to a strategy for a knight or Bishop) in playing the game of high bureaucratic politics. The official line is clear enough: experience (even on the staff of a great official) is a training in statesmanship, and a steady stream of Honours secures good servants for the state.[151]

There are three latent strategies for controlling the powerful ministers on whom the King relied to get his administration done. First is the creation of a situation in which a dangerously powerful official is put under cross-pressure: a *Sajo* (high Gothic military official) has both the Papacy's court and the authority of the Count of the Sacred Largesses (on whom the whole state depended for precious currency) counterposed against him.[152] The crucial institutional factor upon which this and the next strategy are based consists in the fact that all major unresolvable disputes are referred to the King's law court for settlement.[153] The second strategy involves the replacement of a high official if his conduct of his office gives offense.[154] Alternatively a successor known to be inimical to him might be sought.[155] Or he might be shorn of some of his competence by having a (possibly nominally) junior) official take over part of his job.[156] Finally there is the selection of appointees: the key communications post of the Quaestorship is reserved for men who are either young or inexperienced enough (of the wielding of power) not to convert it into a dangerous instrument of power.[157] The Prefecture, which could shape policy in implementing it, went to elderly men, hopefully beyond an age with the energy for indiscretions. If a post showed signs of becoming unduly powerful, an inappropriate appointee[158] would provide the King with a grateful, responsive creature and an occupant who would immobilize the post through frictions caused by his appointment.

Countering strategies are much more limited; the King is at a position of advantage, institutionally, in this game of court and bureaucratic intrigue.[159] The King's strategy of cross-pressuring a post can be utilized to bring a personal enemy to destruction or to disadvantage another group, as follows. Popular disaffection[160] might be stirred to an outburst against the upper orders. A counsellor could then suggest to the King that empowering the appropriate official to deal with the outburst might involve too large a mandate of power. A mediator could then be given part of the additional power. The hapless "appropriate official" is now at the latter's mercy.[161] Or a clash between two spheres of authority could be strategically induced or advertised, leading to a situation in which a new definition of the situation is inevitable, thus benefitting those incommoded by the old definition.[162] The King's second general line of strategy might be

- 113 -

exploited by causing a favourite to be dropped from favour so that you might replace him.[163] This changes the game into the zero-sum variety, where one side gains whatever the other loses; so infighting becomes savage. Alternatively, one might secure one's "own" appointee for a top job,[164] thus compounding one's influence without a war to the knife within one's peer group.

None of these strategies attempt to alter the rules of the game; and, in fact, Cassiodorus' conception of the various posts in the civil bureaucracy is a static one: these posts are not thought to be developing or dwindling in power. First comes the Quaestorship, "not the highest" of posts. It goes to glib, personable men who have been effective as advocates.[165] The appointee is the spokesman for the King.[166] This post constituted the door to royal favour, and conferred real power, via the King's counsel chamber.[167] Not a lot is said of the position of Master of Offices: a learned man gets a (late) promotion to it in one letter.[168] It is a way-station in the official career at Rome — whereas it is (realistically) viewed as the key access post at Constantinople.[169] The top career post at Rome is undoubtedly the Prefecture, upon which "all other posts wait as laqueys."[170] The Prefect is a sort of father figure, provider for the populace and so on.[171] He *must* be a fair and impartial judge.[172] The key post in the King's *entourage* seems to be that of Count of the Sacred Largesses. The latter, as the minister in charge of the supplying of currency, had to be free from avarice.[173] The Urban Prefect's was a prestige post and involved the presidency of the Senate.[174]

Cassiodorus does not speak of intra-bureaucratic feuding, i.e. feuding within the civil bureaucracy, say. But he does provide evidence of some inter-bureaucratic infighting, i.e. conflict between civil and ecclesiastical bureaucracies. This mostly concerns the scope of the law courts of the Bishops; other bureaucracies involved are the *Comitatus* (via the Count of the Sacred Largesses) and the army (via the *Sajo*).[175] To the Head of a *Corps* the King is the all-important factor in the situation. The staff of the *corps* are in the background, and are, if anything, negatively viewed (as a source of informing, disloyalty, and greater expertise). [176] In keeping with this attitude, the calibre of their recruits is regarded as not a matter of moment.[177] Cassiodorus largely ignores ingroups and outgroups;[178] and his ingroup is seen as consisting of competitors rather than comrades, for the passage on loyalty to friends is unique (and probably tongue-in-cheek).[179]

In connection with bureaucratic intrigue, the most frequently recurring concept is that the power of a Head of *Corps* consists in influence with the King, gained by becoming a trusted counsellor.[180] There seems to have been something of a tendency to regard the influence of a persuasive counsellor as entirely controlling the reactions of the counselled: responsibility for a decision taken after counsel is, for instance, externalized upon the counsellor.[181] A counsellor can win a king's "entire" confidence and "rule" him by counselling.[182] This is the picture that a civil administrator has of a military man's influence in counsel; military men saw civilian advisors in the same light.[183]

As such influence could secure the granting of high positions to the counsellor's nominees,[184] the counsellor enjoyed a gatekeeper's strategical controlling position in regard to access to influence.[185] As the King was thought readily to grant his requests,[186] knowledge that a man shared in the royal counsels exposed him to enmity.[187] But enmity could be incurred in other ways too: the King might instruct a capable counsellor to take over part of the official duties of an incapable minister.[188] As favorite, the counsellor was liable to attack from informers, even from hostile subordinates.[189] Well might Cassiodorus depict the paralyzing perplexity of decision-making in such a situation,[190] where he could, furthermore, be followed in his post by a hostile successor.[191]

This is a much more personalized world of bureaucratic intrigue than that which John depicts. In part this contrast reflects the actuality: John *was* one of a group and influenced by trends. He thus had little experience of a courtier's successful special pleading upon a specific occasion and its being immediately translated into action. But, even in Cassiodorus' world of personalities at counsel, there must have been unanticipated consequences; yet that idea is foreign to him. Clearly, then, the contrast partly results from biases in Cassiodorus' perception of situations. Perhaps a greater sophistication in the eastern capital is involved. The cunning and tortuousness ascribed to Constantinopolitans by a Rome now become provincial may thus be a projection of this disparity in sophistication.[192]

Institutional and social cross-pressures were very dimly seen in Cassiodorus' world: a King might be alive to them, but not a subordinate.[193] The ruling forces in Cassiodorus' world are those of enmity and envy, both personalized and much mentioned. The former follows a man, i.e. it is not seen as resulting from the situational pressures at one point in his career.[194] An attempt to change the structure of the bureaucracy, involving a change in the rules of the game of high politics, would, in such circumstances, be so liable to misconstruction as to be too dangerous to contemplate. Hence the Head of a *Corps* would use a courtier's skills, working through the existing administrative machinery. This would seem to indicate that, in the West at any rate, change was induced by the Emperor, not foisted on him by reforming ministers.

Cassiodorus' view of the world is much more sanguine and optimistic than John's, as their respective achievements and placement in the power structure might lead one to expect. Cassiodorus is favorably attuned to change: "continuous new improvements" are thought to be a (highly desirable) characteristic of a key industry of his day.[195] It is "the man devoid of forethought" who "fears change."[196] In his system of causation the working of a beneficent deity is much in evidence. The evidence for this comes not only from the parade of assurances of divine help for, or commands to, various Kings. Such protestations, most invoked when times were most troublous, seem rather to constitute the conscious manipulation of symbols likely to engender group loyalties.[197] More telling are the unconscious assumptions underlying the letters. Humane actions will be rewarded by blessings from Heaven. Miracles occur. Administrators will one day stand before a final judgment. Ill fortune is ascribed to a dimly conceived "Fate." Apparently it could not be associated with Cassiodorus' deity.[198]

There is some inconsistency in regard to views expressed on "the times." A Gothic ruler might well be proud of the love of fair play shown in his reign, and at the achievements which the present generation of Goths, as opposed to their ancestors, had wrought. Cassiodorus had reason to share such views.[199] But as a Roman, the letter writer sees the superior wisdom and science of the ancients, and yearns for a morality worthy of the good old days.[200] However, by and large, Cassiodorus must have identified with the Goths in their sense of achievement.

His imagery, if showing signs of being deliberately varied for stylistic reasons,[201] contains, as dominant themes, power[202] and manipulation of the environment.[203] Catastrophic natural forces do not haunt it. There is a sense of movement and achievement.[204] Possibly this is the shallow view of a conformist. Certainly Cassiodorus conceives of man as "an animal peculiarly fond of approbation," who ought not to shun social gatherings or deviate from social norms, and whose ambitions can only be kept in bounds by fear of punishment — an authoritarian's picture.[205] But such assumptions equipped Cassiodorus with a functional set of values for dealing with subordinates such as John, which is more than can be said of John's in the reverse case. Anyway, such was the value system of my Lord Cassiodorus and his like, the top administrators who bestrode John's world — and that of most other contemporaries, too.

Section 4. The Professional Image of the Bureaucracy

The first problem to be dealt with concerns the historical propriety of the question "How did these men think of their jobs? " To a large extent preoccupation with this issue is a feature of industrial society only.[1] However, it would appear from cross-cultural surveys of bureaucracy that this was in fact an issue in traditional bureaucracies.[2] To assess our writers' views it is proposed to analyze for and compare their attitudes to the public, to consider their views on the responsibilities of (and their criticisms of) the bureaucracy in which they served, and to investigate the cluster of issues at the center of their job preoccupations.

In regard to the public, both writers confront it as authoritarians. As John informs us more than once, he is a believer in one man rule, and a strong man's rule at that.[3] His betters are esteemed: Patricians, e.g. are always spoken of with respect, opposition to them is condemned, and their behavioral code is roundly approved.[4] His inferiors are held in some disdain: the demes (for John, the lower class population of the city) tend to be mentioned in association with (a) pejorative descriptive terms, (b) anecdotes related so as to redound to their discredit, and (c) a need for discipline and direction.[5]

His is a punishment orientation: in a review of the functions of the Censorship, its disciplinary duties almost entirely monopolize his attention; the letting out of contracts is noted only as a brief afterthought.[6] The functions of the Prefect's law court are largely seen as a means of empowering its staff. John pays lip-service to Justinian's reforms aimed at making justice cheap and accessible, but in fact is most concerned at the loss of income involved for the Prefect's staff.[7] He has some feeling for the taxpayer, it is true, but at least as much for the tax extractor (and this in a case of tremendous hardship for the former).[8] In describing the horrors of John the Cappadocian's tax-extracting in his (Lydus') own place of origin, it is a suffering upper class which is selected for commiseration,[9] and he may well be failing to mention collusive activities on their part.[10] Concern for the public cannot be regarded as a major concern of John's: contemporary activities of the lower orders are, except in one instance, unsympathetically noticed in asides, not considered matters of importance.[11]

Cassiodorus' authoritarianism differs somewhat from John's. The only debt of loyalty acknowledged is to the King;[12] as the latter could be a fellow-nobleman raised by the play of chance to the throne (e.g. Theodahad), this loyalty was to the institution, not the individual. As has been shown, Cassiodorus holds high birth in high esteem.[13] Patricians, nobles and senators are repeatedly mentioned with respect and regard. Proportionately, they loom far larger in Cassiodorus' thought-world than in John's. But Cassiodorus adopts a less reverential posture before this highly esteemed group: one could be critical of nobles without impropriety if one were their peer, presumably.[14]

There is a strong suggestion of a code of *noblesse oblige*: a Golden Mean between avarice and profligacy had to be followed,[15] and high status involved the setting of good example.[16] There seems in fact to have been a difference between the attitudes of the nobility of East and West in this regard, the former having less regard for such an obligation.[17] Certainly, for Cassiodorus, the code was strongly felt: he can criticize senators for reacting strongly to scurrilous abuse.[18] In regard to the lower orders, Cassiodorus is less hostile than John, if possibly more patronizing and disdainful.[19] They are seen as a differentiated body, townees (more highly regarded) and rustics, not as John's relatively undifferentiated mass.[20]

There is evidence of a punishment orientation in Cassiodorus' case too. Punishment for crime is light for the esteemed classes, harsh and inexorable for the lower orders.[21] The taxpayer is regarded as a kind of milch-cow, to be well treated in order that more tax may be forthcoming.[22] Where Cassiodorus differs from John is in the fact that he has more regard for the well-being of the taxpayer than the smooth functioning of the tax-extraction machine. There is repeated mention of the need to make concessions in cases of real need;[23] moderation as a tax official, rather than maximal tax revenue obtained regardless of human suffering, is urged upon tax collecting agents.[24]

Both the milch-cow and the *noblesse oblige* concepts seem to be operating here. In regard to the former, Cassiodorus sees a need, to foster commerce, to which John is markedly insensitive;[25] and anomic disturbances are frequently mentioned and their implications keenly felt.[26] In regard to the latter, Cassiodorus effectively defines his concept of "the Public Good," his society was too underdeveloped to have *consensus* on such a concept[27] — in terms which indicate that it was a matter of personal responsibility, for him. His role of Prefect involved paternalism for Italy, a development of his paternalistic concern for his barony at Squillace.[28]

In general outline, the attitudes of the writers are as follows in regard to the responsibilities incumbent upon their bureaucracy and the criticisms which could be levelled against it:

Figure 6.3

	John the Lydian	Cassiodorus
Emphasis on bureaucratic responsibilities	Low	High
Emphasis on criticism of the working of the bureaucracy	High	Low

The disparity in the emphasis which they individually assign to bureaucratic responsibility has already been indicated in the analysis of their attitudes towards the public, where this aspect of their work received relatively little attention from John, whereas for Cassiodorus it wnn n mnjnr innuc

But there is more to it than this. John seems to have difficulty in defining the duties and responsibilities of the Prefecture. In contrast e.g. with the post of Master of Offices, whose functions are clearly and specifically defined,[29] John speaks rather obliquely about the Prefecture. Its functions were those of accountant to the Empire.[30] Characteristically, it is seen as primarily a body whose services enable other sections of the bureaucracy to function,[31] or one upon which falls the duty of keeping up the Public Post.[32] However, John speaks of these duties and responsibilities as a thing of the past, inasmuch as the Prefecture was no longer capable of meeting them.[33] Of old, the contentment of the taxpayer had been the sole aim of the Prefecture, and this was still the case under a good Prefect, but the trend amongst recent Prefects has been away from this aim.[34]

Cassiodorus, on the other hand, has a very clear image of the role and responsibilities of the Prefecture: it was founded by Joseph to see that Italy's peoples were kept provisioned.[35] Obligation to this duty was sincerely felt by him,[36] and underlies his relatively frequent references to such things as commerce and provisioning.[37] The Prefect had to be a judge of complete probity.[38] He ought to care more for the welfare of the taxpayer than that of the tax-extracting machine.[39] "Holy righteousness" was the bounden duty of those employed as the King's ministers, and moderation should be their watchword in interpreting their duties.[40]

To some extent this difference between Cassiodorus and John may reflect the latter's "trained incompetence," as a narrow career-specialist, in thinking in terms other than those of one particular set of vested interests.[41] Coming as a generalist to a series of discrete appointments, Cassiodorus seems to have been more aware of the larger responsibilities of the various sections of the bureaucracy and how these were interrelated. Thus, as *Quaestor* he acted as spokesman for the King, being particularly concerned with the administration of the law, especially in its application to taxation; problems concerning disciplining and large estates were salient. As Master of Offices he was concerned with making the "right" appointments and conciliating opinion among the upper *echelons* of society; the need to encourage city life in the Italian countryside became very evident. As Prefect he was again engaged in conciliating upper class opinion, but had the job of negotiating with his bureaucratic opposite number (the Master of Offices) in Constantinople over international problems; problems of provisioning within Italy loomed large too.[42]

In regard to criticisms of the bureaucracy, however, the position is reversed. John gets down to details and the issues concerned are obviously highly meaningful for him. Criticisms involve minor issues, such as the discontinuance of the practice of the lunch break or of a special type of garb worn in the Prefect's law court.[43] They also involve issues which have really important implications, such as the inadequate training of the current crop of judges in the Prefect's law court; false claims to titles, involving (more) diversions of cash in the "trickle-up" process of extraction; the extension of the *suffragium* principle in the making of appointments; inefficiency caused by job overlaps; and finally the discontinuance of archives, of systems of cross-checking, and of a section of the public post.[44] John's criticisms on the score of inadequate pension provisions have already been noticed.[45]

But what obviously concerns him most deeply, and is the criticism which, after pension inadequacies, is expressed with the most *animus*, is his complaint about the disciplining of the staff of the Prefecture.[46] Reasons for such disciplining are nowhere given, though collusive practices are hinted at; as has been seen, John is very loyal to his ingroup.[47] The bureaucratic world is at the center of John's focus of attention. It belongs to him and his like, is judged on its own terms and in its own interests. John resents outside interference with it. For a department within the Prefect's *corps* to have the task of disciplining members of that *corps* is uncomfortable, but a source of pride.[48] When the Prefect himself disciplines staff *in camera*, it is intolerable.[49] This matter of disciplining touches on one of the nerve centers of the bureaucracy: control of the machinery of discipline gave retrospective control, and was the object of endemic strife as a consequence.[50]

Cassiodorus has little to say by way of criticism of the bureaucracy within which he worked. There is one general remark, that staff could not be trusted to implement instructions faithfully.[51] The force of this remark is borne out by references to specific disciplinary actions.[52] One implicit criticism of detail is made: Cassiodorus evolved stock letters of appointment to save waste of time composing an original letter each time a dignity was conferred.[53] Apart from this, what criticism there is of bureaucratic proceedings concerns how previous kings or the Constantinopolitan Emperor comported themselves towards their bureaucracies. In such cases the fault is felt to lie with the monarch.[54] It is as though Cassiodorus regards the bureaucracy abstractedly, as one might a gardening fork which one uses habitually, pausing only to address oneself to the removal of obstructive objects with which it becomes entangled, or reflecting on how others have used it or one like it. For Cassiodorus the bureaucracy is a means, which he takes for granted, to an end, whereas for John means and ends have become transposed, in a classical instance of bureaucratic goal displacement.[55]

The clusters of issues which form as it were a central core of preoccupations in either writer's case illustrate their different thought-worlds strikingly. These clusters have been constructed by listing the matters most frequently mentioned by either writer, and ranking them in order of frequency of mention, in both cases.[56] Figure 6.4 illustrates (next page).

John's preoccupations are with issues internal to the bureaucracy, and these are seen from a bureaucrat's viewpoint. Cassiodorus, on the other hand, thinks primarily about issues external to the bureaucracy,

Figure 6.4

Issue areas most frequently mentioned

	JOHN	CASSIODORUS
Declining	Perquisites of office	Seeing that the law is imple-
Order	Bureaucratic feuding	mented
of	Work: loads & efficiency	Handling the upper orders
Frequency	Past glories of the *Corps*	Tax extraction without undue
of	Pomp and red tape	severity
Mention		Problems posed by the lower
		orders
		Relations with the church

and bureaucratic interests are only tangentially included in his frame of reference. To some extent this is a function of the *genre* and its subject matter, which differs in either case. The point, however, is that there is a *total* divergence in viewpoint between these two bureaucrats, who are both talking about what the same job is all about. The emergence of two patterns, wholly separate but each individually coherent and consistent, indicates a fundamental difference in the assumptions with which both writers approach their work as bureaucrats. The differences are complementary, from the point of view of a head of state: together they enable such a head to control the bureaucracy by playing off one element against another.

Section 5. Conclusion

Divergences of viewpoint as wide as this mean that this traditional bureaucracy was no monolithic unit. Much has been said of the different worlds in which John and Cassiodorus lived. These were physical, as well as mental. An attempt has been made, in chapter 2, to assess how John perceived his environment. Effectively it comprised France, Italy, the Balkans, Anatolia and Iraq. Spain, North Africa and Egypt are somewhat nebulously attached. This world centers on Constantinople and has a heartland comprising the area around the Black Sea running from the Danube via Constantinople to the Caucasus, and having the Anatolian massif over as far as Syria as its productive center.

Going by Cassiodorus' geographical and topographical references in those letters which have been intensively analyzed, one finds that *his* world centers around an Italian heartland,[1] protected by military holdings stretching across the top of the peninsula and head of the Adriatic from the Midi to the Balkans. This world should center on Rome, to which all of Cassiodorus' loyalties go, but the power of the Goth stronghold in the marshes at Ravenna gives it a second "capital." From a hazily-thought-of point in the East comes the menace of Constantinople, towards which Cassiodorus' feelings are highly ambivalent.

Thus, paradoxically, the junior bureaucrat has the larger overall view of the world in which both bureaucrats were living. But the advantage in breadth of vision is purchased at some cost to the detail of the picture: Cassiodorus' world is the smaller, more intimately known world of the provincial, John's a more superficial metropolitan's view.

Now the inhabitants of these lands appeared in a guise which varied with the writer's viewpoint. For just as there was a difference between the view which each had of his geographical environment, so too did differences exist between their views of their respective institutional environments. Such differences underlie the differing focus of attention already shown in their view of their occupational situations. The array of institutions, and the relative salience of items within that array, varies in each writer's mental image of his social and institutional environment.

From this distance in time one can do no more than attempt an impressionistic survey of such mental images, of course. But close quantitative work on the texts involved does give one a strong impression as to which items were mentioned most frequently and at greatest length (or in exceptionally striking emotional terms). One remembers things which, to one's surprise, one found to be little mentioned, or mentioned with little emphasis. The following brief survey, then, is an attempt to delineate the relative salience of items in each writer's background frame of reference, insofar as this can be ascertained from his habits of bringing up such matters, in and out of season, as he discusses a variety of other things.

For John, in writing the *De Magistratibus*, the civil bureaucracy was ever in the foreground. It was largely made up, in his mind's eye, of the Praetorian Prefecture and the Master of Offices and his men. These two *corps* were involved in cooperation of the most antagonistic nature. The Prefecture was the more salient; and, within it, the departments of its judicial branch. There is conflict here too, between the judicial branch and the financial department of the Prefecture. But the Master's men were only slightly less omnipresent in John's thoughts, especially the Agents, who had preempted the topmost position within the departmental headships of the Prefecture. Lurking in the background, as it were, was the Urban Prefecture, a source of residual conflict for the Prefecture. More remote still was the ecclesiastical bureaucracy; relationships with its various bishoprics occasioned infrequent mention.

Hazily visible, as backdrop to this foreground as it were, are the busy literary and academic circles of Constantinople. Somewhere off in the distance is Rome and wars in north Africa and Italy, in this descending order of what can only be misleadingly described as emphasis. Persia, the Danubian regions and the Caucasus, in this order, are more salient features in this background. But these things are remote from John's central concerns, which are with the Constantinopolitan world of letters.

Cassiodorus' mental landscape has different contours. True, given the nature of his writings, the bureaucracy dominates the immediate foreground. But the configuration of that bureaucracy is different for him. The Praetorian Prefecture is of central importance here, but the Prefecture does not monopolise Cassiodorus' preoccupations. The *Quaestor* of the Sacred Palace is also much in evidence, the Urban Prefect is only just less so. The Master of Offices is also part of this complex of officialdom within Cassiodorus' attention span; so are the King's household staff. All these *corps* are thought of largely in terms of their topmost personnel. They are not seen as antagonistic or in conflict.

Closely connected with this central area of awareness, as it were, and never far from Cassiodorus' thoughts, are the military establishment and the papal hierarchy. Tensions subsist at this level, between all three groups within the apparatus — between civil and military, civil and ecclesiastic, and military and ecclesiastic bureaucracies. Behind these powerful groups one keeps catching glimpses of the Senate, the most respected status group in Cassiodorus' *Who's Who* of Rome. Such, then, are the layers of preoccupations which seem most central in Cassiodorus' background awareness of his *milieu*. In the further background is the Italo-Gothic Kingdom of his much-loved Italy; and in the yet more remote background is the eastern empire. Constantinople is on the periphery of Cassiodorus' attention area. It is subtle and menacing. It houses an eastern bureaucracy with a powerful Master of Offices and a prestigeful Praetorian Prefect. Both foreground and background thus differ in these two writers' thought-worlds.

At John's level, one's whole working life was irretrievably committed in the very act of entering the service. One could not subsequently switch *corps*, and within a *corps* one's training (and investment in seniority) limited one to certain departments only. Personal qualities and efforts could advance one only within his chosen department (or branch of a department). Irrespective of such advance, one's career was made or marred by (a) the ebb and flow of the fortunes of the *corps* to which the department belonged and, equally important, by (b) the relative position won, lost or maintained by his department amongst competing departments within that *corp* at large. Hence John is, by job-conditioning, a tactical thinker. Against his better judgement he was pressured into "the" branch in "the" senior administrative *corps* of the world of his day. He had ample time to see how much better his better judgement had been. The very department which he had intended to join rose to affluence by destroying the fortunes of the branch of the department which he actually joined,[2] while the *corps* of which it was a part displaced his own *corps* and assumed primacy of place. Across his forty-odd years of service, against a politically stable background (effectively only one change of ruler), the whole of his immediate, occupational background underwent continuous and, for him, adverse change.

John's was not a world in which new skills and occupations could be acquired by professional men in mid-career. He did his best to job-hop by transferring to academic circles (after, characteristically, supporting the wrong Prefect). He remained classified with the *corps* into which his initial choice of branch of departments had brought him. Hence his desperate concentration upon the fortunes of the Prefecture, upon which so tragically much depended. Hence too his scant attention to other, for him irrelevant, "outside" bureaucracies — those of the Emperor's household, the military, the Urban Prefect, and even (given his unorthodox religious views) the Church. Political events affecting the East (i.e. that part of Anatolia and its surroundings from which his *corps* drew most of its tax income) loomed large in his attention. But the West did not affect the fortunes of his Prefecture. Hence the official line on Cassiodorus' Goths was uncritically accepted in what fleeting attention he had to spare. The Goths whom Cassiodorus presents as patriotic champions of Italian liberty[3] become "savages," who are "tearing Holy Rome and the surrounding countryside to pieces"; Rome is freed from the fetters they have set upon her, Rome the sufferer of much distress.[4]

At Cassiodorus' level, intermittent service in the civil administrative bureaucracy kept up the nobility of one's family. Nobility was achieved by the securing of a variety of appointments high in the Emperor's, or latterly the King's, service; it had to be kept fresh by each generation.[5] One moved farthest and fastest along the career-line of high offices by a policy of moderation,[6] i.e. by not performing so incompetently as to embarrass the monarch (who had, after all, to provide for certain minimal societal needs), nor so efficiently as to frighten him (he did not far outreach his fellow Goth nobles in power and could ill afford the emergence of a constellation of power at some unexpected point, as this would immediately alter the overall balance of bureaucratic forces). If John's situation encouraged tactical thinking about one's career, Cassiodorus' was an inducement to strategical thinking: he had not only to cope with the problem of how best to manage a given set of circumstances, but with the further problem of choice within a variety of sets of circumstances.

Now, across Cassiodorus' thirty-odd years of service in the bureaucracy, the bureaucracy itself underwent relatively little change, but there was a great deal of change in the political background (effectively, three changes of ruler). Instability in the latter regard only made Cassiodorus' position the stronger: the Goths could not run Italy without a bureaucracy, and this only men trained in the Great Tradition could manage. The Goths lacked the educational traditions which would have enabled them to take over and maintain the sophisticated bureaucratic apparatus which ran the territories which they had conquered. Moreover, without a bureaucracy to centralize the resources of the lands which they had overrun, their state would break up into petty baronies and fall prey to any more well organized neighbor. Rapid changes of kinglets, royal musical chairs, thus made the centralizing services of the bureaucracy increasingly indispensable, and Cassiodorus' prospects ever brighter. Hence liberation from the Goths was a daunting prospect. In the East were boundless reservoirs of Greek-speaking administrative personnel; incorporation within a larger bureaucratic system would inevitably mean changes in the structure of the bureaucracies of the West, especially given the reforming, empire-building Heads of *Corps* encouraged within that larger bureaucracy.[7] Cassiodorus, therefore, watched developments coming from the East very closely.

Cassiodorus was far less totally committed to the administrative bureaucracy than was John: he was a generalist, not a specialist, at home in several major *corps* within it; moreover, service with the bureaucracy was only expected to occupy part of his active career. And Heads of *Corps* were, in the nature of things, far more aware of their bureaucratic opposite numbers than was the case with their respective middle-level staffs, amongst whom were men such as John. Consequently, Cassiodorus was far more aware of "outside" bureaucratic *corps* than was John. Those mentioned are those of the King's household, the military, and the Church. The latter was least affected by the "liberation" of Italy, and it was to it that Cassiodorus gravitated after he had withdrawn from service in the administrative bureaucracy in view of the progress of the war in Italy.

The picture of the Byzantines which emerges from these letters conforms to the sombre expectations which a western bureaucrat would tend to hold. There is little that is favorable: the eastern Court was once admittedly superior,[8] but things had changed for the better in the West,[9] and Cassiodorus affects to regard the two bureaucracies as currently on a level.[10] The easterners are regarded, with traditional ethnocentricity, as a lesser breed, emotional and crafty;[11] they labor under the undue influence of bureaucratic masters.[12] Their cause is unjust and they are basically hostile and covetous.[13] Such is the burthen of the sum total of the fleeting (and often cryptically allusive) references to the Byzantines in the letters.

Finally, we come to the appraisal of the formative influence upon an official of his position within the bureaucratic apparatus. This could shape his views on the larger world outside in at least two major ways. Cassiodorus' attendance in the counsel chambers of power gave him a splendid vantage point from which to watch the play of politics at national and international levels, as it were (e.g. at crises of succession and of the outbreak of war). Hence a wider and more realistic view than John could manage was possible for him.[14] John might be able to accept glib claims that "the Romans...with God at their head...hold the whole world,"[15] but Cassiodorus, who had to put the blunt facts presented by his Goth masters into a Latin that was both stylistically and diplomatically acceptable, knew better. There were two potentially bitterly hostile peoples in Italy,[16] and two potentially equally hostile powers within what had formerly been the one Roman Empire.[17]

John was not so strategically placed, in his middle-level post. His days went by in a blur of work, but it was work on the detail of (part of) the execution of decisions in whose making he had no part, and of whose planning he was not informed. As a cultured man of letters, he was alienated from the Circus, which, with its Blue and Green Factions, was all that remained of the once proud tradition of Graeco-Roman popular government.[18] In contrast to Cassiodorus, John was thus depoliticized: he had a restricted intellectual horizon and range of interests and, outside the area where he disposed of expert knowledge, readily accepted the official version of what was going on in the world of his day.

This was not the only way in which one's position in the bureaucratic apparatus could inform one's views. Besides hierarchical grade, the physical location of one's working environment was all important. Cassiodorus served in the bureaucracy of the West, which was clearly recognized as a separate, if kindred, service in a separate, if kindred, world. Basically, however, Cassiodorus thought of Rome as the one true centre of all that Latinity and the empire represented. For all the material superiority of Constantinople, Cassiodorus' world centred on Rome and Italy. His unconscious assumptions are Italocentric.[19] His notions of his environment sharply, if unconsciously, distinguish between Italy and surrounding areas. Thus, if one goes by simple frequency of geographic references, there are 46 mentions of towns, regions or places in Italy to 15 in the rest of the world, in the three books analyzed. Rome is explicitly mentioned 38 times, as contrasted with 4 mentions of Ravenna and one of Constantinople (these cities were not included in the previous count). His picture of Italy is moreover not merely seen in more detail; it is painted more lovingly.[20] In fact the most emotionally charged descriptive passages in Cassiodorus have to do with Squillace, Rome and Italy — land or people.

For John "Rome" is a less tangible concept. His view of Roman history, upon which his *On the Magistracies of the Roman Constitution* (this, the Greek title of the work, has been Latinized as *De Magistratibus*) is based, is of a (changing) system of government. "Rome" for him is not the Holy City set in a well-loved Italian countryside. It is a set of institutions, founded by Aeneas (who was aided by Tuscan, i.e. Lydian, priests who had come out of John's own home area in the East), and developed by a series of giant historical figures: Brutus the Tyrannicide, founder of the Republic; Caesar, whose reign marks a great turning point in the fortunes of Rome, and Anastasius, the financial and administrative genius.[21] The city Rome is much more salient for John in relation to Constantinople than is Constantinople in relation to Rome in Cassiodorus' case: even in book three of the *De Magistratibus,* which centers squarely on Constantinople, there are five references to Rome, all with some formulaic utterance of respect.[22] In the other books Rome is far more frequently mentioned. But the only extended descriptive passage displaying emotion goes to Constantinople; Rome was not felt as a rival, but as a glorious, if faded, relic of bygone days.[23] This tale of two cities is simply not an issue which engaged John's partisanship. So it is with each writer's attitude to the other's language. For the Italocentric Cassiodorus, arrangements must be made to have seminal works in Greek translated. For John, all educated men ought to know Latin. But this involves no acknowledgement of the seniority of contemporary Rome. Use of Latin as the language of the bureaucracy would give John gigantic career advantages.[24] Moreover John cannot think of "Byzantines" in the same way that Cassiodorus can think of "Romans" (i.e. the original, non-Gothic inhabitants of the peninsula). He has no word for them, sometimes referring to his people as easterners, sometimes as Hellenes, sometimes as Romans.[25]

In contrast to Cassiodorus, John assigns his most emotional passages to things such as pensioning, the disciplining of officials, bureaucratic feuding, and the loss of prestige undergone by his *corps.* All issues so presented involve the Praetorian Prefecture, the most important concern in John's life. John lived in an empire which had seen much change in its territorial boundaries, and change in its capital, its language, religion and ethnic composition. The great unchanging element in this world was the Prefecture. Hence John anachronistically projects it back into an existence at Rome's very beginnings.[26] He cannot conceive of "Rome" without "the (prefectural) Service," in some shape or form. The Prefecture, in his eyes, is more important to the Empire than any other institution. It channels the precious golden lifeblood around inside that system. As the Prefecture was so vital to the administrative machinery, any change it underwent would be widely felt, eventually, throughout the whole apparatus of government. Hence serving this great institution gave purpose and meaning to his life, for all that his personal career prospects were so dismal. Hence, too, his assumption of wide outside interest in the history of his Service,[27] an assumption which speaks volumes about his values and preconceptions.

From Cassiodorus' point of view, Italy had seen the ebb and flow of different rulers and different systems of government. In his day Rome contained two great bureaucracies, one ecclesiastical and one administrative. These were the equal of any similar bureaucracies elsewhere in the world. There was nothing in these institutions that was unique or immune from change. What was unique was Rome and what she stood for, including her great noble families reaching far back across changing political systems and sets of institutions.[28] For Cassiodorus the institutional framework was valued in proportion as it served Rome, the object of his affections and reverence. Hence the bureaucracy in which he served was an important part of his life, but he viewed it as an instrument. When his prospects in serving within it grew dreary, he retired — to serve the Church — and proceeded to produce his life's greatest achievement in a wholly different field, by preserving for subsequent ages the great literature of Rome, which was in his day in imminent danger of extinction.[29] The contrast with John's reaction, under similar circumstances, reveals how different was the meaning of service in the civil bureaucracy in the life and aspirations of the two men.

Thus a metropolitan bureaucrat could well be conditioned by the traditions of the great Service in which he labored to have a wholly different regard for the bureaucratic apparatus than that entertained by a provincial bureaucrat. As bureaucratic apparatus and state could not be dissociated in the thinking of the time, since the two were so interwoven and interdependent, this entailed a different regard for the state. With such divergent views, the bureaucracy could not be a monolithic structure. Such strains and stresses as have been shown here to have existed within the bureaucracy meant internal change, which could only mean extensive repercussions within the society that depended on the bureaucracy. For this traditional society was far from static,[30] as a moment's reflection on the radically different conditions prevailing in the Byzantine Empire one hundred years later indicates: territorial extent, provisioning and administrative system, ruling dynasty, major friends and foes, bureaucratic machinery — all had changed.[31]

FOOTNOTES TO SECTION 1

1. Unless otherwise specified this biography follows Jones, *An Introduction to Divine and Human Readings by Cassiodorus Senator*, pp. 3-42.

2. So Cassiodorus claims at I 4, 146 (n.b.: for precision of reference, Cassiodorus' correspondence, the *Variae*, is cited by book (I), letter

therein (4), and pages of Hodgkin's translation (in *The Letters of Cassiodorus*) — the 146 of the ref. above). The claim may well be part of family mythology: neither Bury *(History of the Later Roman Empire)* nor Jones in *LRE* mention this prefecture.

3. *Var.* I 4, 147.

4. Indicated by the depth of feeling, without parallel elsewhere in his writings, consistently shown in his references to the region: see in particular VII 31-33, 378-83. John the Lydian evinces something of the same feeling towards his birthplace (see chapter 2, end), but lacks the feeling of responsibility for its welfare.

5. The correspondence on which this analysis of Cassiodorus is based comprises books I, VIII and X studied in detail. This selection of books enables one to cross-compare (1) demands imposed by the job and (2) demands imposed by the individual ruler (see Fig. 6.1, below). It follows that any consistently maintained policy — and this desire to further the best interests of Roman civilization within Italy *is* consistently maintained — is independent of either set of demands. One view of Cassiodorus is that he was a "political acrobat," aiming solely at achieving personal distinction and being prepared to serve any ruler in service of this ambition (see G. A. Punzi, *L'Italia del VI secolo nelle "Variae" di Cassiodoro*, 1927, pp. 47-49; Punzi concludes by rejecting this view). Analysis of the motivations of a long-dead historical personality seldom is conclusive. To impute unprincipled self-seeking to Cassiodorus is to ignore the problem that expediency in regard to means which are adopted in order to further a deeply held principle is quite a different type of expediency from that involved in an unprincipled desire for self advancement. Moreover Cassiodorus' actions, when his entire lifetime is considered, indicate a landed

Figure 6.1 (to note 5)

Official position and reign in which books were written

RULING KING	OFFICE HELD		
	Quaestor	Master of Offices	Praetorian Prefect
Theodoric	Book I		
Amalasuntha		Book VIII	
Theodahad & Witigis			Book X

aristocrat's identification with his fellow aristocrats and his estates. This study is based upon this quite general characterization of his motivation. See Jones, *Introduction to Divine and Human Readings*, pp. 9-10 & 17-18 and A. Momigliano, "Cassiodorus and the Italian Culture of his Time," *Proceedings of the British Academy* 41, 1955, pp. 207-45.

6. See Jones, *Introduction to Divine and Human Readings*, p. 19 & n. 1.

7. See Momigliano (*op. cit.*, n. 5), *fin.*

8. There is some uncertainty as to whether Cassiodorus became a monk; probably he did not: see Jones, *op. cit.*, pp. 23-25.

9. Prominent amongst these is the *Historia ecclesiastica tripertita*, promoted by Cassiodorus' interest. Epiphanius compiled this tripartite history of the Church from the histories written by Socrates, Sozemenus and Theodoretus. It is full of mistranslations from the Greek, a language as badly understood in Italy as was Latin in Constantinople: see Jones, *op. cit.*, pp. 28-29 & n. 58.

FOOTNOTES TO SECTION 2

1. See chapter 4, note 4, and text thereto, for discussion of this Great Tradition.

2. On the form of content analysis used, see my study "Construing Literature as History" in *Mosaic* 1, 1967, pp. 22-38.

3. See O. J. Zimmermann, *The Late Latin Vocabulary of the Variae of Cassiodorus, with special advertence to the technical terminology of administration*, Catholic University of America, Studies in Medieval and Renaissance Latin Language and Literature, XV, 1944 (cf. Jones, *An Introduction to the Divine and Human Readings*, pp. 38-39), and A. J. Fridh, "Terminologie et formules dans les Variae de Cassiodore," *Studia Graeca et Latina Gothoburgensia* II, 1956.

4. Riggs' study "Agraria and Industria" (in Siffin, *Towards the Comparative Study of Public Administration*) never fails to delight any newcomers to it, in my experience. The concept "Prismatic Society" is owed to his more recent work, *Administration in Developing Countries* (cited in this book as "Riggs"); see, for example, pp. 122-4; 174-86 & 206-220 there.

5. In particular M. Rokeach, *The Open and the Closed Mind*, pp. 8-11 & 31-53; on the judgmental scale, see C. E. Osgood, G. J. Souci and P. H. Tannenbaum, *The Measurement of Meaning*, U. of Illinois Press, 1957.

6. This is multivariate content analysis. For further details on the method, see my study, "Looking for a Writer's Picture of Reality," in *Revue* 2, 1968, pp. 36-81.

FOOTNOTES TO SECTION 3

1. III 62,3.
2. III 69,2.
3. III 61,6; II 20,2-21,1 partakes of this nature.
4. III 50,4-5; 69,3; cf. 38,3-4. A decidedly recalcitrant spirit in a Head of a *Corps* vis-à-vis the Emperor is lauded at II 17,2. Hence the significance of the remark that Justinian was *not* an Emperor to think of thwarting: III 76,2.
5. At III 75,1-2 John unhesitatingly obeys a Prefect in illegal activities.
6. III 56, 2-4.
7. III 76,10.
8. Rufinus is the classical instance: II 10,3-4; III 7,5; 23,1-3 & 40,2-3. III 17,3 tells of another such case of disciplining an over-powerful minister. On the play of intragovernmental forces in an absolutist autocracy, see Wittfogel, pp. 106-107, 145-47 & 152-60.
9. III 42, 3-4; cf. 68,2-5.
10. Marinus is the arch-villain here: III 49, 1-5 and 51, 2&5.
11. III 56, 2-4; cf. 68, 2-5.
12. III 45,3.
13. III 39,2-4.
14. One such is lauded at II 26,1.
15. III 42,1-2 is a particularly far-fetched instance of this idea; 61,2-4 indicates a shrewd insight into the long-term results of a policy initiated by a Prefect without the Emperor's knowledge.
16. Two "classical" instances, of "good" and "bad" Heads respectively, are presented: Phocas (III 72,2-76,10) and John the Cappadocian (II 21,2-4; III 57,1-58,1; 62,1-5; 64,1; 65,1-5; 68,2-70,2 & 72,1). The "good" Head is everything that is good; the villain the reverse, no allowance — unusually for John — being made for cross-pressures or unanticipated consequences. It requires some such atmosphere as that postulated by Wittfogel (see pp. 152-60) to explain this reaction in John.
17. *Var.* X 31-33, 444-48.
18. X 4, 419-20 & 16,429; cf. also X 20, 432 and Hodgkin's note.
19. I 12, 152; X 5, 421-22; see Wittfogel, pp. 126-36 on "Benevolent Despotism."

20. VIII 20, 367; X 6, 422-23; X 27, 438.

21. Cf. VIII 26, 375; at one time informers were regularly employed as a check on judges: 16, 362; a classical illustration of how a "bad" Prefect typically behaves occurs at 20, 367.

22. *Pref.* 135-7.

23. X 31, 444; *Pref.* 135-6; cf. X 35, 447.

24. Respectively X 31, 444 and VIII 6, 351.

25. See Riggs, pp. 15-19 & 182-84 and n. 57 below on "Overlapping."

26. Cf. VIII 7, 351-2 and X 17, 429.

27. VIII 23, 370.

28. I 4, 141; X 1, 415 & 32, 447.

29. Cf. VIII 26, 374-5 with Hodgkin's note, and see Wittfogel, pp. 78-84 on "Weak Property," and pp. 208-213 (cf. 173-76) on "The Margin of the Hydraulic World."

30. John is far less aware of the succession as a crisis point; but then it was surrounded by fewer hazards in the East, and, in consequence, he experienced fewer successions. See *De Mag.* III 45,1-3 & 51,1-6 plus 55,1-4: a much more stable throne is (unconsciously) assumed in this account.

31. Respectively *Var.* VIII 3, 349; 4, 350; 8, 352 and X 14, 427-8 (striking examples concerning the succession) and *Pref.* 136 & VIII 17, 364 (loyalty to the King).

32. For the attitude of the Senate see VIII 15, 360-61 & X 13, 426-7.

33. X 16, 428-9.

34. X 31, 445.

35. As the monarch strives to project himself as the sort of ruler that his influential subjects wanted (see e.g. VIII 3, 349; 4, 350; cf. X 14, 427-8), the letters are here taken as a projection, in this regard, of the views of those subjects. It is quite clear that they did not wish for a mighty overlord.

36. I 12, 152; VIII 13, 359; X 5, 421-2.

37. VIII 4, 350 (cf. 3, 349, beginning).

38. VIII 9, 352-54.

39. X 31, 444.

40. Instances of the overriding authority of the *Sajo* (effectively, the Gothic equivalent of the Master of Soldiery — see I 24, 157) occur at VIII 24, 371 & 27, 375. Disciplinary measures do not seem to be taken against Gothic notables, though Roman officials can be threatened with

them: I 2, 144; 32, 162; VIII 13, 359 & 18, 366; cf. VIII 26, 375 & 28, 376. The ability of a king to proceed against even Roman subjects who defaulted, however, varied with his power: Theodahad, for instance, had to treat a refractory Senate very gingerly: X 13, 426-7; 16, 429 & 18, 430 (cf. I 30, 161 & 32, 162).

41. VIII 10, 355; 11, 357; cf. 9, 352. At X 31, 444 Witigis expresses the fury of a Gothic noble at the thought that matters of high moment should be decided through consultation with counsellors other than Gothic nobles.

42. VIII 19, 366.

43. X 11, 425.

44. The remarks of the Goth Tulum on his admission to the Senate bring this point home with more force than tact: "Reflect, I pray, that by my accepting it, the genius of the Patriciate is exalted, since none of my fellow-countrymen will hold cheaply that rank in you which he sees honoured in me": VIII 11, 356.

45. See n. 40.

46. I 42 & 43, 167.

47. A particularly touching instance occurs at X 29, 440-41.

48. I 13, 152 & VIII 13, 358.

49. I 42, 167 & X 12, 425. Irregular career patterns gave the king more control over appointees, who were the more dependent upon his favor in proportion as the promotions were more arbitrary: see Eisenstadt, pp. 278-79, and cf. n. 53.

50. He takes it for granted that even the Popes should be the king's appointees and subject to the latter's direction: VIII 15, 360-61; 24, 371; X 19, 431 & 25, 436.

51. Heliodorus (I 4, 146) and Peter the Patrician (X 33, 447).

52. VIII 16, 361-2.

53. *Pref.* 135; VIII 14, 359-60; X 6, 422; a *Quaestor* is informed of his duty to oppose the King if the latter is in the wrong at I 13, 359, an injunction which implies that the King was effectively above the law.

54. I 42, 167; it needed empowering if there was serious work to be done: 44, 168.

55. *Pref.* 134-5; see also VIII 20, 367 & 6, 351 and X 27, 438. In view of VIII 11, 356, however, it must be borne in mind that this preeminence is within the civil bureaucracy, which is inferior to the military in standing.

56. Surprisingly little notice is paid to the status and authority of this post: cf. I 12, 151.

57. *Pref.* 135; I 13, 152; on the concept "Overlapping" see Riggs, pp. 13-15.

58. For the concept see Riggs, "Agraria and Industria," p. 85.

59. To some extent governmental control was in fact tighter in the East, so that the disparity has some factual basis. But the difference in viewpoint is more the result of a much greater realization on the part of Cassiodorus of the cross-pressures in which Heads of *Corps* were involved.

60. For reference groups, see I 13, 152 & 42, 167. Among individuals named from any given class in society, Patricians easily top the list; amongst classes pride of place is held by the Senate. Nobles are frequently mentioned, always favorably (see VIII 17, 364 & 31, 379 and X 11, 425). Cassiodorus seems obsessed by pedigrees (see VIII 16, 361 and cf. X 31, 445), which are for him the crucial reason for advancing of a man to high honours (I 42, 167, VIII 16, 361 and X 11, 424-5). These are clearly the people and issues central to his focus of attention, and their prominence in his thought-world indicates their prime importance for him.

61. "Obviously" because there is a semantic field of technical terms covering the area, indicating its salience in the ancients' thought-system (on the concept "semantic field" see Ullmann, *Semantics: An Introduction to the Science of Meaning*, pp. 244-50). See the discussion of *Sportulae* etc. in chapter 5, note 23 and text thereto.

62. See *LRE*, pp. 484-94, 586 & 791 on *praescriptio fori*; 468-9, 568-9 & 602-5 on *sportulae* and 391-6 & 398-9 on *suffragium*.

63. This point is brought out analytically in the discussion already referred to in chapter 5, note 23 and text thereto.

64. For the terms, see Riggs, "Agraria and Industria," p. 35.

65. Riggs uses the term "prismatic" for this syndrome: see, for instance, pp. 265-85 for a discussion of its operation.

66. The following passages are relevant to the subsequent discussion (italicized numbers indicate special importance): *De Mag.* II 10,5; 15,1; 16,1; *16,3; 17,1;* 29,1; III 9,9-10; 10,3; 11,2-3; 13,1-5; 14,1-2; 15,1-2 & 4; 16,1; *17,3;* 18,1-5; 20,3; 23,2; 24,2; 25,4-5; 38,3-5; *40,4*; 42,3-4 & 5-6; *49,2-5*; 50,2; *50,5*; 65,5-66,3; 76,10; cf. 7,1; 68,4 & 69,3.

67. This is the theme underlying the laments at II 15,1 (cf. 16,1 & 29,1); III 9,9-10; 18,1-2 (cf. 25,3-5); 40,5-6; 49,2-5, and 67,1-4.

68. III 38,3-5.

69. II 10,5; III 23,2 and 40,4 (the only triple repetition in the work).

70. See *LRE*, pp. 833-4.

71. III 50,5 and 38,3-5.

72. John is particularly scandalized at a Praetorian Prefect who voluntarily restricted his area of authority: III 42,3-5.

73. On the results of its importance or lack thereof, see II 16,3; 17,1-2 (cf. 9,1-2); 18,1-5; 23, 1-2; III 25,5; 42,5-6; 49,5; 50,1-2; 66,1-2 & cf. 21,1-2; on its being viewed as a weapon: III 9,10; 17,1-18,2; 40,2-3; & cf. II 16,1.

74. III 13,1-5; cf. 15,2-4.

75. The key passage occurs at III 25,4, but this is merely the most striking of several: see III 14,1 & 15,1 and cf. II 18,3; III 10,1 & 18,5.

76. Some provision (a food allowance) *was* made: III 30,4, but John was not satisfied: III 30,10.

77. The first salary mentioned occurs in John's second year at work: III 27,2.

78. The ideal is suggested at I 15 (4).

79. I 23,3 suggests straitened financial circumstances; II 15,2 implies that he found the cost of living in Constantinople too high. See next note.

80. III 25,1-6; 29,4; 30,1-2 & 10; 66,3-6 and 67,4-6.

81. Contrast III 27,2 with 66,4-6.

82. See II 17,1 where "persons worthy of note" are indicated as desirable recruits; contrast III 2,3. On literary training see III 6,1; 20,7 (cf. 27,4); 28,3 and 54,1.

83. II 18,2-3; III 2,3-5; 9.7; 10,3; 17,3; 20,2 & cf. 14,2. All three qualities are important: see discussion in chapter 5, text to nn. 24-5. John was himself considered a bureaucrat of outstanding merit (III 30,5-8) and had been recruited for his potential (cf. the implications of III 17,3; 26,4 & 67,3, and see the beginning of John's biography in chapter 1).

84. III 9,5-6 & 20,2.

85. III 3,3-5; cf. II 18,2-3 & III 67,3.

86. The implication of III 66,3-67,5.

87. III 27,2-5.

88. He is remarkably objective in regard to a Head of *Corps'* pretentiousness in claiming a larger and more luxurious official residence: II 20,1-21,4.

89. He always speaks of them in the highest terms (I 15(4); III 30,10; cf. 66,3-6 & 67,4-6), as opposed e.g. to the academics (III 47,1; see also 13,4; 15,2 and II 26,4), with whom he also served (III 29,1-4).

90. See the Summary of the Findings of Part One above.

91. On the "constricted personality" of traditional man, see Lerner, *The Passing of Traditional Society*, pp. 48-72 & 98.

92. *Var.* VIII 24, 371-2.

93. The largest cluster of new and much-used subject headings which the content analysis produced concerned the general subject-heading "Law."

94. John is handling the routine, detailed work arising out of the decisions taken, so the more impersonal view of the business of the court as a mere work-flow is understandable. He does not reflect on the effect of his opposition to a Prefect (such as John the Cappadocian) upon the work-output of that Prefect. For Cassiodorus, however, recalcitrant subordinates are a serious factor, to be taken into account in the work situation: see *Pref.* 134; I 2, 143-4; 11, 151 & 35, 163.

95. *Pref.* 134. Cassiodorus also complains of chronic lack of time (*ib.* 134-36): on the unequal distribution of work-loads, leading to overwhelming pressure on a Head of *Corps* in a traditional society, see Riggs, pp. 112-13.

96. Contained in the comment that a *Quaestor* (the King's top legal advisor) should not be dependent on one of his subordinates when he has to perform his duties: VIII 18, 365.

97. A case in point is cited at VIII 16, 362. The contempt was mutual: a Head could not trust his subordiantes to implement his instructions: *Pref.* 134.

98. Hence the (already observed) salience of the Senate in the letters (see n. 60). Significantly, whereas John wrote a history of his branch of the Prefecture as a loving tribute to it (*De Mag.* I 15(4)), Cassiodorus' interest was in having a history of the Church written (see Jones, *Introduction to the Divine and Human Readings*, pp. 28-29).

99. Contrast John's laments re the fading fortunes of the Prefecture (as at *De Mag.* II 5,1; 7,1-3; 10,3-5; 11,1; 16,3-17,2; III 1,1; 7,1; 9,9-10; 13,1-14,2; 15,3-4; 18,1; 19,1-4; 20,5-10; 23,1-2; 25,4-5; 36,1-2; 39,1; 40,1-4; 41,1-3; 42,2 & 5; 45,1; 49,5; 56,2-4; 65,4-66,4 & 67,4 — the dominant *motif* in books 2 & 3) with Cassiodorus' bland assurance that all is as should be with its prestige: *Var. Pref.* 134-5 & VIII 20, 367. Justinian had to raise an outsider, an efficiency expert, from the ranks to get a Prefect who would abandon this languid disengagement and make a career out of reforming the bureaucracy (cf. *De Mag.* III 57,1-3; Anastasius had done the same: 46,1-3 & 49,1-5). Hence the pro-aristocratic John had a double reason for detesting John the Cappadocian, the reforming Prefect in question.

100. The sole case in the letters analyzed in which a loyalty other than that to the king is lauded concerns a case of loyalty towards fellow aristocrats: VIII 17, 364.

101. The case involves a military official overriding the jurisdictional competence of an ecclesiastical official: VIII 24, 371-2.

102. Informing was very adversely regarded by the judges whom it imperilled: VIII 16, 362; cf. 25, 373.

103. Theodahad's resentment is patent, if concealed, in his official letter at X 4, 419-20 (as the sequel proved).

104. I 5, 147; see also 23, 157.

105. VIII 13, 359; 18, 366 & 20, 367.

106. As e.g. at *De Mag.* III 69,2-3.

107. One such case is mentioned at VIII 13, 358.

108. I 22, 156; cf. VIII 20, 367.

109. The issue was much more clear-cut at Cassiodorus' level than at John's, where servicing, rather than decision-making, activities were in progress. For an aspersion on bribery in judges see *Var.* X 28, 433.

110. Reference to pedigree is very frequent in this connection: see I 42, 167; VIII 10, 354; 16, 361; 20, 367; 22, 369; X 11, 424-5 and 29, 440. John would appear also to think of high birth as a qualification for top bureaucratic positions: *De Mag.* III 38, 3 & 5.

111. *Var.* X 11, 424-5; cf. VIII 9, 353.

112. He prides himself on having produced some stock letters of appointment that made less of a chore out of disbursing them: *Praef.* 168.

113. See I 3, 145; 42, 167; VIII 10, 354-6; 16, 363; 21 & 22, 368-9.

114. I 42, 167 & VIII 19, 368. John had availed himself of advancement brought through nepotism (*De Mag.* III 26, 4-27, 2) and seemed to regard this as perfectly fit and proper (cf. III 26,4 & 28,1-2). The lengths of the careers at the two levels presumably accounted for the lesser emphasis on nepotism at John's level: Cassiodorus might reasonably expect the favor of a monarch to be good for three requests for office across a twenty-year period, whereas John had to attain some thirty posts across a career of more than forty years. The former problem called for a courtier's skills, the latter necessitated those of a bureaucrat.

115. See *Var.* X 33, 447 & 34, 448.

116. Training: VIII 21, 368 (and X 31, 444-5: this was hardly a normal "position," but it indicates Gothic views very clearly); training in civil administration is referred to at I 4, 145. Experience: VIII 18,

365; 20, 367 & X 7, 423 (all lawyers).

117. It is not frequently mentioned and always appears in a group of other claims to advancement: cf. I 42, 167.

118. I 12, 151 & 13, 152.

119. Delays: I 42, 167; X 7, 423; inversion of sequence: X 12, 425.

120. On the simultaneous co-existence of feudal and bureaucratic trends within the same society see Riggs, *The Ambivalence of Feudalism and Bureaucracy in Traditional Societies*, Comparative Administration Group, Occasional Paper, 1965.

121. I 41, 166.

122. See *Pref.* 134; VIII 367 & X 438; a classical instance of a Gothic interpretation of a lord's responsibilities to his subjects occurs at X 5, 421. Underlings such as John seem to have had an almost exclusively punishment orientation: see chapter 5, note 8 and discussion thereto in the text; see also the discussion to notes 6 to 11 of section 4 of the present chapter.

123. X 28, 439-40. This is the nearest approach to mention of *suffragium* in the letters studied.

124. See *Pref.* 134, I 2, 143-4; 11, 151; 35, 163 (anxiety in regard to subordinates' implementation of instructions) and 2, 144 & VIII 13, 358 (threats of punishment). John in fact speaks with bitterness of Prefects to whom their staff is "of neither account nor consequence": *De Mag.* III 56, 3-4.

125. Cf. e.g. II 5,1; 7,1-3 (such extended imagery is very rare in John's writings); 16,3;III 9,10; 11,1; 12,1; 18,1; 20,9; 25,5; 45,1; 56,2; 66,3 — passages where striking imagery or unusually emotional language occurs.

126. See n. 99 for their frequency.

127. II 10,2-11(5) & 13,2-3 (cf. III 24,1-25,3 for an actual instance of this general trend); see also II 7,6.

128. II 10,2 & III 40,1.

129. II 10,3-4; III 23,1-2; 40,2-4; 41,3; & cf. 7,5 and 24,1-25,3.

130. The senior *agens in rebus* on the Master's staff in that sub-group was given, as his final career-position, the post of *princeps*. The latter was in, but not of, the office staff of the Prefect, and from this vantage point cross-checked on the activities of all the Prefect's judicial staff. This meant infringement of *praescriptio fori*, of the career-patterns of the Prefect's Men (who lost access to the topmost position open to them) and of the Prefect's absolute authority. From this point on, the two great *corps* were thus in a structurally-caused

state of enmity. For examples of this see: III 21,1-2 & 67,1-4.

131. III 7,1; 9,10 and 24,1-25,5.

132. See the implication at III 17,3.

133. III 67,1-4.

134. The decline of the Prefecture (see n. 99) is seen throughout John's lamentations from the point of view of its judicial departments: the accountancy department was prospering: III 21,2; 36,1-2 & 49,1-5. The records department, for which in particular John exhibits fellow feeling (see III 27,3-5), was totally ruined: III 19,1-4; 20,4-10 & 68,3-4.

135. No reference to them is favorable: III 21,2; 31,1-3; 35,1-6; 36,1-2; 46,2-3; 49,1-5; 50,1 & 57,2. It is difficult to decide whether John felt more dislike towards this group or towards the *principes* from the Master's Men. On the obsolescence of John's professional skills, see III 28,2 & 54,1-2 and cf. II 17,1; 18,2-3; III 3,3-5; 14,2; 20,2; 67,1-3.

136. This authoritarian's picture is more fully discussed in the contrast between John and Procopius in the next chapter. Only key passages are cited here and in the following notes: see II 23,1; III 11,1; 12,1; 20,4; 68,3; cf. II 19,9 & 28,1.

137. See especially II 5,2; III 39,1 & 67,1.

138. II 5,1; 7,3; 11(2); III 41,2.

139. See II 23,1; III 18,1; 40,1; 42,1; 45,1; 46,1; 55,1; 57,1; 71,1 & 76,9.

140. Agents exceed instructions: III 39,4; 46,2-3; 61,6; 62,3; and 69,2-3; unanticipated consequence: III 31,5 and cf. 42,1-2; 67,2-3 & 68,4.

141. This is the implication of anecdotes such as those at III 24, 1-25, 5; 35, 1-36, 2 & 67, 1-4. For an explicit statement, as a perfectly natural viewpoint, of such an attitude, see III 33, 3-34, 5.

142. See II 26, 4; III 13, 4 and 15, 2 (all tales to the discredit of academics) with the conclusive 47,1.

143. It was almost on parity with the Praetorian Prefecture originally (II 9,5); John tells of two contemporary diminutions in its power (II 29,3 & III 38,3-5).

144. III 17,3 & 59,5-6.

145. II 9,2.

146. See biographical sketch in chapter 1, notes 4 and 7, and text thereto.

147. This inconsistency is here taken as the usual authoritarian ambivalence towards figures of authority. On Prefects seen as enemies see II 56,3-4.

148. John's work was composed in retirement after a career whose last stages had been a bitter disappointment (cf. *De Mag.* I 15(4) and III 25,1-6 & 66,5-67,5). Cassiodorus' letters were edited when he was on the verge of retirement and faced with the imminent prospect of seeing the Italo-Gothic state for which he had worked brought to ruin (see biographical sketch in section one of this chapter).

149. On the concept see E. Goffman, *The Presentation of the Self in Everyday Life*, Doubleday Anchor, 1959, pp. 112 ff.

150. Cf. *Var.* VIII 16, 361-3 & X 20, 432 (comparing both with Hodgkin's notes).

151. Respectively VIII 31, 378 (training) & VIII 13, 358 (good servants).

152. The assumption here is that rationality and efficiency are *not* the most salient norms in the value system underlying a *traditional* bureaucracy. On the model assumed, see S. N. Eisenstadt, "Political Struggle in Bureaucratic Societies," *World Politics* 9, 1956, pp. 15-36. For the case under discussion see VIII 24, 371-2 and cf. I 33, 162 & n. 175 below.

153. See I 4, 147; 23, 157; VIII 15, 360-61 & 24, 371-2.

154. VIII 13,358.

155. VIII 16,362.

156. *Pref.* 135.

157. It is thus no accident that Cassiodorus was appointed at such a youthful age; other *Quaestors* too seem to have lacked experience in the exercising of power: VIII 14,359; 18,365 & 19,366; X 7, 422-3; one is even exhorted to the study of law: X 6,422 (& cf. VIII 18,365).

158. Such a late appointment occurred in Cassiodorus' own career: see IX 24,408-12. There is repeated mention of a delay in conferring high positions — a strategy not confined to the Prefecture: I 12,151; 42,167 (cf. 43,167-8). As for inappropriate appointments, at I 42,167 an aged Patrician, who does not seem to have expected it, is appointed Urban Prefect. The King had recently had difficulties with the previous occupant of the post: I 32 & 33, 162.

159. This agrees with Wittfogel's findings on the "absence of effective societal checks" on the traditional autocrat: see pp. 102-108, esp. 106-7. These strategies tended to operate against the interests of bureaucratic strength: see Eisenstadt, pp. 278-9.

160. There is ample evidence of a high level of *anomie* in the Italy of Cassiodorus' day: disturbances: I 3,144; 27,159; 30,161; 44,168; VIII 16,362; dispossessions: I 7,148; 18,154; 38,165; VIII 28,376;

banditry: VIII 27,375-6; 32,380 & 381; 33,381-2 (the latter passage providing a very good explanation of at least one major cause of unrest). In general, on the peasant's outlook in traditional society, see Lerner, *The Passing of Traditional Society*, pp. 73 & 101-103, and Banfield, *The Moral Basis of a Backward Society*, pp. 63-67 (on *la miseria*) — findings which are amply confirmed by other studies on "the Culture of Poverty" (cf. O. Lewis, *The Children of Sanchez*, Vintage, 1961, pp. xxiv-xxviii). Disturbances could thus be readily provoked.

161. Cf. I 20,155; 30-33,161-62 & 42,167. It is not suggested that this is the only way that these letters can be interpreted (the letters are too carefully edited for such prosopographical exercises), merely that the stratagem was practically possible as well as theoretically probable.

162. The classical instance occurs at VIII 24,371-2, which tells of a conflict taken to such extremes that the victor would necessarily become involved in some form of royal displeasure: cf. I 2,143-4.

163. The easiest way to do this was by the laying of anonymous accusations: cf. VIII 16,362; on the strategy of displacement, see X 28,439 & VIII 25,373. If anonymity were not secured and the accusations were not successful, the life the informer took could well be his own: I 9,149.

164. VIII 15,360-61.

165. "Not the highest of posts": *Pref.* 135; eloquent, personable advocates desired: I 12,151; VIII 14,359; 18,365; X 6,422 & 7, 422-3.

166. VIII 14,359.

167. "Door" image: VIII 14,359; cf. *Pref.* 135, VIII 13,358 & 19,366.

168. I 12,151; even in the effusive IX 24,410 the post is hazily defined.

169. Way-station: *Pref.* 138 & I 13,152; see previous and following notes. Under Peter the Patrician the Master's post became the power center of the Byzantine bureaucracy (cf. John, *De Mag.* II 26,1); this fact is clearly recognized by Witigis: *Var.* X 33,447. No such change seems to have occurred at Rome.

170. *Pref.* 134-5; cf. I 3-4, 145-6 & VIII 11,356.

171. VIII 20,367; X 27,438; cf. *Pref.* 134.

172. This theme runs through all the passages mentioned in n. 171; note the implications of the opening sentence of X 28, 438, and I 3, 145.

173. VIII 21, 369.

174. I 42, 167.

175. I 9, 149; VIII 24, 371-2. The Count seems to be involved in another such jurisdictional quarrel at I 2, 143-4. There are a number of instances of the King's humbling the pretensions of Gothic warlords: I 26, 159; 38, 165; VIII 26, 375; 27, 375-6; 28, 376 & X 18, 430.

176. Informing: I 9, 149 (who better could inform at VIII 16, 362 & 25, 373-4?); disloyalty: *Pref.* 134 & VIII 16, 362; expertise: VIII 18, 365; cf. X 6, 422.

177. Cf. I 41, 166.

178. They are mentioned infrequently and in passing, in contrast to John's preoccupation with them. The Constantinopolitans may well have constituted such a group for Cassiodorus, however (see I 16, 153 & 31, 161 — with Hodgkin's notes; cf. VIII 9, 353 — "the Eastern people" — and X 14, 427). John's enemies on the other hand, are largely within the bureaucracies, external foes being far less real.

179. VIII 17, 364; cf. Hodgkins' notes at pp. 362-3, and n. 150 above.

180. It occurs in nine passages (*Pref.* 134 & 135; VIII 9, 353; 10, 354 & 355; 11, 356; X 31, 444 & 445; 33, 447), as opposed to the next most frequent concepts, enmity and envy, with three passages each (respectively I 32, 162; VIII 10, 354; 16, 362 — enmity; I 4, 147; VIII 25, 373 & X 28, 439 — envy).

181. Cf. X 14, 428 & 33, 447. On this point of view, see J. C. Skinner, "Symptom and Defense in Contemporary Greece: A Cross-cultural Inquiry," *The Journal of Nervous and Mental Disease* 141(4), 1966, pp. 481-5.

182. Respectively VIII 9, 353 & 10, 355; cf. X 33, 447.

183. A soldier's influence is presented in a courtier's terms at VIII 11, 356-7, and a courtier's influence in those of a soldier at 31, 444.

184. See VIII 11, 356.

185. On the term, see Easton, *A Systems Analysis...*, pp. 87-96; less technically, B. de Jouvenal, *The Pure Theory of Politics*, Cambridge, 1963, pp. 120-23. But Cassiodorus himself speaks of the Quaestorship as "the door to our Royal favour": VIII 14, 359. Its key strategical position was well appreciated: *Pref.* 135; cf. the implications of the King's words "I have been myself a witness," at X 31, 445.

186. See n. 184 and *Pref.* 136.

187. VIII 10, 354.

188. *Pref.* 135; complete supersession is mentioned at VIII 13, 358.

189. Cf. VIII 16, 362.

190. *Pref.* 134 & 136.

191. Cf. VIII 16, 362 & 20, 367.

192. On Cassiodorus' view of Constantinopolitans cf. I 43, 167, whence it appears that the Court at Constantinople had more prestige. The notions of duplicity (X 14, 427), emotionality (I 31, 161), and undue influence of courtiers (X 33, 447) are — naturally, under the circumstances — implicit (but see Hodgkin's notes). There are further implications of injustice (I 16, 153; X 32, 446), and a suggestion that the Constantinopolitans are effete Orientals (VIII 9, 353).

193. The King is aware that the powerful may constrain his minister to divert grain meant for the relief of the poor (X 27, 4-38), but as a subject Witigis could see nothing of the cross-pressures on Theodahad, attributing his actions to duplicity (X 31, 445).

194. On the prominence of envy and enmity in Cassiodorus' views on causation see n. 180; on enmity striking long after it had originated, see VIII 25, 373; cf. 16, 362.

195. I 2, 144.

196. X 4, 419.

197. The themes most invoked are that the Deity helps the King (I 1, 141; 24, 157; VIII 3, 349; 5, 351; 24, 371; 29, 377; X 3, 417; 9, 424; 14, 428; 18, 430 & 32, 447), and that the King has been given a divine command to do something or other (VIII 5, 350; 6, 351; X 31, 445). These and other themes involving the Deity occur, in by far the majority of cases, in books VIII and X, apropos of Kings whose position is none too secure.

198. Humane action rewarded: X 27, 438; miracles: VIII 32-33, 380-83; the last judgement: X 3, 418; 16, 429; "Fate" responsible for ill fortune: VIII 5, 350 & X 31, 445.

199. Fair play: VIII 28, 376; superior to ancestors: VIII 5, 351 & X 22, 434. However politic, Gothic religious tolerance (cf. X 26, 437) should have conciliated the religiously inclined Cassiodorus, whose faith benefitted thereby.

200. Ancient wisdom: *Pref.* 139; I 46, 170; VIII 30, 377; 31, 379; morality of the good old days: VIII 17, 364 & X 14, 427. But the Goths too thought highly of their ancestors: X 31, 444.

201. The imagery of his similes is very mannered and obviously a conscious stylistic feature, so the careful avoidance of repetition amid such a welter of instances indicates deliberate choice (such avoidance constituted a literary process known as *Variatio*).

202. It is not suggested that these underlying *motifs* are consciously planned. Most striking and indicative of preoccupation with power are the eagle and hawk similes: I 38, 165; VIII 21, 369 & I 24, 158 (with

VIII 31, 379 perhaps indicating some deeply latent rejection of such Gothic symbols?) More fundamental, because more subtle, is his conceiving water in spates as fraught with power, without seeing such power as threatening (as John does): *Pref.* 136 & 139; X 12, 425; 29, 440.

203. Images concern teaching (I 24, 158; 38, 165; VIII 21, 369), healing (I 5, 147; VIII 27, 375), the opening of doors (VIII 14, 359), and cooperation (I 4, 147; cf. X 4, 419 — the "two eyes in unison" idea, & 21, 434 — the idea that nothing is lost by helping).

204. Striking images involve growth (I 12, 151), clearing away dark clouds (VIII 20, 367), and divine inspiration (VIII 2, 348). There is none of the sombre imagery that recurs in John's writings.

205. Approbation: I 13, 152; shunning of society: VIII 31, 378 (so an unknown man is to be shunned at X 33, 447). The "ambition curbed by fear of punishment" theme (X 28, 439) links up with a naive belief in the ease of discovering the guilty (VIII 32, 381). It is not suggested that John is more sophisticated. He has an equally naive belief in the ease of discerning inner human feelings: *De Mag.* III 73, 2. Likewise he considers withdrawal from society abnormal (III 44,3). Such similarity in background beliefs about personality comes from the Great Tradition in which both were educated, and merely highlights the differences in their views of the world about them.

FOOTNOTES TO SECTION 4

1. See S. Nosow & W. H. Form, *Man, Work and Society*, Basic Books, 1962, on "The Meanings of Work," p. 9.

2. Cf. Eisenstadt, pp. 274 & 280.

3. One man rule: I 36,1 & II 7,3 (the context of the former passage indicates his views on the strong man in politics). Expectably, given this acceptance of an hierarchical social ordering, it is worse to kill an *elder* brother (I 5,1), and no title can be more splendid than that of "King" (II 2,1).

4. See I 16,1; 17,1; 38,2; 44,3; III 38, 3-5; 48, 2-5; 72,3. Noblemen are referred to as Patricians or Eupatrids, both words with a highly favorable (and emotional) *penumbra* of associations.

5. See II 15,2; 29,3; 30,6; III 62, 1-2; 70-1,2 & 6; 76, 3-7. The semantic field involving the concept "citizen of lower class status" is overwhelmingly negative in feeling-tone: *demos* is rarely used with favourable connotations (e.g. as "body politic," "citizen body"), more

frequently occurring with neutral ("populace") or negative ("commons") force. Its derivatives, *demotes* and *demodes*, have pejorative significance in John's usage. Much used in this connection is *plethos* in senses varying from neutral to negative ("multitude" to "mob"). *Polites*, "citizen," a word with a favourable *penumbra* of associations, is most used in speaking of Early Rome, a sentimentally seen, favorably viewed period for John; in speaking of contemporaries, it is attached to John's home-townsmen. More usual is the word *hypekoos*, "subject," which has a negative feeling-tone. Snobbery in regard to social inferiors is patent: I 50,4; II 22(2) & III 35,1-6.

6. I 43, 1-4. Eisenstadt says that "by 'punishment orientation' is meant that the norms of the bureaucracy are *imposed* on the population and not fully accepted by it as contributing to its welfare." "Political Struggle in Bureaucratic Societies," *World Politics* 9, 1957, p. 30, note 29.

7. Compare III 1,3 with 14,1 & 25,4-5. See also n. 73 above and discussion thereto in the text.

8. Sympathy for the taxpayer: II 20,3; III 61,7 & 70,1 (cf. 51,5); difficulties of the taxpayer seen merely as something harmful to tax-collecting officials: III 37,3; 44,2; 54,6; 56, 204 (cf. II 29,3 & 30,6 for a similar attitude in regard to penal officials); borderline case between these polar extremes: III 49, 2-3.

9. See III 57, 2-62, 5 & 65, 4-70,1. The amounts involved mean that municipal officials, or at least men of means, are the targets of the tax extraction campaign.

10. His home town is involved and so is he in at least one case: II 57,7. John had been recruited to the Prefecture by Zoticus, a local magnate who seems to have built up something of a bureaucratic clique (Riggs' "clect") within the Prefecture, probably to look after local interests: see note 4 and discussion thereto in the bibliographical sketch in chapter 1.

11. See II 15,2; 29,3; 30,6; III 62, 1-2; 70-1,2 & 6 and 76, 3-7. The exception, 70, 1-6, can hardly be said to be sympathetic towards the lower orders, who are described as "wishing to live in indolence rather than work like prudent men," "the barbaric and merciless multitude," and as "appropriately" punished by having 50,000 of their number massacred.

12. See nn. 28-31 in section three, and discussion thereto in the text.

13. See nn. 110-111 in section three, and discussion thereto in the text.

14. Criticism of the upper orders by inferiors, however, was a different matter. Whether latent (as in the case of informers: *Var.* VIII 16, 362; cf. 25, 373 with Hodgkin's note and I 9, 149), or overt (as with public abuse at the games: I 27, 159-160; 30-32, 161-2 & 44, 168), it was to be repressed.

15. Profligacy is condemned at I 7, 148, avarice at I 35, 163; praise for the observance of the golden mean occurs at VIII 17, 364 & X 3, 417.

16. See I 27, 159; X 13, 426; cf. 5, 421-2.

17. *De Mag.* I 20, 5-7.

18. *Var.* I 30, 161 & 32, 162.

19. *Pref.* 134 & 139. Both writers, incidentally, only criticise the faction of the Greens; this seems to have been the grouping identified with the lower orders. The Blues, appropriately, were associated with the upper class and Establishment. For a full discussion of these factions see G. Manojlovic, "Le peuple de Constantinople," *Byzantion* 11, 1936, pp. 617-716, and F. Dvornik, "The Circus Parties at Byzantium; their Evolution and their Suppression," *Byzantina-Metabyzantina* 1, 1946, pp. 119-33. John's sole mention of factions by colour occurs at *De Mag.* III 62, 1-2; "Greens" are mentioned by Cassiodorus at *Var.* I 20, 155; 27, 159 & 32-3, 162.

20. For the distinction see VIII 30, 378 and 31, 379. Mention of the troubles of the urban population at Rome occurs only in one section of the letters, but these often speak of troubles in the Italian towns and countryside. John's attention, when given to such matters, seems engrossed with troubles among the townee population; rustics are only mentioned at *De Mag.* III 54,6 & 70,1.

21. Punishment for a given crime was less severe if one was of superior social status: see I 32, 162; VIII 38, 378 and X 4, 410-20; cf. the attitude of a Goth noble at having to undergo due process of law in a common court at X 5, 421. This disparity reflects the actuality: the upper class, or *honestiores,* were by law entitled to less severe penalties than the lower, or *humiliores:* see *LRE,* pp. 17 & 519. For the severity of measures disciplining the lower orders, see VIII 32-33, 381-2.

22. VIII 26, 375 — a classical instance of what Wittfogel describes as "the ruler's rationality optimum": see pp. 126-36.

23. I 16, 153; 19, 155; X 27, 438 & 28, 439.

24. I 22, 156; VIII 20, 367; cf. I 14, 152. It is regarded as commendable in a Prefect that taxes were not felt to be as burdensome under his administration: I 3, 145.

25. John tends to look on the taxpayer in the abstract as it were, as an item on a tax-collecting schedule, a producer of tax-input; there is only one detailed reference to commercial interests (*De Mag.* III 61, 7-8; 54,6 contains an oblique reference). For Cassiodorus, commerce has to be considered along with taxation income; the two are integrally connected: see *Var.* I 34, 163; VIII 31, 378-9; 33, 381-83; X 18, 430 and cf. 27, 438 & 28, 439.

26. Banditry: VIII 27, 375-6; 32, 380; 33, 381; dispossessions: I 18, 154 & VIII 28, 376; uprisings: I 20, 155; 27, 159; 30, 161; 32-3, 162; 44, 168.

27. On the absence of *consensus* and effective public opinion in such a society see B. Berelson and M. Janowitz (eds.), *Reader in Public Opinion and Communication*, Free Press, 1953, chapters on "The Concept of Public Opinion in Political Theory" and "Nations and Classes: The Symbols of Identification."

28. *Pref.* 134.

29. *De Mag.* II 26, 1.

30. III 45, 3.

31. II 7, 1-2; in III 45,3 it is accountable to state officials, not seen in a frame of reference in which the general public features. This concentration on regulative rather than servicing functions (for the concepts see Eisenstadt, pp. 277-8 & 292-5) seems to have been the norm in pre-industrial society. N. N Safran ("Theses on Comparative Bureaucracy and Political Development in Western Europe and the Middle East," mimeo, MIT, 1966, p. 2) argues that traditional bureaucracies were *primarily* self-serving. See Constas, "Max Weber's Two Conceptions of Bureaucracy" in the *American Journal of Sociology* 52, 1958, pp. 403-409.

32. See III 61, 6-7 and II 10, 4-5; III 23,2 & 40,3-4.

33. II 7, 1-2 seems to be speaking of the past. So does III 45,3. III 39,1 states that the Prefecture currently has no effective power, and III 56, 2-4 indicates how this has come about.

34. The aim of old: II 20,3; its continuance under a good Prefect: III 76,6; the trend against it: II 21,1; III 56, 2-57, 2.

35. *Var.* VIII 20, 367 and X 27, 438.

36. The letters were composed during his last year as Prefect, and the *Preface* (at Hodgkin's p. 134) indicates Cassiodorus' major preoccupations in that post: these are the provision of justice (so also at VIII 20, 367; cf. X 28, 438) and of adequate provisioning.

37. Commerce: see n. 25 above; provisioning: I 34, 163; 35, 163; X 27, 438; 28, 439.

38. See n. 172 to section three (and n. 36 above).

39. See nn. 23-26 above, and discussion thereto in the text.

40. Righteousness: I 12, 151-2; cf. X 5, 421-2; moderation: I 19, 155; 22, 156; 27, 159; VIII 20, 367; X 3, 418 & 7, 423.

41. For the concept see I. Lewis, "In the Courts of Power," in Berger, *The Human Shape of Work*, p. 138.

42. This survey is based on an in-the-big content analysis of books I, VIII & X bearing on major issues with which Cassiodorus there concerns himself in his capacity as *Quaestor*, Master, and Prefect respectively.

43. Lunch breaks: III 15,3; dress: I 28,5; II 16, 2-3 & III 15,4.

44. Judges: II 18, 2-3; III 2, 3-4 & 14,2; false claims to titles: III 37,3; appointments: III 67, 3-4; overlapping: II 10, 4-5; III 23,2 & 40,3-4; cf. 69,3; archives: III 19,2 & 20,4-8; systems of cross-checking: III 11,2-12,5; public post: III 61,6-7.

45. See nn. 76-80 in section three and discussion thereto in the text.

46. There is a high degree of emotion about the passages concerned: II 21,2; III 16,1-18,5; 57,3 & 65,4-5.

47. It is frankly stated that the law "had good reason to suspect collusion" at III 12,2; see 42,4 (with accompanying editorial note), and the elaborate precautions taken, as indicated by 61,6-7. The biographical sketch indicates how such collusive practices operated: see note 4 to chapter 1 and discussion in text thereto.

48. Discomfort: III 17,1; pride: III 17,2-18,2.

49. See II 17,1; 21,2; III 57,3 & 65,405.

50. See Eisenstadt, "Political Struggle in Bureaucratic Societies," *World Politics* 9, 1956, p. 28.

51. *Pref.* 134.

52. I 2, 143-4; 11, 151; 35, 163; VIII 13, 358.

53. *Pref.* 138.

54. X 7, 423; 31, 444&445; 32, 445-6 and 33, 447.

55. See Eisenstadt, pp. 279-80, on the concept.

56. As the contents of the chapter to this point indicate, the relative salience of these issues is of the order set out in tabular form in Figure 6.4. For statistics underlying what is contended in John's case, see chapter 7, Table 7.2, and comments thereon.

(Apropos of the comparison of the attention areas of John and Procopius : The assessment of Cassiodorus' focus of attention is based on the fact that, in performing the content analysis of his letters, certain cards had to be filled in with exceptional frequency. Interrelated themes were found to be responsible for this indexing phenomenon. These themes made up the issue areas designated in Figure 6.4, and frequency of mention was easily calculated. Thus the issues and their sequence emerged by serendipity effect.)

FOOTNOTES TO SECTION 5

1. Specifically, as *Quaestor* Cassiodorus focuses on the administration of the law and on taxation problems (generally involving large estates); Italy is seen in some detail as a consequence. As Master, Cassiodorus has to secure the acceptance of Amalasuntha and Athalaric; he sees the Goth barons in the Balkan areas around the head of the Adriatic and around the (Gallic) top of the Italian peninsula. But he also performed as Master some of a *Quaestor's* functions, so is still aware of the Italian countryside (a rising wave of unrest there is indicated by VIII 22-33, where attention switches from the succession problems of VIII 1-21). As Prefect, Cassiodorus has to deal with tensions between the Goth (military) capital at Ravenna, the Roman (administrative) capital, and the ill-descried enemy capital of Constantinople.

2. This account follows the biography reconstructed in chapter 1. As to his better judgment: John initially decided to join the *Memoriales* (the group handling the sending out of letters of appointment) of the Master's Men (*De Mag.* III 26,1). He was pressured into the clerical staff of the Prefect's Men. This meant that his best move was into the *Augustales*, the judicial branch of the Prefecture. Then the *Memoriales* effectively secured control of purchaseable offices connected with the *Augustales* (III 67, 1-5), ruining the latters' vested interests in the resale of posts.

3. *Var.* X 14, 428 & 18, 430.

4. *De Mag.* III 55,4; 1,2; 28,4; cf. II 24,5.

5. Office holding was also the major source of income: see Wittfogel, on "Bureaucratic Landlordism": pp. 276 & 297-99, and Riggs, on "Pariah Capitalism": pp. 187-95.

6. The concept *moderatio* has already been discussed at n. 108 in section three (and text thereto). This is a slightly different interpretation, but no inconsistency is involved: it is a basic feature of prismatic society that in it things are other than they seem on the surface, and that their appearance changes as one's viewpoint alters: Riggs, pp.

27-31; 33; cf. 15-16. See also P. Selznik, *The Organizational Weapon*, Free Press, 1960 ed., pp. vi-xi for the type of analytical approach adopted in this study of the operational codes of institutionalised groups.

7. Cassiodorus had a realistic awareness of this: letter X 33, 447 unerringly identifies the key bureaucrat in Constantinople, Peter the Patrician, recently come to power by displacing the Prefecture (*De Mag.* II 26,1). Peter had won his spurs by diplomatic achievements in Italy which were Byzantine in the most offensive sense of the adjective (see Bury, *History of the Later Roman Empire*, vol. 2, pp. 163-4; 168; 172-3 & 206). These happenings took place between 534 and 535, so Cassiodorus could not help but know of them, given his closeness to Goth Court circles.

8. *Var.* I 43, 167.

9. VIII 5, 351 & X 22, 434.

10. I 4, 147.

11. I 31, 161; VIII 9, 353 & 14, 427.

12. X 33, 447.

13. X 32, 446 & 18, 430.

14. If Cassiodorus' career line encouraged thinking in strategic terms, John's more limited choices led him to tactical thinking: see discussion in the text to n. 6 above. On realistic thinking versus the acceptance of myth see section 3, notes 26-34 and 190, and discussion thereto in the text; see also chapter 5, note 11 likewise.

15. *De Mag.* II 24,5.

16. See especially *Var.* I 18, 154; VIII 11, 356; 26, 375 & X 14, 428 — the most telling glimpses of the reality behind the façade; see also VIII 3, 350; 7, 352; 15, 360; 17, 364; 21, 369; X 18, 430; 26, 437 & 29, 440.

17. This emerges in spite of all his diplomatic finesse: see nn. 11-13 above; for actual mention of "two Republics," "an Eastern and a Western world,"and so on, see: I 1, 142; 4, 147; VIII 9, 352; X 19, 431; 21, 434; 22, 434; 23, 436; 25, 436 & 32, 449.

18. This is evident from his fleeting and unsympathetic references to the factional life of the capital: see n. 11 to section 4, and discussion thereto in the text.

19. Striking instances of this occur at X 14, 427; 19, 431 & 32, 446.

20. Expanded or loving descriptions of places only occur when the Italian countryside is concerned: I 27, 159; VIII 4, 350; 7, 351; 10, 355; *31-33, 378-83* & X 19, 431 — where italics indicate the most

striking instances. Nowhere in John's writings is a comparable degree of emotion displayed concerning his native land. The nearest John comes to exhibiting such strong identification is in his description of the destruction wrought to Constantinople by the Nika Riot: *De Mag.* III 70, 2-71, 1.

21. See " 'Roman History' for John" in chapter three.

22. *De Mag.* III 1,2; 22,1; 28,4; 40,1 & 55,1; the passage which is most revealing of John's attitude to Rome occurs at II 30, 1-5. Compare this with the references to Constantinople in book III: 26,1; 38,3; 44,3; 70,1; 70, 3-71,1; 76, 6-9.

23. Contrast III 70, 2-71,1 with II 30,1-5.

24. Relevant passages indicative of the role of Latin as a communications medium within the *corps* of the bureaucracy, and the departmental interests connected thereto, are: II 12,1-2; III 19,2-4; 20,3-10; 27,3-5; 29,1; 42,1-2; 68,1-5.

25. Nationalistic concepts and symbols had not yet evolved: see chapter 2, n. 7 and discussion thereto in the text; cf. also n. 27 to section 4 of the present chapter.

26. II 3,8; 6,1-4; 13,1; 22,1; 23,1-24,5; III 2,1; 3,6; 22,2-3. Since institutions which owed their origin to the Early Principate (as did the Prefecture) were held in little esteem, as having originated in the household staff of a master (II 27,2), it was particularly important that the pedigree of the Prefecture be back-dated into Republican times.

27. On the key functions of the Prefecture see II 7,1-3 (containing the most striking imagery in the work) and 5,1 & 29,1. On expectation of interest in the history see III 9,3 and cf. I 15(4) & II 19,1.

28. On Rome, see X 18,430 & 32,446; on the great families, see his references to the Anicii at X 11, 424 & 12, 426, and to the Corvini at VII 22,369 (illustrative of how family traditions reached back across the centuries via membership of the Senate).

29. See Jones, *An Introduction to Divine and Human Readings*, pp. 27-36, 40 & 47-49.

30. It is, apparently, fallacious to assume that our modern times are unique in regard to the incidence of rapid social change: see R. Grew & S. L. Thrupp, "Horizontal History in Search of Vertical Dimensions," *Comparative Studies in Society and History* 8, 1966, p. 263.

31. See chapter four, Part One, Book One, on the changes intervening between the Proto- and Middle Byzantine periods.

Part Three

Problems in Effecting Change in a Traditional Society:
A Case-study--the Reforms of the Emperor Justinian

Chapter 7
Problems in Effecting Change in a Traditional Society:
A Case-study — The Reforms of the Emperor Justinian

Section 1. Introduction

This study will appraise an attempt at rapid planned change with massive implications for its society in a historical case, namely the reign of Justinian in the sixth century A.D.[1] The changes introduced by this Emperor were unusually wide-ranging, and the reign has been exceptionally well documented by surviving contemporary source evidence. This combination provides probably the best opportunity available in the history of the ancient and medieval worlds for the observation of the problems of producing planned systemic change in traditional, pre-industrial society.

A brief review of the attempted changes and the achievements associated with Justinian's name will bring the background events of the study into focus. Justinian's was an unusually long reign. Not only did he himself rule for a lengthy period (527-565 A.D.), but he seems to have exercised great influence in the previous reign when his uncle Justin was Emperor (518-527). The most striking achievement is connected with his attempt to reconquer some of the former territories of Rome's empire. The achievements of his reign in this regard can readily be seen from map IV, which shows imperial territory before and after his campaigns. Approximately 50 percent increase of territory resulted. The aim most probably was to secure control of commercially vital areas of the Mediterranean shoreline. There is ample evidence of interest in control of strategic commercial areas and of concern with the development of commerce throughout the reign, and no indication of interest in the type of military operations involved in campaigns aimed at conquest of hinterland areas.[2]

In terms of commerce, possibly the most important developments were the introduction of the silkworm to Europe and Western Asia[3] and of an intricate customs system throughout the Empire.[4] Equally significant for commercial relationships was the thorough-going revision of the legal system. A diverse mass of unintegrated legislation had accumulated by the sixth century, as result of the retention of customary practices and the continuous addition of *constitutiones* (as the rulings of the Emperor or of his *quaestor* — an official in charge of legislation and jurisdiction — were known). There had been an attempt in the previous century to make this into a coherent code, as its inconsistencies and contradictions seriously hindered the conduct of business operations. Justinian now caused the production of a unified body of laws, contradictions and inconsistencies being struck out. Also produced were a similarly systematized body of authoritative interpretative rulings and a synopsized handbook for the education of law students — whose educational syllabi were, moreover, subjected to revision and systematization.[5]

These happenings had repercussions upon the civil administration. The more systematic and coherent body of law facilitated administration and speeded it up. It also made it easier to bring officials' malpractices to book. Better facilities for legal training meant an improved supply of lawyers.[6] The developments in commerce resulted in an increase in revenues from (and activity in extracting) customs dues. There were huge army expenses and massive expenditures on building. Hence a much increased need for accountancy skills. Recruitment patterns within the bureaucracy altered accordingly, and groups with different skills (from the *litterati*) were advanced. A new type of Head of *Corps* appears: the "upstart" John the Cappadocian, for instance, or Peter Barsymes. Major and irreversible structural changes occur within the bureaucracy. The power and prestige of the Praetorian Prefecture is brought low. That of the Urban Prefecture grows, with the growing importance of Constantinople. The beginnings of the system of the exarchate appear, when military commanders are given both military and civil authority in their provinces. The civil bureaucracy was in fact never to be the same again.[7]

Justinian aimed at winning back the orthodox Christians of the West from their Arian Vandal or Gothic masters. The war in north Africa probably paid for itself in booty, but money had to come from the East for the campaigns in Italy and Spain. The pressures of war thus exacerbated the religious conflicts in the East, which had been troublesome enough in Anastasius' peaceful reign. For the precarious balance between Orthodox (Trinitarian) and Monophysite (single Godhead) Christianity had been maintained to this point only by dint of devious and unobtrusive policies. The different varieties of Christianity coincided, to a great extent, with differences in the major racial groups, Greek as opposed to Syrian and Coptic, in Anatolia, Syria and Egypt. Linguistic, political and economic interests were heavily involved. The new policy meant a blatant sacrifice of Monophysite to Orthodox interests, as it meant spending taxes, raised largely in Monophysite areas in the East, to finance assistance for orthodox Westerners.[8] Justinian's attempts to breach the gulf which came increasingly to yawn open were disarming, disingenuous — and disastrous in their consequences.

The growth of the metropolis to a hitherto unparalleled position of dominance within the cultural life of the Empire was probably largely due to accident, although certainly Justinian aimed to make it predominant architecturally.[9] Major natural disasters occurred during the reign: earthquakes and outbreaks of bubonic plague. The first outbreak, in Constantinople in 542-3, possibly due to overcrowding, was particularly virulent, and enormous numbers of people apparently died. Population losses owed to these causes, together with the movement of Slavs into the Balkans, which were denuded of defending forces because of the demands for troops in the other theatres of war, brought about major alterations in the population structure of the Empire. Immediately affected, in this reign, was the guild system in which the lower orders were organized. It became less caste-like — one could leave some guilds, now — and thus began basically to alter the structure of urban life among the lower orders.[10]

As is indicated by Figure 7.1 (and by Riggs' comments on prismatic society, noted in earlier chapters), these developments were so closely interconnected that piecemeal change was impossible. Consider the situation insofar as the three bureaucratically organised groups within the apparatus were concerned. There was jurisdictional chaos within the civil bureaucracy as result of the system of *praescriptio fori.* This was accompanied by sinecurism, formalism and other forms of inefficiency. And this was, in its turn, combined with empire-building activities on the part of Heads of *Corps.* This did not make for a docile and efficient servicing instrumentality. Earthquakes and plagues seriously reduced the taxation resources upon which the civil bureaucracy drew, whereas the expansion of trade increased them only moderately. Yet outgoings on buildings and military campaigns were up, and had to be met. The army had to hold the line in the Balkans and against Persia while invading north Africa, Sicily, Italy and Spain. Distant local commanders in trouble-prone areas were given dangerously large mandates of power. Thus an aggressive military policy meant a twofold source of trouble

Figure 7.1   Inter-connection of areas in which change occurred

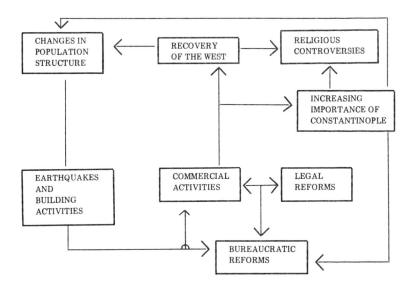

for the civil bureaucracy: it meant heavier taxation *and* expansion of the administrative competence of the military. The civil bureaucracy, accordingly, fought back by retrenching on military expenditures wherever possible.

There was friction, too, between the civil bureaucracy and the Church. For the Church in the East seems to have considerably increased its financial resources and jurisdictional competence, and to have committed huge quantities of the empire's resources to its own building activities. None of this made the tax-man's job easier. There were feuds between Patriarchs, and between orthodox and Monophysite communities. There could thus be no one religious policy agreeable to all. Given all these tensions and cross-pressures, an earthquake in Antioch, for instance, would mean disruption of the administration of Syria, a dropping away in the financing necessary to maintain the military cover for the area, a consequent Persian invasion and then increased alienation within its Monophysite communities.

Obviously it was essential to make maximum use of the resources of the civil bureaucracy, and, clearly, this could not be done without making some changes. Justinian did not shrink from the task. He was a phenomenally hard worker with a passion for order; consequently the changes that he conceived to be required were painstakingly and industriously made. His was a highly literate society at its acme, and the accidents of survival have dealt kindly with its products. So we have to deal with one of the few well-documented periods in the history of the ancient and medieval worlds. Hence it is possible to assess the views of contemporaries on the Emperor's activities.

Section 2. Problems in the Interpretation of the Evidence

Justinian's was a long and eventful reign.[11] It was unique in that it saw the high-water-mark of Byzantine military success and the most complete domination achieved by an Emperor over the Church, indicating imperial control over two of the three bureaucracies on which Byzantine society depended.[12] In many respects — administrative, financial, religious — the reign marked a turning point in the customs and practices of the Byzantine Empire. Hence this study can focus on only one of many possible aspects of the reign, in dealing with problems met in producing change. And the study will have to be selective in regard to what it considers. Consideration will be limited to the reactions of contemporaries to these problems. Their pictures of these things will, moreover, have to be reconstructed only in large-scale, overall terms.

Thus what this chapter aims to do is to set out, hopefully in a fairly objective pattern, the views held by certain contemporaries about these events. As will rapidly become apparent, contemporaries viewed this complex process of interactions in a highly selective fashion. In fact, when writers mention the changes which we are discussing, their preconceptions are such as to make them focus on only a limited part of the complex. Moreover they tend to evaluate happenings from a two-valued (or good/bad) standpoint.

In reconstructing the mood of the times for a given period of classical antiquity, one immediately runs into the problem of securing a representative sample of opinions. All our samples are grotesquely skewed. The voices of antiquity speak to us only in the cultured tones of its small literate class. These men selectively perceive events from the viewpoint of that class, bearers of the Great Tradition of the culture.

The illiterate masses have left virtually no record of their views. This over-representation of the sectional viewpoint of the *élite* is the norm when the mass of the population is not "mobilized." "Mobilization" is a term much used by those who work in communications: it refers to those who take part in the long range communications of a particular speech community; they write, keep written records, transmit messages widely, and to many people, and do so frequently.[13] Mobilization comes with print primarily, and always with telecommunications.

Now a modern historian is confronted by the masses of documents typically generated by a mobilized society, and has to select a representative range of communicators from within this wide choice. But in antiquity communicators of this sort were relatively few (and consequently individually of far greater importance), while the accidents of survival tend to leave a motley array of survivors, even from this few. So the ancient historian may not have enough suitable documents to form a viable sample. He tends to compensate by reading all the documents available. But impressionistic reading necessarily introduces the *modern's* own selectivity in perceiving, to further distort the picture.[14]

The solution for this problem adopted here is that of making a strategic choice of texts and analysing them methodically by the use of content analysis. Three contemporaries, situated at vital points within the communications network of their times, have been chosen. Contemporaries have been chosen because subsequent generations tended to exaggerate Justinian's performance as Emperor: living within a sadly foreshortened empire, they overvalued his military accomplishments. Among contemporaries, it is Justinian, John the Lydian and Procopius who have been chosen.[15]

No one can speak for the Emperor as well as that Emperor himself. John identified closely with his fellow *officiales* of the Praetorian Prefecture; his feelings for his colleagues seem to have been reciprocated; he wrote to advance his and their cause and interests (see chapter 4, n. 19, and text thereto). We can therefore take it that his views represent this sectional interest-group. Procopius was the greatest historian of the sixth century. He was closely aligned with the military aristocracy, for he had served as private secretary to the general Belisarius and written an account of the latter's campaigns. His is a viewpoint of someone outside the central bureaucracy, but close to important decision-makers. All these scholars were, both at the time and subsequently, regarded as exemplars of the literary education of

- 162 -

their times. All are available in translation, so readers can peruse their works to form their own conclusions on the impressions presented here, as my own viewpoint acts, as it were, as yet another perceptual filter, selectively distorting the picture.

Such then are the texts chosen for analysis. To portray the writers' opinions on the topics central to the concerns of this chapter, I have focussed on the following aspects of their perceptions, as these are indicated by their writings. Firstly I have analysed the attitudes of these writers to change, in its social, political and economic dimensions. Then I have identified those parts of the actual changes brought about by Justinian which excite comment, and those which do not. Finally, their reactions to such changes as they have chosen to select for notice are examined, to see what biases are thus exhibited. This appraisal has been carried out by use of the technique of content analysis.

Section 3. Contrasting Contemporary Views

The *Institutes* of Justinian (datable to 21 Nov. 533) are four books ghosted by a committee and edited by the Emperor, who laid down guide-lines for the work throughout. He draws attention to all legal reforms introduced by himself, specifying whether this was on the recommendation of his top legal advisors or of his own initiative, and generally explaining why he made the change. He also writes the introductory headings explaining the philosophy behind the major sections of the work. So it is fairly easy to isolate his views and assumptions on "change," by breaking this concept down into a number of less "fuzzy" concepts or themes, collecting every instance of each of these in the *Institutes*, and then analyzing the emphases or patterns in the resultant data (see Table 7.1).

Procopius was born sometime in the 490's, and probably died after 565; he became personal secretary to a leading general and was close to Court circles. He wrote three surviving works: the *Histories, On the Buildings of Justinian* and *The Secret History*. The latter is undatable, but was probably written after 541. The first of the above works focusses on the wars of the reign; the second is an adulatory "official" picture; the third, a secret document only published long after Procopius' death, is a scathing and abusive attack on the Emperor. It is, in fact, the most vicious piece of character assassination produced by the ancient world. This work has, uniquely in contemporary writings, circumvented the problem that criticism of the Sacred Emperor was

TABLE 7.1
Comparative analysis of perceptions of change

		JUSTINIAN		PROCOPIUS		JOHN THE LYDIAN
Time Focus		PRESENT	Superior in morality and humanity to past.	PRESENT	Worst age known to man. Demons at large	PRESENT	Contemporaries deranged in wits; but (sometimes) seen as prosperous.
		PAST	To be improved on (by implication).	PAST	Firmness and order (by implication).	PAST	Golden Age, from which a decline set in.
Views on Causation			No theories. Some factual assessment of trends — no one "pet" explanation.		Blind, amoral change — or, possibly God has deserted Constantinople and left her to the demons.		Cyclical change; time inherently destructive; "Fortune" has abandoned Rome. *Bouleversement* very sudden.
Views of Tradition			Much confusion, some errors, sometimes inhumane. More wisdom currently available.		No confusion; things fixed firmly in their appropriate places. Preservation J's duty, not change. Anastasius the model emperor.		Antiquity gives status and should not be disturbed.
Views on Innovation			Action not in a spirit of innovation. "Extension of ancient custom" sometimes pleaded.		J. an inveterate innovator, inclined to turmoil, cannot abide firmly by a decision, no sense of the appropriate, inherently treacherous.		The mark of a vainglorious, tyrannical disposition is innovation.
Motivation Ascribed for Changes			To attain efficiency and simplicity of functioning, fewer faults in system, more equity. Aim of surpassing Augustus as a statesman.		Avarice and a lust for human blood. Possibly a demon. Dominated by a woman.		J. aims to summon back the authority which constitutions had of old, or enhance it, or rescue them from chaos, improving efficiency.
Beneficiaries of Change			Those who have to use the courts; especially the less influential and women. No powerful group advantaged, if anything, the reverse.		Justinian and Theodora — but the viewpoint presented is almost exclusively that of the wealthy gentry of office, who have been penalized, the writer avers.		J. has stopped the rot in regard to the prefecture — but not fully.
Effects of Change			By implication, greater efficiency of working, and correction of abuses for the administration.		Confusion and turmoil.		The prefecture is a fallen estate; some of J's ministers have caused disturbances.

SEE TABLE 7.1a FOR SOURCE REFERENCES

TABLE 7.1a

Source references to Table 7.1

COMPARATIVE ANALYSIS OF PERCEPTIONS OF CHANGE

		JUSTINIAN	PROCOPIUS	JOHN THE LYDIAN
Time Focus	PRESENT	I 6.2; II 20.36; III 12.1; IV 8.6; II 6.20,23	PRESENT 8,30; cf. 6.19&26, 24. 12.16; 18,36-37.	PRESENT Deranged: III, 11.1; 20.4; cf. 67.) Prosperous: I 3.5; II 24.5; III 30.9 & 55.1 (all formal praise of Emperor)
	PAST	II 6.7, 10,10; III 2.3,9,4	PAST See ur der Tradition and Innovation (30,34 fin only future reference.)	PAST II 20.3; III 67.1
Views on Causation		Possibly III 2,3 & IV 4,7 are relevant	4,44; 10.9-10, 18, 37 (chance) 6.5-9; 12.1,4ff.; 18, 1&37 (demons)	Cyclical change: III 23.10; cf. Preface, 6 Time: III 39.1; cf. III 19.7 Fortune, etc.: II 12.1; III 40.1; 42.1; 46.1; cf. III 42.1 Suddenness of change: III 76.7; cf. 71.1
Views on Tradition		Proem. 2 (cf. 3); I 5,3; II 13; 13.5; III 1.16; 7, 7.4; II 19.1&2; 20.23; IV 8.6; I 11.12; II 11; IV 1.16	Relevant are: 6.21; 14.1; 6.11; 9.51; 22.38; 29.20. 19.5 (Anastasius)	Preface 5; III 22.2-3; 68.3; cf. I 49.2; II 27.2; III 10.4
Views on Innovation		Not in a spirit of innovation: III 14 Extension of custom: I 6.7; II 6.14; 11.6; 16.1; III 11.14.2 & 19,14; cf. III 23 & 15.3; II 19.6; III 7,4	Innovator: 8.26; 11.1,2; 18,12; 30,21 Turmoil: 18.12; No firmness: 8,24; 22,30; Inappropriateness: 9.53; 11.12; 18,29; 26.15; Treachery: 6.28; 8.22; 13.16; 16.1; 29.1; cf 8,31 & 27,18	II 19.9; cf. I 3.5-6; II 15.2; 28,1
Motivation Ascribed for Changes		I 12.6; 20.5; II 5.5; 7.2; 10.4, 23.7; III 7, 4.21; IV 8; 6.8; I.7; 18.6.1; III Proem. 3; II 20.21; III 8; IV 9.4; 19,13; IV 6.25; III 1.16; 23.1; 29.3; 6.2; 7; III 9.5; 19.1C; IV 6.33; II 7.4; 20.34; II 23.12	Avarice: 6.20; 13.18; Blood lust: 6.24; 11.5; 13.8; 26.2; 'Demons' above; Domination by a woman: 2.36; 4.1; 4.31; 9.30; 10.17; 12.29; 15.10; 17.38; 22.29	I 3.5; II 5.3; 28.1; 29.3; 30.6; III 1.2&3; 38.2
Beneficiaries of Change		I 10; 22; II 8; 13.5; III 12.1; IV 6.29; III 27.7	14.17; 26.3,9; 27.2; 27.25; 27.33; 29.15; 29.27; 10.23.	III 1, 1&3; 39.1
Effects of Change		I 5.3; II 7.3; III 2.7; 7.3; 11.7 (to perfect) cf. I 12.4; 25.13; II 14.1; 19.6; 20.34; III 2.7 (to avoid unreasonableness)	8.4; 9.50; 11.1.2; 14.1; 14.14; 19.8; 7.7; 13.23; 14.1,10&20; 17.24; 28.16; 30.11&14	Fallen estate: II 16.3; III 9.9-10; 14.1-2 Bad side-effects: III 2.5; 56.2; 69.2.3

treason. So it can be less inhibited in passing judgement than the other two. Actually, it turns out to be a rather terrifying picture of the writer's own authoritarian personality overwhelmed by confrontation with massive change. This evidence as to personality structure in its turn suggests the kind of personality systems which we should look for within a society which produced such a man as its best historian — and burned heretics alive.

John the Lydian (490 to about 544, probably) also wrote three surviving works: *On the Months, On Portents* and *On the Magistracies of the Roman Constitution* (see chapter 1, note 23). The latter work is datable to about 554. It is a history of the *corps* within the civil apparatus in which John served. Again we have a unique work: this is the only monograph on the bureaucracy written by a career bureaucrat which has survived from Roman-Byzantine times. As John's *corps* within the civil bureaucracy was the focal point of the administration, his view, that of a senior career bureaucrat, indicates the thinking of a highly influential group.

It immediately appears that Justinian's picture of what he was doing and why he was doing it was strikingly different from that of the other two writers. So much so, in fact, that communications between the *élite* and sub-*élite* of government must be assumed to have been very imperfect. Table 7.1 shows that differences in the individual variables fall into two consistently related patterns. Justinian appears as an efficiency and equity oriented personality, concentrating on the solving of practical problems in a present unencumbered by God or Deviltry. The other two writers both look back to a Golden Past from a present full of unintelligible turmoil, where causation is seen in terms of blind devil-forces and twisted human personalities.[16]

This is a significant finding. In view of the fact that Procopius and John were both members of the sub-*élite* and close to the corridors of power, it suggests lack of communication, as well as *consensus*, between the all important middle *echelons* of society and the apparatus and the Emperor. A basic cause for such lack of *consensus* is not difficult to trace: Justinian, the last Latin-speaking Emperor, came of Latin-speaking peasant stock inhabiting an unsophisticated district in the Danubian regions of the Empire (present-day Uskub). Though his uncle Justin had spirited him away to the metropolis and a proper education, things like his choice in wives and his diction in Greek[17] showed that he was not perfectly assimilated. There is something of a "Two

Cultures" type of gap here; the other writers come from sophisticated, urban, Greek-speaking, middle to upper class stocks. Now, the urge to recover Rome for the Empire would be far less urgently felt in the latters' cases. So the gap between the two parties' view of "the necessary" would widen for reasons such as this.

There is something of the clash between the "official" and the anti-governmental pictures behind these discrepancies, however. Where John the Lydian is reporting in formal adulatory terms, Justinian's picture of the prosperity of the reign appears in John's writings too. Procopius' picture, on the other hand, seems something of a point-by-point rebuttal of the official depiction of the reign and its achievements.

This helps explain the accompanying tables, which show, respectively, which of Justinian's reforms were perceived by Procopius and John (Table 7.2), and the emotions generated by these perceptions (Table 7.3). The tables have been constructed from data generated by two content analyses: the first analyses for all mentions of Justinian and

TABLE 7.2
Aspects of Justinian's government activities
on which the writers comment

*(Numbers refer to the number of times
the author in question mentions a topic.)*

	JOHN	PROCOPIUS
The bureaucracy	24	36
Military matters	11	33
Taxes	3	14
Trade	----	11
Property rights	----	11
Legislation	2	5
Currency	----	3
Building activities	2	3
Relief measures for the poor	----	4
The Church	4	9
Education and literature	3	3
Length of texts in Teubner pages:	170	183

TABLE 7.2 a
Source references to Table 7.2

SUBJECT	PROCOPIUS	JOHN
Bureaucracy	13, 1; 14, 3-5; 14, 11; 15,11; 18,15; 19,4; 20,7; 20,15; 21,9; 21,16; 21,18&20; 22,13; 22,37; 24,30; 26,7; 26,15; 30,8; 30,10; 30,14&16; 30,23; 30,27. *Intrigue involving persons:* 1,14; 6,26; 12,1ff.; 16,28; 20,16&20; 21,6; 22,2&3; 22,22&33-4; 29,1-10; 29,34	*Trends:* I 6,6; II 5,3; 29,1-3; 30,1; 30,5-6; III 1,1; 28,4; 39,1; 55,1; 56,2 *Influence of agents:* II 26,1-2; III 38,3-5; 39,2; 39,4; 57,2; 61,6; 62,3; 69,2-3; 76,7; cf. 70,1-2&75,1 *Side-effects:* III 2,3&5; 56,2; 69,3; cf. I 28,5 & III 54,6
Military	*Destructive wars:* 6,25; 11,10; 18,9; 18,13 & 20 & 22 & 25 & 32 & 38 ff. & 44; *Money for barbarians:* 8,5; 11, 5-9; 11,12; 19, 6&13; 21,36; 30,24; cf. 12,9 & 23,24. *Lack of military pay:* 22,20; 24,1-6 & 7-8 & 13-14 & 18-20 & 21 & 26 & 29. *Personal intrigues:* 4,13; 5,33; 6,27-28; 16,3-6	II 28,2-3; III 1,2; 28,5; 55,2-4; 56,1-2; cf. also II 24,5&29,1; III 54,2-5; 61,8; 70,1 & possibly, 76,6
Taxes	21; 1-6; 22,19; 23,1&6; 23,9; 23,14; 23,21&23; 24,9; 25,5&7; 26,19&21; cf. 22,18	II 15,2; III 51,5; 56,2; cf. however III 39,2&4; 57,2; 62,3&69,2-3†
Trade	20,1; 20,5; 22,18; 25,10; 25,17; 25,21; 25,25; 26,36; cf. 23,14; 26,19&21	

related persons and incidents in the appropriate work of each writer; the second for the manner of presentation of all the "mentions" so discovered.

The focus of interest in both cases is emphatically on the Emperor's

TABLE 7.2 a (continued)

SUBJECT	PROCOPIUS	JOHN
Property holding	8,9; 12,12; 13,4; 21,15; 22,40; 28,9; 29,14; 29,19; 29,24; 30,19; cf.23,9	
Legislation	11,34; 14,5; 14,8; cf. 21,15&29,19	II 15,1; III 1,3
Currency	12,9; 22,38;* 25,12	(III 70,1?)
Building	8,7; 19,6; 26,23	III 71,1; 76,7
Doles	26,8; 26,29; 26,33; 26,43	
Church	11,14ff.; 11,31; 13,4; 13,7; 18,34; 27,10; 27,29; 28,16; cf. 28,9	II 28,3; III 71,1; 76,7; 76,9
Literature & Education	26,2; 26,5; cf. 30,19	III 28,4-5; 29,1-3; 30,9

*The only *factual* statement which subsequent historians have claimed as a falsehood.

†On the psychological and institutional mechanisms involved, see Wittfogel, p. 134.

activities in regard to the bureaucracy and military matters. Here the similarity largely ends, except that both writers devote about the same amount of attention to the Emperor's impact on the literary arts and on building activities. Bureaucratic reform engrosses the largest part of John's attention, as is natural in a writer who was himself a bureaucrat. For Procopius such reform, though very important, merits only a few more comments than those which the Emperor's military activities

TABLE 7.3
Component parts of Justinian's image as a reformer

	JOHN THE LYDIAN	PROCOPIUS
His Aims:	Efficiency 3 Maintenance of (decrepit) institutions 6 To be a model emperor 2	Lust for blood and money 16, Passion for novelty and turmoil 5
His Beliefs:	In benevolence 6 In encouraging literature 3	Improper for subjects to have great wealth 3
His Character:	Not safe to disregard his wishes 1, but can't control all aspects of his agents' activities 10, (and some measures have unfortunate side-effects) 3	Basically treacherous 6, pretends to ignorance of misdoings 5, conflicts with Theodora feigned 6, unstable in holding to a decision 2, can't act at the appropriate moment 5
Dominated by a woman:	Theodora gives timely assistance 1	Thraldom to a vicious female 11
Attitude Towards Various Groups:	Benevolent to lower orders 6	Blue faction favored 3 Against senatorial landlords, the taxpayer, the city poor and the soldiers. For the Church and the barbarians, especially the Huns (frequent references).
Work Habits:	Hard driving taskmaster — to self and others 2	Unnatural activity and abstinence from food and sleep 5
Popular Impressions:	Nothing specific to this	A demon 3

Numbers indicate times that the particular point is the main topic under discussion.
See Table 7.3a for source references.

TABLE 7.3 a (source references)

	JOHN THE LYDIAN	PROCOPIUS
His Aims:	II 30,6; III 1,4; cf. II 29,3&III 38,2. II 5,3; 28,1; III 1,1; 1,3; 39,1; cf. I 3,5. I 3,5; II 28,2-3	6,20; 6,24; 10,21-22; 11,5; 13,8; 13,18; 14,17 & 19-20; 26,3-9; 26,24; 27,2; 27,25; 27,33; 29,15; cf. 13,32; 26,16 & 30,14. 8,24; 8,26; 11,1-2; 18,12; 22,30; 28,16
His Beliefs:	I 6,6; II 15,2; III 39,4; 61,6; 62,3; 69,3. III 28,4-5; 29,1-3; 30,8-9 (an "official" picture)	4,33; 29,24; 30,19
His Character:	III 76,2. II 26,1-2; III 38,3-5; 39,2; 39,4; 57,2; 61,6; 62,3; 69,2-3; 76,7; cf. 70,1&75,1. III 2,5; 56,2; 69,3; cf. 54,6 (& I 28,5).	6,28; 8,22; 13,16; 16,1; 29,1; cf. 27,18. 10,22; 16,10; 17,45; 21,5; 27,22. 10,14; 10,15; 10,23; 14,19; 27,13; cf. 13,9. 8,24; 22,30; cf. 7,7; 13,23; 14,10&20; 16,1. 9,53; 11,12; 18,29; 26,15 & 23-25; cf. 30,17.
Dominated by a woman:	III 69,2.	2,36; 4,13; 4,31; 9,30; 10,17; 12,29; 15,10; 17,38; 22,29; cf. 22,22&33
Attitude Towards Various Groups:	I 6,6; II 15,2; III 39,4; 61,6; 62,3; 69,3.	7,1; 7,41; 29,37. See Table II under Legislation, Property holding, the Church, Doles, etc. On the barbarians, see: 8,5; 11,5-9; 11,12; 19,6&13; 21,26; 30,24; cf. 23,24.
Work Habits:	II 15,2-3; III 55,1.	12,21; 12,27; 13,28-30; 14,3-5; 15,11.
Popular Impressions:		6,5-9; 12,14-32; 18,1&37.

attract; and the cluster taxes, currency, property rights, and lastly trade, if taken together, receives more comments than either of the other two areas. Furthermore, Procopius' comments touch on every major area of the Emperor's activities (see Table 7.2).

The writers' attitudes in their comments are markedly at variance, as Table 7.3 shows. In general, John's picture approaches that which content analysis of the *Institutes* shows the Emperor to have had of his own activities: Justinian is seen as efficiency oriented, benevolent toward his subjects, and bent on preserving or advancing ancient institutions. But John is aware that the Emperor's actions sometimes had unanticipated consequences, and that his agents could act in defiance of their master's wishes and, initially anyway,escape detection. His is largely a friendly picture, of a hard working Emperor aided by an intelligent and public-spirited Empress. As we shall see, however, there are hints that it is something of an "official" picture, i.e., one that could not be charged with the dangerous accusation of criticising the Sacred Emperor. It nonetheless has markedly negative undertones (see notes 29-30 and discussion thereto in text).

Possibly the contradictions are best reviewed in terms of the "psycho-logic" of the "Congruity" or "Dissonance" models.[18] Thus John, for instance, would have (a) his evaluation of Justinian, (b) his judgement on Justinian's attitudes and policy and (c) his own opinion on the best interests of the bureaucracy to bring into some form of harmony. For all indications are that there is a "strain towards consistency" fundamental to our mental economy. The pressure to change one's views is proportionate to the disparity between the positions of a respected source and one's own, combined with the importance of the issue to oneself. Resolution of the tension comes through changing those opinions which are easiest to change, such as weakly held opinions or opinions on peripheral matters. Alternatively one can misperceive the source's position or the situation. On basic issues where emotions run high resolution is generally not of a logical character.

On the other hand McClelland's distinction between the perceptual systems of the efficiency-oriented but basically conformist person and the innovator with a high need for achievement may be behind the differing pictures of what is going on which we receive from John and Justinian respectively.[19] Typically, innovators tend to underestimate others' opinions of the scale and significance of the changes which they contemplate. They view interpersonal relationships on a more impersonal basis. In their attitude to work-tasks they tend to overestimate their own capacities and underestimate the difficulties involved.

Procopius' picture shows a uniformly negatively-perceived Justinian; it has no half-tones, depicting Justinian only in the most sombre of colors. There is evidence of compartmentalized thinking. For instance Procopius holds, inconsistently, that the wily and ruthless Justinian used and then destroyed his agents, while he yet believes that the Emperor was duped with ease and with impunity by his creatures.[20] The writer seems to have projected much of his own confusion into the Emperor's designs. How conscious he was of this, it is hard to say, as his depiction bears all the hallmarks of a highly authoritarian personality: in addition to the above aspects of such a personality, one might cite his emotional anti-feminism, his sexual and other fantasy-projections and his valuation of individuals primarily in terms of granting respect only to high social status. On the other hand the work is something of a *tour de force* in a *genre* which had a long tradition of rather hysterical invective.[21]

Some important things are *not* here. Empathy,[22] for instance, is certainly totally absent in Procopius. What is involved is the ability to put oneself in the other person's position. This does not necessarily mean that one sympathises with him, but rather that one can critically assess the difficulties confronting him and the options open to him in taking the actions which he is under pressure to take. As the discussion to Figure 7.1 (above, p. 154) indicated, there were ample sources for conflict in the cross-pressures working within the apparatus of government; and the disasters arising from natural causes during the reign caused further strain upon, and change within, that apparatus.

There is a psychology of the situation as well as of the person. Consider the keeping of the imperial peace between a Monophysite South, an Orthodox East and a West that was increasingly becoming orthodox with a small "o" as Roman Catholicism gradually emerged — and this with five feud-prone Patriarchs to contend with. Now it is evident that Justinian, like Emperors before and after him,[23] had to temporize for the sake of state interests, so no legitimate conclusions can be drawn, from deviousness in this regard, about his personality. Procopius fails totally to take situational cross-pressures into account and to distinguish public and private aspects of the Emperor's character. This again is a significant finding, being yet another indication that there was a serious failure in communication between the Emperor and the upper *echelons* of Byzantine society, insofar as these are represented in the views of this well-placed and highly esteemed member of that society.

Detailed inspection of what the writers "see" of Justinian's achievement shows this too to have been equally biassed and partial. For instance, Procopius thinks of Justinian's military achievement largely in terms of three issues. The first of these concerns the number of men (Romans, allies and enemies) who met their death as result thereof (10 mentions); the second concerns mishandling of arrangements for pay for the troops (9); and the third concerns squandering of public moneys on bribes to barbarians (8).[24] With some scandals involving high military personnel (3 mentions), this largely exhausts Procopius' comments on this aspect of Justinian's activities. John, on the other hand, either talks in generalities about the extent of the conquests, or mentions specific campaigns and their success. Neither writer mentions Justinian's conquests in Spain, the technical and logistical virtuosity of the planning, the religious crusade aspect of the north African and Italian campaigns, or the overall strategical (and commercial) gains that resulted. John's account is vague and chauvinistic; Procopius, by exaggerated emphasis on negative aspects combined with no counter-balancing assessment of positive gains, provides a grotesque parody of the actuality (source reference in Table 7.1a, above, p. 165).

This is not an isolated phenomenon. This type of biassed selectivity also appears, for instance, in their comments on Justinian's activities as these affect the bureaucracy. John — a shrewd analyst of this topic and of this topic alone — comments on successful reforms (10 passages refer), but qualifies by specifying the great influence of the implementing Head of *Corps* (9 passages) and undesirable side effects (4 passages). Procopius singles out only negative aspects for comment and makes frequent reference to scandalous bureaucratic intrigues (13 out of 36 references). The complex trade-taxation-currency-property rights is presented by Procopius virtually as though he were a spokesman for the landed gentry. It is a uniformly negative depiction, imputing enmity and avarice to the Emperor as motivation, with no suggestion of the abuses that the latter was proceeding against. If one compares Procopius' comments with the contents of the contemporary law codes, however, one finds that imperial legislation shows repeated attempts to cut back the growth of large estates, which were often built up by quite ruthless practices, in order to protect the little man, who was easier to extract taxes from and to conscript into the army.[25] Similarly, to present Justinian's building activities by focussing all of one's attention on a senseless squandering of money on useless buildings on the sea-front around Constantinople (as does Procopius), or in a laudation of the building of the Church of the Holy Wisdom in the rebuilding of Constantinople (which is what John does), without mention of the vital border installations, urban unemployment and its relief by large-scale public works, or rebuilding of earthquake-damaged cities, is seriously to distort the overall picture.[26]

But perhaps the best illustration of such distortion concerns a matter dear to the hearts of both John and Procopius, who had both enjoyed the traditional literary training.[27] John the Cappadocian, Justinian's efficiency expert brought in to improve the Praetorian Prefecture, had simplified and streamlined judicial procedure, to save litigants time and expense. One side effect of this was that certain lucrative and largely ornamental perquisites for rhetoricians (cf. *De Mag.* III 50,5) were done away with. To Procopius this is a striking example of Justinian's desire to destroy the arts which adorned the Empire (*S.H.* 26, 1-2). John sees it as a direct result of the activities of an evil and inefficient departmental Head (*De Mag.* III 66, 1-3; cf. 76, 10), and construes it as the ruination of the staff of the Praetorian Prefecture and of the Prefecture. As two of his special interests are adversely affected, his attitude is negative and highly emotional. Neither writer considers the case which could be made for the measure, and for the cutting back of red tape in general.

Clearly, this lack of *consensus* and empathy among such areas of the sub-*élite* must have had massive consequences for the implementation of Justinian's reforms. In the case of Procopius this can be easily seen. He tells of Justinian's reprisals against senators as a sequel to the Nika Riot, which almost destroyed the Emperor. Procopius is the only source to make such mention of this aspect of the sequel. When he went abroad as personal secretary to a General, the General was one whose loyalty was to fall under the Emperor's suspicion. In conformity with his patently pro-army viewpoint in the *Secret History*, his work on the *Wars* implicitly features his General as true hero rather than the Emperor, and this in a published work. He does not seem to have held high office subsequently, and the only indication of his sympathies in the latter part of the reign is to be found in the unusually detailed catalogue of ways in which the Emperor's reforms affected the vested interests of the landed aristocracy. From Justinian's viewpoint this attitude could be at best construed as passive hostility; this may indeed be the reason why he offered the task of writing a history of his Persian War to (the more amenable) John rather than the obviously more suitable Procopius.[28] Anyway, the Emperor could hardly entrust a position of power to a man with an attitude such as Procopius'. And Procopius seems to be speaking for many others of like mind, such as the landed gentry for instance.

John's case is more complicated. His attitude towards the Emperor is one of some ambivalence: beneath the *façade* required in references to the Sacred Emperor in a published work lurks bitter dissatisfaction with the treatment meted out to him in the Emperor's reforms of the bureaucracy.[29] Now John's identification with his fellow bureaucrats is both pointed and striking, in view of his failure to identify with other (family and academic) special interest groups. And John specifically tells us that many of these colleagues with whom he thus so closely identifies himself experienced like treatment.[30] It looks as though Justinian had to deal with a civil bureaucracy which was basically hostile to him and to his measures below the top *echelon* of new men whom he had brought in to reform it. This would mean crippling obstruction, as the bureaucracy initiated policy as well as implementing it.[31]

Section 4: The Operational Code of the Bureaucracy

The source of discord lay in a conflict deeply woven into the structure and functioning of the bureaucracy. On the one hand, the vested interests and resultant operational code of the bureaucrats were bound up with certain practices: judicial privilege, purchase of office and collection of fees. On the other, the taxpayers' interests were best served by the elimination of these practices. The first encouraged corruption in officials. The second increased administrative costs by facilitating sinecurism. The third added to the costs of tax paying. Moreover these practices inhibited the Emperor's powers in controlling and directing the bureaucracy, inasmuch as they made the taking of disciplinary action, or changing the bureaucratic life-style by promotions or demotions, difficult to effect. An examination in detail will show the ramification of problems involved in this basic conflict of interests.

Possibly the most important of these practices is that known as *praescriptio fori*. By this a bureaucrat, as a defendant, had the right to be tried before his *corps*, his prosecutor having to "follow his court." This meant that if, for instance, a member of the Prefect's staff obtained a special assignment to look into tax collection in a province and committed extortion there, the taxpayer would have to come to Constantinople and arraign him before the Praetorian Prefect, which in effect meant his colleagues the *commentarienses*. Conversely an ex-*Praefectianus*, as members of the Prefect's staff were known, might dispute tax payment in his province of residence, where collection was normally effected by local municipal authorities. The case would then be referred to the central office, and referred and referred.... One year in five, with luck, would see a remission of all outstanding "bad taxes."[32]

The trial would involve numerous expenses, the *sportulae* or "fees" already mentioned, which would price "justice" out of the range of all but the affluent. Even getting one's case admitted would be a costly business, and the subsequent proceedings would be written up in an alien language — Latin — involving further *sportulae* for translations, etc. A taxpayer would thus be prepared to present an official with a *sportula* rather than be involved in a contest of lawsuits.[33]

Under these circumstances control of jurisdiction was vital to a *corps*, for it guaranteed its income of *sportulae* and its privileges in tax evasion. Together these two abuses made for increasing costs of tax collection and judiciary processes. Moreover, since *sportulae* were structurally necessary owing to low official pay and lack of an adequate pensioning scheme, officials were enmeshed in illegalities. So the morality of bureaucratic conduct came to approximate that of a zero-sum game, that is a conflict in which what is lost by one party is gained by the other. So losing had to be prevented at all costs. For the stakes were high, as discipline was administered via these courts. For instance, if another *corps* were to gain control of the jurisdictional matters which should have come up before the law court of one's own *corps*, the entire prospects of one's own *corps* and of all the departments in it could be seriously affected. Inter-*corps* feuding thus took a savage course, the law court being conceived of as a weapon which granted power. John's writings, however, suggest that, up to Justinian's day, the infighting had very largely involved the Heads of *Corps* only.[34]

A way for the career bureaucrat to control the functions of a post lay open in the practice of purchasing an office or the reversion of that office *(suffragium)*. A needy Emperor had only to make an appointment in this way and the position involved continued thereafter as the property of its succession of purchasers. Such a state of affairs led to investment in purchase of offices as a means of speculation. It also led to pluralism, that is to say to the holding of several posts simultaneously, with its inevitable consequences of absenteeism (though five years' absence would lose one one's "job"). Besides this, it led to sinecurism — for posts came to involve little actual work. As working efficiency decreased as result of all of these side effects, they thus led to increases in the establishment. This development was encouraged by the bureaucrats involved, because it provided yet more opportunities for saleable positions. And so the vicious circle was perpetuated. Moreover, purchasers had a vested interest in special types of recruitment as a consequence of all this. Recruits had to come from those of appropriate purchasing power. Thus considerations of specialist training, merit or efficiency receded into the background. Moreover, those with an investment in positions also sought to ensure a particular form of promotion, involving a long career sequence of offices going by seniority, to protect their investments.[35]

Again, this practice as it were compounded the others: for a *sportula* an official would make out an honorific position in the name of the person who had tendered the *sportula* to him. This "purchase" constituted a *suffragium* and conferred a position which, in its turn, gave the purchaser access to rights of *praescriptio fori*. The official would then insert the document conferring the honorific position in a strategic position in an (in)appropriate tray for the Emperor's fleeting signature. Justinian (the Emperor "who never slept"),[36] uniquely, read everything he signed — a practice much disapproved of in some circles.[37]

Now, clearly, such malpractices could not be tackled individually. They constitute as it were an "apparatus culture";[38] that is to say these practices are part and parcel of a bureaucratic life style. They so interlock with a whole configuration of related practices and norms of behaviour that the removal of any one of them as an individual item is virtually impossible. Moreover, the bureaucrats' *esprit de corps* encouraged in them a punishment orientation towards the defenceless lower orders. The latters' subject orientation in any case severely inhibited their inclination to make appeal to the Emperor. Even in the event of a complaint's reaching the Emperor and his acting upon it, his instructions still had to be implemented by the very bureaucrats against whose interests they were directed.[39]

Now there were various types of Emperor. At one extreme was Arcadius — an effete minor dominated by a eunuch chamberlain; Justinian's uncle, an illiterate peasant, unable even to sign his name (some said), had been a similar "good" appointment from the point of view of the bureaucrats involved in the intrigue which unexpectedly raised him to power. Justin, however, had a highly educated nephew and trained the latter to power: this nephew turned out to have a will of his own, and was capable of working 23 hours a day without stopping for meals.[40] Justinian thus provides the classic instance of the other extreme of Emperor. And the insidious web of the bureaucracy was to prove too strong even for him to break through it.

John's *De Magistratibus*, especially its last book, thus gives the career bureaucrat's picture of the great struggle. Content analysis of all changes mentioned as undergone by the administrative bureaucracies in Justinian's reign (see Table 7.4 and its appendages) shows that, for John, these changes were felt to have brought about a drop in status for the Prefect's staff, and were seen as changes, in legal procedures, adversely affecting that body. These matters were very much at the forefront of John's awareness. *Praescriptio fori* and *sportulae* are involved. Changes are seen largely in terms of personalities rather than of issues or policies. Thus major financial reforms are misperceived and misunderstood by being seen as a disconnected scatter of actions performed by individual Prefects, who are appraised with so much emotionality that rational assessment of their long-range or large-scale objectives simply is not possible. Similarly, there is no connection seen between a felt need for a drop in the empire's expenditure, and the Emperor's retrenchment on perquisities and pensions.

This is a tactician's (rather than a strategist's) eye-view of change as it affected the bureaucracy — if not a worm's eye-view — as comparison with Cassiodorus' *Variae* clearly showed (chapter 6). For John is wholly concerned with the impact of these changes upon the career game as played inside his branch of the Prefect's *corps*. So he is blind to the larger implications, for the administrative bureaucracy as a whole, of empire-building moves at strategical points within its system of interacting *corps* and departments. There is something in this of the professional's trained incapacity to see beyond the immediate boundaries of his sphere of expertise;[41] but, as already noted, the constricted

TABLE 7.4
Changes in the bureaucracy attributed by John to Justinian's reign

Priority ranking	Attention Area	Number of times discussed (See 7.4a)	*High degree of emotion shown (See 7.4b)
1	Changes in standing of the Prefect's staff	22	of which 18 passages merit classification as emotional
2	Changes in the administration of the law and in the standing of the Prefect's law court	21	of which 15 as above
3	Alterations in recruitment or career patterns	18	10 passages as above. Emotion is mainly generated when career patterns are disturbed
4	Financial activities	(13)	Possibly 2 passages describable as "emotional". Emotion seems not to be focussed on the issue but on the personalities involved.
5	Activities of individual Prefects —in particular, the Cappadocian's cutback of red tape	8 / 3	All 8 passages are emotion-charged. Negative feelings are more strongly expressed than are the 3 positive ones.
6	Additions to the body of officials	5	—Quite impassionately assessed, by and large.
7	"No pension" type complaints	4	Very strong emotion generated in each case. Imperial retrenchment policies not seen as such.
8	Status gains by Master of Offices	3**	Not to the forefront among John's anxieties: only one emotional passage.
9	Disciplining of his own staff by the Prefect	2	Very strong emotion generated in both passages.

*Passages are taken as falling under this heading if emotion-laden terms, imagery or rhetoric occurs therein.
**Significantly, these are the only comments not directed to the Prefecture, apart from seven general remarks on the law.

TABLE 7.4a
Source-references — by frequency

	GAINS	LOSSES
Standing of Staff	III 59,5-6 (bishop's authority flouted by Praetorian Prefect's agent); 61,6 (cuts back *cursus publicus* and therefore power of Master of Offices)	II 16,3-4; 17,2; 21,2; III 10,3; 14,1; 15,4; 17,1-3; 56,4; 66,5-6; 67,2-4; 69,3.
Common to both ↕	III 38,1-5; 76,10	III 9,9-10; 13,1-5; 25,4-5; 65,4-5; 66,2-3; 68,2-5; see 20,4-10 which means a loss of power to the prefecture
Law & Court of Praetorian Prefect		II 15,1-2; 16,1&3; 17,1; 29,1-2 (means a loss of power). III 11,1-12,1; 14,2; 18,1-5; 19,4; 42,5-6; 66,1-2; cf. III 1,3 (means less litigation for PP's court) & 70,1-2 (Praetors' & Quaestors' courts gain).

3. *Financial officials advanced:* III 10,3; 36,1; 38,1-5, 54,1-2 (46,1-2&49,3-5 refer to Anastasius' reign).
   Recruitment problems: II 17,1; III 28,3; 54,1 (66,4&67,3-5 also refer).
   Career patterns broken: II 18,2-3; III 2,3-5; 9,7; 66,3-6; 67,3-5; cf. 14,2; 27,2; 57,2; 69,3.

4. II 15,2; III 51,5; 54,6; 56,2-4; 57,5-7; 58,1; 59,7-8; 60,1; 61,7; 61,9; 62,1; 68,3-4; 76,7-8.

5. III 76,7; 76,10 (Phocas).
   III 38,3; 61,6; 62,2; 62,3; 68,2-4; 69,2-3 (John the Cappadocian).
   Red tape: III 14,1-2; 25,4-5; 68,3-5; cf. 76,10.

6. II 28,1; 19,3; 30,5-6; see III 70,1.

7. III 25,6; 30,2; 66,3; 67,4-5.

8. II 26,1; III 9,9-10; 67,2-4.

9. *(Disciplining of staff by the Prefect:* II 21,2; III 65,4.)

*There is much overlap between areas 1 and 2; John has difficulty in keeping the subjects "the administration of the law and the Prefect's Court" and "the status of the Prefect's staff" distinct, so interconnected are they in his way of thinking. *Some* overlap will be found between almost any two categories in this table; in keeping with the generally discursive nature of John's writing, he rarely restricts his outbursts of indignation to one topic at a time.

TABLE 7.4b
Source-references (by degrees of emotion shown)

--based on the layout and source citations of Table 4a; specific mention is made of source citations only where this is necessary for clarity.

1/2 etc.: means one out of the two source citations to be found in the appropriate section of Table 7.4a is emotion-laden; this one is then specified.

--*indicates that the passage has to do with John's *bête noire* John the Cappadocian, so the emotion may be generated by him rather than the subject matter.

	ATTENTION AREA		COMMENTARY
	Gains	*Losses*	
1. Standing of Staff	2/2 (both negatively seen — but the Cappadocian is involved).	11/11 II 16,3; 17,2; *21, 2** (striking); III 10,3 (probably) 14,1; 15,4; 17,1&3; 56,4; 66,6 (real issue pay?); 67,4; 69,3.	More emotion generated by losses than gains. John is often blind to the implications of a devious piece of empire-building. With the exceptions of areas 7 and 9, the most memorable passages cluster in these two initial areas.
Common to 1 & 2	1/2-III 76,10 (probably to be so classed).	7/7 III 9,9-10; 13,4-5; 25,4-5; 65,4-5*; 66,2-3; 68,2-5*; & 20,9-10.	
2. Law and lawcourt		8/12 II 15,2; 16,3; 17,1; *III 11,1&2; 12,1* (striking); 14,2; 18,1; 42,5 (probably here); 66,1-2	
3. Breakdown: *Career-patterns*		7/9 II 18,203; III 2,4-5; 66,3-6 (really on pay?); 67,4; see 14,2; 27,2; 57,2; 69,3.	The most salient issue in overall terms is the disturbance of career patterns.
Recruit-ment		2/5 possibly II 17,1 & III 67,5 (really on pensions?)	
Financial officials	1/4 III 36,1.		Two passages are relevant — but they date to Anastasius' reign.

TABLE 7.4b (continued)

ATTENTION AREA		COMMENTARY
4. Financial Activities	3/13 possibly III 54,6 & 56,3-4 (status loss the real issue here?) III 57,6-7; 58,1; 59,7-8; 60,3-4; 61,9; 62,1; 68,4; III 76,7-8	These passages seem to bear rather on a Prefect's implementation of the tax laws than on changes to them: 7 concern the Cappadocian's activities, 1 Phocas'. Classification under 5 possible.
5. Individual Prefects	8/8 (see also *Commentary* to section 4)	The negative passages seem the more emotional. Lamentation is always extensive. In general, a highly emotion-charged area.
Red-tape	3/3 III 14,1-2; 25,4-5; 68,4-5	
6. Additions to officials	0/4	Some remarkably objective appraisals of the usefulness of such additions.
7. No Pension	4/4 III 30,2 surprisingly muted.	Strikingly put. Short excerpts from John are often found in translation in works on Justinian; one of these four passages is generally included in such cases.
8. Status gains by Master of Offices	1/3 III 9,10.	Not central to John's focus of attention; see second point in *Commentary* to section 1.
9. Disciplining	2/2 II 21,2 particularly striking.	In fact, possibly the most emotional passage to be considered here.

NB. Clearly, frequency and emotionality of mention need not be correlated: e.g., subject matter might dictate the former, salience owing to some quirk of John's psychological world the latter. It is not contended that these figures "prove" anything; this way of setting the matter out merely gives clarity to the analysis of a complicated issue, enabling readers to judge the *relative* trends operating there (on this impressionistic and subjective use of statistics see H. R. Isaacs, *Scratches on Our Minds,* New York 1958, p. 27). Accordingly, I have not attempted to rank priorities by weighting and combining frequency and emotionality (see in particular sections 4 and 5), merely listing by frequency. Disparities between the two dimensions do, however, pinpoint strongly held attitudes rather clearly. I am indebted to Barton S. Whaley of the C.I.S. at M.I.T. for calling my attention to the need to control for emotionality when listing frequencies.

personality and empathic ability tend not to coincide. But, for all its distortions, John's picture of what Justinian was doing was probably entertained, as has been argued, by more members of the bureaucracy than Justinian's own picture of what he was doing.

Justinian proceeded as follows.[42] *Praescriptio fori* was sharply cut back. Local cases were not to be appealed below the amount of 750 gold pieces; the office of "Defender of the State" was further empowered to protect the interests of the lower class in such local trials. The staff of the Master of Offices were empowered by Sacred Decrees emanating from the Emperor to transfer cases that had come before the Prefect's Court — from which appeal was now allowed. Not only did the Prefect's Court lose its power of trying members of other *corps*; it now saw its own staff firmly prosecuted within its own walls by a new, unorthodox Prefect. The latter, moreover, followed up tax evaders of high standing who had taken advantage of *praescriptio fori*. Unusually, this reign saw no rebates to such people of taxes on which they had stalled payment.

Sportulae also were hard hit. There were pay raises for provincial governors, who had to take an oath against corruption of the sort entailed in the receipt of *sportulae*. The Emperor made himself accessible to all, perused all documents that went out under his signature and himself read out his own proclamations. The length of the sessions of the Consistory was shortened, the Emperor making many lesser appointments in person in private sessions. Formality and red tape were cut back also in judicial records and generally in the archives and day-to-day business. All these measures cut out stages in the course of conducting business with officialdom that formerly had produced a rich haul of "fees" for the officials involved.

Suffragia fared no better. Sinecures were done away with in the army and civil bureaucracy. These reforms often resulted in real hardship and unfairness, as the lucrative honorific senior posts involved in some of these retrenchments had served to provide a form of lump sum payment in *lieu* of an adequate pension scheme. Expertise, in law and especially in accountancy, was specifically rewarded. Career patterns were broken and new (and, in the eyes of the old guard, unsuitable) personnel advanced. Erring staff were savagely punished, whereas previously only the topmost *echelons* seem to have been in danger from power politics. The *esprit de corps* of the Prefect's Men broke under this concerted attack on its system of privilege.

But these bureaucratic reforms were not in the event just so many changes automatically carried out by the bureaucracy exactly and immediately as the Emperor commanded them. One cannot think of this situation as though the civil bureaucracy were some mere neutral instrumentality — a black box, as it were, into which the Emperor fed instructions from one side to have them come out from the other as accomplished acts. This black box, as shown in chapter 5, was equipped with a scrambling device.

After all, the implementation of reforms lay with the bureaucracy itself, and in particular with the new leadership imported by the Emperor. This new leadership proved as difficult to control as it was vigorous, and it spawned new problems, necessitating further disciplinary actions, while itself dealing with the old ones. Bureaucracies which are neutral, service-oriented instrumentalities with an operational code based on efficiency, economy and rationality are in point of fact only found in certain types of environment. They occur along with particular combinations of political institutions and value-systems. They are found, for instance, in conjunction with legislatures, political parties and an independent press and judiciary. In such cases a governmental bureaucracy cannot aggregate all talent and power to itself, and it is not allowed to act irresponsibly. For the value-system of the host society in which such bureaucratic instrumentalities are found includes what is known as a "market morality," that is to say widespread subscription to the belief that one should treat others with a generalised, impersonal fairness (i.e. without making special arrangements for friends and so on) so that the economic system will work.

This background simply did not exist in sixth century Byzantium.[43] Perhaps an appropriate model for the sixth century situation is the Pacific Islander's definition of health, namely that one strikes a symbiotic balance with one's parasites (i.e. successful cure of one or two varieties may just put the whole remaining horde into action against fresh body tissues).

Specifically, the selling of offices soon came to be practised again. The Vicars, occupants of positions in a lucrative but seemingly largely formalistic career stage, had themselves returned to the Establishment after being initially dispensed with by Justinian. More posts as Praetorian Prefect or Master of the Soldiery were created. The Count of the Privy Purse built himself a departmental empire. If the guilds of city dwellers were at last effectively taxed (via the new customs duty, the Tithe), they managed to secure a system of monopolies for themselves, and, of course, they passed the Tithe along to the purchaser.

But the bureaucracy did not simply adjust by losing perquisites in some areas only to gain them in others. Its balance of cooperating antagonisms shifted, to find a new level. After Justinian, it is true, the literary record is poor, so that when we next see the bureaucratic system, and find it altered, this alteration may have been determined by some other factor. But the change to be described seems to have been effected by the next century. Moreover, it is significant, in view of Justinian's humbling of the Praetorian Prefecture, that the alteration involved the replacement of the system of subordination to a few major Heads of *Corps*, of which that prefecture had been the outstanding example. The new system was based on coordination among a vastly increased number of smaller departmental units.[44] More: the separation of military and civil administration, long carefully nurtured for purposes of internal security, was breached. So it was that the system of administration by prefectures changed into one of administration by themes (compare maps 2 & 6, pp. 180 & 184, Bk. One). Justinian had not meant to weaken the central government's control of the empire. His aim was the reverse: "one Church, one faith, one empire." He aimed to bring *both* empire and central bureaucracy under firmer control. But, unexpectedly, control of peripheral areas began to weaken. The overseas dioceses — Africa, Italy, Spain — resulted in the development of joint civil and military governors or Exarchs. Forty-five years after Justinian's death, the son of one such governor, the African Exarch, was powerful enough to sail on Constantinople and overthrow the Emperor.[45]

Nor was Justinian's playing-off of bishop and local governor without its effect. Bishops in distant provinces, empowered by enactments such as the Pragmatic Sanction, came speedily to serve as focal points for local disaffection: Alexandria provides a striking example.[46] Moreover, the confrontation of Emperor and Church on doctrinal matters had led the latter to new ideas on the subject of independence.[47] Justinian's reign in fact witnessed the high-water mark in imperial intervention in Church affairs. No subsequent Emperor was quite so able to treat the Church as though it were just another section of the apparatus of government. Thus the weakening of power centres in the central administrative bureaucracy had as its unanticipated consequence the development of increasingly autonomous power centres in the ecclesiastical bureaucracy as well as at the periphery of the empire.

The reigns of the Emperors who follow Justinian indicate, in their fading fortunes, that their inheritance was a troubled one. But we can find more immediate evidence about the overall impact of Justinian's reforms upon his subjects from early in his reign. As Emperor he was striving to ameliorate the lot of his subjects. Clearly conscious of the abuses under which they were labouring, he put his sympathy and concern into his frantic work as reforming Emperor. One immediate result was the Nika Riot of 532, the most destructive in Byzantine history. The riot arose out of public dissatisfaction with Tribonian and John the Cappadocian, two of Justinian's most trusted and most senior bureaucrats, both vigorous reformers. It almost cost Justinian his capital, his throne and his life. Behind this outburst was *anomie*, resulting in the violent mass movements that we read about in descriptions of the Green and the Blue Factions. Procopius' account of these makes vivid, if rather horrifying, reading.[48] Perversely, it was precisely those whom Justinian so much meant to help, the lower orders, who were, and felt themselves to be, so very much disadvantaged as result of those attempts to help.

In short, if the reign shows that attempts at large-scale social amelioration were not foreign to the ancient world, it also shows that they were attended by almost as many hazards and unplanned-for consequences as face their modern counterparts. And a major share of the responsibility for the unexpected and untoward consequences which attended upon Justinian's reforms must be attributed to the civil bureaucracy, whose reaction to and implementation of those reforms largely produced the unanticipated consequences detailed above.

FOOTNOTES TO CHAPTER 7

1. The study on which this chapter is based originally took the form of a lecture in the course "Society and Man," provided by the Department of Political Science at M.I.T. as a sophomore course. Hence it focusses very largely on the attention areas, in bibliography and method, of the above course, which were of an interdisciplinary nature. On the concept of traditionalism and the interdisciplinary approach to it, see Riggs, pp. 50-54 and J. Galtung, "The Structure of Traditionalism: A Case Study from Western Sicily," *Journal of International Affairs*, 19(2), 1965, p. 218.

2. Lewis, *Naval Power and Trade in the Mediterranean*, pp. 21-49.

3. On the importance of silk to the commerce (and diplomacy) of

the day see R. S. Lopez, "The Silk Industry in the Byzantine Empire," *Speculum*, 20, 1945, pp. 1-42. For the general background on the Byzantine *solidus* or gold piece, the "dollar of the Middle Ages," see C. Cipolla's survey, *Money, Prices and Civilization in the Mediterranean World, Fifth to Seventh Century*, Princeton, 1956, chapter 2.

4. The reign marked the commencement of what is customarily thought of as a medieval pattern of customs zones in the Mediterranean: see H. Antoniadis-Bibicou, *Recherches sur les douanes à Byzance*, 1963, pp. 39, and 91-95.

5. See *LRE*, pp. 470-9.

6. *LRE*, pp. 481-516.

7. For these points, and for what follows in the text, see the discussion on Justinian in chapter three, Book One.

8. Lewis, *Naval Power and Trade in the Mediterranean*, pp. 6, 21, 49 and 54; see however *LRE*, pp. 964-70. Katz, *The Decline of Rome and the Rise of Medieval Europe*, p. 127, puts the matter in more general terms and in a larger perspective.

9. Rome was reduced to a shell by repeated occupations, now by one side, now by the other, during the war in Italy. Athens had its school of philosophy, suspect for its pagan associations, closed in 529. The law school at Berytus (Beirut) was closed after the destruction caused to the city by the earthquake of 551, and Antioch also received severe setbacks from earthquake and sack. Even Constantinople suffered, from arson, in the Nika Riot of 532. Alexandria alone, of the major cultural centers, went unscathed. It was Justinian's policy, as his building activities show, to increase the glories of his capital. In consequence of all the above developments, the trend towards a one-city, metropolitan culture must have been immensely stepped up during the reign.

10. On the impact of the plague, see J. L. Teall, "The Barbarians in Justinian's Armies," *Speculum* 40, 1965, pp. 305-322; on the demographic alterations caused by the Slav "wedge" in the Balkans, see P. Charanis, "Ethnic Changes in the Byzantine Empire in the Seventh Century," *Dumbarton Oaks Papers* 13, 1959, pp. 36-44. Other important studies on the demography of the period are P. Lemerle, "Esquisse pour une histoire agraire de Byzance," *Révue historique* 219-220, 1958, pp. 32-48 and 74, and D. Jacoby, "La population de Constantinople à l'époque byzantine: un problème de démographie urbaine," *Byzantion* 31, 1961, pp. 81-110, especially 94 and 106-108. On the resultant changes in the guilds, see Lopez, "The Role of Trade

in the Economic Readjustment of Byzantium in the Seventh Century," *Dumbarton Oaks Papers* 13, 1959, 76-8 (cf. also n. 3 above).

11. Justinian exercised very considerable influence during the reign of his uncle; Procopius actually dates his reign from Justin's accession: *S.H. (Secret History)*, 6, 19; cf. 8, 4 and 9, 50. This gives a total of (9 plus 38) 47 years' authority as a ruler — the longest reign in the early Byzantine period, and one of the longest reigns in the whole of Byzantine history. Other reigns of superior or comparable lengths are those of Basil II — 62 years (but jointly, nominally anyway, with Constantine VIII), and Constantine VII Porphyrogenitus — 47 years (but jointly with Romanus I for 25 of them) in middle Byzantium, and John VI — 47 years (but with a gap in the middle) in late Byzantium.

12. Military success: see how the boundaries of empire shrink back on the maps which date after his day. On Emperor-Church relations: see F. Dvornik, "Emperors, Popes and General Councils," *Dumbarton Oaks Papers* 6, 1951, pp. 1-26, especially p. 21, and E. Kitzinger, "The Cult of Images in the Age before Iconoclasm," *ibid.* 8, 1954, pp. 87, 94-7 and 124-8; Bury, *History of the Later Roman Empire 395-800*, vol. 2, chapter 11, and, in general, the discussion in chapter three, Book One.

13. The point is well made by Riggs; see "Agraria and Industria," Siffin, *Toward the Comparative Study of Public Administration*, pp. 52-57, on "The Ideological Framework," and 73-81 on "Communications Networks" and "mobilization" (p. 74).

14. On selectivity in perception see section 2, "Perception, Memory and Motivation" in E. E. Maccoby & co., *Readings in Psychology*, Holt, Rinehart & Winston, 1958, especially pp. 47-54, and H. D. Lasswell's classic "Why be Quantitative?" in Berelson and Janowitz's *Reader in Public Opinion and Communication*, pp. 265-77. On assessing the mood of a period see R. E. Lane and D. O. Sears, *Public Opinion*, Prentice Hall, 1964, especially chapter 2, "Portrait of an Opinion."

15. Respectively: *The Institutes of Justinian* (translated by J. B. Moyle), 1955; Procopius, *The Anecdota* (cited in this study as *S.H. — Secret History*), vol. VI of the Loeb series (translated by H. B. Dewing), 1960; and John the Lydian's *On the Magistracies of the Roman Constitution*, translated in Book Three of this work.

16. If, in reading the *Secret History*, one rates its views against Adorno's F-scale, the authoritarianism of its writer becomes very strikingly apparent. Some of its statements even read like those of the questionnaire! The F-scale examines a man's views on "proper" attitudes — in religion, to parents, tradition, his betters and inferiors; on

ingroups and outgroups in general; on toughness in war and so on, and on the place of women and sexual behaviour in general. See T. W. Adorno & co., *The Authoritarian Personality*, Wiley, 1964, chapters 7 (especially) and 19. For the significance of "compartmentalised" thinking, time-focus and so on (the basic infrastructure to Table 7.1 - on change, in other words), see Rokeach, *The Open and Closed Mind*, pp. 31-53. On the inter-connection of authoritarian personality systems and traditionalism, see Hagen, *On the Theory of Social Change*, part II, chapters 4-7.

17. *S.H.* 14, 2 and 3.

18. See R. Brown & co., *New Directions in Psychology*, Holt, Rinehart & Winston, 1962, pp. 14-82, especially 79-82. The model might be represented:

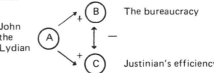

(Here arrows indicate views, plus signs a favourable orientation, the negative sign an unfavourable one.) Cf. Lane and Sears, *Public Opinion*, chapter 5, especially pp. 44-53.)

19. McClelland, *The Achieving Society*, pp. 226-28; chapters six and seven contain relevant material. It is *not* here suggested that Justinian was an entrepreneurial type; the point is rather that a highly innovative personality differs markedly, especially in traditional cultures, from his more conformist contemporaries; in such a way, in fact, as to cause the one difficulties in understanding the other, and *vice versa*. See Hagen, *On the Theory of Social Change*, chapters 5 and 6.

20. On the former view see *S.H.* 10, 20-23; 16, 6-10; 21, 3-6 & 9-15 (cf. also 29, 13 & 27); and on the latter, 8, 22; 13, 10-11 & 18-20 (cf. also 14, 16-22). On "compartmentalized thinking" and its significance, see n. 16.

21. A good example of the distortions in presentation which could be caused by the form of presentation required by a *genre* in this literary age is analysed by A. D. Cameron, "Christianity and Tradition in the Historiography of the Late Empire," *Classical Quarterly* 14, 1964, pp. 316-28.

22. On the crucial importance of this factor for change in traditional society, see Lerner, *The Passing of Traditional Society*, pp. 43-75, especially 47-52 & 69-75.

23. The Emperor Zeno (474-491) had issued a compromise statement known as the *Henotikon* in an effort to bring unity to warring Church factions; Anastasius (491-518) had been required to give undertakings that he would not allow his Monophysite leanings to influence him in his activities as Emperor; Heraclius (610-641) was to issue the *Ekthesis* and evoke the theory of Monotheletism in an attempt to bring reconciliation: see Ostrogorsky, *History of the Byzantine State*, pp. 59, 61-62 & 96-97. On the importance of such matters in contemporaries' belief systems, see Barker, *Social and Political Thought in Byzantium*, pp. 7-15 and esp. 34-42; on the salience of religious issues in the life, thought and literature of Byzantium, see Hussey, *The Byzantine World*, pp. 100, 105, 124 & 139-40, and Jenkins, p. 25.

24. Some idea of the biassed nature of these charges can be obtained by consulting C. D. Gordon, "Procopius and Justinian's Financial Policies," *Phoenix* 13, 1959, pp. 23-30.

25. See e.g. Diehl, *Byzantium, Greatness and Decline*, pp. 152-3 and 69 respectively.

26. Justinian's great Church of the Holy Wisdom in Constantinople remains to this day one of the architectural wonders of the world. Procopius does not mention it. On the *limes* system (fortified frontier lines or zones), an essential part of Byzantine military strategy, see Lewis, *Naval Power and Trade in the Mediterranean*, pp. 27-29.

27. On this see Browning, "Byzantine Scholarship" in *Past and Present* 28, 1964, pp. 3-20. The part that such a tradition-bound system would play in producing the "constricted personality" of traditional man is obvious. Semantic problems are involved too, as focussing on the "model" language of the past left the society with only bygone concepts with which to conceptualize a rapidly changing world: see Barker, *Social and Political Thought in Byzantium*, pp. 1-8 & 42-45, esp. 1-3; cf. also Ward and Rustow, *Political Modernization in Japan and Turkey*, pp. 444-47. There is in fact evidence that increases in powers of conceptualization broaden political horizons and contribute even more than the spread of empathy in producing ability to appreciate the position of an alien political group: see H. Inglehart and R. Schoenberger, *Communications and Political Mobilization*, mimeo, American Political Science Association, Washington AGM, 1968.

28. A suggestion of Rubin's: see *Das Zeitalter Justinians*, p. 169.

29. Most clearly seen in John's sense of grievance over lack of provisions for his pension: III 25, 6; 29, 2-4; 30, 2; 66, 3 & 5; 67, 5; cf. I, 23, 3. But even the formal laudation of the Emperor at the beginning

of book three has critical undertones: it is brief and immediately followed by oblique criticism: cf. III 1, 1-4 (esp. 4) & 2, 3-5. Equally significant is his hero-worship of Phocas (III 72, 2-76, 10), a member of the aristocracy, whom Justinian seems to have been forced to accept in place of John the Cappadocian (the Emperor's choice and John's *bête noir* — cf. II 20, 2; 21, 1-4; III 57, 1-62, 5; 64, 1; 65, 2-5; 68, 2-70, 1; 72, 1) as result of the Nika Riot: cf. pp. 41 & 55 with 368 in vol. II of Bury, *History of the Later Roman Empire*, and see Procopius' *S.H.* 13, 6-8.

30. On his family see III 26, 1 & 4; 27, 1-2; 28, 1 (the only references — contrast his contemporary, the writer Agathias); his attitude to his fellow academics appears most strikingly at III 47, 1 and to his fellow members of the Prefect's staff at I 15 (4); III 30, 10; cf. 27, 5. For the comment that his own experiences were shared by many, see III 66, 3-6 & 67, 4 (*esprit de corps* appears strikingly in the following passages: II 17, 1; 18, 2-3; III 2, 3-5; 14, 2; 67, 1-3).

31. There was now no constitution involving a popular assembly with voting rights.The old Republican magistrates of Rome had long since become little more than municipal officials; the Senate was largely a rubber-stamping device. Effectively, the civil apparatus ran the government, under the Emperor's direction. Technically there was an Imperial Council for high-level decision-making, but (a) this comprised many imperial (Court) officials and senior bureaucrats and, anyway, (b) it too largely rubber-stamped "recommendations" made by the Emperor on the advice˙of relevant bureaucratic Heads of *Corps*: see *LRE*, pp. 321-65, esp. 338-40.

32. On *praescriptio fori* see *LRE*, pp. 484-94 (cf. also 494-9). The method of tax evasion outlined in the text was but one of the many ways in which, by a species of progressive taxation in reverse, as it were, the lower *echelons* of society, who were least able to pass the tax burden along to others, came to be the victims of "extraordinary" taxes whenever these were levied: see *LRE*, pp. 463-69.

33. On *sportulae* see *LRE*, pp. 496-99; 602 & 605; 644-6 (military); 909 (ecclesiastical). For John's views (approval of the practice), cf. *De Mag.* III 14, 1; 23, 1; 24, 2; 25, 4; 27, 1; cf. also 8, 7; 10, 1; 13, 3-4; cf. 65, 4-5.

34. Concept of the law court as a weapon conferring power: *De Mag.* II 15, 1-2 and 16, 1 & 3; 17, 1-2; III 9, 9-10; 14, 2; 19, 4; 25, 5; 42, 5-6; 49, 3-5. Infighting to secure control of areas of competence: III 7, 5; 23, 2-3; 40, 2-4 (Rufinus); III 38, 3-5 (Gabriel and John the

Cappadocian) — the move at III 61, 6 is an attack by the Praetorian Prefect on the Master of Offices; see also II 26, 1-2 (Peter the Patrician), III 42, 4 (Demosthenes); III 76, 10 (Phocas) and, in general, II 29, 1 & III 40, 1-2. Other *corps*, and even departments from other *corps*, invade the sphere of authority of the Prefect's Men at III 9, 9-10 (the Master's Men); III 10, 3 (the *a secretis*) & III 67, 2-4 (the *Memoriales*). According to Hodgkin (*The Letters of Cassiodorus*, p. 112) the *scrinarii* to whom John refers are also the Master's Men. If this is so, it does much to explain the bitterness in John's animadversions upon them; but the key passage does not appear to substantiate Hodgkin's contention: see III 35, 1-36; 2 & 37, 1(-4) and Bury, *History of the Later Roman Empire* vol. 1, p. 443, n. 2. In general, on this topic see *LRE*, pp. 489-90. Trials having serious consequences within the ranks of the Prefect's staff were something of a breach of conventions: II 21, 2; III 57, 2 & 65, 4.

35. See *LRE*, pp. 391-400; 603-5; 641 (military); 909-910 (ecclesiastical); cf. R. Guilland, "Vénalité et favoritisme à Byzance," *Revue des études byzantines* 10, 1953, pp. 35-46. John seems to disapprove of *excessive* purchasing prices: III 67, 1-4; he seems more concerned with the maintenance of career lines: II 18, 2-3 and III 2, 3-5. But he approves of pluralism, a practice engendered by the *suffragium* system: III 27, 1-5.

36. So Procopius, *S.H.* 12, 27; 13, 28-30; 14, 11 (cf. 12, 21); John also seems to be referring to this view of Justinian at *De Mag.* II 15, 2-3 and III 55, 1.

37. Most strikingly, Procopius': 14, 3-5 (cf. 14, 12); Justinian seems even to have read out his own proclamations (*ibid.*, 14, 3), an act which must have cut back collusive malpractices even further.

38. The term is an adaptation of O. Lewis' concept "the culture of poverty" (see *The Children of Sanchez*, pp. xxiv-xxvii) and is used to suggest this interlocking effect, which Lewis has demonstrated so graphically.

39. The syndrome is delineated in Banfield, *The Moral Basis of a Backward Society*, pp. 85-104. A detailed and thorough-going analysis (upon which many of the present writer's assumptions are based) will be found in Riggs' discussion of "Prismatic Society" in *Administration in Developing Countries*, pp. 99-237; see especially 222-37. For the concept "subject orientation" see Almond and Verba, *The Civic Culture*, pp. 17-18. It involves a passive attitude toward governmental activity and lack of sophistication in dealing with authority while

matters are still at the decision-making stage.

40. On Arcadius and other such "good" Emperors — "good" from the point of view of the military men or bureaucrats aiming to control them — see *LRE*, p. 173; on Justin, *ibid.*, 267-9. Justinian's tireless energy occasioned much comment from both our writers: Procopius, *S.H.* 12, 27; 13, 28-30 & 14, 11 (cf. 12, 21; 14, 3-5 & 12); John *De Mag.* II 15, 2-3 & III 55, 1.

41. On this "counter-world" created by the psycho-logic of an occupational vested interest group, see Berger, *The Human Shape of Work*, pp. 227-38.

42. This reconstruction is based upon an extensive collation of the actual changes (not motives) ascribed to Justinian in contemporary sources, as these are reported in modern specialist authorities. Many of these changes are mentioned by John or Procopius, but their interpretation of them is such as to obscure any kind of overall view.

43. See n. 39 and discussion thereto in text; Lerner, in *The Passing of Traditional Society*, pp. 83-103, well illustrates the complex of interacting factors involved. S. M. Lipset's "Methodological Appendix" (pp. 72-75 of *Political Man*, Mercury 1959) goes into this problem of multi-variate correlations. On the concept "market morality" and its significance, see McClelland, *The Achieving Society*, pp. 291 & 374.

44. On the nature of the change, see Bury, *The Imperial Administrative System in the Ninth Century*, pp. 19-20 & 80-82; on its date, see Diehl, *Byzantium: Greatness and Decline*, pp. 64-65.

45. On the joint military and civil governorships, see *LRE*, pp. 282 & 656; on Justinian's place in this gradual evolution, see Karayanopoulos, "Contribution au problème des 'Themes' byzantins," *L'Hellenisme contemporain* pp. 480-3 and Bury, *A History of the Later Roman Empire (395-800 A.D.)*, vol. 2, chapter 13.

46. On the bishops, see *LRE*, pp. 291 (the Pragmatic Sanction), 480 and 492. On the resultant buildup of their authority, see Monks, "The Church of Alexandria and the Economic Life of the City in the Sixth Century," *Speculum* 28, 1958, pp. 349-62. It is here assumed that traditional societies are not either purely "feudal" or purely "bureaucratic," but that both tendencies coexist simultaneously, and are advanced or retarded accordingly as favourable circumstances arise: see Riggs, *The Ambivalence of Feudalism and Bureaucracy in Traditional Societies*, Comparative Administration Group, Occasional Paper, 1965.

47. While prepared to accept the Emperor's chairmanship and convening of meetings, because modelled on the Princeps-Senatus

relationship of the early Empire (the formative stage of the Church's growth as an institution), the bishops were not prepared to be dictated to in doctrinal matters, and the first stirrings against such intervention seem to have come in Justinian's reign: see Dvornik, "Emperors, Popes and General Councils" in *Dumbarton Oaks Papers* 6, 1951, p. 21; *LRE*, p. 297, and Ostrogorsky, *History of the Byzantine State*, pp. 71-2.

48. The riot: John, *De Mag.* III, chap. 70 & 71; *De Ost. Proem.* 8B; Procopius, *S.H.* 12, 12 & 19, 12; *Buildings*, I 1, 20; *Wars*, I 24, 1 ff.; the factions: Procopius, *S.H.* 7, 1-8, 1; cf. also 9, 35-46 & 10, 15-19. On the level of *anomie* in the community, cf. Diehl, *Byzantium: Greatness and Decline*, pp. 139 & 141 — where the contemporary comment that life without the Hippodrome would be "virtually joyless" calls strikingly to mind Banfield's comments (*The Moral Basis of a Backward Society*, pp. 63-67) on *"la miseria,"* or Lerner's findings in *The Passing of Traditional Society*, pp. 73-4 & 101 103. On the factions, the work of G. Manojlović ("Le peuple de Constantinople," *Byzantion* 11, 1936, pp. 617-716), though old, is well worth reading as a comprehensive and insightful account; see also note 19 to section 4 of chapter 6.

BIBLIOGRAPHY
FOR
BOOKS ONE AND TWO

BIBLIOGRAPHY

T. W. Adorne & co., *The Authoritarian Personality*, Wiley, 1964.

H. Ahrweiler, *Byzance et la mer*, Paris, 1966.

G.A. Almond & S. Verba, *The Civic Culture*, Little, Brown, 1965.

S. Andrzejewski, *Military Organization and Society*, Routledge & Kegan Paul, 1954.

H. Antoniadis-Bibicou, *Recherches sur les douanes à Byzance*, Colin, 1963.

W. Ashburner: see *(The) Farmers' Law*.

E. Badian, *Foreign Clientelae*, Clarendon, 1958.

R.H. Bainton, *Early Christianity*, Van Nostrand, 1960.

E.C. Banfield, *The Moral Basis of a Backward Society*, Free Press, 1958.

W.C. Bark, *Origins of the Medieval World*, Doubleday, 1960.

E. Barker, *Social and Political Thought in Byzantium from Justinian to the Last Palaeologus*, Clarendon, 1957.

N.H. Baynos & H. St L.B. Moss, *Byzantium*, Oxford U.P., 1961.

B.R. Berelson & M. Janowitz (eds), *Reader in Public Opinion and Communication*, Free Press, 1953.

P.L. Berger (ed.), *The Human Shape of Work*, Macmillan, 1964.

A.E.R. Boak, "The Roman *Magistri* in the Civil and Military Service of the Empire," *Harvard Studies in Classical Philology* 26, 1915, 73 ff.

—————, *The Master of Offices in the Later Roman and Byzantine Empires*, University of Michigan Studies, Humanistic Series XIV, N.Y., 1924.

—————, *A History of Rome to 565 A.D.*, Macmillan, 1954 reprint: see : *(The) Book of the Prefect*.

A. Boddington, "Sejanus: Whose Conspiracy?" *American Journal of Philology* 84, 1963, 1-16.

(The) Book of the Prefect, translated by A.E.R. Boak, in *Journal of Economic and Business History* 1, 1929, 597-619.

G. Boulvert, *Les esclaves et les affranchis impériaux sous le Haut-empire romain*, Aix-en-Provence (doctoral thesis), 1964.

A.B. Bozeman, *Politics and Culture in International History*, Princeton U.P., 1960.

R. Brown & co., *New Directions in Psychology*, Holt, Rinehart & Winston, 1962.

R. Browning, "Byzantine Scholarship," *Past & Present* 28, 1964, 3-20.

A.R. Burn, "*Hic breve vivitur*," *Past & Present* 4, 1953, 1-31.

J.B. Bury, *The Imperial Administrative System in the Ninth Century; with a revised text of the Kletorologion of Philotheos*, Franklin, N.Y., no date.

—————, *A History of the Later Roman Empire (395A.D. to 800A.D.)*, Macmillan, 1889.

—————, *A History of the Later Roman Empire from the Death of Theodosius I to the Death of Justinian*, Dover reprint, 1958.

—————, *The Invasion of Europe by the Barbarians*, Russell & Russell, 1963 reprint.

Cambridge Ancient History, Cambridge U.P., 1934 ff.
Cambridge Medieval History, Cambridge U.P., 1966.
A.D. Cameron, "Christianity and Tradition in the Historiography of the Late Empire," *Classical Quarterly* 14, 1964, 316-28.
T.F. Carney, "The Picture of Marius in Valerius Maximus," *Rheinisches Museum für Philologie*, 105, 1962, 289-337.
————, *Roman and Related Coins in the Courtauld Collection*, University College of Rhodesia & Nyasaland, 1963.
————, "Construing Literature as History," *Mosaic 1*, 1967, 22-38.
————, "The *Helops*," *Phoenix* 21, 1967, 46-64.
————, "The Political Legends on Hadrian's Coinage: Policies and Problems," *The Turtle* 6, 1967, 291-303.
————, "Looking for a Writer's Picture of Reality," *Revue* (of the International Organization for Ancient Languages Analysis by Computer) 2, 1968, 56-81.
R. Carpenter, *Discontinuity in Greek Civilization*, Cambridge U.P., 1966.
Cassiodorus: see L.W. Jones *(Divine and Human Readings)*, & T. Hodgkin *(Letters)*.
H. Chadwick, *The Early Church*, Pelican, 1967.
M. Chambers (ed.), *The Fall of Rome: Can it be explained?*, Holt, Rinehart & Winston, 1963.
P. Charanis, "Monastic Properties and the State in the Byzantine Empire," *Dumbarton Oaks Papers* 4, 1948, 51-119.
————, "Economic Factors in the Decline of the Byzantine Empire," *Journal of Economic History* 13, 1953, 412-25.
————, "Ethnic Changes in the Byzantine Empire in the Seventh Century," *Dumbarton Oaks Papers* 13, 1959, 25-44.
————, "The Transfer of Population as a Policy in the Byzantine Empire," *Comparative Studies in Society and History* 3, 1961, 140 ff.
————, *The Armenians in the Byzantine Empire*, Bertrand, Lisbon, 1963.
C. Cipolla, *Money, Prices and Civilization in the Mediterranean World, Fifth to Seventh Centuries*, Princeton U.P., 1956.
C.N. Cochrane, *Christianity and Classical Culture*, Galaxy ed., 1957.
D.J. Constantelos, *Byzantine Philanthropy and Social Welfare*, Rutgers, 1968.
Constantine Porphyrogenitus, *De Administrando Imperio:* G. Moravcsik (ed.) & R.J.H. Jenkins (transl.), Budapest, 1949.
————, *De Cerimoniis:* transl. A. Vogt, Budé, 1935-40.
H. Constas, "Max Weber's Two Conceptions of Bureaucracy," *American Journal of Sociology* 63, 1958, 400-409.
M.E. Cosenza, *Official Positions after the Time of Constantine*, Columbia (diss.), 1905.
F. Cottrell, *Energy and Society*, McGraw-Hill, 1955.
J.A. Crook, *Law and Life at Rome*, Cornell U.P., 1967.
F. Cumont, "Lydus et Anastase," *Byzantinische Zeitschrift* 30, 1929/30, 31-35.
H. Daniel-Rops, *The Church in the Dark Ages*, Dutton, 1960.

E. Dawes & N.H. Baynes (transl.), *Three Byzantine Saints: Contemporary Biographies of St. Daniel the Stylite, St. Theodore of Sykeon and St. John the Almsgiver*, Blackwell, 1948.

C. Dawson, *Religion and the Rise of Western Culture*, Doubleday ed., 1953.

H.A. Deane, *The Political and Social Ideas of St. Augustine*, Columbia U.P., 1963.

A. de Grazia, *Politics and Government*, Collier, 1962.

B. de Jouvenal, *The Pure Theory of Politics*, Cambridge U.P., 1963.

H.B. Dewing: see Procopius.

C. Diehl, *Byzantium: Greatness and Decline*, Rutgers, 1957.

B. Diener, *Imperial Byzantium*, Little, Brown, 1938.

Digenes Akrites: see Mavrogordato.

S. Dill, *Roman Society in the Last Century of the Western Empire*, Meridian reprint, 1960.

F. Dölger, "Nochmals zur Abfassungszeit von des Johannes Lydos περὶ ἀρχῶν," *Philologische Wochenschrift* 62, 1942, 667-9.

G. Downcy, *Constantinople in the Age of Justinian*, U. of Oklahoma Press, 1960.

A.M. Duff, *Freedmen in the Early Roman Empire*, Heffer reissue, 1958.

F. Dvornik, "The Circus Parties at Byzantium; their Evolution and Suppression," *Byzantina-Metabyzantina* 1, 1946, 119-33.

————, "Emperors, Popes and General Councils," *Dumbarton Oaks Papers* 6, 1951, 1-26.

D. Earl, *The Moral and Political Tradition of Rome*, Cornell U.P., 1967.

D. Easton, *A Systems Analysis of Political Life*, Wiley, 1965.

S.N. Eisenstadt, "Political Struggle in Bureaucratic Societies," *World Politics* 9, 1956, 15-36.

————, *The Political Systems of Empires*, Free Press, 1963.

————, *Essays on Comparative Institutions*, Wiley, 1965.

————, "Political Orientations of Bureaucracies in Centralized Empires," pp. 216-250 of the foregoing.

W. Ensslin, "Zur Abfassungszeit von des Johannes Lydos περὶ ἀρχῶν," *Philologische Wochenschrift* 62, 1942, 452-4.

(The) Farmers' Law, translated by W. Ashburner in the *Journal of Hellenic Studies* 30, 1910, pp. 85-108 & 32, 1912, pp. 68-83.

R. Fiennes, *Man, Nature and Disease*, Signet, 1964.

E.M. Forster, *Alexandria: A History and A Guide*, Doubleday, 1961.

T. Frank, *An Economic Survey of Ancient Rome*, Pageant Books issue, 1959.

A.J. Fridh, "Terminologie et formules dans les *Variae* de Cassiodore," *Studia Graeca et Latina Gothoburgensia* II, 1956.

E. Fromm, *The Fear of Freedom*, Routledge & Kegan Paul, 1960.

J. Gagé, *Les classes sociales dans l'empire romain*, Payot, 1964.

J. Galtung, "The Structure of Traditionalism: A Case Study from Western Sicily," *Journal of International Affairs* 19, 1965, 218 ff.

E. Goffman, *The Presentation of the Self in Everyday Life*, Doubleday Anchor, 1959.

C.D. Gordon, "Procopius and Justinian's Financial Policies," *Phoenix* 13, 1959, 23-30.

————, *The Age of Attila: Fifth Century Byzantium and the Barbarians*, University of Michigan, 1960.

(The) Greek Anthology, translated by W.R. Paton, Loeb, 1916-1918.

R. Grew & S.L. Thrupp, "Horizontal History in Search of Vertical Dimensions," *Comparative Studies in Society and History* 8, 1966, 258-64.

R. Guilland, "Les eunuques dans l'empire byzantin," *Etudes byzantines* 1, 1943, 197-238.

————, "Vénalité et favoritisme à Byzance," *Revue des études byzantines* 10, 1953, 35-46.

E.E. Hagen, *On the Theory of Social Change*, Dorsey, 1962.

M. Hammond, "Composition of the Senate A.D. 68-235," *Journal of Roman Studies* 47, 1957, 74-81.

————, *The Antonine Monarchy*, American Academy in Rome, Papers & Monographs 19, 1959.

E.R. Hardy, *Christian Egypt: Church and People, Christianity and Nationalism in the Patriarchate of Alexandria*, Oxford U.P., 1952.

A. Harnack, *The Mission and Expansion of Christianity in the First Three Centuries*, Harper, 1962.

A.F. Havighurst (ed.), *The Pirenne Thesis*, in the series 'Problems in European Civilization,' Heath, 1958.

F. Henschen, *The History and Geography of Diseases*, Delacorte, 1966.

P.K. Hitti, *History of the Arabs*, Macmillan, 1961.

T. Hodgkin, *The Letters of Cassiodorus*, London, 1886.

L. Homo, *Roman Political Institutions from City to State*, Routledge & Kegan Paul, 1962 reprint.

L.L. Howe, *The Praetorian Prefect from Commodus to Diocletian* Chicago, 1942.

J.M. Hussey, *The Byzantine World*, Hutchinson, 1967.

H. Inglehart & R. Schoenberger, "Communication and Political Mobilization," mimeo of a paper to the 1968 meeting of the American Political Science Association.

H.R. Isaacs, *Scratches on Our Minds: American Images of China and India*, Day, 1958.

D. Jacoby, "La population de Constantinople à l'époque byzantine une problème de demographie urbaine," *Byzantion* 31, 1961, 81-110

R.J.H. Jenkins, *Byzantium: The Imperial Centuries A.D. 610 to 1071*, Weidenfeld & Nicholson, 1966.

John the Lydian, *De Magistratibus*: see Book III of this volume.

C. Johnson, *Revolutionary Change*, Little, Brown, 1966.

A.H.M. Jones, *The Greek City from Alexander to Justinian*, Clarendon, 1940.

————, "Inflation under the Roman Empire," *Economic History Review* 5, 1953, 293-318.

————, *Studies in Roman Government and Law*, Blackwell, 1960

————, *The Later Roman Empire 284-601: A Social, Economi and Administrative Survey*, Blackwell, 1964.

E. Jones, *Towns and Cities,* Oxford U.P., 1966.

L.W. Jones, *An Introduction to Divine and Human Readings by Cassiodorus Senator,* Columbia U.P., 1946.

T.B. Jones, *The Silver-Plated Age,* Coronado, 1962.

P. Joubert, *Byzance avant Islam sous les successeurs de Justinian,* Picard, 1951.

E.A. Judge, *The Social Pattern of Christian Groups in the First Century,* Tyndale, 1960.

Justinian: *The Institutes of Justinian,* translated by J.B. Moyle, Clarendon, 1955 ed.

————, *The Digest of Justinian,* translated by C.H. Monro, Cambridge U.P., 1904 & 1909 (two vols.).

W.E. Kaegi, *Byzantium and the Decline of Rome,* Princeton U.P., 1968.

D. Kagan (ed.), *Decline and Fall of the Roman Empire: Why did it collapse?* Heath, 1962.

J. Karayannopoulos, "Contribution au problème des 'thèmes' byzantins," *L'Hellenisme contemporain* 10, 1956, 455-502.

S. Katz, *The Decline of Rome and the Rise of Medieval Europe,* Cornell U.P., 1955.

Kautilya, *Arthashastra:* see Shamasastry.

E. Kitzinger, "The Cult of Images in the Age before Iconoclasm," *Dumbarton Oaks Papers* 8, 1954, 82-150.

Kletorologion: see Bury.

R. Klotz, Lydos no. 7, Pauly's *Realencyclopädie* 26, 1927, columns 2210-2217.

W. Kunkel, *An Introduction to Roman Legal and Constitutional History,* Clarendon, 1966.

O. Kuntz, *Tiborius Caesar and the Roman Constitution,* University of Washington Press, 1924.

G.B. Ladner, "Origin and Significance of the Byzantine Iconoclast Controversy," *Medieval Studies* 2, 1940, 127-49.

————, "The Concept of the Image in the Greek Fathers and the Byzantine Iconoclastic Controversy," *Dumbarton Oaks Papers* 7, 1953, 1-34.

R.E. Lane & D.O. Sears, *Public Opinion,* Prentice-Hall, 1964.

J. LaPalombara (ed.), *Bureaucracy and Political Development,* Princeton U.P., 1963.

H.D. Lasswell, "Why be Quantitative?" pp. 265-77 in Berelson & Janowitz, *Reader in Public Opinion and Communication.*

————, *Politics: Who gets What, When, How?* Meridian, 1962 ed.

P. Lemerle, "Esquisse pour une histoire agraire de Byzance," *Revue historique* 218, 1958, 32-74.

P. Leon, "The *Imbecillitas* of the Emperor Claudius," *Transactions of the American Philological Association* 79, 1948, 79-86.

D. Lerner, *The Passing of Traditional Society,* Free Press, 1958.

W.R. Lethaby & H. Swainson, *The Church of Sancta Sophia,* London, 1894.

A.R. Lewis, *Naval Power and Trade in the Mediterranean A.D. 500-1100,* Princeton U.P., 1951.

I. Lewis, "In the Courts of Power," pp. 132ff. of Berger, *The Human Shape of Work.*

O. Lewis, *The Children of Sanchez,* Vintage, 1961.

A.W. Lintott, *Violence in Republican Rome,* Clarendon, 1968.

S.M. Lipset, *Political Man,* Mercury, 1959.

R.E. Lopez, "The Silk Industry in the Byzantine Empire," *Speculum* 20, 1945, 1-42.

———— "The Role of Trade in the Economic Readjustment of Byzantium in the Seventh Century," *Dumbarton Oaks Papers* 13, 1959, 69-85.

———— & I.W. Raymond, *Medieval Trade in the Mediterranean World,* Columbia U.P., 1955.

K. Lynch, *The Image of the City,* M.I.T. Press, 1960.

D. McAlindon, "Senatorial Opposition to Claudius and Nero," *American Journal of Philology* 77, 1956, 113-33.

———— "Claudius and the Senators," *ibid.,* 78, 1957, 278-87.

D.C. McClelland, *The Achieving Society,* Van Nostrand, 1961.

E.E. Maccoby & co. (eds), *Readings in Social Psychology,* Holt, Rinehart & Winston, 1958 ed.

M. McLuhan, *The Gutenberg Galaxy,* U. of Toronto Press, 1962.

R. MacMullen, *Soldier and Civilian in the Later Roman Empire,* Harvard Historical Monographs 52, 1963.

————, *Enemies of the Roman Order: Treason, Unrest and Alienation in the Empire,* Harvard U.P., 1966.

————, "Rural Romanization," *Phoenix* 22, 1968, 237-41.

W.H. McNeil, *The Rise of the West,* Mentor, 1965.

G. Manojlovic, "Le peuple de Constantinople," *Byzantion* 11, 1936, 617-716.

F.B. Marsh, *The Reign of Tiberius,* London, 1931.

H. Mattingly, *The Imperial Civil Service of Rome,* Cambridge U.P., 1910.

———— *Roman Imperial Civilization,* Arnold, 1957.

———— *Christianity in the Roman Empire,* Norton, 1967.

J. Mavrogordato (ed.), *Digenes Akrites,* Clarendon, 1956.

R. Meiggs, *Roman Ostia,* Clarendon, 1960.

M. Mercier, *Le feu grégois,* Paris, 1952.

R.K. Merton & co. (eds), *Reader in Bureaucracy,* Free Press, 1952.

F. Millar, *The Roman Empire and Its Neighbours,* Weidenfeld & Nicolson, 1966.

A. Momigliano, *Claudius: The Emperor and his Achievement,* Clarendon, 1934.

———— "Cassiodorus and the Italian Culture of his Time," *Proceedings of the British Academy* 41, 1955, 207-45.

————, *The Conflict between Paganism and Christianity in the Fourth Century,* Clarendon, 1963.

E.R. Monks, "The Church of Alexandria and the Economic Life of the City in the Sixth Century," *Speculum* 28, 1958, 349-62.

C.H. Monro: see Justinian.

G. Moravsik: see Constantine Porphyrogenitus.

H. St L.B. Moss, *The Birth of the Middle Ages 395-814,* Oxford U.P., 1935.

J.B. Moyle: see Justinian.
H.J. Muller, *Freedom in the Ancient World*, Bantam, 1964.
————, *The Loom of History*, Galaxy, 1966.
L. Mumford, *The City in History*, Secker & Warburg, 1961.
S. Nosow & W.H. Form, *Man, Work and Society*, Basic Books, 1962.
Notitia Dignitatum: see Seeck.
J.D.A. Ogilvy, "The Stirrup and Feudalism," *U. of Colorado Studies*, Series in Language and Literature no. 10, 1966, 1-13.
P. Oliva, *Pannonia and the Onset of Crisis in the Roman Empire*, Prague, 1962.
C.W.C. Oman, *The Art of War in the Middle Ages*, Cornell U.P., 1953 reprint.
S.I. Oost, "The Career of M. Antonius Pallas," *American Journal of Philology* 79, 1958, 113-39.
C.E. Osgood & co., *The Measurement of Meaning*, U. of Illinois Press, 1957.
G. Ostrogorsky, "The Byzantine Empire in the World of the Seventh Century," *Dumbarton Oaks Papers* 13, 1951, 1-21.
————, "Byzantine Cities in the Early Middle Ages," *ibid.*, pp. 45-66.
————, *History of the Byzantine State*, Blackwell, 1956.
H.M.D. Parker, *A History of the Roman World A.D. 138-337*, Methuen, 1958 ed.
————, *The Roman Legions*, Heffer reissue, 1958.
W.R. Paton: see *The Greek Anthology*.
Paul the Silentiary, *Description of the Church of St. Sophia:* see Lethaby & Swainson.
A. Pauly, G. Wissowa & co., *Real-encyclopädie der classischen Altertumswissenschaft*, Druckenmüller, Stuttgart, ed. 2, 1894 foll.
T. Pekary, "Studien zur romischen Wahrungs- und Finanzgeschichte, von 161 bis 235 n. Chr.," *Historia* 8, 1959, 443-89.
C. Pharr: see *The Theodosian Code*.
H. Pirenne, *Mohammed and Charlemagne*, Meridian ed., 1961.
Plutarch, *Life of Cato Minor*.
K. Polanyi & co. (eds), *Trade and Market in the Early Empires: Economics in History and Theory*, Free Press, 1957.
Procopius: *History of the Wars; Secret History* and *On the Buildings of Justinian*, translated by H.B. Dewing, Loeb, 1914-40.
Michael Psellus, *Chronographia:* see Sewter, *Fourteen Byzantine Rulers*.
G.A. Punzi, *L'Italia del VI secolo nelle "Variae" di Cassiodoro*, Roma, 1927.
L.W. Pye, *Communications and Political Development*, Princeton U.P., 1963.
————, *Aspects of Political Development*, Little, Brown, 1966.
L.W. Pye & S. Verba (eds), *Political Culture and Political Development*, Princeton U.P., 1965.
R. Rémondon, *La crise de l'empire romain de Marc-Aurele à Anastase*, Paris, 1964.
D.T. Rice, *Art of the Byzantine Era*, Praeger, 1966.

F.W. Riggs, "Agraria and Industria: Toward a Typology of Comparative Administration," pp. 23-116 of Siffin, *Toward the Comparative Study of Public Administration.*
——— *Administration in Developing Countries: The Theory of Prismatic Society,* Houghton Mifflin, 1964.
——— "The Ambivalence of Feudalism and Bureaucracy in Traditional Societies," Comparative Administration Group, Occasional Paper, 1965.
——— "The Comparison of Whole Political Systems," (mimeo) Center for Comparative Political Analysis, U. of Minnesota, 1967.
——— "Bureaucratic Politics in Comparative Perspective," *Journal of Comparative Administration* 1, 1969, 5-38.
M. Rokeach, *The Open and Closed Mind,* Basic Books, 1960.
M. Rostovtzeff, *The Social and Economic History of the Roman Empire,* Clarendon, 1957 ed.
B. Rubin, *Das Zeitalter Justinians,* De Gruyter, 1960 (vol. 1).
S. Runciman, *Byzantine Civilization,* Methuen, 1961.
N.N. Safran, "Theses on Comparative Bureaucracy and Political Development in Western Europe and the Middle East," mimeo, M.I.T., 1966.
E.T. Salmon, "The Roman Army and the Disintegration of the Roman Empire," pp. 37-46 in Chambers, *The Fall of Rome.*
H.H. Scullard, *Roman Politics 220-150 B.C.,* Clarendon, 1951.
——— *From the Gracchi to Nero,* Methuen, 1963.
O. Seeck, *Notitia Dignitatum,* Minerva reprint, 1962.
A. Segré, "Studies in Byzantine Economy — *Iugatio* and *Capitatio,*" *Traditio* 3, 1945, 101-127.
G.L. Seidler, *The Emergence of Western Europe,* Pergamon, 1968.
P. Selznik, *The Organizational Weapon,* Free Press, 1960 ed.
K.M. Setton, "The Importance of Land Tenure and Agrarian Taxation in the Byzantine Empire from the Fourth Century to the Fourth Crusade," *American Journal of Philology* 24, 1953, 225-59.
E.R.A. Sewter, *Fourteen Byzantine Rulers,* Penguin, 1966.
R. Shamasastry (translator), *Kautilya's Arthasastra,* Mysore, 1929.
W.J. Siffin (ed.), *Toward the Comparative Study of Public Administration,* Indiana U.P., 1957.
W.G. Sinnigen, *The Officium of the Urban Prefecture during the Later Roman Empire,* Papers & Monographs of the American Academy in Rome XVII, 1957.
G. Sjoberg, *The Preindustrial City Past and Present,* Free Press, 1960.
J.C. Skinner, "Symptom and Defense in Contemporary Greece: A Cross-cultural Inquiry," *The Journal of Nervous & Mental Disease* 141, 1966, 481-5.
R.E. Smith, *Service in the Post-Marian Roman Army,* Manchester U.P., 1958.
P.A. Sorokin, *Man and Society in Calamity,* Dutton, 1942.
F. Stark, *Rome on the Euphrates,* Murray, 1966.
C.G. Starr, *Civilization and the Caesars,* Cornell U.P., 1954.
E. Stein, "Introduction à l'histoire et aux institutions byzantines," *Traditio* 7, 1949-51, 95-168.

Suetonius, *Life of the Divine Claudius*.

C.H.V. Sutherland, *Coinage in Roman Imperial Policy 31 B.C. – A.D. 68*, Methuen, 1951.

R. Syme, *The Roman Revolution*, Clarendon, 1952 reprint.

————— *Tacitus*, Clarendon, 1958.

H.O. Taylor, *The Emergence of Christian Culture in the West*, Harper ed., 1958.

J.L. Teall, "The Grain Supply of the Byzantine Empire 330-1625," *Dumbarton Oaks Papers* 13, 1959, 87-140.

————— "The Barbarians in Justinian's Armies," *Speculum* 40, 1965, 305-322.

(The) Theodosian Code, translated by C. Pharr, Princeton U.P., 1952.

E.A. Thompson, "Peasant Revolts in Late Roman Gaul and Spain," *Past & Present* 2, 1952, 11-23.

H.F. Tozer, *A History of Ancient Geography*, Biblo & Tannen, N.Y., 1964 reprint.

S. Ullmann, *Semantics: An Introduction to the Science of Meaning*, Blackwell, 1962.

A.P. Vacalopoulos, *History of Thessaloniki*, Institute for Byzantine Studies, Thessaloniki, 1963.

F. van der Meer, *Augustine the Bishop: Church and Society at the Dawn of the Middle Ages*, Harper ed., 1965.

A. Vogt: see Constantine Porphyrogenitus.

K. von Fritz, *The Theory of the Mixed Constitution in Antiquity*, Columbia U.P., 1954.

————— "Tacitus, Agricola, Domitian and the Problem of the Principate," *Classical Philology* 52, 1957, 73-97.

C. Wachsmuth, *Ioannis Laurentii Lydi liber de Ostentis*, Teubner, 1897.

F.W. Walbank, *The Awful Revolution: The Decline of the Roman Empire in the West*, Liverpool U.P., 1969.

G. Walter, *La ruine de Byzance 1204-1453*, Michel, 1958.

————— *La vie quotidienne à Byzance au siècle des Comnènes (1081-1180)*, Hachette, 1966.

R.E. Ward & D.A. Rustow, *Political Modernization in Japan and Turkey*, Princeton U.P., 1964.

M. Weber, "The Essentials of Bureaucratic Organization: An Ideal-type Construction," pp. 18-28 in Merton & co., *Reader in Bureaucracy*.

T.D. Weldon, *The Vocabulary of Politics*, Penguin, 1953.

R.G. Wesson, *The Imperial Order*, U. of California Press, 1967.

L. White, *Medieval Technology and Social Change*, Clarendon, 1962.

Ch. Wirszubski, *Libertas as a Political Ideal during the Late Republic and Early Principate*, Cambridge U.P., 1960.

K.A. Wittfogel, *Oriental Despotism: A Comparative Study of Total Power*, Yale U.P., 1957.

E.R. Wolf, *Peasants*, Prentice-Hall, 1966.

Q. Wright, *A Study of War*, U. of Chicago Press, 1965 ed.

R. Wünsch, *Ioannis Lydi de Mensibus*, Teubner, 1898.

————— *Ioannis Lydi de Magistratibus Populi Romani*, Teubner, 1903.

O.R. Young, *Systems of Political Science,* Prentice-Hall, 1968.

O.J. Zimmermann, *The Late Latin Vocabulary of the Variae of Cassiodorus, with Special Advertence to the Technical Terminology of Administration,* Catholic U. of America, Studies in Medieval and Renaissance Latin Language and Literature, XV, 1944.

H. Zinsser, *Rats, Lice and History,* Bantam, 1967.

INDEX TO BOOKS ONE AND TWO

Note: Page references to Book Two are preceded by (II)

Basil II 152-57, 161, 163, 168.
Behavioural code of the bureaucracy (II) 82, 83, 88, 91, 92, 103, 104, 105, 107, 108, 109, 110, 119, 126, 133, 134, 137, 185. See: *litterati*, Value systems.
Belisarius (II) 15, 162.
(the) "Best" *(optimus)* princeps 60, 71-72. See (the) Autocrat's position, Care-taker *princeps*, Court, Dominate, Maximum and minimum *princeps*, Principate.
"Black box" (II) 91-92, 185; cf. 176. See: Behavioural code, Unanticipated consequences.
boethura (II) 8, 9, 14.
bucellarii 121. See: *comitatus*.
Building operations 15, 99, 115, 123. See Crucial resources.
Bureaucracy 1 (definition), 2, 3-4 (difficulties in interpreting). See: Administration and Politics, A-political servicing instrumentality, Apparatus bureaucracies, Balance of power, Caesaropapism, Camarilla, Clerical and Sub-clerical staff, Countervailing power, Dynamic equilibrium, Environmental influences, Establishment, Goal displacement, Law courts, Morale in the bureaucracy, Political culture, Political process, Politics of administrators, Super-departments, Surveys of developments in and theories on bureaucracy, Trained incapacity, Unanticipated consequences.
Bureaucrats' concerns 147-48, 159, 161, 164. See: Bureaucratic ethics, Bureaucratic malpractices, Estates, Recruitment, Titles.
Bureaucratic Ethics 117-18, 120, 161, 171. See: Behavioural code and Bureaucratic friction points.
Bureaucratic feuding (II) 78, 82, 83, 88, 89, 90, 107, 109, 111-12, 114, 121, 123, 125, 127, 130, 138, 139, 141, 159-60, 177, 186, 192-93.
Bureaucratic friction points 18-19, (145-) 47, 148-49, 157, 161.
Bureaucratic life cycle 16-17, 59.
Bureaucratic malpractices 123-24, 128-29, 141, 154, 160, 167. (II) 9, 13, 83, 89, 102, 106, 120, 136, 150, 159, 175, 176, 178, 193. See: Behavioural code, Formalism, Operational code, *praescriptio fori, sportulae, suffragium*, Trickle-up and Trickle-down taxation.
Bureaucratic politics 19-20, 56, 111, 125 and Table 1, 135, 143, 144, 148-49, 151, 153, 157-60, 161, 163, 164, 167. (II) 112-15, 125-26, 151. See: (the) Autocrat's Position, Bureaucratic friction points, Camarilla, Dynamic equilibrium, Eunuchs, Inner court, Overlapping spheres of competence, Political culture, Political process, Politics of Administrators.
Bureaucratic power 19-20. See: Apparatus bureaucracies, Autocrat's position, Camarilla, Property holding.
Bureaucratic responsibilities (II) 78-79, 119-20, 140, 149-50. See: Aristocratic code, Behavioural code, Service orientation.
Byzantium & the Byzantines (II) 29, 87, 127, 129, 152. See: the East, Greek.

caballarius 142.
Caesar (II) 32, 35, 37, 38, 40, 48, 49, 54, 57, 58, 68, 128.
Caesaropapism 101, 121-24, 167; cf. 150, 165.
Camarilla 19, 112, 153, 158. See: Autocrat's position, Coups, Court, Inner court, Palace intrigues, Praetorianism, Succession.
cancellarius (II) 5, 8, 14.
Careers 30, 40-41, 52, 54-55, 56, 59, 65-66, 70-71, 94, 147. See: the Establishment.

Career sequence inside *officium* (II) 5, 9, 13, 113, 125, 139, 140, 178, 180, 181, 193; cf. 105, 110.

Caretaker Emperor 79-80. See: (the) "Best" *princeps*.

caritas See: Concepts.

Cassiodorus (II) 37, 40-41, 45, 55, 67, 69, 73, 77-78, 84-85, 86, 87, 89, 90, 91, 97-99, 101, 102, 104-5, 108-111, 112-17, 124, 126-30, 130-32, 138, 145, 149-50, 152, 179.

catepan 155.

Centurionate 33-34.

Change (views on) 23. (II) 160, 163, 164, 167, 172-73, 190.

Change (to the bureaucracy) (II) 79-81, 91, 102, 112, 114, 116, 130, 153, 158, 160, 161, 168, 173, 174, 176, 179, 180, 186.

charisticium 166. See: Estates.

chartularius (II) 3, 7.

Chronology (II) 35-37, 41-42.

Church (II) 25, 49, 68-69, 81, 98-99, 112, 114, 122, 124, 125, 127, 129-30, 135, 160, 161, 170, 175, 180, 186, 189, 191, 194-95; cf. 73, 77-78, 85.

Citations (II) 52, 64, 65, 71-72.

(the) "Classics" of John's day (II) 47-49, 55, 61, 72; cf. 66, 75.

Claudius 43-52.

Clerical & Sub-clerical Staff (in the Late Republic) 30; (in the army of the Late Republic (34-35); (in the Principate) 39-40; (in the army of the Principate) 39, (in the third century) 71; (Militarization of) 64-65, 71; (Dominate) 94, 107, 110-11, 113-14; (in the sixth century) 118.

Client-relationship 22, 160. See: Feudalism, *pronoia*.

Code of the bureaucracy. See: Behavioural code.

Coinage 36-37, 51, 57, 68-69, 89, 92, 95-96, 113, 162. See: Financial Institutions, Minting, Pay-scales, Trade.

comitatenses 97, 144.

comitatus (retinue) 13, 92-92. See: *bucellarii*.

comites (II) 8, 11, 17.

Commander of the Key 142.

commentarienses (II) 3, 4, 5, 8, 12, 14.

Communications 15, 22, 55-56, 62, 75, 114, 127, 140, 164. See: Gate keeping, Mobilization, Public opinion, Public relations.

Concepts of importance (Bureaucracy) 24; (*caritas*) 74, see 155; (Demand overload) 136; (Image) 142, 151, 172; (Municipality) 59; (Pagan) 129; (State) 24. See: Change, Corporation, Counter-world, *pronoia*, Public Good, Theories on bureaucracy.

Confiscations 14, 48, 67, 69, 73, 96, 166. See: Property holding, Trade.

Consistory. See: Council.

Constantine 89-101, 111, 120, 125; (II) 35, 37, 38, 39, 50, 53, 57, 60, 111, 128.

Constantinople & Constantinopolitans (II) 3, 13, 26, 29, 32, 39, 41, 44, 45, 47, 48, 50, 52, 53, 79, 87, 98, 99, 114, 115, 120, 121, 122, 123, 124, 128, 129, 137, 144-45, 151, 152, 153, 158, 159, 177, 186, 187.

Content Analysis (II) 43, 85, 101-3, 133, 138, 150-51, 162, 163, 167-68, 172, 179; cf. 26.

Controls on bureaucracy 18, 119, 142-43, 146-47, 153, 154-57. (II) 78, 82, 91, 92, 109, 111, 112, 120, 138, 140, 172, 176, 179, 186, 194. See: Countervailing power, Cross-checks, Law, Recruitment.

cornicularius (II) 4, 5, 7, 8, 14, 17.

Corporations 100, 115; cf. 151, 156.

Council (of *princeps*) 41-42, 44, 55, 70, 92-93; cf. 174.

Count of the Sacred Largesses (II) 114, 144.

Countervailing Powers 5, 6, 17, 27, 41, 44, 82, 93, 101, 121, 154, 155-56, 162. (II) 113, 142. See: Balance of Power, Bureaucratic politics, Controls on bureaucracy, Cross-appointments, Cross-checks, Estates, Law Courts, Overlapping of functions, Overlapping spheres.

Counter-world (view) 49-50, 61, 62, 74, 75-76, 99, 101.

Counts 93, 97, 111, 121. (II) 39. See: *comites.*

Coups 153. See: Court, Praetorianism.

Court (II) 9, 10, 15, 88, 114, 124, 127. See: *comitatus,* Palace.

Court (intrigue) 71, 72, 80, 93, 147. See: Inner Court, *palatini.*

Courtier's skills (II) 114, 115, 116, 139, 143, 144.

Criteria for comparing bureaucracies 10-11, 23, 154. See: Crucial resources/ facilities, Theories on bureaucracy.

Criticism of the bureaucracy (II) 119, 120-21, 150.

Cross-appointments 107, 110-11, 146.

Cross-checks upon officials 146, 148-49. See: Overlapping Spheres.

Cross-pressures (II) 115, 145, 160, 173. See: Countervailing powers, Overlapping of functions.

Crucial resources/facilities 13-15, 35-42, 47-48, 154. See: Building Operations, Communications, Decision-making, Man-power resources, Taxation.

curae epistolarum (II) 4, 5, 14.

curiales 95, 96, 99-100, 108, 115, 123. (II) 13, 39. See: Local Government.

Decision-making 42, 43, 44-47, 52-54, 55, 59-60, 61, 70, 72, 75, 99-100, 102, 119, 146, 148-49, 150-51, 157-59, 165, 167. (II) 176, 179, 192, 193. See: Demand overload, Gate-keeping, Jurisdiction, Law Courts, Legislation, *praescriptio fori.*

Definition of bureaucratic duties (II) 119-22, 149-50.

Deity (II) 116, 145.

De Magistratibus (II) 10-12, 16, 17-18, 19, 36-37, 45, 65, 75, 101, 166.

Demand overload. See: Concepts.

De Mensibus (II) 10-11, 16, 18, 19, 36-37, 65, 166.

Dioceses 90-91.

Diocletian 89-98, 99.

De Ostentis (II) 10-11, 12, 16, 19, 45, 65, 166.

deputatus (II) 5, 8, 14.

Developmental trap (II) 91-92. See Bureaucratic malpractices.

dignitas ("Dignity" or high office) (II) 7, 87, 105, 109, 110, 113, 126, 139.

Disciplining the bureaucracy 18. See: Controls on bureaucracy.

Disciplining of bureaucrats (II) 121, 150, 176, 177, 180, 183, 184, 193.

Domestics 97, see table 2, 154, 162.

Dominate 90-94, 97, 102.

Donatives 48-49, 53, 63-64, 67, 68.

dromos. See: Public Post.

Dukes 97, 155, 162, 163.

Dynamic Equilibrium 2; cf. 5.

Hadrian 52-61.
Head of Corps (II) 77-79, 82, 86, 89, 90, 91, 97, 103-6, 107, 108-11, 114, 115, 116-17, 118, 120, 122, 126-27, 139, 144, 174, 175, 177, 186, 192, 193.
Hebrew (II) 47, 49, 65, 66-67.
Hephaestus (II) 11, 17, 57.
Heraclius 149, 150, 169, 172.
"History" for John. (II) (Contemporary) 35, 36, 37; (Dominate) 35, 36; (Principate) 35, 36, 40; (Republic) 35, 36, 37, 39, 40; (Rome, Regal) 35, 36, 38-39, 73; (Greece) 62, 73, cf. 62-63.
Homer (II) 48, 49, 54, 57, 60, 74.
Household of the Emperor (II) 40-41.

Ideal (Weberian) Type Bureaucracy 20, cf. 27-28.
illitterati (II) 4.
Image. See: Concepts.
Images (of persons and institutions) (II) 86, 123-24, 127, 166, 167, 170, 172, 174, 175-76, 179-83, 190. See: "World" of a bureaucrat.
In-built sources of friction within bureaucracies 79-80. See: Bureaucratic friction points.
Inflation 96.
Inner Court 19, 42. See: Council of princeps.
instrumentarius (II) 5, 8, 14.
Italy and the Italians (II) 25, 26, 28, 32, 98, 119, 120, 123, 124, 128, 148, 151, 152-53.

John the Cappadocian (II) 10, 11, 13, 14, 15, 16, 18, 63, 88, 89, 118, 133, 138, 158, 175, 180, 180-82, 187, 192-93.
John the Lydian. (II) (Autobiographical details) 12; (Books) 10-12, 56; (Bureaucratic concerns) 79-82, 106-8; (Career) 9-12, 15, 16, 17, 77, 84, 111-12, 125; (Christianity) 10-11, 16, 39, 4950, 69; (Confusion in thought) 108; (Death) 12; (Historical error or confusion) 40, 44; (Identity) 29, 31-32; (Marriage) 9, 14; (Metaphors) 29, 31, 40, 112, 140; (Origins) 3, 13, 176, 194; (Overclaiming for bibliography) 30, 48, 51, 56-61, 64-66, 68, 71, 73-75; (Retirement) 107-8, 135; (Stereotyping) 32, 39, 103; (Travels) 3, 11, 12, 16, 29-30, 32-33; (Writing habits) 19, 36-37, 63-66, 71-72.
Judicial branch of prefect's officium (II) 4, 8, 51, 83, 111, 123, 140-41, 177. Jurisdiction 42, 44-47, 56, 59, 75, 76, 114, 119, 123, 150-51, 165. See: Decision-making, Law.
Justin (II) 86, 157, 166, 179, 189, 194.
Justinian 121-31. (II) 10, 11, 14, 15, 39, 45, 49, 51, 54, 56, 57, 58, 72, 79, 81, 86, 88, 90, 91, 99, 101, 117, 133, 138, 157-61, 162, 163, 164, 166, 167, 172-76, 178, 179, 184-87, 189, 191-92, 193, 194.

Latin (II) 3, 15, 39, 47-48, 52, 53, 61, 68, 72, 74, 127, 129, 132, 166, 177.
Law Courts 18, 21; ("Classical" age of Roman Law) 55, 59-60; (Dominate) 93; (Late classical age) 70; (Law courts in Republican Rome) 30, 78; (Law in the early Principate) 42; (Seventh century) 148-49; (Eleventh century) 164. See: One Law for the Rich....
Law (II) 51, 69-71, 78, 107, 108-9, 113, 114, 116, 117, 120, 122, 137, 139, 145, 150, 151, 157-58, 174, 175, 177, 179, 181, 184, 188, 192-93.
Legislation 42-43, 112, 117. See: Decision-making, Law courts.
Levels of Analysis 4, 10-11, cf. 18.
Library facilities (II) 53-54, 56-62, 73.
limitanei 96, 114. See: *ripenses*.
Literary Circles (II) 52, 55-56, 64-66, 72.
Literary Tastes (II) 55-56, 64-66, 72-73, 77, 84, 100.
litterati (II) 4, 7, 13, 14, 47, 52-53, 64, 83, 84, 89, 91, 100, 108, 158, 175, 191. See: Strategic learning.
Local government 32, 51, 57, 59, 68, 71, 72-74, 95, 119. See: *curiales*,Property holding.
logothetes 145, 146, 158, 163.
Lords of the Border Marches 142.
Loyalty (II) 103, 104-5, 114, 118, 134, 139, cf. 97, 98.

Machinery of Government. (available to these bureaucracies) 12-13, 137; (of the late Roman Republic) Diagram 1, 29, 30, 35; (of the Principate) 38, Diagram 2; (of the Dominate) Diagram 4, 104-5.
magistriani Master's Men (II) 3, 4, 83, 107.
Man-power resources 14. See: Crucial resources
Maps (II) 21-28, 29, 30.
Marcus Aurelius 61, 67.
Marinus 12, 82, 127.
Master of Offices 92-93, 107, 112, 114, 119, 145, 146, 148. (II) 106, 111, 119, 120, 123, 135, 151, 180, 181, 183, 184, 193.
Master's men (II) 111-12, 114, 123-24, 140, 141, 143, 151, 193. See: *magistriani*.
Masters of the Soldiery 97, 110-11, 121, 148.
matricularius (II) 5, 7, 14.
Maximum & minimum *princeps* 51, 79-80, cf. 60. See: (the) "Best" *princeps*.
Mediterranean (II) 31.
memoriales (II) 3, 7, 12, 151, 193.
Mercenaries 121, 160, 162.
mesazon (Prime minister or Vizier) 164.
Middle-level officials — attitudes (II) 77-79, 83, 86, 103, 106, 109, 110, 115, 117, 120, 122, 125, 127-28, 138, 139, 140, 166, 176.
(the) Military (II) 124, 125, 127, 158, 159-60, 161, 169, 174, 186, 189, 194. See: *sajo*.
militia (II) 7. See: (the) Service.
Minting 36-37. See: Coinage, Financial institutions.
Missions 115-16, 149-50.
Mobilization 127, cf. 13. (II) 162, 189.
Models (II) 92-93, 102, 142, 172, 190.
moderatio (II) 109, 126, 139, 151-52.

Monastic movement 100, 123, 124-25, 150, 151, 158, 166, 167, cf. 156. See: Alienation, Estatism, Schism.
Monophysitism (II) 50, 69, 158-59, 160, 173, 191.
Morale in the Bureaucracy 125, 145, 149.

Nationalistic concepts (II) 129, 153. See: Constantinople, (the) East, Greek, Italy, Rome, West.
Need for achievement (II) 172-73, 190.
Nepotism (II) 139.
Nero 48, 50, 52, 57.
Nika Riot (II) 10, 14-15, 41, 153, 175, 187, 188, 192, 195.
Nobility 35, 51, 60, 82, 98. See: (the) Establishment.
Notaries (II) 6.
numerarii (II) 4, 5, 7.

Official Positions. (late Republic) 29, 32, 33-34; (early Principate) 38-39, 44-47, 49; (mid Principate) 53-54, 55-59, 61; (Third Century) 64-67, 69-71, 74-75; (Dominate) 93-94, 95, 96-98, 99-100, 101; (Overall 102, 107, 108, 110-11, 113, 114. (II) 90; (Justinian) 118, 120, 121, 122; (Seventh Century) 142, 143, 144, 145, 146-50, 172; (Eleventh Century) 154-57, 160, 162, 164-66. See: (the) Establishment.
officium (II) 4, 5, 108. See: Praetorian Prefecture
One Law for the Rich.... 77.
Operational code of the bureaucracy (II) 176-79, 192-93. See: Behavioural code.
Overlapping Spheres of Competence/Functions 5, 13, 41, 56, 69-70, 81, 92-93, 107, 125, 145, 146, cf. 6. (II) 106, 111, 136, 181. See: Countervailing power, Cross-appointments, Formalism.

Pagan. See: Concepts.
Palace. See: Court.
Palace intrigues 153. See: Camarilla, Coups, Court, Praetorianism, Succession.
palatini 98, 108, 114, 118, 144. See: Court.
patrimonium 36. See: Financial institutions.
Patronage. See: Client relationship.
Pay scales 49, 56, 58, 64, 78, 94, 122, 139 & Table 2, 144. See: Coinage, Donatives, Pensions, Salary, sportulae.
Pensions 59. (II) 17, 72, 83, 85, 107-8, 111, 120, 137, 180, 183, 184, 191. See: Pay scales.
(the) People (II) 39, 43, 117-18, 122, 128, 146-47, 148, 152, 159, 170, 174, 178, 187, 188-89, 193, 195.
Persia (II) 25, 28, 29, 32, 40, 44, 90, 124, 159, 176.
Peter Barsymes (II) 158.
Peter the Patrician (II) 10, 15, 16, 17, 41, 50, 53, 54, 57, 135, 143, 152, 193.
Philadelphia and its inhabitants (II) 3, 13, 29, 30, 32, 54, 118, 147.
Phocas (II) 10, 14, 15, 17, 18, 69, 88, 89, 133, 181, 183, 192, 193.
Pirenne Thesis 149-50.
Plague (II) 15, 41, 159, 188.
Plato (II) 50, 54, 57, 60, 70.
Pluralism 14-15, 17, 23, 83, 108, 111, 178, 193. See: Schism, suffragium.

quaesitor 120, 145.
quaestor (II) 106, 113, 114, 120, 124, 135, 138, 142, 151.
quaestor of the Army 121.
quaestor of the Sacred Palace 93.
Quotations. See: Citations.

Rationality 20, 23, 164. See: Efficiency, Ideal type, Inner court, Overlapping spheres, Recruitment.
Recruitment 17-19, 23, 119. (II) 108, 110, 114, 137, 158, 178, 180, 181. See: Appointments, Controls on bureaucracy, (the) Establishment, Great Tradition, Inner Court, Sub-*élite*.
Reference works (II) 37, 65. See: the Law, Ptolemy, Specialist treatises.
regendarii (II) 4, 5, 8.
res privata 67-68. See: Financial institutions.
Rhetoric (II) 15, 52, 175.
ripenses 97.
Rome and the Romans (II) 26, 32, 39, 40, 41, 44, 45, 79, 87, 114, 115, 123, 124, 125, 128-29, 130, 148, 151, 153, 167, 188.
Romulus (II) 37, 38, 128.
Rufinus (II) 39, 43, 88, 133, 192.

sacellarius 146.
sajo (II) 113, 114, 134, 144.
Salaries 33, 37, 59, 117, 118, 119, 142. See: *sportulae*.
Schism 100-1, 103, 107, 114-15, 123-24, 138, 149, 151. See: Alienation, Monasteries.
scholae 97, 118. (II) 4, 5, 7, 14.
School texts (II) 37, 48, 55, 61, 65, 67, 74-75.
scrinarii (II) 5, 7, 193.
Secretariate 41, 44, 55, 56, 91-92, 146.
Senate (II) 39, 43, 106, 110, 114, 124, 132, 138, 170, 175, 192.
Septimius Severus (& the Severan dynasty) 62-76, 98.
(the) Service (II) 50, 100, 129, 130, 153. See: *militia*.
Service orientation (II) 66, 83, 90, 91, 92, 107, 108-9, 114, 118, 140, 148-49. See: Bureaucratic malpractices, Law, Punishment orientation.
Side effects (of changes to a bureaucracy) (II) 174, 175. See: Unanticipated consequences.
Sinecures (II) 9, 83, 108, 111, 176, 178. See: *suffragium*.
Social forces (II) 39, 40, 44, cf. 66. See: Authoritarianism, Great men.
Source materials. (ancient) 2-3, 20, 27, 52, 129, 170-71, 190, 192, cf. Appendix B; (modern) 3, 129, cf. 192.
spatharius 111.
Specialist treatises (II) 52, 55-56, 65, 73.
sportulae 117. (II) 3, 11, 78, 82, 106, 107, 108, 109, 139, 177, 178, 179, 184, 192.
State. See: Concepts.
Status system of bureaucracy 57-58, 93-94, 108, 113, 147-48. See Establishment, Strata, Titles.
Strabo (II) 30, 67-68.
Strata. (within the bureaucracy) 18; (in the late Republic) 30; (in the early Principate) 50-52; (in the middle Principate) 8, 52-54, 57, 58; (in the third century) 64-65, 70-71, 72, 73; (Dominate) 94, 95, 130; (in the sixth century)

123; (in the seventh century) 142, 147, 148, 150, 151; (in the eleventh century) 157-60. See: (the) Establishment, Nobility, Provincials.
Strategic Learning (II) 66, 76, 87.
subadiuva (II) 5, 8, 14.
Sub-*élite* 17-18, 154.
Subject/citizen (participation) orientation 21.
(the) Succession 19, 43, 52, 60, 157-59, 163. See: (the) Autocrat's Position, Camerilla.
suffragium 118, 120, 160, cf. 122, 166. (II) 78, 106, 108, 109, 110-11, 140, 178, 184, 185, 193. See: Absenteeism, Pluralism, Sinecures.
Super-departments 19-20, cf. 125, 171.
Supernumeraries (II) 5, 7, 14.
Surveys. (of developments within and among the bureaucracies) 4-10; (of traditional vs. industrialized views on bureaucracy) 21-23. See: Balance of power.

Taxation 14, 20, 56-57, 65, 68-69, 73, 94-95, 96, 102-3, 108, 109, 110, 113, 116, 155, 159-62, 163, 164. (II) 78, 81, 117, 118, 119, 120, 122, 147, 148-49, 151, 158, 159, 161, 172, 174, 176, 177, 184, 192. See: Trickle-up and trickle-down taxation.
Tetrarchy 90-91.
Themes 121, 139, 142, 144, 146, 154-56, 162.
Theodahad (II) 86, 104, 118, 131, 135, 139.
Theodora (II) 10, 15, 16, 69, 86, 170, 172.
Theodoric (II) 86, 97, 98, 131.
Theodosius I the Great 102-8.
Theodosius II 108, 112-14.
Theories on bureaucracy 4, 11, 20. See: Concepts of importance, Criteria for comparing bureaucracies, Crucial resources/facilities, Ideal type, Levels of analysis.
Time focus (II) 166, 190.
Titles 57-58, 94, 108, 120, 147-48, 164, 165.
Trade 14, 82, 116-17, 138, 143-44, 145, 152, 155-56, 162, 173, cf. 163, 168. See: Coinage, Confiscations, Countervailing Power, Taxation, Wantlessness of the impoverished.
Traditionalism (II) 81, 102, 117, 130, 138, 143, 153, 157, 185, 187, 190, 191, 194.
Trained incapacity 161. See: Trained incompetence.
Trained incompetence (II) 43, 75, 120, 150, 179, 194, cf. 96. See: Strategic learning.
Trickle-up & trickle-down taxation 23, 113. (II) 106. See: Taxation.

Unanticipated consequences 118-19, 125, 127. (II) 79, 80, 81, 82, 87, 112, 115, 172, 186, 187. See: Black box, Side effects.
Unrest 120. See: Alienation, Anomie.
Urban Prefect 39, 44-47, 56, 70, 81, 93, 98, 120, 145. (II) 106, 112, 107, 114, 124, 125, 135, 142, 158. See: Eparch.

Value Systems (II) 47, 52, 72-73, 83, 107, 116-17, 129-30, 178, 185, 193. See: Behavioural code.
Varangian Guard 154.
Vergil (II) 48, 49, 54, 57, 60, 74.

- 219 -

"Wantlessness of the impoverished" 27.
(the) West (II) 28, 32, 40, 73, 79, 105, 116, 118, 126, 127, 128, 158-59, 173.
Witigis (II) 15, 86, 104, 115, 131, 135, 145.
Working conditions (II) 83, 87, 107, 109, 111, 120, 122, 138, 150.
"World" of a bureaucrat (II) 1-2, 21, 28, 29, 41, 56-61, 65-66, 77-78, 79-82, 102, 107, 121-30, 179-84.

Zoticus (II) 3, 9, 12-13, 14, 16, 86, 147.

BOOK THREE

John the Lydian
On the Magistracies of
the Roman Constitution
(De Magistratibus)

TABLE OF CONTENTS

INTRODUCTION

This is, I think, the first complete translation into English of John the Lydian's *On the Magistracies of the Roman Constitution.* The scant attention this work has received is possibly a fitting comment on its merits as a piece of literature: artistic scintillation is not a major characteristic of the work, though it does fitfully sputter into an acrid glow in the occasional passage of vituperation. However, the work is of considerable historical value. Not only is it the only record of the Roman and Byzantine bureaucracy to the sixth century A.D., written by a bureaucrat, that survives, but it provides a contemporary's comments on the emperors from Anastasius to Justinian. As the latter's bureaucratic reforms adversely affected the writer's retirement, in which the work was written, marked personal bias is evident. Owing to this bias and to the schematic arrangement of subject matter, the work is particularly well suited to the application of content analysis, and reveals much of importance about the world of a sixth-century Constantinopolitan.

Of the writer's background the following details emerge from the work: John was born in 490 A.D. in the township of Philadelphia lying below Mount Tmolus in Lydia (some fifty miles inland from present-day Izmir in Turkey), probably of well-to-do parents. At twenty-one he went to seek his fortune in the capital, Constantinople. A post with the *memoriales* seemed to promise the best career, but, while furthering his literary education pending establishment with them, a relative from his home town, the Praetorian Prefect Zoticus, prevailed on him to enter the staff of that prefecture. As the prefecture was in decline, this point of entry was not to lead to a strategically situated position within the power-mechanism of the bureaucracy, a fact which probably accounts for the ambivalence in John's attitude to the civil service, evident in spite of the departmental loyalty that grew upon him. However, in the short run, the decision paid off well: after a highly profitable year as a minor official during his kinsman's term of office as prefect, John was advanced with unprecedented rapidity to the post of First *Chartularius* to the Assistants to the *ab actis*. Then followed a busy period during which he seems to have held several minor posts simultaneously, making himself something of a reputation for industry and literary gifts. He rose to the *a secretis* and made an advantageous marriage through the intermediacy of the ex-prefect Zoticus. But by now men with training in finance seem to have begun to be preferred to those with literary training for advancement, and John left the prefect's legal service to practise teaching. Though he was allowed to stay on the establishment while so doing, reforms within the bureaucracy meant that he had no chance of the final post abounding in perquisites which, in the absence of a system of superannuation, officials such as John had been counting upon to finance retirement. Some consolation seems to have come from the esteem in which he was held in a society which admired literary gifts in its administrators, but the penury that would accompany his retirement cast a blight upon the latter part of his career. His retirement seems to have been spent in writing and to have been beset with worries, probably of a financial nature.

Internal evidence dates the composition of the work to the period from 551 to before 565, book three (and probably the whole work) being written after 554. It is not a well finished piece of work and may possibly not have received its final editing. It would appear that from John's orthograph version a majuscule copy was made in the seventh century. Both are lost. To judge from references to it, the work was little studied in medieval Byzantium. Extant is a tenth-century minuscule manuscript (the *Codex Caseolinus*), containing the copyist's and a second script. The latter appears to be that of the eighteenth century Greek Scholar to whom we owe a manuscript (the so-called *Codex Atheniensis*) discovered c. 1852 and obviously based on the *Codex Caseolinus*. The text has suffered in its descent to us: it has been damaged at beginning and end and has lost some folios within the body of the work, as its occasional citations by other sources show. Moreover, at many points the writing is difficult to make out, owing to erosions or stains caused by wine spots. It might not be inappropriate to mention at this point the fact that the original, tenth-century copyist made many mistakes over word-inflections in copying. Hence editors of the text have asked that, in view of the difficulty of establishing a text, an understanding view be taken of possible infelicities in their work. Prudence compels the translator to the same course: the dictionaries available (H. G. Liddell & R. Scott, rev. H. S. Jones, *A Greek-English Lexicon*, 1940; E. A. Sophocles, *Greek Lexicon of the Roman & Byzantine Periods from B.C. 146 to A.D. 1100*, reprint of 1887 edition;

D. Demetrakos, *Mega Lexicon holes tes Hellenikes Glosses*, 1958) are meant to cover classical Greek literature, Byzantine religious literature and the whole of Greek literature respectively. John's writings, however, abound in bureaucratic jargon, words often having their meanings extended to senses not recorded in the dictionaries. A special glossary had to be built up to cope with the resulting semantic problem; its completion was not effected till translation was finished, so earlier parts of the translation may still need some re-phrasing.

The text translated has been that of R. Wuensch (Teubner, Leipzig 1903) used in conjunction with that of I. Bekker (in the *Corpus scriptorum historiae Byzantinae*, Bonn 1837) and with its Latin translation of I. D. Fuss (of 1812 vintage, appended to Bekker's text and apparatus). The scholarship of these men and their personalities reach out from their editions and compel admiration. My debt to them is enormous; my hope is not to have followed too unworthily in their footsteps. Relatively few scholars have worked on this text; all, given its unsatisfactory condition, have made emendations. Some fresh emendations underlie this translation, and it is hoped that they will appear in an appropriate specialist journal in due course. It did not seem appropriate to include discussion of them in this work, which is already encumbered by the notation involved in providing a comprehensive system of reference.

This translation will mostly be used by students of history and, possibly, government, who will require a precise system of reference. Hence sentences in the chapters have each been numbered. Where stylistic affectations lead to sentences of a chapter in length, the main clauses have been numbered, going by obvious breaks in the flow of the narrative or argument. The latter numeration is indicated by bracketing the number involved. It sometimes seemed advisable to disembarrass unusually discursive sentences of some of their asides by relegating these to footnotes. Such relegation has been marked by a letter (a, b, c and so on) so as not to add to the number of numerals on the page. If the footnote comprises a whole sentence, the number of the sentence within the chapter follows the letter referring to text above. Sometimes the insertion of an explanatory note by the translator seemed to be called for: in such a case an asterisk has been used. The text is equipped with references to book, chapter and sentence at the top of each page, so that a glance at any pair of pages reveals the full extent of text covered by the translation on those pages.

A quick perusal of any review of the state of theory on bureaucracy (e. g. S. N. Eisenstadt, "Bureaucracy and Bureaucratization" in *Current Sociology* vol. 7, 1958, pp. 99-165) indicates the many differing viewpoints from which one can approach this topic. There is much divergence in the interpretation of the source evidence on Justinian: as ways of representing polar extremes in conceptualizing the emperor one might suggest the images of the bull in the china shop and the blow-fly in the spider's web respectively. Much of this has clearly been caused by historians who have not explicitly spelled out how they assume a bureaucracy to work in an agricultural society. Experience gained by working on this author with seminar and tutorial groups suggests that F. W. Riggs' study, *Agraria and Industria* (in W. J. Siffin, ed., *Towards the Comparative Study of Public Administration*, 1957), is particularly helpful in this respect. My debt to this scholar is immense and I am glad to acknowledge it out of gratitude; for semantic reasons too I should indicate that this translation has been informed by insights provided by Professor Riggs' work.

The historical reference work basic to this translation is naturally A. H. M. Jones' monumental *The Later Roman Empire 284-602*, 1964. Some references to particularly useful or meaningful studies will be found in the footnotes. There is no intention of providing a bibliography here, but for those wishing to acquire something of a feeling for the environment in which John produced his work, G. Downey's *Constantinople in the Age of Justinian* (1960) is recommended as an excellent complement to John's writings.

It is impossible fully to acknowledge one's intellectual debts in regard to an undertaking of this sort. I have tried to do so in cases where I have been conscious of them and would like to make known my gratitude to the students and other members of the 1964 tutorials and the 1965 seminar on this work. The History Department of Sydney University has provided a stimulating intellectual background, and its head, Professor J. M. Ward, has given generously in encouragement and moral support as well as in research facilities. For all of this I am very grateful indeed. My thanks also go to Antoinette Sliteris, secretary to the Ancient History group, for her cheerful and painstaking work on typing and layout, and to Walter Stone for being an understanding publisher of the preliminary trial edition of this work (Wentworth Press of Sydney, Australia, 1965).

This is the point where, as writer of an introduction, I have to say that I alone am responsible for any errors and sins of omission or commission. Obviously.

T. F. Carney

John the Lydian
De magistratibus

PREFACE

It is common knowledge that those who were subsequently 1
rulers of the Roman state were initially priests. Tyrrhenus, the
man who induced the Etruscans,[a] as they were then called, to
move to the West out of Lydia, taught them the mysterious
Lydian rites and, as it turned out, their name was changed to
Tuscans on account of their thyoscopy*. I know that I made a
detailed reference to this matter in the first book of the study
which I have written, called *On the Months*. It was from Tuscans 2
that King Numa took over the official regalia of their rulers and
introduced it into public life — as he also took over from Gauls
weapons that were difficult to fight against. Witnesses to this are 3
Capito and Fonteius, based upon the most learned Varro — all
Romans; after whom the famous historian Sallust gave a lucid
account in the first book of the *Histories*. Consequently, what 4
remains to be done is to give an account of the civil powers,
because they changed from a priestly nature to a civilian
character. So let no one think that I am at variance with what the 5
ancient sources record, unless by chance, on a premise that is in
conflict with sound logic, he should, out of envy, alter the
grounds for praise. That a certain Gracchanus wrote of old about 6
these matters too, is recounted by the compilers of law codes, as I
am aware. But this book is probably nowhere extant; Time has
assuredly hidden it in oblivion too, as well as having brought it
into being.

---

[a] They were a Sicanian race.

* Lydus posits an etymological connection between words which might be
transliterated as thyoskopia and Thuskoi. Thyoscopy means "inspecting of
victims' entrails."

BOOK ONE

As I am attempting to make a clear deposition on the   1.1
magistracies of the Roman state, it has occurred to me that it
would be worthwhile giving the account a preface commencing
from the eldest and most honoured statesman of all. This was   1.2
Aeneas who, on account of his handsome appearance and
strength of both mind and body, was thought to be the son of a
superhuman being.

Well then, from Aeneas' arrival in Italy to the building of the   2.1
city of Rome, 439 years passed, according to the Romans Cato
the Elder and Varro; but according to Africanus, Castor and the
disciple of Pamphilus* it was 417. From the founding of the city to   2.2
the expulsion of the kings 243 years ran their course. The years   2.3
under the consuls until the first Caesar ran to 465 — or 466,
according to some authorities. From Caesar to Constantine 375   2.4
years elapsed. From the latter to the death of the emperor
Anastasius 224 years and seven months elapsed, from which one
could subtract nine years during which Constantine was in fact
emperor in holy Rome. Actually the period from the building of   2.5
this blessed city tots up to 215 years and seven months. So one   2.6
could work it out that from Aeneas to the death of the good
Anastasius there were in all 1,746 years and seven months, as is
the Greek view, based upon all the writers in either language.
After putting this truthfully in this fashion, it is time for me to   2.7
make a clear statement on the magistracies of our state, the
subject as announced.

Well, with his brother Remus, Romulus, at the age of   3.1
eighteen, built Rome, the mother of the empire. The name of   3.2
their rule was what Latins term regal, i.e. tyrannical. For the
styling royal is not, as some suppose, indicative of a
constitutional Roman principate. For this reason it was not
retained, after the expulsion of the kings, as current usage

---

* Eusebius.

amongst the Romans, even though they were subject to a   3.3
monarchical type of authority. The title of a constitutional
princeps means one thing, that of a tyrant another — and that of
an *imperator* means something else again. As to how, I will soon
say. A *princeps* is one who, chosen as first citizen by the vote of 3.4
his own citizens for an elevated position — a sort of pedestal as it
were,ᵃ attains a position superior to other men. A characteristic   3.5
peculiar to a *princeps* is that he never disturbs a single one of the
laws of the state but sedulously preserves the status of his own
constitution through the principate. He does nothing arbitrarily
outside the law, and ratifies by his own vote policies that are
favoured by the best men in the state, displaying for the citizenry
the affection of a father as well as that of a leader. He is the sort
of statesman that God and the prosperity of the age have granted
our generation. A tyrant will not treat those who fall beneath his   3.6
sway like this, but will act without consideration, as far as his
power permits, if he does want to do anything, neither seeing fit
to respect the law, nor submitting to councilling in legislation,
but being activated by his own impulses. For the habit of a   3.7
princeps is what the law is, whereas a tyrant's law is what his
habits suggest.

The title Caesar (that is *imperator*) is not indicative of a   4.1
princeps' position nor again of that of a tyrant. It is rather that of
an absolute ruler and of absolute authority, authority so to
handle disturbances which arise against the commonwealth as to
produce a better state of affairs, and to give instructions to the
army as to the way in which battle should be fought against the
enemy.ᵇ That the name *imperator* or Caesar does not mean a   4.3
princeps' position, is immediately evident from the fact that both
the consuls, and after them the Caesars, took the name of the
so-called *imperator* as a title in their official styling. The Caesars 4.4
as rulers do not seem to have used the official regalia of tyranny,
attending the Roman senate in a purple robe and nothing more

---

a As Sophocles said of Ajax "he had the firm pedestal of Salamis by the
sea."

b (4.2) For *imperare* is the Latin for "to give commands"; hence
imperator.

elaborate, and also directing the forces under arms as *imperatores*, as stated.[c] The name Caesar is indicative of a line of descent from 4.6 the first Caesar, as is that of the Fabii, Cornelii, Flavii and Anicii, this being an earlier convention conceived among the barbarians. For the Egyptians called their kings Pharaohs after the first 4.7 Pharaoh, and Ptolemies after the first Ptolemy.

This kind of orderly behaviour on the part of the Caesars was 4.8 preserved among the Romans until Diocletian. He first set a diadem made of precious stones on his head, adorned his clothing and feet with gems, and turned to a royal style of behaviour, or, to tell the truth, that of tyrant, burdening the land with taxes after carefully surveying it.

So Romulus was a tyrant, in the first place because he slew his 5.1 brother — his elder brother at that, and because he acted without rhyme or reason in dealing with matters that came up. Hence he 5.2 was also called Quirinus, i.e. *Kyrios** — even if Diogenianus the lexicographer should think otherwise. For it is not shown that Romulus or those around him did not at that time know the Greek language — I mean Aeolian,[d] for Evander and the other Arcadians had gone to Italy at some undefined date and spread the Aeolian tongue among the barbarians.[e] Tyrants like to have 5.5 themselves called *Kyrios* and *dominus* but not king.[f]

---

c (4.5) Hence Romans called a Caesar a *princeps* also, that is supreme head of the entire state.

d As is asserted by Cato in his work on Roman antiquities and also by Varro, a man of the widest scholarship, in the Preface of his work dedicated to Pompey.

e (5.3) The etymology invoked by the grammarians, when compared with this view is, if you will excuse my saying so, forced. (5.4) They would have him to have been so named after Cures, a small Sabine town, although he was not sprung from there but was born on the Palatine Hill beside the banks of the Tiber and brought up there.

f (6.1) The position of a Caesar is superior to a king's position, because of old it had it within its power actually to confer kings upon the peoples.

* Greek for "master."

It was a hateful thing and foreign to Roman freedom of   6.2
speech to call the man in power *dominus* and not *princeps*,
because the name *dominus* was common to these rulers and to
those who owned a single slave, whereas that of *princeps*
belonged to the former alone. It is patently obvious that it was   6.3
the Roman custom to dub those who had won their way to a
tyranny *dominos*, as for instance Sulla and Marius, and to call
tyranny *dominatio*. Consequently the distinguished position of a
princeps is belittled by base flatterers when in their ignorance
they introduce the idea that a *princeps* is first man among slaves.
That this is true can be deduced from the following facts also.   6.4
Once Augustus — or perhaps Tiberius, his successor — was called
dominus by one of the flatterers. He got to his feet and dismissed
the meeting, deeming it below him, as he put it, to converse with
slaves. But, since the insulting word had already, before
Justinian's reign, been brought into use as though in honorific
usage, our most mild emperor in his clemency allowed himself
even to be called *dominus*, i.e. kindly father, although he
surpassed in moderation every emperor who ever ruled. Not that
he rejoiced in the title; no, rather he was embarrassed at giving
the impression of not granting an audience to those who thought
they were doing him honour.

Concerning the official regalia of the rex.

Even before Romulus, the official symbol of kingship among   7.1
Latins was an enclosed throne and as garb the *trabea*, as it was
called among them. What its nature was, I will state a little
further on. Hence the Roman poet, when describing the court of   7.2
Latinus in the seventh book of the Aeneid, records a throne and a
trabea. Romulus had a crown also and a sceptre with an eagle   7.3
atop it, and a thick white upper garment reaching to his feet. This
had stripes of purple webbing running down from the shoulders
in the front to the feet,9 and crimson sandals. According to
Cocceianus* the name of the sandal was a buskin. This garb   7.4
consisting of the so-called *toga* was common both to the *"rex"*
himself and to the citizenry in time of peace. But the *trabea* was a

---

9 The name of the garment was a toga, i.e. a covering — from the word
tegere, with an interchange of letters; for such is the Latin for "to cover."

* Cassius Dio.

paratura, i.e. official dress, for the *rex* alone. It was a tunic or   7.5
wrap of semi-circular form which, the story goes, Agathocles the
tyrant of Syracuse was the first to devise. The throne they used
to call a *solium* in their native tongue instead of a *sellion*, by
interchange of letters, as the Roman Asper claims. Or again, on
another interpretation, they used the term *solium* instead of
solidum (i.e. all of one piece). For they would carve out a thick   7.6
log into the shape of a small chest or chair and make a raised seat
for the royal presence in which the king's person was protected as
though in a sort of chest, with no junction or added piece of
wood at the back and at either side, to connect chair and backing,
as it was one complete whole, all of one piece. Hence they used   7.7
to call the king's *solium* a throne.

In addition to this Romulus was preceded by axes — twelve,   8.1
to correspond to the number of the vultures which he saw when
he was commencing to lay the foundations of the city. When the   8.2
rex Tarquinius Priscus later defeated the Tuscans and Sabines in
war, to the insignia of the kingship were added longish spears,
likewise twelve in number. These did not have blades at their
extremities but dangling crests. The Romans call these *iubae*, the
barbarians *tufae*, the Roman word having suffered some slight
corruption. In addition to these were *vexilla* (i.e. long spears with
bunting hanging from them) — they call them *flamula* from their
fiery colour   concerning which I have given sufficient account in
my work *On the Months.*

Such were the insignia of the monarchy of that time. As to   9.1
the men serving under arms, the Roman Paternus speaks as
follows in the first book of his *Tactics* (his own words in
translation): "Romulus advanced decurions to look after the
sacred insignia; also he conferred upon these men the name
centurions of the infantry groups. For there were 3,000   9.2
shield-bearing infantry, and Romulus put a leader over each
century.* (Greeks call him a *Hekantontarches*, Romans a
centurion.) Consequently the centurions in all were thirty in
number and there were also as many maniples (i.e. standard
bearers). From the army he set aside three hundred *scutati*"h —   9.3

h A little further on there will be an account of what a "clipeate" and of
what a "scutate" soldier is.

* Squad of one hundred men.

the Roman term for shield-bearing infantry — "for a bodyguard. He also added three hundred troopers to his forces, handing over responsibility for these to a certain Celerius (such was the man's name). Because of this, by a part for the whole process of thinking, the whole battalion thereupon acquired the styling *celeres*. As the cavalry force was composed of three centuries, he distinguished these by three further stylings, appointing them *Ramnes, Titienses* and *Luceres.*"[i] 9.4

But it is time to state how a *scutum* differs from a *clipeus*. 10.1
Well, *scutum* is what the Romans call what is at once strong and 10.2
spare — what Greeks call tough (i.e. sturdy, as Aristophanes puts it in the *Acharnians*: "tough old fellows, men who fought at Marathon, hard as oak"). Hence the Romans call garments that 10.3
are tough and waterproof and light *scutulata* And such is the 10.4
make-up of the shield; for it is light, being plain and spare, but very strong and not easily permeable to blows. *Clipeus* is the 10.5
Romans' name for the oblong shield, from its concealing and covering its bearer. For it is a characteristic peculiar to the Greeks 10.6
alone that they use very round shields in war, whereas the custom of barbarians is to use oblong shields. To meet the battle pressing hard upon them their practice is to lift up their oblong shields and use them as cover.

There is also another form of shield, a smaller one, which the 11.1
people beyond the Danube, not having the ability to fight on foot, carry on horseback, as the Scyths carry their targes.[j] Besides 11.2
these the ancients had — it does not now exist — an *ancile*, a form of small shield, from which they even called women captured in war *ancillae*. For, when a woman chanced to please him, the 11.3
soldier would cover her with the *ancile* in the attack so that she should not be harmed by anyone, being as it were kept under protection by her saviour.[k] *Ancilia* — from a Greek, specifically 11.5

---

i I have given the reasons for these names in my depositions called *On the Months*.

j People in Italy call this a *parma*.

k (11.4) In this way the name *servi* too is given by people of Italy to slaves — from their having been preserved from the consequences of war. Those who are not captives in war but, although free as to the status that life has allotted, become slaves as result of indigence, are called *famuli* (because famine is called *fames*).

an Aeolian, expression — means as it were "smooth all around";
the Amazons' targes were of such a kind.

Equipment at that time was uniform for all the Roman army: 12.1
a copper helmet, a breast-plate made of mail, a short broad sword
hanging at the left thigh; two javelins with broad-bladed tips in
the right hand, black leggings of woven stuff and, for the feet,
sandals which Greeks call *arbylai*, Romans *garbola* and *crepidae*.*
Not a silly or a thoughtless term: Terentius — the one with the
cognomen Varro[l] — wrote that according to the statuary Aeneas
came to Italy of yore in such a garb (he had seen a statue of him,
he said, carved out of white stone at a fountain in Alba). And it is   12.2,3
quite literally true. For the Roman poet introduced him, so
garbed, wandering with Achates in Libya in the first book of the
Aeneid. In time of peace they put on long flowing garments made
of wild beasts' pelts, which hung from their shoulders down as far
as their calves, adorning the parts on them where the feet and tail
had been and calling them *globae* (i.e. skins, because it was a
Roman custom to describe skinning as *globare*). And it was not   12.4
merely the soldiery who were customarily clad like this when
under arms; the *imperatores* too were so clad.

But since nowadays the soldiery imitates the barbarians and   12.5
the latter imitate them, only among the palace guards[m] has this
type of dress remained, one which, as I said, took its origin from
Romulus who followed Aeneas. For Romans were not permitted   12.6
to put on barbaric dress. Suetonius records this in his work on   12.7
Augustus, for he says that, upon seeing certain Romans in the
hippodrome dressed in a way that tended towards the barbaric,
Augustus complained angrily. The sequel was that although those
against whom he complained instantly laid aside their barbaric
dress, they had difficulty in gaining recognition from Caesar.
Well, such was Romulus' army.

---

l The additional styling "Varro" means "manly" in the Celtic language, and
"Jewish" according to the Phoenicians, as Herennius claims.

m These are called *excubitores,* i.e. vigilant guards, among Romans.
Tiberius Caesar was the first man after Romulus to think of having them.

* The Greek word means a strong shoe coming up to the ankle; *garbolum* is
its low-Latin equivalent, and a *crepida* is a latinized form of a Greek word
for a sandal.

I 13.1 —

The so-called *attentiones*, my guess is, were devised to serve   13.1
the *reges* — for the fetching and carrying of necessaries, just as
night carriages were devised to cope with furniture and other
items which are useful for sleeping arrangements. The great   13.2
Cicero records this name in the speech against Verres, calling the
household servants of the *reges* "*attenti*" from their paying
attendance and obedience. For *attendere* is the Roman word for
"to show a keen, competitive spirit."

First Position to be created: the Master of Horse

Well then, as I stated, the infantry force was put by Romulus   14.1
under the command of the centurions and the cavalry force under
that of Celerius, who had formerly led the whole army. He bade
Celerius exercise control over the entire force, its fortunes and its
management, with the result that the monarchy held nothing else
but the crown back from the authority of the Masters of Horse,
an authority which was not answerable to the monarchy itself.
This official position was available to and under the *reges* and the   14.2
dictators too, all of them, and after that the Caesars had it (after
they had changed the name of the Master of Horse to that of
Prefect). The jurist Aurelius bears witness to this, speaking as
follows (in his own words in translation): "It is necessary to state
briefly whence the Praetorian Prefect took his origin. It was, most   14.3
assuredly, from the Master of Horse. For it is handed down in all
the ancient sources that it was in the latter's place that the
Prefect was created. In ancient times, entire control over affairs
was entrusted in an emergency to one dictator or another. Each   14.4
selected for himself a commander of the cavalry, a partner as it
were in his position of authority and management of affairs.
When power later devolved upon the *imperatores*, the Praetorian   14.5
Prefect came forward in a like manner to the Master of Horse. He   14.6
was given greater power than the Master of Horse had been given,
both in the management of affairs and in the disposition and
training of the armies and all administering of correction, and
progressed to such a degree of eminence that nobody could
initiate moves for an appeal against, or in any way impeach, a
judgement reached by him."

This is what the jurisconsult says. But you must realise that,   15.1
although it has been conceded that a Praetorian Prefecture is, as it

turns out, senior to and more important than the other magistracies, it was both necessary and fitting as well to extend the account to cover all of the establishment and powers of the prefecture. Anyhow, it was not at the outset but in the time of 15 (2) Augustus, as I said, that the prefecture was created, in place of the Master of Horse. So it will be sufficient, until I come to that point, to mention its antiquity and its origins in its infancy. Then, 15 (3) after the description of the older magistracies, in the opening remarks on Augustus' principate,[n] I will give a detailed, orderly description of all the functions of the prefecture and those which were gradually taken from it, and then also an account dealing with the establishment — truly a very great one — which comes under its jurisdiction.[o] And I can do so, because my knowledge of it is not second-hand but comes from having looked after its business by personally working at it.

In doing this I am offering a thank-offering, like a beloved 15 (4) object that gets dedicated, to the senior members of the staff, who gave me splendid support and who also, next to God who is master of all, provided me with honours as reward for my work, a dignified retirement and a better lot in life.

Second Institution to be created: the Patriciate.

It is quite clear that elders, one hundred in number, for all the 16.1 *curiae* (i.e. tribes) were selected by Romulus to look after public affairs. He called them "Fathers"; people in Italy called them *"Patricii"* (i.e. men of noble lineage). After the rape of the Sabine 16.2 women he gave them the additional styling *conscripti* (i.e. enlisted — hence it is *patres conscripti* that the Roman governing class is still called today), and included another thirty *curiae*, an equal number of centurions and another three hundred troopers from the Sabine people in the numbers of the Roman army. Consequently there were in all six thousand infantry and six hundred cavalry. This number was later preserved by Marius when 16.3 he fashioned the so-called legions (i.e. picked men). The emperor Leo was the first, when establishing the so-called Excubitors to

---

n From which, as I said, the magistracy took its beginning.

o I too, as things turned out, was one of its staff.

act as guards of the side-entrances to the palace, to form them, according to time-honoured tradition, into a force of not more than three hundred.

Official dress for the Fathers — or Patricians — consisted of double-folded mantles or *chlamydes* * which came down from the shoulders to the knees, girt up with golden brooches, russet in colour, conspicuous by a purple stripe down the middle,p and *paragaudas*, tunics with a pattern of spear heads, with a purple edge, wholly of white, with sleeves (they call these sleeves *manicae*).q There were white leggings, covering the whole leg, foot and all, and a black sandal, a sandal-sole quite without a top. This held the heel fast with a sort of tiny projecting rim and the toes at the front in the same way. Leather thongs were drawn from either side towards the ankle bones beneath the arch of the foot, meeting one another towards the ball of the foot and binding the foot so that very little apart from toes showed through the sandal at front or back, whereas the main part of the foot was visible because of the legging. They call this the *campagus* from its being used for the *campus*, i.e. the plain, even nowadays. For it was when they were in the plain that the Romans carried out the elections of their *mag*-istrates, and for this purpose they used to dress themselves in this sort of sandal. This *campagus* belonged to the Tuscans formerly, claims Lepidus in his book on priests.

17.1

17.2

17.3

17.4

17.5

The patricians never went forth on foot; furthermore they did not go out on horseback either — I make the point because they were commonly believed to do so — but in official carriages, with their chairs being set on high. Four mules drew the carriage, which was of Corinthian copper and which had a mass of figures and engravings of old-fashioned appearance carved upon it. Yoking horses to the carriage was not permitted except in the

18.1

18.2

---

p They used to call them *laticlaviae;* the *chlamydes* they called *atrabatticae* from their colour, because grey with them is termed *ater.*

q This sort of tunic the man in the street is wont to call a *paragauda.* For all that, the *paragauda* is a form of tunic of ancient origin, an official form of dress for Persians and Sauromatians, as has been stated by Diogenianus the lexicographer.

* Another name for a mantle, or cloak, of no one set length.

case of the king alone, as processing in a horse-drawn carriage was a triumphal rite. They used to call the carriages *burichallia*, from the oxen which drew them. If oxen were not used, since there was not a heavy load on it, they used to entrust the yoke to mules.

Why the Romans call the official designations of positions of honour "titles."

Titus Tatius, when leading the Sabines, as I have just stated, after uniting with the Romans, so unified the pair of peoples that they were no longer spoken of as two but as one, in fact only as the Roman Republic. And because this statesman had the name Titus Tatius, they spoke of the official designation of nobility as a title, employing the word as a diminutive, from the first Titus; and they spoke of those who were of noble lineage as Tituses, according to the Roman writer Persius.   19.1

19.2

So much for titles. Of all types of honour the noblemen of Rome believed that the first and foremost was the good reputation deriving from favours bestowed. The more persons they had under their patronage, the greater they believed their glory to be by contrast with those who had fewer such persons. A witness to this is the Roman Juvenal, who states that among the ancients the fame that came from favours done took pride of place before consulships and triumphs, and also before brave deeds performed in war. The people who were brought under their patronage they called in their native tongue *clientes* — for *colientes* ʳ by an interchange of letters. It was with every sign of deference and in a self-effacing way that they made presents of their gifts, so that liberal treatment of friends became called liberality. No one who had the luck to become on familiar terms with a nobleman had need of another man, after that, to come to his assistance for the whole of his life; for a nobleman thought it a disgrace and a departure from the way of life proper to him if any friend of his should be reduced in any way to have recourse to another man. A dim trace of this practice was preserved until recently among the Romans. The leading men in Rome used to   20.1

20.2

20.3

20.4

20.5
20.6

ʳ I.e. those who did them honour and who displayed affection towards them.

send those most suitable for the task out around Ostia — a city
lying at the mouth of the Tiber — to lay hold of the strangers
who were putting out to sea as though they were a sort of
splendid prey and to bring them to them before the other
notables could do so. To ensure free giving completely without
niggardliness, the outer doors of the residence of the dignitary
were opened to all. No guard or janitor prevented anyone who
asked to do so from coming in. The nobility themselves appeared
with their wives and children before the strangers and requested
people whom they had never seen before to put their trust in
them. This sort of benevolence came in a like fashion to our   20.7
Rome also and then did not become established, since the
notables among us kept their displays of the superiority of their
fortunes to themselves.

Why Romans have two or three or more names.

Even before Romulus one might find the kings of the   21.1
country-side bearing the additional title *Silvii*, from Silvius
Aeneas, descendant of the first Aeneas. For the people of former 21.2
times had their dwellings in the woods and held the nomadic way
of life in high regard. So they called themselves *Silvii* in their
grave way, since even their kings themselves did not think it
unbecoming to pasture herds and gather wealth from them.
Hence also amongst them wealth is spoken of as *pecunia.* Thus   21.3
antiquity knew Evander of yore, him from Tegea, as being
accompanied by dogs. And it was not merely upon men that the   21.4
additional styling of *Silvius* was put, but upon women too, as on
Rhea Silvia and Ilia Silvia. After the birth of Rome and the rape 21.5
of the Sabine women, king Numa was first to go by a two-fold
name, being addressed as Pompilius Numa (of these names the
one was Roman, the other Sabine). Before him you would not   21.6
find that Romulus, or anyone at all before the union of Sabine
women to Romans, possessed another name besides his own
proper name.

At that time it was a distinction keenly sought amongst them   22.1
to have the exalted styling of a name drawn from another stock.
As it went on, however, time introduced fresh *cognomina*,
coming at one time from the Trojan nobility, at another from the
so-called Aboriginals or autochthonous people of the
country-side. In fact we know that Cethegus claimed to trace his

line from those original inhabitants — Cethegus who attended the market place without a stitch of clothing, with only a rough toga around his chest, although he was decorated with the distinctions of senatorial status. Then again time also introduced *cognomina* derived from a man's habits or his disposition, as in the case of Publius Valerius Publicola. Of these names, the first two indicated his distinction in coming, as I said, from Roman *and* Sabine stock, the third showed his disposition, arising out of his affection for the commons. Possibly what is needful is to record   22.2
not a lot but a moderate number of incidental details of this type — because I have not got leisure to digress upon this line of enquiry, which is one that is enough, even by itself alone, to occupy the largest book.

Well then, Proculus was their name for the child who was born   23.1
while his father was abroad; Postumus for the child born after his father's death; Vopiscus for the child who was one of a pair of twins that had been conceived and who survived while the other twin perished; Caesar for the child who had been taken to safety from his mother's womb which had been cut open after her death; Flaccus for the child with rather large ears and Naevius for the one with birth marks. And there is the name Lucius Licinius Crassus. Of these names the first indicates the child born while the sun was rising, the second the child with hair that curled at the tip, the third the child who is fleshy and well-grown. For   23.2
Crassus, among people in Italy in a more distant age, was the name for the person who was naturally stout of build, while Pinarius was the name for the starveling, Statius for the one of good stature, Faustus for the one who is fortunate, Flavius for him who was kindly disposed, Gaius (i.e. Gaudius) for him who was joyful, Tiberius for him who was born beside the river Tiber, Titus for him who was descended from Tatius the Sabine, Appius for him who dwelt on the Appian (it is a famous road), Servius for the one who was saved though his mother died in her pregnancy, Nero for the one who was strong (from the Sabine dialect), Naso for the one who had a fine nose, Tucca for the one who ate flesh,[s] Varus and Blaesus for the person with mis-shapen legs, Serranus for the one who farmed (from the verb for

---

[s] The man in the street of our day has put the name Zikkas upon this fellow.

"sowing"), Augustus for him for whom the omens were good, Vitellius for the one who was golden-coloured in appearance,[t] Varro for the one who was Jewish according to the Phoenicians, or manly according to the Celts.

A man could gather many things of this nature together at his 23.3 leisure, if his lot should chance to be to live his life through in a carefree fashion without having work to do and if he did not indulge in the sort of foolish pastimes over which I toil away night and day, despite my being involved in countless worries!

Third Institution to be set up: the Quaestors.

The testimony of ancient sources confers credibility upon a 24.1 writer. Well, Junius Gracchanus in his work *On Authorities* speaks 24.2 in these words about the *quaestor*, as he is called among the Romans: "They were created by the vote of the people. After the 24.3 experience of these, the *rex* Tullus decided that the office of the quaestors was a necessary one. Consequently the majority of historians have ascribed to him alone the creation of this type of office. It was from their investigatory duties that the quaestors 24.4 acquired this name of theirs, according to Junius, Trebatius and Fenestella." And, after another passage: "Later however the 24.5 white-robed quaestors of the emperor were selected. These officials busied themselves solely with the reading of the imperial documents. They scrutinised in person even the decisions emanating from the whole body of the senate over the matter of people who were being advanced to positions of rank." This is 24.6 what Junius says; but the jurisconsult Ulpian, in his book *De Officio Quaestoris* (viz. "Concerning the Quaestor's Establishment") speaks at quite sufficient length about quaestors.

I think it is worth while making the enquiry as to what a 25.1 *quaestor*, as opposed to a *quaesitor*, is, and as to what the meaning of the word is when it is written with a diphthong, as opposed to that which is written simply.* Well, a quaestor is the 25.2

---

t The Romans call the yolk of an egg *vitellus*.

* Latin -ae- transliterates into Greek -ai- (e.g. quaestor to kuaistor). But in late Greek the -ai- diphthong sometimes was represented by an "e" sound; hence Lydus takes pains to distinguish quaero and queror later in this chapter.

one who makes investigations — from *quaerere* (i.e. to make
enquiries); what are known as Inspectors among Greeks were
termed *quaestores* among Romans. A *quaesitor* is the man who   25.3
exacts penalties. The former word is dissyllabic among Romans,
the latter trissyllabic. It is upon Minos the Cretan alone (him who   25.4
was believed to have become an avenging judge, according to the
myth, of the spirits in Hades) that the Roman poet has put the
name of *quaesitor* in the sixth book of the Aeneid. Hence   25.5
Romans decided to call judicial retribution *quaestio* and the
officials who administer the punishments *quaestionarii*. For the   25.6
quaestor is an investigator in money matters, whereas the official
with the name that is extended by the additional syllable
investigates legal charges. Both words will be written with a
diphthong (even if a treasurer is meant, because among Romans
assessable income is called *quaestus*). But when the word is not a   25.7
diphthong in its opening letters but is written with a simple
vowel, it means neither of the things mentioned but indicates, by
the way it is written, the querulous person who speaks words of
ill omen. For their word for "I find fault with" is *queror*, a
common verb indicative of a feeling of distress coupled with
doing something about it, and for "fault-finding" it is
"querimoniae" or *"querelae."*

So that I should not accidentally give the impression, by using   26.1
technicalities, of playing subtle tricks with the truth, let us learn
from those who have made these things their business. Well then,   26.2
the jurisconsult Gaius in the study that he wrote entitled *Ad
legem XII tabularum* (i.e. "On the Law of the Twelve Tables")
speaks as follows (his own words in translation: "When the public
treasury came to increase, quaestors were created to look after it,
getting their name from the acquisition and protection of its
monies. But since the magistrates were not allowed to pass   26.3
sentence against a Roman citizen where the death penalty was
concerned, *quaestores parricidii* were instituted, as it were, to
investigate and adjudicate on those who had slain citizens."
Romans call both the slayer of a parent and the slayer of a citizen   26.4
by the same name, parricide, for they term both of these
categories of people *parentes*. They make the following sort of   26.5
distinction concerning the latter term. By compressing the first
syllable and making it short they indicate a "parent," and by
lengthening it a "subject" is indicated.

I 27.1 —

In the two hundred and forty third year of the consular 27.1
epoch, in the consulships of Regulus and Junius, when the
Romans had decided to make war upon the allies of the Epeirote
Pyrrhus, a fleet was brought into being and the so-called *classici*
(i.e. naval commanders) were instituted, twelve quaestors,ᵘ as
paymasters and collectors of money as it were. This type of 27.2
practice in revenue collection was preserved both by the consuls
and by the praetors when on service outside the state boundaries.

It is an easy matter to find out about the quaestors attached 28.1
to the palace from the jurisconsult Ulpian. He speaks of them as
follows in his single volume book on the quaestor's
establishment: "However the *candidati Caesaris* were selected as
the quaestors, for they devoted themselves solely to the reading
out of the books in the senate and attended to the Emperors'
correspondence." "*Candidati*" is what the Romans usually call 28.2
people dressed in white. No one came to perform the reading,
whatever kind it was, and especially if it were in the presence of
the emperors, unless he was dressed in white. "*Candidati*" was 28.3
also the name for those who were intending to stand for office to
govern the provinces, because they too appeared in public dressed
in white, showing thereby that they wished to hold a magistracy.
As witness to this is anyone who is not unacquainted with Roman 28.4
history. The fact that no magistrate wore any other garb besides 28.5
that worn at festivals is very well known to everyone. And this
practice prevailed not in Rome alone but also in the provinces. I
myself remember personally, while the curial councils
administered the cities. When these were done away with, minor
varieties of customs slipped away along with the main practices.

Such was the number of magistrates that guided Rome's 29.1
affairs under the *reges* for the two hundred and forty three years
for which the *reges* ruled, according to the tradition of general
history. And after that the name of freedom shone forth as
though in darkness.

---

u I have already defined the difference between a *quaestor* and a *quaesitor*.

— 24 —

On the Consulship and the Official Regalia connected with it.

Greeks call the high and mighty *hypatoi,** not making out the   30.1
true significance of the name; for the word *consul*, as the nature
of the word has revealed to Latin speakers, indicates not the
highly placed but the president of a council. For Poseidon was   30.2
thought by them to be Consus, and the former was a clandestine
deity living below the surface of the sea and, as it has pleased the
poets to put it, an Earth-shaker and Earth-quaker. This term   30.3
"clandestine" means "something which has escaped notice."
From this point of view, councils and secret plans are called
consilia among Latin speakers, from *condere* (i.e. to hide); and
the man who hides his thoughts is called a *consul* from his taking
forethought and vigilant planning, keeping his own council, in the
public weal. Hence also the ancients' name for the festival known   30.4
as the "hippodrome festival" is "*Consualia*"; for legend speaks of
Poseidon as God of the horse race.

So much for the Latin name for the consuls. But there must   31.1
be some modest account of Brutus, since absolutely everyone
knows the names of those who were the first to become consuls.
Junius was the statesman's proper, personal name. People called   31.2
him Brutus, in the way they had of appending a *cognomen*, as a
result of the foolishness which he affected. For the Italians of old
spoke, in the language of their country, of the stupid man as
brutus — from the brutishness of his wits. This Brutus, as I said,   31.3
while play-acting at being a simpleton, was searching for an
opportunity of thrusting Tarquinius, who was the harshest tyrant
ever, from his position of authority. But while he was delaying in   31.4
Athens over the laws, in company with those whom the Romans
had sent along with him for this purpose, he kept asking the deity
to show him a way, and to participate with him in achieving this
aim, of deposing Tarquinius. The divine power gave him an oracle
stating that, if, when he set foot upon his native land, he were not
to stand on ceremony but to take his mother in his arms in a
hearty embrace, he would attain his goal. And in fact when he   31.5
returned to Rome and embraced the earth — which is mother of
everything — he did free Rome from tyranny, devising a

---

* The play on words cannot be reproduced as *hypatos* means "highest" as
an adjective and "consul" as a substantive.

magistracy known to no other people — even if Daniel, the most
holy of the Hebrew prophets, does record that there were once
consuls among the Assyrians. For he did not name them such in   31.6
the Hebraic tongue, as Aristaeus says. It was the translators,
represented in Ptolemaeus' work, of the holy scriptures who once
used the term *hypatoi* instead of "men of power" and "members
of the council." This though Rome's empire was not yet at that
time in evidence and attracting admiration from all because of the
novel greatness of that empire. So much for these matters; now   31.7
the symbols of consular office must be described.

Consuls wear a white toga that reaches to their feet and a   32.1
*colobus,** moderately girt up in comparison with the toga, with a
broad purple stripe; they have a distinctive purple stripe on either
shoulder, in the case of the toga, at the front; in that of the
colobus at the back too; and they have white sandals.ᵛ Also a   32.3
white kerchief worn on the right hand side and made out of linen
was official dress for the consuls. This they termed a *mappa* or
faciolis in the language of the country, because amongst them
facies is the name for the face. There were axes preceding them,   32.4
lifted on high; and a mass of men carrying rods, from which were
fastened thongs that had been dip-dyed scarlet, in memory of the
dictator Serranus. As a wood-cutter in the forests the latter
naturally carried an axe; with this and a rod fastened to the reins
so as to drive the oxen drawing his cart, he changed his abode to
assume office over the Romans, as Persius the Roman satyrist
says. Or the practice may also have been due to the fact that an
axe is indicative of power. In addition to these trappings there is a   32.5
chair — the Romans call it a *sella* — made of ivory. After his
election, with the consul seated on this the citizens used to put
longish poles beneath it and carry him.

In order that the consul's authority might not become   33.1
something that could not be made to yield (because of the power
being vested in one man), two consuls were created and only for a
year, as has been said, Brutus, the champion of liberty, and with

---

v [32.2] [Such a sandal, an] *aluta,* is the Roman name for the hide that
has been treated with alum, because amongst them this astringent is called
alumen.

* An outer garment without sleeves, a sleeveless tunic.

him Publicola — the name means "the demagogue." They had the authority to write laws and also to manage the wars at their own discretion, inasmuch as the management of the whole state had been firmly delegated to them. When Brutus' life came to an end   33.2 they honoured the corpse with public mourning and called their wives *Brutae* after him because of his modest way of life. The other consul, who still survived, was first to honour his fellow with a lament at the grave-side. The funeral oration is termed   33.3 *nenia* amongst them, a word of Greek rather [than Roman] derivation: for Greeks call the last of the chords on a lyre the *nete*.

Fifth Instititution to be created: the Ten Leading Men and the City Prefect.

Gaius the jurisconsult records after the magistracy of the   34.1 quaestors that of the ten-man board, in the following words (in translation): "A great deal of confusion concerning the laws, since these had not been set down in writing, took place in public affairs as result of the strife between the magistrates and the people. So, by a decision of senate and people together, all the magistrates were deposed and they handed over the task of taking care of the constitution to ten men alone." The latter, history   34.2 says, sent Spurius Postumius, Aulus Marcius and Publius Sulpicius to Athens. But as the mission lingered there for a period of three   34.3 years, until they might acquire the rest of the Athenian laws also for the Ten Tables, the people put forward ten men to manage affairs in their stead. The first of these was styled the Guardian of the City (the City Prefect, as we would put it). As official regalia   34.4 to denote his power he had twelve rods.* It was not so for the rest; they each had one and only one arms-bearer. But city   34.5 prefect had a staff of men dressed in togas, men to carry the *fasces*, fetters and all the other insignia of office that we are used to.[w] The Bureau of Works, which did not exist from the outset,   34.7 was assigned by Augustus to the magistracy when he built the basilica in Rome, as Suetonius, the man of letters, said.

---

w (34.6) This staff was maintained by those who owned fertile holdings. Hence they also got the name of "of the glebe," because the Romans call friable (i.e. fertile) land "glebe."

* The Latin word for these is *fasces,* a technical term which is employed from this point in the translation.

I 34.8 —

But when the magistrates whom I have mentioned became 34.8
puffed up with arrogance and began to live in a tyrannical
fashion, the people grew alarmed, quit the city and settled round
the hill called the Aventine.ˣ The people remained there biding 34.9
their time, out of resentment at very many things but especially
on account of Verginius and his daughter who had just then been
done grievous violence. But I think that the story is well known.

These men were magistrates — unless you are not prepared 35.1
also to count as magistrates the *pontifices* (i.e. chief-priests), as
they used to call them, who were wardens of temples. For it was
in response to their opinions and decisions that the men of
antiquity used to write their laws and regulate the prices of goods
on the market. Hence it is *aediles* that the clerks of the market
who regulate buying and selling are, as it happens, still called even
today, in accordance with the Roman name — *aedes* — for
temples. After the deposition of the kings and the institution of 35.2
the consuls, upon the occurrence of rioting, as has been stated by
the historians writing in the other language, for nearly fifty years
military tribunes took charge of affairs. Then the state went
through a troublesome period involving five years' anarchy. After
that it came to pass that three law-givers and judges were created
— for a brief time, as a result of the civil strife.

Sixth Institution: the so-called Dictatura.

So it was in this way that the Romans, with their affairs in 36.1
confusion, came to agree on creating the so-called *dictator*. For
"the rule of many is not a good thing." Now they were worried 36.2
by anxiety on two counts (whilst also being afraid of the name of
"king") — that they might unwittingly fall in with a new Tarquin
or be torn asunder by a multitude of quarrelling magistrates. And
that is why they decided, as has been stated, to create the
so-called *dictator* (i.e. *interrex*), his tenure of power being
circumscribed to six months only. And at this point it is, I feel, 36.3
proper to explain the name "*dictator*" for the Greeks. Well then, 36.4
in their native tongue the Romans so term the monarch for a
season, the one who is not created to put the affairs of his
subjects in order by the writing down of laws, inasmuch as he is

---

ˣ The place takes its name from one of the sons of Hercules, as the Roman
bard has related.

going to be stripped of his office in a short time. For a 36.5
dictatorship is what they call the power that is not absolute but
granted for a short time to effect the improvement of affairs, so
that, when affairs that were not in a state of calm have been put
to rights by the exercise of reason alone, thereafter the man who
has been advanced to the dictatorship returns again to his
previous station. For the *dictator* quitted his office immediately 36.6
he had attended to the parts of the body politic which had been
ailing.

Well, as first dictator the Romans appointed Titus Marcius, 37.1
who established two consuls as soon as he took over in office. He 37.2
did not however define a time at which the consular elections
should be held.ʸ He entrusted the honour of consular office to its 37.3
holders for a year only, since Romans everywhere are fond of
rotation of office. All of the symbols of position were the 37.4
dictator's, the crown excepted: the twelve axes, purple, throne,
spears and all the official regalia by which the *reges* used to be
distinguished. As first Master of Horse he created Spurius Cassius 37.5
as his lieutenant, just as Romulus had created Celerius tribune in
charge of the cavalry. There preceded him longish *fasces* without 37.6
crests, a practice which even nowadays, though not understood, is
still preserved. When the generals of the cavalry journey forth, 37.7
they are no longer preceded by their lictors as of old; the custom
is for one ensign, in the rear, to bind longish *fasces* up into a
uniform shape and carry them (and he does not know the reason
for carrying them but is just following custom). All of the 37.8
magistracies of the state were under the power of the Master of
Horse, and it was not allowable for anyone, while the Master was
holding trials, to move for an appeal against him. But none of the 37.9
dictators held on to the power of this monarchy for more than
six months, often, in fact, for much less, even for one single day.
It is no difficult task to recall the particulars of the individual 37.10
dictators, both in regard to how many there were and as to how
long they existed.

First as dictator was Titus Marcius, the man who advanced the 38.1
men who had been consuls before him, Titus and Valerius, to the
consulship once again. When a disturbance of the peace took

ʸ The election of a consul in the month of January is a practice of later
date.

place and the consuls abdicated, the dictator created others in
their stead on the first of September. In the seventeenth year of   38.2
consular government, when a major conflict occurred between
the senate and the populace, the multitude created two tribunes.
The sequel was that these were arbiters for the common people
and controlled the market. These tribunes, puffed up with
insolence, had the effrontery to carry measures against the very
patricians themselves. In the twenty-third year of the rule of the   38.3
consuls, the *imperium* was split into three parts, between the
consuls, the city prefect, and the populace. The consuls
administered the wars, the populace served on the campaigns, but
the prefect, with the name *custos urbis* ("Guardian of the City"
as it were), protected the city. In the twenty-eighth year of the   38.4
rule of the consuls, when the populace and the senate were at
variance, Aulus Sempronius was nominated dictator. After
appointing Gaius Julius from the senate and Quintus Fabius from
the populace as consuls, he laid down his dictatorship. Again, in   38.5
the forty-eighth year of the consuls a dictator, Gaius Mamercus,
was created. But when the populace began being restive once   38.6
more, three military tribunes were created. When they set affairs
tossing and turning, Titus Quinctius was nominated dictator. In a
mere thirteen days he laid his office aside with the conflict
quieted. In the seventy-fourth year of consular government, when
the Etruscans were disturbing the commonwealth, because of the
importance assumed by the war there was a dictator — Marcus
Aemilius — nominated. After him, Publius was nominated and he
laid his office aside within a mere sixteen days, after having
brought the war against the Etruscans under control. When the
populace again created military tribunes and the senate opposed
this, Quintus was nominated dictator. He effected a reconciliation
within the city in eight days and then terminated his office. After
him came Publius Cornelius Cossus, and after him Titus
Quinctius.

After the one hundred and thirty-sixth year of consular   38.8
government, at the beginning of the one hundred and third
Olympiad, the city underwent a time of anarchy that lasted for a
period of five years. When consuls were once again elected, there   38.9
were instituted, from among the patricians, four aediles, two
quaestors, a praetor (i.e. a general), *legati* (i.e. lieutenant
generals), and twelve military tribunes, because of the fact that it

was expected that Alexander of Macedon would make an
expedition against Rome. In a panic the Romans voted that   38.10
Papirius Carbo as praetor should meet Alexander, and created
augurs and *pontifices*. It is a clear sign of expectation of defeat
when those with war in prospect take refuge in prayers. In the   38.11
two hundred and sixty-third year another praetor was instituted,
the so-called *praetor urbanus* (the latter is their word for "civil")
and the so-called *peregrinus* (i.e. one who looks after strangers). It
was when the people were divided up into four factions and
thirty-five wards that three further praetors were added to those
recorded above. In the two hundred and ninetieth year of   38.12
consular government, when Hannibal darted in upon Italy, on
account of the seriousness of the war, there was set up not only a
dictator but a pro-dictator too, a Master of Horse and
counter-vailing Master of Horse, with the idea that, with another
of them to follow his colleague's decision, he should not bring
ruin upon the state out of individual self-will.

These are the only dictators or *interreges* recorded by Roman   38.13
history. After them Gaius Julius Caesar, after embarking on the
war against the senate and Pompey that was so deadly in its
effects upon the commonwealth, constituted himself sole ruler by
his own act, employing Lepidus as Master of Horse.

The Censorship

From the beginning the populace, in fact quite simply the   39.1
whole citizen body, used to go out on campaigns, even the priests
themselves going forth against the enemy. Everyone kept himself   39.2
in food. Accordingly, it became necessary for the Romans to
create what was called among them censors, officials who
registered the wealth of the citizenry with a view to expenditure
incurred in war. For the treasury did not up to this point furnish
the soldiery with supplies for war as it does nowadays, as it did
not have tax-payers up till this time. This is the reason why Greek   39.3
translates *censor* as "assessor."

At this point it was that Titinius the Roman comic poet put a   40.1
play on the stage at Rome. Plays were divided into types,   40.2
[tragedy and comedy; of these tragedy is itself divided into two
types,] the *crepidata* and the *praetextata*. Of these the *crepidata*

has a Greek, the *palliata* a Roman theme. Comedy divides into   40.3
seven types: *palliata*, *togata*, Atellane, *tabernaria*, Rinthonian,
planipedaria and miming. A *palliata* is the comedy with a Greek
theme, a *togata* is the one with a Roman theme, set in ancient
times. An Atellane comedy is the one put on by the so-called
exodiarii; a *tabernaria* is a comedy which is presented on a stage
or in a theatre; a Rinthonian comedy is the play with a foreign
origin; a *planipedaria* is named after the dress worn; a miming
comedy is the only one that is preserved today; it contains no
artistry and moves the multitude by mere slapstick.

Since my feeling is that it is necessary not to hasten over the   41.1
account, I will add this point too. Rhinthon, Sciras, Blaesus and   41.2
the other playwrights we know to have been men who expounded
teachings of no small importance in lower Italy, and especially
Rinthon, who was the first man to write a comedy in hexameters.
It was by taking him as his starting point that the Roman Lucilius
first wrote a comedy in heroic verse. After him and those who   41.3
followed him, whom Romans term satyrists, the new school,
which strove after the characteristics of Cratinus and Eupolis,
employed Rinthon's metres and the biting wit of those
mentioned above and established satyric comedy more firmly.
Horace, who did not go beyond the formal rules, and Persius,
who wished to imitate the poet Sophron, surpassed the faint
reputation of Lycophron. Turnus, Juvenal and Petronius violated   41.4
the laws of satire by indulging incontinently in abusive attacks.

So much for ancient comedy and tragedy.   42.1

With Fortune's causing Rome's affairs to prosper mightily, as
consequence, as you would expect, came faults and, in particular,
profligate behaviour. As result, after the legislation of the Twelve
Tables, Rome also enacted the law concerning profligate
behaviour, a law established at Corinth of old. Title or heading of
the law was *De nepotibus*, i.e. "Concerning Profligates." As the   42.2
meaning of this word in Latin has two-fold significance,[z] I would
like briefly to indicate the difference. *Nepos* ("the youthful son")   42.3
is a name derived from the Greek for grandson, as Philoxenus has
well said. But *nepos* is also a name for "a profligate," and this
usage too is figurative. In an investigation perhaps one ought to   42.4

---

z For they call both grandsons and profligates alike *nepotes*.

concede to the Greeks that in their native tongue the Romans call the scorpion *nepa*, i.e. "that has been deprived of its feet," [a] as a result of that which, in the course of nature, happens to the beast. For in the winter season the scorpion, as you would 42.5 expect, himself too, like the other reptiles, lies in the earth overcome with torpor, eating nothing but the earth. Well, when 42.6 he has exhausted all the edible earth around him on himself, the scorpion fastens upon his own legs and devours them all without feeling it. When spring summons him up, along with the other 42.7 insects, to the light of day in accordance with the laws of nature, he grows new feet and, going to the mint plant, by merely touching its herbage, recovers his savage sting and up comes his tail to cover him from above, just as is the case with a snake and fennel.[b] For these reasons the Romans call spendthrifts* *nepotes* 42.8 — those who as it were ruin their own limbs.

Such is the sort of thing that, in an aside from my objective, I 43.1 would say about this subject.

The censors were, as it happened, pretty severe and ruthless, being both relentless and unyielding in their ways, to profligates; position in society and rank did not rescue the guilty. Of the 43.2 truth of this contention history is witness, and she says: "Appius Claudius was first to be created censor. This magistracy was 43.3 among the most important. Its duties were to investigate and also to pass judgement on the lives led by the citizenry, and to apply punishment, with power to do anything, to those who sinned. No one was outside the range of the censor's authority." The censors 43.4 were also responsible for seeing to the city's amenities through public works.

---

a For Romans use the syllable *"ne-"* in a negative fashion as do Greeks with *nelipos, nechytos, negretos, nedymos.* [I.e. barefoot, full-flowing, unwaking, sweet (the second and fourth terms are not instances of the usages posited) — Ed.]

b Hence Romans call mint *nepeta.*

* Lydus employs the term *scorpistes* to convey the sense spendthrift; as with the term for "ruin" (*diaphthoreus* — corrupter and consumer of), it is charged with two meanings simultaneously, but these cannot be translated by one English word in the former case.

Tribunate

Well, with the censors troubling the populace and proceeding   44.1
somewhat sharply against the citizenry, and since the
money-lenders were particularly inexorably disposed in their
dealings with debtors, the people created two tribunes in its own
interests, Gaius Licinius and Lucius Albinus, to act as arbitrators
for the multitude and supervise the market. These tribunes wore   44.2
short swords at their belts and had publicly-owned slaves to
attend upon them. They used to call these *vernaculi*.c Over this   44.3
matter the populace went beyond the bounds of moderation; it
ordained by law that even the patricians themselves should be
summoned to trial by the vulgar. As a sequel the consul, wooing
the mob, brought in a law that the magistrates should not be
allowed to punish* a citizen without a decision on the part of the
tribune.

Then, when once again the leading citizens were at variance   45.1
with the multitude, by a decision taken in common they removed
the consuls and entrusted the reviewing of the common interests
to ten legislators. From the sixtieth year of consular government   45.2
for fifty years public affairs were in confusion, what with the
creation, at one time of military tribunes, and at another of
interreges. Then the treasury for the first time distributed to the   45.3
soldiery, who formerly used to maintain themselves in wartime, a
monthly allowance on a definite basis. From this point the state   45.4
had the misfortune to undergo anarchy for a period of five years.
Once again consuls were created, then four aediles from the
patricians and two quaestors and the one praetor; and the
populace in turn created five augurs and four *pontifices*. In the   45.5
two hundred and sixty-third year under the consuls the other
praetor was created so that he could provide arbitration for
foreigners. The praetors did not exceed an annual term in office.   45.6
Up to the time of Caesar consuls administered warfare and the   45.7
civil magistrates looked after home affairs.

---

c The name indicates slaves who have been born within the household.

* There is some disingenuousness in Lydus' wording, the neutral "punish"
being selected (instead e.g. of "execute" or "scourge") to show popular
action the more unfavourably.

When were the so-called capita *first distributed to the soldiery and what is the meaning of the name* capitum?

In the city's three hundred and sixty-fifth year, under the consuls Lucius Genucius and Quintus Servilius, when the Romans were engaged in war with their neighbour Veii, it became necessary for them not merely to carry on through the summer but actually to spend the winter also alongside their enemies. This was when it was first decided that the treasury would make provision for the soldiers to meet expenditure on horses as well, by means of the so-called *capita.*d As the populace from the first used to go on campaign en masse, they decided to form a force of troops that would have definite organized sections and be in a state of preparedness: there were to be tactical units of three hundred shield-bearing infantry (they call them cohorts), *alae* — their word for troops of horse* — of six hundred cavalry, *vexillationes* of five hundred cavalry, *turmae* of five hundred mounted archers and legions of six thousand infantry and a specified force of cavalry.

46.1

46.2

Detachments in the legions are as follows:*   46.3

alae of six hundred troopers;
vexillationes of five hundred troopers;
turmae of five hundred mounted archers;
legions of six thousand infantry.
Tribunes (commanders of units from the electoral wards);   46.4
ordinarii (corps-commanders);
signiferi (standard bearers);
optiones (special duties or clerical staff);

---

* The Greek word used would be transliterated as *ilae.* In this account Lydus anachronistically attributes to the Republican army formations which only emerged under the Empire, at this point and in what follows.

* On these terms, see J. Marquardt, *De l'organisation militaire chez les Romains,* 1891.

** *Two leaves are missing from the MS; the greater part of the following discussion on praetors has thus been lost.*

d Such was their name for the baskets made out of switches — from *capere,* i.e. *"to contain."* Hence, using a diminutive form, the Romans speak of
d Such was their name for the baskets made out of switches — from *capere,* i.e. "to contain." Hence, using a diminutive form, the Romans speak of *"capitula"* in their native tongue.

vexillarii (ensigns);
mensores (camp-surveyors);
tubicines (trumpeters for the infantry);
bucinatores (trumpeters for the cavalry);
cornicines (horn-blowers);
andabatae (troops completely armoured in mail);
metatores (land-surveyors);
arquites and *sagittarii* (archers and arrow-bearers);
praetoriani (men under the command of the Praetorian Prefect);
lanciarii (javelin-throwers);
decemprimi (decemvirs);
veneficialii (men assigned to give medical attention to the veterans);
torquati (collar-bearers; those who wear the necklace);
bracchiati or *armilligeri* (men who wear bracelets);
armigeri (weapon-bearers);
munerarii (men who give gladiatorial displays);
deputati (men who have been appointed for a specific task);
auxiliarii (shield-bearers);
cuspatores (military police).[e]
Imaginiferi (image-bearers); 46.5
ocreati (infantry with their calves covered in steel greaves);
armatura prima (light armour, first class);
armatura semissalia (light armour, superior class);
hastati (spear-bearers);
tesserarii (the men who make the pass-words known to the mass of the troops at the time when the pass-word is due);
draconarii (standard bearers);
adiutores (adjutants);
samiarii (those who polish the weapons);
vaginarii (scabbard-makers);
arcuarii (bow-makers);
pilarii (javelin-men);
verutarii (quoit throwers);
funditores (slingers);
ballistarii (artillery-men).[f]

---

e For Romans call logs of wood tied to the feet *cuspi, custodes pedum* as it were — i.e. stocks and foot-fetters.

f A *catapeltes* is a form of engine for sieges, and is called a "Wild Ass" by the generality.

Vinearii (men who man the mantlets in attacking a wall);   46.6
primoscutarii (those who cover their fellows with their shields;
they are termed *protectores* nowadays);
primosagittarii (archers, first class);
clibanarii (soldiers clad all in mail).g
Flammularii (those upon the tips of whose spears strips of   46.7
crimson cloth are fastened);
expediti (men girt up for action, stripped down, ready for battle);
ferentarii (mounted javelineers);
circitores (those who circle round the troops while they are
fighting and supply them with arms, since they are not yet
knowledgeable enough to do battle);
adoratores (veteran *tirones*, concerning whom a detailed
exposition is, I think, necessary).

*Adorates*h is the Roman name for honorably discharged   47.1
soldiers and *veterani* is their name for those who have grown old
under arms. Witnesses to this are Celsus, Paternus and Catiline
(not the conspirator but another) and, before these, the first Cato
and Frontinus; after these comes Renatus. These are all Romans.
Among Greek writers are Aelian, Arrian, Aeneas, Onesander,
Patron, and Apollodorus in his *Siege Operations*; and after them
come the Emperor Julian in his *Science of Mechanics*i and the
famous Claudian, the poet from Paphlagonia, in the first book of
his laudatory odes on Stilicho. *Tirones* is what they call the lowly   47.2
— such as are, as it happens, the so-called Triballi in our day. This
was how Arrian described the Bessi in his work on Alexander. For   47.3
it is because of poverty and nothing else that the so-called *tirones*
give themselves to become the servants of those who serve as
proper soldiers. They are emphatically not worthy, at this stage in
their careers, to be called soldiers or fully to be classed in the
category of soldiers at this point, both because of the beggarliness
of their position in the community and their lack of battle skill
and experience. For none but the well born were allowed to fight

---

g The Romans call iron coverings *celibana,* a variant of *celamina.*

h For *adorea* amongst them is the name for fame gained in war, deriving
from the wheat given as a mark of respect at one time to those whom they
honoured.

i Of which Frontinus makes mention in his *De officio legati,* i.e. *On
Generalship.*

in battle for their native land. Diodorus, indeed, in the second 47.4
book of his *Historical Library*, says that Solon enacted for the
Athenians a law of the following nature, which he had learned in
Egypt: that their body politic should be arranged in three parts —
into that of the well born, who busied themselves with
philosophy and literature; second section was that of the farmers
and warriors together, and the third that of the artisans and
industrial workers. The section of the community that came after
these was held in no honour. From it the more useful,
presumably, served their time amongst the good farmers and the
valorous warriors, being taught how to make war and to farm
while they were subject to the latter. Men of this sort were called
tirones by people in Italy, the term deriving from the distresses
and suffering experienced in being subject to another man.* As 47.5
the Romans emulated Athens in everything, they too arranged
their populace in this fashion. This is also the reason why they 47.6
called their tribal wards *tribus*, the word coming from the
distribution of the body politic into three parts.

These troops were brigaded as an additional force, some of the 48.1
historians assert, by Marius — the one who later became a tyrant.
Those who from the outset were in the train of the Master of 48.2
Horse, all alike received the styling of *promoti*, being
systematically organised into four ranks of position: *biarchi,
ducenarii, centuriones* and *centenarii*** ....

....

" . . . . from all of these, ten tribunes, two consuls, eight praetors 48 (3)
and six aediles alone remained to manage the city." Such is 48 (4)
Pomponius' account, which, it appears, shuns the multitude and
diversity of historical facts. Ulpian however, in his work entitled 48 (5)
The Protribunalia, has gone in detail right through the accounts
which concern the praetors, terming some of them "tutelary,"
others *fideicommissarii*. Since these matters have already been
studied once, I have decided not to record them in my account.

---

* The etymology cannot be brought out in English; it depends on the
words *tiro* — which Lydus here spells as *teiro* — and *teiresthai,* "to suffer
distress."

**Two leaves are missing from the MS; the greater part of the following
discussion on praetors has thus been lost.

All this number of magistrates from the beginnings of the 49.1
Roman state down to Titus' most mild reign are, I have found,
recorded in the history books. So I will put an end to my account
of them. For I have decided not to record mention of Domitian's 49.2
twelve city prefects and certainly not of the revolutionary
changes brought in by Bassianus (also known as Caracalla).
Features that are introduced by emperors who have ruled badly
must be given scant attention, even if the features are good by
general standards.

Concerning the Prefect of the Night Watch

The Treveri, a Gallic people, who dwelled by the banks of the 50.1
Rhine (where, too, the city of Treveri is situated),ʲ once, in the
time of Brennus, as they wandered here and there through the
Alps, were brought out into Italy through the trackless,
thorn-covered wastelands, as Vergil says. Thereupon, by actually 50.2
coming through the sewers, they seized Rome and even the
Capitol itself. This was the occasion on which, when the geese in
the temple had been alarmed by the appearance of the barbarians
in the dead of night, the general Mallius on being awakened — he
was near the geese — thrust the barbarians from the Capitol and
laid it down that the Romans were to hold a festival and
chariot-racing in honour of the geese, whereas the dogs were to be
done to death when the sun was in conjunction with Leo in the
zodiac. As result of these things' happening in this way at that 50.3
time there was a law laid down — the one which brought into
existence the keepers of the night watches. And, so far as length 50.4
of time of establishment is concerned, I ought to have made
mention of these officials before now. But since it is not
customary to number this department among the magistracies of
the state and since the organization and corps of officials was
really devised for its servicing functions, it was reasonable to put
it on one side, at any rate until some sort of final stage of the
discussion on the magistracies. These men do not merely keep the 50.5
city unharmed by attack or stealthy onset on the part of a foe
and free from disturbance from mischief originating within the
city's own population, but they also aid those whose property is

---

ʲ In our day the people of Italy call them Sygambri, the Gauls call them
Franks.

being damaged by an outbreak of fire. Witness to this is the   50.6
jurisconsult Paul, who puts it like this (his own words, in
translation): "the three-man organization was created by the
ancients to deal with out-breaks of fire. They were actually
spoken of as 'the nocturnals' from the facts of the situation.
Both the aediles and tribunes associated with them and made a   50.7
college (another way of saying organization) which resided by the
city gates and walls, so that, if the need for it summoned, they
were easily found and assembled at speed." Such is Paul's   50.8
account. That the account is a true one, can be seen even today,   50.9
since incidents of this nature are always happening throughout
the city: those of them who by chance have been found in time,
shout out in the ancestral language of the Romans *"omnes
collegiati!"* — that is to say "All members of the company
assemble at the double!"

By the time these institutions had been brought into being in   51.1
this way, the city's seven hundred and sixth year had gone by,
and Caesar as sole ruler brought all the magistracies to a stop and
took upon himself alone the powers that had been wielded by the
whole set of magistracies. After lasting for three years, Caesar   51.2
himself was struck down in the senate; but thereupon his place as
Caesar was assumed by the young man who was his nephew, after
whose reign control devolved upon the Caesars.

BOOK TWO

On Caesar and Caesar's Official Regalia.

Those who venture upon tyranny at any time are not only a   1.1
disgrace to their own times but also a source of ruin for posterity,
since they leave behind for the citizenry those who eagerly aspire
to evil. For instance, after the assistance of Marius' having set   1.2
himself up as tyrant, Sulla rose up and became a tyrant in
opposition. As result of their conflicts with one another, the
Roman state, which was the object over which the tyrants were
quarrelling, was mangled. Marius, at the outset, had the upper   1.3
hand over the Sullan forces. But, as chance was eager to make
away with both of them, first one, then the other kept winning to
power. The result was complete destruction for each of them.
Marius, upon being worsted, was cut to pieces by Sulla, whereas   1.4
Sulla perished miserably, from an infestation of worms which
burst out on him, after his victory — getting nothing out of the
victory but the styling "Fortunate." While Sulla was still alive   1.5
Pompey came to associate with him, was highly impressed by him
and became his son-in-law, taking his daughter Antistia in
marriage, and was completely Sulla's man. Though he was in the   1.6
beginning struck with passion for Pompey, by the time that his
daughter Julia[a] had died, Caesar embraced the opposite faction,
began to do honour to Marius, and was captivated by his ways.
Well, they were both brought into conflict with one another as   1.7
though they were heirs of the tyrants. Every people that existed
in the East was with Pompey; all the barbarians that lived towards
the setting sun and the North were on the side of Caesar — and of
his army at the same time. The sequel is well known.

---

a He had, as it happened, given her in marriage to Pompey.

Caesar became master of all. When he went up to Rome, in his   2.1
triumph over three hundred captive kings, he did not consent to
accept the styling of king — though what could be more
splendid? — or rather of any monarch. He sought some other
honour, and one that fortune had not known. For, as he was   2.2
driving from the Capitol to the Senate after his triumph, one of
his army officers ran out and, without his foreknowledge, set a
crown about his temples. Caesar seized it with his own hands and
hurled it off, exclaiming angrily, as though supposing that he
would undergo outrage if he, who had enslaved so many kings
and taken lady luck herself captive, should be called king. Full of   2.3
his good fortune in this fashion, he grudgingly consented to be
styled at one and the same time God, High Priest, Consul, Sole
Ruler in Perpetuity, First Citizen in Rome and Guardian of Kings
Everywhere, Master of Horse, Father of the Fatherland, General,
Protector of the City and Foremost among the Tribunes. He put
on raiment indicative of all these titles. Its name was the
triumphal regalia — and it was no easy matter to invent a name
for the garments that would have so many shades of meaning. It   2.4
was a tunic, of purple within, all gold on its outer surface, as
though composed of beaten gold. It had a *lorus* on its upper parts
— this is the name by which Romans like to call gold-work
shoulder straps. After his example the custom prevailed that the   2.5
Roman Emperors should wear this garb whenever they triumph
over captive kings. This was well illustrated in our own day when
Gelimer the king of the Vandals and of Libya with his whole
nation was made by God a prisoner of war for our empire. For it   2.6
could not be that the victor should be dressed in a like fashion to
the vanquished — who was wearing the purple.

For three years Fortune laughed at such acts of insolence in   2.7
Caesar. Then Nature convinced him that he was mortal.

After him Octavian, who was his nephew by his sister, Atia by   3.1
name, and his adopted child, inherited the honoured position of
emperor. He requested not to be styled a god, but rather
"divine," presumably from pious modesty, and this honorific
styling was conferred upon all of his successors. One styling is the   3.2
perquisite of those who are sons by blood, the other of those who
become so by adoption, the title being conferred upon emperors
for honorific purposes — or rather for purposes of blasphemous

flattery. But he was not for the moment able to employ the   3.3
official regalia which the mighty Caesar had employed, primarily
because he had Antony and Lepidus as partners in his position of
command. He was quite young and wearing the *bulla*, as it was   3.4
called by the Romans,b when he was thought worthy of the title
of Caesar. It is from this that even now those who are being   3.5
promoted to the throne do not have the insignia of this office
conferred upon them until the army commanders, by putting a
necklace round the candidate's neck, declare him worthy of the
throne, demonstrating that he is a Caesar just like the young
Caesar and worthy of the honour and styling of the first Caesar.
For, just as there is a Persian custom to advance the child born of   3.6
the king to rule over them, so there was of old a Roman custom
not to put imperial power into the hands of any chance person
but only into those of the descendants of Caesar's line.

Well, the young Caesar was in an ambivalent position, neither   3.7
having possession of the entire honour conferred by imperial
power (because of his partners in office) nor, of course, without
his share, but having the advantage over them given by the name
Caesar which his uncle had conferred upon him before he died,
after resolving to leave him as his heir. When Lepidus died and   3.8
Antony inclined towards Cleopatra, spurning Fulvia, the sister of
the young Caesar, who had been living in wedlock with him up to
that point, he took Egypt and Antony with it, and put a stop to
Rome's internal strife. Thereupon he too became filled with his
own importance and assumed the styling of god — he who but
lately used to act with moderation. He accepted temples that
were dedicated in his honour and appointed a Chief-priest as
though he had forced his way into the ranks of the gods, after
appointing himself to be foremost among the priests of the gods
who were believed in at that time. He employed all the official
regalia which his father had employed, and all the troops and
staff establishments and bodyguards that Romulus and all who
came after him up to that point had employed, with only one
change — that of Master of Horse to Prefect. The Prefect he
honoured with a sumptuous chariot made of silver, and he
assigned a staff of civilians to serve under him, calling them
Augustales after himself. I will speak of these men shortly after
this, in the section on the staff establishment of the prefects.

---

b I.e. a gem.

However, he treated the citizenry mildly, so that the Romans 3.9
said of him in their native tongue: *utinam nec natus nec mortuus
fuisset.* For they used to wish that he had not been born because
he and he alone firmly established the rule of the Caesars; and
likewise, they wished he had never died, because of his mildness
and at the same time because of his abrogation of the civil wars.
For after him no civil war was kindled.

He used to wear the garb, in time of peace, of a *pontifex* — 4.1
the name stands for chief priest, connected with bridges — of
purple, reaching to the feet, priestly, ornamented with gold, and a
cloak likewise of purple, which had pleats of gold at its
extremities. He used to cover his head, for the reasons which I
gave in the treatise *"On the Months"* which I have written. For 4 (2)
the wars he wore *paludamenta*: these are scarlet mantles of
double thickness, spun from top-quality raw silk, caught up at the
shoulders by a golden brooch inset with precious stones. We call
this a *fibula* as Italians do, but people in the palace even
nowadays speak of it, with a sort of special term, as a *cornucopia.*
At festivals he would wear the *limbus* — this is a purple cloak 4 (3)
which covers the body down to the feet, with a Meander pattern;
on the shoulders it has a brilliant array of golden *tabulamenta* —
that is to say material woven into piping — and a *paragauda*
embroidered with a golden letter gamma (in other words a tunic
with little "gamma" figures in gold embroidered upon it); from
the border at the feet and the bottom end of the garment, on
both sides these little figures trick out the tunic with gold to form
a letter gamma. In the senate he would wear a mantle of purple 4 (4)
(of course) and, at the edge of the border near the wearer's feet,
bedecked with outlined squares of pure gold — the court
functionaries call these squares *"segmenta"* instead of "gold
hemline embroideries"; the generality call those on the mantles of
private individuals *"sementa."* This mantle is "bracteolate,"
gemosa and "lanceolate" (words for covered with gold plaques,
set with precious stones and ornamented with embroidered
spear-heads). He also wore the rest of the emperor's official
regalia, concerning which I presume a detailed description to be
excessive and so I omit it, since the narrative leads me next, in the
interests of order, to a description of what was once the first of
offices.

Concerning the Praetorian Prefecture.

One could find sufficient evidence of the distinction of the 5.1
office, and of the fact that it came second in importance to the
throne alone, even in the mere murky shadow which is all that it
seems nowadays to preserve. For it is in the nature of mighty
institutions that they can be comprehended even from their
ruined state itself. Time is dreadfully adept at eating away and 5.2
bringing down things whose lot is to have a beginning and an end
as well. But the emperor's excellence is so great that institutions 5.3
that have come to ruin in the past are eagerly awaiting a rebirth
by his intervention.

Well, the magistracies developed in the way I have already 6.1
described until the period of dominance attained by the first
Caesar. The latter, coming with Fortune's help to control affairs,
radically changed the entire organisation of the state, leaving the
consuls nothing but the name, as an indication of chronology
presumably. Assigning the entire army to be subject to his own
command, he gave his successors the choice of bringing to an end
any wars that cropped up either by their own efforts — but only
if they should not prefer a life of ease — or through the agency of
generals of their own choice, or through that of delegate-generals
(called "legates" by the Romans). Only to the Master of Horse,
who was Lepidus during Caesar's sole rule, did he leave power
with a larger sphere of authority. After him Caesar Octavianus, as
has been stated, appointed this official as his Prefect, not merely
controlling the court but also an entire army and a staff of
civilians which he had not disposed of before. In a short time the
expression became perverted as result of careless usage and he
came to be called *hyparch* instead of *hipparch*. At Rome — where 6.2
alone it is the custom to call the court the palace — he came to be
customarily called Caesar's Prefect, as being next in standing after
the emperor; on the other hand in the *castra* (this was the
customary Roman name for encampments struck in a war) it was
Praetorian Prefect, i.e. officer in charge of the *praetorium*. It was
their practice to call the general's quarters struck on enemy
territory the *praetorium*, even if by chance the emperor himself
should happen to bivouac there. Moreover I have found a 6.3
compelling reason to explain why the title "Praetorian" was also
added to the styling of the prefect. It was so that the magistracy

should be one of those which had some specific sphere of authority, and that it should not seem to have a preeminence that was not indicated by a name and be synonymous with the city commander (who also, it has already been demonstrated, was called a prefect, being styled the *praetor urbanus* previously). Further, while dedicating his *Lives of the Caesars* in his writings to Septicius (who was prefect to the praetorian cohorts in his day), Suetonius shows that the latter was at the time prefect of the praetorian brigades and leader of the battle array. Consequently, one might take it that the prefect of the court (which I have shown to be often termed *praetorium* too) has been well named not only in the singular but also in the plural. For not only is he termed prefect of the *praetorium* but also prefect of the praetorians, i.e. commander of the praetorian sc. "brigades," or "cohorts," or "armies" or "forces." 6.4

Well, you would not be out of order in giving the above as reasons for the styling conferred upon the office, which is a sort of ocean of state business, 7.1
"from which flow all rivers and every sea."
For the other official bodies of the constitution clearly stand in relation to this one, which is truly the magistracy of magistracies, somewhat as sparks do to a raging fire. Without it they would never have been able even to exist; and likewise neither they 7.2 themselves, nor of course those which function beneath them as a sort of as it were establishment, would be able to maintain their coordination, if the prefecture were not to provide the expenses for the offices themselves and those who direct them. Here is a 7.3 parable: a man has a magnificent bowl, made out of silver, which has come into his possession not as result of his own initiative but from his ancestors. Now, being gradually drawn into poverty, he breaks it up, thinking little of its strength and beauty; and, fashioning many a fragile little pots out of it, he fancies having a great deal of silver of a cheap nature rather than a magnificent antique piece in one piece. In the same way, with the greatest office broken up, many a — perhaps unnecessary — office has sprung up, fortune having become rather displeased with the poet who said:
"The rule of many is not a good thing:
let there be one ruler."

For the so-called army commanders possess the honorific 7.4
position of *comes*, of long standing and as their sole distinction.
Hence antiquity knew men holding secondary army commands as
comitiani also. Italians call friends who accompany one abroad 7.5
comites and the emperor's entourage is called by the one word
comitatus. The department of the so-called *magister* is not an 7.6
office of such standing, but is a very important one nonetheless
and ranks high near that of the prefect in distinction and power. I
will speak of it towards the end of this historical account. For, as
it is of more recent origin, it ought not to be reckoned in with the
senior offices but given the placing which time has assigned it.

Notwithstanding this, the consulship as an honour has 8.1
achieved a transcendent position and has surpassed all
magistracies. In power it is inferior to the prefecture but in
prestige it is superior. For the latter magistracy administers the
whole state, providing nothing from its incumbents' own
resources but seeing to the distribution of public resources. But
the former pours forth abundant wealth upon the citizenry like
snow-flakes, from private resources, and gives its name to the
year, keeping contracts from going astray; as to the rest, it does
not undertake warfare but is the mother, as it were, of Roman
liberty. For it is opposed to tyranny and while that prevails, does 8.2
not support it. And that is why Brutus, the avengor of chastity
and champion of freedom, caused the honour of the consulship
to flash forth while simultaneously Tarquinius the tyrant
perished. Our father and at the same time most gentle emperor is
a consul, for as long as he acts as one, for setting matters to rights
and conferring gifts upon the citizenry; he becomes a consul in
garb, whenever he consents to adorn an occasion, defining
consular honour as a rank superior to that of emperor.

According to what has been previously stated, it was to the 9.1
throne alone, from the beginning, that the prefecture yielded
pride of place, getting a meed of honour equal to that of the
throne. This fact can be inferred directly from the emperor's
position. For when the council is being convened — of old in the 9.2
so-called "senate" (council of the elders, as it were), nowadays in
the palace — the foremost men of the armies there represented,
advancing some considerable distance from their proper seats,
acknowledge the prefecture by falling to their knees. And the

prefecture deems those that approach it as worthy of a kiss, so that it may serve the army. Caesar himself, that is to say the emperor of the Romans, leaves the palace and approaches on foot, in person acknowledging the prefect. When the emperor has gone in and is closeted with the prefect, total security measures prevail, which allow no magistrate to go within after the prefect, nor, even when the meeting has broken up, do they allow any member of the council to withdraw before the prefect. This 9.3 practice was firmly preserved until the time of Theodosius The Young. The latter, as he was young and lacked the strength to do honour to the prefecture by going forward in person as was customary, set up a statue and ordained that the image instead of himself would acknowledge the prefect.c The urban prefect too 9.5 receives this honour, being considered worthy of equal honour because of the similarity of his styling to that of the senior magistrate. The prefect used to wear a sword at his belt from the 9.6 beginning, as he would, having authority over arms too. This can be found out with your own eyes here and now, if you are fond of antiquities and cross over to Chalcedon and closely examine the statue of the prefect Philip. Romans call the sword worn 9.7 under the belt the *sica*, whence butchers are called *sicarii* and the food made from flesh that is cut up fine is called *sicata*.

But "everything fated to begin has an end," in the poetic 10.1 adage. For when Constantine — and Fortune too — had gone 10.2 from Rome, and after the forces which used to guard the Danube had been scattered about lower Asia by a decision of the emperor, the treasury suffered the loss of Scythia and Moesia and the revenues from those provinces, because the barbarians from over the Danube, with no-one to withstand them, swept down on Europe. With the peoples of the East burdened with immoderate taxation contrary to long-standing practice, it came to be necessary for the prefect no longer to exercise control over the court and the forces under arms (the former was handed over to the so-called Master, the latter were granted to the recently established generals) and, while administering the East as well as lower Asia and all that went with it, to be called for the future Prefect of the East. But there was no breaking-up of the power of 10.3

---

c (9.4) With the correct pronunciation changed, the populace calls the sceptre the *persikion*, because among the Romans "in person" is put *"per se."*

the magistracy until the time of Arcadius, the father of Theodosius the Young. In his day it came about that his prefect Rufinus, who had the name "insatiable" put on him, in pursuing a tyranny, missed his objective — fortunately for the best interests of the commonwealth — but brought the magistracy catastrophically down in ruins. For the emperor forthwith took 10.4 from the magistracy the power which it had derived from weaponry, and thereafter the supervision of the so-called *fabricae* (that is, armouries) and that of the public post and all other supervisory functions, out of which the so-called *magisterium* was comprised. But there were difficulties in working a procedure 10.5 whereby the prefect maintained the public horses and the personnel in charge of them in the provinces while other officials possessed the rights to dispose of them and administer them. So a law was laid down ordaining that the prefect was to retain the task of looking after the Public Post, but that the chief of the *frumentarii* — his styling nowadays is *princeps*, as it happens — should always be present at the law court held by the praetorian prefect, should make a host of inquiries and find out the reasons why many people are provided by the prefecture with the so-called official authorizations and use the *cursus publicus.*d These inquiries were made although the so-called *magister* is also the first to sign the official authorizations for the use of the *cursus.* As to the fact that such is the case, you can find it out 10.6 from the actual ordinance, which is in the Theodosian Code of old but has been passed over in the new code.

With the prefecture being in this way as it were brought down 11.1 step by step, the sovereign put the military registers under the counts and generals, as they were then called, and the palace service lists under the official at the head of the force of Court functionaries (I am going to speak of him at the end, as I promised). This official too, like the army commanders 11 (2) mentioned, came to have magisterial position largely because of the losses suffered by the prefecture — for expensive buildings, on being broken up, provide sufficient materials for many a man to build his home therefrom. While it happened to be the case that 11 (3) the emperors went to the wars in person, the prefecture had a

---

d Because of this he got the name *curiosus* too — a word meaning officious. And this official was not the only one to be so styled; all the officials who were in charge of public horses in the provinces got the styling.

certain power and influence, if not as great as it had been, in excess, however, of all the other magistracies. But from the time when Theodosius the First, making provision for the indolent dispositions of his own children, put a curb on valour by *legislation*, prohibiting, through them, a Roman emperor from going forth to the wars — from then on matters concerning wars became the field of the generals and the administration of palace business that of the *magister*. The result was that the prefecture had no other business than the mere supervision of the expenditures which must in fairness arise in connection with officials in commands connected with itself, as I said, and in connection with those, of course, whom those officials had been appointed to control.

11 (4)

11 (5)

If one were prepared to take into account also the conjectures arising out of predictions which some call oracles, the words once spoken by the Roman Fonteius have come to pass. He is the source for the tale about certain couplets, supposedly given to Romulus once in the ancestral language, which openly foretold that Fortune would depart from the Romans at the time when they should themselves forget their ancestral tongue. The oracle, as it is termed, has been included by me in my work *"On the Months."* Prophecies of this sort have assuredly come to fulfilment. For a certain Egyptian, Cyrus, who is even nowadays admired for poetical skill, while administering the urban and the praetorian prefectures simultaneously and being expert in nothing besides his poetry, presently broke with the ancient customs without a qualm. And when he proclaimed his decrees in the Greek tongue, along with the Roman speech his magistracy cast its status away too.

12.1

12.2

On the Official Regalia of the Praetorian Prefecture.

Well, as I said, when the office of *hipparch* was removed from the magistracies by Augustus' doing and the praetorian prefect inherited the latter's power, naturally the prefecture grew to greater proportions, for to its control of weaponry was also added the management of political affairs. Nonetheless some traces of the office of *hipparch* remained adhering to the prefecture, a certain slight change coming over it. The prefect began to wear a

13.1

13.2

mandyes of the Coan variety.^e The *mandyes* is a species of short 13.3
mantle, called *mantion* by the generality, which does not fall
further from the shoulders than the knees. *Segmenta* were not
put on the *mandyes* — but it has what we call *tablia* (i.e. stripes
sewed on the hem) — for when *segmenta* were put on, it was not
allowable for anyone but the emperor alone to wear it.^f So much 13.5
for the mantle. There was a *paragauda*, a tunic of purple, and a
belt of purple leather, glued on to itself, worked into a delicate
hem at the edge of the ribs, with a kind of little crescent-shaped
ornament on the left side made out of gold, and on the other a
sort of tongued-fastening or strap passing through a buckle. This
too is made of gold and fashioned into the shape of a bunch of
grapes, for the reason which I have narrated in my *"On the
Months."* This strap passing through the buckle is brought round
from the right and, on being applied to the crescent-shaped
ornament, makes a girdle for the wearer that will not slip, since a
brooch, itself too of gold, pins into the leather and fastens the
bunch of grapes to the crescent. The Romans call it a *fibula* in
their ancestral tongue and they call the belt a *balteus*; the gear of
the girdling device as a whole the Gauls call a *cartalamos*. Witness 13.6
to the fact that this is not a Roman word is the Roman Varro in
his fifth book *On The Latin Language.* He there distinguishes the
sort of word which is Aeolic and that which is Gallic — and that
one is Tuscan, another Etrurian, in the confused medley of words
from which the currently prevailing Latin language was made up.

Such was what was called among them the *paratura* (i.e. 14.1
official garb) of the prefecture; and there was a carriage, of the
kind we are used to, and caskets. The latter is their name for what
is known to the man in the street as the *calamarion*. It is for mere
pomp that it has been fashioned into such a shape and gilded, for
it was supposed to contain a hundred pounds of gold. Another 14.2
deep receptacle, made of silver, serves their court as a receptacle
for common or garden ink. The custom is to call it a *calliclion*,

---

e (13.2) For it was on that island *alone* that the deeper dye of purple hue,
which was in former times publicly esteemed, was produced. The dye that
was as it were imperceptibly tinctured towards a flame colour and not of a
very deep hue was a discovery of the Parthians' — the reason why skins
dyed a flame colour are, as it happens, actually called "Parthian."

f (13.4) *Segmenta* are what the Romans are wont to call garments with a
design in gold at the hem, as I have already stated.

i.e. a little hollow, from *calyx*. And there is a *cantharus* (that is a sort of basin), made of silver, on a silver tripod, and a goblet, put there for the purposes of those pleading cases within a stipulated time before the court. Although I feel that it will be tiresome to go on at length about this, I am forced of necessity to take up the account, saying this first, that there are still even today three ships at the disposal of the prefecture for voyages across the straits from the imperial city to the neighbouring mainlands. People of a more bygone age called them *barcae* in the ancestral   14.3 language (instead of dromons), *celoces* (i.e. swift sailing ships − because the word "swift" was for them *celer*), and *sarcinariae* (the word for merchantmen − because burdens are termed *sarcinae* in their language). So much, in general, for that. Let us   14.4 return to the subject.

There was a law − yes, and it has recently fallen into   15.1 desuetude − that those who were pleading their cases in the provinces, after appeal from decisions of the prefecture, might send them up again, within a fixed time, to the prefecture, according to the law governing appeals; and that those who were pleading their cases before the more old-fashioned courts might appeal from their verdicts to the emperor's court. The former were to be called *temporales* (for "having a time-limit"), the latter *sacrae* (i.e. sacred, because of their being, as I said, sent up to get a hearing from the emperor on appeal). This was a very   15.2 great source of respect and admiration and evidence of a constitution with every blessing. A Roman emperor submitted to the undertaking of the duties of a lowly judge, possibly even enduring the passing of judgements on business in a very shabby law case, as our most mild emperor does because of his love for his subjects, although for the most part keeping tireless vigil against the foe and taking pains to brave the first danger on our behalf. Or he would do so if the populace, enflamed by discord sent by God, did not make peace more dangerous for us. To deal with this discord the public treasury has to meet a heavier expenditure to guard the peace than for restraining our foes. Hence the source of the so-called "new" expenditures and restricted availability of necessities. For, granted that indolence   15.3 proved the undoing of emperors who have reigned in the past, how could this emperor have been idle, since he neither gets complete relaxation in sleep, nor does he touch solid food, for sustenance's sake, so as to eat his fill?

Well, since this sort of practice had earlier already broken down into wanton behaviour, and since previous officials had spurned, along with weaponry, even the supervision of public affairs itself (insofar as pleading was concerned), a law became current that the prefect should hear cases concerning the Sacred Dispositions — a fact which suffices to show, even after the change, the sacredness once inherent in him. For the prefect appeared upon the bench clad in white and his staff were likewise garbed in befitting fashion; even those themselves responsible for the law-suits were well attired and silence covered the court room. Present were the most distinguished barristers clad in attire worthy of a festival, the tripod in the middle of the audience-chamber with the *cantharus* suspended within it, and the goblet stationed beside it.9 And the style of pleading by the litigants was in every way on the high level appropriate to a sacred judge.   16.1   16.2

With all of this in ruins not even a trace of its dignity remained from then on in the court-room, since the councillors sit merely in a hole-and-corner court, amid the laughter of the bystanders as though at a pantomime, hearing a limited number of cases. There is no staff nor means of telling the time of day, as formerly there had customarily been. For the officer in charge of the staffh would stand at the head of the retinue while the prefecture was transacting business, and gravely cast down upon the floor all of a sudden, with a stately sound, some small silver balls of expensive make, bearing writing indicating the hours of the day in Roman numerals and characters. The ball that was cast down upon the marble indicated the hour of the day.   16.3   16.4

When this spectacle, dignified and so becoming, had been brought to an end, with the prefecture as it were either not even being seen at all on the judicial bench or, in accord with the laws   17.1

---

g After being filled with water, at a certain point, by means of this goblet, the *cantharus* gave as much time for the termination of the case as it took for the hollow of the *cantharus* to be set free from use, with the water that was in it being filtered out via some form of water-clock release.

h They called him a *subadiuva* (i.e. an assistant).

of the Cappadocian — about whom I will speak later — going unobserved in some bed-chamber, no person worthy of note from that point on came forward to join its staff, as it was so disregarded and as it brought shame rather than any honour upon anyone taking up service. So its business collapsed along with the collapse of the prefecture, and the first of offices, the one that used to stand above the others, came to be more disparaged than any other, being haled to Court without ceremony in any old order. And yet formerly the prefecture never made its appearance in the so-called *silentia* at Court unless it was after all the council had proceeded in before it, when, as has already been stated, it was last of all the magistracies to enter and first in coming forth, with the emperor's statue, in place of his person, escorting it. Because of this it was the chief of the so-called *silentiaries*[i] who was sent early in the morning by the Court to the prefecture. He would fall on his knees and urge it to come to Court. The prefecture then bestirred itself, grudgingly and deeming the inconvenience below its dignity.

17.2

It remains to give a detailed account of the prefecture's staff, to enumerate the numbers and nature of the personnel lists from which it is composed, and its customs and laws. For I am convinced that already not even a memory survives of those practices that have recently vanished. For people who are uneducated (inasmuch as they have obtained *no* previous experience of a court of law) come rushing in to deal with matters that were once cautiously undertaken after prayer by men of the greatest experience, who had already attained a dignified and stately age. For there was a law — not of mere word of mouth but formally prescribed — allowing no-one to advance quite to the office of the assistant until, graced by dignity accruing to his house and a preparation in the liberal arts, after nine years' distinguished service as a secretary, and after proceeding through the whole range of experience in affairs and exchanging the impetuosity that comes from youth for reasonableness, he should seem worthy of an honour of such dignity, involving no small honour and an emolument that sometimes brings in a thousand gold pieces.

18.1

18.2

18.3

---

i He is called the *admissionalis*.

But perhaps the more intelligent of my readers will, not 19.1
unreasonably, make objection, saying: "Why on earth, after
promising to talk about the official regalia of the prefecture, have
you not also made mention of standards, axes and rods? For 19.2
these were the insignia of the Master of Horse of old, and it was
in his place that the first of the emperors or Caesars appointed
the Praetorian Prefect." Well these *were*, I admit, the 19.3
distinguishing tokens of the praetorian prefects until Domitian.
But the latter, after appointing a man by the name of Fuscus to 19.4
head the prefecture, came near to wiping the memory of the
Master of Horse clean away, by not leaving axes, standards or
even the so-called rods to the office.j Because he was of 19.9
vainglorious disposition, Domitian rejoiced in innovations. It is
the peculiar characteristic of tyrants to upset long established
customs. For this reason he not merely deprived the praetorian 19.10
prefecture of the honour which it had formerly possessed but in
fact dissipated the power of the urban prefecture also, at least in
so far as it fell to him to do so, by appointing twelve urban
prefects instead of one, ostensibly to go with each region of the
city of Rome.

There was no established official residence, initially, for any 20.1
of these magistracies — not in the first imperial city nor in ours —
as there is at present. No, it was at his own seat that the man who
was administering the office did business. This remained the case 20.2
right up to the time of Leo in our life-time. In his reign
Constantine, a man of aristocratic lineage, himself too from
Mazake (but possessed of *good* qualities proportionate to the bad
ones of the Cappadocian) — whose literary education was very
good and surpassed those who were at that time most esteemed
among the Italians — while holding the high office of the

j (19.5) The rod which is at present borne by the *princeps* preserves
nothing else but its styling from antiquity. (19.6) Of old and nowadays, in
the military service units, the chief of the so-called *Biarchi* bears a switch
twined round a rod made of silver, in honour of the once esteemed
Dionysos, as has been adequately related for you in the book *"On the
Months."* (19.7) But time with its changes has left an axe only to the
consul and the consular magistrates in the provinces, perhaps out of a sense
of embarrassment at taking this mark of distinction too from the
honorable office of consul. For the rest, only the Caesar himself, as is well
known, possesses standards. (19.8) What their nature is I have made clear
in the book *"On the Months."*

prefecture, built a most distinguished building for doing business in, putting Leo's name upon it; and he also had the latter's accession portrayed in a mosaic in it. He built this place himself, as I stated, at his own expense, since he lived hard by the spot and was grandfather to Rufus, the prefect in our time, and left it to the prefecture as an unpretentious and modest place of business, having built it to serve the needs of his successors in the prefecture in course of time, a deed entirely worthy of approbation. The foremost office, the one that stood out above the others and yielded pride of place to the throne alone, did its business at that time in a little building. So neglected, among people of a more bygone age, was concern with luxuriousness; their sole enjoyment was in the contentment of the taxpayer. 20.3

Later on Sergius, a professor from among the rhetoricians of the judicial branch and an object of veneration to the good Anastasius because of his rhetoric, by loading the building spoken of with an upper chamber as an official residence, paid no regard to moderation and introduced greater luxury, with the prefecture already in decline, not foreseeing — for it is not in human nature to calculate what is to come — that he was building a lair for the Cappadocian. With the building's *bathing-room* he was satisfied, observing moderation in this respect at any rate. But when the Cappadocian — I will state who he is a little further on — fell on the prefecture, he handed the dwelling place of the magistracy, old and so dignified, over to his troupes of servants. He himself made his lair in the upper storey, with urine and excrement covering the sleeping quarters; he used to sprawl naked upon the couch, commanding everyone from his staff to stand before his bedchamber as though they were base household slaves, while he himself selected those it pleased him to select and placed them outside to be punished by the most bestial of his household slaves, barbaric and wolfish in spirit and name alike. Well, with eccentric prodigality, he changed the old bathing-room into a steading for draught animals and gave it over to a small faction for their herds of horses. Another bath he set hanging in the air, and, by making the water in its natural form flow upwards by compression to irregular heights, he took baths in it in the fashion that has already been dramatically told. Then he used to gulp down the products of the air, land and sea alike, all with wines brought from every quarter of the world, while being debauched 21.1 21.2 21.3 21.4

by countless sexual promiscuities. From the spot where this took place, while personally binding a light summer garment around his head, as though it were a mantilla, so that it fell over his cloak, and wrapping his hair up in the veil (like Pompey's parasite in Plutarch, or, to tell the truth, like the Bedouin rulers), he would be carried over to the courts of the home which he had personally built for himself. If one wanted fully to recount the wastefulness of these and the munificence of his buildings, you would not go wrong in describing as modest residences fit for philosophers the mausoleums and pyramids and so on — all that is recorded by writers in descriptions of Egyptian excesses — of Sesostris, Amasis and all the rest put together.

It remains, in accordance with my former announcement, to talk about the staff, of what its nature once was under the Master of Horse and what it became after him under the Praetorian Prefect; about the staff registers, stylings and duties; about the customs, contracts and the words upon the documents that are drawn up — in a word about all that, though preserved to our time, with the prefecture having undergone a decline and the establishment which served it having come to ruin along with it, has also perished. The object is that the actual memory of its good qualities should not also, along with the traces of ancient customs that survived, meet wholly with obliteration, by not being even recounted in literature. To begin with I will talk about the remainder of the magistracies in the state. After that I will set forth a special account of the staff — for it is not seemly to count along with the magistracies the people who are subject to them. 22.1

[22.2]

Concerning the Master of the Divine Offices
(i.e. officer in charge of the establishment at Court)

Everything that exists both comes into being and exists in accordance with the nature of the Good. That which exists is as it is; but that which develops is not always in existence nor uniform in being but goes through coming-into-being into decay and then turns back from that to coming-into-being, and is imperishable in regard to existence but rather subject to diversity in regard to its undergoing changes. A returning to itself is in the object's essence and is produced by decay, since Nature of her own accord watches over it and guides it forth again to manifest existence, 23.1

according to the laws laid down by the Creator. This is the   23.2
meaning of the story concerning the original form of the
constitution which we have now, in the case of which we know
that the power of the Master of Horse came into being, as has
been said, before any other office did; and next, that when that
magistracy was wiped out by time, it was transformed into the
office of prefect. After this office had taken the commonwealth   23.3
over, once again the imperial power came around to the need for
the Master of Horse. And forth there came into public life, or
rather there was brought forward by the nature of events, the
office which had previously been wiped out by another styling, in
no point wanting in its own basic essence but strengthened by
greater power and by the addition of properties which had not
been there formerly.

Let no one start away at the novelty of the name. If you were   24.1
to take a proper look into the matter, you will find that even the
actual name of the magistracy is not at variance with the
magistracy in itself. The *rex* or monarch always had his Master of   24.2
Horse, who led his cavalry force and was at the head of his entire
household. Consequently what is spoken of in the more recent
terminology as the *magister* is simply the Master of Horse.
Possession of greater power has been responsible for the change
of name. The name Master of Offices signifies nothing else but   24.3
the Comptroller of the Court registers, as I have already said, in
which both the cavalry and infantry forces of the emperor pass
under review, combining into ten thousand fighting effectives.
This was the only special function that the Master of Horse   24.4
possessed. The *magister* has more, since the imperial power has
been elevated to such an eminence. For in those days the Romans   24.5
only held Italy whereas, now, with God at their head, they hold
the whole world, land and sea, all at once.

As to who was first given the name *magister*, I cannot say, as   25.1
history is silent. Before Martinianus, who was *magister* under
Licinius, history does not record a title for anyone else. After this   25.2
man had served as *magister* under Licinius, Constantine, after
gaining sole possession of the entire control over the empire,
appointed Palladius as Master of the Court. Palladius was a man
of sagacity and had previously brought about friendship between
Persians and Romans under Galerius Maximianus by means of

embassies. But for anyone who desires to find out the *magistri* who succeeded one another up to our own day, sufficient information will be found in Peter, always a writer of high purpose and a safe guide in general history (see his writings on the so-called *magisterium*).   25.3

Well, the power of the magistracy advanced to greater heights. For the Master is entrusted to have, as coming under his jurisdiction, not only the embassies sent by the various classes, the public post, the dignified multitude of those called *frumentarii* of old but nowadays *magistriani*, and manufacture of and power over weapons, but also control of political affairs. An outstanding example is this man Peter the Great, who is second to no one in any respect as far as good qualities are concerned. For he maintains the Court and watches over it and does not spurn the Roman tradition of majesty, which, though it nearly perished through the fatuity of his predecessors, stands reinstated by him, as you would expect from a man of wisdom who has always devoted himself to books. The laws he knows as well as any man, for he was brought up amongst them from his earliest years and he acts as advocate for anyone who needs him. He has been shown to be of the greatest stature as a magistrate, displaying a lofty authority in keeping with his power, and to be a penetrating judge who knows how to make absolutely just decisions, since chance conjunctures of events do not in any way make him make concessions. He is a mild and kindly man but not easy to push around, and he does not go outside the law to meet requests, but is steadfast and at the same time takes forethought for the things that his visitors will urge. He spares no time for idleness, spending his nights on books, his days on business. Even the journey itself from his home to the Court he does not simply waste in social intercourse, engaging those who spend their time on these things on inquiries concerning word-meanings and explanations of matters belonging to the more remote past. For him no time is free from concern with learning, with result that those who teach literature fear a meeting with him, for he involves them in difficulties and awkward questions in the course of gently showing them up, in moderate terms, as only being said to be but not really being the sort of men that report commonly says they are. As for me in particular, conversation with him makes my head spin quite a little: I am glad for his sake that he is a good   26.1   26.2   26.3   26.4   26.5

man and at the same time a gentleman with no affectation or drivel; but he flings at me, as has indeed been stated, ideas of great importance, by putting forward as subjects for enquiry none of the things that I deem myself to know about and introducing topics that are completely unheard of. Consequently what I pray for most vehemently of all is that he should not, as has been his practice, pose for me some impossible subject for debate.

On the Prefect of Scythia and the Praetor and Quaesitor Justinianus

General history records so many magistrates as legally recognised at Rome from the beginnings of the Roman constitution to the death of the emperor Anastasius. The *comes largitionum* (as Italians say, instead of the official in charge of the emperor's treasuries) and the *comes privatarum* (for the official in charge of the dues accruing in some way or other to the emperors as individuals) no one would even number in a catalogue of magistrates but, arising from the whim of the imperial authority, they have an origin that is new-fangled — and obscure. Such is the case of the so-called *patrimonius* (i.e. guardian of the wealth that accrues to the emperor in some private capacity or has come by chance from his ancestors). This official — and he too was not numbered among dignitaries before this — was raised up by Anastasius, always a sensible man, in his concern, as was his wont, about provision of an examination of accounts for the tax-collectors, so that they might not have trouble because of confusion as to spheres of authority. 27.1 27.2

Although after him Justin lived at peace and brought in no innovations, the next emperor, who was Justin's nephew, in his eagerness to preserve everything that was of use for the commonwealth and aiming to summon back all of the lofty authority of the form it had possessed of old, first of all hit upon the so-called Prefect of Scythia. Being a wise man and having discovered from books how materially prosperous and strong in arms the country is now and has long been[k], he thought fit, as he 28.1 28.2

---

k It was first captured, along with Decebalus who had led the Getae, by the great Trajan, who brought in for Rome, as Crito maintained — and he participated in the war — five million pounds of gold and twice as many of silver, without goblets and gear — these went beyond the bounds of estimation — herds and weapons, and over five hundred thousand of the most valiant fighting men along with their arms.

personally was in no way inferior to Trajan, to preserve the north, which was already at times turning restive, for Rome. And it was no wonder that everything went according to his prayers. For he not merely rivalled Trajan in his feats of arms but outrivalled Augustus himself in his piety towards God and the moderation of his way of life, and Titus in gentlemanliness and Aurelius in brilliance of mind. **28.3**

Well, as I have just stated, Justinian created a prefect to supervise the troops in Scythia, assigning to him three provinces, the most flourishing of all: Cerastis (the Cyprus of nowadays; it changed its name under the influence of Cypris who, according to legend, was venerated in the island) and all of Caria, along with the Ionian islands. These but recently used to fall under the jurisdiction of the first of offices, like all the other islands, but the emperor thought it proper that they should be taken from the prefecture and come under the jurisdiction of the Prefect of Scythia. He set a special tribute aside for the Prefect's law-court, and a whole staff establishment. It was as though it was a spark from the volcanic craters on Lipara that he kindled from the prefecture. And he contrived many advantages for the commonwealth all in the one action. The greatest and second **29.1**
greatest Authorities had immoderate burdens lifted from them by the emperor, acting in person and alone, when he distributed assignments involving administration of affairs among many officials in posts of command. Further, he made their commands easy for them to manage and moderated the frantic pressure on the hard workers. Thinking the task skimped if he did not also rid the city prefecture of substantial burdens, he introduced the urban praetor among the magistrates (in this too faithfully imitating Titus), because he thought that the prefect of the city had enough to cope with in the discord among the demes, which kept everything in agitation. And with these officials — or rather before them if you consider the antiquity of the office, as I said before — he introduced the so-called *Quaesitor* (i.e. the most awesome investigator into capital charges). **29.2** **29.3**

Concerning the Constantinian and Justinianic Praetors and the Magister Census.

The monad is an archetypal form, and an instance of the monad is uniqueness. And such, in the beginning, was believed to **30.1**

be the position of our beloved city, for Rome at that time had
outstripped all in preeminence. Consequently Constantine never,   30.2
according to the evidence, termed it the new Rome prior to the
consecratio[l] carried out there, but called it too a camp, like the
other country towns. You would be in command of the proof of
this if you were to read Constantine's *Discourses*, which he
personally wrote in his native tongue and left to posterity. Well,   30.3
judging the latter city to be an image, an imperfectly seen
conjectural example, of the former, he was of opinion that two
praetors were adequate in view of the moderate numbers of
inhabitants and the small press of business. So, of the serried   30.4
array of the praetors at Rome, he appointed the *tutelarius* and
the *fidei commissarius*, giving the former the styling
"Constantinian" and calling the latter the *magister census*.[m] And
he established that a *scriba* (i.e. secretary) should serve the former
and a *censualis* (i.e. preserver of antiquities) the latter. Our Rome,   30.5
which has gone beyond the jealousy of a rival and which has also
brought the first Rome into obscurity, taking its power away, in
the opinion of the Most Excellent Justinian stood in need of the
introduction also of an urban praetor. So he created one, giving   30.6
the post the dignity of being called by his own name, for he
wished to deal with the transgressions of the populace and at the
same time he wisely lightened the city prefecture of excessive
functions of supervision.

---

l This is what Romans call deification.

m That is "magistrate in charge of the original contracts" — because people
call the register of antiquities a *census,* and that of current business a
regesta.

BOOK THREE

As the law of history has, as I think, been observed, and, as   1.1
was previously announced, the civil magistracies have passed
under review, there has come to me the idea of suspending to the
history a book on its own, a singleton, about the greatest
establishment, that of the first of magistracies. Through this book
one might dimly see mirrored the splendid disciplined system
which prevailed in the praetorian prefecture of old. Although this
had almost collapsed in ruins, our noble emperor did not allow it
to be completely obliterated; he maintains and as it were holds
together ancient institutions which are crumbling away through
age. Through him the state is greater in extent than it was not   1.2
long ago, since Libya has been restored to us,[a] and Rome herself,
the mother of our civilization, delivered by the sweat and effort
of the empire from the fetters and the power of barbarians. All   1.3
the institutions of distinction which ever graced the constitution
have been preserved with enhanced authority. The laws have been
delivered from a confused state of over-burdened chaos; what is
just is readily discernible, and the litigious regret their former
burning of the midnight oil over contentious points, since no
chance of making a fight of it is left for the future because of the
clarity of the laws. The good qualities of the sovereign are beyond   1.4
any praise. But it is time for me to proceed to my aim with the
narrative.

---

a No small acquisition, in fact the greatest part of Europe — for it shares
the west with the latter, whereas the east in its entirety is constituted by
Asia alone.

Well now, the staff which obeyed the authority of the Master   2.1
of Horse was, once upon a time, a force of armed men to a man.
The names given them, in general, were *promoti,* a styling which
is subdivided into four categories, *ducenarii, centenarii,*
centurions and *biarchi.* Concerning these terms I would have
given an explanation along the lines handed down by the
tacticians, but for the fact that I would be forced to go beyond
the limits of my subject. Of this styling, that of the *promoti* I   2.2
mean, there are still even today traces recorded by the so-called
*matrices.*b But when the magistracy assumed another form thanks   2.3
to Augustus, as has often been stated, there were added to it the
so-called *adiutores,* i.e. assistants. And this is the only styling that
is recorded by the *probatoriae*c which are provided by the
emperors for men proceeding to appointments in the services. For
formerly an applicant for any of the service-belts* did not simply
gain permission to gird it on, without having previously
demonstrated that he was suitable to have it.d But nowadays the   2.4
man in the street calls them *privatoriae* in an ignorant conjecture
with hints at the truth, by introducing thereby the idea of the
status of a mere private person. For there is no difference   2.5
between a private person and a man who insinuates himself into
any of the services by styling alone. I do not say that state affairs
have not assumed a better and more productive form as result of
the care taken by the sovereign, but that these people are coming
forward for public work although they are not of the proper
background.

Now generally in all the registers bearing the emperor's   3.1
signature *adiutores* were of old entered up in the fore-front of the
battle-line. The expression is as follows: *et collocare eum in
legione prima adiutrice nostra***— "and you should station him in

---

b Another word for the muster-lists of the registers.

c I.e. letters of appointment and recommendation.

d For *probare* is the Roman term for adducing proof to show what the
essence of a thing is.

* The phrase "to put on the service belt" meant "to take up an
appointment in the military service" initially, then later came to be applied
to the civil service also (cf. the English "take silk," and see R. MacMullen,
Soldier and Civilian in the Later Roman Empire, 1963, p. 180).

** The Latin actually means: "and to place him in our Legion I Adiutrix."
"Entrance into the office meant enrollment in a mythical First Adiutrix
Legion (as entry to a provincial governor's staff lay through a mythical
'cohort')" — MacMullen, p. 71.

the first legion assisting us," so to speak. Hence the official who   3.2
heads the whole register even nowadays is termed the
cornicularius, viz. the man on the wings or the front-line fighter.
For the supreme commander, namely a prefect or the Caesar, was   3.3
in the middle of the army when battle was joined. The further   3.4
styling *imperator* was common to these officers, as I said. It is not
the sole property of the emperors, but belongs unconditionally to
the one to whose lot it has fallen to manage the war as
commander-in-chief. In the mid-most position was, as has been   3.5
stated, the *imperator* — as Frontinus says. On the left wing was
the Master of Horse, or rather the Prefect; on the other were the
praetors and legates[e] (terms for generals and envoys). Although   3.6
the so-called legion comprised up to six thousand infantry in
numbers,[f] as I said, the *cornicularius* was allocated to the first
position. For this reason he is even now at the head of the whole
staff, since, for the reasons which I have given, it has been
decided that the prefect should no longer go to the wars.

The others then being all *adiutores*, the prefect gives   4.1
permission under his own signature to the man who is going to a
position in the service to be entered under the classification that
the man himself may choose. The titles to be found in all the   4.2
registers on the establishment are as follows: the *cornicularius* is
first. He is conspicuous by the splendid distinction of the title
styled *comes*; this although he has not yet retired from the service
and come by length of service to the conferment of honours by
the emperor in the endowment of the so-called codicils (another
name for writing-tablets) — a privilege this enjoyed by no leading
official in other service groups. After the *cornicularius* came two
primiscrinii, whom Greeks call first in the establishment, two
commentarienses,[g] two *regendarii*, who direct the public post,

---

e The latter the consuls used to leave behind in place of themselves, at the
point when their period of tenure of the consulship was at an end, to be in
charge of the army until the arrival at the theatre of war of the consul to
be.

f There were only ten legions in all in the beginning, apart from cavalry —
Roman, auxiliary, belonging to cohorts and *turmae* and the rest of the
forces, and then again that of the mercenaries also.

g Such is the name customarily given to those assigned to direct those who
enter up the public records.

III 4.2 —

and two officials styled *cura epistularum** for the Pontic Diocese.

Perhaps a man might not be asking an irrelevant question if he 5.1
werc also to enquire the reason why, when all the dioceses have
the officials called *cura epistularum*, they have not been allocated
to the Bureau for Constantinople and the Bureaus for Weaponry
and of Works. Obviously the Bureau for Constantinople is a 5.2
matter for the Diocese of Thrace and that for Works is a matter
for any other provinces at all in which restorations of public
works might chance to occur. As these are very discontinuous, it
is through the agency of the *cura epistularum* in the
aforementioned dioceses that the orders for payment of the
expenditure disbursed from the public treasury take place. The 5.3
Weaponry Bureau does not have a *cura epistularum* because the
contributions that it has coming from the provinces are fixed, I
mean bow-strings and horns and so on, and, to meet needs which
crop up in wartime, it services orders to deliver the above.

The crowd of short-hand writers is large, in fact beyond 6.1
number, and they have ample opportunities for work that will net
them a profit. Those of this group who have more literary
training and who moreover are equal to the work to be done are
collected together in fifteen conventicles, which people call
scholae. Those who have demonstrated their expertise in practice
proceed to the corps of the *Augustales* (that is, if they want to do
so), and arrive at the final career stage of the position of
cornicularius — but only after the *boethura*, as it is termed. Those (6.2)
who stay at the writing tablet are advanced to the final career
stage of a position as *primiscrinius*. A more detailed account of 7.1
this topic will be given in the proper place.

After the officials assigned to servicing functions of a literary
nature come the so-called *singulares*, skilled officials who are
despatched to the provinces to deal with public affairs. Although
from the first they handled the affairs which were most vital and
which had a contribution to make which actually influenced the
whole state, at the point when the prefecture was beginning to
decline the so-called *magistriani* with their pompous verbiage
slipped in. The officials under discussion got the name *singulares*, 7.2

* Secretariate. On these officials see W. G. Sinnigen, *The Officium of the
Urban Prefecture during the Later Roman Empire,* American Academy in
Rome, Papers & Monographs XVII, 1957, pp. 10-69, especially 63-69.

as it happened, from the fact that they used to set out for the
provinces on a single post-horse.[h] For it is the custom of the
people of Italy to call a man on his own a *singularis*. After these   7.3
officials come the *mancipes*, the producers of the bread made for
commons and slaves. Subject to them are the bakers and the
officials generally called the Boards of Revenue-collectors, who
tend to all those who in any way whatsoever are considered to
have a right to have food provided at public cost. Romans call
them *rationales*, because amongst them the word for accounts is
rationes, but the Greeks have changed their name to Catholics
because of their untiring attention to details of any and every
kind in dealing with the public accounts. Next come the public   7.4
buyers of corn, whom the historian Victor, in his *"History of the
Civil Wars,"* knew to have been styled *frumentarii* formerly
because they used formerly to look after the provisioning of the
Palace with corn. But when Rufinus at this time caused the   7.5
downfall of the office of prefect by aiming at a tyranny, these
officials too were involved in destruction along with him. Last of   7.6
all are those who formerly ranked amongst the first (in as much
as they originally served the Master of Horse), the *ducenarii,
biarchi, centenarii* and centurions. I have already given the Greek
names for all of these.* That they did in fact belong to the staff
of the Master of Horse can be inferred from the codicils that
concern them published by the Court, which speak of certain
ranks of dignitaries but not about these officials.

Such is the nature and the size of the section classifications in   8.1
the registers covering the prefecture. I do not mention *cursores* —   8.2
i.e. couriers — for they get released from the service upon going
into the Court. *Applicitarii* and *clavicularii*[i] however, upon the

---

h Or, rather, with one trace-horse, I mean.

i Of these the former is merely the name for the beadles who arrest those
who are kept under constraint on account of criminal charges, the latter
that for those who put the fetters upon the arrested.

* Not in the text now extant; possibly the discussion occurred in the
section lost at I 48,2. The names are those of n.c.o. army ranks, transferred
across to the appropriate civil service grades. In ascending order of
seniority they run: *biarchi; centenarii* and *centuriones; ducenarii* (see
Jones, *Later Roman Empire*, pp. 578, 599 and 634). The *ducenarius* was
an official of some considerable importance.

termination of their menial tasks — *not* a service appointment or an elevated position — act as criers. They serve as attendants for the *commentarienses*, as the Roman establishment list termed the keepers of public records, as I said. Just as the *nomenclatores*   8.3
fulfil a function, and single out the advocates, calling them out by name, so these attendants service suits involving criminal charges. The *nomenclatores*, according to Aemilius in his *"Commentary*   8.4
on the Histories of Sallust," are officials who name and announce the *togati* — another word for barristers. *Togati* is the Roman   8.5
term for those who are not on military service but are dressed in *paenulae* and assist the speaker in the presentation of his case by speaking for a fee. Since they always attend court, devote themselves to their books, and never cease to work on difficulties in the law codes, those who are pleading a case before a *pedaneus* — the name for a petty judge — call them in to have their advocacy when the finding is due. For this reason they are called   8.6
advocati, i.e. called to give assistance, to this very day. I make no   8.7
mention of *turmarii*, for I have already, when I mentioned them before, recorded that they were in attendance on the Bureau of the *subadiuvae*, and serviced the *completiones* (i.e. complete writing-up) of the records of verdicts as well, securing for themselves considerable sums by way of recompense, of so extensive a nature was the abundant and profitable business that was being done. In addition to the above, stewards of the imperial   8.8
palace, case-carriers and criers undertake servicing functions, but fall under other sectors of the bureaucracy.

On the short-hand writers and Augustales

It has been stated previously that the corps of short-hand   9.1
writers was one body in the beginning but that it has been divided into two sections and final career stages. One group of them pass   9.2
their time without leaving their writing tablets and proceed to the position of *primiscrinius* as their final career stage. The other group transfers into the section comprising the *Augustales*, and, completing their service appointments more speedily than the short-hand writers, they progress to the dignity and rank of a *cornicularius*. So that what lies behind this distinction should not   9.3
be incomprehensible to outsiders — for in fact the public daily, out of a feeling of ignorance, makes enquiries — unsuccessfully — being confused over the stylings I have mentioned — I will set

forth an account of the reason for the cutting of the one body
into two. The short-hand writers, like the tribunes, must serve   9.4
many years in order to complete their service appointment (for
the fact is that there are great numbers of them, as in the case of
the tribunes). If by some chance the lapse of years summons   9.5
them to the conclusion of their labours, they are worn out by old
age. This is quite the wrong time of life for hard work. So it is   9.6
reasonable that, as they are not up to the services called for from
the more highly ranked positions — with which those with the
resources of bodily youth and experience in affairs to support
them are only just able to cope without running risks — they
require assistants. Originally each one of them picked out three   9.7
officials, the best in all respects, from the short-hand writers.
And, what is more, only those who were qualified by experience
and literary training were allowed to carry out the business of the
court of justice. Nowadays however the custom of selection has
gone by the board; but the number is still preserved even now. As   9.8
result it comes about that six Assistants attend upon the Bureau
of the *Ab actis*, that of the *commentariensis*, and that of the
primiscrinius, since, as has already been shown, the law involves
retirement from the service at the rate of two men each year from
the ranks of the short-hand writers. You inevitably infer, upon   9.9
observing the great numbers of the Assistants, how important the
court of justice was and the limitless amount of business
transacted there in former times. At present however, since the   9.10
citizenry do not have matters to settle at law, no incentive urges a
man into the service of the prefecture, for the judges everywhere
are being ruined, whereas the *magistriani*, possibly out of
contumacy — I beg pardon for the remark, but make it because
they are fond of bandying words around — take the suits away to
other judges, who excellently suit the tastes of the litigants, by
means of the so-called Sacred Decrees.

Since formerly considerable profits — and those not gained on   10.1
war-service, plus most outstanding honours, along with really
effective power, fell to the lot of the Assistants in the bureaux
mentioned, it was only natural that, when they had had their fill,
they should deem it unworthy of them to go back again to the
writing tablet and the modest status that comes when no profits
are made. Hence, at their request, a law was laid down by   10.2
Arcadius, ordaining that a special, wholly distinct Board of

officials, thirty in number, who had already by this stage in their careers given conspicuous service as Assistants, was to be organized by the prefecture to look after its business for it. For it 10.3 was no easy matter either, at that time, with the emperors hearing suits as well as the senate, for all those giving service to be of the highest quality. Consequently a further fifteen officials, taken from those who were themselves the more mature men, of superior experience and length of service, were specifically assigned to the emperors to append signatures in the emperor's name.j These officials head the section comprising the *Augustales.* For the officials who have recently grown up beside them, the *A secretis* as their name is, were not as yet in existence, as enquiries dealing with money matters were on a very modest scale since the emperors heretofore used to go off to the wars and those who governed the prefectures used to apply their vigilance to the laws not to thefts. Upon the board of the thirty aforementioned 10.4 officials the law set the title of "the *Augustales.*" This was not an adventitious nor a new-fangled name. The law recalled the styling of the first of the emperors, who, as I have repeatedly stated, first organized the praetorian prefecture and then handed down a decision that those on its establishment should be called *Augustales* from his own title.

Concerning the primiscrinii and the presentation of documents in the old days.

With the greatest part, perhaps indeed all, of the traces of the 11.1 wisdom of the ancients wiped away, one cannot continue to remain without tears when one realizes from what is set out below how formerly the law preserved freedom for the citizenry and how numerous were the blessings from which people of our day have gradually been excluded through the derangement of the wits of the ruled. The custom of old was that no business 11.2 should be transacted outside the Precincts of Justicek so that there might be no wrong-doing of the sort that arises from insult or injury caused to the taxpayer. After the decision on the opinions had been made, as the law required, the law was that the

j These officials are known even nowadays as *deputati.*

k This is called a *secretum,* i.e. undisturbed and venerable through silence, and the like of it no longer exists in any shape or form.

assessors who sat on the advisory council of the magistracy, men of very great legal learning, should first read out the opinions, subjoin them to the so-called *schedarion* (termed *recitatum* amongst the people of Italy)[l] and give them for a signature on the part of the magistracy to the officials appointed for this function.[m] Then after that, when the so-called clean sheet was read out in the due fashion by the secretaries and in this way dismissed from court in favour of the *litigator* (i.e. the man standing by to get judgement), the secretary made a synopsis of the force of the transaction in Latin and kept this by him to prevent an audacious addition to or subtraction from it. After   11.3 this had taken place, the man involved in the case took the judgement and, amazed at the punctilious accuracy of the court, approached the *primiscrinii*, whose duty was to assign a debt collector to deal with decisions that had been handed down. The latter, through the officials assigned to assist them, scholars who used to set problems concerning literary questions to the very teachers themselves, completed the process by appending an additional note, in words stately with the weight of all the awesome power represented by the writer, on the back of the record of the verdict by the name of the official who completed the filling in of the document.

I have an impulse to weep when I see the force the law had   12.1 and how the devil has pared off and taken all the good qualities away from us. For the law suspected, and not without reason,   12.2 audacious acts of collusion, on the part of those giving assessors' opinions, with their officials who completed the filling-in of the documents, collusion against those with whom they were dealing. So it decided to pass word around through the agency of those who served justice, in severe terms containing threats of penalties, to those in positions of trust; and that the same decree should be written up to bring disgrace upon the debt-collectors who got up to all kinds of acts of audacity in the provinces. For in granting   12.3 authority to act, as it were, to the heads of the department in which the official sent out to see to the entering-up in full of the assessors' decisions happened to be established, the Assistant used

---

l Viz. collated material.

m These officials go by the name of *Cancellarii* in the courts of justice. I will speak about them towards the end of the work.

the following words, in writing: *Facite...** As one might say in   12.4
translation: "To the departmental heads:[n] So that he may not
suffer by default in regard to his rank, put the following man in a
separate category out of ranking order from the present day until
the following day, in the consulship of N here — if, that is, he is
of the orthodox faith, initiated into the divine mysteries, not
under a requirement to make a payment to the treasury, and not
connected by kinship with the man who has disregarded the tax
demand: and, of course, if he has not, within the past year, been
given a position of trust in this province to deal with public or
private affairs. This is however to be effected in such a way as not
to transgress against the force of practice as enjoined by the law."
With these words the Assistant of the *primiscrinius* used to   12.5
safeguard all those who were engaged in transactions. In
conjunction with him the *princeps*, in his capacity as chief
official,[o] and in conjunction with these officials, the *cornicularius*
— inasmuch as he keeps watch over the enforcement of the law
and is responsible for all the business that is being transacted —
by personally appending a signature, granted their great authority
to the decisions that had been handed down.

So extensive was the business that was conducted in those   13.1
days that it would be difficult to survey and synopsise it in ten
books. And what harm is there in lingering over the narrative to   13.2
illustrate the subject under discussion? So great was the mass of   13.3
business being transacted that the whole year was not adequate
for the Assistants to complete it, with the result that, after the
end of the so-called *boethura*, they had a place set aside for them
in the middle of the entrance of the Praetorian Court near the
Bureau for Europe wherein they assembled and completed
business that had been commenced during their year of duty.
Even the officials who had recently retired from serving as   13.4
Assistants to the Bureaux currently assisting administration

---

n As I said, of the establishment to which the official entrusted with the
assessors' decisions happened to belong.

o It is not the proper occasion at this point to speak about this official. For
he is not himself part of the establishment, but comes up from the
magistriani, when he attains a certain rank, to what were once the most
important courts of justice. I will set out his history a little further on.

* Seven lines of Latin have been lost from the MS.

worked on this business, getting no small recompense in profits out of it. Those who had ended their service before them or still earlier used to flock in there and were entrusted with the most important and distinguished of the requisitions coming under the magistracy's competence and all the others, which some other official had not been able to bring to conclusion. And even when the time for abstaining from work came they did not set it aside and keep it free of inquiries into literary matters, what with the famous academics in the schools of letters flocking to them and joining in their investigations into terms whose meaning was not known. But all this died away to such an extent that, with the   13.5 place henceforth inactive, the so-called *exceptarii* (i.e. receivers of corn) entered possession of the bureau, after the disappearance of its once admired occupants.

Many, indeed beyond count, are the distinguished institutions   14.1 of its former solemn splendour that have perished. The officials of the prefecture's establishment have got actually to ask those who do business with them for paper. Formerly the custom was not merely not to undertake such shabby transactions but, further, to expend the most transparent sheets of all upon the business being handled, with the scribes being as distinguished, in proportion, as the parchments. Then both practices vanished. The officials exact a payment in copper currency, a very modest charge which does the prefecture no credit, in their penny-pinching. They issue fodder, not paper,* with written characters that are shoddy and smell of poverty. All of these   14.2 practices have perished along with the prefecture and departed on a road over which there is no return, because of the following facts. There are no lawsuits among the citizenry, ruined as they are by poverty. Also, what business does chance to be brought before its court is running a risk, partly because of inexperience on the part of the staff belonging to the court, partly through appropriations practised by younger officials now and again when, out of puerile wilfulness, they throw off the controls exercised by men who are held in the highest honour. So much   15.1 for the customs concerning clerical matters.

---

* Presumably, very poor quality papyrus: the fibrous nature of paper made from this plant would contrast strikingly with well-prepared vellum.

A mass of *ducenarii* serves the tribunal of the *primiscrinii*, giving them every assistance in dealing with the legal inquiries arising from unwritten requisitions (which used to be called joint writs). Next to the boundless profits that were introduced as result of the exactions of paper, this business has produced the most important turning point in its finances for the department headed by the *primiscrinius*. For the prefect, doing business from 15.2 the dead of night until the break of day, busied himself vigilantly during the night on legal enquiries. After which, through the time of the day customarily allocated to work, he spent his time on public business and on the questions put to him by the legal advisors, both those involved in teaching and those concerned with *ex parte* applications. The time towards evening he assigned to the discharging of the so-called joint writs. By doing this he satisfied all the desires of those ministering to justice, of the litigants who had the luck to get business transacted that needed transacting, and of those who were quit of their suits. None of 15.3 these prefects allowed himself to make concessions in court or to be slack because of pressure of work. The prefect decided the sphere of competence of his magistracy with discretion, knowing that his jurisdiction was over free men and also that it did not extend to cover everything. He used continually to give breaks from their work to his staff, by providing them with what is nowadays already unknown even by name: *monomissa*. This was the name given by a by-gone age to the break given every day at mid-day to the staff. For the people who ran the administration in those days knew — they were wise and educated men — that night has been provided by nature for rest and day for work, and they thought it against God's will that those who passed the night working hard on state business should also be penalized by losing their respite from work after sunrise — a short one, indeed. But, 15.4 as if their change of status for the worse was not enough, the *primiscrinii* even had the consolation and honour accruing from their style of dress taken from them. Their being deprived of this solace constituted a hazard for the courts of law, as I said.

Concerning the Commentarienses

Two is the number of the *commentarienses* themselves also, as 16.1 I have already stated, as it happens. These are the officials whom time has brought from employment as short-hand writers. They too, like those before them, have six Assistants currently working under them, brought in from the department comprised by the *Augustales*. These are men of unflinching devotion to duty who make no bones of a severity that befits the law and with them in fact resides all the power of the magistracy. These were the officials who brought the criminal trials before the court of justice. In attendance on them, as I have stated previously, were the *applicitarii* and *clavicularii* with a multitude of beadles who kept the court in a turmoil of fear, what with their iron fetters and the varied array of their instruments for inflicting punishments and floggings. When they had deployed their retinue of *ducenarii*, even without the authority of the law, they were enough to teach transgressors to behave themselves.

16.2

I am aghast, when I bring the subject up and let my mind run back to those men, at the nature of the fear felt towards the *commentarienses* among all those who had any sort of leading position on the prefect's staff, but especially among the *scrinarii*, and at how everyone who fell in with a *commentariensis* journeying on his route, rated contact with him highly. For they were the agents who attended to matters not merely when the prefect's feelings had been aroused but also when the emperor's ire had been incurred. For instance, I personally remember serving as a supernumerary *chartularius*,* as this official was termed, to the *commentarienses* just at the time when the Emperor Anastasius was moved to anger against Appion, a most outstanding man who had been his partner in the emperorship, at the time when Cavades the Persian was enflamed with hostility. Leontius, a man of the greatest learning in the law, was administering the prefecture. The emperor in his wrath entrusted the confiscating of property and sentences of banishment, the measures involved in bringing home his displeasure, to the prefecture alone and to no other magistracy. In carrying out this commission such mastery and so much eager skilfulness was exhibited by the *commentarienses* of that time, in conjunction with entire honesty and restraint from any kind of sharp practice aiming at speculation, that the emperor, in admiration of the fine

17.1

17.3

*Aide to the assistant to the Head of Department (i.e. the *commentariensis*).

qualities of the men at that time in the service, entrusted to them all the affairs that cropped up.P By "them" I mean the *commentarienses* of the prefects. This was in spite of the fact that Celer, the closest of all the emperor's friends, was at the emperor's side and carrying out the duties of the so-called *magister* with distinction.

This state of affairs too has been brought to an end, through divine and human intervention; for what remains is "of neither account nor consequence." But no less of an ornament to the dominance maintained by the bureau through change after change was the tremendous authority of the councils, as they were termed. For when the prefect desired to turn an official of some sort or a certain citizen over to the law, either at the prompting of the emperor or because he was himself stirred to action by the dictates of the law, he took the *commentariensis* as a private secretary and entrusted to him the steps that had to be taken. The latter, without attracting the attention of the guilty person, brought in to act with him that one of his own *chartularii* who was at one and the same time the most trustworthy and the most distinguished in standing. The *commentariensis* then dictated the official letter, in weighty Latin, in the presence of members of his staff, entrusting to an official who was most trustworthy and simultaneously of distinguished standing the commission, as though he were a penal official, of bringing the individual against whom displeasure was felt before the tribunal. But when the emperor's clemency and, further, the affection felt by the officials for the citizenry secured a pardon for the condemned, it was natural that the individual who was set at liberty should make no secret of his debt of gratitude to the intermediaries in what he actually did to recompense them.

And there was, generally, associated with the bureau of the council the so-called *instrumentarius,*q to append signatures to and complete the forms recording its decisions. An area has, from long ago, been set aside for him in the Hippodrome, to the South below the Emperor's tribunal, extending all the way to the

18.1

18.2

18.3

18.5

19.1

---

p Amongst these he also entrusted them with the bringing home of his displeasure to Macedonius, at that time bishop of the imperial city, on the grounds that the latter had kept excluding discussions concerning innovations in dogma.

q I.e. the Keeper of the Public Records of the court of justice.

so-called Sling. All the business transacted since the reign of   19.2
Valens in what were then the most important courts of law is
preserved there, and if you go to look up the records they are as
readily available as if the transactions had happened to occur
yesterday. The *instrumentarius* too has vanished and his seat   19.3
remains empty and has passed to mere slaves, who await
occupants for it. For, since no legal finding takes place — or   19.4
anything else requiring transactions, as you would expect — or is
set in motion in the court of justice, how could the official
himself be thought to be necessary for business?

Concerning the Ab actis.

Ab actis is the name of the department. It indicates, when   20.1
translated, the official concerned with financial transactions, as *A
pigmentis* indicates the officials over the spices, *A secretis* those
in charge of secrets,[r] and *A sabanis* those over the baths of the
Court. The *Ab actis* themselves too are two in number. Time by   20.2
degrees summons them, like those before them, from the
short-hand writers. Six officials, men of hard-working disposition,
of the utmost discretion, and still in their full vigour, come from
the division comprised by the *Augustales* as "Assistants,"
nominally, even today. Their duties are to handle cases at law   20.3
which involve finance.[s] Serving them are the *nomenclatores*,
whom I have already spoken of as criers and conveners, once
upon a time belonging to senators but nowadays to advocates in
the law courts. There was a law[t] that all their transactions were   20.4
published by the *chartularii* who were in attendance upon them
(these too came from among the short-hand writers) in the
so-called *regesta* or *cottidiana.*[u] The departmental   20.5

---

r It is *not adsecretis* as laymen would have it, unwittingly, with the letter
"d," adding the preposition on.

s Another way of saying to examine them carefully and bring them before
the tribunal to be judged.

t I say "was" for it no longer exists, as it has of late been ignored as result
of silliness, or, truth to tell, derangement of the wits.

u Another term for daily; *regesta* is what Romans decided to call the books
in which they entered up events in course of occurrence, because *res gestae*
is their name for affairs of state. From this record a man making
investigations at any time into business transacted at any time had easy
short-cuts for making his enquiries. The *regesta* and *cottidiana* by
themselves enabled one to make out the significance of what had been
done.

instrumentarius, after receiving these from the *Ab actis,* indicated the year and the consul in an abridged formula for purposes of speedy reference, and was done with his work, all in a trice. This practice, an admirable token of well ordered behaviour, was zealously observed. Every appropriate period of time was entered up in the daily record. Not even the days which might not be used for business were omitted by those writing up the record; on the contrary, they even wrote up the reasons why it came about that these days were days of inactivity. Now this practice 20.6 deserved admiration, but the copying out of decisions as done by the so-called *personales* was justly deemed beyond any praise. For 20.7 the findings of the trial were written up periphrastically in Latin by the Assistant with the best literary training, in such detail that even if by chance it ever happened that the finding was lost, it could be established again just from the paraphrase and as it were outline by itself. I myself personally remember an incident of this nature. A finding had been introduced, but there was no evidence 20.8 at all of the details of the trial that led to making it. When the so-called *personalis* had been brought before the prefecture, the finding was confirmed, no part of it proving deficient. And who 20.9 would not be reduced to tears upon coming to recall the high praises used of the prefect's staff and this kind of token of its high qualities by the great Sergius, the most fair-minded Proclus and the greatest polymath Trebonian? Of these the former has had no equal as prefect, and the latter pair, on becoming quaestors, have added to the splendours of the constitution. Along with them in praising the prefecture went all of the barristers of their day to a man.ᵛ This was the state of affairs 20.10 once. Nowadays it not only does not exist but is not even thought worth remembering at all, for reasons which I have given more than once.

After the *Ab actis* comes the *Regendarius.* He is nominally 21.1 even nowadays in charge of the task of looking after the official letters allowing use of the *cursus publicus.** But he does nothing, for the Master of the Court has filched from him all competence

---

v Concerning the latter I think it better to maintain silence rather than to praise them in terms more splendid than they merit.

* The Public Post, comprising an express post and a slow wagon post. Warrants allowed use of its facilities for persons travelling: see Jones, *Later Roman Empire*, pp. 830-34.

in the matter. After him come the officials of the *Cura*
epistularum of the dioceses. They merely write out the decrees
that come in to the public treasuries, and are, apart from this
function, thought little of. The so-called *Trakteutai* have stolen
their entire area of competence by appending to the order to
make payment the official instructions which *they* determine —
especially since the time when the *scrinarii* made bold to bring
the prefecture under their own control. Thus one comes to the
end of the collegial groups for staff of literary training within the
establishment. *Ducenarii, centenarii, biarchi,* and *adiutores,* and
the rest of the branches of the establishment, after completing
the servicing functions prescribed for them by the law, arrive at
whatever culminating position in the Service that chance gives
them. The so-called *Thekophori,* who carry the prefecture's
effigies on its standards, and the *Diaetarii** are enrolled in
different departments within the staff establishment from those
in which they fulfil their duties.

Since all (I think) of the personnel-lists — unless I have made
some mistake — have been reviewed in my account it remains
once again to bring the *cornicularius* into view in my history, like
a venerable leader, at the end. For, since he is the unifying
element behind the whole establishment, he ought to illustrate
both its beginning and its end as well. Mere considerations of time
alone are sufficient to win credence for the case of the
cornicularius: for over one thousand three hundred years he has
been the leader of his section, and it was at the actual building of
Holy Rome that he appeared upon the scene. For he was in
attendance from the outset upon the Master of Horse (and the
latter upon the *rex* of that time). Thus from the very beginnings
of the Roman state one can find evidence for the *cornicularius,*
even if nothing but his styling has been left to tell us about him.
For, from the time when Domitian, after creating Fuscus[w]
Praetorian Prefect upon his own assumption of the role of
Augustus, showed that the honoured position of the Master of
Horse was unnecessary by himself leading the armed forces,
everything underwent a change.

21.2

21.3

21.4

22.1

22.2

22.3

w Such is the name Romans have for the man with a swarthy skin.

* Stewards of the imperial palace.

So then, business of any nature that was conducted before the   23.1
prefects was arranged by the *cornicularius* alone and he obtained
the income from it to recompense himself. This practice,
prevailing from Domitian till Theodosius in our day, was altered
because of the tyrannical powers built up by Rufinus. For a law   23.2
was laid down by the Emperor Arcadius, in his alarm at the
power potential acquired by the prefecture, to the effect that the
*Princeps** of the staff of the Master [of Offices] should proceed to
the most important courts of law. He was to conduct a prying
and officious investigation into the significance of what was being
done in those courts and to find out the reasons that lay behind
the granting of official letters allowing access to the Public Post.
And after that Rufinus, after he had taken a trip, of his own   23.3
initiative, to the East, scourged and deposed the so-called Count
of the East, in return for his having ventured to vie with the
prefecture in standing. Arcadius' statute, as I said, was recorded
in the old Theodosian Code, but those who established the recent
Code passed it by, on the grounds that it seemed to them to be
superfluous.

So then the *Princeps* of the *magistriani* was in attendance on   24.1
what were once the most important courts of law and he had
nothing but his styling. So he made propositions to the
cornicularius of the prefect's staff of the time so that the latter
would give him some entrée to the business proceedings. They
agreed on the following arrangement, and the *Princeps* prescribed
it: that one pound of gold should be paid each month by him to
the *cornicularius*, after the usual amounts had been given
automatically to all those on the establishment who customarily
received some share of its revenues. When they had made this   24.2
arrangement, the *cornicularius* on that occasion received his
twelve pounds of gold from the *Princeps* without any shortfall.
Doing him all honour, he conceded to his superior the right to
bring into court cases involving records of verdicts concerning *ex
parte* applications. But he preserved for himself, as well as the
privileges accruing from his high rank and other sources of gain,
the practice of completing current business by appending his own
signature — and this business brought him in an income of at least
a thousand gold pieces.

---

* The most distinguished person (on the staff).

The sequel "I could not recount further without tears," as 25.1
Euripides says in the *Peleus*. For, with all these perquisites by this 25.2
time already done away with, just as the others too had been, I
also personally shared in the results of the mental derangement of
the time, since I came to the topmost limit of the rank-positions
in the Service and got nothing from it but the title. And I make 25.3
no blush in invoking Justice as witness to the fact that I am
telling the truth. Not so much as one obol did I get from the
Princeps or from the so-called *completiones*,* to my knowledge.
Where was I going to get it from? Of old the custom was that 25.4
thirty-seven gold pieces were provided for the prefect's staff, to
meet the expenses of a petition connected with an *ex parte*
application, by those who introduced such a petition, in what
were then the most important law-courts, however they
introduced it. Afterwards however a payment in coppers,× a very
moderate amount, was made as a contribution, as though in pity,
in a shabby fashion and not as a regular thing. Again, how is the 25.5
Princeps bound to give what was once given by him to the current
cornicularius? He does not even have the memory that would
be evoked by at least a bare name recalled to him; nor, further,
does he go through with attendance at the court of law — for no
official of any high position does his service in the court. I feel 25.6
regret, when after the right time to have done so has passed, I
reflect on what I ought to have been reflecting about. For what
purpose have I spent such a long time as clerk of the court of law,
since I got nothing from it by way of recompense? Was it right
that this has happened to me after I had embarked upon public
service of this type? Consequently, it is no hardship to recount in 25.7
the narrative the full tale of my story from its beginnings up to
this point.

When I was in my twenty-first year, in the consulship of 26.1
Secundianus,** I came from my native Philadelphia below Mount
Tmolus, which is situated in Lydia, to this blessed city. After I
had turned the matter over a great deal in my mind, I decided to
go the *memoriales* of the Court and put on the belt for a service

---

x I mention this because it was not gold.

* Fillings-out of forms etc.

**511 A.D.

career among them. So that I should not seem to be causing the   26.2
time until I took up an appointment to be wasted, I decided to
attend a philosopher's school. Agapius was the man at that time;   26.3
on him the poet Christodorus, in his single volume on the
disciples of the great Proclus, remarks as follows: "Agapius was
last in time but first of all." At his lectures, after learning the
main points of the teachings of Aristotle, I had the luck also to
hear something about Platonic philosophy. But chance, with a   26.4
view to impelling me rather into this service, advanced Zoticus, a
fellow-citizen of mine and a man who gave me no little
encouragement, to the praetorian prefecture under Anastasius,
the most mild of all the emperors. Zoticus, who had the power
not merely to urge but also to compel me, put me on the staff
among the short-hand writers of the prefecture. In this position
Ammianus, a very equitable man who was my father's nephew,
was, as it happened, serving with distinction.

So that I should not chance to pass my time in idleness, the   27.1
prefect showed me every way of making money, with the result
that, in the course of the whole of his term of office — and it was
one of moderate length and went little beyond the year — I made
a gain of not less than a thousand gold pieces in a temperate
fashion. Well, as you might expect, I was grateful — what else   27.2
could I be? So I recounted a short encomium to him. In pleasure,
he bade me to take from the table a gold piece for each line of
verse. And the officials invited to serve as Assistants by the
so-called *Ab actis* sent for me and took me on — an
unprecedented occurrence — into the position of First
Chartularius. This although the other *chartularii* had been only
two in number, already old men on attaining the position, and
though formerly it was after making the Assistants a gift of gold
that they got on to their staff establishment. This was not all;
they also gave me a fixed salary of twenty four gold pieces a year.
In like fashion, while doing the so-called *personalium* and   27.3
*cottidianum*ᵞ in return for this pay, I began composing
suggestiones. The following is the explanation of what these are:
from the beginning all those serving, in what was once the first of
magistracies, as Assistants to the bureaux currently involved in
administration were distinguished for a high level of education,
but vied to excel in the Latin language; for it was, inevitably,

---

ᵞ I have only just given an account of these.

essential for them. Well then, when a suit involving the right of appeal chanced along and then was referred to the senate for amendment, the Assistant who was superior to the others drew up the so-called *suggestio*^z for its hearing in the senate so excellently as to amaze the senate's *Quaestor* and the officials known of old as *antecessores* but nowadays known as Writers of Rescripts. With God's help and with the enthusiasm which arose from the encouragement given me on all sides helping me not to feel the labour involved, I not only carried out the services spoken of above in the bureau but actually also served as secretary among the short-hand writers, and, further, acted as Assistant to other short-hand writers in the Precincts of Justice which are called the *Secretum*. A major incentive was the reputation which accrued because of the work done and also the abundant encouragement given while engaged upon it. As result of this work I moved on apace, as though furnished with wings, to the so-called *A secretis* of the Court.

27.4

27.5

In response to the suggestions made to him by Ammianus, a good and moderate man in all respects and of a scholarly, philosophical way of life, Zoticus actually procured me a wife, who brought me a dowry of one hundred pounds of gold and who was, moreover, superior to any woman ever admired for her moral fibre. As I expected that things would go far better for me as time went on, I held back from forming keen attachments towards the Court and made the whole of my life over to the Service. Well, when public affairs had been reduced in all respects to the state the narrative has recorded and furthermore since fortune was, as she had not heretofore, exhibiting displeasure towards men of letters, I fell to hating the Service, and gave myself over wholly to books. The emperor, who had come to know of my unremitting literary labours, first of all deemed me worthy of addressing an encomium to him, in the very presence, as it happened, of senior statesmen from the elder Rome, who always have the study of literature to heart, even in this distress that they are suffering. After this had taken place, he bade me also to write the history of the war against the Persians, which had been auspiciously handled by him, on the occasion when,

28.1

28.2

28.3

28.4

28.5

---

7 Another name for an official elucidation.

while they were harassing the city of Daras,[a] the enemy fell back from it with no small losses, not advancing against it again.

So then, in writing an imperial edict to the prefecture about   29.1
me, the Emperor employed the following words: "We can testify
that the most learned John's training in literature, accuracy over
points of grammar, charm and facility in poetry, and
encyclopaedic knowledge of other kinds are very considerable;
and that it was in order by his labours to make the Latin language
more revered that he actually chose, although his service career in
the law-courts of Your Eminence was proceeding in due order, to
practice the life devoted to books in place of that career, and
wholly to dedicate himself to literature. Well then, that the   29.2
scholar who has progressed to such heights of virtuosity should be
left unhonoured is, We deem, unworthy of Our times; so We
charge Your Eminence to grant him this wish at public expense.
The aforementioned most learned gentleman is to rest assured   29.3
that We will not stop at this but will also honour him with
dignities and with Sacred Largesses of greater amounts, because
We deem it inappropriate that such linguistic facility should be
thought worthy of such meagre requital. We commend him,
should he impart to many others also a share in the training that
is his." After the official who was at that time managing the   29.4
prefecture of the city had confirmed this edict and had
designated for me a place set aside for teachers in the Court of
the Capitol, I did my teaching while retaining my establishment
in the service, and was led on to entertain great notions.

However, via the grades and avenues of rank in the serivce,   30.1
without any set-back, with time speeding by un-noticed as it
were, I came up to the end of the service career. As far as   30.2
financial reward went, I was passed over as though I did not even
have a place in the service. But I did get honour and the respect
of the mighty and, a thing which is of course most pleasant of all,
I passed my life in a relaxed atmosphere. Justice, wise in all   30.3
things, soothed and encouraged me in a proper fashion; made of
me an object of respect for those in the service, as I have said, and
one not unworthy of honour in the sight of the authorities. This
is evident from the decree that was brought out concerning me

---

a This city had been set at the enemy's throat by the great Anastasius.

when I went to the Court after relinquishing the belt denoting my
official position. In the first place, when I mounted upon the   30.4
tribunal of the prefecture — you know, in accordance with that
custom of giving thanks to one's superior and laying down one's
office — the prefect,b as a mark of honour, got to his feet and
warmly returned my salutation. After embracing me, the first
thing he did was to give me with his own hands the order
requiring delivery of an allowance in provisions, with an
expression of his gratitude. Then, after countless expressions of
praise, with the entire staff in attendance, he read out a decree
which went as follows: "The most learned John — for he takes   30.5
pleasure in this designation rather than in the official titles which
have accrued to him from the honours which he holds — has
already before this showed himself in the best of all things — We
mean in education and literature — a man of such a stamp that it
is not he alone who is an object of admiration, but many another
also — those, that is, who are the product of his teaching. But,   30.6
thinking it to be a small matter, apparently, that he should be
honoured for literary pursuits alone — and yet what would
anyone deem more important than these? — he has also
participated in public affairs. In his service in Our Courts of law   30.7
he maintained a single even tenor through everything, always
following his own example and teaching through what he actually
did that a nature that is good and that is able to put forth service
of a superior type whatever way of life it may turn to, does not
abandon its native advantages, but renders its good qualities more
respected by providing those qualities with the embellishments
conferred by literature and public affairs. Well then, with a   30.8
splendid reputation made in all these fields, John, a man of the
greatest distinction, after proceeding right through both the
career positions and the work involved in Our courts of law, will
hasten to follow our great Emperor, and will enjoy greater
blessings from that course. For the Emperor, of course, in   30.9
addition to his other excellent qualities, is a lover of literature as
well, time having done well to bring this about for Our
generation, namely that the serious bent of Him who reigns over

---

b He was the good Hephaestus, a fine gentleman whose name by itself was
evidence of his high birth. For Hephaestus, the first king of Egypt
according to the Siceliote [Ed.-Diodorus Siculus (I 13,3)], was his
ancestor, widespread belief maintained.

us might bring all the rest of the official order also to some
greater level of distinction."

    After receiving this honour, in place of a great deal of money,   30.10
from the court of law, in procession behind my associates, men
who were in every way most dear to me, I went back into the
Court. I had served in all forty years and four months. After
receiving from the sovereign the title customarily conferred upon
those who complete their service, I proceeded once again to my
books.

*On the Scriniarii of the Dioceses, those of the Military Bureau,
the Bureau of Provisions and the Cancellarii.*

    If someone were to go over Roman history closely in its   31.1
entirety, he would not find the name of the *scriniarii* anywhere
before the reign of Constantine. He will find *scrinium* and *scriba*   31.2
and their derivatives, of course, but he will not find the styling
scriniarii anywhere. So then they were unknown, in the first   31.3
place, in public life, and they are not a part of the establishment
of the Master of Horse nor, of course, that of the prefects. It was   31.4
as private individuals that they came forward, because their
services were indispensable, to deal with public business. I will tell
you how this came about. Constantine the First, as has been said   31.5
before, without intending to do so, caused the Roman state to
lose Scythia and Moesia and the tribute from those regions, by
dispersing over Lower Asia the forces guarding the bank of the
Ister in the North, out of fear that a tyranny might arise there. It   31.6
seems a good idea to digress briefly from my objective and say a
few words about the name of the river. For we find one and the
same river sometimes being called the Ister and sometimes the
Danube. Consequently explanation will be necessary.

    From the mountains of Raetia[c] both the Rhine and the Ister,   32.1
springing from one source, discharge themselves into the sea,
neither of them without changing its name. For the Rhine, as it   32.2
runs through the entire interior of Gaul[d] does not merely, in

---

c Which are part of the Celtic mountain-land according to Caesar in the
first book of the *Gallic Journal* which he wrote.

d Which is divided into three regions, Celtica, Germania and Gallia.

conjunction with the Rhone, irrigate the land; it also protects it by keeping it free from invasion. Towards the end of its course,   32.3 roughly speaking, its flow glides into the river Meuse, which debouches into the northern ocean over towards the West, and it drops the name which it had in the beginning and, merging with the Meuse, streams with the latter into the bays around the British Sea. The Ister lets her sister river Rhine go her own way as   32.4 the latter withdraws towards the setting sun and goes her own separate way towards the East. As far as Pannonia[e] and Sirmium[f]   32.5 it keeps the same name. But, as it winds its way around Thrace, it loses its former name among the people of that land, getting called the Danube instead. The Thracians have put this name upon it because it is as result of the boundless waste of waters stretching below it that the air, it is believed, meeting the mountains to the North and the North-North-Westerly Wind, is made pretty well always cloudy and responsible for causing them continual heavy rains (*Danubius* is what they call a bringer of clouds, in their native language). This disquisition upon the rivers,   32.6 in a digression as it were, is based on Samonicus the Roman historian, who held discourse with Diocletian and the elder Galerius concerning enquiries into abstruse matters.

Well then, Constantine, as I said, lost Scythia, and Moesia too,   33.1 and the tribute from these areas. After proclaiming all of Syria,   33.2 and Palestine,[g] as provinces he found it necessary to create a Prefect of the East too (in addition to the Prefects of Libya, Galatia, Illyria, and Italy) because he was considering, as the Emperor himself says in his own works, a surprise attack upon the Persians. For Constantine knew well, as he was a great man   33.3 for literary education and constant practice in weaponry,[h] that it was not easy to overcome the Persians in war otherwise than by an assault which poured over them out of the blue. A treatise on   33.4

---

e Which Greeks have termed Paeonia, inventing the name for purposes of euphony and to avoid a barbaric word-form.

f The flourishing city that once was under Roman rule and is now under that of the Gepids.

g It is one country and is generally mentioned in reports as a unit.

h A man was not created Emperor of Rome unless he happened to be someone outstanding for the instruction he had received in both fields.

this subject in a single volume has come down from Celsus the Roman tactician. He shows for all to see that the only way Persians will surrender to Romans is if all of a sudden the Romans fall upon their land as darkness does. The reason he gives is a sensible one. It is of the following nature.

The entire Persian citizen body, and in fact their whole race, is 34.1 wont to set out for war as the Romans too used to before the organization of the legions, as they were called, that was effected by Marius.[i] For it is evident that the Persians do not maintain 34.3 specific bodies of troops in a state of mobilization so as to be ready to do battle, as the Romans do. Consequently they need 34.4 time to get an army together and to assemble finances adequate to meet the demands imposed by the war. And so it is 34.5 appropriate, says Celsus, to make an unexpected attack on them, and especially by way of Colchis, as an area to accommodate the opening stages of the invasion.[j] For the rugged terrain is hard for the Persians, who are cavalry-men, to operate over. This was the reason why Corbulo in Nero's reign seemed to them irresistible. For by forestalling their raids, mounted in the Persian deserts by way of Hyrcania, he deprived them of the victory they achieved by fleeing. The result was that, having been caught in a narrow pass,[k] they retreated in flight to Antioch[l] on the river Mygdonius and nowhere else. This city too they abandoned when the Romans thereupon fell upon them like a tornado.

Well, having come to this way of thinking and having created a 35.1 Prefect of the East, Constantine gave him a staff of accountants to deal with the tribute. These were men who were held in respect and who had had training in the finer points of accountancy. Now it was wearing the garb of a layman that they 35.2 attended upon the court of justice, with nothing else but their accounts in their hands and under the title of *scrinarii.*[m] And this

---

i 34.2 But *they* cleave a human being in two and march the army between the two parts of the body.

j Lazica is what the people of our day call this area, taking the name from a leader.

k This was how it appeared to the Persians with their vast numbers.

l The Persians changed its name to Nisibis after they had captured the city.

m I.e. Archivists, because *scrinium* is the Roman name for the lattice-work chest.

remained the only title by which they were called. They were 35.3
not, of course, classified as belonging to the Service and did not
move from the status of private citizens, as the ancient *matrices*
inform us. But in the reign of Theodosius the First, when they 35.4
saw that they were being passed over whereas members of the
established civil service were at that time administering state
affairs, after enrolling themselves as a body and taking up a
collection in gold for *douceurs*, they submitted a request to the
Sovereign that they be put on the establishment. After succeeding
with their petition and securing for themselves the *probatoriae*, as
they were called, they were advanced to the classification of
Adiutores (i.e. Assistants), on equal terms with the other staff.
But although they purchased the name *Augustales* at an immense
price, until the time of Leo they were regarded as though not
even members of the Service, as far as concerned those on the
establishment. For Rome in ancient times did not even know of 35.5
their existence. This is the reason why, even nowadays, when the
prefecture goes in procession to the tribunal, they tag along
yielding place to bring up the rear. The Establishment alone, in
straight files, rank on rank, provides the escort for the Prefect.
Consequently they embellished the Placoton, as it was called of 35.6
old, near the city's sun-dial, setting up a statue in honour of the
emperor, of wrought silver throughout, on a column.[n] The 35.7
monument has in our day and age advanced in importance to be
one of the more useful public-works in the city; the column,
standing in front of the public building in the so-called
Hebdomon, boasts the statue of our most mighty emperor.

Well, the fortunes of the *scrinarii* went from strength to 36.1
strength, starting from Zeno's reign, in proportion as those of the
prefecture went into decline. Amongst many others, Polycarp was
snatched up from their ranks by Anastasius to become prefect.
Then Marinus too formally took over the entire administration of
affairs. This man himself was also, as it happened, one of the
scrinarii of Syria. And after this pretty well no-one save them
alone succeeded to the office. This being so, because of the
dropping away in tribute, the fortunes of the prefecture were
brought to a complete breakdown. For these men became 36.2

---

[n] As I found it recorded in the archives of the public *instrumentarius*.

cancellarii, logothetes* and governors of the sacred and of the public exchange. And yet long-standing practice held that no-one should be promoted to the position of serving as a *cancellarius*, as the official was called, save only those of the *Augustales* and the short-hand writers who were held in high esteem, since there were two *cancellarii* alone that were recognised by the law-court. These men actually had one gold piece each day specifically assigned to them as pay by the treasury. The reason for their styling was as follows.

Formerly in courts of law there was nearly always — as is the case even nowadays in the rural courts — a partition, or one might term it a barrier, made out of wood. This was composed of long laths, set in a criss-cross pattern atop one another and making diamond-shaped apertures for looking through (like the reticulation of a net). This stretched right across the middle of the court, separating the presiding official from the people brought before the court. A *cancellum* is what the Romans call this, using a diminutive word form, i.e. a little net.º At this dividing partition stood two *cancellarii*, one at each side. They took their name from the facts of the situation. Since no-one had the hardihood — and, what is more, it was not permitted — to touch the tribunal, it was through these officials that the documents for signature were brought up to the prefect and also that the laying of information concerning facts necessary to the case was carried out. But as, even before our day, in a very large number of cases the title had been abused, the treasury withheld its contribution — but then pretty well everyone however peripherally associated with the law-courts goes by the name of *cancellarius* nowadays. And they are not the only ones; no, even the people who handle the exchange of copper money in the provinces assume the title of *cancellarii* — in order that they may increase the exchange rates for the provinces with impunity.

Such is the story behind the confused state of affairs among officials of this type also.

37.1

37.2

37.3

38.1

---

o Because, in the original form of the word, they call nets *casses*, calling them *cancelli* in the diminutive form.

* Intendants of finance.

To the *scrinarii* there have also been added the officials in charge of the instrumentality which looks after the soldiery (i.e. that which sees to allowances of provisions). This was not because these too were a part of the court of law, as it was constituted of old. No; it was due to the fact that, after the praetorian *scrinarii* had been superseded, it came about that the service list on which these other officials were registered was made an effective part of the establishment. Through the good qualities of an Emperor 38.2
what had been believed to have been devised to do despite to others was shown as being beneficial when well administered. Now the wheat fund originally came under the city prefecture, 38.3
but was taken from it as result of the autocratic powers exercised by that blackguard of a Cappadocianᵖ — on whom I will speak a little further on. By his own unaided efforts Gabriel, while city prefect, restored authority over this matter to his court of justice. For the emperor is wont, being a gentleman and of liberal views, to show respect for those who vie with him, insofar as it is possible for them to do so, in breeding, way of life and munificence. But when the aforementioned Gabriel laid down his 38.4
office, once again the task of looking after the corn supply returned to the more important court of justice. Consequently it was shown up quite clearly to all that the emperor had made a concession to Gabriel because he was pleased with him, as well he should have been. For it could not but be that Gabriel, being a 38.5
man of parts and without a peer for good qualities, should experience preferential treatment on the part of an emperor who did honour to justice, love of God and distinction of lineage.

It remains then, to give the reasons for the diminution in 39.1
authority undergone by the prefecture and for this striking change in its circumstances, even if, fortuitously, the prefecture itself is still nowadays, to outward appearances (owing to the ceaseless efforts of the emperor), both more important and more distinguished than it really deserves to be. For it is not functionally attached to the state as a whole, because the emperor did not raise it quite to eminence and firmly-based power combined when he gave it its decorative features, although he inspected it very fully while he was at it. Nor is it functionally attached to the distinguished institutions which it possessed

---

p For he imagined that he ought, also, in addition to his transgressions against the provinces, to bring the emperor's city beneath his sway.

originally, in that it did not take them over when it got a supplementary grant of distinctions. Well anyway time, which is inherently destructive, has either completely obliterated the majority of the distinguished institutions, which were at one and the same time useful and decorative, maintained by the establishment under the prefect's instructions, or has brought about such an extensive change in them as to preserve for the future only a faint hint of its once admired position. For the prefecture stood firmly based upon its own powers, but its establishment, what with the vicissitudes undergone by the prefecture on the one hand and its own remissness on the other, kept slipping close to complete ruin, if God and our famous Emperor, good in all respects, did not render assistance. If   39.2 perchance at any point, out of my keen interest in the freedom which we all enjoy, one of those who have not carried out their magisterial functions in accordance with the directives emanating from our noble emperor should be touched upon in somewhat bitter fashion as the narrative gently unfolds, it is not to the magistracies themselves but to the officials who have not utilized them properly that those who have wise insight into public affairs should relate the expression of displeasure. For it is not only   39.3 castigation of bad officials that has been ventured in the account; there has been praise of good ones too, even if it has not measured up to their deserts. As result of this those officials who   39.4 do not know the bounds within which they should keep their magisterial activities will be ashamed to commit outrages upon people's liberties and to work havoc among the citizenry. But those who are eager to rival the emperor's mild rule will hasten at a brisk pace to attain to his other virtues too. But it is time to tell   39.5 the full story, giving the reasons why the fortunes of the establishment have been reduced to such a low ebb.

When Constantine, as I said, had gone from Rome — and   40.1 Fortune with him, and when all the forces which used to keep guard on the Danube had been scattered about Lower Asia at the emperor's decision, the treasury suffered the loss of Scythia and Moesia and the revenues accruing from those regions; for the barbarians from beyond the Danube, with no-one to withstand them, swept down upon Europe. As the peoples over towards the East had been given a heavy burden of tribute to bear, it proved necessary that the prefect should no longer be in charge of the

Court and the armed forces (of which the former had been
handed over to the Master, as he was termed, the latter had been
officially assigned to the recently created generals) but that he
should go by the title of Prefect of the East. None the less,
though it was waning day by day, the effective authority of the
prefecture lingered on until the reign of Arcadius, father of
Theodosius the Young. In this reign it came to pass that Rufinus,
him who was dubbed insatiable,q in aiming at despotic power,
missed his goal − fortunately for the best interests of the
commonwealth − but sent the prefecture hurtling down into a
yawning abyss. For the emperor's immediate reaction was to strip
the magistracy of the power accruing to it from controlling
weaponry; subsequently he took away authority over the
so-called *fabricae* (i.e. manufacturing of arms), the task of looking
after the Public Post, and the rest of its authority − and it was in
these functions that the so-called *magisterium* was comprised. But
there were difficulties in working a procedure whereby the
prefect maintained the public horses throughout the provinces
and the personnel in charge of them, while other officials
possessed authority over them and the right to dispose of them.
So a law was laid down ordaining that the prefect was to retain
the task of looking after the Public Post, but that the chief of the
*frumentarii*r should always attend upon the court of justice run by
the Praetorian Prefect and should make a host of inquiries and
find out the reasons why there are many people, provided by the
prefecture with the so-called official authorizations, using the
Public Post.s This took place although the so-called *magister* also
used to sign the official authorizations for the use of the Post
first. That this was so can be made out from the actual ordinance,
which was put in the old Theodosian code but which has been
passed over in the new one.

Well with the prefecture being in this way as it were brought
down step by step, the Sovereign put the military personnel-lists

40.2

40.3

40.4

40.5

41.1

---

q Rufinus was Arcadius' Praetorian Prefect.

r This official nowadays, as things have turned out, is called the *Princeps* of
the *magisterium*.

s Hence he was also given the name *curiosus* (viz. officious) − and not he
alone but also all those as well who were in charge of public horses in the
provinces.

under the counts and generals, as they were called at the time, and the staffs established in the palace he put under the official at the head of the force of Court functionaries. And the latter himself too, just like the army commanders mentioned, was to no small degree set up as a magistrate by the diminutions in power which the prefecture underwent. For expensive buildings, on 41.2 being broken up, provide sufficient materials for many a man to build his home therefrom. While it happened that the emperors 41.3 went out in person to the wars, the prefecture had some power and influence — if not actually as great as it had been, in excess however of all the other magistracies. But when it came about that the last Theodosius attained the throne while quite a young child and, in accordance with a piece of legislation of his father's, was not allowed to be present at the wars, and when this was prohibited by a law of general application, which forbade a Roman emperor to set out for war, naturally matters connected with the wars came to be the sphere of the generals and matters concerning the palace that of the *magister*. Consequently the prefecture had no other function thereafter save only the task of looking after expenditure, a task which naturally accrued to it because of the necessities of the case, which involve both the officials which it had itself produced as off-shoots and further, those individuals whom these officials had, of course, been established to govern.

If one were prepared to take into account also the conjectures 42.1 based upon the prophecies, which some people call oracles, what was once said by the Roman Fonteius has come to pass. For he claims, and he cites some verses, allegedly given to Romulus once upon a time in the ancestral language, verses which are clearly prophetic, that Fortune is to desert the Romans at the time when they shall themselves forget their ancestral tongue.† Divine 42.2 prophecies of this sort have assuredly come to fulfilment. A certain Cyrus, an Egyptian who is even today famous for his poetry, simultaneously administering the prefectorial duties of the city *and* praetorian prefecture and knowing nothing beyond his poetry, presently had the hardihood to transgress ancient custom, and proclaimed his decree in the Greek language. Along with the Roman language the magistracy also cast its standing away. For the emperor was prevailed upon to write with his own 42.3

---

† The so-called oracle was inserted by me into my work *"On the Months."*

hand a law that stripped the prefecture of all authority. For the magistracy which but recently of its own initiative both lightened tribute and made additional grants to the cities for foodstuffs, lighting, shows and renovations of public works, was not capable hereafter (and did not dare to do so) of making anyone a grant of at least some tiny recompense. Demosthenes in our time, and he 42.4 was himself a prefect at that, brought it about that not even under instructions in writing from the sovereign, unless a pragmatic* law was there as guide, did the prefecture have permission to make a contribution to the citizenry. He thus not merely was on guard against personally conferring benefits upon the tax-payer but precluded others also from so doing for the future. As the prefecture had by this time suffered the loss of its 42.5 actual façade of status as well, it followed, for those who were pleading cases at appeals, that they came to despise the court of justice, which, compared with what had been customary, was entirely ham-strung. A law determined that this should be the 42.6 case. For the emperor, in his kindliness, did not forebear to deprive those engaged in pleading their cases before the law of the hopeu that came from the possibility of making appeal.

This is the full extent of what I have to say in my lament over 43.1 the prefecture. But nothing will prevent me from recording, in 43.2 outline as it were, the gradual diminution which its power underwent. For one would not have clearly indicated what was taken away, unless one had previously enumerated the powers which, formerly present, were subsequently removed. Well, after 43.3 Theodosius and the moderate Marcianus came Leo. Finding the wealth which Attila, the enemy of the Roman empire, was to have taken,v his head swollen by power, Leo decided to make war on the Vandals, a German race which had trekked from the arctic regions into Spain, passing through the Pyrenees, and from there had invaded Libya. Well, upon countless warships (the sort that 43.4 people call Liburnian galleys) he embarked a host such that Time, for all its length, has never yet cast wondering eyes upon its like.

---

u Namely that, foreseeing an appeal, the judges would perhaps look into their cases impartially.

v It was more than a thousand hundred-pounds-weight gold bars.

* I.e. a law issued under imperial edict. The precaution shows the prevalence of forged documents emanating from the bureaucracy.

He thus brought the prefecture into most dire straits, by putting it under strain and compelling it to meet the expenses of four hundred thousand fighting men engaged upon a battle to be fought overseas, going to the difficult terrain of a land that was made into a stronghold by harbourless roadsteads, and matched with the might of barbarians whose wealth no words could match. There was expended upon that ill-fated war, after 43.5 Basiliscus assumed the leadership in the dreadful business, sixty-five thousand pounds weight of gold and seven hundred thousand of silver; and of horses, weapons and men as many as you might well estimate to have died across the time known to man.

After all this came the wreck of the entire state. For since the 44.1,2 money in the treasury, and all that which the emperor had in his privy purse, was not enough to meet requirements, the entire complements of the campaign forces perished in the failures of the war. Not to make a long story of it, as result of this dreadful debacle the Exchequer became no longer able to meet the demands it had to meet. But it made additional expenditures, ahead of time, upon state business, expenditures that involved sums that had never been planned for — by the tax-payer, that is. The result was that the difficulties which faced the treasury were boundless. But time would fail me, if I were to try to enumerate 44.3 the misfortunes of the state as it collapsed in Leo's reign. Along with the domestic disaster of the time, when the public buildings were consumed by fire, were mingled the misfortunes brought by the wars of the time and by countless other disasters. In consequence the wretch himself — the emperor, I mean — breaking down under the misfortunes that had fallen to his lot, not merely quitted the Court — with phantoms haunting him as though he were an Orestes wanting in manhood — and dwelt elsewhere, but even came seriously to consider quitting the city itself, the city whose streets are lined with gold. And one man could have brought down an empire as great as this one, had not God preserved for the city this mighty power which He has given it.

Leo eventually passed away, but the prefecture went under in 45.1 the flood that he had caused, for Zeno after him gradually made away with the power that had been his kinsman's. He was a 45.2

coward, or rather a miserable kind of fellow, and bought his way out of wars, since he could not bear to look at a battle even in a picture. He compelled the prefect to purchase peace with a lavish expenditure of gold, while he busied himself with confiscations of the property, and encompassing the downfall, of the state's magistrates. He too, for all that, met with an ill-starred end. After 45.3 such a flood of misfortune had been poured over that one of the magistracies which had formerly enjoyed prosperity, Fortune smiled, a little smile but a sincere one: she set Anastasius over the citizenry, who were in the grips of the death-wish. Anastasius explored every way of paying off the deficiency in public means. Like some *paterfamilias*, after firmly ear-marking for the *essential* routine outgoings, he kept requiring accounts for expenditures and meeting them fairly, shunning excess. He did not act as once did Nero and his ilk. They ran up immoderate expenses, but as for accounts, not even as much as a mention did they think fit either to extract from the prefecture or to render to it, supposing that gold was coming streaming out for them in rivers, or possibly in a complete sea.

But all the same, in a grudge felt even against the aims of the 46.1 administration, Fortune proceeded to hamstring the state. Although the curial corporations used to administer the cities, 46.2 maintain the soldiery, and in reality manage public business, a certain Marinus from the so-called *scrinarii* of the Eastern diocese cunningly insinuated himself into the emperor's confidence and prevailed upon him to entrust the entire state to him in his capacity as collector of taxes, undertaking to show a profit in gold for the emperor. Actually, however, the fellow was 46.3 something of an extortioner like Taulantius of Epidamnus in Illyria.w And there was a good deal of talk about over-anxiety for gain, involving imputations against Anastasius. As consequence there were even some verse couplets posted up in the Hippodrome by the populace criticizing him (for there was an iron statue dedicated to him in the Hippodrome). The verses, of a 46.4 character known to the Romans as slanderous and to us as blasphemous, went as follows:

---

w Durrachium is what the Cretans, who founded a colony there, termed it, taking the name from Durrachus who was king of Crete at the time, as the Roman writer Lucan asserts in the second book of his *Civil Wars*. Or was it the Corcyreans, Corinthian colonists, as the historian has it?

III 46.4 —

Of iron is this your statue,
Emperor world-devouring;
cheaper than a copper you,
we put it up as being.

For: blood spilt, and poverty devouring;
anger too, and hungriness;
To: that which destroys everything,
Your Money-Grubbingness.

A Charybdis devouring have they dedicated,   46.5
for Scylla, set close by;
a fierce one, who raw-flesh masticated,
Anastasius here, nearby.

Even you should shake and quake,   46.6
Scylla — in your mind and wits,
Lest even you may him a meal make,
bronze goddess, chewed to...threepenny bits.

There are slanderous remarks recorded by the ancient sources   46.7
concerning almost all the inhabitants of Europe on the score of
excessive fondness of money, both in their manner of acquiring
and in that of spending what surpluses they had. But the Epirotes
were especially criticized, since they were colonists who had
come from Syria, as Polemo revealed in the fifth book of
explanatory notes on the composition *"On the Civil Wars"* by the
Roman writer Lucan.×

Well, this was the sort of man the emperor was. And in other   47.1
matters he was wise and well-educated, fair and active too, with
it; lavish in his generosity and with his temper under control, he
showed due respect for literature. So much so that, when he
wanted to provide teachers of literature with a career stage to
round off their time in the service with an elevated grade, it was

---

× (46.8) Hence it is also called Palestine [Ed.-Apparently in error for
Palaeste: cf. Lucan V 460 and Caesar *BC* III 6,3.] by the ancients. Herod
once built the city of Nicopolis there, in honour of Augustus, by Cape
Leucas and the Bay of Actium where the latter had defeated Cleopatra,
with Antony in her train.

their inability to agree[y] that prevented the move. He was, then, a   47.2
good man as I have said and let no suppliant go away with a
frown on his face. Consequently no city, fort, mess, harbour or
any place at all in the whole Roman state went without its share
in the grants made by him if it had need of one. Because he alone,   47.3
after Constantine, lightened the tribute collected from men's
souls, if only in part (for he did not manage it fully), may he find
God kind to his sins, whatever they may have been — and he
committed some, for he was human. Though Anastasius'   47.4
achievements in the service of the common good were many,
beyond number in fact, one alone will suffice as an illustration of
their nature: the city built by him beyond the Euphrates.[z] If God
had not, through the agency of Anastasius, pressed this home into
the throat of the Persians, they would long, long ago have
over-run all the Roman domains that are near their borders.

But it will do no harm also to recall one deed of his that was   48.1
done in secret and goes unremarked even now. For one ought to
put into the account mention of one of the great man's private
good qualities as well. Paul, a patrician, son of Bibianus, who was   48.2
of most distinguished rank, lived in his reign. He made even those
among previous consuls who had been renowned for their
open-handedness — any of them, ever — pale into insignificance
by his feats of generosity. Paul, who proved useful to Anastasius   48.3
in regard to matters of a private nature, owed a Zenodotus (who
also was numbered among the consuls but had only the honorific
rank) an irredeemable amount of money, coming in all to a
thousand pounds' weight of gold. As Paul was despondent as to   48.4
paying off the debt, Zenodotus, making a loud outcry, besought
Anastasius to look after his interests. Anastasius, realizing that   48.5
Paul did not have adequate resources to pay the debt off nor
Zenodotus to cede it to him, gave him two thousand pounds'
weight of gold, one thousand for the creditor, the remainder —
and it was as much as this — as a free gift for Paul.

But I am going to return, in telling my story, to Marinus. Well,   49.1,2
being a Syrian and — naturally — a scoundrel, after he took over

---

y It is the make-up of the academics, because of their lack of practical
experience, to disagree amongst themselves.

z Daras is what the people of the region call it; the City of Anastasius is
what people call it, after him, amongst us.

the taxes, he brought about the undoing of the local councils of all the cities by selling the citizenry to any chance person, provided only that the latter would promise him a bigger return. In place of the local town councillors who had from the first carried the tax requisitions into effect he created the so-called *vindices*.ᵃ When they took the tax-payer over, these people treated the cities no better than enemies. And the emperor came 49.3
to be tremendously wealthy if ever a man was — and Marinus along with him. And so did all those who made no bones of their allegiance to Marinus. But an all-embracing lack of resources and profound poverty made away with public business, since the prefecture from then on, after the fashion of a petty judge, dealt only with law-suits of a private nature. Marinus however made a 49.4
display of respecting it and gave the appearance of doing the prefecture honour, siklfully dissociating himself from the ill-will produced by this turn of events. After this, with the public 49.5
monies falling as it were into the sphere of competence of other officials and not being collected via established procedure, the establishment of the prefecture began to slip somewhat and entered into an era of poverty. For what resources were left to it when all it did was to provide all the servicing for the law-suits of private individuals?

Well, since its business had fallen away in this fashion under 50.1
Marinus, the emperor decided to come to the support of the prefecture, now that it had fallen on evil days, by conferring another honour upon it. The cream of the barristers, that is, were 50.2
advanced by him to that magistracy; and on one occasion, when he was being importuned by his lady wife Ariadne to entrust the office to Anthemius, the son of the Anthemius who had been Emperor in Rome, he expressed displeasure, and did so with the remark that no one but men of literary training could fitly hold the office of prefect. The degree of respect in which he held the 50.3
prefecture can be recognized from the following incident. A 50.4
certain Hermias, who was on the staff of the *scrinarii* of Lydia, came under castigation, with Sergius, who was administering the prefecture at that time, expressing disapproval. The emperor, on 50.5
being importuned by Hermias' mother, made every effort in exhorting the prefect not to press his case against Hermias. But the latter kept all the time prevaricating, and the emperor kept

---

ᵃ Such is the name by which people in Italy customarily call God.

deferring to him, paying scrupulous attention both to the prefecture and to Sergius' distinguished status. But for all that the emperor prevailed, since he was urging a plea that had justice on its side. Then, since the aforementioned men of repute kept taking over the office one after the other, he granted that those who were most distinguished for speaking among the so-called *Augustales*, and moreover analogous members from the corps of short-hand writers, should be in attendance in public *auditoria*, should present speeches and demonstrate the skill they had in speaking — and should receive considerable honours for it.   50.6

Such were the sort of practices which went on at that time.   51.1
The emperor was living a life of fastidious refinement; he was   51.2
wealthy, thanks to Marinus' sharp practices, and he prided himself upon the acclamations accorded him by the consuls. A   51.3
profound peace enervated the entire state and not least its soldiery, for everyone alike emulated the indolent way of life passed at the emperor's Court and made the emperor's way of living their own. And so to Anastasius' life came an end that was   51.4
a chaotic one, what with the disturbances arising from matters of dogma and those caused by Vitalian. When Justin came to the   51.5
throne,[b] Marinus, and all those who had received their advancement at the hands of Anastasius were removed. As henceforth rulers did not have sources of gain available on the former scale,[c] all Anastasius' wealth, which when taken all together, amounted to countless tens of thousands of pounds' weight of gold,* trickled away. A host of wars shook the Roman   51.6
empire, with Persia demanding the much talked-about expenses for the Caspian Gates. The story about these expenses is as   51.7
follows.

Towards where the sun rises under the constellation Leo,   52.1
there where the Caucasus Range is narrow at its source, towards the north wind by the Caspian Sea, the foothills of the Caucasus

---

b He was a man not versed in affairs and he knew absolutely nothing besides his skill, gained by experience, at arms.

c This was so because they abandoned the abuses that were being practised upon the citizenry.

* 320,000 pounds weight (reputedly, but this is probably a wild exaggeration), the largest treasure ever amassed by a Byzantine Emperor.

Range form a natural divide and have made an entrance for some barbarians, unknown to us and to the Persians, who live around the Hyrcanian Sea. Making raids through this pass they used to ravage both the lands to the East, which belonged to Persia, and those to the North, which belonged to Rome. While Artaxata and 52.2 the regions still even further beyond that were in Rome's possession, the Romans withstood the invaders, as they were on the spot, But when they had been forced out of these places — and all the others which they lost under Jovian, the Persians did not prove equal to the task of protecting both their own territories and those which had of old belonged to Rome, and chaotic fighting continually held the Armenias belonging to either side* in a grip which could not be endured. Consequently there 52.3 was an agreement made, after the Roman campaign under Julian miscarried, between Sallust, who was prefect, on our side, and the most outstanding of the Persians, and later Isdigerd. It was to the effect that, sharing the expenses, the states together should build a hill-fort at the point of entry mentioned above, and set it up to provide the region with military help aimed at restraining the barbarians who came pouring down through the pass. But since 52.4 the Romans were hard put to deal with the wars fought for the West and the North, the Persians were compelled, in as much as they were more exposed to the barbarians' onsets, to build a hill-fort against them at that point — they called it Biraparah in their native tongue — and station forces there. And enemies do not affect an entrance.

Availing themselves of this pretext the Persians set upon 53.1 Rome, gradually spreading out over the Syrias and Cappadocias. They asserted of course that they had been wronged and had been deprived, in the expenditure incurred over the joint project, of the amount which was payable by Rome. Consequently Sporacius, the first of that name, was sent off by the elder Theodosius to hold talks with the Persians. Through the influence his money brought and his opportunist's facility in speaking, he almost persuaded the Persians that, if Rome as it were complied with them, they should keep the peace, with Rome subject to tribute, and live as friends. The projected arrangement lingered on until it came to Anastasius in our day, being the object of talks

---

* Armenia was divided between Rome and Persia, thus constituting *two* states of Armenia.

and decrees and, in a word, not being acted upon. In Anastasius'   53.2
time a war ensued when the aged Coades led the whole of Persia
against Rome. And though the Romans were capable of winning
by main force, because of the profligate and affected way of
living of Areobindus,[d] the last of that name, and the inexperience
and cowardice of the generals Patricius and Hypatius, they were
at first worsted when the Persians suddenly poured over them.
Afterwards, however, when they had put the Persians on the run
and had set Amida, which had been captured, free again, the
Persian king instigated talks with Celer, who was Anastasius'
Master of Offices, on the subject of Biraparah, on the lines
previously indicated, and on that of the expenses incurred in
connection with it by Persia on her own. And the wrangle came   53.3
to an end when certain modest concessions were made by
Anastasius to Coades. For Anastasius' generous and well-ordered
personality dutifully endured the loss that was made to secure
peace.

Such then is the account found in the Roman historians on   53.4
the subject of the Caspian Gates. In his *History of the Alans* and
especially in the eighth book of his *Parthian Wars* Arrian goes
right through it in greater detail, for he had visited the place in
person as was natural since he was in charge of the country itself
under the good Trajan. This was the type of commander that that
emperor had under him; men who both by their words and their
deeds brought the state on to the tremendous fame achieved in
that reign.

So much for Persia. But, as countless other wars kept being   54.1
kindled, after this a man of literary training had no means of
entering the prefecture. There was need of money: nothing of   54.2
what needed doing could be done without it. Not to omit   54.3
anything that might lead to the breaking up of the previous state
of well-being, tremors which set the ground leaping and caused it
to gape apart brought Seleucus' city of Antioch down in ruins
right from its foundations, covering the city with the hill that had
towered over it. The result was that no trace was left on the spot
that could distinguish mountain from city: all that there was was
a woodland glen and crags which had once cast their shadow

---

d He was fond of singing, flute-playing and the dance.

across the river Orontes as it went gliding by the city. Well, a 54.4
countless amount of gold had to be showered by the prefecture
upon carrying away, as an intermediary measure, the mounds
which had been heaped up by the ruins and which had piled up
and massed to form a towering piece of broken terrain. For it was
dangerous to leave the capital city of Syria lying demolished to its
foundations. As result of a great deal of labour, an unstinting 54.5
expenditure of money and the deployment of all the crafts, the
city grew up again as though from the nether world. But when
Justin met his end, the evil genius Chosroes came through Arabia
with a countless host and fell upon the Syrias. The recently
demolished city itself, which appeared to him as an easy prey in
as much as it was not fortified, he took in war and burned to the
ground, doing countless people to death. The statues, however,
with which the city was adorned, he seized without scruple as
booty, along with slabs of marble, precious stone and pictures: it
was the whole of Syria that he carried off to Persia as plunder.
There was not a farmer or a taxpayer left for the treasury. Tax 54.6
payments did not come in for the empire, and the prefect was
compelled to maintain the soldiery and to meet all the customary
expenses for the state as well. This was in spite of the fact that he
had not merely suffered the loss of the tribute revenue coming in
from Syria (and this on its own was of crucial importance for the
authorities) but was in addition compelled to meet countless
further expenses as well, in connection with those of the cities
which had been captured and the tax-payers who made voluntary
contributions.e

With the state being tossed about by such billows and squalls 55.1
of misfortune, as a countervailing influence to the slackness that
had prevailed of old Fortune brought assiduous industry to the
fore by putting Justinian, the most indefatigable of all emperors,
in charge of the commonwealth. He used to think that something
was somehow lost from his own life unless everyone was, like
him, working without respite and doing battle on the state's
behalf in order to take not merely that which had once belonged

---

e If it happened anywhere that someone had escaped from the fetters of
the Persians and was wandering in the deserted wastes that had once been
eagerly sought-after properties. [Ed.— Payment of the appropriate tax on
these would confer ownership: opportunity was apparently taken to
transfer to less-heavily taxed land.]

to Rome and then been lost through indolence on the part of previous generations, but, further, that which belonged to the enemy, in addition to the above. Well, he overwhelmed Persia and 55.2 the ruthless Chosroes, first by gold, then, when the latter renewed the fight, with steel as well. But as to the Vandals,[f] he suddenly 55.3 poured over them in war; in a mere two months he both captured them and, after capturing them in war, displayed them to the imperial city — Gelimer in person along with the notables among his race[g] and his lady wife, children and huge riches, as though it were the most worthless of slaves that he was handing over to act as slaves for Rome. As this appeared a small achievement in his 55.4 eyes, he assailed the Betae, who were tearing Holy Rome and all the countryside belonging to her to pieces and maltreating the original Roman patricians, carried them off as booty, their kith and kin and all, and put them on display with their despotic master. For Rome he preserved what was Rome's.

But when he threatened to keep a watchful eye on the 56.1 Sygambri[h] too, Choesroes once again, as though no agreement had been recently reached, suddenly poured his troops forth over the Syrias since the Roman forces were fighting for both Libya, where stability was being disturbed by the Getae, and since the Colchians and the Caucasus were being troubled by Scyths, and Thrace by wild-beast-like creatures countless in their numbers. The emperor proved capable of coping with all the wars, as 56.2 though it were one that he was fighting: but the prefecture was beset by a tempest that was to prove fatal, since the citizenry renounced their immoveable property, through destitution, and since the tax-collectors were no longer able to bring in the tax revenues for the authorities, as tax-payers did not exist. But, for all this, servicing of expenditures as immense as those outlined and as inexorable had to be done by whoever was prefect. So 56.3 naturally, following one after another in a succession that was at one and the same time rapid and, of necessity, heavy-handed, they broke the magistracy to bits. Their staff was "of neither 56.4

f A Germanic race which was stripping Libya bare by its depredations.

g The barbarians called these Asdings.

h They are called Franks after their leader, nowadays, by the people living around the Rhine and the Rhone.

account nor consequence," and its ruination was complete. For when those who comprise an institution are destroyed it cannot but be that what they comprise is destroyed.

In a way the evil power is putting me under duress, forcing me to recall misfortunes beyond number. A certain John, whose place of origin was Mazaca — the city had its name changed to Caesarea by Tiberius Caesar when, by a ruse, he summoned Archelaus, the king of the Cappadocians, to Rome and kept him there[i] — this fellow came originally, as I said, from there. While on the establishment of the *scrinarii* of the magistracy attached to the local military command he craftily (as you would expect in a Cappadocian) insinuated himself into favour with the emperor and was admitted to close association. Upon announcing that he would achieve things which surpassed belief on the state's behalf, he was advanced to become one of the logothetes. Then from there, as though it were a stepping stone, he proceeded on to the *illustres* as they are called; and, since it was not yet recognized what sort of a man he really was, in one fell swoop he was spirited away to the high honour of prefectural office. Afterwards the emperor, a good and fair ruler, did not allow himself to entrust the magistracy to blackguardly officials, since he had by that time learned and discovered from the facts of experience that: —

57.1
57.2

> Cappadocians are ever a worthless lot:
> but if a Service job they've got
> they're more so — and a haul
> to make, they're most worthless of all.
>
> But now, should a mighty man's palanquin
> twice or thrice their grasp come within,
> well then, with every minute
> their worthlessness grows more infinite.

---

i Cappadocia, which was not so originally, Tiberius first made into a province that paid tribute to Rome.

It was in this fashion then, as I have just said, that the villainous   57.3
Cappadocian won to power. He then proceeded to cause
misfortunes that were felt by the general public. Firstly he set out
chains and shackles, stocks and irons. Within the praetor's court
he established a private prison there in the darkness for the
punishments that were inflicted upon those who came under his
authority — like a Phalaris — craven coward and only to his slaves
a man of very great power. There he shut in those who were being
subjected to constraint. He exempted no-one, whatever his
station,* from torturing. He had no compunction in stringing up,
without holding an enquiry, those against whom the only
information that had been laid was that they possessed gold, and
they were either stripped of all they possessed or dead when he
let them go. To this the populace is witness, but I personally have   57.4
knowledge of it because I was an eye-witness and was present at
what was done. And I will tell you the ins and outs of it. A   57.5
certain Antiochus, who was advanced in years at the time when
this happened, was named by an informer, telling his tale to John,
as being the possessor of some gold. So John arrested him and   57.6
hung him up by the hands, which were fastened by strong, fine
cords, until, after denying the charge, the old man was a corpse
when he was freed from the ropes that bound him. Of this   57.7
murder I was an eye-witness, for I had known Antiochus.

Well now, as a deed this one was, for the Cappadocian, the   58.1
most moderate of all his doings — and would that he had at least
been on his own in his tireless preoccupation with wrong-doing!
But just as Briareus of mythology is said by the poets to have
innumerable hands, so this infamous scourge had countless
ministers of evil. It was not merely in the imperial city that he
operated; no, to every place and land he sent off men like
himself, raising, like a well-bucket and windlass, the coppers that
had escaped notice up to this time. From the mass of these agents   58.2
I will recall one by way of illustration of the bestiality of the rest.
He was a man with the same name as the Cappadocian, closely   58.3
related to him, a man whose evilness, with its dire consequences,
surpassed anything you could imagine. He too was himself a
Cappadocian and his bodily make-up in itself revealed the

---

* The status of an *honestior* was theoretically supposed to exempt its
holder from physical torture as part of court proceedings except in cases of
treason: see Jones, *Later Roman Empire*, pp. 519-20.

bestiality of his spirit. For he was a very fleshy type of man with 58.4
a face that ran prodigiously to flesh: his jaw-line was bloated out
to an unsightly width with rolls of excess meaty flesh, and
because of the weight of the flesh under the skin the sack of
tissue hung down from his face like a cloak. "Embroidered
curtain-jaw" was what the populace dubbed him. This Cerberus 58.5
with his saw-like jagged teeth was a common source of ruination
for everyone; but my home-town of Philadelphia he chewed up
into such small pieces that after he had finished, being stripped
bare not merely of money but also of people, it did not have
resources thereafter that permitted any form of opportunity to
change its circumstances for the better. For when this person, 58.6
nothing but a devil from the nether world, had been informed
that, as Euripides puts it, "the Lydians have lands that are rich in
gold," bringing in a massed pack of beasts and a force of
Cappadocians, he fell upon the country, assuming no
commonplace or moderate styling but that of Praetorian prefect.
Then during his stay in this country he left none of the poor
wretches who dwelt in the land with an implement of any kind,
or a spouse, a maiden or a young boy that went unharmed and
escaped ruination. In the punishments undergone by the guiltless
he went on like a Phalaris; in murdering his hosts as a Busiris, and
in his acts of indolent wantonness like a Sardanapallus.

Would that these acts alone had been the most extreme of 59.1
those for which he was principally responsible in dealing with the
citizenry; and would that he had not also been responsible for
acts of terrorism outdoing those of tragedy! Well of course I
shudder at the thought of giving a full account of the majority of
his foul deeds — and they are endless, so much so that they alone
would make the largest books look sorry — but of one act of his,
done for gain, I will at this point tell the tragic story in my
narrative. A certain Petronius in my home-town of Philadelphia — 59.2
a man of some note, distinguished by his breeding, property and
education — this Petronius had in his possession as an heirloom a
jewel of great price; both for its beauty and at the same time for
its size, the stone drew all eyes among the general public. The 59.3
Cyclops seized this man Petronius, clapped him in irons and had
barbarians flog him, stripped of his clothes, without mercy, after
he had shut him up in the shed for the mules.j When *this* became 59.4

---

j People in Italy call this a *stabulum*.

known "up rose the city in a panic and clapped hands to eyes" and the populace wailed aloud, for it dared neither give help to the man being cut to ribbons nor dissuade the vengeful spirit of the Cappadocian. But the Bishop of the city, with all the priests 59.5 accompanying him, took up the divine writings themselves and ran to the Cappadocian, because he had the idea that he would prevail upon him through these. But our Salmoneus,* looking straight at men and God, bade them go on the stage and do their business; and he refrained from none of all the things which are lasciviously done in the so-called bawdy-houses when men are talking lewdly. Unveiled and visible to all, there at the scene were 59.6 God's emblems; and the priest, who had been a victim of the outrage along with them, raised a wail of bitter lamentation upon seeing the godhead so contemptuously dishonoured. Petronius 59.7 however, putting God before his personal property, sent home and fetched all that he had, along with it also the jewels I mentioned; these possessions he cast in Cyclops' courtyard. Then 59.8 taking some gold he settled it, as an interest-bearing deposit, upon the men who had inflicted the punishment on him (on the grounds, presumably, that they had worn themselves out labouring over him) to produce *sportulae.* k

As this seemed to be a modest exploit, Cerberus decided to do 60.1 some murdering too. Well then, a certain Proclus, a soldier with 60.2 an honourable discharge from the army raised and stationed locally, was required to bring in twenty pieces of gold to him. As Proclus did not have it, he put him under duress and blunted all the instruments of torture upon the sinews of the wretched pauper. The latter thereupon, neither being able to bear to keep on living nor being allowed to die, sought death by a trick. Accordingly, he took the executioners and announced that he 60.3 would hand over the twenty gold pieces, as he was being forced to do so, if so be they would follow him till he got to his lodgings. When he got there he went within while his guards kept watch outside, fastened a noose round his neck, and made away with his life. Afterwards, when he did not come out, the 60.4

---

k This is the name the Romans have for a tip.

* A king of Elis who pretended to be Zeus; amid his display of simulated thunder and lightning the real Zeus smote him with a thunderbolt, according to the myth.

III 60.4 —

executioners let themselves in. When they saw him strung up,
they hurled his corpse into the market-place, trampling it
underfoot, asserting roundly that they had been deceived. His
property they plundered, not even allowing, out of consideration,
a miserable shroud for a burial.

Busying himself with feats of this nature the Laestrygonian*   61.1
— or, better, "the infanticide, despoiler of my native land" as the
well known writer Lycophron puts it — kept up the sack of Lydia
for a whole year. Deeming it a mean and shoddy accomplishment,   61.2
if it were only the — formerly fortunate — Lydians that he
subjected to his wrong-doings, he decided to extend his ungodly
activities simultaneously over the whole diocese comprised by the
massif of Asia. A law passed long before ruled that a broad road   61.3
and a fast one should be laid down concurrently in the provinces.
Of these the broad one was used by wagons, the fast one by
teams of horses.¹ As the peninsula was pretty well entirely under   61.4
the authority of the Cappadocians it was not easy for news of
what happened over towards the East to be brought up, with all
possible speed, to those responsible for the state, since sometimes
the latter were engaged in bringing the very seas themselves under
control by armed warfare. By the fast road at any rate the   61.5
burthen of a piece of information reached them before it had
become public knowledge. This institution, which exercised such   61.6
a wholesome influence on public life, Broad-jaw decided to wipe
out with a piece of information which he himself laid, by
prevailing upon the prefect his kinsman (and kindred spirit in his
bestiality); for as he saw it, the service rendered by the Public
Post was in excess of needs. He did not realise, being more
stone-blind than Niobe herself, the usefulness of the
instrumentality. The prefect, without the knowledge of the
sovereign — for he of course did not allow mistakes that would
bear hard on the public — did away with this adjunct to the state
too. Because of this people's produce, going unsold, grew rotten   61.7
within on the farms, with the province of Asia all but dislocated.
So the land-owners who had to raise and pay the taxes were
ruined, when gold was demanded from them by the collectors of

I Post-horses is what the authorities have called them and I think I have set
out the reason why in my book "On the Months."

* A member of a race of cannibal giants encountered by Odysseus.

tribute in place of their produce. For they could neither sell their produce, as they were settled far from the sea, nor were they allowed, as of old, to employ it to pay the treasury. On top of this were also to follow changes in deployment of the military forces settled in the locality. These were effected by the commonwealth at the dictates of necessity. The result was that, as this chance factor too led to the crops remaining in the country, while the taxes had been changed to taxes in gold, the crops were ploughed back into the land every year. Would that this fellow had in fact been the only one gnawing away — and that this had been the only province gnawed at! And would that it had not been the case that others such as he — and worse than he — came to every city, and country too, trying to draw up the pennies howsoever they might have been buried in the earth, with a host of stony-hearted implacables and massed packs of Cappadocians trailing after them!

So then, incalculable riches were gathered together by the prefect, epitome of justice. As consequence this encouraged him actually to try for a despot's power. The more audacious part of the populace was with him and assisted in what was entrusted to them. Well, when he was cultivating this group and associating with it, he began to think that he would not persuade it that he was a keen admirer of the dash cut by the group unless he went over in person to the East, put on clothes of a bright green colour and of a brilliant hue, and thus became conspicuous in everyone's eyes.* Well, the sort of things that he did in regard to the Cilicians and the size of the load which he forcibly added to the taxes in despite of the emperor's intent to show kindliness are known to absolutely everyone. When he came back to us, upon seeing oceans of wealth flowing around him, he swept all he had made boon companions of (even the cooks!) precipitately into the foremost of the high positions which the state afforded. The consequence was that no-one, even among the slaves he had acquired by purchase, was left to go without a long purse and honours which a town-councillor would have prayed to get. He personally lived a life of wantonness. He bathed together with

61.8

61.9

62.1

62.2

62.3

62.4

---

* The cities were currently split into warring factions which bore the colours blue or green; the latter colour seems to have been associated with the more humble elements of society and the monophysite faith, whose major centres lay in the eastern provinces.

III 62.4 —

young boys not of an age to shave, and not yet looking masculine
because their bodies were smooth, and with the licentious
element among the prostitutes. He showed his lechery both by
perpetrating and submitting to acts of venery. He had a pallor
that came from both afflictions, and drank heavily of unmixed
wine on such a lavish scale that he would be carried, limbs
asprawl, in a litter by his naked companions when he piled wine
on wine to go with the food he had eaten. Neither the strait lying   62.5
beneath the city nor all the Hellespont put together completely
satisfied his luxurious tastes. Further, no pheasant could do so,
nor could the *Lelops*, multi-coloured fish, worth their weight in
gold, that were captured in the open sea. So it was to the Black
Sea that those who danced attendance upon his luxurious tastes
turned. No fish was left unsought in the sea, no bird went
unhunted in mountain or in grove. The river Phasis* in its
entirety failed to afford sufficient fare for his festivities. As
consequence the pheasants departed, not trusting themselves to
their instinctive flight from spot to spot; by a show of wings as
though by due process of voting to take to the air they decided to
get out of the way of the gluttony of Cappadocians.

Now that by chance the fish the *Lelops*** has come to be
mentioned, I will set down what is known to me about it. It is a   63.2
fish that is soft to the touch and translucent, so that it seems to
have body tissue that is like frozen liquid and clear as crystal, not
solid and full of sinews. It brings its young forth alive and as it
were chews the cud. Its natural habitat is in spots that are   63.3
well-favoured; taken thence it was to the accompaniment of
flutes and cymbals that the fish was served up to the Romans, so
Athenaeus asserts. When swimming, it screens its eyes with the   63.4
barbels it has growing along its sides. An *elops* is what Aristotle and   63.5
all the natural scientists call it, and so does Aristophanes of
Byzantium in his abridged work on the characteristics of fish. But
the Romans call it the *aquipenser*, for the reasons which they
have themselves given in their writings. Cornelius Nepos and the
poet Laberius, a pair of Romans, assert that a certain Optatus, a
captain in the Carpathian fleet and a member of the household of
the emperor Claudius, brought these fish out of the southern sea

---

* The pheasant, much prized as a table-bird, came from this region.
** On this passage, see Carney, "The *Helops*" in *Phoenix* 21(3), 1967,
46-64.

and introduced them all over the length and breadth of the sea off Ostia and Campania.

Something on these lines must suffice as far as the fish is concerned. As the Cappadocian made his way up to the city — or rather was escorted back in — there were to be seen in ranks about him girls with their limbs draped in the *sandyx* openly revealing "what ought to be hidden from the eyes of men." For a short while I will drop the subject under discussion and try to put into words just what the *sandyx* really is and what sort of garment was used by the Lydians of old. The Lydians, who were of old rich in gold, had a passion for using abundant gold, in all the quantity that the river Pactolus, along with the river Hermus, lavishly supplied them, to produce smocks that were actually inter-woven with gold,[m] and not only these but also the garments called *sandyces*. These were smocks, an invention of theirs, the most transparent ones being of linen, and they used to dye them with the juice of the plant the *sandyx*.[n] With these to conceal their naked bodies, the women of the Lydians seemed to have nothing save air alone draped about them, and enticed the men who gazed on them by a beauty that flouted the dictates of propriety and modesty. It was a smock of this kind that Omphale dressed Hercules in, once upon a time, when she made him effeminate through his shameful passion for her. Hence Hercules was also referred to as Sandon, as Apulelus the Roman philosopher reports in the work entitled *"On Love,"* and Suetonius too before him in his work *"On Famous Courtesans."* Hence, I think that *sandon* is even nowadays a name that bears a note of disparagement, although the generality thinks that it is from their being made out of linen that they go by the name *sandons* (as though for *sindons*).*

This is the sort of thing that one might mention in a digression, as it were; but, for my part, I am going to go back to the subject of the Cappadocian. He used to be enticed by the

64.1

64.2

64.3

64.4

64.5

64.6

65.1

65.2

---

m A witness to this is Pisander, who talks of "Lydians with their golden smocks."

n The colour of the plant is flesh-colour.

* Lydus has been using the term *sindon* for linen to show the etymology; the play on words is untranslatable in English.

allurements of prostitutes, while being borne along by other prostitutes who appeared naked, with licentious kisses that compulsively urged him to have intercourse with them forthwith. Limbs asprawl, he partook of both the foods and drink that were 65.3 held out to him by other male wantons. These refreshments were in such enormous quantities and contained so many dainties as to cause him to vomit, when his mouth could make room for no more and acted like a drain cutting a swathe out of the hearth, and causing no little danger to the parasites, as they slid out of the way, from the glistening mass of bits of mosaic work! This was how he used to carry on in his rottenness, running day into night, so that an end was brought to his junketings by the star that heralds the day and business commenced with the evening star. In order that there might not by any chance be a hindrance 65.4 to his idle pleasures, he foreswore the Precincts of Justice° once and for all, only forebearing to put in an appearance there when, unstable from the excess of food he had eaten, he selected the most distinguished men on his staff for punishment. Judges were 65.5 created by him to hold court in the emperor's cloister, with result that, while the latter were listening to the law-suits that concerned money matters, he was busying himself with the matters of which I have just spoken.

Well, after this the advocates too felt no enthusiasm for 66.1 embellishing their advocacy with rhetoric capable of persuading a magistrate of the highest competence, since after this no business was transacted at the *secretum* — no plea in intercession, or *ex parte* petitions, or matter for elucidation, or task of assessment, or effecting of equality in tax distribution — or anything else at all. Consequently then none of the speakers who formerly were accustomed to be highly esteemed for their speeches on such matters spent their time on them for anyone. Whom was an 66.2 advocate to defend, or on what grounds was he to lay claim to plaudits, when there was not even a witness or, in a word, anyone capable of forming a judgment in praise of the fashion in which the law-courts were conducted? This was the cause of the ruin 66.3 that came to the prefect's staff, and, as they had no business to do, an unseemly air of desolation made the court tarnished and there was tearful lamentation on the part of those who had

---

o The *secretum* is what people call these in the courts of law.

reached the end of their service careers, since they were going to
be brought to destitution in their old age. So naturally no one   66.4
reported for entry to the service, although formerly it had been
the custom that over a thousand short-hand writers each year, on
beginning their service, secured a considerable income for those
who were retiring from work,* and especially for the
matricularius as he was called.ᵖ I was personally involved in this   66.5
debacle for I did not even make my daily expenses in fulfilling
my service tasks. As truth is my witness, I do not know of one   66.6
short-hand writer who served out the official year required to
complete the appointment. The reasons for this were diverse. In
the first place there was the complete penury in which the
prefecture operated. Then there was also the fact that gaining of
access to the *probatoriae* as they were called was difficult to
effect. I will tell you how this came about.

Of old the custom was that five gold pieces should be   67.1
provided to the *memoriales* for a letter of appointment to the
rank of Assistant, though the letter was despatched, even then, to
be dealt with under the authority of the prefect. This was when,
as the myth would have it, people were basking in the sunshine of
the Golden Age. But nowadays when it is not possible even to
find a name for our day and age that is capable of showing the
depravity which is prevalent in it, they have decided that the
letter of appointment should be given out to these people for
twenty gold pieces. But when they realised that no one was   67.2
prepared, or rather that people were not able, to provide
themselves with a letter of appointment at such an enormous
price, they extorted a pragmatic edict in their own interest which
allowed no one without a letter from the emperor to go over into
service under the prefects. The business as a whole, however, had   67.3
the effect of disgracing the prefecture, since originally the law
had allowed it at its own discretion to enlist whomsoever it
wished among the short-hand writers of the court of justice.
Many a man, as I know personally, entered the service as result of
being talked about and both distinguished himself and completed
his career in the service with honour. As this mode of entry too   67.4

---

p Viz. the Keeper of the Personnel Lists.

* One sold one's position to one's successor on retiring.

was of course closed after this, the fortunes of the staff on the prefect's establishment went completely to ruin. But the department constituted by the so-called *matricularii*, having been torn up by the roots, was completely destroyed. What need of words, when all of these men alike, after the end of their service careers, dragged out the remaining period of their lives suffering in shameful poverty? Now I retired from the service after 67.5 attending to its business for forty years — and getting nothing out of it besides the styling appropriate to my final career point. And 67.6 it would be a good thing to close at this point, for this tragic business would be enough to show the truth of the end of the book. However there is another tale also on which I believe I ought to touch.

There was a law of old that every piece of business, however 68.1 transacted, done by the prefects and perhaps also by the other magistrates, should be promulgated in Latin. When this law was broken, as has been stated — the sequel would not have occurred without this — the course of the decline of the prefecture proceeded apace. The transactions which concerned Europe all preserved their form as of old, of necessity, because of the fact that its inhabitants, in spite of being Greeks for the most part, spoke the Latin language, and especially those who were in the public service. This practice was changed by the Cappadocian into 68.2 an old-wife-like, mean form of announcement. This was not because he was anxious to make his meaning plain, but so that the announcements, being easily accessible and open to all, should cause no difficulty for those who were trying, in conformity with his schemes, to carry out projects which were absolutely not their business. In his deeds, writings and 68.3 innovations and in the disturbances of every sort which he caused to time-honoured customs, it was not to the appropriate over-seers of the regions[q] or to revenue collectors, as custom would have demanded, that he gave the transactions requiring forms to be filled out, so that nothing that was in contravention to the law should occur. No; he personally gave orders that it was through men from his own household that the receipts should be filled in, himself assuming responsibility for the expenses customarily provided for the regular officials assigned to filling out the documents. Then when, as result of the reckless issuing of 68.4

---

q People call these *Trakteutai*, i.e. Regional Governors.

documents that were not as they should have been, very
considerable difficulties arose for the tax-payer, *he* expressed
displeasure and imposed death sentences upon those who did not
understand the consequences of discharging documents without
duly checking them and in a casual fashion. A custom became
prevalent as result of him: all officials, to meet a situation that
has cropped up, write and fill in and discharge documents on
matters about which they are completely in ignorance. Formerly
these things were hedged about with safeguards in countless ways
— by the *cottidiana*,^r as they were called, of the *Ab actis*, and by
the bureaux appropriate to the matter dealt with, and also by the
officials themselves who got an income from them. Why should I 68.5
discourse at length? Everything has completely collapsed,
preserving no recognizable traces of their former perfection.

After this blackguard of blackguards, enemy of the laws, had 69.1
gone on like this, God turned his attention to him, for he had
decided that the person responsible for the wrong-doings should
be hoist to his own petard, to persuade him that "there is a
justice and a nemesis that brings evils home to roost." The 69.2
emperor, gentlest of souls, knew nothing of these happenings. On
account of the Cappadocian's unrestricted power everyone,
although subject to his injustices, spoke highly of the scoundrel,
and their praises for him were loudest of all when in the
emperor's presence — for who would have ventured to bring up
even his mere name without a word of praise? Only the
emperor's wife, the superior in intelligence of any man ever, who
was maintaining a vigilant watch out of sympathy for those to
whom injustice was being done, finding it intolerable to watch
inactively any longer as the state foundered, armed with accounts
that told no ordinary tale, she went over to the emperor and
informed him of everything that had up to this time escaped his
notice, of the fact that there was a risk that not merely would the
citizenry come to ruin amid the wrongs being perpetrated but
also that the empire itself was near to being brought down. Well, 69.3
as you would expect, the emperor, being a good man and slow to
requite evil, was in the toils of a perplexing situation that was
impossible to resolve; he did not even manage to find a way of
removing the subverter of the state. And this was what he really
was, inasmuch as he had wickedly mis-managed public affairs and

---

r I.e. the Daily Record of Proceedings.

had set the revenues in a dizzy whirl of perplexity and unintelligible confusion by mixing all up together the so-called taxes that were set by imposition. The result was that there was never any end to his holding of the prefecture; and none of the officials from the senate, nor in fine anyone working upon the provision of justice, dared to undertake his administrative duties. But all the same the Emperor came to the aid of his subjects as far as humanly possible.

*The tax-payers by this time had no resources, not even those 70.1 which had been passed over when taxes were taken from them. This was because of their being compelled to carry food to Constantinople and being used as forced labour, with the work involved in this. And it was because their women-folk, with children at the breast, while carrying loads and fetching their produce long distances from the hinter-land to the sea, died en route, unpitied and unburied. Also the people exacting the revenues demanded a huge range of taxes of divers names** (*censualia*, holographic, curial, homodule, *contributaria, afanticia*, abandonments, civil, fiscal, deputed, *recollocata*, concerning relegations, *refusa*, *keratismoi*, discounts, exchange-rates, interest-rates, endomatic, metatoric). And, after the pitiless exaction of these taxes in the current coin, countless other evils sprang up for the tax-payers, as though from a hydra, to tower above them (purchased positions held in joint ownership, ... members of the emperor's retinue who had favourites, monasteries that were utterly neglected, gold of a pale colour). And, finally, it was because of the armies permanently quartered on them, and the plundering expeditions that went off booty-laden, undertaken by the protecting forces against the very people whom they were looking after; and because of the

---

* The text of section one of this chapter is very faulty.

** Respectively: pertaining to the census; pertaining to wills written entirely in the same hand; concerning members of municipal councils; on lands subject to the same servitudes; concerning joint tax contributions; concerning derelict lands; taxes abandoned by a defaulting land-owner; pertaining to residents in towns; appertaining to the treasury; pertaining to emphyteutic leases (?); to do with reassessments (?); pertaining to the properties of those banned; refunds (?); losses incurred at the exchange of currency of small denomination; discounts; exchange and interest-rates; on fees paid at court; on lodgings — where (?) means that the sense is difficult to make out.

extortion and rape practised, as they passed through the
provinces, by all the campaign forces which had, as chance
dictated, to set out for the wars.[s] Well then, because of these
reasons — or, rather, desperate conditions — they one and all left
the lands that had supported them. Wishing to live in indolence
rather than to work like prudent men (as well they might, as they
had not even been given a chance to do the latter), they filled the
imperial city up with useless mobs. And the law was much in
evidence; in view of the countless numbers of offences it was
extended to keep up with their multitude. The result was that
even the magistracies which had previously been in obscurity,
praetors and quaesitors, were advanced to prominence, in
accordance with the usage once prevalent at Rome, as I have
already recounted. As the latter conducted their prosecutions
into the wrong-doings perpetrated by the populace rather harshly,
the multitude rose up and, united into a singleness of purpose
that was to have dire results, burned almost the entire city. The
Cappadocian disappeared. But the fire, getting going upon the
entrances to the Court, spread from there to the main church,
from where it spread to the council chamber built by Julian,[t] and
from there to the forum which people call Zeuxippan after king
Zeuxippus.[u] After whole constructions of this huge scale had
turned into flames, there was looting of the colonnades which
went straight through the city to the Forum of Constantine, with
the graceful contours of their large and beautiful columns[v]

70.2

70.3

s For this reason the citizenry reckoned that a barbarian invasion was a less
serious matter, so far as it was concerned, than the sojourn of its own
troops.

t This is the building called the Senate, after the Assembly of Augustus.

u Under whom, in the thirty-eighth Olympiad, the Megarians sent out a
colony to Byzantium. They called the forum by this name in his honour,
just as the Megarians who settled Cyzicus named the colonnades after
Charidemus. The latter is recorded to have ruled over Greece, as Castor has
laid down in an abridged chronicle. I mention this because the public bath
has been given the name Severan after Severus, the Roman commander,
who built the baths because he was having trouble with a disease affecting
his joints while he stayed on and on in Thrace on account of the civil war
he was fighting with Niger.

v The Campanians are said to have built these in gratitude towards
Constantine, coming from Parthenope (the Naples of our day) and what
was once Dicaearchia (and is now Puteoli) to Byzantium in gratitude, as
has been stated, towards the emperor.

providing shade for the high street. Well, also reduced to ashes —   70.4
it was inevitable — were the buildings adjoining Middle Street to
North and South. The city was turned into a mountainside with
black, beetling hills, as on Lipara or at Vesuvius; ash, smoke and
an acrid smell from the materials that were reduced to ashes made
it uninhabitable, inspiring a piteous fear in those who beheld it.
The populace, or rather the barbaric and merciless multitude, was   70.5
reduced in numbers by appropriate punishments resulting from
this "victory,"* up to almost fifty thousand being destroyed
indiscriminately by the sword. But the city lay in ruins, a
terrifying spectacle what with the fires, heaps of rubble and
unsightliness of the remains. But God — for the task was one he   70.6
alone could do — gave consolation to such a mighty .....**

...... but all the same with God's help the emperor's destiny   71.1
prevailed over all the heaped ruins — and quickly. And it was a
better and more beautiful city that was seen, powerful and secure
at the same time. It was as though, from an amorphous mass, the
creator were once again, as he did of old, summoning all this
world of ours up to the light of day by the unaided power of his
will.

Well, this was the end of the first tenure of the post of Chief   72.1
Robber by the villainous Cappadocian. In compensation for the   72.2
evil, God lavished his goodwill upon the disaster-stricken
community. Phocas was a patrician, grandson of the most   72.3
fair-minded Salvius and son of Craterus, who surpassed all men in
piety. After attaining the foremost eminence among the
silentiaries of the Court, as they were called, and excelling any
man who had ever been admired for greatness of spirit by his
bequests, which were beyond counting, he proceeded to become
one of the Fathers of the State, as he deserved. Being proud of his
wealth and coming to the assistance of those who made requests
of him, of his own accord he was parsimonious only to himself.
His way of life and abstemious ways in taking sustenance were to   72.4
extreme as to be accounted mean by those whose circumstances
were exceedingly straitened. In keeping with his ample personal   72.5

---

* From the cry ("*Nika!*" "Conquer"/"Victory") of the rioters, these were
known as the Nika Riots. Lydus is alluding to this.

** Seven lines of text have been lost at this point.

fortune was the hospitality which he gave his friends in his home, but he personally partook only of the enjoyment experienced by his guests. For he was a dignified man with excellent taste, not an exhibitionist. From this alone ....*

..... and to spin plots; he was embarrassed at making the request, though he was in want of necessities. He groaned and made lament and, from the tears with which his eyes were heavy, it was clear, even to people totally unacquainted with him, that he was in distress. Phocas happened to catch a glimpse of this man. Being a good man and able to comprehend grief of soul when it was recognizable, with nothing more than despondency of the features to go by, he put off saying anything to him. Sending for me^w and wanting me to do him a good turn, he asked me to give some thought to the question of someone to teach him the Latin language. It was a Libyan that he was after. For the latter, he claimed, spoke more volubly than the Italians. When one of the company brought up mention of Speciosus he rose to his feet and, directing his entreaties at both the speaker and myself, urged us to effect a meeting with him. I brought Speciosus to him with all speed, thinking the request an unexpected piece of good luck. I knew the man, you see. Phocas took him aside on their own; falling to his knees and staying there, with earnest entreaties couched in sober terms he asked Speciosus to impart to him some of the linguistic knowledge he himself had. Taking me aside for a moment from the talking that was going on, he requested me to take a hundred gold pieces, which were to be given to Speciosus. I of course did so and, giving them to Speciosus as the teacher's fee, as it is called, I prevailed upon him to attend more frequently upon our subject, a good man through and through. Speciosus presented himself early in the morning — what else was he to do? — waiting expectantly in front of the fore-court of the man who had, as he thought, required him to do so. But Phocas sent for him and solicitously besought him not to wait upon him until he should personally give express instructions and request him to be with him.

73.1

73.3

73.4

73.5

73.6

w He did so because he thought fit to be more fond of me than of the others, being under the rather mistaken impression that I had no trifling acquaintance with certain minor matters to do with literature.

* 32 lines of text (=one page of the *codex*) have been lost at this point.

Thereafter Speciosus, inferring the mode of presentation required 73.7
from the period allowed for thinking about it, ceased to wait
upon him. For Phocas, who was very well educated in both
languages, was not concerned to secure instruction in those
matters where he had a remarkable knowledge compared to the
generality of people.

And you can guess, from the correctness of Phocas' behaviour 73.8
where fellow humans were concerned, at how great his piety
towards the deity was.

Near Pessinus, a city in Galatia — the spot got the name, as it 74.1
happened, from the fact that a countless number of Gauls from
round the Rhine fell there,* when they attacked the country
under the leadership of Brennus, being under pressure to claim
the country which bore the same name as they did.ˣ Well then, at (74.2)
this place there was a temple that was dedicated to the
Immaculate Host of Holy Angels of the God that None may
Name. When Phocas found out — it was common knowledge — in
connection with this sanctuary, that a certain Ellamus was
holding twenty pounds of gold, having donated it to the deity on
one condition, namely that the priests should have an additional
income of eighty gold pieces for the church, he made haste to
befriend these strangers.

**Such then were the little ruses which he adopted in the city. 75.1
But every year he kept secretly pouring out gold to pay ransoms
for prisoners of war. He was reduced to tears whenever anyone
recounted to him the story of an enemy inroad and abduction of
prisoners of war. And I am not afraid to invoke Truth as witness 75.2
that I am speaking truly. I know that, in his absence, I received
from his chamberlains gold on just such a scale, for the multitude
of people being ransomed. When his philanthropy in this 75.3

ˣ This is what the Roman writers Fenestella and Sisenna say; it is
quotations from these writers that Varro reproduces in his books "On
Human Affairs" (I have not to date seen the books).

* Lydus uses the word *Pesein* to indicate an etymological connection with
the place name (Pessinon); the play on words cannot be brought out in
translation.

** The text of the two final chapters is full of gaps and has been massively
supplemented by emendations, not always convincingly.

direction developed to excessive lengths, he sold his clothing. Putting to the sum as much as he possibly could, he sent it off for use as compensation in requital of these ransoms. He adopted the son of Theoprepes and spared no pains to bring him up to make these matters his over-riding concern. The latter completely 75.4 outdid his father, who was getting on in years and bore witness to what was going on, as the latter had prayed that he would. In consequence the father acknowledged his gratitude to the deity, inasmuch as though he was physically nearing his end, his reputation for piety was going to be immortal because of the doings of his son.

As Phocas was a man of such sterling qualities the emperor 76.1 gladly urged him, going to much trouble to do so, to display the liberality of spirit that was his in public for all to see, to accept the task of looking after public affairs and to set his guiding hand upon the helm of government, now that the whole state was foundering under its misfortunes. Reluctantly — for it was not 76.2 safe to push aside a request that came from an emperor of such calibre — Phocas undertook the heavy duty. But for all that he was afraid and his brain reeled at the magnitude of fearsome prospects — when he saw the hand of God before him eager to help him. For when he succeeded to the position and came 76.3 forward to make an appearance before the Court, as soon as he was raised into the state carriage, the entire citizen body and people of all age-groups and sexes, all together, raising their hands to heaven, sent up hymns of gratitude to God, mingled with their tears, for having deemed them, as they lay prostrated by countless evils, worthy of such a tremendous act of providence. God saw fit to give mankind proof of his intentions: He showed 76.4 that He was party to what was going on and that it was by His councils that blessings were in train. For as the Prefect stood 76.5 before the state carriage, some blackguard strung an arrow to a bowʸ and shot at him. The arrow fell short. Phocas himself, by coming off unscathed, gave clear proof of being a human under protection by divine providence. After this incident the populace 76.6 ceased its armed disturbances. They sang songs in honour of the mightiest of emperors. Their happiness, shown in contentment and revelry, did not die quickly away, although the change from most violent disturbances and fears to song and dance had been a

ʸ The citizen body still practised the use of arms.

sudden one. Abundance of necessities of every type returned to   76.7
the city, as everyone, wherever they had gone to to hide and flee
from the danger, came pouring into the city without fear and in
good cheer, bringing with them every kind of thing in plenty. For
already everyone expected that there would for the future be no
harm done to and much profit for the citizenry as they went
about their way of life, one in which there would be a spate of
good things. In these circumstances the Emperor, with the same
man as prefect, commenced enthusiastically to build the temple
of the Mighty God. A river of money came flowing, poured forth
to meet the vows made by the emperor and the justice shown by
the prefect. Well, four thousand pounds of gold were at once   76.8
poured by the prefect into the work being done on the holy
building, with no injustice being suffered by anyone and without
the contriving of ways to turn the prosperity that had come along
to ungodly use. For the prefect took pleasure in being held in
high repute for striving to honour God and seek earnestly after
piety. One cannot be surprised that, with God to hand,   76.9
everything should turn out to be to hand for men who attribute
the abundance of good things to him rather than to human
cleverness.

The prefect's staff took fire, just as though someone were   76.10
pouring oil with a lavish hand on to a fire that was on the point
of dying out. There was a bustle that came as a joy to those doing
business; gains that were modest and welcome in the eyes of the
law accrued to those serving the prefecture, and the Precincts of
Justice were opened up. Orators began to be famous for their
speeches; publishing of books and keen rivalry about them began
recurring as part of the whole life-style of the state; the ..... *

---

* The MS breaks off at this point.

GLOSSARY OF BUREAUCRATIC JARGON

GLOSSARY

For ease of reference a list of explanations of important terms in John's bureaucratic jargon is appended herewith:

a secretis: secretaries to the Consistory or Imperial Council.

ab actis: heads of the prefectural department which administered civil law suits; next to *commentarienses* in status.

adiutor: assistant; a vague term. It can mean the assistant to the *princeps officii* i.e. the *primiscrinius.* It can also mean the aide to the *promotus* or head of department (an *ab actis,* for example). It may however also mean an assistant within the department in general, either clerical (an *officialis*) or sub-clerical (an *apparitor*) in grade.

agentes in rebus: initially imperial couriers, these men became secret service men under the direction of the Master of Offices; an ex-agent was always chosen as *princeps* of the prefectural staff, as a security measure.

apparitor: an attendant of sub-clerical grade, who served an official of the prefecture.

augustales: the 30 senior men of the clerical grade within the prefecture.

cancellarius: the door-keeper of a judicial official of the prefecture; the controller of access to the latter's court.

chartularius: clerk to the aide to the departmental head.

commentariensis: heads of the prefectural department which administered criminal law suits and prisons. Senior in status to all other departments.

cornicularius: second of the *primates officii* or officials in charge of the prefecture (these were respectively the *princeps,* the *cornicularius* and the *primiscrinius*). Saw to the conducting of all court-cases by the prefecture.

cottidianum: day book of proceedings of the court of the prefecture.

cura epistularum: heads of the prefectural departments which handled the budgetary correspondence with the dioceses.

curiosi: secret service agents sent out to inspect the working of the "public post."

deputatus: one of the 15 most senior *augustales* from whom aides to departmental heads were chosen; he could sign in *lieu* of his head of department.

ducenarius: highest ranking member of the secret service *corps*; serves in the department of the *commentariensis;* a *magistrianus.*

exceptor: a short-hand clerk, clerical grade, prefectural staff.

litterati: those men of the clerical grade of the prefecture who had an extensive background training in literature.

magister officiorum: the Master of Offices; in charge of many branches of the central administration, including the public post and secret service, the central secretariate for imperial correspondence, the *memoriales,* and the state factories.

magister militum: Master of the Soldiery; one of seven army commanders (two of whom resided in Constantinople, the others in the dioceses) in charge of infantry and cavalry units of the central strategic reserves or *comitatenses.*

magistriani: members of the various staffs subordinate to the Master of Offices.

matricula: the rolls of the prefecture certifying membership of its establishment of *officiales.*

memorialis: on the staff of the Master of Offices, these officials acted as secretaries for the Imperial Council and issued *probatoriae* to the middle ranks of sections of the civil bureaucracy and the army.

militia: the civil bureaucracy (the military service was styled *militia armata*) or service therein.

notarius: officials in charge of the secretariate of the Imperial Council, these men kept the records of all grants of high dignities and commissions.

numerarius: one of the two heads of the financial bureaux, the *scrinia,* of the prefecture.

officialis: a civil bureaucrat serving in an *officium.*

officium: the office staff serving a civil or military official at the administrative level.

personale: an index of cases, under the names of the litigants concerned, which had come before the prefect's court.

praefectiani: members of the staff subordinate to the Praetorian Prefect.

primiscrinius: the third of three *primates officii,* this official appointed those who were to execute decisions of the prefecture.

princeps officii: the head of the staff of the Praetorian Prefect and most senior of the three *primates officii.* This official decided which cases would appear before the Prefect's court, supervised the staff-rolls and exercised general surveillance over the prefecture. This post was reserved for retired agents of the Master of Offices.

probatoria: imperial sanction permitting entrance to the civil bureaucracy.

regendarius: head of the prefectural department which controlled the issue of warrants allowing use of the facilities of the public post.

regesta: register of official business.

scholae exceptorum: the divisions or groups into which the short-hand clerks of the prefecture were organised.

scriniarii: the financial clerks serving the accounting *bureaux* of the prefecture; their departmental heads, the *numerarii,* were chosen from among their number.

scrinia: John most often seems to refer, by this term, to the 8 *bureaux* which handled the financial affairs of the prefecture.

singularis: a mounted messenger serving an *officium.*

suggestio: an official report or account.

tabularii: accountants on the *officium* of a governor.

trakteutes: a provincial governor.